ALSO BY BENJAMIN M. FRIEDMAN

Day of Reckoning:
The Consequences of American Economic Policy Under Reagan and After

The Moral Consequences of Economic Growth

The Moral Consequences of
Economic Growth

BENJAMIN M. FRIEDMAN

ALFRED A. KNOPF   NEW YORK   2006

THIS IS A BORZOI BOOK
PUBLISHED BY ALFRED A. KNOPF

Copyright © 2005 Benjamin M. Friedman

www.aaknopf.com

Knopf, Borzoi Books, and the colophon are registered trademarks of
Random House, Inc.

A portion of this work previously appeared in *The Atlantic Monthly*.

Library of Congress Cataloging-in-Publication Data
Friedman, Benjamin M.
The moral consequences of economic growth / Benjamin M. Friedman.—1st ed.
p. cm.
Includes bibliographical references and index.
ISBN 0-679-44891-8 (alk. paper)
1. Economic development—Moral and ethical aspects. 2. Income distribution.
3. Political participation. 4. Democracy. I. Title

HD82F7168 2005

174—DC22   20045040792

Manufactured in the United States of America
Published October 25, 2005
Reprinted Two Times
Fourth Printing, February 2006

For B.A.C.

Contents

PART IV

DEVELOPMENT, EQUALITY, GLOBALIZATION,

AND THE ENVIRONMENT

PART V

LOOKING FORWARD

Preface

Morality has many dimensions. In some contexts, the actions and attitudes we recognize as moral are mostly a matter of individual behavior. Personal honesty, fair dealing, family bonds, and loyalty to friends and co-workers would be on almost everyone's list. Religious belief and practice would be on many people's. Many would also add, now in a negative sense, aspects of sexual behavior, or use and abuse of drugs and alcohol.

This book is about how economic growth—or stagnation—affects the moral character of a *society*. But here as well, what constitutes a moral society is a matter of many dimensions, and a question to which different people bring different conceptions.

The concept of a moral society that I take as the benchmark for examining what difference economic growth makes is the image held out by the Enlightenment thinkers whose ideas were key to the creation of America as an independent nation and have remained central to Western thinking ever since. Its crucial elements include openness of opportunity, tolerance, economic and social mobility, fairness, and democracy. Surely there are other valid conceptions of the moral society as well; but these are the characteristics that I keep in mind throughout, and against which I measure the progress or retreat that economic developments help bring about. I make no attempt here to argue *why* these characteristics of a society are desirable, much less moral. I take them to be so for the reasons Locke and Montesquieu, Adams and Jefferson, and political thinkers both theoretical and practical ever since, have recognized.

This book could have been written from any of a number of familiar viewpoints, and not just because different people might conceive the moral society differently. Beginning from the same benchmark, a historian, a philosopher, a psychologist—not to mention a theologian—could well treat this subject, and presumably would treat it differently. Although I have drawn on these disciplines along the way, I have nonetheless written from the perspective of an economist. After more than half a lifetime of study and research into policies designed to keep output and employment as close as possible to an economy's existing potential, and to help that potential expand over time, I wanted to be able to say why this matters for countries (like my own) where the average income is already high and most people enjoy a comfortable standard of living. That is where this inquiry starts.

And, of course, I have written also from the perspective of my time and place. One of my Harvard colleagues with whom I once discussed in some detail the hypothesis about economic growth and moral progress that I advance here, a distinguished European scholar a decade and a half older than I, commented that only an American—and at that, only an American of my generation—would write a book expressing such an optimistic perspective on economic growth from a moral point of view. If this is right, I gladly accept that identification as well.

BENJAMIN M. FRIEDMAN

Cambridge, Massachusetts
July 2005

PART I

IDEAS, THEIR ORIGINS, AND THEIR IMPLICATIONS

Chapter 1

What Growth Is, What Growth Does

Economic growth has become the secular religion
of advancing industrial societies.

—DANIEL BELL
The Cultural Contradictions of Capitalism[1]

Are we right to care so much about economic growth as we clearly do?

For citizens of all too many of the world's countries, where poverty is still the norm, the answer is immediate and obvious. But the tangible improvements in the basics of life that make economic growth so important whenever living standards are low—greater life expectancy, fewer diseases, less infant mortality and malnutrition—have mostly played out long before a country's per capita income reaches the levels enjoyed in today's advanced industrialized economies. Americans are no healthier than Koreans or Portuguese, for example, and we live no longer, despite an average income more than twice what they have. Yet whether our standard of living will continue to improve, and how fast, remain matters of acute concern for us nonetheless.

At the same time, perhaps because we are never clear about just why we attach so much importance to economic growth in the first place, we are often at cross-purposes—at times we seem to be almost embarrassed—about what we want. We not only acknowledge other values; as a matter of principle we place them on a higher plane than our material well-being. Even in parts of the world where the need to improve nutrition and literacy and human life expectancy is urgent, there is often a grudging aspect to the recognition that achieving superior growth is a top priority. As a result, especially when faster growth would require sacrifice from entrenched constituencies with well-established interests, the political process often fails to muster the determination to press forward. The all too frequent outcome, in low- and high-income countries alike, is economic disappointment, and in some cases outright stagnation.

The root of the problem, I believe, is that our conventional thinking about economic growth fails to reflect the breadth of what growth, or its absence, means for a society. We recognize, of course, the advantages of a higher material standard of living, and we appreciate them. But moral thinking, in practically every known culture, enjoins us not to place undue emphasis on our material concerns. We are also increasingly aware that economic development—industrialization in particular, and more recently globalization—often brings undesirable side effects, like damage to the environment or the homogenization of what used to be distinctive cultures, and we have come to regard these matters too in moral terms. On both counts, we therefore think of economic growth in terms of material considerations *versus* moral ones: Do we have the right to burden future generations, or even other species, for our own material advantage? Will the emphasis we place on growth, or the actions we take to achieve it, compromise our moral integrity? We weigh material positives against moral negatives.

I believe this thinking is seriously, in some circumstances dangerously, incomplete. The value of a rising standard of living lies not just in the concrete improvements it brings to how individuals live but in how it shapes the social, political, and ultimately the moral character of a people.

Economic growth—meaning a rising standard of living for the clear majority of citizens—more often than not fosters greater opportunity, tolerance of diversity, social mobility, commitment to fairness, and dedication to democracy. Ever since the Enlightenment, Western thinking has regarded each of these tendencies positively, and in explicitly moral terms.

Even societies that have already made great advances in these very dimensions, for example most of today's Western democracies, are more likely to make still further progress when their living standards rise. But when living standards stagnate or decline, most societies make little if any progress toward any of these goals, and in all too many instances they plainly retrogress. As we shall see, many countries with highly developed economies, including America, have experienced alternating eras of economic growth and stagnation in which their democratic values have strengthened or weakened accordingly.

How the citizens of any country think about economic growth, and what actions they take in consequence, is therefore a matter of far broader importance than we conventionally assume. In many countries today, even the most basic qualities of any society—democracy or dictatorship, tolerance or ethnic hatred and violence, widespread opportunity or economic oligarchy—remain in flux. In some countries where there is now a democracy, it is still new and therefore fragile. Because of the link between rising or falling living standards and just these aspects of social and political development, the absence of growth in so many of what we usually call "developing economies," even though many of them are not actually developing, threatens their prospects in ways that standard measures of national income do not even suggest. But the same concern applies, albeit in a more subtle way, to mature democracies as well.

Even in America, I believe, the quality of our democracy—more fundamentally, the moral character of American society—is similarly at risk. The central economic question for the United States at the outset of the twenty-first century is whether the nation in the generation ahead will again achieve increasing prosperity, as in the decades immediately following World War II, or lapse back into the stagnation of living standards for the majority of our citizens that persisted from the early 1970s until the early 1990s. And the more important question that then follows is how these different economic paths would affect our democratic political institutions and the broader character of our society. As the economic historian Alexander Gerschenkron once observed, "even a long democratic history does not necessarily immunize a country from becoming a 'democracy without democrats.' "[2] And as we shall see from our own experience as well as that of other countries, merely being rich is no bar to a society's retreat into rigidity and intolerance once enough of its citizens lose the sense that they are getting ahead.

The familiar balancing of material positives against moral negatives when we discuss economic growth is therefore a false choice, and the parallel assumption, that how we value material versus moral concerns neatly maps into whether we should eagerly embrace economic growth or temper our enthusiasm for it, is wrong as well. Economic growth bears moral benefits as well, and when we debate the often hard decisions that inevitably arise—in choosing economic policies that either encourage growth or retard it, and even in our reactions to the growth that takes place apart from the push or pull of public policy—it is important that we take these moral positives into account.

Especially in a work focused on the positive link between economic growth and social and political progress, it may seem strange to think that America, now so preeminent across the world in economic terms, faces any significant threat in this regard. One country after another—including even China and Singapore, which thus far have hesitated to liberalize politically—has adopted American approaches to the management of its economy, based on free enterprise, private initiative, and mobile capital. Why would ongoing economic growth not therefore herald an era of further social and political progress that would reinforce the openness of American society and otherwise strengthen and broaden American democracy?

One concern is simply that the robust growth of the latter half of the 1990s may prove to have been only a temporary interlude, a "bubble" as many disappointed stock market investors now regard it, between the stagnation that dominated most of the final quarter of the twentieth century and further stagnation yet to come. But even the prosperity that America experienced in the late 1990s bypassed large parts, in some important dimensions a clear majority, of the country's citizens. Jobs were plentiful, but too many provided poor wages, little if any training, and no opportunity for advancement.

Economic progress needs to be broadly based if it is to foster social and political progress. That progress requires the positive experience of a sufficiently broad cross section of a country's population to shape the national mood and direction. But except for a brief period in the late 1990s, most of the fruits of the last three decades of economic growth in the United States have accrued to only a small slice of the American population. Nor was that short period of more widespread prosperity sufficient to allow most American families to make up for the economic stagnation or outright decline they endured during previous years. After allowing for higher prices, the average worker in American business in 2004 made 16 percent *less* each week than thirty-plus years earlier.[3] For most Americans, the reward for work today is well below what it used to be.

With more and more two-earner households, and more individuals holding two jobs, most *families'* incomes have more than held their ground. But nearly all of the gain realized over these last three decades came only in the burst of strong growth in the late 1990s. Despite mostly low unemployment, and some modest growth in the U.S. gross domestic product—

and despite the increased prevalence of two-earner families and two-job workers—the median family's income made little gain beyond inflation from the early 1970s to the early 1990s.4 For fully two decades most Americans were not getting ahead economically, and many of those who did were increasingly hard-pressed to keep up even their meager progress. This was not the kind of broadly based increase in living standards that we normally conceive as "economic growth."

Even for many families in the country's large middle-class majority, economic prospects have become increasingly precarious in recent decades. Young men entering the American job force in the 1970s started off their working careers earning two-thirds more, on average, than what their fathers' generation had made starting out in the 1950s. By the early 1990s young workers were starting out at one-fourth *less* than what their parents' generation had earned.5

It is not surprising, therefore, that even as they expressed confidence that the U.S. economy would continue to expand, throughout this period Americans in record numbers also said they had no sense of getting ahead personally and that they feared for their children's financial future. Even in the late 1990s, with the surge in both the economy and the stock market in full bloom, more than half of all Americans surveyed said they agreed that "The American dream has become impossible for most people to achieve." More than two-thirds said they thought that goal would become still harder to attain over the next generation.6

The disappointment so many Americans felt at failing to achieve greater advances—and that many feel today—is grounded in hard reality. So is the sense of many young Americans that their prospects are poor even at times when the economy is strong. Our citizens applaud the American economy, especially in years when it prospers, yet even then they fear that the end of the American dream lies ahead. They do so because in the last generation so many have failed to experience that dream in their own lives.

The consequence of the stagnation that lasted from the mid-1970s until the mid-1990s was, in numerous dimensions, a fraying of America's social fabric. It was no coincidence that during this period popular antipathy to immigrants resurfaced to an extent not known in the United States since before World War II, and in some respects not since the 1880s when intense nativism spread in response to huge immigration at a time of protracted economic distress. It was not an accident that after three decades of progress toward bringing the country's African-American minority into the mainstream, public opposition forced a rolling retreat from affirmative action programs. It was not mere happenstance that, for a while, white supremacist groups were more active and visible than at any time since the 1930s, anti-government private "militias" flourished as never before, and all the while many of our elected political leaders were reluctant to criticize such groups publicly even as church burnings, domestic terrorist attacks, and armed standoffs with law enforcement authorities regularly made headlines. Nor was it coincidental that the effort to "end welfare as we know it"—a widely shared goal, albeit for different reasons among different constituencies—often displayed a vindictive spirit that was highly uncharacteristic of America in the postwar era.

With the return of economic advance for the majority of Americans in the mid-1990s, many of these deplorable tendencies began to abate. In the 2000 and 2004 presidential campaigns, for example, neither anti-immigrant rhetoric nor resistance to affirmative action played anything like the role seen in the elections in 1996 and especially 1992. While hate groups and anti-government militias have not disappeared, they have again retreated toward the periphery of the nation's consciousness. Even so, much of the legacy of those two decades of stagnation remains. While it has become commonplace to talk of the importance of "civil society," many thoughtful observers increasingly question the vitality in today's America of the attitudes and institutions that compose it.7 Even our public political discourse has lately lost much of its admittedly sparse civility, foundering on personal charges, investigations, and reverberating recrimination.

It would be foolish to pretend that all these disturbing developments were merely the product of economic forces. Social and political phenomena are complex, and most have many causes. In the 1960s, for example, conventional thinking in the United States interpreted the wave of student uprisings on college campuses across the country as a protest against the Vietnam War. No doubt it was, in part. That simple view failed, however, to explain why other countries not involved in Vietnam had much the same experience (in some cases, for example France, even more so) at just the same time. The political and social changes that have been underway in America in our era have multiple roots as well.

But it would be equally foolish to ignore the effects of two decades of economic stagnation for a majority of the nation's citizens in bringing these changes about. And it would be complacent not to be concerned now that the economy's prospects are in question once again. As we shall see, the history of each of the large Western democracies—America, Britain, France, and Germany—is replete with instances in which just this kind of turn away from openness and tolerance, and often the weakening of democratic political institutions, followed in the wake of economic stagnation that diminished people's confidence in a better future. In many parts of Europe, the social and political consequences of the transition from the postwar economic miracle to today's nagging "Eurosclerosis" are all too evident.

In some eras, both in our own history and in that of these other countries, episodes of rigidity and intolerance have been much more intense and have borne far more serious consequences than anything we have seen recently. But then some past eras of stagnation or retreat in living standards have been much more pronounced as well. At the same time, periods of economic expansion in America and elsewhere, during which most citizens had reason to be optimistic, have also witnessed greater openness, tolerance, and democracy. To repeat: such advances occur for many reasons. But the effect of economic growth versus stagnation is an important and often central part of the story.

I believe that the rising intolerance and incivility and the eroding generosity and openness that have marked important aspects of American society in the recent past have been, in significant part, a consequence of the stagnation of American middle-class living standards during much of the last quarter of the twentieth century. If the United States can return to the rapid and more broadly based growth that the country experienced during the first few decades after World War II—or, more recently, the latter half of the 1990s—over time these unfortunate political and social trends will continue to abate. If our growth falters, however, or if we merely continue with slower growth that benefits only a minority of our citizens, the deterioration of American society will, I fear, worsen once more.

The importance of the connection between economic growth and social and political progress, and the consequent concern for what will happen if living standards fail to improve, are not limited to America and other countries that already have high incomes and established democracies. The main story of the last two decades throughout the developing world, including many countries that used to be either member states of the Soviet Union or close Soviet dependencies, has been the parallel advance of economic growth and political democracy. As recently as the 1970s, fewer than fifty countries had the kind of civil liberties and political institutions that we normally associate with freedom and democracy. By the close of the twentieth century there were nearly ninety.[8]

Not surprisingly, the countries where this movement toward freedom and democracy has been most successful have, more often than not, been countries where average incomes have risen during these years. As we shall

see, the specific context of developing economies creates several reasons for
this to be so. To be sure, there are highly visible exceptions—China, Singapore, and Saudi Arabia, to name just a few—and discrete transitions in
countries' political systems usually exhibit other complexities as well. But
taken as a whole, the experience of the developing world during the last two
decades, indeed since World War II, is clearly more consistent with a positive connection between economic growth and democratization than with
the opposite.

For just this reason, concern that the robust expansion many developing countries have enjoyed for some years may abate is likewise not a matter
of economics alone. We know that new democracies are fragile democracies. They have neither the appeal of historical tradition nor much record of
concrete accomplishments to give them legitimacy in the eyes of what may
still be a skeptical citizenry. Economic growth, or its absence, often plays a
significant role in spawning not only progress from dictatorship to democracy but also the overthrow of democracies by new dictatorships.

It is too soon to judge whether the financial crisis that beset some of the
most successful developing economies in Asia and Latin America at the end
of the 1990s marked the beginning of a new era of slower growth—due, for
example, to global excess capacity in many of the industries in which these
economies compete—or merely a warning to avoid risky financing structures and eliminate wasteful corruption. Either way, what should be clear
is that the risks these countries face, if their growth in the early decades of
this century is disappointing, are as much political and social as they are
economic. The brutal violence suddenly inflicted on Indonesia's Chinese
minority when that country's economy stumbled was only one demonstration of the dangers inherent in falling incomes. For the same reason, the
frequently expressed fears of what an economic collapse would mean for the
still tenuous and highly imperfect democracy in Russia also deserve to be
taken seriously.

Concerns of a graver nature surround those "developing countries"
where there is little actual economic development. In much of Africa, but
elsewhere as well, living standards are stagnant or declining. In many such
countries the familiar claim is that proper institutions—rule of law, transparency, stable government that is not corrupt—must be in place before
economic advance is feasible. But if it takes economic growth to make these
institutions viable (they go along with a democratic society although they
are not identical to it), seeking to implant them artificially in a stagnant
economy is likely to prove fruitless.

The link between economic growth and social and political progress in the developing world has yet other practical implications as well. For example, the continuing absence of political democracy and basic personal freedoms in China has deeply troubled many observers in the West. Until China gained admission to the World Trade Organization, in 2002, these concerns regularly gave rise in the United States to debate on whether to trade with China on a "Most Favored Nation" basis. They still cause questions about whether to give Chinese firms advanced American technology, or let them buy an American oil company. Both sides in this debate share the same objective: to foster China's political liberalization. How to do so, however, remains the focus of intense disagreement.

But if a rising standard of living leads a society's political and social institutions to gravitate toward openness and democracy—as the evidence mostly shows—then as long as China continues its recent economic expansion, Chinese citizens will eventually enjoy greater political democracy together with the personal freedoms that democracy brings. Since 1978, when Deng Xiaoping's economic reforms began, the Chinese have seen a sevenfold increase in their material standard of living.[9] The improvement in nutrition, housing, sanitation, and transportation has been dramatic, while the freedom of Chinese citizens to make *economic* choices—where to work, what to buy, whether to start a business—is already far broader than it was. With continued economic advance (the average Chinese standard of living is still only one-eighth that in the United States), broader freedom to make political choices too will probably follow. Indeed, an important implication of the idea that it is in significant part the *growth* rather than just the level of people's living standards that matters for this purpose is that the countries in the developing world whose economies are actually developing, like China, will not have to wait until they achieve Western-level incomes before they experience significant political and social liberalization.

If this conclusion seems optimistic, that is because it is. Traditional lines of Western thinking that have emphasized a connection between material progress and moral progress (as the philosophers of the Enlightenment conceived it) have always embodied a powerful optimism about the human enterprise. The real dangers that accompany stagnating incomes notwithstanding, many of the predictions as well as the implications for public policy that follow from this connection encourage such optimism and are, in turn, sustained by it.

In arguing that rising living standards nurture positive changes in political institutions and social attitudes, it is important to be clear that practically nobody opposes economic growth per se. Rather, a seriously credible warning of the end of economic growth would prompt real consternation, as indeed occurred in the wake of the energy price increases of the 1970s and, far more so, during the depression of the 1930s.

Greater affluence means, among many other things, better food, bigger houses, more travel, and improved medical care. It means that more people can afford a better education. It may also mean, as it did in most Western countries during the twentieth century, a shorter workweek, which allows more time for family and friends. Moreover, these material benefits of rising incomes accrue not just to individuals and their families but to communities and even entire countries. Greater affluence can also mean better schools, more parks and museums, and larger concert halls and sports arenas, not to mention more leisure to enjoy these public facilities. A rising average income allows a country to project its national interest abroad, or send a man to the moon.

All these advantages, however, lie mostly in the material realm, and we have always been reluctant to advance material concerns to the highest plane in our value system. Praise for the ascetic life, and admiration for those who practice self-denial, has been a continual theme in the religions of both West and East. So have warnings about the dangers to man's spiritual well-being that follow from devotion to money and luxury, or, in some views, merely from wealth itself. Even the aristocratic and Romantic traditions, which rest on the clear presumption of having wealth, are nonetheless dismissive of efforts to pursue it.

Further, even when people plainly acknowledge that more is more, less is less, and more is better, economic growth rarely means simply more. The dynamic process that allows living standards to rise brings other changes as well. More is more, but more is also different. The qualitative changes that accompany economic growth—including changes in work arrangements, in power structures, in our relationship to the natural environment—have nearly always generated resistance. The anti-globalization protests in the streets of Seattle, Genoa, and Washington, D.C., and even on the outskirts of Davos, reflect a very long-standing line of thinking.

More than two centuries ago, as Europe was embarking on its industrial revolution and Adam Smith and his contemporaries were analyzing and celebrating the forces that create "the wealth of nations," Jean-Jacques Rousseau instead admired the "noble savage," arguing that mankind's golden age had occurred not only before industrialization but before the advent of settled agriculture. Seventy-five years later, as prominent Victorians were hailing the "age of improvement," Karl Marx observed the raw hardships that advancing industrialization had imposed on workers and their families, and devised an economic theory of how matters might (and in his mind, would) become better, together with a political program for bringing that supposedly better world into existence. Although communism is now mostly a relic where it exists at all, romantic socialism, combining strains of Marx and Rousseau, continues to attract adherents. So do fundamentalist movements that celebrate the presumed purity of pre-industrial society.

The Club of Rome's influential *Limits to Growth* report and the "Small Is Beautiful" counterculture of the 1970s, mounting concerns over the impact on the environment of economic expansion, especially since the 1980s, and most recently the anti-globalization movement mounted in opposition to the World Trade Organization and against foreign investment more generally, are all echoes of the same theme that are thoroughly familiar today. Environmental concerns in particular have expanded from their initial focus on the air and water to encompass noise pollution, urban congestion, and such fundamental issues as the depletion of nonrenewable resources and the extinction of species. In recent years the force of competition in global markets and the turmoil of an unsettled world financial system have inflicted visible hardships on large numbers of people both in the developing world and in countries that are already industrialized, just as they have created opportunities and given advancement to many others. As in the past, the plight of those who are affected adversely—Indonesians who faced higher food prices when their currency plunged, Argentinians who found their savings blocked when the country's banking system collapsed, textile workers throughout the developing world who cannot compete with low-cost factory production in China—has led not just to calls for reform of the underpinnings of economic growth but to outright opposition.

What marks all these forms of resistance to the undesirable side effects of economic expansion or of the globalization of economic growth is that, just like earlier strands of religious thinking, in each case they are accompanied by a distinctly moral overtone. Ever larger segments of our society accept that it is not just economically foolish but morally wrong for one generation to use up a disproportionate share of the world's forests, or coal, or oil reserves, or to deplete the ozone or alter the earth's climate by filling the atmosphere with greenhouse gases. While pleas on behalf of biological diversity sometimes appeal to practical notions like the potential use of yet-to-be-discovered plants for medicinal purposes, we also increasingly question our moral right to extinguish other species. Opposition to the global spread of markets is often couched as much in terms of the moral emptiness of consumerism as the tangible hardships sometimes imposed by world competition and unstable financial systems.

But if a rising standard of living makes a society more open and tolerant and democratic, and perhaps also more prudent in behalf of generations to come, then it is simply not true that moral considerations argue wholly against economic growth. Growth is valuable not only for our material improvement but also for how it affects our social attitudes and our political institutions—in other words, our society's *moral* character, in the term favored by the Enlightenment thinkers from whom so many of our views on openness, tolerance, and democracy have sprung. For reasons that we shall explore, the attitude of people toward themselves, toward their fellow citizens, and toward their society as a whole is different when their living standard is rising than when it is stagnant or falling. It is likewise different when they view their prospects and their children's with confidence as opposed to looking ahead with anxiety or even fear. When the attitudes of the broad majority of citizens are shaped by a rising standard of living, over time that difference usually leads to the positive development of—to use again the language of the Enlightenment—a society's moral character.

Hence questions about economic growth are not a matter of material *versus* moral values. Yes, economic growth often does have undesirable effects, like the disruption of traditional cultures and damage to the environment, and yes, some of these are a proper moral concern that we are right to take into account. But economic growth bears social and political consequences that are morally beneficial as well. Especially for purposes of evaluating different courses for public policy, it is important that we take into account not just the familiar moral negatives but these moral positives as well.

It is no less essential to understand the proper relationship between public policies and private initiatives regarding economic growth. Here, too, positive *moral* consequences of rising living standards significantly change the story.

A commonly held view is that government policy should try, insofar as it can, to avoid interfering with private economic initiative: the expectation of greater profit is ample incentive for a firm to expand production, or build a new factory, while the prospect of higher wages is likewise sufficient to encourage workers to seek out training or invest in their own education. The same reasoning applies to private decisions on saving, starting a new business, or adopting a new technology. The best that government can do (so the story goes) is minimize the extent to which taxes, or safety regulations, or restrictions imposed for the sake of national security blunt these market incentives. The "right" pace of economic growth is whatever the market—that is, the aggregate of all private decisions—would deliver on its own.

But this familiar view too is seriously incomplete. To the extent that economic growth brings not only higher private incomes but also greater openness, tolerance, and democracy—benefits we value but that the market does not price—and to the extent that these unpriced benefits outweigh any unpriced harm that might ensue, market forces alone will systematically provide too little growth. Calling for government to stand aside while the market determines our economic growth ignores the vital role of public policy: the right rate of economic growth is greater than the purely market-determined rate, and the role of government policy is to foster it.

As we shall see in some detail for the United States, there are many ways by which the government can foster economic growth, given the political will to carry out such policies. Except for a few years in the late 1990s, we have been systematically under-investing in our factories and productive equipment. Just as important, we under-invest in our nation's human resources and we misuse what we do invest. Removing these impediments to our growth would be highly desirable. But finding the will to do so depends, in part, on popular understanding of why growth is so important in the first place.

It would be a mistake, however, to believe that only market incentives and government economic policies are important for achieving economic growth and with it the positive influence on social and political development that follows from rising living standards. While economic growth makes a society more open, tolerant, and democratic, such societies are in turn better able to encourage enterprise and creativity and hence to achieve ever greater economic prosperity. Alexis de Tocqueville, visiting America in the 1830s, remarked at length on how the openness of this new democratic society seemed to spur effort: economic advance was open to all (he was thinking only of white males), and in a classless society rising economically meant rising socially. The resulting *opportunity* to achieve and advance, Tocqueville observed, created in turn a sense of *obligation* to strive toward that end. As we look back nearly two centuries later, it is also self-evident that removing forms of discrimination that once blocked significant segments of the population from contributing their efforts has further enabled the American economy to harness its labor resources and its brainpower. On both counts, the openness of our society has helped foster our economic advance.

America is perhaps the preeminent historical example of such reciprocity between social and political openness and economic growth. Taken as a whole, our nation's history has predominantly been a mutually reinforcing process of economic advance (as we shall see, sometimes interrupted) and expanding freedom (also sometimes interrupted). The less fortunate experience of some other countries, most notably those in sub-Saharan Africa since the end of the colonial period, suggests the same reciprocity at work but in the opposite direction. Many governments there were at least formally democracies when the colonial powers departed, but in time they became corrupt and oppressive dictatorships. In parallel, what had been reasonably functioning economies stagnated and then declined.

As we shall see, however, while the evidence suggests that economic growth usually fosters democracy and all this entails, it is less clear that open societies necessarily experience superior economic growth by virtue of their democratic practice. A mobile society, with opportunity for all, obviously encourages economic enterprise and initiative. But democracy is often contentious, even chaotic, and not every aspect of the untidy process of self-government is conducive to economic expansion. Experience clearly suggests that the *absence* of democratic freedoms *impedes* economic growth, and that the resulting stagnation in turn makes a society even more intolerant and undemocratic. The evidence to date suggests that this kind of vicious circle, as has occurred in some African countries, for example, is more powerful than the analogous virtuous circle in which growth and democracy keep reinforcing each other.

A further potentially important influence on economic growth—and one that is especially pertinent to the argument advanced here about the broader consequences of rising living standards—is a society's moral ethic. When people decide how much to save, what size house to buy, whether to accept a new job, or whether to get more education, they normally respond not just to personal economic incentives narrowly construed but to established moral values and social presumptions. Businesses too are rarely the single-minded profit maximizers portrayed in economics textbooks. Whether companies regularly launch new initiatives, whether they act with loyalty to their workers and respect toward their communities, even whether they obey the law, also reflects the broader culture of which they are a part. All societies develop moral norms—against violence, favoring family bonds, against theft, in favor of truthfulness—as a partial substitute for what would otherwise be hopelessly pervasive regulation aimed at getting people to behave in ways that may be of little or no direct benefit to themselves but nonetheless make everyone better off. Such norms are no less important in the economic sphere.

Indeed, they may be more so. Laws and regulations are typically less effective when the desired behavior requires *taking* initiative or action, as opposed to *refraining* from unwanted action. Even in highly developed, well-organized societies, it is far easier to devise laws that discourage murder and theft than laws that encourage helpfulness to one's neighbors. Especially when it comes to the creative impulse that results in enhanced economic productivity, laws and regulations are particularly useless. As we have learned from many countries' experience, regulations limiting how much sulfurous smoke manufacturers can release into the air, or restricting the pollutants we can dump into the water, are often reasonably effective. By contrast, a law requiring businesses to innovate, or otherwise become more productive, would be pointless.

It is not surprising, therefore, that many cultures, especially Western societies in the modern era, have developed *moral* presumptions in favor of precisely those aspects of personal behavior that lead to greater productivity and economic growth. Hard work, diligence, patience, discipline, and a sense of obligation to fulfill our commitments clearly make us more productive economically. Thriftiness fosters saving, which enhances our productivity by making capital investment possible. Education likewise increases our individual capabilities as well as our stock of public knowledge. Such behavior brings benefits that accrue directly to those who conduct themselves in that way, and we value them partly on that ground. But in each case our society also regards these qualities, or actions, as *morally* worthwhile.

A hundred years ago Max Weber argued that what he called "the Protestant ethic"—an ethic in the sense of an inner moral attitude—had importantly spurred the development of capitalist economic growth by fostering just these aspects of personal behavior. Weber overlooked other religious and ethnic groups (Jews and overseas Chinese, to cite just two) who share many of the attitudes toward personal behavior, and much of the economic success, that he associated with northern European Protestants. Moreover, even for the European Protestants whom Weber studied, there is reason to wonder what was influencing what in the rich interplay between religious and economic developments. Many other influences, of course, quite apart from ethical norms, affect economic growth as well. But the fundamental point remains: that certain characteristics of personal behavior are important for economic growth, and that when these characteristics acquire moral status the resulting ethic encourages people to behave accordingly.

For our society's moral values to nurture the behavior that spurs its economic growth seems especially apt if, as I argue here, rising living standards in turn make our society more open, tolerant, and democratic. Because we value these qualities in moral terms rather than market terms, market forces on their own produce insufficient growth. Some further impetus is required. Weber argued that familiar moral principles foster economic growth. My argument here goes further: economic growth not only relies upon moral impetus, it also has positive moral *consequences*. That we may depend at least in part on moral means to satisfy our moral ends, even when the link that connects the two is economic, has a particularly satisfying resonance.

Chapter 2

Perspectives from the Enlightenment and Its Roots

There are four distinct states which mankind pass thro: — 1st, the Age of Hunters; 2dly, the Age of Shepherds; 3dly, the Age of Agriculture; and 4thly, the Age of Commerce. . . . It is easy to see that in these severall ages of society the laws and regulations with regard to property must be very different.

ADAM SMITH
Lectures on Jurisprudence[1]

[T]he spirit of commerce brings with it the spirit of frugality, economy, moderation, work, wisdom, tranquility, order, and rule. . . . [E]verywhere there is commerce, there are gentle mores.

MONTESQUIEU
The Spirit of the Laws[2]

In the Indian summer days of late September 1850, Londoners saw a wondrous structure rising up on the edge of Hyde Park: a building, mostly of glass and steel, that eventually covered seventeen acres and in parts ascended to a height of over one hundred feet. The Crystal Palace, built specially to house the Great Exhibition of arts and manufactures from Britain and other nations, opened on May 1, 1851. And on display inside, in keeping with the marvel of engineering that proudly housed them, were mostly—to put the matter bluntly—gadgets: tiny scissors and a penknife with fifty-one blades; centrifugal pumps and ornamental street lamps; medical instruments, agricultural implements, and safety devices for coal miners; marine engines, locomotives, and a "Great Hydraulic Press." There was even a "Model Dwelling House" consisting of four self-contained flats, designed personally by Prince Albert, the Great Exhibition's royal patron and guiding spirit.[3]

All of these exhibits served to demonstrate the myriad ways in which advancing technology had improved the everyday lives of British subjects, as well as citizens of other lands throughout the world, during the first half of the nineteenth century. But more than that, as everyone also understood, the Great Exhibition and especially the Crystal Palace itself were an exuberant celebration of the idea—indeed, the ideal—not just of scientific and therefore material progress but, far more important, of progress in social, civic, and moral affairs as well. A giant olive tree planted inside the Crystal Palace symbolized the further extension of this progress to the establishment of world peace.

Not long after the Crystal Palace exhibition, the same confidence that new technology not only was raising people's living standards but in so doing was improving their lives in more fundamental ways was on display in America as well. The 1876 Centennial Exhibition in Philadelphia showed off the newest advances in communication and transportation: essential ingredients in the effort, then in full vigor, to build a unified nation spanning a continent three thousand miles across. So too did the 1893 World's Columbian Exhibition, held in Chicago—in the midst of an economic depression, as we shall see—to mark the 400th anniversary of Columbus's arrival in the New World. Along with such outstanding Midway attractions as the world's first Ferris wheel (designed especially for the Chicago exhibition by a young engineer from Pittsburgh with the appropriately patriotic name George Washington Ferris), the Syrian-born dancer popularly known as "Little Egypt," and scientific novelties like Charles Yerkes's telescope and Thomas Edison's Kinetoscope (the forerunner of the modern motion picture camera), the Columbian Exposition prominently displayed Pullman locomotives, American Bell telephones (visitors to the exhibition witnessed the first long-distance call from the Midwest to the East Coast), and the first all-electric kitchen.[4]

Such ideas were hardly limited to the English-speaking world. Just as

Britain's Crystal Palace had its Great Hydraulic Press, and America's Centennial Exhibition its steam engine that powered all of the devices in Machinery Hall, the central item on display at the Paris Exhibition of 1900 was a giant dynamo, forty feet tall. Henry Adams, who had observed at first hand much of the development of both America and Europe in the latter half of the nineteenth century, described this colossus in his autobiography as "a symbol of infinity," "ultimate energy." More than that, Adams wrote, it was "a moral force. . . . The planet itself seemed less impressive, in its old-fashioned, deliberate, annual or daily revolution, than this huge wheel, revolving within arm's-length at some vertiginous speed. . . . Before the end, one began to pray to it."5

Despite the shock of World War I and the trials of the Great Depression, the same ideal of technological progress giving rise to human progress in broader dimensions was likewise readily visible at the 1939 New York World's Fair and, even more so (not surprisingly, in the aftermath of World War II), its successor held in 1964 in Flushing Meadows. At the 1964 fair, any visitor who spent more than just a few minutes in the "Progress Pavilion" sponsored by the General Electric Company clearly sensed that the progress being celebrated extended far beyond the televisions, toasters, vacuum cleaners, and the host of other physical objects on display. Similarly, when Ronald Reagan, evolving from his career as an actor, appeared on television in GE commercials proclaiming "Progress is our most important product," most American viewers understood that he was associating the company's contribution to society with more than just the products it manufactured and sold.

Today the same presumption of a connection running from technological progress to material progress to progress in more fundamental, indeed moral dimensions of human life is evident at Disney World's EPCOT (the acronym stands for Experimental Prototype Community of Tomorrow) in Orlando, Florida. At Disney World, however, the physical symbolism achieves yet further resonance. Spaceship Earth, an eighteen-story-tall geodesic sphere covered in silver, houses a ride through the history of communication. The hydroponics ride displays techniques for growing edible plants in water. The juxtaposition of these and other extravaganzas of scientific futurism with the nineteenth-century-like Main Street and Frontierland and the fairytale Fantasyland, in Disney's nearby Magic Kingdom—all linked by a mass transit monorail that is itself an important part of the overall effect—manages to celebrate simultaneously both the traditional belief in the moral value of progress and the nostalgia for a vanishing past that so often accompanies that belief.

The heady days of the Crystal Palace and of America's Centennial Exhibition may have been the high tide of the Western world's belief in the *inevitability* of progress, but this period was certainly not the origin of the *idea* of progress, nor was it the first time a society had concluded that its material and moral advancement were linked. The concept of human progress, including the belief that progress in one dimension is related to progress in another, has a well-established place in traditional Western thinking.

Faith in progress has hardly been a constant. At times during the last century, it has become commonplace, even fashionable, to deride the very notion of progress. This was many thoughtful people's response to the horrors of two world wars as well as the Nazi Holocaust. More recently, a different but in some ways parallel skepticism about the idea of progress has grown out of the increased awareness of environmental consequences of economic development, fears of depleted resources, and the tensions associated with the new economic globalization. But even these shifts in the public mood have themselves been, in no little part, a response to readily visible economic disappointments, further illustrating the power of changing material circumstances to influence not only prevailing attitudes and institutions but even how people view their society's fundamental evolution.

Belief in one or another form of progress, and even the notion that different aspects of progress might be somehow related, have appeared and reappeared in Western civilization for a very long time.[6] But the specific idea that rising living standards cause public attitudes and political institutions to evolve in ways that improve the moral character of the society, together with some concrete explanation of how this process comes about, was primarily a product of the remarkable efflorescence of new thinking in the eighteenth century that those who observed it soon came to call the Enlightenment.*

Inspired by the ongoing series of scientific advances that had begun

---

*The reverse idea—that positive moral conduct leads to favorable economic outcomes—is much older. An obvious early example, with the causal process attributed to divine intervention, is from Deuteronomy (11:13–15): "If you will earnestly heed the commandments I give you this day, to love the Lord your God and to serve Him with all your heart and all your soul, then I will favor your land with rain at the proper season—rain in autumn and rain in spring—and you will have an ample harvest of grain and wine and oil. I will assure abundance in the field for your cattle. You will eat to contentment."

during the Renaissance, fascinated with the unfolding discovery of entire new continents inhabited by "exotic" peoples, and keenly aware of the revolution in economic production and organization that was just getting under way in their own time, Enlightenment thinkers could not help but address the notion of progress. And when they did, the questions foremost in their minds often bore directly on what the economic changes then gaining momentum all around them meant for society more broadly: Was further progress also in store for government institutions and social relationships? Does progress, whether economic or political or social, continue indefinitely, or is there a limit, perhaps corresponding to the concept of the millennium in familiar religious doctrines (although many of the most prominent thinkers of the time were not particularly religious men)? Above all, is progress inevitable? And if not, what does a society, or even an entire civilization, have to do to achieve it?

The same questions are no less important today. Indeed, in light of the failure of confidence that global economic tensions as well as internal strains within our own society have brought, they may well be more so. As we shall see, there is good reason to think that economic growth figures centrally in the answers. But to arrive at a specific, coherent idea linking progress in one realm to progress in others, the Enlightenment figures who addressed these questions began with something else: "science." As the Crystal Palace exhibition and its many successors suggest, the role of expanding knowledge in accounting for nearly all dimensions of human progress has remained central in Western thinking ever since.

Today most citizens of economically advanced countries, if asked for evidence demonstrating that people are now better off in some fundamental sense than in earlier times, would probably point first to scientific advances and especially to the achievements of modern medicine. Diseases like smallpox, tuberculosis, and polio, which within living memory killed or maimed millions, are now largely under control or even eliminated. Since the discovery of penicillin and other modern-era drugs, countless infections that were life-threatening have shrunk to the level of minor inconveniences. (Economic historian David Landes began his classic treatise, *The Wealth and Poverty of Nations*, with the vignette of Nathan Rothschild, then "probably the richest man in the world," dying of just such an ordinary infection in 1836.)[7] Surgery now repairs once deadly bodily damage like a ruptured appendix or a blocked artery, and often successfully removes malignant tumors, while treatments like radiation and chemotherapy can sometimes overcome other cancers. Still other medications allow patients to live with the symptoms of illnesses that remain resistant to cure (Parkinson's disease and Crohn's disease, for example). Equally important, within just the last generation advancing knowledge has shown how to reduce the risk of remaining major killers like heart disease, and even some forms of cancer, simply by changing one's everyday routine.

In the eighteenth century virtually all of these medical advances still lay in the future. But the thinkers of the Enlightenment drew much of their basic confidence in the existence and inevitability of human progress from the undeniable advance of knowledge generated by scientific discoveries visible in their own day. It was then barely 200 years since Copernicus had revolutionized man's concept of the universe by showing that the earth revolved around the sun rather than vice versa. Early in the seventeenth century Galileo's telescope had literally provided an entirely new view of the moon, and of earth's fellow planets, and soon afterward Leeuwenhoek's microscope had done the same for the world of tiny organisms. By the beginning of the eighteenth century, Newton had developed and systematized theories of such fundamental yet everyday phenomena as motion, gravity, and light. Along with Leibniz, he had also taken mathematics, the oldest and purest form of exact scientific thinking, to the point of developing modern calculus. And along the way, numerous pioneers—among them Boyle, Huygens, Kepler, Pascal, Halley, and Hooke—had achieved discoveries that today still rank among the great advances in science and mathematics.

The thinkers of the mid-eighteenth century also stood barely 250 years from a time when the existence of the Americas was unsuspected among Europeans and even knowledge of China and Japan was more a matter of rumor than substantiated observation. Although Columbus had crossed the Atlantic before 1500, and Magellan sailed from the Atlantic into the Pacific in 1520, the exploration and discovery of the New World as well as Africa, the Pacific, and East Asia continued on for centuries. Indeed, Captain James Cook's discovery of Australia in 1770 was a contemporary event for most of the major Enlightenment figures. Moreover, it was clear at the time that much still remained unknown. The first attempt to cross and systematically map the interior of the North American continent above the Rio Grande did not come until the Lewis and Clark expedition, just after the turn of the nineteenth century.

To be sure, many philosophers had long believed that knowledge expands over time. Greeks such as Aristotle and then Romans like Lucretius had written in explicit terms about the cumulative, progressive way in which the ideas advanced and discoveries made by one individual, or in one age, became the foundation for those that follow.[8] Early in the seventeenth century Francis Bacon's writings had focused squarely on the irreversible growth of scientific knowledge as the fountain of progress in the world, forcefully arguing that it was the possession of greater knowledge, not any change in nature or inborn abilities, that explained why people thought and acted differently than they had in earlier times. Soon after, René Descartes further argued that this all-important accumulation of knowledge was but the logical result of the application of rational thinking.[9] More than any other book or essay, Descartes' *Discourse* on the scientific method, first published in 1637, became a kind of philosophical handbook for thinkers not only in his own century but in the next as well, serving as their defining statement of faith in the powers of reason.

By the middle of the eighteenth century, people no longer had to take these ideas on faith. The series of dramatic discoveries that led up to and continued into their own time was proof enough of the value of the scientific method and of Descartes' expansive claims on behalf of "reason." It had also become clear that this advance in knowledge not only occurred in the realm of abstract thought but that many new discoveries and inventions also bore far-reaching practical consequences. Distant colonies and transoceanic trade had come to play a major role in European economic activity. New crops, most importantly the potato, had visibly increased the productivity of agriculture. Other crops that would not readily grow in European soil— sugar, cotton, tea, tobacco—were now widely available as imports.[10] At the same time, mechanical devices like Thomas Newcomen's steam engine, first introduced in 1712 and revolutionary for being driven by power other than wind, water, or human or animal muscle, were beginning to expand the manufacture of textiles and other consumer goods. New instruments, like John Harrison's clock that kept precise time at sea and thereby enabled sailors to calculate longitude, were revolutionizing navigation. The link between advancing knowledge and changes in the conduct of everyday life, especially including economic life, was easy for anyone to see.

Further, it was also clear that this enormous expansion of knowledge occurring in their own time was cumulative. Europeans now knew with certainty that the New World existed. Their knowledge of how to calculate longitude, or construct a steam engine, or grow hybrid crops, was not likely to disappear. As a result, insofar as key aspects of how their society functioned depended on this new knowledge, the society had become *permanently* different.[11]

Finally, for most of these eighteenth-century intellects, there was also no doubt that the direction of these historic changes driven by expanding knowledge was for the better. Even the vocabulary commonly used to describe what was happening—"discovery," "advancement," "progression," "improvement"—carried an immediately positive connotation. By the middle of the eighteenth century the notion of progress was evident even in the titles that the intellects of the day chose for what they wrote: "A Philosophical Review of the *Advances* of the Human Mind" (Turgot, 1750); "The *Progress* of Society in Europe" (James Robertson, 1759); "A View of Society in Europe, in Its *Progress* from Rudeness to Refinement" (Gilbert Stuart—the Scottish philosopher, not the American painter—1778); and, most famously, "Sketch for a Historical Picture of the *Progress* of the Human Mind" (Condorcet, 1795) (in each case, my italics).

But just how did all this turn into a theory that claimed a causal link from *economic* progress—or, to be complete, from scientific and economic progress—to positive change in the political institutions and social attitudes that the thinkers of this era regarded as the essence of the moral realm? To most of the Enlightenment thinkers, the fact that advances in human knowledge plainly bore implications for economic activity was interesting, but it was not the most important part of the story. The more compelling question was how the advance of knowledge and the resulting change in economic circumstances in turn affected the institutions and conduct of civil society more broadly. In the event, the Enlightenment thinkers developed one account of how economic change affected the society's institutional structure, including in particular its laws and governing institutions, and a separate explanation of how economic change also affected attitudes and behavior at the individual level.

Although other, more broadly conceptual influences on this line of inquiry were also at work in the background (as we shall see), the most significant spur to eighteenth-century speculation about how economic change might affect a society's political institutions was a line of questioning that grew out of the earlier discovery of the previously unknown American continents and, in particular, of the equally unknown peoples living there. The American natives had been an object of intense fascination from the very beginning of Europe's knowledge of the New World. Popular interest quickly focused on nearly every facet of their seemingly strange existence: their dress, racial features, weapons, housing, their exotic foods and use of tobacco, the size and degree of permanency of their settlements, and their ways of organizing and governing their communities. As time passed, the more superficial aspects of this fascination faded, but interest in the more substantive characteristics of the "Indians' " lives and society, including in particular their arrangements regarding property and governance, remained strong.[12] (The Indians' property arrangements were an especially important issue, with obvious implications for the moral validity of the Europeans' right to claim the new lands that they explored and settled.)

Knowledge of the American natives prompted the essential question of what relation these "new" peoples bore to the Europeans themselves; in particular whether, in them, the Europeans were getting a glimpse of their own past. Had the Europeans' own ancestors, at some point beyond either history or memory, lived like the latter-day native Americans? And if so, then what accounted for the progress—most Europeans had no doubt it was progress—of their own society from that earlier stage to its very different level of contemporary development?

By the eighteenth century it was accepted that, far enough back, Europeans probably had lived much like the American Indians of the current day—or, as John Locke nicely put it, "in the beginning all the World was *America.*"[13] (More specifically, the Indians' way of governing themselves "is still a Pattern of the first Ages in *Asia* and *Europe.*")[14] Hence speculation about the Indians was not merely an anthropological study motivated by curiosity about a wholly different society but also, in part, a historical inquiry into the origins of modern Europe. But what, then, might account for the transition from bands of hunters who presumably lived in small communities, mostly without property or permanent places of settlement, to the mighty civilizations of Greece and Rome, and on to the world of nation-states governed from grand eighteenth-century metropolises like London, Paris, Amsterdam, Madrid, Vienna, and Venice?

As not infrequently happens when a line of intellectual inquiry is of sufficiently broad interest, and the influences shaping how people approach it prevail widely, the answer to this question that developed through the successive contributions of any number of thinkers reached fruition at about the same time, and in almost the identical form, in the teaching of two individuals: Adam Smith, who was lecturing first at Edinburgh and then at the University of Glasgow, and Anne Robert Jacques Turgot, at the Sorbonne in Paris.[15] Working independently (although both presumably were influenced by the writings of the seventeenth-century German scholar Samuel Pufendorf), Smith and Turgot arrived at a theory that combined two key elements now so familiar that it almost seems odd to point to their origins in the thinking of specific individuals: First, they claimed that economic forces, primarily arising from expanding populations, tend to cause societies to evolve through a series of stages in which the main economic activity is initially hunting and gathering, then shepherding, then farming, and finally "commerce."[16] Second, they saw that these different forms of economic activity in turn create different needs that the society's political and legal institutions naturally adapt in order to meet. The theory posited by Smith and Turgot therefore placed the evolution of economic activity at the center of human society's ascent from primitive origins to advanced civilization.

Moreover, what made this novel idea a theory of progress, rather than merely a historical account of a sequence of events that had occurred, was the supposition that each of these distinct economic stages contained the mechanism leading to the next—once knowledge had adequately advanced—so that the resulting progression was a matter not of chance but necessity. In each case the driving force was economic scarcity, created by the pressure of expanding population against the limited productivity of land and other resources: hunting animals and gathering fruits and berries may have sufficed to feed small groups but in time the game ran thin, there were too few nearby bushes and trees to provide for everyone who needed to eat, and it became too difficult to keep moving the entire group from place to place in search of food. The natural solution, once the know-how was in hand, was to capture some animals and breed them. Hence shepherding began. After more time passed, however, the tension between expanding population and limited pasturage, again together with development of the required knowledge, led people to plant and tend crops rather than simply rely on whatever grew on its own. In this way agriculture developed. Finally, as both population and knowledge expanded further, people found it advantageous to engage in more specialized activities like blacksmithing, weaving, and carpentry. Doing so enabled them to be more productive, but no longer self-sufficient, and therefore they traded their wares. "Thus at last the age of commerce arises."[17]

In effect, Smith and Turgot had anticipated the problem of overpopulation that Thomas Malthus was to raise at the end of the eighteenth century.[18] But unlike Malthus, they were confident society would solve it. Indeed, in their thinking, pressure due to population growth was not a cause for despair but—always together with the advance of knowledge—the chief engine behind economic and consequently moral progress. For Smith in particular, the idea that this natural progression culminated with specialized production and therefore voluntary exchange, the two defining elements of what he and his contemporaries called "commerce," was especially important, since these two features of modern economic life opened the way for the "division of labor" that he so famously saw as the basis for continually advancing economic productivity.

Most important of all, however, was the fact that this process, driven by the underlying engine of economic change, necessarily led to political and social advance. Bands of wandering hunter-gatherers need few laws regarding property and little structure for governance. But with the advent of shepherding, questions like who owns which animals, and who has rights to what pastures, assume primary importance. Farming places yet greater burdens on social and legal systems, in that cultivating crops requires sustained effort over substantial periods of time and people therefore want to know what claim they will have on the eventual produce. (As several of Smith's and Turgot's contemporaries pointed out, it was not a coincidence that in the Roman pantheon Ceres was the goddess of agriculture and also of laws and lawgiving.) The need to protect domesticated animals or crops also places more burdens on the community's defenses, and hence creates a greater demand for common action.[19] Finally, commerce—again meaning the voluntary exchange of specialized goods produced by different people— in turn requires an even more complex legal and institutional infrastructure, typically involving standardized weights and measures, the enforcement of trading agreements, and (in order to avoid the cumbersome nature of barter transactions) the use of money. Moreover, at each stage of the entire process, as increasing economic productivity makes it possible for more and more people to live in one place, questions of government and social relations necessarily become more complex.

From the engine of economic change made possible by expanding knowledge, therefore, Smith and Turgot conceived a theory of social and political progress—*moral* progress, to use the Enlightenment term—that explained how a society not only might, but with expanding knowledge necessarily would, advance from a condition like that of the American Indians to the achievements of eighteenth-century Europe. In contrast to earlier ideas that attempted to account for why such different societies existed by focusing on static factors like different countries' climates, or different peoples' supposed racial characteristics, or various accidents of their respective national histories, Smith and Turgot offered a dynamic theory showing how any society with access to the right knowledge would progress from one condition to another over time. The more advanced among contemporary societies had evolved in this way, and in the future others, still comparatively primitive, would as well. (More than 200 years later, the ongoing discussion of prospects facing today's developing economies continues to reflect this assumption.)

In this view what progressed, as knowledge advanced and economic conditions changed, was the society, not the basic needs and desires of the individuals in it. Although a few Enlightenment thinkers also believed that the human species itself advanced over time (even though Darwin did not publish his theory of evolution until 1859), the link between economic and social progress posited by Smith and Turgot did not rest on any presumed change in human nature. Rather, this entire line of thought was in part a response to Montesquieu's earlier despairing of the prospects for republican government on the ground that citizens lacked sufficient "virtue" to allow it to succeed. Society progressed, according to Smith and Turgot, and individuals behaved differently, because *conditions* were different—specifically, their extent of knowledge and their economic circumstances.[20]

To be sure, not everyone took such a positive view of the rapidly changing European society of the eighteenth century, and those who disagreed typically saw the contrast between their own world and that of the American natives in a different light. Romantics like Jean-Jacques Rousseau regarded the Indians as "noble savages" whose way of life was to be prized, even envied.[21] Chafing in the last decades of France's pre-revolutionary *ancien régime*, Rousseau admired what he saw as the remarkable individual freedom the Indians enjoyed, as well as the extraordinary degree of equality among a people with few material possessions and little formal hierarchy for governance. He therefore concluded that the peak of human social development had occurred shortly after the emergence of semipermanent settlements but before the advent of sustained agriculture, and therefore before the evolution of private property and the legal and institutional structures that notion entails.

To Rousseau, this stage of society, which must have occurred very early in European development but nevertheless corresponded closely to how he saw the contemporary American Indians, was "altogether the very best man could experience; so that he can have departed from it only through some fatal accident, which, for the public good, should never have happened." By contrast, after the development of agriculture, "equality disappeared, property was introduced, work became indispensable, and vast forests became smiling fields, which man had to water with the sweat of his brow, and where slavery and misery were soon seen to germinate and grow up with the crops." Not only were people worse off individually, but social conflict was inevitable as well: "one man could aggrandize himself only at the expense of another." And he went on to discuss "dominion and slavery," "usurpations by the rich, robbery by the poor," "avarice, ambition, and vice"—all ending in "perpetual labour, slavery and wretchedness."[22] Rousseau's ideas clearly echoed the classical notion of a golden age in the distant past, from which modern society had descended rather than progressed. And although he was not a religious man (he was in some ways intensely antagonistic to organized religion), his ideas resonated as well with the biblical account of man's fall from the Garden of Eden.

Others—including, somewhat oddly, Denis Diderot, the editor of the grand *Encyclopedia* that more than any other single project exemplified the Enlightenment emphasis on knowledge—also admired and even envied the "noble savages." To these skeptics, the Indians' society was a new world not just in the sense that it was newly revealed to them but because, in the historical perspective that they and Rousseau shared with Smith and Turgot, this way of life was nearer to how they believed human society began. Those who saw European luxury as corrupting, and especially those who had confronted the political oppression of eighteenth-century monarchies (the French government burned Diderot's first major work and later imprisoned him for writing another), thought that the Indians' society was not just "newer" but morally superior to their own. To them, moral progress therefore bore an inverse relationship to economic progress and the advance of knowledge. As we shall see, echoes of this romantic view have often appeared, and in various forms they remain familiar today.

But the dominant perspective of the Enlightenment thinkers was one of progress—observing it, explaining it, celebrating it. Instead of idolizing the earliest stages of human existence, or lamenting some long-lost golden age, they acknowledged and appreciated the distance traveled over successive eras, and they looked forward to greater advances to come. And significantly, although their starting point was the role of knowledge and their ultimate concern was the character of society in the broadest terms, the fulcrum of their theory of progress was economic arrangements. The causal mechanism that Smith and Turgot posited led from scientific change to economic change to moral change. As Auguste Comte, a French philosopher who carried the tradition of the Enlightenment into the nineteenth century, succinctly summarized the core idea, "all human progress, political, moral, or intellectual, is inseparable from material progression."[23]

The question of what to make of the primitive peoples found in America, and what implications followed from their property arrangements, may have been the most immediate spur to the development of the Enlightenment concept of progress, especially in the specific form in which Smith and Turgot conceived it, but broader intellectual forces were at work as well.

The Renaissance, for example, had reintroduced—after centuries of mostly static thinking on such matters—the basic idea of human society as an organic entity subject to change and development over time. But while the Renaissance gave the Europeans a renewed consciousness of their history, it also left them too much in awe of their newly rediscovered classical heritage to allow much aspiration for further progress. (If the art, literature, philosophy, and government of Greek and Roman times had represented the apex of human achievement, then merely regaining that high ground was ambition enough.) By the eighteenth century, however, the Renaissance too had become part of Europe's heritage, rather than a constraint on new thinking. As a result, as people witnessed the ongoing series of new scientific discoveries and inventions, and saw for themselves the practical application of many of these advances, they were free to suppose that the progress they were experiencing in their own day might—indeed, would—continue.

A deeper resonance underlying the development of the Enlightenment idea of progress came—oddly, for what were mostly not religious men—from the realm of religion. The promise of a "millennium," literally a thousand-year period of what amounted to the reign of heaven upon earth, had been central to Christian thought from its earliest days. (Before Christianity emerged, Jewish messianism had embodied many of the same notions, though without the limit of time.) But in the period leading up to the middle of the eighteenth century there was a changed sense of what the millennium meant and what it might imply for people actually living in the present day. Men like Smith and Turgot lived in a world in which the role of religion was both important and pervasive, and they may well have been influenced by major currents in the religious thinking of their day.

To early Christians, the millennium promised in the biblical Book of Revelation (and before that, the "fifth kingdom" foretold in Daniel) was part of a straightforward description of how human history would play out: After a period of intense struggle between the forces of darkness and of light, involving ever more acute tribulations and afflictions of the faithful, the power of evil would be "bound" and a heavenly utopia would prevail on earth for 1,000 years.[24] Then, after another brief period of intense conflict, the Kingdom of God would be established and human history would end. But the thousand years of earthly utopia—the reign of the New Jerusalem—was to be very much a part of human history. Indeed, the author of Revelation clearly looked for the apocalypse to occur, and then the millennium to begin, shortly after his own time.[25]

By the beginning of the fifth century, however, not only had these events not come to pass but the Roman empire had adopted Christianity as its official religion. Christians no longer felt oppressed by the existing civil authority. While they may have continued to long for the triumph of good over evil, the overthrow of the established world order no longer seemed necessary, or even helpful, to that end. Perhaps in response to these changed circumstances, St. Augustine developed a new, allegorical interpretation of the apocalypse and the subsequent millennium.

According to Augustine, these events referred solely to man's spiritual development, not events in the temporal world. The bliss of the millennium was to consist in only the soul's relationship to God.[26] Augustine's views soon became the generally accepted Christian belief, and (in an interesting coincidence) remained so for approximately the next thousand years.[27] In parallel, to the extent that secular thinkers during the Middle Ages and the Renaissance addressed the idea of human "progress," they conceived it either as cyclical, as numerous Greeks of the classical era had suggested, or, worse yet, degenerative (again, the descent from a long-ago golden age).[28]

Soon after the Reformation, however, thinking—in particular, among Protestants—began to change again. As early as 1545, Martin Luther wrote an introduction to Revelation in which he accepted the idea that the book conveyed a valid, albeit highly symbolized, prophecy of actual events to come. (In an earlier introduction to Revelation, written in 1522, Luther had held the book to be "neither apostolic nor prophetic.") Why the new attitude? One possibility, suggested by religious historian Ernest Tuveson, is that by the middle of the sixteenth century it was apparent that the Protestant reformers would remain outside the Roman Church, rather than prevailing within it: "The reformed groups . . . were encompassed by powerful enemies, and it must have seemed that the preponderance of world power was with the enemy."[29] Hence a divinely ordained overthrow of existing authority was (once again) not just desirable on practical grounds but in the interest of furthering what the reformers took to be true religion. Returning to the pre-Augustinian worldly prophetic interpretation of the apocalypse would therefore have had substantial appeal.

It was in England, however, a century later, that the revival of prophetic millennialism took a further turn that set the tone not only for the Enlightenment view of progress but for much of Western religious thinking on the subject that has come down to the present day. To be sure, religious tensions remained: not just between Protestants and the Catholic Church but, within the Protestant movement, between the English Puritans and the established Church of England. (In the first half of the seventeenth century, that important struggle led to the Puritan emigration to North America and then, in rapid succession, the English Civil War, the execution of King

Charles I, and the establishment of the short-lived Protectorate under Oliver Cromwell.) But by this time it was clear that the Protestant Reformation, while not universally triumphant, was healthy and durable. Moreover, the geographical discoveries and scientific inventions of the past two centuries, together with their practical consequences, were as visible to theologians as to everyone else.

Joseph Mede, a distinguished biblical scholar at Cambridge in the first half of the seventeenth century, took the lead not only in reinterpreting the apocalypse and millennium as foretelling real-world events but also in turning toward a decidedly optimistic rendering of the prophecy itself. To Mede, the progress of both worldly and religious history represented not a decline, or even a never-ending cycle, but the gradual defeat of evil and the realization of the Gospel in human life: highlighted in most recent times by the invention of the printing press (which was crucial for spreading God's word), the Reformation, the defeat of the Spanish Armada, the establishment of a Protestant succession in England following the death of Elizabeth I, the failure of the "Gunpowder Plot" to destroy the Houses of Parliament, and the Puritan Revolution. Moreover, the Revelation of St. John, read independently from the burden of Augustine's interpretation, was clearly an account of forthcoming human history, not just a spiritual allegory. Far from a message of decay and decline, the true import of Revelation was to guarantee both religious and secular progress. The world was already a better place than it had been, in both realms, and there was—inevitably—a better world yet to come.[30]

The idea that progress, including worldly progress, not only existed but was inevitable, was a major step toward Enlightenment thinking in general but more specifically toward the kind of theory that Smith and Turgot conceived, with its account of a built-in process that naturally led society from one "mode of subsistence" to the next, and with all the positive political and social consequences that ensued from those economic transitions. Even so, there remained a very great distance between the Smith-Turgot theory—or, for that matter, any hypothesis built around a purely human dynamic—and the direct attribution of human progress to the acts of a divine Providence.

The pivotal religious thinker whose ideas began to bridge that gap was Thomas Burnet, active at Cambridge at the very end of the seventeenth century and into the eighteenth. Burnet added to what Mede and others had contributed the further idea that human progress not only is inevitable but, even though divinely ordained, nonetheless operates within the world of natural forces, including human agency. Perhaps not coincidentally, Burnet was a physician and scientist as well as a theologian. While he accepted the validity of a forthcoming apocalypse and millennium (now interpreted according to Mede's ultimately optimistic rendering), the active mechanism he thought would bring these events about was not divine intervention but "nature."

To be sure, all of human history remained an expression of divine will, in that nature itself had been shaped by God at the creation. But once the machine was set in motion, Burnet argued, no further intervention was involved. (As the religious historian James Moorhead put it, "God did not work by coups de main.")[31] In parallel to the prevailing Calvinist view of the predestination of individual souls to be either saved or damned, therefore, Burnet posited that human history too, both religious and secular, was "foreordained," neither requiring nor admitting specific acts of Providence after the initial creation of the world. Hence God, while acting to redeem history, nonetheless works *within* history.[32] In time, this new conception became the conventional view across a broad range of Protestant thinking, at least among the educated leadership.[33] By the middle of the nineteenth century when fascination with mechanical gadgets was at its height, the idea had further developed into the familiar metaphor of God as a watchmaker, designing and creating the world according to his divine plan but thereafter leaving it to run without further interference.

In the meanwhile, religious thinking in both England and America pushed the millennialist ideas of Mede and Burnet still further toward the point from which Smith and Turgot began. Jonathan Edwards, for example—the Northampton, Massachusetts, theologian and preacher who in the 1730s and 1740s spurred the movement that Americans called the "Great Awakening"—likewise thought that progress involved the entire scope of human life, and that progress was foreordained and therefore inevitable. World events were outward signs of God's influence on spiritual affairs, acting in human history. Moreover, the concept of inviolable laws of nature, even of an automated, mechanical universe, in no way implied that God's involvement was any less immediate.[34] In his views on how "nature" brought progress about, Edwards carried the theological study of millennialism to a point from which the secular concept of inevitable progress held out by the thinkers of the Enlightenment might proceed.[35]

Edwards's writings, and those of sympathetic followers in the latter half of the eighteenth century, marked a fork in the road of Christian thinking about the millennium promised in Revelation. Edwards believed that the Protestant church had already suffered its worst persecutions. But how could further human progress occur, and the millennium begin (as he thought it would, within only a few hundred years of his own time), without the apocalyptic struggle between good and evil? Or, even more so, without the return of Jesus?

Although the term was not in use before the nineteenth century, the path charted by Edwards and his followers developed into what in time became known as *post*millennialism: "post" in the specific sense that the Second Coming was now taken to occur not before but *after* the millennium, so that the kingdoms of this world were destined to *become* the kingdom of Christ.* But in time, postmillennialism became more than a matter of dating the Second Advent. It also implied an understanding of history as gradual *improvement* according to the laws of nature as viewed through science, and faith in an orderly *ascent* of mankind *into* the golden age.[36] Indeed, as early as the end of the seventeenth century some Protestant thinkers were beginning to suggest that the apocalypse had already occurred, so that in the future progress might proceed without further significant interruptions.[37] Over the course of the nineteenth and twentieth centuries, the postmillennialist view spurred by Edwards (from the earlier base established by Mede and Burnet) became ever more secularized, to the point at which the seemingly oxymoronic label "civil millennialism" became just as familiar if not more so.[38]

Already by the time of Smith and Turgot, however, more than a century of evolving debate had laid an ample religious foundation for believing that worldly human progress was inevitable, and that the process that drove it forward—whatever that might be—operated within the world of natural forces potentially subject to scientific analysis and explanation. Edwards, for example, according to his recent biographer George Marsden, "was as eager as anyone to find God's hand in history or nature, but he also expected God to work through secondary, or natural, causes." He also regarded political life, including the dealings among nations, as an integral part of the millennial process.[39]

---

*The alternative view, *pre*millennialism—which, as the name implies, anticipates the Second Coming *before* the 1,000 years of heavenly bliss could begin—retained a more explicitly religious character. Premillennialism did not lend itself to a belief in human progress, and many of its strongest nineteenth-century adherents, like the Mormons and the Shakers, sought to separate themselves from what they saw as the advance of evil (which in time would precipitate divine intervention). In time, postmillennialism—"millennial optimism"—became the prevailing view among the "mainline" Protestant denominations, especially among the more educated leadership, while premillennialism appealed to evangelical denominations but also maintained its hold on parts of the laity in mainline churches. To the extent that the beginnings of this distinction were already in place by 1750 or so, Smith would presumably have been more subject to influence by the views then current among the educated clergy.

Moreover, even the specific approach of conceiving of that progress in "stages" was resonant not only of classical writers like Hesiod but also of recent religious thinking. Burnet, for example, thought that God created progress by fixed cultural stages, from the "primitive" to the "philosophical."[40] Before Burnet, another English Puritan, Richard Baxter, had likewise argued that the Kingdom of God grows by stages.[41] Perhaps most explicitly, and also nearest in time to Smith and Turgot, Jonathan Edwards argued that the progress of the world took place in set stages, and that "there is in *each* of these Comings of Christ an ending of the old, and a beginning of new heavens and a new earth."[42] It remained to be said just what the successive stages of human progress were, and to specify the dynamic process that propelled human history from one stage to the next, and that is precisely what Smith and Turgot did.

Even the essential role that Smith and Turgot assigned to the advance of knowledge as the necessary vehicle that enabled man to make the transition from each "mode of subsistence" to the next likewise reflected both the theme of the secular Enlightenment and important strands of religious thinking, especially among the English Puritans. As religious historian Charles Webster has argued, "It is not an exaggeration to claim that between 1626 and 1660, a philosophical revolution was accomplished in England. . . . [A] period of spectacular scientific advance coincided with the economic, political and religious changes of the Puritan Revolution."[43]

Clergymen like Burnet and John Beale—and, more famously, scientists like Robert Boyle (of Boyle's law, which relates the volume of a gas to its pressure), Isaac Newton, and in the next century Joseph Priestley (the discoverer of oxygen, but a clergyman as well)—thought that to advance human understanding of nature was a fundamental element of religious experience, a way of seeking to know the works of God. Puritans were instrumental in the founding of the Royal Society in 1660, and a disproportionate number of the society's early fellows were Puritans, including many Puritan clergy.[44] The millennium might be inevitable, but the Puritans nonetheless felt an urgent need to strive to bring it about. Expanding the frontiers of knowledge was central to that effort. Hence scientific research (along with education, as we shall see) took on religious significance.[45] For Smith and Turgot to place advancing knowledge alongside growing hunger as the twin ingredients of their theory of human progress was characteristic of Enlightenment thinking. But it fit with the religious currents of their day as well.

The cultural historian Robert Nisbet proclaimed that "we cannot appreciate the origins of the modern, secular idea of progress in the eighteenth century and after apart from such millennialist revivals in Christianity as that of the Puritans in the seventeenth century."[46] Similarly, Tuveson concluded that "the idea that progress is the 'law' of history . . . was religious before it was secular."[47] These remarks apply not merely to the Enlightenment idea of progress, as these historians so forcefully argued, but also to the specific form of this idea that placed economic change at the center of the process that leads from progress in human knowledge to progress in society's governing institutions.

In the Enlightenment frame of reference, this advance in society's laws and institutions was, in itself, moral progress.[48] But further lines of Enlightenment thinking connected the economic changes that Smith and Turgot emphasized—and especially the development of "commerce"—to moral progress in other contexts as well, including the posture of nations in their dealings with one another and, even more so, the conduct and attitudes of individual citizens. Previous thinking, in both religious and classical republican traditions, had regarded "trade" as pernicious, at best a morally regrettable necessity. Smith, and many of his contemporaries, disagreed.

The idea that having a commercial economy induces a nation to act morally, or that participating in commercial activity causes individuals to do so, has often attracted sharp disagreement. Some people today would immediately reject either proposition. (Witness the view of commercial nations underlying the anti-globalization movement, or the attitude toward businessmen and financiers on display in a novel like *The Bonfire of the Vanities* or a film like *Wall Street*.) But as we shall see, more often than not social attitudes do shift in a morally positive direction when people have the sense of getting ahead economically, and vice versa when they are falling behind. And at least in regard to the domestic policies of nations, here as well there is evidence that economic growth is, on balance, conducive to democratic political change while stagnation or decline is not. These notions too have roots in Enlightenment thinking.

As Adam Smith in particular was (and remains) known for recognizing, what he and his contemporaries called "commerce" bore far-reaching implications. This new way of organizing economic activity combined two features that together created a powerful engine for generating the "wealth of nations." First, the *specialization* of what each individual personally contributed to the society's output of goods and services made each worker's labor, and therefore the entire economy, more productive. And second, the *voluntary exchange* of different goods and services, produced by different people, allowed individuals' own self-interest to steer their productive efforts in directions that would best deliver the products others wanted.

Moreover, unlike the gains that ensued from one-time transitions, like that from shepherding to farming or from farming to commerce, in principle there was no limit to the advance in productivity that increasingly specialized division of labor, guided by the incentives underlying voluntary exchange, could achieve. Even though the Enlightenment thinkers saw commerce as the ultimate stage of economic organization—they did not dwell on such later concepts as the distinction between the industrial sector and the service sector, much less foresee today's postindustrial "information economy"—they could anticipate, therefore, that under the right conditions living standards might continue to improve if not indefinitely then at least for the foreseeable future.[49] Indeed, Smith intended *The Wealth of Nations* as, partly, an instruction manual showing how any given commercial nation's wealth could be made to increase. (Montesquieu, by contrast, had attributed nations' different levels of wealth to such factors as climate.)

This bold new concept had strong moral content. For the first time people saw the possibility of acquiring wealth in a way that need not be inherently exploitive. At the individual level, the idea of voluntary exchange was that in any transaction both parties expected to come out ahead. But the same point applied even more strikingly at the level of the entire society. The route to national wealth was commerce, not conquest.[50]

For the first time, therefore, people now thought it possible for a nation to gain wealth without resorting to war, pillage, slavery, "tax farming," or any of the other morally objectionable means through which one people had historically improved their material well-being primarily by exploiting another.[51] Through commerce, one country, entirely on its own, could continually raise its average standard of living. Or, if two countries engaged in trade, both could benefit. Smith clearly intended his central idea in *The Wealth of Nations* to apply to the international context as well, and early in the nineteenth century David Ricardo worked out in some detail how two countries could engage in mutually beneficial trade by exploiting their respective "comparative advantage." (As we shall see, by mid-century Britain had removed its grain tariffs in favor of free trade.)

It is not surprising that the Enlightenment thinkers also extended their enthusiasm for the moral implications of "commerce" to what this form of economic activity meant for individual behavior and moral conduct. After all, Adam Smith thought of himself not as an economist—there was no such term then—but as a moral philosopher, and his other great work, written seventeen years before *The Wealth of Nations*, was titled *The Theory of Moral*

Sentiments. (The modern image of Smith as concerned with material ends alone is simply incorrect.) Smith and his contemporaries were deeply concerned with how both the "character" of societies and the "manners" of individuals were shaped.[52]

In the same way that Smith and Turgot saw the successive transitions from one "stage of subsistence" to the next as the origin of progress in laws and institutions, numerous Enlightenment thinkers thought of the advent of "commerce"—still a recent development in their own day—as conducive to individual moral improvement. A crucial implication of commerce was to sweep away the traditional moral problems associated with self-interest in economic activity. Smith's central point in *The Wealth of Nations*, which Bernard Mandeville had anticipated more than sixty years earlier in his *Fable of the Bees*, was that when economic activity is guided by commerce, the public interest is advanced not despite but *because of* individuals' self-interest.

Rather than worrying about how to suppress individuals' insatiable appetites, as the Stoics of ancient Greece had done, or simply railing against them as countless religious sects had, Mandeville, Smith, and their followers believed that commerce would harness those appetites to serve the society as a whole.[53] Just as insatiable curiosity drove the quest for scientific discovery, insatiable material wants drove the economic machine. The answer to the medieval religious injunction that all economic activity must be for the common good was that, under the arrangements imposed by commerce, economic activity driven by self-interest *was* for the common good.[54] In the absence of individuals driven by "virtue," commerce offered an economic system that mimicked what a society of virtuous individuals would do. The result was, in cultural historian Christopher Lasch's apt phrase, "the moral rehabilitation of desire."[55]

Further, many of the thinkers of the eighteenth century believed that the mere practice of participating in voluntary commercial exchange—an inherently social act, in that it necessarily involved two or more parties—fostered an improvement in personal behavior.[56] Smith frequently hailed the advantages of commerce for this purpose, especially in encouraging individual self-control. Montesquieu, writing just a few years before Smith and Turgot conceived their theory based on successive stages of subsistence, declared "it is an almost general rule that everywhere there are gentle mores, there is commerce and that everywhere there is commerce there are gentle mores," going on to conclude, "Commerce . . . polishes and softens barbarous mores."[57] Joseph Priestley thought that commerce "tends greatly to expand the mind and to cure us of many hurtful prejudices."[58] William

Robertson, like Priestley a clergyman but also principal of the university in Edinburgh, wrote that commerce "softens and polishes the manners of men. It unites them. . . . It disposes them to peace."[59] Even the fiery radical Thomas Paine, whose tract *Common Sense* helped inspire the American revolutionaries, went on to say in *The Rights of Man* that commerce "is a pacific system, operating to cordialise mankind. . . . The invention of commerce is the greatest approach towards universal civilization that has yet been made by any means not immediately flowing from moral principles."[60]

As Paine's remarks in particular suggest, a part of what compelled this admiration for the moral improvement inherent in commercial activity was the presumption that it tended to prevent wars.[61] To the extent that observers in the eighteenth century thought of commerce as a new way for a society to gain wealth, and therefore as a substitute for war and plunder, the point may have seemed obvious. Even though history includes plentiful examples of armed conflicts driven at least in part by commercial interests—most recently, the 1991 Persian Gulf War, fought over control of the Kuwaiti oil fields[62]—the idea that countries with commercial economies based on free markets do not go to war with one another continues to have widespread currency today.[63]

But the Enlightenment thinkers also saw that commerce rewarded such personal traits as reliability, order, and discipline, not to mention an inclination to be helpful and friendly toward one's fellow citizens. In a commercial world it was in people's self-interest to adopt these and other similar personal characteristics, conducive to success.[64] (Anyone who ever tried to make a purchase in a Moscow shop during the Soviet period would immediately understand Montesquieu's argument.) Wholly apart from their advantage for gaining economic success, however, qualities like reliability and discipline also bore moral content. Hence, far from abandoning the classical goal of instilling "virture," as Smith's critics argued, in the eyes of Montesquieu and other similar thinkers commerce led to its own version of virtue.

For much the same set of reasons, the Enlightenment view of commerce also saw this way of conducting economic activity as fostering tolerance and even democracy. Because people had an economic incentive to buy from the cheapest supplier, or sell to the highest bidder, irrespective of religion or political affiliation, commerce helped to break down group prejudice. Further, because many commercial transactions require bargaining and eventual compromise, engaging in commerce was a kind of conditioning for participation in a democracy. (As we shall see, Tocqueville later observed that Americans' proclivity to join many kinds of private associations served a similar purpose.)

In the same spirit of Smith's and Turgot's assumed progression of economic activity through successive stages, the Enlightenment thinkers even
reflected on the usefulness of commerce, in comparison to economies based
largely on shepherding or farming, for fostering greater equality. Antoine
Barnave, a French philosopher active at the time of the Revolution, wrote:
"It is a definite principle that where the only revenue is that of land, the big
holdings gradually engulf the small ones; while where there exists a revenue
from commerce and industry, the labor of the poor gradually succeeds in
winning for them a portion of the lands of the rich."[65] In short, commerce
was an agent of opportunity, democracy, and equality.[66]

Here too, in the implications that they drew from economic change for
improved individual behavior no less than for progress in political institutions, the largely secular minds of the Enlightenment had a solid and long-
standing foundation of religious thinking upon which to build.

One of the most important ways in which the Reformation helped pave
the way for the Enlightenment was in the emphasis that Protestantism,
especially the strands associated with John Calvin and his followers, placed
on the life and behavior of the individual. A strong sense of what constituted
morally appropriate personal conduct, in settings including family, workplace, and congregation, was a central element of the approach to life that
these new religious denominations and sects espoused. They aspired to
carry human society to new heights not just by reforming the church and
the institutions of the state, but also through their individual conduct and
example. While the English Puritans and their spiritual descendants saw
secular progress as inevitable, at the same time human effort directed
toward bringing that progress about was a moral imperative. Moreover, as
Max Weber famously emphasized, these early Reformed Protestants saw
both material prosperity and the religious and moral higher state that they
sought as desirable, and even tended to conflate the two. The Puritan
"saints," as they called themselves, took it as their collective duty to reform
society and thereby create the new Christian Commonwealth. And they
also strived individually to achieve material prosperity.[67]

A central tenet of Calvin's own belief, likewise accepted by his followers, was that individual men and women were predestined either to be
among the spiritually elect or not, and that their own behavior in itself
therefore had no effect on that outcome.[68] The Westminster Confession,
the authoritative Puritan creed of 1647, declared, "By the decree of God,
for the manifestation of His glory, some men and angels are predestined

unto everlasting life, and others foreordained to everlasting death. . . .
Those of mankind that are predestinated unto life, God before the foundation of the world was laid . . . hath chosen . . . out of His mere free grace and
love, *without any foresight of faith, or good works, or perseverance in either of
them*" (my italics).[69] But although a person's actions therefore had no *causal*
effect on his soul's ultimate fate, proper conduct and worldly success were
nevertheless taken to be *indications* of an individual's divine favor, and hence
of spiritual salvation.

Economic success was not excluded. The "theater of glory" that God
had created left room for many forms of human creativity. Especially in the
eyes of Calvin's followers, including the Puritans in particular, economic
prosperity was an outward sign of inward grace. Rejecting the doctrine of
St. Jerome and St. Augustine (among many others) that having wealth was
unjust and that men could acquire wealth only by exploiting other men,
Calvin wrote that "Riches in themselves and by their nature are not at all to
be condemned; and it is even a great blasphemy against God to disapprove
of riches, implying that a man who possesses them is thereby wholly cor-
rupted. For where do riches come from, if not from God?"[70] More succinctly, "Adversity is a sign of God's absence, prosperity of his presence."[71]
(As we shall see, these ideas have frequently reverberated in American political debate in later times.)[72]

The key concept that lent moral content to an individual's *economic*
endeavor, in this line of thinking, was the idea that everyone—not just the
clergy—had a calling. Although the notion of individual "callings" outside
the church was originally Luther's, Calvin and his followers developed the
idea well beyond what Luther had suggested, and they assigned it a much
more central place in their code of individual behavior. Fulfilling one's
appointed duty in worldly affairs was an explicitly moral undertaking. As a
result, everyday activity, importantly including activity devoted to being
economically productive, took on a religious significance.[73]

The central idea, as Weber described it, was that "The only way of living acceptably to God was not to surpass worldly morality in monastic
asceticism, but solely through the fulfillment of the obligations imposed
upon the individual by his position in the world. That was his calling."[74] In
America, Cotton Mather wrote that "Every Christian ordinarily should
have a calling . . . some settled business wherein . . . he may glorify God by
doing good for others and getting of good for himself."[75] (Weber took the
thoroughly secular Benjamin Franklin as the "ideal type" of what he called
the "Protestant ethic," but he could just as well have pointed to Mather or
Jonathan Edwards.)[76] Horatio Alger's earnest declaration, several centuries

after Calvin, that all honest work is respectable was an unmistakable echo. It is also no accident that the standard word still used in English to describe one's means of earning a livelihood is "vocation."

The importance attached to each individual's meeting the obligations of his or her calling provided a religious underpinning for admiration of the very qualities of personal behavior that Montesquieu and others later concluded that "commerce" induced: industriousness, discipline, honesty, sobriety, patience, and thrift. The concept of the calling also lent moral justification to the advancing specialization that Adam Smith and his contemporaries saw as the key source of advancing economic productivity: in contrast to the traditional view that an individual was not a morally complete being unless he were self sufficient, or at least had some finished product to show for his labors, even someone whose only task was to perform one mechanical operation among many in a complex production process—Smith's famous example of the "division of labor" was work in a pin factory—was meeting his moral obligations if that was his calling and he attended to it dutifully and well.

The same moral endorsement also applied to the energy, initiative, and enterprise that in time proved so important for commerce to succeed, since the millennium these Protestant thinkers envisioned was worldly as well as religious. Mankind's progress toward the millennium was inevitable, but still that progress had to be earned in any specific age. Just as the belief in predestination and the emphasis on morally proper conduct existed in tandem, Reformed Protestant thinking likewise sustained both a belief in the inevitability of the millennium and the keenly felt obligation to reshape the world so as to bring it about—in political philosopher Michael Walzer's words, "the sharp, insistent awareness of the need for and the possibility of *reform.*"[77] And just as the individual's path to salvation was more a process than a single, finite experience, worldly progress toward the millennium required constant, ongoing effort and the process of getting there was, in many ways, as important as the outcome.[78]

The result was what many later observers called "the *doing* tradition" in Puritanism.[79] Bunyan's *Pilgrim's Progress*, and countless other Puritan tracts and parables, made clear that the historical necessity of progress was no ground for complacency. As Joseph Mede's Cambridge contemporary John Preston put it, "this life is the time of striving,"[80] and the competition of commerce imposed on every individual the need to strive. Further, as Smith later argued, under conditions of market competition this individual striving resulted in promotion of the common good. "Commerce" required great energy, but to Calvin and his followers the energy was moral as well as physical.

A further feature of Reformed Protestant thinking that opened the way for the ideas that came to full flower in the Enlightenment was the emphasis not just on science and the need to expand the frontiers of human understanding, but education more broadly. Literacy was central, a necessity if lay church members were to read the Bible and perform their daily devotions. But higher education mattered too. Because of the preeminence that the English Puritans attached to the sermon in their regular worship services, and the responsibility they gave to individual preachers to interpret holy scripture (in both England and America, Puritan ministers were normally appointed to congregational pulpits for lifetime tenure), this emphasis was partly an understandable consequence of the need for an educated ministry. Further, because the Puritans wanted their clergy to be open to talented individuals regardless of the condition of their birth, that education also needed to be broadly based.[81] The Puritans who came to America made the founding of schools, and even a college (Harvard) modeled on Oxford and Cambridge, one of their earliest priorities.[82]

As we shall see, in time America led the way first in providing universal free public education, then in extending that public education through high school, and finally in pioneering mass higher education. To be sure, part of the motivation for doing so was economic. Part, too, reflected the widely accepted need for an educated citizenry to make the new nation's experiment in democracy work. (As John Adams wrote, "whenever a general knowledge and sensibility have prevailed among the people, arbitrary government and every kind of oppression have lessened and disappeared in proportion.")[83] But there was an underlying strain of religious motivation as well. As the eighteenth-century American theologian Samuel Hopkins put it—Hopkins was Jonathan Edwards's protégé, and his earliest biographer— "knowledge, mental light, and holiness, are inseparably connected; and are, in some respects, the same."[84]

These lines of religious thinking not only survived the transition to the more secular age that followed but, as Weber and others have emphasized, played a major role in shaping the secular world to come. It is not necessary to accept wholesale the link asserted in *The Protestant Ethic and the Spirit of Capitalism* to know that hard work, discipline, patience, and thrift are conducive to productivity in a market economy, or to recognize that education and scientific research contribute to economic productivity even in an increasingly postindustrial world. And clearly, both religious and secular reformist movements have had a major impact on political and social institutions throughout the Western world and beyond. The crucial contribution of each of these lines of thinking that preceded the Enlightenment was, from this perspective, to invest these *worldly* activities, at the individual as well as the community level, with *moral* force.

What remains unclear is the extent to which the religious thinkers of this pre-Enlightenment era intuitively understood the economic importance of what they consistently set forth as straightforward moral injunctions guiding individual and community behavior. Calvin himself took a highly favorable view of "commerce," wrote intelligently about economic matters, and even used commercial metaphors to describe moral behavior.* (In one example, "Those who expend usefully what God has deposited with them are said to trade. For the life of the godly is aptly compared to business, since they ought to deal with one another in order to maintain their fellowship; and the industry by which each person carries out the injunction laid on him and his very calling, the capacity of doing right, and his other gifts, are regarded as merchandise, since their purpose and use is to facilitate intercommunication among men.")[85] Similarly, Calvin's definition of money as "a medium for reciprocal communication among men, principally used for buying and selling merchandise" would command approval among today's advanced economic theorists.[86]

But regardless of whether the support that Calvin and his followers gave to the advance of commercial and in time industrial activity was deliberate, the Reformed Protestant denominations clearly accepted, rather than resisting, the key institutions of the dynamic economic world that was then evolving, including specialization, trade, wage labor, and credit. As the British historian R. H. Tawney put it in his classic work *Religion and the Rise of Capitalism*, "It is not that they abandon the claim of religion to moralize economic life, but that the life which they are concerned to moralize is one in which the main features of a commercial civilization are taken for granted."[87] This congruence between the new morality and the emerging

---

*At the same time, however, Calvin also believed that because of the "epistemic hold" that sin exerts on man, as a consequence of the fall from Eden, humans are apt to have a distorted view of what is in their interest, often putting what they see as their self-interest before the interest of others and even before the love of God. Calvin used commercial imagery to describe these ideas also. In a way that parallels later ideas about the need to conduct economic competition within a framework of appropriate legal constraints, Calvin saw the resolution of this conundrum in the use of "the law" to structure human functioning, including freedom and commerce, and to constrain individual behavior. These more fundamental ideas also provide the setting for Calvin's views about the "calling."

new structure of economic activity aided the successful spread of Reformed Protestantism, in the same way that (as Weber argued) it provided support for the successful advance of commerce itself.

Indeed, the resonance that these religious thinkers posed between the economic and the moral spheres extends further. A central thrust of their doctrines, whether deliberate or not, was to lend *moral* support to secular activities and forms of worldly behavior that were conducive to advances in the society's material standard of living. If rising living standards in turn exert a positive effect on the attitudes and institutions that form a society's moral character, however, then the very economic activities for which this line of religious thinking provided moral support ultimately help to foster superior moral outcomes.

But were any of these elements of Enlightenment thinking, and its roots, really an account of the consequences of economic *growth*?

The idea that economic progress is a (or perhaps even the) source of a society's moral progress does not necessarily say anything very directly about economic growth in the modern sense of a sustained increase in per capita incomes and living standards. Indeed, the account of the influence of economic change on laws and governing institutions given by Smith and Turgot, and also the claims of Montesquieu and his followers about the positive implications of "commerce" for individual behavior, lend themselves more immediately to the interpretation that what matters in this regard is not rising living standards but rather the level of economic development—or, as Smith put it, the "stage of subsistence": once a society has taken to farming, and both the principle of private property and the requisite legal structures have emerged, these institutions are unlikely to wither even if the society remains an agricultural economy indefinitely and its people's productivity and incomes increase no further. Similarly, once a society has moved on to economic specialization and commercial exchange, and has developed the institutions that this more complex way of carrying out economic activity requires, arrangements for standardizing transactions or for enforcing agreements would likewise seem secure even without any ongoing rise in productivity and incomes. And the same is true for the advances in political structures that evolve once greater productivity has enabled larger groups of people to live together.

It is unclear whether the thinkers of the mid-eighteenth century even understood the concept of economic growth in the modern sense of sustained increase over time. Smith in particular, and many of his contemporaries as well, saw that a nation's "wealth" could be great or small depending on a host of circumstances—per capita income was far higher in England than on the continent—and the point of Smith's famous book was that at least some of the circumstances that cause a nation's wealth to be greater were within its power to choose. Even so, that still does not resolve the question of whether what was at issue was a once-and-for-all transition from small wealth to great, consequent upon the transition to "commerce," or a sustained increase that would continue indefinitely once a commercial economy was in place.

One might suspect that the technological advances like the steam engine and the flying shuttle, which were beginning to be put to work by the middle of the eighteenth century, would already have suggested to thoughtful observers that increases in productivity would be ongoing. Although Smith did not dwell on technological change per se, the key element he emphasized in the advance of productivity—specialization (the "division of labor")—was likewise a process that, in principle, could continue indefinitely. Some historians have even argued that in England the idea of sustained increases in productivity and therefore in living standards had begun to take hold as early as the seventeenth century.[88] The more prevalent view today is that even though wages and living standards had been rising in England for some time, a real industrial revolution had not yet gotten underway when Smith published *The Wealth of Nations*, in 1776, and so neither he nor anyone else could possibly have understood the concept of sustained increase in per capita income as we know it.[89]

Regardless of whether Smith and Turgot conceived of economic growth in the modern sense, however, their account of how scientific progress led to economic progress, which in turn led to moral progress, nonetheless points to a role for rising incomes even if this was not what they had directly in mind. The driving force in their theory of economic and therefore political development was scarcity, in particular the scarcity created by growing population, and scarcity is largely in the eye of the beholder. As we shall see, whether people perceive their economic circumstances at any specific time as a matter of scarcity or abundance depends heavily on what they have come, from past experience, to regard as customary.

There may have been times when peoples advanced from hunter-gatherers to shepherds, or from shepherds to farmers, quite literally to avoid starvation as expanding populations strained their existing food supplies beyond the barest survival level. But it is equally possible, indeed far more likely, that the desire not just to eat enough to stay alive but to eat "better"—or dress more warmly, or have better shelter against the weather—provided the impetus that drove the key economic transitions from which Smith and Turgot drew such far-reaching moral implications. If so, then the force behind these transitions was, in part, a matter of people's comparing their current standard of living against that of the not so distant past. And for the great majority of people in any society, that comparison is very much a matter of economic growth.

Even this more growth-oriented retelling of the Smith-Turgot story, however, stops short of relating rising incomes directly to moral progress. Even if the desire for growth is what lies behind the movement of society from one "stage of subsistence" to the next, in their account it is still the transition from stage to stage, rather than any increase in living standards within any one stage, that brings about advances in the society's laws and governance.

A more direct role for economic growth in affecting these institutions, once an economy's productivity has advanced beyond the survival level, arises from the freedom that people then have to choose how to spend their waking hours. As Smith and his contemporaries repeatedly emphasized, the advances in productivity that came from adopting shepherding, or farming, or ultimately from specialization and commerce, meant that less human effort was necessary to feed and clothe and shelter a given population. The simplest way for society to reap the benefit of this increased productivity would have been for every individual to spend fewer hours laboring at agriculture and related employment. But that would have been inconsistent with the idea of specialization. The more practical response, in their eyes, would have been for some people to continue to work at these activities full-time, freeing others to do something else. Either way, somebody—maybe everybody—would have time for other pursuits.

And the Enlightenment thinkers had no doubt that at least some of these other pursuits—education, reading, developing the arts, discussing either political ideas in general or what was specifically best for people's own communities, even directly participating in self-government—would contribute to the advance of society's institutions. In the words of John Millar, a Scottish contemporary of Smith's, "According as men have been successful in these great improvements, and find less difficulty in the attainment of bare necessaries . . . the most important alterations are produced in the state and condition of a people; . . . men, being less oppressed with their own wants, are more at liberty to cultivate the feelings of humanity; . . . and the various rights of mankind, arising from their multiplied connections, are recognized and protected."[90] Smith had expressed much the same idea in *The Theory of Moral Sentiments:* "Before we can feel much for others, we must in some measure be at ease ourselves. If our own misery pinches us very severely, we have no leisure to attend to that of our neighbour."[91]

It could also happen, of course, that as productivity rose people would continue to devote themselves exclusively to economic labor, producing not just foodstuffs but ever more elaborate clothing and housing as well as an expanding array of luxuries. But most Enlightenment thinkers strongly rejected this possibility, arguing that people would instead choose to enjoy some part of the fruits of their advancing productivity in reduced hours of labor. And as daily hours of work decreased, at least for some but perhaps for all, time spent participating in the society's governing institutions would increase. (As Montesquieu and other eighteenth-century theorists of government were well aware, part of what made Athenian democracy possible was that its citizens did no work: Athens was a slave society.)

In reasoning this way, Smith and his contemporaries anticipated much of the thinking about political democracy that emerged over the next century, especially in response to "the American experiment." Tocqueville's observations on Americans' astonishing proclivity to participate not just in politics but in clubs and societies and associations of every kind ("not only commercial and industrial companies in which all take part, but associations of a thousand other kinds, religious, moral, serious, futile, general or restricted, enormous or diminutive"), and his emphasis on that participation as an ingredient important for the success of American democracy, sound like an empirical confirmation of Smith's and Millar's ideas on the importance of leisure pursuits—which, in a way, they were meant to be.[92] Throughout the nineteenth and twentieth centuries, whenever reformers planned would-be utopian communities, they gave prominent place to such group activities to fill people's leisure time.

More recently, sociologist James Coleman and political scientist Robert Putnam have emphasized exactly these ways of building the "social capital" on which a successful democracy relies.[93] Indeed, as Putnam has suggested, making Tocqueville's argument in reverse, the fact that in the last generation or so Americans have greatly reduced their participation in such leisure-time groups may have much to do with today's sense of the declining adequacy of American democracy. To extend this idea also to embrace Smith's argument in reverse, this decline in participation may itself have been a response to many Americans' feeling the need to work more in order to make up for stagnating wages, even though basic biological survival is hardly threatened.[94]

The further implied role for economic *growth*, within Smith's and Turgot's account of the link between economic and moral progress, is therefore that the perception of rising living standards affects how people use the time that advancing productivity frees them to spend away from work—if they choose to do so. Smith and the other Enlightenment thinkers assumed that people would so choose in the wake of a transition from one economic "stage" to the next. But because the transition from shepherding to farming, or from farming to commerce, presumably raises people's living standards, thinking about their spending less time at work as a result of these transitions leads to much the same implications as thinking of their doing so as a result of advancing living standards.

But there remains a crucial difference: each of the successive transitions that Smith and Turgot described occurs only once for any society. Does the society's moral progress stop in between? And after the transition to the final stage has taken place, is that progress then over? In particular, are we to think that because our own society's transition to "commerce" occurred long in the past, the Enlightenment claim for our moral progress no longer applies?

The importance of economic growth in this process is that it can account for continuing economic *and* moral progress not only between transitions but also after the transition to the final "stage" of economic development (if indeed there is such a thing). If incomes stagnate in these circumstances, in time people will no longer regard their current living standard as high, and they will be less inclined to devote themselves and their resources to the pursuits that Smith and other Enlightenment thinkers associated with society's moral improvement. By contrast, if productivity and therefore living standards continue to rise, then the social and political advance that the Smith-Turgot theory associated only with distinct economic transitions will follow anyway, as a consequence of rising prosperity.

Smith, Turgot, and their contempories did *not* put forth this idea about the role of economic growth. Nor, for that matter, did Monetesquieu and his followers relate the development of honesty, discipline, and reliability to rising incomes. They thought of these improvements in individuals' behavior and attitudes, as well as the implications they drew for equality and democracy, as a consequence of "commerce" itself, rather than any ongoing advance of living standards that resulted from this new way of organizing economic activity. But the integrated view of scientific, economic, and moral progress that these Enlightenment thinkers so powerfully advanced certainly leaves a place for economic growth to play such a role in the processes they had in mind, and taking rising incomes into account in each case only reinforces the original argument.

Chapter 3

Crosscurrents:
The Age of Improvement and Beyond

[T]he history of our country during the last hundred and sixty
years is eminently the history of physical, of moral, and of
intellectual improvement.

THOMAS BABINGTON MACAULAY
The History of England[1]

It was seventy-five years from the publication of *The Wealth of Nations* to
the Crystal Palace exhibition. The fascination with which citizens of the
rapidly advancing Western economies viewed technological progress, beginning sometime in the first half of the nineteenth century, was by then easily
understandable. It also turned out to be insightful.

Despite such important developments as the first steam engine and the
flying shuttle in the first half of the eighteenth century, followed in the
1760s by James Hargreaves's spinning jenny and Richard Arkwright's water
frame, neither Adam Smith nor his contemporaries had focused on technological progress as a central force expanding production and raising living
standards.[2] Only in retrospect, some decades later, did the extraordinary
industrial implications of these inventions become apparent. True, Smith
took note of the still new "factory system" at the very beginning of his book.
But the opening chapter, with its famous description of a pin factory, was

titled "Of the Division of Labour," and the point of the discussion was to illustrate the importance not of technical progress but of specialization, whereby each worker performed, over and over, a single element in a multi-step production process.[3] (The fact that Smith chose the example of pins rather than textiles, which in time became the center of the Industrial Revolution, further reflects his failure to foresee the eventual implications of continually advancing technical progress.)

By early in the next century, however, the power of new technology had become evident. James Watt had developed his improved steam engine in the 1760s, but only in the 1780s was it adapted to rotary motion and thereby made suitable for driving industrial machinery.[4] Other inventions that vastly increased productivity in textile manufacturing—Samuel Crompton's spinning mule (called a "mule" because it combined elements of Hargreaves's jenny and Arkwright's water frame), Edmund Cartwright's power loom, Eli Whitney's cotton gin—likewise came after *The Wealth of Nations* but before the turn of the nineteenth century. Further, with steam power it was no longer necessary to locate factories on rivers. Industrial production could therefore become an urban activity. The scientific inventions of an earlier age, like Galileo's telescope or Leeuwenhoek's microscope, had expanded knowledge, but not the possibilities for economic production. By contrast, the contributions of Watt, Crompton, Cartwright, and the other inventors of this new era did just that, though it took time for these new devices to become widely used, and more time still for the full implications of their use to become widely understood. Britain's production of cotton textiles had risen more than two-and-a-half-fold in the half-century leading up to 1820. By the time of the Crystal Palace exhibition, just thirty years later, it had more than quadrupled from there.[5]

A parallel process took place in the production of iron and the manufacture of ironware machinery. In the 1780s Henry Cort had perfected the process of refining coke-smelted pig iron, thereby opening the way for the large-scale manufacture of machine parts with the strength and resilience to withstand industrial-level, power-driven, repetitive motion (thus permitting, in effect, the use of machines to make other machines). During the first quarter of the nineteenth century, Britain's production of pig iron rose from 125,000 tons to 455,000. By mid-century pig iron production was 2.7 million tons.[6]

The steam engine also revolutionized transportation. Robert Fulton began steamboat service, on New York's Hudson River, in 1807. The first regular rail service opened in 1830, between London and Liverpool. Samuel Cunard initiated transatlantic steamboat service in 1840. Meanwhile, the development of cheap, efficient transportation powered by steam greatly extended the range over which farmers could ship to the cities what they grew, and factory owners could now send their products to far-flung markets. A further implication of the transportation revolution, therefore, was an increase in the economically feasible size of cities. Between 1800 and 1850 the population of greater London grew from just over 1 million to nearly 2.7 million. By 1900 it was 6.5 million.[7]

At the time of the Crystal Palace exhibition, however, the great expansion in both railroads and steamships was yet to come. The turning point was the advent of dramatically cheaper steel, first made possible by the Bessemer process in 1856. In the United States, within a decade both steelmaking and railroad construction surged, not only transforming the nation but providing jobs and incomes to fuel what became a general economic expansion. At the same time, the substitution of steel for iron also made steamships both lighter and stronger, giving them greater range, more power, and larger carrying capacity. Cheap steel also made easily affordable to the average family such standard household items as scissors, razors, and guns. By the end of the century it had revolutionized construction by making skyscrapers possible, along with wonders like the Eiffel Tower and the Brooklyn Bridge. But in 1850 all this lay in the future.

Even without the enormous expansion that would follow from cheap steel and railroads, however, by mid-century the standard of living in Britain had improved dramatically, and for most people the way of life had changed in other ways as well. Even by Adam Smith's time, British living standards had reached the point at which most residents, most of the time, could look forward with confidence to getting enough to eat.[8] Seventy-five years later, many people felt a real sense of affluence.

With some lag, the same phenomenon occurred in some other parts of western Europe, and especially in the United States. By the end of the nineteenth century, per capita income in America had caught up with, and surpassed, that in Britain. But at the time of the Crystal Palace exhibition, British subjects knew that not only had their incomes on average been rising but their standard of living stood well above that of any other nation in the world. They also knew technological progress was the chief reason.

This realization bore important implications. A fundamental objection to the view of Smith, Turgot, and the other Enlightenment thinkers who so praised the effects of "commerce" was that the economic specialization inherent in ever greater division of labor robbed workers of their economic independence and thereby—or so the idea went—stunted their moral capacities. To Smith, this specialization was the key to enhanced productivity and therefore greater national wealth. But it also rendered people economically dependent on one another (the blacksmith cannot eat iron, and plow horses cannot pull wearing shoes made of wheat). This dependence was the very basis of much of what Montesquieu, Paine, and many others of their day saw as the civilizing and democratizing influence that flowed from commerce in the first place. The further question was whether at the same time that dependence undermined workers' ability to be fully developed moral beings, and full citizens of a democracy.

Far from resisting this argument, Smith made it forcefully. As he put it, the problem facing "the man whose whole life is spent in performing a few simple operations" is that he "has no occasion to exert his understanding, or to exercise his invention in finding out expedients for removing difficulties which never occur." The result is that "he naturally loses, therefore, the habit of such exertion, and generally becomes as stupid and ignorant as it is possible for a human creature to become. The torpor of his mind renders him, not only incapable of relishing or bearing any part in any rational conversation, but of conceiving any generous, noble, or tender sentiment."[9]

To Smith, concerned as he was with "sentiments" like generosity, nobility, and tenderness—this was, after all, the subject of his first book, *The Theory of Moral Sentiments*—the corrosive effect of economic specialization on the character of the individual worker was bad enough. But he also saw dangerous implications for the society as a whole, including the impairment of its prospects for sustaining a democracy and even of its ability to defend itself militarily: "Of the great and extensive interests of his country he [the specialized worker] is altogether incapable of judging; and unless very particular pains have been taken to render him otherwise, he is equally incapable of defending his country in war. . . . His dexterity at his own particular trade seems, in this manner, to be acquired at the expense of his intellectual, social, and martial virtues."[10]

Not surprisingly, since he was such a champion of the division of labor, Smith had a solution for this problem. Notwithstanding his popular image today as an opponent of government and government institutions, in this instance he was clear not only on what to do but on who should do it. "[I]n every improved and civilized society this is the state into which the labouring poor, that is, the great body of the people, must necessarily fall, unless government takes some pains to prevent it." Going on to refer to "the gross ignorance and stupidity which . . . seem so frequently to benumb the understandings of all the inferior ranks of people," Smith concluded, "[t]hough the state was to derive no advantage from the instruction of the inferior ranks of people, it would still deserve its attention that they should not be altogether misinstructed. The state, however, derives no inconsiderable advantage from their instruction."[11] Along the way Smith offered a set of detailed recommendations for a universal public school system.[12]

The importance of substituting technical progress for ever greater division of labor as the origin of ongoing economic growth (to call it that), as the nineteenth century developed, was therefore twofold. First, to the extent that it was advancing technology that made individuals more productive, they could continue to perform work in which there was room for thought, discretion, initiative, and creativity. The atrophy of mental faculties that even Smith had feared need not occur. And second, the requirements of an ever more highly technological economy further reinforced the importance of education, which Smith had proposed as an antidote to the "stupidity" and "torpor" resulting from excessive division of labor, but which many others had also conceived as a way of fostering economic mobility and democracy.

As larger scale production became more commonplace, and the factory system increasingly replaced individual artisanship, a growing share of the industrial labor force in Britain as well as America now worked for wages. But wage labor meant more than just economic specialization. Unlike the blacksmith, who at least produced a finished horseshoe on his own, or weavers who made finished cloth, factory workers carried out individual tasks that contributed to producing something only in the context of the entire corporate effort. These workers had nothing to which they could point as their own product, and certainly nothing tangible to offer for exchange. They simply sold their labor in return for wages. Traditional republican ideas, recently championed most prominently by Thomas Jefferson in America, held that economic independence was essential to citizenship and participation in self-government.[13] Could democracy survive in a world increasingly worked by wage labor?

To make matters worse, the conditions under which workers supplied wage labor in the early days of the Industrial Revolution often seemed to violate the principle of voluntary exchange that was so central to the Enlightenment thinkers' conception of "commerce." Many workers' only choice was to work at the wage offered or starve, along with their families. Indeed, an active debate questioned whether wage laborers were better off than plantation slaves.

Defenders of commerce addressed the problem of "wage slavery" by pointing to the essential opportunity, under democratic political and social institutions, for talented and energetic individuals to advance to a higher condition. The lack of independence inherent in wage labor therefore was, or at least could be, only temporary. Even in the Britain of Smith's day, some factory laborers had become foremen, owners, or, on occasion, large-scale entrepreneurs. Even more so in the nineteenth century, and especially in America, there was always the possibility of rising above wage labor. As historian Frederick Jackson Turner's "frontier hypothesis" later emphasized in retrospect, the availability of open land on favorable terms meant that any free laborer in America who accumulated modest savings could achieve economic independence (though certainly not freedom from hard work) by moving west.[14] Abraham Lincoln, speaking in 1856, put the point concisely: "The man who labored for another last year, this year labors for himself, and next year he will hire others to labor for him."[15] In what sounded very much like Smith's reference in *The Wealth of Nations* to "that disgraceful degree of poverty, which, it is presumed, no body can well fall into without extreme bad conduct," Lincoln also argued that in America the only reason for a worker's failure to rise out of wage labor would be his "dependent nature," or perhaps "improvidence, folly, or singular misfortune."[16]

Even so, by the middle of the nineteenth century in Britain, and well before the end of the century in America, it was clear that the factory system was here to stay and that many if not most working people would in fact work for wages. Hence it was important to ensure not only that they received the skills necessary to make upward mobility a realistic prospect but also that the moral capacity and potential for citizenship even of those who remained wage laborers would become fully developed nonetheless. On both counts, the role of education was crucial.

The emphasis on the opportunity of individual workers to advance, an aspect of democracy that became a major theme in Western and especially American thinking in the nineteenth century, fit naturally with the Enlightenment idea that economic conditions determined how societies developed their political and social institutions. Turgot, for example, had speculated that among ordinary workers there were always some of genuine "genius," and that the crucial question was whether society was organized in such a way to allow that genius to become fertile and be discovered. (What would have happened, Turgot asked, if Racine had been brought up as a plow boy? Or if Corneille had been born the son of illiterate Indians in French Canada?)[17] Beyond the obvious implications for these naturally talented individuals themselves, it was in *society's* interest to create the opportunity for every person's genius, regardless of the circumstances of birth, to reach fruition. Claude Adrien Helvetius, a Frenchman writing not long after, made the same argument in a more lofty way that resonates with discussions of mobility and opportunity today: "all men . . . have in them the *physical power* to raise themselves up to the *highest ideas*; . . . the *differences in intellect* which we observe among them depend on the *different circumstances* in which they find themselves placed, and the *different education* which they receive."[18]

As the nineteenth century progressed, the emphasis on knowledge and education, both as vehicles for fostering individual mobility and as the key to exploiting new technology for the benefit of society as a whole, became ever more widespread. As the English historian Asa Briggs pointed out, the "folk heroes" of mid-century Britain were mostly engineers, including many of modest social origins: George Stephenson, who built the original London–Liverpool railway; Joseph Whitworth, whose work opened the way for mass production by making possible the precise manufacture of metal products with interchangeable standard parts; James Rendel, the chief engineer in charge of building the Birkenhead docks and the Portland harbor; and many others.[19] Indeed, the Crystal Palace exhibition—including both Joseph Paxton's marvelous building and the exhibits inside it—was in large part a way of showing off British achievements in the fields of civil and mechanical engineering.

In America the importance that the Puritans had attached to education for the non-elite easily outlasted the Puritans themselves. As early as the 1820s, a loose coalition of businessmen, intellectuals, and workingmen's groups, especially in New England, launched a vigorous campaign for universal public education. In 1834 Pennsylvania became the first state to provide it. In 1839 Horace Mann established, in Massachusetts, the first state "normal school" for the preparation of teachers, and in 1852 Massachusetts became the first state not just to provide free public education but to make school attendance compulsory (for ages eight through fourteen). By the end of the nineteenth century, all states in the East and Midwest had followed, and the public high school movement was also well underway.

In the meanwhile, not only did the creation of private colleges and universities (which began in colonial times) continue, but especially after 1862, when the Morrill Act provided federal land grants for the purpose, state institutions of higher education proliferated as well. In light of the importance of technology and technological progress—which by now nearly everyone understood and accepted—the primary stated purpose of the land grant colleges and universities was to provide instruction in "agriculture and the mechanical arts." But their curriculum soon expanded to encompass the liberal arts as well. Within a few years, these new state institutions were democratizing American education by serving thousands of students who could not afford private college tuitions. And throughout the century, the quest for education extended still further, as libraries, lyceums, athenaeums, mechanics' institutes, chautauquas, and public lectures offered adults opportunities for learning nearly everywhere in America.

Even as technological progress gradually took the place of mere division of labor as the perceived source of economic growth, however, important strands of thought in the nineteenth century rejected the basic idea that the development of the economy in this way represented "progress" in a broader social, political, or moral sense. Even Tocqueville, who in other ways was so enthusiastic about the vitality of American democracy, and so optimistic about its prospects, expressed serious concern about the dangers of what he saw happening in the young nation's emerging manufacturing industries.[20]

Using language that consciously echoed Smith's, Tocqueville acknowledged that ever greater division of labor would dull workers' mental faculties and destroy their economic independence. (As if to make sure no one missed the unstated reference to Smith, Tocqueville asked, "What can be expected of a man who has spent twenty years of his life making pins?")[21] But he then went on to argue that a further effect of the division of labor was to create a separation between men who, in principle, were fellow citizens of the same democracy: "While the workman concentrates his faculties more and more upon the study of a single detail, the master surveys an extensive whole, and the mind of the latter is enlarged in proportion as that of the former is narrowed. . . . This man resembles more and more the administrator of a vast empire; that man, a brute." As a result, "The master and the workman have then here no similarity, and their differences increase every day."[22]

Under these circumstances, Tocqueville was skeptical that actual opportunities for mobility would prove sufficient to preserve the "equality of condition" that he took to be the essential characteristic of a democracy. To be sure, he saw the risk of *downward* mobility as ever present ("the rich are constantly becoming poor. . . . Their relative position is not a permanent one"). But *upward* mobility was a different matter: "The poor have few means of escaping from their condition. . . . Thus the elements of which the class of the poor is composed are fixed." He concluded that "if ever a permanent inequality of conditions and aristocracy again penetrates into the world, it may be predicted that this is the gate by which they will enter."[23]

Still other negative aspects of the new economic progress caused deep concern as well. The Industrial Revolution brought real physical hardship to large numbers of workers, including children who labored for lengthy days and under dangerous and unhealthy conditions that today are prohibited in all advanced industrialized countries (and increasingly so in the developing world).[24] The required movement of workers to locations where economic activity was becoming centralized under the factory system broke apart many families and uprooted still more from their traditional homes. Even "commerce" itself—the system of voluntary exchange of both goods and labor at market-determined prices—supplanted long-standing relationships that had previously bound landlords and tenants, masters and servants, and tradesmen who formerly dealt with one another as a matter of loyalty or even simply habit. Dickens's *Hard Times*, which appeared in Britain almost simultaneously with the Crystal Palace exhibition, gave as clear a view as any of the nasty underside of the "progress" that the rest of society was celebrating.

These harsh realities provoked two separate lines of reaction, each of which has continued to resonate ever since. One, drawing on eighteenth-century concepts of what it meant to be a fully developed moral being, was romantic and even aristocratic. The Romantic movement of the nineteenth century had a widespread and profound effect throughout the arts, literature, and philosophy. But Romanticism was also a social and political movement, addressing the real concerns of the time. Critics like Thomas Carlyle in Britain, and Ralph Waldo Emerson and Orestes Brownson in America, expressed a longing for what historian Peter Laslett later called "the world we have lost."[25] Like Montesquieu and Smith, they sought a society molded by honor and republican "virtue" (Emerson often spoke of "character"), but like Rousseau they instead saw the advance of commerce corrupting these values. Their point was not to deny the benefits of the material progress that scientific advance and industrialization had brought, but to lament the parallel emergence of what Carlyle called the "cash nexus" in place of a social system in which lasting personal relationships had assumed more importance than transient connections based on momentary market advantage. As Dickens described the harsh new model of human relations, "Nobody was ever on any account to give anybody anything, or render anybody help without purchase. Gratitude was to be abolished, and the virtues springing from it were not to be. Every niche of mankind, from birth to death, was to be a bargain across a counter."[26]

Not just Dickens but other novelists too—Elizabeth Gaskell in *North and South*, Anthony Trollope in *The Way We Live Now*, George Eliot in *The*

Mill on the Floss—expressed the same romantic longing for a vanishing way of life (the "South" of Gaskell's title) that had embodied different values. Others objected to advancing modernization more on aesthetic grounds. In contrast to the popular admiration for the new railroads, art critic John Ruskin wrote, "All traveling becomes dull in exact proportion to its rapidity. Going by railroad I do not consider traveling at all; it is merely 'being sent' to a place, and very little different from becoming a parcel."[27] Even some of the leading writers on "political economy," as the subject was then beginning to be called, expressed views that echoed those of Dickens and Gaskell. John Stuart Mill, for example, wrote in his classic *Principles of Political Economy*, "I confess I am not charmed with the ideal of life held out by those who think the normal state of human beings is that of struggling to get on; that the trampling, crushing, elbowing, and treading on each other's heels, which form the existing type of social life, are the most desirable lot of human kind, or anything but the disagreeable symptoms of one of the phases of industrial progress."[28]

In the nineteenth century, as again is true today, the concern at the heart of this Romantic strain of thought was not just the material hardship imposed on individuals but the consequences for society at large as increasingly individualistic, market-driven interactions—again, "commerce"— broke down social bonds, family ties, and even patriotism. The cogent elements of concern in this regard, however, often were (and today still are) hard to disentangle from a nostalgia that implicitly posed as a benchmark for comparison an idealized past that never quite existed.[29] And in some cases the expression of this nostalgia sought (as today it seeks) to undermine even the most fundamental underpinnings of the entire idea of progress, as both the Enlightenment thinkers and their successors conceived it, by questioning the very notion of objective scientific reality.[30]

The other important line of reaction against the advance of "commerce" in the nineteenth century was that of Karl Marx. In contrast to the Romantics, who longed to return to an earlier time, Marx readily acknowledged the progress represented by commerce and, like Smith and Montesquieu a century before, on occasion even waxed enthusiastic about these advances. In *The Communist Manifesto*, for example, he and Friedrich Engels wrote that "The bourgeoisie. . . has accomplished wonders far surpassing the Egyptian pyramids, Roman aqueducts, and Gothic cathedrals; it has conducted expeditions that put in the shade all former Exoduses of nations and crusades."[31]

Also like Smith—and here he struck the same chord as did the Romantics—Marx saw the ever advancing division of labor as a force with devastating consequences for what Smith had called "the labouring poor, that is, the great body of the people" and what Marx simply called "the proletariat." But Marx drew a far different conclusion from the plight of the poor than had Smith. While Smith had worried about the possible "stupidity" and "torpor" of laborers' minds, he was nonetheless confident of a rising standard of living even for the working poor. Marx, writing at a time when industrial hardship was widespread, warned instead of "the enslaving subordination of individuals under the division of labour." Indeed, "the man who possesses no other property than his labour power must, in all conditions of society and culture, be the slave of other men."[32]

While Smith had sought to address the problem he identified by means of education, and the nineteenth-century devotees of the "cult of progress" saw technological advance as powerful enough to solve any such problems without requiring significant government intervention, Marx was convinced that neither education nor technology represented a satisfactory answer. Rather, he saw the plight of ordinary workers, *under existing political institutions*, becoming steadily worse. In this respect, the same concept of a continually cumulative process that was so important to the earliest notions of the advance of knowledge, and to Smith's ideas about the division of labor and also to the subsequent nineteenth-century belief in technical progress, was a crucial feature of Marx's thinking as well. In Marx's case, however, it led him to think that the plight of the working masses would worsen without limit. The implication he drew was that the existing economic and political system would therefore collapse.

In the end, the overriding difference between Marx and Smith was therefore that Marx believed industrial capitalism—a specific form of what Smith had called "commerce"—would not prove to be the ultimate way of organizing economic activity. Something else, in particular communism, would take its place. The contemporary political system, in Britain based on a highly limited form of democratic government, would likewise give way to the "dictatorship of the proletariat." To Marx, neither the shift from agriculture to commerce that Smith and Turgot had emphasized nor Britain's bloodless political revolution of 1688, which was so dear to the Whigs of the nineteenth century, was the end of the story. A further transition was still in store, and much of Marx's revolutionary writings were addressed to the question of how it might come about.

Marx, therefore, was also a believer in progress: at the economic, political, and moral levels.[33] He thought, however, that future progress would take place only after the (presumably violent) overthrow of the existing economic and political structure.

History, of course, took a different path. As we shall see, economic inequality in Britain reached its peak within a decade or two after *The Communist Manifesto* was published in 1848. The Second Reform Act, which greatly expanded the scope of British democracy, was passed in 1867, the same year in which the first volume of *Das Kapital* appeared. By the time the second volume was published in 1885 (posthumously; Marx had died two years earlier), the creation of the basic social insurance institutions of a modern welfare state was well underway in Germany. And by the end of the century it was clear that the living standard of the working poor, in the industrialized European countries as well as in America, far exceeded what it had been at mid-century.

As Britain's national enthusiasm for the Crystal Palace exhibition suggests, however, neither Marx nor the Romantics represented the main course of nineteenth-century thinking about the connection between economic progress and society's moral progress. To the contrary, prevailing attitudes toward what was happening in both the economic and the political sphere more typically reflected the combination of complacency about existing institutional arrangements, faith in technological progress, and confident expectation of future social improvement that in retrospect seems characteristic of so much of nineteenth-century thinking. (Especially in Britain, the historians and other writers who expressed this view eventually became known as "Whig historians" for their firm commitment to the principles established by England's 1688 revolution, and their resulting support of the Whig Party in their own day.) By the mid-1800s, prosperous people in both Britain and America were firmly committed to their respective countries' prevailing political structure. Potential social and political reforms continually arose on the national agenda, and many were adopted. But unlike in continental Europe, where violent revolutions frequently occurred—1830, 1848, and so on—the prevailing sentiment in both Britain and America was strongly anti-revolutionary.

Instead, faith that social progress could and would continue to take place within the existing overall political system accompanied the belief that technical progress, and therefore economic growth in the modern sense, would continue under the overall system of "commerce." The favorable political developments of the recent past seemed to offer confirmation of that confidence. Just as the religious thinkers of the seventeenth century and later many of the key Scottish Enlightenment figures had drawn reassurance from such events as the Protestant succession after the death of Elizabeth I and the Whig revolution of 1688, by the mid-nineteenth century their successors could take similar heart from the abolition of the slave trade and then of slavery itself, the reaffirmation of democracy in Britain by the Reform Act, the spread of public education (especially in America), and the establishment of amicable relations between Britain and both America and France in their post-revolutionary forms. Indeed, although Britain's expanding world empire involved the country in an endless series of military actions in faraway places (revolt in Jamaica, insurrection in Canada, the Afghan War, the First Opium War in China, wars against the Maoris in New Zealand), at the time of the Crystal Palace exhibition Britain had been at peace with America and with the rest of Europe since the final defeat of Napoleon in 1815.

The British historian who most exemplified the spirit of the age was Thomas Babington Macaulay, who, among many other aspects of a strikingly varied career, also served as a Whig member of Parliament and, for nearly two years, secretary of war. Macaulay's classic *History of England*, published between 1849 and 1855, addressed only the period since the Whig revolution of the 1680s. But it richly expressed the sense of grandeur with which he and his contemporaries viewed the breadth and extent of the progress they saw all around them.

After listing at the outset some of the "disasters mingling with triumphs, and great national crimes and follies" that his account would cover, Macaulay went on to write, "Yet unless I greatly deceive myself, the general effect of this checquered narrative will be to excite thankfulness in all religious minds, and hope in the breasts of all patriots. For the history of our country during the last hundred and sixty years is eminently the history of physical, of moral, and of intellectual improvement." And he dismissed as simply wrong the classical idea of secular decline: "Those who compare the age on which their lot has fallen to a golden age which exists only in their imagination may talk of degeneracy and decay: but no man who is correctly informed as to the past will be disposed to take a morose or desponding view of the present."[34]

Indeed, Macaulay was acerbic in his dismissal not only of Romantic nostalgia but also of claims, like those underlying Marx's dire predictions, that the working population had become worse off: "It is now the fashion to place the Golden Age of England in times when noblemen were destitute of comforts the want of which would be intolerable to a modern footman, when farmers and shopkeepers breakfasted on loaves, the very sight of which would raise a riot in a modern workhouse, when to have a clean shirt once a week was a privilege reserved for the higher class of gentry, when men died faster in the purest country air than they now die in the most pestilential lanes of our towns, and when men died faster in the lanes of our towns than they now die on the coast of Guiana." But he also flatly rejected the presumption that his own age represented the apex of development in any of these dimensions, writing, "We too, shall, in our turn, be outstripped, and in our turn envied."[35]

It is especially interesting that Macaulay and his contemporaries, writing just before Darwin's publication of *The Origin of Species* in 1859 exploded the idea altogether on scientific grounds, were already so contemptuous of the notion of a past golden age that held such great appeal for the nineteenth-century Romantics (as it had for Rousseau a century before). Moreover, Macaulay was also clear that the advances in knowledge and therefore in society that he and his contemporaries were celebrating were by no means the end of the story: "From the great advances which European society has made, during the last four centuries, in every species of knowledge, we infer, not that there is no room for improvement, but that, in every science which deserves the name, *immense improvements may be confidently expected.*"[36] And elsewhere, "We rely on the natural tendency of the human intellect to truth, and on the natural tendency of society to improvement."[37] By Macaulay's time the link between expanding knowledge and social progress, about which Smith and Turgot and other thinkers of the Enlightenment had theorized, had come to seem self-evident.

It was natural that Americans too, having traveled so much greater a distance in establishing a new nation with a new form of government, and settling a vast continent, would have much the same view. Historians like Francis Parkman wrote muscular narratives of the early exploration and settlement of North America, while William H. Prescott produced equally striking accounts of the conquests of Mexico and Peru. But among American historians the most eloquent spokesman for the "Whig" point of view—although the label made no real sense in the American context—was George Bancroft, a Bostonian who, like Macaulay, also had a political career. (Bancroft was originally a Democrat, and in the 1840s he served as secretary of the navy and then minister to Britain. He broke with the Democrats over slavery, however, and after the Civil War he served in the Johnson and Grant administrations as minister to Prussia and then Germany.) Bancroft's nine-volume *History of the United States: From the Discovery of the Continent* was the first history of America with national scope and amplitude, and it occupied much of his effort over a span of four decades.

In his introduction to the opening volume, published in 1834, Bancroft began by celebrating America's "precedence in the practice and the defense of the equal rights of man," going on to say that "The sovereignty of the people is here a conceded axiom." In America, "Prosperity follows the execution of even justice; invention is quickened by the freedom of competition; and labor rewarded with sure and unexampled returns. . . . Every man may enjoy the fruits of his industry; every mind is free to publish its convictions." Far from resisting the influx of immigrants (as we shall see, a recurrent focus of contention in American politics throughout much of the nineteenth and twentieth centuries), Bancroft welcomed both their numbers and their diversity: "An immense concourse of emigrants of the most various lineage is perpetually crowding our shores, and the principles of liberty, uniting all interests by the operation of equal laws, blend the discordant elements into harmonious union."

After going on to give examples of the kinds of physical expansion and economic and intellectual advance just then underway, Bancroft drew the comparison that made the notion of progress seem so real and so dramatic to Americans of his day: "And yet it is but little more than two centuries since the oldest of our states received its first permanent colony. Before that time the whole territory was an unproductive waste. Throughout its wide extent the arts had not erected a monument." The aim of his *History* was "to explain how the change in the condition of our land has been brought about; and, as the fortunes of a nation are not under the control of blind destiny, to follow the steps by which a favoring Providence, calling our institutions into being, has conducted the country to its present happiness and glory."[38]

Here, with the nineteenth-century addition of a belief in ongoing scientific advance and its practical application, was the full development of a worldview that firmly linked economic and moral progress. At its center was an unmistakable image of economic growth.

Bancroft lived to see his *History* through a new edition nearly fifty years after he began the great project. Writing now from the perspective of the late nineteenth century, he chose to add to his earlier introduction only two sentences, hailing the nation's passage through the crisis of the Civil War and otherwise reaffirming its continuing progress: "The foregoing words, written nearly a half-century ago, are suffered to remain, because the intervening years have justified their expression of confidence in the progress of our republic. The seed of disunion has perished; and universal freedom, reciprocal benefits, and cherished traditions bind its many states in the closest union."[39]

The distinguished British economist Alfred Marshall cautiously summarized where matters stood at the end of the century in his *Principles of*

Economics, the classic treatise that served as the subject's basic text for more than a generation (and also first popularized the new name: "economics"). As if to answer directly the concerns voiced by both Marx and Smith, Marshall wrote, "The hope that poverty and ignorance may gradually be extinguished, derives much support from the steady progress of the working classes during the nineteenth century. The steam-engine has relieved them of much exhausting and degrading toil; wages have risen; education has improved and become more general . . . while the growing demand for intelligent work has caused the artisan classes to increase so rapidly that they now outnumber those whose labour is entirely unskilled." As a result, "a great part of the artisans have ceased to belong to the 'lower classes' in the sense in which the term was originally used; and some of them already lead a more refined and noble life than did the majority of the upper classes even a century ago."[40] In so naturally identifying both poverty and ignorance as the evils to be overcome, and a "refined and noble life" as the presumed object of proper aspiration, Marshall was implicitly confirming just how close the link between economic and moral progress had come to appear.

As Macaulay's appeal to "all religious minds" and Bancroft's reference to "a favoring Providence" suggest, the nineteenth-century perception of progress as both unified and inevitable also had its religious underpinnings. As the years passed, in both Britain and America, it became ever more difficult to distinguish religious thinking about world affairs from the secular view of progress.

For example, a magazine article bearing the title "Laws of Progress," which appeared in 1853, asked "what preceding age can compare with ours, in general knowledge and enjoyment of the rights of man, the principles of representative government, the true theory of social happiness, embodied, for example, in the British and American constitutions, the true landmarks of progress?" The author went on to identify technological progress as the fount of both material advance and a "nobler" life: "In physical science, not merely abstractly but in practical applications universally familiar, but not the less wonderful, by which the comfort of all is greatly increased, and abridgments of labor are multiplied, leaving more time and energy to be devoted to nobler purposes the pre-eminence of this period is almost universally allowed."[41]

Apart from the puffy language and tangled syntax, the author might well have been either Macaulay (the successive volumes of whose great *His-*

tory were only then just being published) or Bancroft. In the explicit connection running from "physical science" to "comfort" to "nobler purposes," it could even have been Smith. In fact, the article, which was anonymous, appeared in America, in the *Presbyterian Quarterly Review*. And it went on to relate these happy developments to the realization of God's purpose on earth.

As we have seen, well before the era of industrially applicable technology, the English and American Puritans had felt a keen affinity to scientific inquiry, and the central role of technological advances in spurring the Industrial Revolution opened a natural avenue for technology to take on a religious connotation in countries with Reformed Protestant traditions. Shortly before the turn of the nineteenth century, just as the practical implications of Watt's steam engine and of the textile-making machines invented by Arkwright, Hargreaves, and Crompton were becoming widely recognized, the American theologian Samuel Hopkins hailed labor-saving devices and other technological and material improvements as part of his vision of an ever better future in his classic work, *A Treatise on the Millennium*.[42] After the turn of the century, references to "comfort" and "convenience" increasingly figured in religious thinkers' ideas about the millennium and man's progress toward it.[43]

Similarly, ever since millennialism had again become not just an abstract notion of eventual spiritual development but a set of expectations about the course of worldly affairs, the spreading of knowledge and the particular role of communications and transportation in bringing about the unity of mankind—presumably under the banner of Christianity—were also prominent elements in Protestant religious thinking. Inventions like the telegraph, and later on the telephone, bore recognizable religious overtones, just as the printing press had several centuries before. (The laying of the first transatlantic cable, in 1858, was an event of particular religious significance for some Protestant groups.)[44] Especially in America, where physical distances were so great, developments like the steamboat and the railroad did as well.

The postmillennialist vision in particular—the belief that the return of Jesus would not occur until after the millennium, so that the promised period of earthly bliss would still be a part of human history as we know it—lent itself to a belief not just that secular progress was inevitable but that it had religious meaning and importance as well. In both Britain and America, the nineteenth century was the period when such thinking flourished, especially among the educated Protestant elites. The religious language in which Macaulay and Bancroft sometimes clothed their ideas about the progress their respective countries had made expressed a central aspect of the ethos of their age, their education, and their social standing. They did not emphasize the connection because, in the society in which they lived, it was taken for granted.

Technological and material advance, however, was not all that mattered. Postmillennialism also lent itself to a belief in the religious value of social reform. While the millennium and the subsequent return of Jesus were inevitable, it was still incumbent upon Christians to strive to hasten this much desired evolution. Eliminating evil in the world was a way of setting the stage for the millennium's dawning.[45] Not surprisingly, the profusion of social reform movements throughout the nineteenth century likewise took on a religious connotation: the abolitionist and temperance movements especially so, as well as many others in areas including education, hygiene, and democratic government.

America was a particular focus of this blurring of secular progress and the realization of religious aspirations. Many people of the time saw America, with its democratic form of government, its personal freedoms, and its seemingly unlimited natural resources, as both the philosophical and the physical realization of the Enlightenment.[46] (Many still do.) But from the earliest days of Puritan immigration, many had also attached a religious—in particular, a millennialist—significance to the colonization of unknown lands, the building of a new nation, the conquering of a vast continent, and, increasingly in the nineteenth century, the emergence of both agricultural and industrial strength on a scale that led the world's economic development.

The early Puritans had spoken of their "pious errand into the wilderness," a "mission" to create a Christian Commonwealth in the New World to serve as a "beacon" for others to follow—to establish, if not St. Augustine's City of God, then at least John Winthrop's City upon a Hill.[47] The rich tradition of personal liberty (for male citizens) that developed during the colonial era, and became enshrined in the Bill of Rights, likewise resonated with the emphasis on the individual that was so central to Reformed Protestant thinking.[48] The development of universal public education reflected not only the Puritans' emphasis on science but also the more general Protestant commitment to direct knowledge of scripture by the laity. The extended project of spreading European civilization (and Protestant Christianity) across an untamed continent had obvious religious overtones as well.

So too did the remarkable effusion of human energy that this endeavor required. The chronic "restlessness of temper" and "feverish ardor" that Tocqueville observed in how Americans in the early republic went about their business (as we shall see) seemed to reflect the kind of dedication to one's calling that the early Reformed Protestants had made central to their ideas about how to live one's life. In the context of the mighty challenges that Americans were continually meeting and overcoming, national striving became an extension of personal salvation. "A man at ease was a man lost" in Calvinist thinking, and the circumstances of early America made it hard to settle into either ease or complacency.[49]

Such resonances had led American religious thinkers of the eighteenth century, even before the Revolution and the establishment of the new republic, to see their new world as the center from which spiritual salvation would emanate. The Great Awakening of the 1740s had led many, including Jonathan Edwards, to think that what was happening in New England marked the beginning of an era of worldwide revivals. Edwards, who believed that God worked through favored nations, thought it likely that "this work of God's spirit . . . is the dawning, or at least a prelude, of that glorious work of God, so often foretold in Scripture, which . . . shall renew the world of mankind." He went on, "And there are many things that make it probable that this work will begin in America."[50]

These ideas gained renewed force in the first half of the nineteenth century as populist evangelical religion played a major role in what amounted to a reinventing of America.[51] Westward expansion, which had always had religious overtones, now became Manifest Destiny.[52] The eighteenth-century idea of an "American experiment" now became, in many eyes, the belief that God had chosen America as the nation through which to work his will, no less than he had long ago chosen the ancient Israelites. Americans and others too came to see the United States as a "redeemer nation," guiding the path toward the millennium. As Ernest Tuveson nicely put it in his book bearing that title, "The United States hardly needed to identify itself as the appointed agent of the Apocalypse; it seemed as if the stage manager of Providence had summoned the American people from the wings of the stage of history."[53]

Herman Melville combined the language of the Hebrew Bible and of early Calvinism in expressing this idea, just at the nineteenth century's midpoint, in *White-Jacket* (which preceded *Moby-Dick*): "we Americans are the peculiar, chosen people—the Israel of our time; we bear the ark of the liberties of the world. . . . God has predestined, mankind expects, great things from our race; and great things we feel in our souls." Indeed, America was more than just the new chosen nation: "the political Messiah . . . has come in *us*, if we would but give utterance to his promptings."[54] Soon thereafter the bloody trials of the Civil War, which many Americans also saw in explicitly religious terms—recall the words of the "Battle Hymn of the Republic"—further purified the chosen nation and its people, just as the American Revolution had done nearly a century earlier.55

In time, the explicit expression of this millennialist interpretation of secular progress faded, but the religious undertones remained. As popular literature like the Horatio Alger novels made clear, education was seen in the first instance as the route to worldly advance, including success in business. But the religious connotation of knowledge as an element of salvation remained strong as well. The Bible said that "poverty and disgrace come to him who ignores instruction," and so even the secular advantages of getting an education had ample religious imprimatur.56

At the same time, especially in America, Calvin's belief that riches came from God took ever greater hold on popular attitudes in an era when new industries and new railroads were not only raising living standards generally but creating concentrated wealth on a scale never before seen. Russell Conwell, the pastor of Philadelphia's Baptist Temple, declared that "there is not a poor person in the United States who was not made poor by his own shortcomings, or by the shortcomings of some one else."57 Later on, William Lawrence, the Episcopal bishop of Massachusetts, would write that "in the long run, it is only to the man of morality that wealth comes. . . . Godliness is in league with riches."58

Conwell was an especially illustrative example of the combination of secular foreground and religious backdrop that was so characteristic of ideas about the unity of "progress" in the late nineteenth century. In addition to his church role, Conwell founded Temple University, and for many years he served simultaneously as pastor and university president. His unique distinction, however, was to have delivered thousands of times, all across America, a motivational address titled "Acres of Diamonds." (The title refers to the story of a young man who traveled the world in search of riches, only to return home and find "acres of diamonds" in his backyard.) In what amounted to an extreme simplification of Adam Smith's vision of how competitive markets harness individual self-interest for the common good, Conwell advised that the way to get rich was to think creatively about how to improve the lot of one's fellow human beings. And in an echo of Horatio Alger's theme of "luck and pluck," Conwell affirmed that while not everyone *would* get rich, in America anyone *could*. As he told the listeners at each performance of "Acres of Diamonds," "[T]he opportunity to get rich, to attain unto great wealth is . . . within the reach of almost every man and woman who hears me speak tonight, and I mean just what I say."59

Conwell's theme also had a moral component that clearly drew on familiar elements of Protestant religious thinking. While only a few would actually succeed in getting rich, the idea that the path to riches lay in improving the lot of one's fellow citizens meant that everyone had a positive obligation to seek to do so. The central message of "Acres of Diamonds" was that "you ought to get rich, and it is your duty to get rich."[60] And among those who succeeded in doing so, almost all were men of moral standing: "ninety-eight out of one hundred of the rich men of America are honest. That is why they are rich."[61] Nor did Conwell ignore the principles of asceticism in personal life that Weber, writing contemporaneously, emphasized as central to the economic implications of the "Protestant ethic." While getting rich was much to be desired, in "Acres of Diamonds" Conwell condemned lavish consumption. (He also warned of the damage a rich man would do to his children by leaving them large amounts of money; the unstated implication was that the only proper use of wealth was philanthropy.) But *economic* effort, and the material progress that it brought, were central to the vision of *moral* progress.

By late in the century, the ever greater blurring of the religious and the secular in American attitudes toward progress, at least among the educated elites, prompted a reaction in the form of the Social Gospel movement.[62] As postmillennialism—by now often called "civil millennialism"—had faded into a general metaphor for perpetual temporal improvement, the human journey had become a goal in itself and the idea of a final destination had largely disappeared from view. The Social Gospel movement was an attempt to restore an explicit role for Protestant Christianity. Its leaders shared the same concerns with the problems of temporal society, and the same focus on social reform, but they sought a renewed motivation drawn from the teaching of Jesus as seen through the mainline Protestant churches. As we shall see, the Social Gospel movement gained further strength after the turn of the twentieth century and became a significant force for American social reform in the years immediately before World War I.

Even without this late-century revival, however, it was clear that religious underpinnings had long been an essential foundation beneath the nineteenth-century belief in progress, including especially the ultimate unity of material progress and moral progress. As Tuveson has argued, "The most important contribution of the millennialist idea was the confidence that mankind can and will climb at last into a Golden Age. That contribution originally was religious, and the idea of progress in English-speaking countries probably has never wholly lost its religious coloration."[63]

. . .

Attitudes toward the connection (or lack thereof) between material and moral progress have continued to evolve to this day. But the dominant lines of thinking developed in the Enlightenment and then elaborated during the nineteenth century have continued to define the basic questions at issue.

Over time the balance of optimism or pessimism about prospects for human progress, and also the public sense of a connection between the economic and the moral dimension in this regard, have often shifted in response to the improvement or stagnation of the society's living standards. As we shall see, America's protracted agricultural depression of the 1880s and early 1890s was the backdrop to the declinist views of Brooks Adams and the industrial pessimism of Henry George. It was also during this difficult period that Frederick Jackson Turner offered his new interpretation of American history, which differed from the traditional "Whig" view (as expressed by Bancroft) by identifying free land rather than technological progress as the engine of America's economic and moral development, and therefore held out a pessimistic prospect at the vanishing of "the frontier." At the same time, writers of American fiction took a harsh view of what "commerce" (by now rendered as "business") meant, both practically and morally.

A parallel erosion of confidence and optimism occurred in Britain, and under similar economic circumstances. In his famous poem "Locksley Hall," first published in 1842, Tennyson had articulated the spirit of the Crystal Palace era, writing "Forward, forward let us range, Let the great world spin forever down the ringing grooves of change." In "Locksley Hall Sixty Years After," published in 1886, he squarely rejected that earlier optimism: "Gone the cry of 'Forward, Forward,' lost within a growing gloom; . . . Let us hush this cry of 'Forward' till ten thousand years have gone."*

---

*Earlier in "Locksley Hall," Tennyson's more famous lines had envisioned a utopian future, including myriad human advantages and even universal peace:

> For I dipt into the future, far as human eye could see,
> Saw the Vision of the world, and all the wonder that would be; . . .
> Till the war-drum throbb'd no longer, and the battle-flags were furl'd
> In the Parliament of man, the Federation of the world.

By contrast, parts of "Locksley Hall Sixty Years After" even echoed the social discontent of Marx:

> Is it well that while we range with Science, glorying in the Time,
> City children soak and blacken soul and sense in city slime?
> There among the glooming alleys Progress halts on palsied feet,
> Crime and hunger cast our maidens by the thousand on the street.

Other British writers, of both fiction and social commentary, reflected a similar change in attitude. In a lecture that he delivered two years before his death in 1895, the great biologist T. H. Huxley looked back at the spirit of optimism and faith in progress that had characterized so much of British thought earlier on and, in what became one of his most famous remarks, wrote that "One does not hear so much of it as one did forty years ago; indeed, I imagine it is to be met with more commonly at the tables of the healthy and wealthy, than in the congregations of the wise."[64]

By contrast, the literature of the early years of the twentieth century, when economic growth was strong and the prospect of world war yet unseen, was positive and optimistic. Even prospects for world peace seemed bright. As late as 1910, with large-scale naval building programs well underway in both Britain and Germany, the Anglo-American economist and peace activist Norman Angell dismissed the idea of war among countries bound by extensive commercial and financial ties as a "great illusion." In his classic book bearing that title, Angell argued "that military and political power give a nation no commercial advantage; that it is an economic impossibility for one nation to seize or destroy the wealth of another, or for one nation to enrich itself by subjecting another." Instead, "wealth in the economically civilized world is founded upon credit and commercial contract."[65]

Reflecting the same faith in progress that had been so typical of the nineteenth century, but now in an age that had more nearly come to terms with Darwin, Angell went on to claim "that human nature is not unchanging; that the warlike nations do not inherit the earth; that warfare does not make for the survival of the fittest or virile; that the struggle between nations is no part of the evolutionary law of man's advance."[66] The war that followed soon thereafter falsified the pacifist prediction that Angell drew from his ideas, but in many ways the war's aftermath confirmed the central tenets of his thinking: the defeated nations suffered economically, but the victors did not prosper.

The shock of World War I was all the greater against the background of precisely the belief in the unity and inevitability of progress that had held sway in Western thinking since the Enlightenment. As cultural historian Paul Fussell has argued, "the Great War was . . . a hideous embarrassment to the prevailing Meliorist myth which had dominated the public consciousness for a century. It reversed the idea of Progress . . . the collision was one

---

Robert W. Hill, Jr., *Tennyson's Poetry* (New York: Norton, 2nd ed. 1999), pp. 119, 121, 554, 559.

between events and the public language used for over a century to celebrate the idea of progress."[67] Oswald Spengler's *The Decline of the West* appeared, in Germany, in the midst of that country's postwar economic and political chaos.

The Great Depression that followed a decade after the war was a shock as well. The spectacle of seemingly intractable worldwide economic decline undermined the very basis for a concept of human progress that had made economic advance the mechanism connecting scientific progress to moral progress. The most immediately threatening manifestation of the depression was mass unemployment, and as we shall see, President Franklin D. Roosevelt explicitly framed the loss of the opportunity to work in moral terms. But the loss of confidence in future economic growth was also a major theme in the reaction to the protracted decline.

The prominent American economist Alvin Hansen, reaching back to Marx's and John Stuart Mill's notions of a "stationary state," suggested that the United States had become a "mature economy" with little potential for further growth.[68] (At the end of *The Decline and Fall of the Roman Empire*, which appeared in the same year as Smith's *The Wealth of Nations*, Edward Gibbon had nicely summarized the Enlightenment view of what these later economists would call a stationary state: "All that is human must retrograde if it does not advance.")[69] Marxian ideas returned to fashion in a much more general way in the 1930s, and in the early 1940s widely respected non-Marxist thinkers like the economist Joseph Schumpeter and the theologian Reinhold Niebuhr advanced their own largely pessimistic views about the prospects for progress in general and capitalism in particular. Even as late as the early 1950s, American writers like Walter Lippmann were expressing what now seems in hindsight a remarkable degree of pessimism.[70]

But the intellectual tide changed once the reality of postwar prosperity became apparent, and by the late 1950s and especially the 1960s— in the United States, before the disappointments of Vietnam and then Watergate—a renewed optimism emerged that resonated strongly with earlier strands of thinking about the nature and causes of progress. As sociologist Daniel Bell put it, by the 1960s faith in economic growth as a "social solvent," providing the wherewithal to correct whatever needed fixing in the world, had become "the secular religion of advancing industrial societies: the source of individual motivation, the basis of political solidarity, the ground for the mobilization of society for a common purpose."[71]

The traditional faith in scientific advance as the fountain of economic and therefore moral progress likewise flourished anew in this time of prosperity and general optimism. When President John F. Kennedy proposed

a manned moon landing as a high-priority goal of American national policy, and the project succeeded within a decade, the bold endeavor captured
the popular imagination. Most Americans instinctively understood that
advances in scientific knowledge were the basis of gains in economic productivity, and in retrospect the chief surprise in this regard was how rapidly
many of the space program's technological achievements—fuel cells, computer hardware, communications satellites, even equipment for monitoring
human cardiovascular function—found practical commercial applications.
But beyond the scientific excitement and whatever anticipation the public
had of direct economic benefits, the popular enthusiasm for space exploration carried an echo of the traditional assumption that the advance of
knowledge, working in significant part through economic channels, would
lead in time to a morally improved society.[72]

Beginning in the 1970s, after the Organization of Petroleum Exporting
Countries (OPEC) raised oil prices and a pervasive economic slowdown
ensued, the "limits to growth" (as the Club of Rome report famously labeled
the issue) again became the object of intense concern. So did the "cultural
contradictions of capitalism," in the apt phrase that Daniel Bell used as the
title of his widely read book.[73] By 1982 the American Academy of Arts and
Sciences sponsored a volume of essays titled *Prosperity and Its Discontents.*
Joel Colton, of the Rockefeller Foundation, would begin his foreword
to the book by asking: "What has happened in our day to the idea of
progress—the belief in the continuing improvement of the human condition? To contemporary ears it has a hollow ring."[74] The chapter on economics, written by the distinguished economist Moses Abramowitz, was titled
"The Retreat from Economic Advance." (In contrast to the pessimism of
the 1930s, however, none of these lines of argument drew in any significant
way on Marxist thinking. Well before the Soviet Union collapsed, that
country's increasingly obvious economic weakness, together with the widespread discontent in the USSR's Eastern European satellites, had left Marx's
economic ideas largely discredited.)

At the same time, strains of the Romantic disenchantment expressed
more than a century earlier by Carlyle and Emerson also reappeared. Much
of this new Romanticism had been a reaction against the strains of globalization, including the failure of many developing countries to advance as
rapidly as some had hoped, and also a familiar nostalgia for traditional ways
of life in an era of modernization. But parts of the Romantic reaction also
focused on America, addressing mounting concerns over the deterioration
of the family as an institution and of individual values more generally.[75]
Reactions to corporate "downsizing"—not just because new ways of doing

business have caused widespread personal hardship, but also for the effect they have had in eroding long-standing notions of loyalty between employee and employer—have echoed the concerns expressed 100 and 200 years earlier. In the financial world, the emergence of "transaction banking" in place of the more traditional "relationship banking" has prompted similar reactions. Even the movement to undermine the foundation of traditional views of progress by questioning whether there is such a thing as objective scientific reality once again gained some renewed currency during this period of slower growth.

Ironically, just as the absence of economic growth was fostering skepticism about progress and heightening the appetite for nostalgia in America and the other traditional Western democracies, the collapse of the Soviet Union and its European empire was stimulating a new confidence in prospects for economic advance, as well as the development of civil democracy, in parts of the world where that belief had long been banished. As stagnation finally gave way to a burst of renewed growth in the United States, beginning in the mid-1990s, American attitudes likewise became more positive. The source of much of this renewed growth in new information technologies reinforced the familiar theme of science as the starting point for the chain leading to economic and then broader progress.

In the meanwhile, however, the "Asian" financial crisis of the late 1990s (which affected much of Latin America as well) prompted fresh concerns about many of the more successful economies in the developing world, and the dismal plight of many African countries has continued to worsen. And in the United States and elsewhere, the attacks of September 11, 2001, and the resulting fears of an ongoing struggle with an amorphous but deadly international terrorism, have raised yet a new specter confronting both the economic and the political and social prospects of the democratic West.

As the tortuous history of attitudes toward progress over the last century and continuing into our own time reveals, not only do broadly understood ideas of progress assign a central role to economic advance but they depend on rising living standards for their ability to generate widespread appeal. The point of this look back at earlier perspectives on economic and moral progress is not to imply that the connection between economic growth and the advance of openness, tolerance, and democracy argued in what follows—or, conversely, the effect of economic stagnation in leading to social retreat and political rigidification—is identical to any, much less all, of these earlier lines of thought. But there are similarities, and some of the resonance runs deep. The long history of thinking about progress, both material and moral, provides a supportive tradition for what is a new idea in some respects but a very old idea in many others.

One important question left unresolved in that tradition, however, is whether progress—again, both material and moral—is inevitable. (Millennialists certainly thought so.) As we shall see, there are plausible reasons why a rising standard of living, broadly distributed across a society, fosters positive developments in spheres of life beyond economics, and there is much evidence to indicate that rising living standards have just these consequences. Moreover, in America as in most other Western societies, there is substantial agreement that these very features of social and political development constitute a significant part of what is morally desirable. Is there then a moral imperative to seek economic growth in order to promote these ends? Or can citizens have confidence that economic growth, and the moral progress that a rising standard of living implies, will occur on their own?

Ample experience shows that at least over time spans that are easily long enough to affect profoundly the lives of individuals as well as the existence of nations, neither economic nor moral progress is to be taken for granted. Progress may or may not be inevitable, but it is surely not without interruption. Within the lifetime of any person, or any generation, whether progress occurs depends in large part on the choices and actions people take, both individually and collectively. As we shall also see, for the aspects of progress that are measured in economic terms, that includes economic policy.

Chapter 4

Rising Incomes, Individual Attitudes, and the Politics of Social Change

[A]fter a time new riches often lose a great part of their charms.
Partly this is the result of familiarity.

ALFRED MARSHALL
Principles of Economics[1]

Men do not desire merely to be *rich*,
but to be *richer* than other men.

JOHN STUART MILL
On Social Freedom[2]

It is not hard to see that a strong economy, where opportunities are plentiful and jobs go begging, helps break down social barriers. Bigoted employers may still dislike hiring members of one group or another, but when nobody else is available discrimination most often gives way to the sheer need to get the work done. The same goes for employees with prejudices about whom they do and do not like working alongside. In the American construction boom of the late 1990s, for example, even the carpenters' union—long known as a "traditional bastion of white men, a world where a coveted union card was handed down from father to son"—began openly recruiting women, blacks, and Hispanics for its apprenticeship program.[3] At least in the workplace, jobs chasing people obviously does more to promote a fluid society than people chasing jobs.

But low unemployment is not the same as economic growth. Jobs can be plentiful even as wages decline and living standards stagnate, as was the case in the United States much of the time from the early 1970s through the early 1990s. Economic growth means rising incomes and improving living standards, and over more than just the few years of the typical business cycle. This can happen only when there is a sustained advance in productivity, and productivity growth need not bring low unemployment. Indeed, as the experience of one industry after another has shown, beginning with the introduction of power looms to replace hand weavers at the outset of the Industrial Revolution, when an economy achieves productivity gains by adopting new technologies the immediate result is often to eliminate jobs (but also to push up the wages of those still working) for some time thereafter.

Moreover, while eradicating job discrimination is surely important, creating an open, tolerant, democratic society requires much more. Issues of social prejudice, of how generously the society deals with its unfortunates, of who goes to school with whom, even of who gets to vote, have all been central to the turmoil and change that America has experienced over just the last century. Elsewhere, the story has involved not just exclusion and intolerance but outright persecution and religious and ethnic warfare.

For economic growth to foster greater tolerance and fairness and democracy, therefore, the mechanism at work must cut deeper than just the difference between tight and slack job markets. What matters is how rising incomes shape the perspective and attitudes of those who earn them, and their families, and how the resulting impact on enough individuals' attitudes in turn brings about change in a country's political institutions and social dynamics.

At first thought, the notion that people are more inclined to be generous, or tolerant, or democratic when they are getting ahead may seem obvious. But different reactions are no less plausible. Why don't rising incomes merely intensify the competition to be richer than everyone else? Why don't they generate increased disdain for whoever falls behind, or a feeling that only the most successful should have a say in the nation's affairs? Why then does economic growth more typically have just the opposite effect?

The key is that while everybody of course wants to have more income so as to enjoy a higher standard of living, better health, and a greater sense of security, our sense of what constitutes "more" for any of these purposes is mostly relative. Whenever people are asked how well off they think they are, they almost always respond by comparing their lives to some kind of reference point.[4] Further, whether most people think what they have or how they live constitutes "more" or "less" depends on how their circumstances compare to two separate benchmarks: their own (or their family's) past experience, and how they see people around them living.

The principal driving force underlying the positive influence that economic growth has over people's attitudes, and through the political process therefore over the character of their society, is the interaction between how each of these two respective points of comparison affects people's perceptions. Obviously nothing can enable the majority of the population to be better off than everyone else. But not only is it possible for most people to be better off than they used to be, that is precisely what economic growth means. The central question is whether, when people see that they are doing well (in other words, enjoying "more") compared to the benchmark of their own prior experience, or their parents'—or when they believe that their children's lives will be better still—they consequently feel less need to get ahead compared to other people. If so, then the reduced importance they attach to living better than others leads in the end to more wide-ranging benefits, for the society as a whole, whenever general living standards are increasing.

Happiness depends, of course, on more than just money and the things money can buy. In surveys, most people say that their sense of satisfaction with their lives depends most on the strength of their family relationships and personal friendships, or their health, or their education, or their religious attachment, or their feeling of connection to a broader community beyond their own family, or their sense of being engaged in purposeful and productive work, or even on their everyday work environment.[5] In many surveys the single most important influence on adults' happiness is whether they are married. (People who are, or who are living together as if they were, are typically happier.)[6] People with "extrovert" personalities also tend to be happier on average, perhaps simply because they have more friends.[7]

Money matters too, however. People with more income typically enjoy not just a higher standard of living in terms of food, clothing, and housing but also better health (in part because of better access to medical care, but also because they drink and smoke less and get more exercise). They also have better educations and a stronger sense of security in the face of major life uncertainties. Familiar popular images of the business rat race notwithstanding, people with higher incomes on average also have more leisure time, and they mostly spend it in activities that foster the friendships they then say (in surveys) matter far more than money. Having at least some financial resources is even helpful in maintaining marriages, perhaps because it allows young couples to live on their own instead of with their parents.[8] At any given time, within a given country, people with lower incomes are far more likely to say that they are unhappy.[9]

But the essential point is that how much income it takes to enjoy advantages like these is a relative matter, and the most obvious benchmark people have in mind when they draw such comparisons is their own past experience. People who live better now than they did before, or better than they recall their parents living, are likely to think they are doing well. Those who look back on better times—better for them and their families, that is—think they are not. As a result, psychological studies have repeatedly confirmed that people's satisfaction depends less on the *level* of their income than on *how it is changing*.[10] But rising incomes are, in turn, what economic growth is all about.*

Moreover, most of the time economic growth provides people not only with higher incomes that enable them to buy more of whatever they had before, but also with much that is new or improved. New products and new ways of organizing productive activity are usually the essence of what creates economic growth: within the last century, for example, first automobiles and airplanes, then television, and then consumer electronics appeared, while at the same time work on farms and in dirty factories increasingly gave way to cleaner, less physically demanding jobs in modern manufacturing facilities and in the rapidly expanding service sector. With economic growth, people are also typically aware that their lives are qualitatively different.

There is also plenty of evidence, however, that as time passes and people get used to circumstances that once seemed new and different, the benchmark against which they compare their current situation adjusts to reflect their more recent custom.[11] Abraham Lincoln remarked, when a friend asked him why he paid no attention to the death threats he frequently

---

*The idea that satisfaction depends primarily on changes in economic well-being (to the extent that economic factors are important in this regard) is hardly new. Adam Smith observed that "all men, sooner or later, accommodate themselves to whatever becomes their permanent situation." Hence "between one permanent situation and another, there [is], with regard to real happiness, no essential difference" (*The Theory of Moral Sentiments*, p. 149). Moreover, Smith claimed no originality for this view but attributed it to the Stoic philosophers of ancient Greece.

received as president, "there is nothing like getting used to things."[12] In just the same way, most Americans today do not derive much satisfaction from continually reminding themselves of the gap by which their current living standard—or, for that matter, their scientific knowledge or their cultural attainments or their awareness of the broader world—exceeds what was common fifty or a hundred years ago. People do look back to make comparisons, but not that far back. Even the winners of multimillion-dollar lottery jackpots typically experience only a short-lived euphoria, after which they soon get used to their new wealth and the lifestyle it has made possible.[13]

Economic growth matters because it enables the majority of a society's population to feel better off compared to benchmarks that are still recent enough to be meaningful. But once growth stops—no matter how high people's incomes have risen—it is only a question of time before habits adapt and the sense of heightened well-being dissipates. Not only does a better standard of living come to seem familiar and customary, so too do changes like improved working conditions, fewer hours on the job, and superior medical treatment. Only if growth and change persist will people continue to feel better off.*

Adam Smith, writing more than two centuries ago, before anyone had grasped the possibilities for a permanently rising standard of living that technology was just then beginning to create, nonetheless understood the difference that rising incomes make: "[I]t is in the progressive state, while the society is advancing to the further acquisition, rather than when it has acquired its full complement of riches, that the condition of . . . the great body of the people, seems to be the happiest and the most comfortable. It is hard in the stationary, and miserable in the declining state." As a result, he concluded, "The progressive state is in reality the cheerful and the hearty state to all the different orders of society. The stationary state is dull; the declining melancholy."[14]

What makes this aspect of economic growth all the more important is that people respond differently to hopes of having "more" than to fears of having

---

*This same basic human reaction to past progress—the tendency to ask what have you done for me *lately*?—is of course familiar in many other contexts as well, very often to the chagrin of those whose hard work and sometimes whose genius have been responsible for the earlier advances that made possible what everyone now simply accepts as the norm. In areas of endeavor ranging from business to politics, the civil rights movement, science, and even artistic achievement, an all too common figure is the pioneer of one era whose accomplishments are taken for granted in the next.

"less." Over time people's happiness may return to its usual level after either an improvement or a deterioration in their economic circumstances, but at least when people contemplate such prospects *beforehand*, fear is stronger. One of the "deepest instincts of man," wrote Oliver Wendell Holmes, Jr., is that "a thing which you enjoyed and used as your own for a long time . . . takes root in your being and cannot be torn away without your resenting the act and trying to defend yourself, however you came by it."[15] Or as Tocqueville observed, explaining what made the Americans he saw in his travels so energetic, "the most imperious of all necessities [is] that of not sinking in the world."[16]

This reluctance to give up whatever people already have concretely in hand pervades human attitudes toward matters including wealth, income, lifestyle, risks to health or even life, and even seemingly trivial aspects of everyday occurrences. The basic point is that what people think depends on what they have.[17] Attitudes toward a job that pays $53,000 a year (about the median income today for American families), versus another paying, say, $10,000 more, are very different in a family with a current income of $40,000 than in a family whose income is $70,000. For exactly the same reason, most stock market investors regard missing out on a potential gain as nowhere near as painful as actually incurring a loss.[18]

Even in responding to hypothetical questions, most people not only show that losses loom larger than gains but also display a clear preference for whatever situation the questioner establishes, explicitly or perhaps more subtly, as the status quo. (This pattern of behavior is part of what enables political pollsters to engineer the results their clients want, and also why people's choices on what kind of medical treatment to seek—whether to operate on a tumor, for example—differ depending on whether the probabilities involved are framed in terms of the odds of survival or the odds of mortality.) In the typical response, people resist the idea of losses from whatever is the presumed status quo more than they value gains beyond it. For example, if told that they will receive $1,000 and then asked to choose between getting an additional $500 for sure or a fifty-fifty gamble on getting nothing or another $1,000, most people will choose the sure $500. But if told that they will receive $2,000, and asked to choose between a sure $500 *loss* and a fifty-fifty chance of *losing* $1,000 or nothing, most people will choose the gamble. The two situations, however, are identical.[19]

In an entirely different context, most people, if told that a potentially cancer-causing chemical may soon begin leaking into their local water supply from a nearby industrial dump, will favor aggressive and, if necessary, costly measures to stop the leak. But if told that their water supply has recently been discovered to have been contaminated by this substance, which has been leaking into it for some time, the same people will be much less eager to spend money to get rid of it. The hypothetical risk of cancer in the two situations is the same. But in the first instance this risk is presented as something new, while in the second it appears to be part of people's existing circumstances.[20] (In an especially tragic example of this psychology at work, featured in Jonathan Harr's book *A Civil Action*, families in Woburn, Massachusetts, refused to move from a neighborhood that had become contaminated even after the hazard had become apparent and some of their children had developed leukemia.) At the opposite extreme of importance, many people become surprisingly attached to trivial physical objects, even if they have owned them for only a very short time.[21]

This tendency for people to become strongly attached to whatever they currently have bears far-reaching implications. On the positive side, it helps give our lives stability. Most people do not spend each day dissipating their emotional and intellectual energy by endlessly reconsidering whether they are pursuing the best possible career, or living in the best possible house, or whether they are married to the best possible life partner. Nor do they keep changing jobs or swapping houses just because whichever situation looked slightly less preferable last month now seems a bit more so. Over time people become attached to the job, the house, the spouse, and the friends they have. It may be true that in many settings "the grass looks greener" elsewhere, but when it comes to actually making a switch, the *dis*advantages normally loom much larger than the advantages. Most people simply do not reshuffle their basic life arrangements with every minute change in their daily circumstances.

In other contexts—especially including situations in which people have to compromise in order to reach agreement with one another—the proclivity to form strong attachments to whatever they have or whatever they are accustomed to doing can be more problematic. For example, most people would be irate if their city government forced them to move to a new house to make way for a new road, even though the city paid them "full market value" for their old one. Full market value may be what the house is objectively worth to someone who has never lived in it, but to the family that lives there it is worth far more. For much the same reason, bargaining between labor and management over such issues as work rules is often much more difficult than even well-informed outsiders expect. Each side places greater value on whatever it is asked to give up than the corresponding value placed on that concession by the other side (or by an unbiased third party). As a result, each side thinks it is getting the short end of the bargain, and it is hard to reach an agreement unless the new work rules improve productivity sufficiently to provide a substantial premium for each side.[22]

Because of this fundamental asymmetry in how most people perceive gains and losses, a steady rate of economic growth affects people's attitudes differently than the same average growth but with pronounced ups and downs along the way. Because losses provoke a stronger reaction than gains, people's discontent in downswings is likely to be more intense than the satisfaction they take in expansions.[23] Sizable business cycle swings, therefore, are likely to detract from whatever feeling of satisfaction people take from a country's longer-run trend of economic growth.

Economic growth itself, however, whether steady or irregular, crucially affects people's attitudes toward matters including equal opportunity and economic mobility. Because fear of moving down the economic scale is more compelling than the opportunity to move up, the prospect of mobility is naturally threatening. But in a stagnant economy, where one person's gain is necessarily someone else's loss, people who get ahead are perceived not only as doing so at other people's expense but as directly disadvantaging others. As a result, the people who strongly support expanding opportunities in a stagnant economy are mostly either those who have little to lose because they are starting off near the bottom of the economic and social ladder, or those who think that their particular circumstances make them especially likely to benefit from specific new developments. Neither group is likely to be the dominant force in any society. Usually people at the bottom have both economic and political influence that is disproportionately weak compared to their numbers, and most new developments bring likely losers as well as likely winners. Stagnant economies, therefore, do not breed support for economic mobility, or for openness of opportunity more generally.

Indeed, in societies where the prospect of economic growth seems sufficiently remote that people believe it is possible to get ahead only by taking away what others have, moral and legal impediments to individual efforts to achieve economic or social advancement are often no more than part of keeping the peace. In the absence of any concept of potential growth, even the accumulation of wealth from the productive use of capital is often an object of suspicion. Until the Industrial Revolution gave people the idea that economic growth was possible, "usury" laws that prohibited even ordinary lending at interest, as well as sumptuary laws forbidding people to wear clothing or live in houses "above their station," were familiar in most Western countries. Positive measures to promote economic mobility were simply absent, and discrimination based on birth was the norm.

By contrast, under robust economic growth the fundamental asymmetry between "more" and "less" takes on reduced importance because, for most people, downward mobility—should that be someone's lot—does not mean "less" but merely not as much "more" as they might otherwise enjoy. Over a far broader range of the income distribution, therefore, people in a growing economy will be willing to accept enhanced mobility, and they are willing to accept measures like anti-discrimination laws, or special education programs for children from low-income families, designed to make actual mobility greater.

Apart from looking back at their own experience, the other obvious benchmark against which people compare their standard of living is how people around them live.[24] This too has potentially important implications for both the causes and the consequences of economic growth.[25] The desire to get ahead compared to other people, just like the desire to advance beyond one's own prior experience, creates a motivation for economic effort that persists no matter how high living standards rise. Even citizens of high-income countries still have an incentive to work, to invent new technologies, and to create new enterprises. The difference is that when people judge how well off they are by comparing their own circumstances to what they see around them, raising everyone's living standard together leaves no one feeling better off than before. When incomes across the entire spectrum rise, people's sense of what it means to be rich or poor simply adjusts in step.

There is ample evidence that people think this way, at least in part. Beginning in 1952 the Gallup poll regularly asked Americans, "What is the minimum amount of money a family of four needs to get along in this community?" Over the next quarter-century—a period of rapid growth, over which incomes on average rose by more than 50 percent even after allowing for higher consumer prices—the average response to the question roughly tracked the rise in average income. In 1952 the perceived minimum "to get along" was 42.7 percent of the average after-tax income for a family of four. Twenty-five years later it was 41.3 percent, nearly unchanged.[26] Families whose income had risen merely in step with the country's average saw no improvement compared to what they regarded as the required minimum for merely getting along. Only after the rise in incomes slowed, beginning in the late 1970s, did the perceived minimum needed to get along decline as a share of average income. (By 1986, the last year Gallup asked this question, the average response was down to 36.3 percent of average income.)

The force of comparing ourselves against other people is apparent in other ways too that bear more closely on social and political issues. Today an

American family that is at the borderline of the bottom one-fifth of the nation's income distribution has an income of $24,100 per year—nearly three-fifths greater than the median income of *all* American families in the early years of this century after allowing for higher prices.[27] Moreover, this favorable comparison does not take account of programs like food stamps, Medicaid, and government housing assistance, on which many bottom-fifth families now draw.[28] But because its income is small compared to what other Americans make today—the median income for all families is now $52,700—not only does the family that earns $24,100 think of its living standard as low, but the American body politic as a whole finds it unacceptable and therefore provides funding for various forms of public assistance on which such families can rely.

What it means to be poor is, to a surprisingly great extent, a matter of social comparisons. Even our sense of the basic physical requirements of life—the most obvious example is food—heavily depends on what we see around us. As economist Amartya Sen has pointed out, although physical well-being increases with nutrition over a fairly wide range, in fact people can survive with very little nutrition. Hence "there is difficulty in drawing a line somewhere, and the so-called 'minimum nutritional requirements' have an inherent arbitrariness."[29] Even Karl Marx, who predicted that recurring crises of capitalism would drive workers' wages to the "subsistence" level, nonetheless acknowledged that over time the accepted notion of what that meant would move upward.[30]

Precisely because being poor is largely a relative matter, most countries other than the United States do not define an absolute "poverty line" but instead merely report how many families or individuals live on incomes below some stated fraction of the national average. In 1995 a panel commissioned by the Joint Economic Committee of Congress recommended that America also adopt an official poverty concept that would change over time in relation to a measure of average income.[31] (Before the establishment of a fixed poverty line in 1965, successive widely recognized measures of "minimum subsistence budgets" did generally increase over time, although not as rapidly as the rise in average income.)[32] Adopting a flexible, relative standard of this kind would probably increase the current estimate of poverty in America. At the same time, many Americans who fall below today's recognized poverty line—$19,200 for a family of four—would be considered extremely well off if they lived in some other country.[33] The point is, they don't.[34]

Thinking in terms of such comparisons is relevant not just in regard to the bottom of the income scale, but to how people assess their well-being more generally. Ever since the 1870s, for example, the British have seen both their economic preeminence and their leadership in world affairs continually eroded by the advance of other countries. One result has been more than a century of analysis of Britain's "decline."[35] Yet Britain's per capita income was one-third *higher* (after allowing for inflation) on the eve of World War I than in 1870, it was more than half again higher in 1960, and since then it has more than doubled again. The much lamented decline has only been in relation to other countries that grew even faster.[36]

Moreover, there is reason to think that the tendency to look over one's shoulder in just this way may well have intensified in recent years, at least in the international context. In a widely publicized study carried out in the late 1950s and early 1960s, researchers asked citizens of more than a dozen countries whether they were happy with their lives.[37] As expected, people's responses indicated that those who were better off tended to be happier than the poor *within* any one country. But the surprising result was that, on average, the citizens of poor countries were no less satisfied than those of rich countries. Germany's per capita income was four times Yugoslavia's and fourteen times Nigeria's, but Germans, Yugoslavians, and Nigerians were all, on average, about equally happy.[38]

By contrast, when new researchers carried out a similar study a quarter-century later, the results were dramatically different. Now the Swiss, Norwegians, and Canadians were distinctly more satisfied than the Germans and Belgians, and they were more satisfied than the Italians and Spaniards, who in turn were more satisfied than the Greeks and Portuguese. The alignment with per capita income was not perfect (the Irish, for example, stood out by being much happier than their comparatively low average income level alone would have suggested), but it was very close. Citizens of richer countries, on average, now professed to be distinctly happier than those of poorer countries.[39] Still more recently, surveys conducted in a wide range of countries, including many in Africa, Asia, and Latin America, as well as new countries that until 1990 were parts of the Soviet Union, have likewise shown that people on average are more satisfied with their lives in countries where per capita income is higher.[40]

The most plausible explanation for this puzzling change is that while people in the pre-television era mostly compared themselves to their fellow countrymen, and felt either satisfied or frustrated depending on whether their own circumstances matched what they saw at close hand, once a new generation grew up watching TV it began to look at matters differently. What people see on television every day, even if it reflects the lives of citizens in other countries, may provide a standard of comparison that seems more relevant than what they may know about the lifestyle of those among their own fellow citizens whom they rarely if ever see. When residents of cities like Athens or Lisbon, for example, watch programs depicting urban life in Lyon, Stuttgart, and Los Angeles, what they see may well matter more to their sense of themselves than their impressions of conditions in the rural villages and farms of the Greek or Portuguese countryside.[41] John Steinbeck, looking back on his years as a young man in pre-television California, made the same point: "[W]e had no envy of the rich. We didn't know any rich. We thought everyone lived the way we lived, if we thought of it at all."[42] The same unawareness is hard to imagine today.

The importance of social comparisons as a benchmark for thinking we are well-off goes far beyond issues of either poverty lines or cross-country investigations. This aspect of human nature is both more pervasive and more personal than that. As Daniel Bell explained, in Adam Smith's view "it is not economic motivation that prompts a man to work, but status, respect, esteem, moral mettle, qualities which would enable him to be a man of worth and dignity."[43] Maintaining self-esteem—as Thorstein Veblen put it, echoing Smith, striving "to stand well in the eyes of the community"—is a basic drive of every individual.[44]

The result, in Veblen's words, is "a desire to live up to the conventional standard of decency." But "conventional" ends up meaning what everybody else has. The standard to which people aspire is "flexible . . . infinitely extensible."[45] And it refers not just to a person's overall standard of living but even to specific aspects of the houses where people live, or the cars they drive, or the food they eat and the clothing they wear. Moreover, the comparisons that matter are specific to both time and place. (In Adam Smith's famous example, although people of an era earlier than his had no linen, "in the present times, through the greater part of Europe, a creditable day-laborer would be ashamed to appear in public without a linen shirt." Smith went on to discuss footwear. In England, he wrote, leather shoes were necessary for "the poorest creditable person of either sex" to avoid shame in public, whereas in Scotland they were necessary to even "the lowest order of men" but not to women. In France "they [were] necessaries neither to men nor to women.")[46]

In some cases, though, the drive for self-esteem makes things desirable not because everyone has them but precisely because everyone doesn't— indeed, can't. Front-center seats at the theater provide a better view, and perhaps even better acoustics, but part of their attraction may also be the sense of being where everyone else would like to be. In the same way, highly selective colleges and universities presumably do provide greater educational opportunities, but part of the allure of Harvard or Swarthmore also depends on the distinction conveyed by having been selected to go there. As Veblen argued in his classic theory of "conspicuous consumption," because of the importance for self-esteem of one's position relative to others, what matters is not merely to meet and exceed society's norm but to be *seen* to do so.[47] More recently, economist Fred Hirsch has suggested that as general living standards in a society improve over time, and increasing numbers of people are able to satisfy their basic material wants at an ever higher level, these "positional goods"—things that remain scarce by their very nature— take on ever greater importance.[48] Once again, the implication is that raising everyone's living standard together does not help people feel better off compared to one another.

It may for a while, of course. Because perceptions do not always keep up with reality, sometimes people lack an accurate basis for comparing their incomes or living standards to what others have. Widely shared increases in living standards, therefore, may temporarily lead people to think they are getting ahead of their neighbors because the benchmark they have in mind reflects their observations of how other people have lived in the recent past. Such misperceptions are especially likely to occur when everyday life patterns are improving because of the introduction of new consumer goods, or a shift from one kind of work to another, or a change in how people live more generally. Many families no doubt thought they were among the first in their neighborhood to have a CD player, or in an earlier era a color television set, without realizing how many others had beaten them to it. Other families probably had the same feeling about moving to the suburbs, or sending a child to college, before they realized how many others were doing the same thing. But in time perceptions catch up, and the inescapable truth remains that economic growth cannot raise up everybody compared to everybody else.

The fact that people have two potential benchmarks by which to assess their current standard of living is of crucial importance to the way in which economic growth versus stagnation affects people's attitudes toward openness, mobility, and tolerance. The relationship between economic growth and the development of social behavior and political institutions that the experience of many different countries reflects, suggests that these two ways of gauging our economic well-being are substitutes for each other—in other words, the sense of doing well according to one benchmark lessens the urgency we feel to do well according to the other. In particular, when people know they are moving ahead compared to their own past experience, they feel less need to get ahead of other people too.[49]

And here economic growth enters the picture. By continually giving most people a sense of living better than they or their families have in the not very distant past, sustained economic growth reduces the intensity of their desire to live better than one another. Economic growth satisfies the form of people's aspiration for "more" that *is* possible for everyone to fulfill. In doing so it reduces the urgency that they attach to the form of that aspiration that, while perfectly understandable for each person individually, is nonetheless an obvious impossibility for the society as a whole.

When an economy stagnates, however, the importance people attach to living better than others against whom they naturally compare themselves is more intense. The fact they cannot do so, or at least on average cannot, then takes on heightened importance in their eyes. The resulting frustration generates intolerance, ungenerosity, and resistance to greater openness to individual opportunity. It also erodes people's willingness to trust one another, which in turn is a key prerequisite for a successful democracy.[50]

Mobility, either economic or social, is inherently threatening because it means the possibility of movement either up or, more to the point, down, compared to the prevailing norms for the society as a whole. But when the average income in an economy is stagnant, people who allow others to get ahead of them are not only falling behind in relative terms but also losing ground compared to their own past living standard. They lose out from the perspective of both benchmarks. When the economy is growing, however, and per capita income is rising, those who fall behind compared to others can still be moving ahead—and if growth is sufficient, moving ahead solidly—by the standard of their own experience.

For example, today the average family in the fifth decile of the American income distribution (that is, in the 10 percent of families who are just above the median) has an annual income of $58,800, while the average family in the sixth decile (the 10 percent just below the median) earns $47,400.[51] If real incomes in the United States were to resume growth at 3 percent per annum—the average rate at which the median income advanced from the late 1940s through the early 1970s—and if incomes across the economy retained their current relationship to one another, then a family that slipped from the fifth decile to the sixth over the course of the next fifteen years would nonetheless be earning $73,900 in today's dollars: more than one-fourth again as much as its income today. To be sure, getting full advantage of the 3 percent increase would be preferable, and presumably there would also be some additional satisfaction from keeping pace with the general advance rather than falling behind in relative terms. But even that down-wardly mobile family would still enjoy a very large gain from today's level.

By contrast, even at 1 percent per annum growth—well above the rate at which the median income has grown on average since the early 1970s—dropping from the fifth to the sixth decile over the next fifteen years would mean earning only $55,100 in today's dollars, $3,700 *less* than what the aver-age fifth-decile family has to live on today. And if incomes were to stagnate altogether, as happened from the early 1970s through the early 1990s for most Americans near the middle of the country's income distribution, falling back by that one decile would mean earning $11,400 less. It is easy to see why the slower the increase in incomes overall, the more urgent is peo-ple's need to maintain or even enhance their position compared to others in order to ensure that they are still getting ahead compared to their own past experience. With faster economic growth, however, people have less incen-tive to resist opening the society in ways that may allow others to move ahead.

Aspirations and fears of this kind can be especially powerful when peo-ple contemplate prospects for their children. Most adults know there is lit-tle they can do to bring about a major improvement in their own economic prospects. Except for the small handful of unusually successful entrepre-neurs, or a few lucky lottery winners, by midlife most people's career trajec-tory is pretty much set.[52] How much they will earn during the remainder of their working lives depends more on the accidents of personal health and corporate downsizing than on any new financial success their own ini-tiatives might bear. But even those who see little prospect for any significant improvement in their own economic circumstances may nonetheless harbor quite different ambitions—and, more strongly, anxieties—for their chil-dren. Many families' circumstances change enormously from one genera-tion to the next, and so for most adults the possibility that their children will either move ahead or fall behind is far greater. Their beliefs about which is more likely (the fact, for example, that so many Americans today think attaining the "American dream" will become more difficult in the next gen-eration) are a powerful source of motivation shaping their social and politi-cal attitudes.

On the surface, this line of reasoning would seem to suggest that it is primarily people near the top of a country's income ladder (or at least in the upper half) who face the greatest threat from enhanced economic mobility, and who are therefore most likely to resist an open, mobile society when-ever economic growth slows or disappears. After all, people who start at the top have the most to lose from anything that might shake up the existing hierarchy. Those nearer the bottom have a greater probability of benefiting than of losing from increased mobility. Yet as we shall see—prime examples include the Populists in late-nineteenth-century America and the Ku Klux Klan in the 1920s—it is more often people in the lower half of the income distribution, not the very poor but semiskilled workers and struggling small proprietors, who react most defensively when an economy stagnates.

One explanation for this apparent contradiction is simply that people with lower incomes are closer to the level at which a significant decline in their economic circumstances would seriously threaten their way of life or, in the days before widely available government assistance, perhaps even their survival. In a mobile society, people in lower-income groups may have a greater probability of moving up than down, but for them the consequences of moving down would be disastrous. As we have seen, opinion surveys consistently show distinctly lower levels of personal happiness among people with extremely low incomes.[53] (F. Scott Fitzgerald seems to have gotten the matter exactly backward in his famous quip that the rich are different. In this respect, at least, the survey evidence shows it is mostly the *poor* who are different.) Most people who stand economically just above that level of extreme unhappiness are all too aware of what it would mean to fall back.

Another explanation, however, is that people in higher-income groups do not merely have higher incomes. They also typically have more control over their lives and personal circumstances, including influence and authority in the social as well as political spheres. Although they were less likely to be either Populists or Klansmen, upper-income Americans in the 1880s and the 1920s may well have been no less eager to defend their position in a stagnant economy. They merely had different ways of doing so.

Moreover, in both of these episodes from the American experience, an important part of the story was also the impact of migration, including immigrants from abroad in both the 1880s and the early 1920s as well as southern blacks moving north in the latter period. When a society is regularly receiving newcomers, economic mobility means more than merely rearranging the rankings among those who already have positions in the existing income distribution. Openness and tolerance then bear also on the opportunities extended to people who do not yet have a place in the hierarchy at all, or at least who did not until very recently. In America of the 1880s and the 1920s, as today both here and in many other countries, new arrivals primarily strove for jobs, housing, and status by competing against native-born citizens from the lower parts of the income distribution.

Even those whose position at the starting gate may seem to give them much to gain from more open opportunity and increased economic and social mobility, therefore, may nonetheless perceive that they too have much to lose—at least much that matters to them. And as we have seen, what makes matters worse is that the fear of falling back is more compelling than the prospect of moving ahead. The result is that when economic growth gives way to stagnation, people's attitudes toward openness and mobility in their society harden accordingly.

How, then, do the differences in individuals' attitudes that follow from economic growth rather than stagnation make an entire society—say, a country like the United States—more open, and tolerant, and democratic? Through what route do they bear consequences for a nation's legislation and other public policies? And how do they affect the private behavior of its citizens in ways that ultimately shape the society's moral character?

Issues like openness and tolerance are in the first instance a matter of making good the basic principle of equal opportunity, which in turn holds out the prospect of real economic and social mobility. Many people also care about other characteristics of their society, like whether the outcomes of even a completely open competition seem fair, or to what ends their society deploys its resources. In all of these regards, whether incomes are advancing or stagnant powerfully influences people's attitudes, and for much the same reason.

Most people, at least in modern Western societies, presumably favor equal opportunity and fairness in the abstract sense that they would certainly support furthering these aims if doing so implied no risk, and no other cost, to themselves. But in practice, taking steps to move a society toward greater fairness or more equal opportunity typically does impose risks, as well as costs, on at least some people. The importance of economic growth for this purpose is that rising incomes make people more willing to accept these risks and costs in the interest of what they take to be a better society for themselves as well as others.

In the case of equal opportunity, for example, the obvious risk that increased mobility imposes on many people is that they may decline in the economic and social hierarchy. Indeed, sometimes the anxiety created by the risk of not keeping up can be so great as to make greater opportunity for advancement seem like a misfortune rather than an advantage. In one well-known illustration, soldiers who served in the Army Air Corps during World War II enjoyed distinctly greater opportunities for promotion than those in the Military Police. Yet the MPs reported they were mostly content with their promotion prospects, while members of the Air Corps were less satisfied with that aspect of their assignments. A plausible interpretation of this puzzling contrast is that when advancement is sufficiently widespread, people stop asking what is special about the fortunate few who get ahead and instead wonder what is wrong with those who don't. Under those circumstances, the fear of *failing* to advance becomes the dominant attitude.[54] As historian William Freehling likewise observed about attitudes among middle-class whites in the American South in the early nineteenth century, "The apparent ease of entrance into the upper crust made failure to do so more galling."[55]

Especially when incomes overall are stagnant, the opportunity for some to get ahead also often creates intense resentment of those who do. Edmund Burke, defending the pre-revolutionary regime in France as a form of "open aristocracy" analogous to England's, hailed "the ease with which a commoner could obtain a title by securing one of the official posts that automatically ennobled their holders." By contrast, Tocqueville argued that "Far from reducing the dislike of the nobility by their 'inferiors,' the practice of ennobling commoners had the opposite effect. The envy with which the newly made nobleman inspired his former equals intensified their sense of being unfairly treated." According to Tocqueville the result, which is thoroughly familiar in the modern context as well, was "more animosity towards the recent creations than towards the old nobility."[56]

Because not everyone enjoys the same opportunities for advancement to begin with—that was partly the point of Tocqueville's remark—efforts to make life's chances more equal impose different risks on different people. Today making opportunity more equal for all of a country's citizens often means breaking down existing racial, ethnic, or gender discrimination. What then matters for those who have *not* faced such bias in the past is mostly the increased risk of losing out to people whom active discrimination previously excluded from competition for the better jobs or better housing, or from preferred places in the economic and social hierarchy more generally. Experience suggests that most people are more willing to support antidiscrimination policies and to accept the risk that their advantage over others might erode if they are confident that, even if this should happen, their own living standard will rise over time nonetheless. Economic growth creates that confidence, and thereby makes the personal risks that come from eliminating unfair discrimination more readily acceptable.

Making opportunities more equal also usually entails costs. In America many children from low-income families begin school significantly underprepared to develop the learning skills or even the basic social disciplines that will enable them to do well in school, to proceed to higher education (in many cases, just to finish high school), and to go on to even an average-paying job thereafter. As a result, children from low-income families dispro-portionately grow up to be low-income adults. The problem is all the more acute in urban areas, among nonwhites (especially blacks), in families where the parents themselves have little education, and in situations in which only one parent (or maybe neither) is present at home.

Most Americans accept the notion that the disadvantages these children suffer—as of their very first day of school—are not their own fault. They therefore support, in principle, making these children's opportunity to learn and succeed more nearly equal to that of other children. But as a practical matter, providing those enhanced opportunities is expensive. Greater finan-cial support for schools in areas with larger numbers of "at-risk" children, redistribution schemes whereby a state's high-income school districts subsi-dize low-income districts, and early-intervention programs like Project Head Start are all efforts aimed at overcoming the disadvantages these chil-dren face. Each requires tax financing, however, and in each case the people who pay most of the extra taxes are not the parents of the children to be helped.

Making educational opportunities more equal therefore imposes a direct cost, mostly on people who do not expect that they or their children will benefit in any direct way from the programs they are asked to finance. (In time they may benefit indirectly from reduced exposure to crime and lower law enforcement costs in their community, and even more indirectly from enhanced productivity of the economy's workforce.) Moreover, these costs come in addition to the risk of greater competition, perhaps not for themselves but for their children, from other families' children who other-wise might not finish high school or attend college, and so would not be eli-gible for the desirable jobs they want their own sons and daughters to get. It is hardly surprising, therefore, that public support for programs like Project Head Start—or, in an earlier era, racial integration of the public schools—is likely to be stronger when incomes in general are rising and the people who will have to bear the necessary costs approach these burdens with a secure sense of getting ahead themselves.

Questions about the fairness of economic outcomes are clearly different from questions about opportunities. Americans in particular have tradition-ally emphasized equality of opportunity rather than equality of outcomes, whether the competition is economic, athletic, or academic. Most Ameri-cans are comfortable with the idea that winners are winners and also-rans come behind, and that life rewards the two differently whatever the nature of the contest. Socialist egalitarianism has never attracted much of a following in this country.[57]

When it comes to the question of what to do about outcomes that seem so bad as to be intolerable, however, the considerations at work in shaping people's attitudes are much the same as for questions about opportunities. Most Americans favor, at least in principle, government programs like food stamps and subsidized medical care, as well as shelters, soup kitchens, and other private charity efforts, that prevent the plight of their most unfortunate fellow citizens from becoming even worse. Indeed, much of the harshest criticism of such programs on grounds of principle (as opposed to cost) rests on the idea not that it is wrong to limit the range of economic misfortune but rather that many programs intended to do so create perverse incentives and therefore ultimately make the poor even worse off.[58]

These seemingly contradictory public attitudes—support in principle for alleviating extreme negative economic *outcomes*, even in a country where the emphasis has always been on equality of *opportunity*—suggest that questions about outcomes are partly questions about opportunities in another guise. People recognize that today's unequal economic outcomes are in part the product of the unequal opportunities of some time in the past. For the same reason that they support steps to make opportunities more equal for children today, most people favor at least some minimal assistance for today's adults who faced these same disadvantages when they were children.

But even where misfortune is merely the result of bad luck, or even lack of talent or energy or discipline, most people are still reluctant to allow the condition of other human beings in their society to sink too low on the economic scale. Americans have never been enthusiastic about limiting how high the living standards of the most fortunate few can rise. Setting a floor at the other end of the scale is a different story. Most Americans apparently agree with Samuel Johnson's maxim that a decent provision for the poor is the true test of civilization. Even as the United States was acting to end the long-standing right to federal welfare assistance without time limits, in 1996, opinion polls made clear that few voters regarded homelessness, malnutrition, and lack of basic medical care as acceptable conditions for citizens of America at the end of the twentieth century.

But maintaining even a modest floor under people's circumstances is expensive, and so here too economic growth makes a difference. Groceries bought with food stamps and surgery performed under Medicaid cost money. So do the shelters and soup kitchens run by the Salvation Army, and the free food and clothing that neighborhood churches give away. Whatever they may think about the abstract principles involved, at a practical level people are more willing to pay taxes or contribute to charity for these purposes when they are living better than they did in the past, and when they confidently expect to live still better in the future. It should have been entirely predictable, therefore, that Americans' early postwar enthusiasm for public assistance to the disadvantaged, just like their support for affirmative action programs aimed at redressing past discrimination, would ebb once the incomes of so many of the middle-class taxpayers who had to meet the costs of that assistance stagnated.

The difference between economic growth and stagnation likewise affects how the society divides its available resources between what people spend on their own private activities—for food, clothes, cars, houses, entertainment, vacations—and what they devote to more public undertakings like parks, sports facilities, orchestras, libraries, and the like.[59] To be sure, the size of a city's basketball arena and the quality of its philharmonic have little direct bearing on openness and tolerance. But public facilities and institutions of this kind do extend the range of potential human experience available to many if not most citizens. Moreover, as Tocqueville first emphasized, the participation that these public activities foster itself strengthens the underlying democracy.[60] It is hardly surprising that most people are more willing to support such public endeavors too when their incomes are rising.

The point is not that every citizen, or even every taxpayer, uniformly changes his or her mind about school integration, English classes for new immigrants, or food stamps and Medicaid, depending on whether that person's family income is rising. Public decisions in a democratic society do not require unanimity. What counts is the extent of popular support or opposition for an idea, and, what is often just as important, the intensity with which people are for or against it. Economic growth matters for both.

Many political questions in a well-functioning democracy are decided when only a relatively small number of voters change their minds. If a large majority were clearly in favor of some piece of legislation, or some administrative policy, in most cases it would already have been acted on. Especially on matters that are not simple yes-or-no questions—how generously should public schools be funded? how progressive should tax rates be?—the prevailing policy usually strikes some kind of rough balance that leaves voters about equally divided on whether to press further or step back. (The inability to reach this kind of compromise is what makes issues like abortion in America, or language in Belgium or Canada, so divisive.) Most of the people who favor either increased or reduced school funding, or a more or a less progressive tax system, rarely if ever change their attitude. But a change of heart among a relative few, who stand on either side of the current status quo but in the broader political context occupy the middle ground on the issue, is usually what moves public policy.[61]

Changing economic circumstances not only bear on people's attitudes on any specific issue but also affect how people strike a balance among the different, and often conflicting, objectives they favor. There is no contradiction in the fact that most citizens care about many different aspects of their society, including different questions of public policy, and that any one individual's preferences on different issues are often in tension with one another. Many people want a higher standard of living for themselves and also want a fairer, more open society. Many want lower taxes and also want better schools and more police protection. Economic growth versus stagnation matters in the political arena in part because the difference affects the priorities people set among their conflicting objectives. As a result, such basic determinants of political outcomes as which groups in the society are actively engaged on which issues, and who is forming coalitions with whom, depend in part on whether people are enjoying rising incomes and are confident about their economic future.

Economic growth also matters because it affects how intensely people care about what they favor or oppose.[62] The democratic political process is a matter of how much people care, no less than what they care about. Even if nobody ever actually changes his mind about whether Project Head Start, or a new baseball stadium, or an anti-discrimination law is worth supporting, the democratic process will still respond if rising incomes lead those who say yes to increase their enthusiasm and their active engagement on the issue while those on the other side become less resolutely opposed.[63]

A similar process, in which sheer numbers obviously matter but the intensity of people's concerns does as well, is at work in private society too. Openness and tolerance are more than just a question of government policies. Whether private employers shun hiring blacks or Hispanics, whether landlords try not to rent apartments to Catholics or Jews, whether private clubs and business organizations discriminate in ways that are unrelated to their inherent purpose, does not necessarily depend on any given individual's changing his or her mind. Prejudice or the lack of it is only one attitude among many that most people bring to their own actions and to the organizations to which they belong. What matters is the importance they attach to these feelings, compared to many others.

The same is true of private generosity. How much the nation's churches, synagogues, and private charities can do to help society's unfortunates depends not only on how many people contribute their money and their time, but also on how great a commitment each supporter makes. The same forces that influence who chooses to participate actively in the political arena likewise help determine who donates time or money to private causes, and in what amounts, and to which ones. With rising incomes—not simply a high average level of income, which after a while comes to seem customary and in time is taken for granted—more people feel able to contribute both time and money. And among those who do so, rising incomes also allow people to feel able to do more.

As we shall see, the historical evolution of social and political institutions in America as well as in other leading Western democracies is consistent with just these kinds of relationships between economic growth and popular attitudes. So are the differences that exist today in the political rights and civil liberties enjoyed by citizens across a much broader range of societies around the world. The same relationships are also clear from comparing people's responses, in different countries, in opinion surveys. In each case, the predominant tendency is for economic growth to render a society more inclined toward openness, tolerance, mobility, and democracy.

But each of these different forms of evidence also clearly shows that economic growth or stagnation normally affects a society's character with respect to such issues only with the passage of time. In part, this dynamic reflects the familiar process by which public attitudes build for some time before they result in new legislation or other changes in government policy. In addition, however, once individuals have formed their basic attitudes about such matters, they are normally very slow to change them.

The World Values Surveys, which have been conducted in many different countries for more than thirty years, provide especially striking evidence of the strong tendency of social attitudes, once formed, to persist over time.[64] The initial finding from these surveys was a sharp difference in attitudes between people who had reached young adulthood before and after World War II. In all six countries surveyed in 1970 (all in western Europe), people who had grown up in the economically depressed conditions of the interwar years cared more about goals like maintaining a high rate of economic growth than did those who had come of age during the widespread prosperity of the 1960s. Correspondingly, the younger generation ranked goals like protecting free speech much higher than did the older generation. Even though by 1970 both older and younger Europeans had lived through more than two decades of postwar prosperity, the attitudes of the older generation continued to reflect their very different experience as young adults.[65]

Subsequent surveys through the 1990s showed that the difference first identified in 1970 was not just a one-time phenomenon associated with the cataclysm of World War II. From year to year, people's attitudes do change depending upon their country's most recent economic growth performance and, even more so, how fast prices are rising. But the differences in attitudes between one age group and another—those who reached young adulthood in the 1930s versus the 1950s, or in the 1950s versus the 1970s—have persisted over time. (Further, the differences in attitudes between the old and the young are systematically stronger in countries where the average rate of economic growth since World War II has been greater and the gap between the prewar and postwar experience is therefore more striking.) The clear implication is that people take on certain basic attitudes in young adulthood, depending in large part on the economic conditions that they experience in these formative years, and then largely retain those attitudes throughout the remainder of their lives.[66]

As Ronald Inglehart, the political scientist who first studied these surveys, summarized the main thrust of his findings, "There is a fundamental difference between growing up with an awareness that survival is precarious, and growing up with the feeling that one's survival can be taken for granted."[67] But even the very notion of economic survival, as we have seen, is flexible. It depends on what people have known, or what their families have known, before.

The chief import of these findings is that the experience of economic growth or stagnation leaves its mark on a society for a long time thereafter. The experience of widely shared economic growth therefore creates a legacy from which a society can benefit—socially, politically, morally—for decades. And conversely, a significant stretch of years during which incomes stagnate imposes a burden that may well persist long after an economy has once again begun to grow.

PART II

DEMOCRACY IN AMERICA

Chapter 5

From Horatio Alger to William Jennings Bryan

If I were to inquire what passion is most natural to
men who are stimulated and circumscribed by the obscurity
of their birth or the mediocrity of their fortune, I would
discover none more peculiarly appropriate to their condition
than this love for physical prosperity. . . . The love of
well-being has now become the predominant taste of the
nation; the great current of human passions runs in that
channel and sweeps everything along in its course.

ALEXIS DE TOCQUEVILLE
Democracy in America[1]

To observe how economic growth or stagnation has influenced a country's social and political development over time, the first place to look is the United States. Not only has this country's long-term record of growth and expansion been the world's foremost, but Americans have always attached a particular importance to getting ahead economically. Tocqueville, visiting the United States when it was still a new nation, described with fascination the "restlessness of temper" with which ordinary citizens went about their business. "It is strange," he remarked, "to see with what feverish ardor the Americans pursue their own welfare. . . . Everyone wants either to increase his own resources or to provide fresh ones for his progeny."[2] Tocqueville's description still fits many if not most working Americans today. At the beginning of the twenty-first century, workers in America on average put in far more hours on the job than in any other industrial country, even including Japan, and the fraction of the American population participating in the formal workforce stood near a record high.[3] Further, the Americans who put in the most hours are, on average, those who already enjoy the highest rate of pay.[4]

The emphasis Americans have traditionally placed on economic advancement—and, in consequence, the opportunity for economic growth or stagnation to make a significant difference for the country's moral character—is not hard to explain. The distinguishing feature of the American experience, emphasized by Tocqueville but in fact dating from much earlier, was classlessness: "equality of condition," as Tocqueville and others of his era called it. Indeed, this new form of human society so impressed Tocqueville that for the opening sentence of *Democracy in America* he wrote, "Among the novel objects that attracted my attention during my stay in the United States, nothing struck me more forcibly than the general equality of condition among the people." He went on to elaborate the "prodigious influence" that such equality exerted: "it creates opinions, gives birth to new sentiments, founds novel customs, and modifies whatever it does not produce."[5]

If the absence of formal distinctions based on birth still seemed novel to a European visitor in the early nineteenth century, it was even more so a hundred years before, and it powerfully affected American citizens' attitudes then too. As an English visitor in the 1760s observed, "Everybody has property, and everybody knows it."[6] By opening the opportunity for advancement, classlessness heightened the incentives—indeed, it acted as a discomfiting spur—prodding economic effort. Classlessness therefore provided an impetus for the unprecedented economic growth that America as a whole has enjoyed over a span of more than two centuries. At the same time, however, the underlying intense concern of individuals for personally getting ahead exposed Americans all the more to frustration and resentment at times when their hopes were disappointed.

It is important to be clear about what classlessness means for this purpose. As Abraham Lincoln acknowledged in one of his debates with Stephen Douglas, the authors of the Declaration of Independence did not mean "to say all men were equal in color, size, intellect, moral developments, or social capacity."[7] Nor did anyone think that all citizens would have equal incomes, own the same acreage, live in identical houses, or enjoy the same overall standard of living. (Americans' incomes and living standards were rapidly becoming more *un*equal in the first half of the nineteenth century.)[8] Nor was the idea that everyone literally faced an equal opportunity to advance in these respects—although a large element of openness of opportunity, especially with the passage of time from one generation to the next, was certainly an important part of what people had in mind.

"Equality of condition" instead conveyed both something less and something more. It meant that regardless of whatever material advantages the owner of thousands of acres might enjoy compared to the ordinary working tradesman, the two were *conceptually* on the same footing in this new society. Even more so, it meant that, unlike in European societies, the successful tradesman who had risen from poverty was in no way inferior to the man who had inherited land or other wealth. There was no reason in principle why the workingman and the landowner might not exchange positions over time, and in fact many did so.[9] The likelihood that their sons might trade places was all the greater.

As historian Gordon Wood described the concept in his classic analysis of the American Revolution, "Equality became so potent for Americans because it came to mean that everyone was really the same as everyone else, not just at birth, not in talent or property or wealth, and not just in some transcendental religious sense of the equality of all souls. Ordinary Americans came to believe that no one in a basic down-to-earth and day-in-day-out manner was really better than anyone else."[10] Especially at the time of Tocqueville's visit, with Andrew Jackson in the White House—the first American president not of English descent (he was Scotch-Irish), not from the Atlantic seaboard (he was from Tennessee), and without any formal education—the classlessness of the new nation must have seemed more real than ever before.

In the absence of aristocratic class designations such as in Europe, with only the rare few able to become military heroes like Washington or Jackson, and with such personal accomplishments as higher learning neither particularly visible externally nor practically accessible on a wide basis anyway, material success—personal economic advancement—became the chief way an American could distinguish himself in the eyes of his fellow citizens. With no obstacle to prevent any individual (among white males) from earning, consuming, and accumulating more than his neighbors, the result was, as Tocqueville characterized it, "a kind of virtuous materialism."[11] And beyond that, in David Landes's words, "self-esteem, ambition, a readiness to enter and compete in the marketplace, a spirit of individualism and contentiousness."[12]

Other powerful influences have also led Americans to place special emphasis on getting ahead economically, further reinforcing the influence of economic growth or stagnation on American life. From the very beginning America has been, in a very real sense, a nation of immigrants. Individuals who were willing to leave behind all that was familiar to go establish a new existence an ocean away no doubt were more inclined to "restlessness of temper" than the average human being of their day. And for most of those who came, the desire to improve their material lot was clearly the dominant motive for making that break. In time those who had immigrated themselves came to be far outnumbered by the children and further descendants of earlier immigrants. (When Tocqueville visited, about one in ten Americans were foreign-born, nearly the same as the foreign-born fraction today.)[13] But the culture and values that successive generations of immigrants established has remained central to the American myth throughout.

In addition, the "American experiment," including in particular the creation of the modern world's first democratic republic, was self-consciously a product of the Enlightenment, with its acceptance of the possibility—in many eyes, the inevitability—of human progress. As we have seen, the thinkers of the Enlightenment saw scientific advance as the chief source of humanity's upward course, on both the material and the moral plane. The same attitudes and assumptions that led philosophers to foresee the overall betterment of mankind, and statesmen to devise a new government "in Order to form a more perfect Union," led such early leaders as Alexander Hamilton, Henry Clay, and Lincoln to favor "internal improvements" like canals and turnpikes as a means of fostering economic expansion and widening citizens' opportunities. These ideas also motivated ordinary individuals to believe they could raise themselves in a personal sense. Individual material advancement and the moral improvement of society as a whole were entirely in harmony. The ethos of "progress" encompassed both.

The religious thinking of such crucial early groups of Americans as the Puritans in New England, the Dutch in what was to become New York, and the Quakers in Pennsylvania further reinforced the secular notion of progress drawn from the Enlightenment. Strict Calvinist doctrine, as we have seen, held that individuals were predestined for heavenly salvation, or they were not, irrespective of their earthly achievements. But worldly success nonetheless provided an outward sign that a man was among the spiritual elect, and it therefore served both to reassure the successful individual and to shape his co-religionists' attitudes toward him. More broadly, as Weber emphasized, Calvinist thinking recognized honest work as a calling, thereby elevating what was formerly an embarrassing practical necessity to the status of a moral imperative. As Cotton Mather put it to his fellow colonists in his aptly titled tract, *A Christian at His Calling*, "Be a master of your trade; count it as a disgrace to be no workman."[14] Especially in America, work was no longer a humiliation but a display of moral worth, and economic success grounded in hard work even more so.[15]

The subsequent development of America, both economically and politically, continually reinforced this early emphasis on economic progress for the individual as well as the nation. The struggle to extract a livelihood from the raw wilderness, the close connection between economic self-sufficiency and the drive to national independence, the progressive advance toward both political and economic mastery of a vast continent, the repeated absorption of successive waves of immigrants, and the dependence of continued economic growth on scientific and technological progress once the physical frontier had vanished, all fostered the belief that achieving economic progress—again, for the nation and for individual citizens—was not just possible but a positive obligation.* As a result, Americans have consistently interpreted freedom itself at least partly in terms of their dedication of energy toward economic ends and their ongoing success at that endeavor.[16] And at times when that effort has faltered, frustration and resentment have been natural consequences.

How, then, have eras of economic growth or its absence, during the course of America's history, influenced the development of popular attitudes that in turn have led to important social, political, and legislative changes? In what ways have Americans responded when growth has slowed, or even stopped altogether, for more than the span of an ordinary business cycle? And what has happened at times when the rise in incomes and improvement in living standards have been strong and sustained? In each case, what groups have then emerged on the leading edge of the nation's political decision making, and in what directions have they pushed the national debate? Who entered into new coalitions with whom? Most important, what changes in private social behavior or public policies followed? In sum, to what extent does the

---

*As the historian David Potter wrote, "American society . . . especially needed men who would accept the challenge of mobility. . . . In a country where the entire environment was to be transformed with the least possible delay, a man who was not prepared to undergo personal transformation was hardly an asset. Hence mobility became not merely an optional privilege but almost a mandatory obligation, and the man who failed to meet this obligation had, to a certain extent, defaulted in his duty to society" (*People of Plenty*, pp. 96–97).

American experience indicate that a sustained advance in standards of living fosters openness, tolerance, mobility, fairness, and a strengthened commitment to democracy? And to what extent has stagnation led instead to inwardness, defensiveness, and rigidity of the nation's social and political structure?

These questions suggest a conceptual framework like that of Figure 5.1 for evaluating the relationship between our economic and our social and political experience. If economic growth indeed fosters a more open and tolerant society, while stagnation has the opposite effect—as a careful consideration of the motivations underlying individuals' behavior suggests—recognizable eras in America's past should fall mostly to the upper left (growth promotes openness) or the lower right (stagnation creates rigidity) in this tableau. Is this a fair description of what our history shows?

	Responses to *Growth*	Responses to *Stagnation*
Movement *toward* openness, tolerance, mobility, fairness, democracy	✔	
Movement *away from* openness, tolerance, mobility, fairness, democracy		✔

FIGURE 5.1

Effects of Economic Growth or Stagnation

What is at issue here is broad trends, economic as well as social and political, not day-to-day or even year-by-year events. As we have already seen, popular attitudes toward such fundamental matters as democracy and tolerance change only slowly in response to economic influences. And once individuals' attitudes shift, it takes yet more time before they coalesce into a meaningful social force, much less into effective political action. Moreover, once public attitudes toward such issues shift ground, they typically do not readily reverse themselves. Social and political movements, once initiated and especially once organized, tend to take on a life of their own, and they often persist long after the conditions that prompted their creation have disappeared.

The ups and downs of the usual business cycle, therefore, are mostly beside the point for purposes of gauging the effect of economic growth or stagnation on the development of a society's character. What matters is not so much how people's incomes and living standards compare to the year before, or even the year before that, but whether the average citizen can see evidence of progress over the last decade or even the last generation: whether people have a sense of getting ahead compared to how their parents lived, and whether their experience gives them confidence that their children will do even better.

It is also important not to look exclusively to economic forces to account for specific political events or social developments. To be sure, distinct economic episodes like a bout of high unemployment or rapid inflation, or a stock market crash, sometimes have immediately visible political consequences. The popular vote in American presidential elections, for example, often depends heavily on the pace of business expansion in just the year or so prior to the election.[17] But events like the outcome of a particular election, or the passage of specific items of legislation, also hinge on influences of all kinds—most obviously war and peace, but also corruption and scandals, cultural developments, diplomatic relations, and of course personalities. Just within the post–World War II period, who could understand the election of 1952 without knowing about the Korean War and the earlier collapse of Nationalist China? Or the 1968 election without Vietnam? Or 1976 without Watergate, or 1980 without the Iran hostage crisis? Or 2004 without the September 11 (2001) attacks and the war in Iraq?

Underlying economic forces may shape the rise of a social or political movement over time, but the catalyst that brings that movement to the center of public attention and makes it a potent force in the society is just as likely to be something else that occurs on its own timetable, quite unrelated to the nation's economy. The most one can expect of the relationship between economic growth and the society's broader course of development is a general coherence over significant periods of time, not precise correspondence between every political or social event and the latest economic news.

Seeking that coherence in the American experience would be problematic for the years before the Civil War, for two reasons. Most important, hard information about the American economy in the antebellum era is altogether too scant to admit reliable inferences distinguishing specific periods of stronger growth from times of economic weakness.[18] Moreover, a single issue—slavery—dominated much of the country's politics during a large part of the early life of the republic. (The Missouri controversy of 1819–20, the Nullification Crisis of 1832–33, the Texas annexation debate in the early 1840s, the agitation surrounding the 1850 Fugitive Slave Law and the 1854 Kansas-Nebraska Act, and most obviously the secession crisis of 1860–61 were in each case either directly or indirectly about the slavery question.) The place to begin, therefore, is the late 1860s, when America had left slavery in the past and from when the necessary data, even if in incomplete form, exist.

Since 1869 the American economy has expanded more than seventyfold even after allowing for higher prices. Railroads, electricity, telecommunications, automobiles, airplanes, atomic power, miracle drugs, and microelectronics have changed the way of life of substantially all of the nation's citizens. Along the way, the evolution of economic production from agriculture to industry and, even more so in our own era, to services has changed how Americans work.

Part of America's economic growth over this period of one-and-a-third centuries reflects the increase of the country's population from just 39 million to 294 million, the result of both natural growth and immigration. But even on a per capita basis Americans' real income rose more than tenfold, from just over $3,400 to nearly $40,000 in today's dollars: an average growth rate of 1.8 percent per annum.[19] If the normal span between generations is twenty-five years, each generation's standard of living has, on average, surpassed its predecessor's by more than 50 percent. Moreover, because incomes have become more equal over this period—incomes in America were probably more unequal in the late nineteenth century than at any time before or since—the pace of growth experienced by the typical American has been even greater.[20]

This impressive growth has been far from steady, however. Along the way there has been not only the year-to-year fluctuation of ordinary business cycles but lengthy stretches of either rapid growth or outright stagnation. A nation's sense of well-being does not stem from the public's study of the national income statistics but from individuals' awareness of what is happening in their own lives. At some times along the way most Americans have been able to look back and know that they were living better than their parents did, that their career prospects outstripped their parents', and that prospects for their children seemed even better. At other times few Americans have had that sense of progress. What is at issue here is the social, political, and moral consequences of these contrasting economic eras.

. . .

The first years following the Civil War were strong economically for the recovering United States. After a brief recession due to demobilization and the end of wartime production, business outside the South surged. The demands created by the war had already spurred the development of industries that produced goods like munitions, uniforms, and boots. Now industrial activity expanded rapidly, not just in older manufacturing centers like New York, Boston, and Philadelphia but in the Midwest as well. Chicago in particular, but also Cincinnati, St. Louis, Milwaukee, and other newer cities developed significant industrial employment during this period. At the same time, both domestic and foreign demand for American agricultural produce was generally strong.

Before the Civil War, America's leading industries had been cotton textiles, lumber, and boots and shoes. By 1880 machinery manufacturing was in first place, followed closely by iron and steel production. The English inventor Henry Bessemer had developed his more efficient process for decarbonizing iron in 1856, and as soon as the war ended Alexander Holley started putting up Bessemer plants in America. Andrew Carnegie began to convert the Pittsburgh ironworks to steelmaking in 1868. American steel output, which was essentially zero in 1860 and still just 69,000 tons in 1870, grew to 1.2 million tons by 1880. Other technological advances opened new opportunities as well. In 1875 Alexander Graham Bell demonstrated how electricity could carry sound. Thomas Edison demonstrated the first commercially successful electric lamp in 1879.

Transportation facilities were also expanding rapidly, as the growing nation spread across the continent. The Union Pacific and the Central Pacific completed America's first transcontinental rail line in 1869. By the early 1870s the railroads were laying more than 6,000 miles of new track per year on average, compared to barely 2,000 miles per year in the decade just before the war. Railroad construction absorbed half of the production of the country's iron and steel industry, and directly employed one out of every ten members of the country's nonfarm paid labor force.

The bubble burst, albeit only temporarily, in 1873. A financial panic in Europe caused German investors to cut off lending to Jay Cooke's Northern Pacific Railroad.[21] Soon lending dried up for other railroads. Defaults by those that had borrowed heavily during the heady years of rapid expansion in turn caused some prominent American banks to fail, thereby setting off a more general banking panic in the United States that promptly led to a more widespread business downturn. Railroad construction in particular fell back to prewar levels and did not recover until the end of the decade.

Economic activity in other spheres recovered soon enough, however, and between 1873 and 1880 America's total economic production expanded between 40 percent and 50 percent (depending on which among the various estimates for this period is the most accurate). Real income per capita had advanced by an extraordinary 5.2 percent per annum on average in the few years leading up to the panic of 1873, but the increase was still a very healthy 3.1 percent on average from then to the end of the decade.[22] Incomes were still becoming more unequal during these years, and so the income of the average citizen—the median income—was presumably rising somewhat more slowly than this. (There are no reliable data on median income in the nineteenth century.) Even so, with such extraordinary growth of incomes overall, even the typical American no doubt experienced healthy economic gains.

In the immediate post–Civil War years, therefore, times were good, especially outside the South. Americans could look both to their personal economic circumstances and to national accomplishments like the completion of the transcontinental rail line to see clear evidence of tangible progress. The ceremonial driving of a golden spike where the eastbound and westbound tracks finally met, at Promontory Point, Utah, symbolized the understanding that this progress meant prosperity. As Henry Adams wrote, "for the first time in history, the American felt himself almost as strong as an Englishman." Within a decade William Gladstone, then between his two stretches as Britain's prime minister, would write, "America is passing us as if in a canter."[23]

The most visible expression of this spirit of economic optimism and national confidence was the Centennial Exhibition held in Philadelphia in 1876. Closely modeled after London's Crystal Palace exhibition of a quarter-century earlier, the Centennial Exhibition exuberantly celebrated the nation's economic advance and gave pride of place to showing off technological progress. New devices on display included Edison's "quadruplex" telegraph, Bell's telephone (which, surprisingly, failed to attract much attention), George Pullman's "Palace Car," and George Westinghouse's air brake. The main attraction was George Corliss's forty-foot-tall steam engine. With the display also of works by such American artists as Winslow Homer and Louis Comfort Tiffany, and further exhibits contributed by fifty foreign countries, the Centennial Exhibition was a bold statement of Americans' national pride and their confidence in their future.[24]

The same optimistic spirit found voice at the individual level as well.

Horatio Alger's stories, which began to appear in book form in 1868, told of one penniless urchin after another who found bountiful opportunity and took advantage of it. *Ragged Dick*, Alger's first novel and by far his biggest seller, featured an uneducated (and not very well scrubbed) New York City shoeshine boy who transforms himself into "Richard Hunter Esq." by a combination of honesty, hard work, and good luck. Alger's attitude toward hard work—"All labor is respectable . . . and you have no cause to be ashamed of any honest business"—echoed not just Calvin and Mather, as we have seen, but also Tocqueville (whose *Democracy in America* included a chapter on "Why Among the Americans All Honest Callings Are Considered Honorable").[25] Alger's explicit connection of luck and moral rectitude also resonated with the religious concept of worldly success as a sign of pre-destined membership in the spiritually elect.[26] His next book, *Luck and Pluck* (which in time became the overall title for the series), seemed to sum up all that was necessary to succeed according to the upbeat attitude of the era.[27]

At the same time, Americans were not hesitant to turn to government, especially state and local government, for economic or social help. By 1870 states spent ten times as much on poor relief as a decade earlier. The pension system established after the Civil War, for disabled veterans and veterans' widows, represented America's first large-scale effort to address poverty at the federal level. Changes adopted in 1879 made the program much more attractive, and as a result new claims for a place on the rolls rose for a while to over 10,000 per month.[28]

Public spending on education also increased rapidly during this period, as the value placed on education—reflected clearly in Alger's novels—came to be widely accepted. Virtually all of this activity was by state and local governments, as hostile opposition easily blocked all efforts to establish a school system at the federal level. Business, in contrast, was less reluctant to accept federal help. In the decade ending in 1872, more than 100 million acres of United States government–owned land and more than $100 million in government bonds and loans went to support the rapidly growing railroad industry.[29]

Although the overwhelming majority of newly enfranchised black citizens still lived far outside the mainstream of American life—most remained in the South, where they had until recently been slaves—at least at the national level America in the 1870s continued to take steps toward opening opportunities regardless of race. In 1870 Congress made interference with voting rights a federal crime. Two additional laws passed the next year provided the machinery for curbing violence directed at blacks by the Ku Klux Klan and other such groups active in the South. Nor did these laws remain unenforced. Within a year federal prosecutors had obtained thousands of indictments and hundreds of convictions, with multiyear sentences for the most prominent offenders. President Ulysses Grant also deployed the army to suppress groups of vigilante night riders.

The Civil Rights Act of 1875, sponsored in Congress by Massachusetts senator Charles Sumner but passed only after his death, began by asserting that "it is essential to just government that we recognize the equality of all men before the law and hold that it is the duty of government in its dealings with the people to mete out equal and exact justice to all, of whatever nationality, race, color or persuasion, religious or political." The law's practical object was to further the program of the three post–Civil War constitutional amendments by forbidding discrimination based on race in a wide variety of public and private activities.[30] It required equal accommodations for blacks in public facilities, specifically banning discrimination by inns, transportation facilities, and "theaters and other places of public amusement." (Sumner's original bill had also forbidden segregation in public schools, but the version finally passed did not.) Violations were a federal offense, punishable by fine, with offended parties explicitly entitled to bring suit in the federal courts. The new law also forbade discrimination in selecting citizens for jury duty.[31]

In sum, the decade and a half following the Civil War brought exuberant economic growth that meant rapidly rising incomes for most Americans, and the dominant themes in American life during this period were an awareness of progress and an appreciation of individual opportunity, as well as support for efforts to make opportunities broader. But then growth gave way to stagnation, and the nation's mood as well as its politics changed along with the economy. The 1875 Civil Rights Act—as it turned out, the last civil rights bill Congress would pass for more than eighty years—was one of the first casualties. There were many others.

Even during this period of rapid economic advance, a major anomaly was that most prices were falling. And in what was still a largely agricultural economy, farm prices were falling especially rapidly. Between 1870 and 1880 the economy-wide average price level declined by 16 percent, and wholesale farm prices by 28 percent. This deflation continued through the mid-1890s, by which time prices overall had fallen yet another 23 percent and farm prices another 43 percent. Wheat dropped from an average price of $1.12 per bushel in the early 1870s to 50 cents or less in the mid-1890s, and corn from 48 cents per bushel to 21 cents. Cotton fell from $9.71 per pound in 1876 (the earliest year for which consistent data exist) to $4.59 in 1894. By the early 1890s farmers in some western states were burning their nearly worthless corn for fuel.

More to the point, business overall expanded much more slowly in the 1880s than earlier on. Between 1880 and 1890 Americans' real per capita income grew on average by just .4 percent per annum (versus almost 4 percent in the 1870s).[32] Then, after a few strong years at the outset of the 1890s, what was not much of an expansion to begin with collapsed altogether. An even more severe banking panic than had occurred twenty years earlier set off an especially steep downturn, widely known at the time as the Great Depression. Failures of both banks and businesses proliferated. By the end of 1893, the Erie Railroad, the Northern Pacific, the Philadelphia and Reading, and the Atchison, Topeka and Santa Fe, together with 500 banks and 15,000 other businesses, were bankrupt. Unemployment rose from just 4 percent on average during 1890–92 to over 18 percent in 1894, and remained well above 10 percent for several years thereafter. By 1895 per capita income had fallen below the level of fifteen years earlier.[33]

Popular discontent was widespread, and some of the expressions it found were violent. A strike in 1892 against the Carnegie Steel plant in Homestead, Pennsylvania, which began as a management lockout, led to an armed battle between strikers and company-hired Pinkerton forces that left sixteen dead and over 150 wounded. Two years later a strike against the Pullman Sleeping Car Company led President Grover Cleveland to call in the army to protect the railroads. At the same time some hundreds of unemployed men led by Ohio businessman Jacob Coxey—the group was popularly known as "Coxey's Army"—marched on Washington to seek assistance in the form of new federally financed road construction and other public works projects. Altogether, during the course of 1894, seventeen such "industrial armies" marched on the capital.[34]

The political protest movement was even more widespread in farm areas. The Grange (the Patrons of Husbandry), founded in 1867 primarily as a social organization, evolved into an agrarian protest movement only after farm prices began to fall. Similarly, the Farmers' Alliance, founded in 1877, began to grow in earnest only in the mid-1880s. By 1885 there were hundreds of sub-alliances in the plains states, as well as the all-white Southern Farmers' Alliance and the Colored Farmers' Alliance in the South. Both resentment and activism increased further after 1887–88, when a speculative rise in land prices (despite falling crop prices) collapsed, ruining farmers who had borrowed to buy additional land.

Between 1880 and 1895, real income per capita in America grew by only .7 percent per annum. With increasingly unequal distribution, it is likely that at least half of all Americans realized no gain in income or even a modest decline over this period. Suddenly Horatio Alger's vision of ample opportunity for anyone with "luck and pluck" seemed no longer to describe the reality, much less the mood, of the time. In its place Americans turned to calls for radical economic change, like Henry George's 1879 *Progress and Poverty* (which had looked to a single tax, on land, as the answer to the country's problems), and utopian visions of the future like Edward Bellamy's ironically titled *Looking Backward*, published in 1888.

In contrast to Alger's ready acceptance of the moral rectitude of economic effort in general and commerce in particular, the popular literature of America now portrayed the rise of capitalistic competition, and especially the shift from farming to business, as a source of moral degradation. In William Dean Howells's novel *The Rise of Silas Lapham* (also ironically titled), published in 1884, the title character initially appears as the product of an Algeresque success story, his good fortune the result of hard work, family-oriented virtue, and a significant element of luck. But after he moves his family from their Vermont farm to set up in business in Boston, and further seeks to live in the city's newly fashionable Back Bay neighborhood, Lapham undergoes both a financial and a moral decline. Among other misfortunes, his fine new house on Beacon Street burns down because his Vermont-manufactured paint turns out to be flammable, thus making the point that men who thrive in the country cannot be transplanted to urban life. At the end of the story Lapham salvages what is left of his fortune and his soul only by returning to Vermont, thereby regaining his "manhood which his prosperity had nearly stolen from him."[35]

Howells's 1890 novel, *A Hazard of New Fortunes*, again portrayed the moral decline inherent in the move from rural farming to business in the city. This time Howells was even more explicit about the incompatibility of urban commerce with moral values, as well as about the threat that many saw in the capitalist system. Of one central character he wrote, "His moral decay began with his perception of the opportunity of making money quickly and abundantly, which offered itself to him after he sold his farm. . . . He devolved upon a meaner ideal than that of conservative good citizenship, which had been his chief moral experience."[36] Another character complains of the apparent whimsy and caprice of business: "Here I am, well on the way to fifty, after twenty-five years of hard work . . . I may have my work taken away from me at any moment by the caprice, the mood, the indigestion of a man who has not the qualification for knowing whether I do it well or ill."[37]

A third character echoes a concern that Bellamy had expressed, just two years earlier, for the direction of the American economy and American society—but with an even sharper focus on capitalist commerce—lamenting "how the spirit of commercialism had stolen insidiously upon us, and the infernal impulse of competition had embroiled us in a perpetual warfare of interests, developing the worst passions of our nature and teaching us to trick and betray and destroy one another in the strife for money. . . . Affairs could not remain as they were."[38] Earlier on, the same man also asks, "How can a businessman whose prosperity, whose earthly salvation, necessarily lies in the adversity of someone else, be delicate and chivalrous, or even honest?"[39] The thought that operating a business might generate economic gain not only for the owner but also for employees and customers seemed utterly foreign. (Not surprisingly, the economy pictured in Bellamy's utopia included no merchants, shopkeepers, bankers, or lawyers.)

Although incomes on average remained high by historical standards, and even rose modestly, a sustained era of sluggish growth was clearly leading many Americans to believe that the country's best years were already in the past. In 1893 historian Frederick Jackson Turner first advanced his "frontier hypothesis," arguing that the distinctive character Americans recognized in their nation's experience was a consequence of the pioneer attitudes molded by the opportunity and challenge presented by the ever present but ever receding frontier. The implication was ominous. As Turner noted in the opening paragraph of his essay, in 1890, for the first time, official maps of the United States showed no frontier.* By 1895 Brooks Adams would despairingly title his new history *The Law of Civilization and Decay*. As Bellamy wrote in *Looking Backward*, "We felt that society was dragging anchor and in danger of going adrift. Whither it would drift nobody could say, but all feared the rocks."[40]

But the absence of significant growth in most citizens' incomes, not just over one or two years but for the better part of a generation, affected more than just America's mode of literary expression. In the last two decades of the nineteenth century, relations between whites and blacks (especially the newly freed slaves in the South), government social policies, public attitudes

---

*Turner quoted the superintendent of the census for 1890: "Up to and including 1880 the country had a frontier of settlement, but at present the unsettled area has been so broken into by isolated bodies of settlement that there can hardly be said to be a frontier line. In the discussion of its extent, its westward movement, etc., it can not, therefore, any longer have a place in the census reports." Turner went on, "This brief official statement marks the closing of a great historic movement" ("The Significance of the Frontier in American History," p. 199).

toward immigrants as well as native-born citizens of different religious groups, and economic policy more generally, all reflected the difference in attitudes that accompanied protracted economic stagnation.

The aspect of American life in which the most lasting deterioration occurred was race relations. It is one of the unfortunate coincidences of United States history that what was at the time the most pronounced period of economic stagnation since the founding of the republic set in just as Reconstruction ended and the federal government finally withdrew its troops from the defeated southern states.[41] Moreover, the depression hit the South, with its mostly agricultural economy, especially hard.

No one will ever know whether the country's race relations, both in the South and elsewhere, would have taken a different course had economic times been better during this key period. No doubt some reaction by the reempowered white majority was inevitable regardless of economic conditions. But as C. Vann Woodward, one of the most distinguished historians of the American South, has argued, economic forces played a role too: "[T]he South toward the end of the 'nineties was the perfect cultural seedbed for aggression against the minority race. Economic, political, and social frustrations had pyramided to a climax of social tensions. No real relief was in sight from the long agricultural depression of the 'nineties, an acute period of suffering that had only intensified the distress of the much longer agricultural depression."[42] The consequence was segregation of blacks and whites in practically every aspect of everyday life, the systematic disfranchisement of black voters, and appalling racial violence.

One reason for believing that the frustrations born of hard economic times contributed to the rise of formal discrimination in the South is that although the former Confederate states regained full political independence with the end of Reconstruction in 1879, it was not until the 1890s that most of them began to adopt what in time became their all-pervasive "Jim Crow" legislation. By the end of that decade, however, most southern states had made it illegal for blacks to ride with whites in railroad cars, and some had also segregated railroad station waiting rooms as well as city streetcars. The other southern states followed soon thereafter. Northern and western states, which had far smaller black populations, did not adopt the same kind of Jim Crow laws, but blacks were hardly on an equal footing outside the South either.

Similarly, the devices used to deny voting rights to most black citizens—property and literacy qualifications, the poll tax, and white-only primaries—

were mostly adopted beginning in the 1890s. In Louisiana, for example, more than 130,000 blacks were registered to vote in the 1896 election. By 1904 there were just 1,342.[43] In his widely publicized "Atlanta Compromise" address of 1895, Booker T. Washington in effect proposed the wholesale withdrawal of blacks from southern political life.[44] Because blacks and poor whites together comprised a clear majority in the South, in cooperation they could have shaped the policies of most states to their advantage. Instead, black-white conflict left southern political power mostly in the hands of the white elite. (The same restrictive election laws that disfranchised almost all blacks did the same to about half of the whites—the poorer half.)

During much of this period, the Supreme Court consistently supported states' ability to impose virtually whatever system of race relations they wanted short of reinstituting slavery. In 1883 the court held that the Fourteenth Amendment prohibited racial discrimination by states but not by individuals.[45] Since no states yet had segregation laws, this ruling effectively gutted the most important parts of the 1875 Civil Rights Act. In 1890, the Court further ruled that a state (in this case, Mississippi) could constitutionally impose segregation on railroad carriers, and in 1898 the court approved a set of Mississippi measures designed to deprive blacks of the vote.[46] Most famously, in its 1896 *Plessy v. Ferguson* decision, the Court set forth the "separate but equal" doctrine that laid the basis for more than a half-century of legal segregation in America.

Apart from race relations, the consequences of nearly two decades of stagnant incomes for much of America's population in the late nineteenth century were as much a story of what didn't happen as what did. In the sphere of economic and social policy, for example, one of the most interesting questions about this era is why the United States failed to follow Germany's lead—and, to a lesser extent, that of other countries as well—in establishing a system of public social insurance. As we shall see, in the 1880s Germany under Bismarck pioneered the development of nationwide health insurance, "old age and disability" insurance, and workers' accident insurance.

These measures hardly went unnoticed in the United States. In 1891, just two years after Bismarck's system was fully in place, the U.S. commissioner of labor sponsored a detailed study of the subject by John Graham Brooks, a former Unitarian minister then working as a freelance labor analyst and popular lecturer. The government published Brooks's study in 1893 under the title *Compulsory Insurance in Germany, Including an Appendix Relating to Compulsory Insurance in Other Countries in Europe*. Other studies, and much discussion, followed.[47] The idea even entered the popular literature of the day. Bellamy's *Looking Backward*, for example, approvingly described a system in which "the nation guarantees the nurture, education, and comfortable maintenance of every citizen from the cradle to the grave."[48]

Yet despite the flurry of interest, the only visible public policy successes of America's late-nineteenth-century reform movement were the safety and workmen's compensation laws that state legislatures began to enact; and even these measures faced a hostile environment in many states' supreme courts. The nascent American labor movement either ignored or opposed initiatives to create a broader social insurance system along the lines of Germany's.[49] In this area as well as others, an effective coalition capable of bringing about such reforms simply did not come together. In contrast to both earlier times and later, few among the country's economic and political elites were seriously interested in reforms of this kind. Even apart from the division between whites and blacks (cooperation like that between the Southern Farmers' Alliance and the Colored Farmers' Alliance was the exception, not the rule), the nation's growing urban mass workforce and its deeply troubled agrarian interests faced their own separate problems.

Moreover, the idea of direct measures to alleviate the plight of the disadvantaged and the unfortunate ran counter to the newly ascendent spirit of social Darwinism, most prominently represented in America by the Episcopal priest and Yale professor William Graham Sumner. In his widely read 1881 essay, "Sociology," Sumner wrote, "if we should try by any means of arbitrary interference and assistance to relieve the victims of social pressure from the calamity of their position we should only offer premiums to folly and vice and extend them further."[50] As that decade's economic decline turned into outright depression, views like Sumner's, especially among the nation's elites, were a further impediment to the formation of any effective coalition advancing social reforms.

Instead, the greatest political force that emerged from the hardships of the 1880s and the first half of the 1890s was populism, and in the end the populists chose a different agenda.

Today's familiar image of the late-nineteenth-century American populists mostly recalls the effort to replace the gold standard with a bimetallic monetary system based on both gold and silver, including, most vividly, William Jennings Bryan's electrifying challenge, "You shall not crucify mankind upon a cross of gold." The pro-silver movement was indeed a central element in the populist program, and the silver question was the dominant issue in the 1896 election. (It was one of the rare times in American history that a presidential campaign has focused so intensely on a single financial issue.) But Bryan ran as a Democrat—he gave his "Cross of Gold" speech to the Democratic Party's nominating convention in Chicago—and at least until it endorsed Bryan in the 1896 election, the People's (or Populist) Party stood for much more than just free coinage of silver. Viewed as a social movement, not just an organized political party, the populists always did.

Late-nineteenth-century populism was in large part an expression of the anxieties and frustrations created by the hard economic times that persisted for nearly a generation leading up to the mid-1890s. The populists perceived, more or less correctly, that an easier monetary policy, together with the likely devaluation of the dollar that would inevitably follow, would stimulate economic activity, halt or reverse the continual overall fall of prices, and arrest the sharp decline of prices on agricultural products and other goods that the United States traded internationally.[51] At the same time, many populists also simply failed to understand the distinction between a general deflation and the declining *relative* price of agricultural goods, and looked to free silver coinage out of mistaken assumptions. (The vast expansion of land under cultivation, not only in America but in countries such as Australia, Canada, and Argentina, was a significant depressant to farm prices during this period.)

The populists also correctly perceived that the most immediate impediment to easier money was the gold standard, to which the United States had returned (after the hiatus caused by the Civil War) in 1879. The regimen of the gold standard in effect linked a nation's money and credit to the available supply of gold. Because world gold supplies had hardly grown since the great California finds at mid-century, money and credit remained tight in the United States, even through the most stubborn phases of the 1893 depression. But America had ample silver.[52] If the Treasury would only mint into money the silver presented to it—or, equivalently, issue silver certificates that would circulate as money—all would be different.[53]

A free silver policy therefore made good economic sense for the groups in American society that provided the core support of the populist movement. Westerners, especially those from mining states, stood to gain immediately if the Treasury purchased silver at what would have been, under most forms of the silver coinage proposal, a price well above market.[54] Borrowers, who in a world of continually falling prices had to repay their mortgages and other obligations in ever more valuable dollars, would have benefited from an end to tight money and deflation. (A standard Populist election slogan was, "We Are Mortgaged. All But Our Votes.")

Farmers and manufacturers would gain from the reversal in the relative price of the goods they sold, although manufacturers, who enjoyed substantial tariff protection especially after 1890, had less to gain from a dollar devaluation.[55] For all these reasons the West, the South, and the agricultural states of the Midwest were natural areas of populist strength. By the mid-1890s, free coinage of silver had become "the great panacea of discontented agrarians."[56]

But populism was more than just agitation for free silver—or, for that matter, other specifically economic proposals like taxing high incomes or somehow reining in the power of the railroads (which farmers believed, mostly incorrectly, were overcharging for transporting their produce to market).[57] The populists sought to preserve the agrarian and small-town economy, and the way of life based on it, that had been America's past. They were angered by perceived exploitation, and emboldened by a sense of moral superiority. Populism was, correspondingly, an expression of resentment as well as resistance to the advance of the capitalist, industrialist, and therefore more urbanized economy that was to become America's future.[58] (While it had never occurred to any of Horatio Alger's heroes to seek success by taking up farming, happiness for Dorothy in L. Frank Baum's *The Wizard of Oz*—which has often been read as a populist, free silver allegory—meant getting back to her Aunt Em's farm in Kansas.)* In their specific policy proposals and even more so in their broader social and cultural agenda, the populists represented a turning backward: a closing of American society, a defensive rigidification, and in many ways a retreat from tolerance, in the face of continual economic disappointment. With the pervasive economic frustration of the time, they were not alone.[59]

The most obvious reflection of the desire to close American society was nativism. After a brief decline during the Civil War, the flow of new immigrants to the United States had returned to about the pace that prevailed in the 1850s. On average from the end of the war through 1879, America received 275,000 immigrants per year. And at least until the depression hit

---

*The allegory to the 1890s monetary controversy is lost on anyone who knows *The Wizard of Oz* only from the 1939 film, in which Dorothy's shoes, which hold the hidden power, were made into "ruby slippers." In Baum's book the shoes are silver. The film is at least faithful to the book in that the regimen that represents staying on the gold standard, and that therefore ultimately proves useless, is still to "follow the yellow brick road." Hugh Rockoff gives a detailed discussion of other elements of the possible allegory in "The 'Wizard of Oz' as a Monetary Allegory" (*Journal of Political Economy*, 1990). It is far from certain, however, that Baum actually intended his book to be read in this way; Ranjit Dighe, for example, argues not in *The Historian's Wizard of Oz: Reading L. Frank Baum's Classic As a Political and Monetary Allegory* (Praeger, 2002).

in 1893, slow economic growth certainly did not make America any less attractive. Between 1880 and 1893, 520,000 immigrants arrived per year on average. Then, as now, native-born Americans were concerned that newcomers might take away jobs, or at least drive down wages, by being willing to work for less than what natives considered their due.

The anti-immigrant bias of the time was not just a matter of numbers and wages, however. After all, 520,000 new immigrants per year in the 1880s, when the population was 60 million, was smaller in percentage terms than the 260,000 immigrants per year that America had received in the 1850s, when the population was just 25 million.[60] Even in the 1830s, the 60,000 immigrants per year that America received hardly constituted a small number compared with a population of only 15 million. America had always attracted, and economically absorbed, plenty of immigrants.

There were two important differences. First, beginning in the 1880s immigrants to America were no longer overwhelmingly from northern Europe. Russia, Poland, Italy, Greece, the Balkan countries, and ethnically distinct components of Austria-Hungary all became major sources of immigration to the United States in the late nineteenth century. And not only were these immigrants mostly not Protestants, many were not even Catholics. Greek and Russian Orthodox, and Jews, were now arriving in America in significant numbers.

Second, unlike in earlier decades, by the 1880s fewer immigrants were moving directly to a livelihood on the farm. In part this change simply reflected the more urban orientation of these new arrivals and the desire of ethnic groups to stay together rather than live among strangers. More importantly, by the 1880s the continent was becoming more settled. Many newer immigrants now congregated in New York, Philadelphia, Chicago, and other rapidly growing American cities simply because the economic opportunities to be gained by dispersing across the country no longer seemed so attractive.

While the anti-immigrant sentiment of the late nineteenth century was partly if not mostly due to hard economic times, it was also an expression of religious and ethnic intolerance as well as of opposition to advancing urbanization. The new Statue of Liberty (completed in 1886) may have proclaimed America's welcome to the world's "huddled masses" and "wretched refuse," but popular magazines of the day like *Harper's*, *Life*, and *The Atlantic Monthly* were full of ethnic jokes and slurs.[61] Beginning in the 1880s, these sentiments led to a tightening of immigration standards, mostly in the form of various exclusion restrictions. Over time, convicts, the insane, alcoholics, and those with diseases were all excluded. After riots protesting the use of

Chinese labor for railroad construction, Chinese immigrants were excluded altogether. An 1885 act outlawed immigration of contract labor—an interesting step for a country that, at its outset, had attracted so many indentured servants. Admitted immigrants were also subject to a head tax. In 1897 Congress passed legislation calling for a literacy test for all immigrants, but President Cleveland vetoed it. (After several more attempts, Congress enacted a literacy requirement, overriding President Woodrow Wilson's veto, in 1917.) Also beginning in the 1880s, some of the largely agricultural states adopted legislation prohibiting "aliens" from acquiring land.[62]

Except for the exclusion of the Chinese, none of these measures referred explicitly to race, religion, or ethnicity. But such prejudices were clearly a large part of the underlying motivation. Many Americans feared that new arrivals were diluting the racial purity of the country's (white, northern European) population, with deleterious consequences both physical and moral. The utopia Bellamy described in *Looking Backward* was in the process of achieving "race purification"—indeed, "the salvation of the race"—through successive generations of "sexual selection." The visible result, Bellamy claimed, was "not only a physical, but a mental and moral improvement."[63]

The Jim Crow laws and immigration bars enacted hardly capture the flavor of the racism and widespread anti-immigrant—and anti-Catholic, anti-Semitic, and anti-ethnic—feeling of the time. The 1880s saw a rise in vigilante violence in rural areas, including not only lynchings in the South but also beatings, murders, and arson by such groups as the Bald Knobbers in the Ozarks and the White Caps in Kentucky. Colorful populist figures like "Pitchfork" Ben Tillman, the founder of the Farmers' Association who served as governor of South Carolina from 1890 to 1894 and then as a United States senator, and Tom Watson, a widely read newspaper man and onetime congressman from Georgia who ran for vice president on the Populist ticket in 1896, were outspoken white supremacists.[64] Tillman publicly defended lynching, called for repeal of the Fifteenth Amendment (which had given the vote to blacks, including former slaves), and advocated the use of force to disenfranchise blacks in the meanwhile. In 1895 he called a convention to rewrite the South Carolina constitution, declaring that "the sole cause of our being here" was to deny blacks their voting rights.[65] Watson regularly devoted his speeches and newspaper editorials to sensational attacks on blacks, Catholics, Jews, and foreigners. The American Protective Association, an anti-Catholic organization founded in Iowa in 1887, spread especially rapidly once the 1893 depression set in and claimed to have 2.5 million members nationwide by the mid-1890s.[66] Anti-Semitic propaganda was sufficiently widespread among populists by 1896 that William Jennings Bryan felt obligated to disavow it during his campaign for the presidency.[67]

Especially among the late-nineteenth-century populists, anti-Semitism in particular was not just freestanding bigotry but, in their minds, an integral part of their quest for free coinage of silver.[68] The populists saw eastern financial interests' adherence to the gold standard as the result of a conspiracy masterminded by the hated British, and especially the Rothschilds. Mary Elizabeth Lease, the famed populist orator from Kansas (and for whom, in some interpretations, Dorothy in *The Wizard of Oz* was a symbol—Lease was often called "the Kansas Cyclone"), denounced President Cleveland, who supported the gold standard, as "the agent of Jewish bankers and British gold."[69] Her 1895 book, *The Problem of Civilization Solved*, was full of racist and anti-immigrant theories. Other pro-silver polemics were also plainly anti-Semitic.[70] The most widely read free silver tract of the time, *Coin's Financial School* by William Harvey, was not, although the book's illustration of the "English octopus," with tentacles stretched over the entire globe, was prominently labeled "Rothschilds."[71] But Harvey also published a novel, *A Tale of Two Nations*, that was replete with Jewish villains (prominently including Baron Rothe, the mastermind of a plot to destroy the United States by demonetizing silver). Other widely read populist fiction of the day, like Ignatius Donnelly's *Caesar's Column*, was likewise deliberately and explicitly anti-Semitic.[72]

Beyond their prejudices against Catholics, Jews, and foreigners (especially the British), the populists of the late nineteenth century exhibited a view of the world as not just hostile but deliberately, indeed apocalyptically, so.[73] If honest workingmen, and farmers in particular, were no longer getting ahead, specific acts by identifiable groups and nameable individuals must be responsible. The distress that the populists and their constituents saw and suffered personally simply could not, in their eyes, be the outcome of impersonal economic forces. Imposition of tight money via the gold standard was only a part of a much wider conspiracy of malevolent forces bent on the overthrow of American civilization.

As we shall see, the tensions that the populists faced when confronted by the modernization of their nation's economy, and the consequent transformation of the country's way of life, were far from unique. Many countries throughout the developing world face similar challenges of modernization and industrialization in our own era. But the experience of America in the late nineteenth century, as well as that of other countries today, also makes clear that these challenges are easier to face when modernization goes along with rising incomes. Modernization creates problems; rising incomes offer the wherewithal to solve them, while fostering the spirit for doing so. In the face of economic stagnation, the desire to turn back the clock and the tendency to seek out scapegoats are all too familiar.

In the case of late-nineteenth-century America, the sourness and paranoia bred of economic stagnation in the end prevented the populists from achieving the goals they articulated that would have strengthened American democracy and advanced economic fairness (and, later on, did). Many populists favored such measures as direct primaries and popular election of United States senators. Most favored an income tax. Some also favored women's suffrage (although for many populists the appeal seems to have rested on the assumption that the only women who would actually vote would be native-born white Protestants).74 William Jennings Bryan was a tireless advocate for all of these measures. Yet none of them advanced during the populist era.

Instead, the populists came to focus their political energies ever more narrowly on the single agendum of free silver coinage, if not as the panacea that would cure all of the country's evils then at least as the absolutely necessary first step. Bryan made the connection clearly, in his speech to the Chicago nominating convention, by asserting that with free silver "all other necessary reforms will be possible." By contrast, "until this is done there is no other reform that can be accomplished."75

After Bryan lost, in 1896 and again in 1900—and after an economic revival brought a new era of rising incomes—what lingered on of the populist movement was mostly the residual sentiments of religious and ethnic bigotry, hatred of foreigners, and fear of things urban and ideas modern. Ben Tillman remained in the Senate until he died in 1918, continuing to the end as an enthusiastic champion of the Jim Crow regime. Tom Watson openly used his newspaper to incite the lynching in 1915 of Leo Frank, a Jewish factory manager convicted (wrongfully, as it later turned out) of raping and murdering a teenage female Christian employee, and then to spur the revival of the Ku Klux Klan.76 His activities gained him enough renewed notoriety to win election to the Senate two years before his death in 1922. Bryan remained active in American politics the longest of any of the old populists, briefly serving as secretary of state under Woodrow Wilson. He spent his last years working as a paid booster for Florida land sales and campaigning to bar non-Christians from teaching at American universities. His last public act—in 1925, just days before he died—was to lead the prosecution of young John Scopes for teaching Darwin's theory of evolution at a high school in Dayton, Tennessee.[77]

But the inwardness, defensiveness, and even paranoia that many Americans displayed at the end of the nineteenth century, the antipathy to change and the intolerance of anyone not like themselves, were not unique to populism. They were, to a large extent, the product of the economic stagnation that America faced in that era. And as we shall see, these same strains have resurfaced, in one form or another, at other times when Americans' economic aspirations have met sustained and systematic disappointment.

The early years of the twentieth century were a different story, however.

Chapter 6

From TR to FDR

There is no good reason why we should fear the future, but there is every reason why we should face it seriously, neither hiding from ourselves the gravity of the problems before us nor fearing to approach these problems with the unbending, unflinching purpose to solve them aright.

THEODORE ROOSEVELT
1905 Inaugural Address[1]

The parallel paths of economic growth or stagnation, and of movements in American politics and social relations either toward or away from an open, democratic society, continued into the twentieth century. In narrow political terms, populism as a nationally organized force disappeared surprisingly quickly after the 1896 election, and within two years the silver issue lost much of its relevance anyway. Poor harvests in Europe boosted the demand for American farm products and helped lift their prices. In 1898 pioneer prospectors discovered gold along the Klondike River in Alaska, and related finds in Canada's Yukon Territory followed soon after. In the meanwhile, the new cyanidation process developed by Scottish chemist John Stewart MacArthur had greatly increased production from the Witwatersrand gold fields in South Africa. With world gold supplies expanding once again, the gold standard—which Congress reaffirmed in 1900—was no longer a hard constraint limiting American money and credit. Deflation gave way to inflation, and by the eve of World War I prices overall had risen by 40 percent to 50 percent, just about back to where they had been in the early 1880s.[2]

The return of sustained economic growth squelched populism just as economic stagnation had given birth to it.[3] Although the business cycle continued to produce recessions every few years, most prominently in 1907, the period stretching from 1896 until the beginning of World War I was, on the whole, one of solid economic expansion for the United States. Led by technological change that made possible precision standards of production and therefore interchangeable parts, whole new mass production industries developed, some on a huge scale. By 1913 Ford Motor Company was shipping almost a quarter-million new cars per year.

Other forms of technological progress were also important in stimulating America's renewed economic expansion. As the Siemens open-hearth furnace replaced the Bessemer converter, steel production soared from 4 million tons in 1890 to 31 million in 1913. Printing and publishing became the nation's third largest manufacturing industry at the turn of the century. After 1900, shipbuilding and electrical machinery manufacturing also joined the top ten. By 1910 the United States had finally become a consistent net exporter of manufactured goods. By 1914 more than 8 million Americans worked in manufacturing, compared to 4 million in 1890. At the same time, the westward movement of industrial activity continued. By World War I the Midwest was clearly the center of gravity of American manufacturing.

With the country's population increasingly dispersed across the continent as well as increasingly urbanized (by 1910, 37 percent of Americans lived in cities or towns of over 10,000 and 22 percent lived in cities of over 100,000), all this expansion of production required corresponding advances in transportation and distribution. New railroad construction, which had fallen below 2,000 miles of track laid per year for a while in the 1890s, returned almost to the 6,000-plus rate of the early 1870s. The manufacture of railroad cars, including the recently developed refrigerated car for shipping meat products, grew into another of the nation's biggest manufacturing industries. Large urban-based retailing firms—Macy's and Gimbel's in New York, Wanamaker in Philadelphia, Marshall Field in Chicago, Woolworth and the Great Atlantic and Pacific Tea Company (in time, simply the A&P) practically everywhere—flourished along with mail-order firms like Sears, Roebuck. Within the cities, "skyscrapers" increasingly dominated the new urban landscape.[4]

With all this dynamic activity, American economic output more than doubled between 1896 and 1913 even after allowance for rising prices. The war boom then boosted output by yet another 20 percent by 1918. Record-level immigration after the turn of the century helped to swell the population, as did declining mortality rates (especially among nonwhites) due to improved sanitation. But jobs were plentiful, incomes rose rapidly except during the occasional business downturns, and the resulting recessions were short-lived. Unemployment, which had still been above 14 percent in 1896, declined to 4 percent by 1901 and fluctuated around that level until World War I. It then fell even lower, reaching just 1.4 percent in 1918. The United States also ran a large positive balance of foreign trade throughout this period.

Even as the country's population surged from 70 million in 1896 to nearly 100 million in 1913, real per capita income grew on average by 2.3 percent per annum, and from 1914 through the end of the war the pace was even faster.[5] These gains were not limited to the rich or the otherwise lucky few. Further, during these years many of the newly introduced consumer products were becoming widely affordable. Ford, which introduced the Model T in 1908, reduced the price of a reliable "touring" car from $900 the next year to just $400 in 1917.[6] Over those same ten years, the average annual wage of an American manufacturing worker rose from $550 to almost $900. Overall, from the late nineteenth century to the end of World War I, within one generation, Americans' average standard of living had jumped by nearly two-thirds.

The change from economic stagnation to sustained growth brought a similarly profound change in the nation's social and political life. New groups took on leadership, and they brought new attitudes. Not every family was prosperous, of course, and not everyone who had held populist sympathies changed his mind. But the intensity of the resentments upon which populism had drawn abated with the resumption of generally rising incomes, and different voices attracted the public's support.

The successors to the populists as the principal force driving America's social and political agenda, especially after the turn of the century, were the progressives. While drawn from different bases—the populists' main support had been in America's small towns and rural areas, including farmers in particular, while the progressives were more likely to be urban, including large numbers of middle-class professionals and even some members of the upper-income elite—the two movements were nonetheless similar in several important ways. Like the populists before them, many of the early-twentieth-century progressives felt the anxiety and frustration of watching others pass them by in economic importance and social prestige as America underwent far-reaching transformations. (Walter Weyl, an insightful observer of contemporary political and social trends, wrote, "We are developing new types of destitutes—the automobileless, the yachtless, the Newport-cottageless. . . . The discontent of today reaches very high in the social scale.")[7] Like the populists, progressives feared and resented the growing economic power of big banks, big railroads, and big business in general. And like the populists, the progressives worried that these mighty commercial interests were not only seizing economic power but undermining America's individualism, political freedom, and democracy.

But the progressives acted against a different economic backdrop, and their agenda took on a very different flavor. The populists, weighed down by the pervasive symptoms of a stagnant economy and frustrated by continually unsuccessful efforts at personal advancement, sought to turn back to an earlier, simpler America. The progressives, invigorated and emboldened by the signs of economic growth and technical progress all around them, sought instead to go forward and shape the future to their liking.

In place of the monetary cranks, anti-Catholic and anti-Semitic bigots, and nostalgic secular pessimists of the 1880s and 1890s, the groups who came to the fore in American life after the turn of the twentieth century looked to advocates who focused on specific, concrete problems and offered practical solutions. Rather than grand utopian visions or apocalyptic international conspiracy theories, the public now wanted to read the "muckrakers' " gritty and often narrowly focused accounts of what was wrong here in the United States and, even if only implicitly, what could be done about it. Upton Sinclair's *The Jungle* exposed the unsanitary and unsafe conditions in the Chicago meatpacking industry. Lincoln Steffens grimly described America's urban slums, and the plight of those who lived there, in *The Shame of the Cities*. Frank Norris, in his books *The Octopus* and *The Pit*, cast a harsh light on the powerful monopolies with which midwestern grain farmers had to contend (the titles referred, respectively, to the Southern Pacific Railroad and the Chicago Board of Trade). Louis Brandeis's *Other People's Money* mobilized opinion against the power of large banks, and monopolies more generally, and with its title coined a phrase that still resonates in the securities markets today. Ida Tarbell's *History of the Standard Oil Company* detailed the accumulation and abuse of power by America's most visible monopoly.[8]

Americans' taste in fiction changed as well. Unlike Howells, Baum, Hamlin Garland, and others who had either glorified the virtues of rural and frontier life or, at the least, expressed moral unease toward the nation's fast-growing cities, new writers like Willa Cather took a harsher—today's reader would say more realistic—view of life on America's farms and in small towns. In a series of novels beginning with *O Pioneers!* and *My Ántonia*, Cather drew on her childhood in Red Cloud, Nebraska, to hail the hardy courage of life on the prairies, while reaffirming that in this setting the hardworking and the morally upright get ahead. But she also depicted the prairie farmers' life as physically bleak and culturally restrictive. Edith Wharton, in *Ethan Frome*, likewise wrote of the grim side of New England farm life. At the same time, Edgar Lee Masters's *Spoon River Anthology* and Sherwood Anderson's *Winesburg, Ohio* poignantly dramatized the loneliness and limitations of small-town midwestern life. And novelists who examined America's urban society—for example, Wharton in *The House of Mirth* (the nation's number-one best seller for months after it appeared in 1905)— disparaged as spiritually empty the continual pursuit of money for its own sake, and expressed longing for a life of greater meaning.

Even in its fiction, however, a dominant theme of the Progressive Era was that problems have causes and those causes, once understood, invite solutions. Theodore Dreiser, for example, in his 1912 novel, *The Financier,* distinguished sharply between private profit-seeking activity that does and does not promote the public good. His underlying argument, repeatedly illustrated by showing how rational human beings respond to the opportunities and constraints they face, was that a free market economy can produce growth that is equitable and sustainable only within a framework of appropriate social norms as well as government regulation. The book's title character continually succumbs to temptations that Dreiser implies society should not place before him in the first place, and takes actions that new regulations and better enforcement of existing laws would preclude. The attention-grabbing incident that opens the story presents the idea starkly: the lobster in a pet store tank eats the squid—only because, as Dreiser makes clear, there is no other food.

Many of the authors of the Progressive Era, like their predecessors a generation before, did wistfully lament much of the change they saw America undergoing. As Anderson wrote in *Winesburg, Ohio*, published in 1919, "The coming of industrialism, attended by all the roar and rattle of affairs, the shrill cries of millions of new voices that have come among us from overseas, the going and coming of trains, the growth of cities, the building of the interurban car lines that weave in and out of towns and past farmhouses, and now in these later days the coming of the automobiles has worked a tremendous change in the lives and in the habits of thought of our people of Mid-America." As a result, "Much of the old brutal ignorance that had in it also a kind of beautiful childlike innocence is gone forever."[9] In explaining the motivation that drove one of his most powerfully acting characters, Anderson went on to describe the then recent past as "[t]he beginning of the most materialistic age in the history of the world, when wars would be fought without patriotism, when men would forget God and only pay attention to moral standards, and when the will to power would replace the will to serve and beauty would be well-nigh forgotten in the terrible headlong rush of mankind toward the acquiring of possessions."[10] Leaving aside only the reference to "brutal ignorance," the sentiments were much the same as in the populist era.

But Anderson's response, like that of his contemporaries, was neither to paint small-town life as what it was not, nor to seek to reverse the flow of time in America. One of the most memorable vignettes in *Winesburg, Ohio* ends as a hardworking and apparently attractive young woman weeps, and "turning her face to the wall, began trying to force herself to face bravely the fact that many people must live and die alone, even in Winesburg."[11] And in a more sophisticated echo of Horatio Alger's emphasis a half-century before on the opportunities presented instead by urban America, the book ends as the young newspaper reporter who has been at the center of its series of loosely connected stories leaves Winesburg, a "young man, going out of his town to meet the adventure of life." He dozes off as the train pulls away, "and when he aroused himself and again looked out the car window the town of Winesburg had disappeared and his life there had become but a background on which to paint the dreams of his manhood."[12]

The fiction of the era also reflected a renewed confidence in the ability of economic growth to provide opportunities for social mobility. Edith Wharton's *The Age of Innocence*, not published until 1920 but clearly an attempt to look backward over what had happened in recent decades, at first portrays the resistance that members of the old elite mount against the newly successful. But in the end, the son of the story's principal old-wealth character, Newland Archer (his first name makes him emblematic of America), marries the daughter of the man who was once the "upstart." Thinking back on the changes between the social attitudes of the day and of his own youth, Archer hails the new era's sense of confidence: "The difference is that these young people take it for granted that they're going to get whatever they want, and that we almost always took it for granted that we shouldn't."[13] Yet another theme reflected in *The Age of Innocence* is the Progressive Era trend for high-minded men of old wealth and social prominence (like Theodore Roosevelt) to enter politics as reformers.

Not coincidentally, Americans in the first two decades of the twentieth century also showed renewed interest in Alger's works, which now found a broader readership than they had in his own lifetime. In the same spirit of seeking self-improvement with an eye toward personal advancement, in New York in 1912 Dale Carnegie began conducting educational courses for business and professional men and women. (Women would most surely not have been included a generation earlier.) The Carnegie program, centered on an hour and a half lecture entitled "How to Win Friends and Influence People," soon spread to other cities as well.

Developments on the more formal intellectual plane likewise echoed the theme that individuals, acting alone or in concert, could shape their own destiny. Widely read academic thinkers of the period like Lester Frank Ward rejected the social Darwinism of the late nineteenth century, with its implication that men and women were helpless creatures of the economic analog to nature. Taking their cue from the new muckraking journalists and political reformers, they argued instead that political and legal instruments were available to change the economic system. The plain implication was that society should go ahead and do so.

Perhaps the strongest sign that a new, activist moral outlook had taken hold in this era of growth and progress was the growing strength of the Social Gospel movement within American Protestantism. As the religious historian Henry May has described them, Social Gospel spokesmen "sought, however unsuccessfully, for concrete measures of improvement and listened, however critically, to contemporary proposals for change. . . . The Social Gospel, full of optimism for the American future, sacrificing only a minimum of individualism to the urgent demand for social action, was a middle class creed."[14]

The Social Gospel movement also had its reflection in the fiction of the day. The first Social Gospel novel to be widely read was Charles Sheldon's *In His Steps* (1897), which described the transformation of a fictional town whose leaders approached every public matter by asking "What would Jesus do?" The most successful of the Social Gospel novelists was Winston Churchill (not Britain's prime minister to-be, but an American cousin) whose principal works like *The Inside of the Cup*, *A Far Country*, and *The Dwelling Place of the Light* appeared in the half-decade before America entered World War I. In 1912 Walter Rauschenbusch, one of the movement's major figures, noted the remarkable change that had occurred in Americans' outlook toward social reform, and especially toward the Social Gospel movement, just since the turn of the century. "All whose recollection runs back of 1900 will remember that as a time of lonesomeness,"

Rauschenbusch wrote. "We were few, and we shouted in the wilderness."[15]
The new era was different.

With the change from stagnation to growth, Americans' outlook was
different even if many citizens saw the nation as beset by many of the same
problems as before: If businesses in some industries were colluding to
monopolize markets and block new competitors, the solution was to break
up the combinations that enabled them to do so. If powerful firms were
recklessly endangering their customers or their workers, regulation should
provide protection for the powerless. If large private interests commanding
vast resources were preventing American democracy from functioning as it
should, then new political rules, written into the Constitution if necessary,
were the answer. Even the progressives' less successful efforts—most spec-
tacularly, the prohibition of "intoxicating liquors"—reflected this same
approach of identifying specific problems and proposing concrete solutions.

It is easy enough to imagine the populists' having held any or all of
these positions, and in many instances they had. But in the new climate of
growth and progress, both the tone and the specifics of the progressives'
agenda were different. For example, the Pujo Committee hearings in
Congress in 1913 vigorously attacked the New York "money trust" (consisting principally of the First National Bank, the National City Bank, and
J. P. Morgan & Company), and later the same year Congress established the
Federal Reserve System as the nation's new central bank. But the apocalyptic view of the world as dominated by hostile financial conspiracies and the
fixation on currency arrangements as a universal panacea, both of which had
so dominated populist discussion of such issues, were missing from these
new, activist endeavors. So too was the anti-urban, anti-intellectual character of so much of the populists' thought and rhetoric. To the progressives,
the money trust was an economic and hence a political problem. The new
central bank was a concrete, practical solution.

Racism, ethnic bias, and nativism remained, to be sure, but the progressives' program reflected these prejudices in different ways than had the
populists'. Although no one challenged the "separate but equal" doctrine of
Plessy v. Ferguson, and there was no new civil rights legislation, at least the
legal separation of blacks from whites advanced little further. Racial zoning
was a particular case in point. By 1910 numerous southern cities—first Baltimore, then Atlanta and Greenville, North Carolina, then others—had
moved to segregate housing by race, designating specific city blocks for
blacks and others for whites. Richmond, Winston-Salem, and several other

cities achieved the same purpose as an adjunct to existing miscegenation laws, prohibiting any person from living in a block where the majority of residents were those "with whom the said person is forbidden to inter-marry."[16] New Orleans did not formally ban interracial housing but instead enacted a law that, implausibly, required an individual to gain consent of the majority of people already living in an area before establishing a residence there. But in 1917 the Supreme Court ruled against Louisville's residential segregation law and, in so doing, held all such attempts at racial zoning unconstitutional.[17]

As incomes rose and unemployment declined, many Americans' concerns over having to compete with foreigners lessened as well. With immigration reaching over a million per year on average in the decade before World War I, the progressives worried no less than the populists had about the dilution of traditional American values and lifestyles.* The progressives, however, mostly addressed the problem by seeking not to exclude immigrants but to "Americanize" them. (In 1915, cities across the country held "Americanization Day" celebrations on the Fourth of July.) Apart from the extension to Japanese and Korean laborers of the long-standing bar to Chinese immigrants, in 1908, there were no new anti-immigrant measures between 1896 and World War I. Immigration restrictions were simply not on the progressives' agenda.

Nor was walling off the American economy in other ways. Theodore Roosevelt's initiative in quickly recognizing Panama's independence from Colombia and then launching the Panama Canal project was a dramatic assertion of American interest in world trade, as well as world affairs more generally. (The broader turn toward imperialism, with the country's partic-ipation in the Spanish-American War and the consequent role of the United States in Cuba, Puerto Rico, and the Philippines, had already occurred under McKinley.) With the Underwood Tariff Act of 1913, Congress reduced import duties for the first time since the Civil War. The decision to enter World War I, in the first year of Wilson's second term as president, seemed to put isolationism firmly aside.

. . .

---

*Because return migration was also large during this period, the gross inflow of a million-plus per year overstates the net immigration to the United States. Moreover, despite the massive influx of immigrants to American cities, the share of the U.S. urban population that was foreign-born declined during the early twentieth century because so many native citizens also flocked to the cities.

The progressives' agenda was instead a combination of anti-monopoly activism, protective regulation as a counterweight to unrestrained big business, and measures to strengthen—the progressives would probably have said restore—American democracy. In each of these areas, the progressives prevailed by, in effect, attracting to their cause the "swing voters" whom the advocates of reform in the populist era had failed to capture.

Key court decisions before the turn of the century had largely emasculated such earlier legislation as the 1887 Interstate Commerce Act (originally intended to make the railroads' freight-hauling rates more favorable to farmers) and the 1890 Sherman Antitrust Act. Renewed activism under the Republican Roosevelt and then the Democrat Wilson put new life in the antitrust movement. In 1906 the Hepburn Act reinforced the Interstate Commerce Commission's power to rein in the railroads.[18] At the same time, the courts too began to adopt a different view toward antitrust matters. In 1914 Congress further buttressed the anti-monopoly movement by passing both the Clayton Act, which prohibited such anticompetitive practices as price discrimination and interlocking corporate directorates, and the Federal Trade Commission Act.

The most famous pieces of regulatory legislation during this era at the federal level were the Meat Inspection Act and, even more so, the Pure Food and Drug Act, both of which Congress passed in 1906 partly in response to the uproar created by publication of *The Jungle* earlier that year. But labor safety codes, workmen's compensation laws, and restrictions on the exploitation of child and women's labor were also important parts of the agenda of the time. Much of this activity advancing the regulation of business took place at the state and even the local level.

For example, although the Illinois Supreme Court in 1895 had struck down that state's law limiting the workday for women, beginning with Massachusetts and Pennsylvania in 1900 an increasing number of states nonetheless began to enact their own versions of such legislation. In 1908 the Supreme Court cleared the way for these laws by unanimously ruling in favor of Oregon's ten-hour law for women.[19] California's law, passed in 1911, limited women's work to eight hours per day and forty-eight hours per week, applicable across a broad range of industries and occupations. New York, where organized agitation for such measures had begun a decade earlier, finally acted after the tragedy of the Triangle Shirtwaist fire that same year.[20] By the end of the 1910s, forty-one states had passed legislation regulating women's work hours.[21] In addition, beginning with Massachusetts in 1912, fifteen states (plus Congress legislating for the District of

Columbia) also enacted minimum wage laws for women during this period. In 1916 the campaign against labor market exploitation returned to the national stage, as Congress passed the Keating-Owen Child Labor Law, barring from interstate commerce any goods produced by children under age fourteen working more than eight hours per day or more than six days per week.[22]

The same concern for protecting the interests of women and children led to change in other ways as well, again prompted by coalitions of progressive reformers often acting through private civic organizations. Between 1911 and 1913 twenty state legislatures authorized local government authorities to make regular payments—typically called "mothers' pensions," or in some cases "widows' pensions"—to impoverished mothers of dependent children. By 1920 forty states had such provisions. An important force behind the mothers' pension movement was the effort of organized women's associations, state by state, in conjunction with the work of activist social reformers like Jane Addams of the settlement house movement.[23] During the late 1910s many of America's cities also shut down what had openly been active red-light districts.

In 1912 the federal government established the Children's Bureau to investigate the welfare of children and promote new programs for ensuring children's well-being. A large part of the underlying motivation was the characteristically Progressive Era recognition that because childhood was when people developed into citizens, ensuring children's welfare was an appropriate object of national concern. Much of the active political impetus behind the creation of the Children's Bureau came from the National Child Labor Committee, a private civic organization founded in 1904 (and given a congressional charter in 1907) for the purpose of promoting "the rights, dignity, and well-being of children and youth" in the workplace. For ten years beginning in 1906, the committee employed sociologist Lewis Wickes Hine to travel across the United States studying the conditions of child labor and taking what became his famous photographs of children in factories, sweatshops, farms, and coal mines.[24]

For largely the same reasons, the early twentieth century was also when the idea of mass high school education first took hold in America, or anywhere else for that matter, since no other country underwent a similar change until several decades later. Indeed, the very notion of a secondary school with a standardized curriculum was an American creation of this period. Although the United States had become the world leader in educational enrollment rates by the middle of the nineteenth century, the great majority of citizens at best completed grammar school. In most parts of the country a high school education typically suggested that a young man or woman was from a well-to-do family. As late as 1890 only 3 percent of American youngsters earned high school diplomas. Between 1900 and 1920 the graduation rate went from 6 percent to 18 percent, while enrollment rose from 11 percent to 35 percent.[25] Not surprisingly, the more prosperous states led the way. Most states during this period added to their constitutions a provision promising a free public education, and states with large rural populations passed "free tuition" laws allowing students who lived in districts without a high school to attend one elsewhere at no expense.[26]

Especially in urban areas that received large numbers of immigrants, the public schools increasingly took up the task of "Americanizing" the newcomers. But the emphasis on building citizenship was broader than just language instruction, and the standard curriculum soon came to include courses in American history and "social studies." As John Dewey, the leading American thinker of the day on education, argued, in a country increasingly populated by Irish-Americans, German-Americans, and Italian-Americans, "The point [was] to see to it that the hyphen connects instead of separates."[27]

The expansion of public education led to other changes as well. Earlier on, the tiny minority who attended high school did so mostly to prepare for college. Now many boys and girls sought a secondary education that would lead directly to employment. (It was at this time that the new "English" curriculum, often including training in manual and technical arts, first supplemented the old Latin-based curriculum.) Meanwhile, as in the case of mothers' pensions and child welfare programs, the taxes that paid for the public schools came mostly from property owners and other middle- and upper-income citizens. Hence the high school movement represented another form of redistribution carried out by state and local government.

Congress during this period was also concerned with the welfare of citizens at the opposite end of the age spectrum. A 1906 amendment to the existing veterans' pension laws specified that any veteran age sixty-two or over should automatically be deemed to have a permanent specific "disability" and therefore be eligible for pension benefits. Further legislation passed over the next few years increased benefit levels for veterans as well as surviving dependents.

The progressives also succeeded in significantly reinforcing American democracy at both the government and private levels. Here too the differences that came with economic growth are instructive. For example, advocates of broader democracy, including the populists, had long favored direct popular election of United States senators instead of their selection by state legislatures as originally specified in the Constitution. The motivation, in part, was to make the Senate more responsive to democratic forces and less subject to influence—including bribery—from moneyed interests. After the turn of the century, some states in effect adopted this reform on their own by establishing preferential primaries to guide their legislatures' selection. But it was not until 1912, well into the new era of rising incomes, that Congress approved what became the Seventeenth Amendment. The direct election amendment then quickly received the necessary approval of three-fourths of the states, and it became part of the Constitution the next year.

Other changes intended to reinforce the functioning of democratic government—direct primaries, initiative and referendum, recall of elected officials—flourished at the state level during the progressive period. These measures too were consistent with the populists' agenda, if not actually a part of it. But it was not until the Progressive Era, with the change of outlook and emphasis that accompanied rising incomes and living standards, that these efforts to strengthen democracy attracted enough support to go forward. More specifically, the progressives' crusade against "machine politics" was emblematic of the difference between their approach and that of the populists. Both movements recognized the dangers to democracy posed by the political exploitation of new, often illiterate, immigrants. But while the populists' reaction was to want immigrants kept out, the progressives turned to such devices as the secret ballot to prevent them from being exploited.

The effort to extend democracy by allowing women to vote was also very much a part of the progressives' agenda.[28] Here too actions by individual states led the way, although little real momentum was evident until 1910. With a final boost from the remarkable phenomenon of women in large numbers going to work in weapons factories during World War I, the Nineteenth Amendment, barring suffrage discrimination "on account of sex," received congressional approval in 1919 and final ratification by the states in 1920.

The Progressive Era also saw the establishment of many of the private civic organizations that went on to play a major role in American society throughout the twentieth century, reinforcing what Tocqueville had seen as the uniquely participatory basis for democracy in a nation of "joiners."[29] The National Association for the Advancement of Colored People was founded in 1909, and the Boy Scouts of America in 1910.* By that time the General Federation of Women's Clubs had over 1 million members. By the end of the decade the NAACP had 220 chapters, including more than 150 in the South, and more than 90,000 members.[30] The first modern Community Chest organization was established (in Cleveland) in 1913. The American Association for Community Organizations, the predecessor to the United Way, was formed in 1918. The League of Women Voters was founded in 1920.

Many of these new civic groups were especially important in forming the coalitions that fostered specific reforms. The National Congress of Mothers, established in 1897, played a large part in the campaigns that led to establishment of the Children's Bureau in 1912, as well as the creation of separate juvenile courts in most states. (In 1924 this group became the National Congress of Parents and Teachers, today's PTA.) The National Consumers League, founded in 1899, was a significant force in the push to enact child and women's labor laws. (Since 1992 it has sponsored the National Fraud Information Center.) Still other organizations, such as the American Association for Labor Legislation, which was particularly effective in promoting state-level workmen's safety laws, were active and important in American civic society at the time but have since given way to successors.

Part of the inspiration for this great florescence of civic organizations was the realization that the far-reaching transformation America had undergone in the latter decades of the nineteenth century—industrialization, urbanization, national expansion, large-scale immigration from outside northern and western Europe—had rendered obsolete, or at best less effective, earlier ways of providing for popular democratic participation and hence for creating among citizens a feeling of connectedness to the nation's affairs if not outright influence. Farmers' associations, neighborhood churches, and New England–style town meetings no longer served the needs of many of the nation's citizens. Emboldened by the spirit born of economic prosperity, and drawing on the wherewithal that prosperity provided, America in the Progressive Era re-created its supply of what sociologists and political scientists now often call "social capital."[31]

---

*The immediate spur to the founding of the NAACP was a 1908 race riot in Springfield, Illinois. The point is not that racial tension or even racial violence disappeared (they plainly did not), but that in the Progressive Era the response elicited was positive action in the form of a new, nationally based civic organization.

In the new era of rising incomes, the country also took its first step toward more explicit redistribution via taxes. The constitutional amendment that authorized Congress to impose an income tax provides yet another instance of the difference that follows with economic growth. Before the free silver issue so completely preempted their agenda, the populists too had favored introducing an income tax to supplement the federal government's reliance on tariffs and land sales as sources of revenue. In the midst of the economic stagnation of the late nineteenth century, however, the idea had failed to come to fruition.[32] By contrast, after more than a decade of sustained growth, Congress overwhelmingly approved the Sixteenth Amendment in 1909 (the vote was 77–0 in the Senate and 318–14 in the House), and by 1913 the necessary three-fourths of the states had ratified it.

As we have seen, the attitudes of ordinary people toward their fellow citizens—admiration or resentment of those who are more successful, a sense of opportunity or gnawing frustration over its absence—change markedly depending on whether incomes in general are rising. What the Progressive Era also showed is that attitudes looking down can be just as subject to such influence as those looking up. As Richard Hofstadter concluded, "One of the primary tests of the mood of a society at any given time is whether its comfortable people tend to identify, psychologically, with the power and achievements of the very successful or with the needs and sufferings of the underprivileged. In a large and striking measure the Progressive agitations turned the human sympathies of the people downward rather than upward in the social scale."[33]

Woodrow Wilson, in his first inaugural address, articulated just that viewpoint, beginning by making the connection to the nation's economic growth fully explicit: "We have been proud of our industrial achievements, but we have not hitherto stopped thoughtfully enough to count the human cost, the cost of lives snuffed out, of energies overtaxed and broken, the fearful physical and spiritual cost of the men and women and children upon whom the dead weight and burden of it all has fallen pitilessly the years through."[34] It was against the background of solid economic growth that the progressives succeeded in this regard where the populists had failed.

Business faltered after World War I, however, and the country's mood soon soured once again. America suffered four separate recessions between 1918 and 1927, and a fifth, which soon turned into full-scale depression, set in just two years later. The first of these postwar downturns (which actually began a few months before the war was over) was brief and mild. But the second, which commenced in early 1920, abruptly ended the era of sustained prosperity that had lasted since the mid-1890s.

The primary cause of the downturn was the sudden loss of the stimulus that wartime government spending had provided, together with a sharp decline in foreign demand for American products. Within a month of the Armistice the War Department had canceled nearly half of its $6 billion in outstanding contracts,[35] and within a year it had discharged one-third of the nation's 12 million uniformed servicemen. Federal spending shrank from $18 billion in fiscal year 1919 (25 percent of that year's national income) to $6 billion in 1920, and just $3 billion in 1922. The government's budget shifted from a deficit of more than $13 billion in 1919 to a small surplus in 1920. At the same time, American exports fell from over $8 billion in 1920 to less than $4 billion two years later. And because foreigners who no longer needed a wartime safe haven were now taking their gold out of the United States, instead of bringing it in, the Federal Reserve System tightened monetary policy and interest rates rose.

The total output produced by American industry promptly fell by one-third. Production of iron and steel fell by nearly two-thirds. Although homebuilding remained strong, investment in new factories and machinery, which had surged as industry scrambled to meet the huge domestic and foreign demands of the war years, declined rapidly. With factories not hiring and the military continuing to demobilize, unemployment rose to just under 5 million, or almost 12 percent. As a result of the business downturn, together with continuing tight money and high interest rates, more than 500 banks failed in 1921.

Meanwhile, in a sudden and extreme return to the conditions of the 1880s and early 1890s, prices declined precipitously. In 1921 wholesale prices fell 37 percent, including declines of 21 percent for metals, 34 percent for food products, and 43 percent for finished textiles. And as had happened earlier, key farm products sustained some of the biggest declines. Corn dropped from $1.52 per bushel to 52 cents, wheat from $2.46 to $1.21, and cotton from $35.34 per pound to $15.89.

For the most part, these rapid price declines were simply a reversal of the wartime inflation, and in most cases only a partial reversal at that. At no time throughout the 1920s did wholesale prices overall fall back to the level that had prevailed on the eve of World War I. Nor did farm prices, although the prices of some products (corn, for example) did so briefly. But consumer prices did not decline to prewar levels either, and especially for farmers, living standards clearly worsened. The average net income of American farmers declined from $1,400 in 1920 to barely $500 in 1921. Farm foreclosure rates rose to 10.7 per 1,000 on average in the first half of the 1920s and 16.7 in the second half, compared to just 3.2 per 1,000 during the Wilson years. Especially in America's rural areas and small towns, strains of the populism of thirty years before emerged once again.[36]

Although the 1920s began with an economic decline that depressed Americans' real per capita income to levels that had prevailed shortly after the turn of the century, the period was hardly a time of continual stagnation. New industries based on new technologies fueled a series of irregular growth spurts punctuated by successive downturns, and from 1923 until 1929 unemployment averaged just over 3 percent. In some industries, manufacturing in particular, wages rose strongly. The rapid spread of the automobile not only required industrial production on an unprecedented scale—iron and steel, rubber tires, plate glass windows, casting dies for large parts and precision machinery for small ones, not to mention assembly of the finished cars—but also transformed how people lived. Those changes in turn greatly expanded demands for factory products of all sorts, along with the need for paved roads, filling stations, and roadside restaurants and inns. In 1928 Americans bought almost 4 million new cars, and at the end of the decade one American in five owned one.

Spreading electrification and new inventions to exploit it changed people's daily lives as well, creating demand for other new factory products. Stoves, toasters, washing machines, and even vacuum cleaners all became standard household appliances. So did refrigerators, and as more families bought them their purchases of food products also changed. (The Piggly Wiggly chain, founded in Memphis just before America's entry into World War I, pioneered the concept of the self-service grocery store, which in time evolved into today's supermarket.) By the end of the 1920s, more than two-fifths of American households had telephones. Although the nation's first commercial radio station, Pittsburgh's KDKA, had commenced broadcasting only in 1920, by the end of the decade more than one-third of all American households owned a radio. Public discussion as well as much popular writing about America and the American economy referred repeatedly to the "New Era" that had begun.

These dramatic changes in lifestyle, the growing employment that went into producing new consumer goods, and especially the contrast to the severe depression that set in once the decade ended, have all lent to the 1920s a lingering image of robust prosperity in American historical memory. The lavish consumption of the Jazz Age rich and would-be rich, the apotheosis of movies as not just an increasingly popular form of entertainment but a whole new culture, the national celebration of feats like Charles Lindbergh's solo transatlantic flight, and even the boisterous celebrity of sports heroes like Babe Ruth, Jack Dempsey, Bobby Jones, and Bill Tilden, all contributed to the prosperous image of the "Roaring Twenties." So too, in a different way, did the stories—often fondly exaggerated, especially after the crash—of taxi drivers and elevator boys speculating on the stock market.

But despite these appearances, the average American made little real progress during the 1920s. Only a tiny minority could aspire to the life of flapper girls and glittering parties that F. Scott Fitzgerald depicted in his novels, and relatively few enjoyed the gains created by rising stock prices. There was plenty of work, but wages were stagnant or declining for farmers, miners, and ordinary workers in many industries. Although wages rose in manufacturing, especially for the highly skilled, because of new labor-saving technologies the number of workers employed in the nation's manufacturing sector declined.[37]

Of the eleven years between the end of World War I and the final predepression peak in 1929, Americans' real income per capita rose in four (one of which was 1929), declined in three, and remained approximately unchanged in the other four. Between 1918 and 1929 real income per capita rose on average by just 1 percent per annum, only two-fifths the rate of advance that had prevailed over the previous two decades.[38] Because inequalities were widening once again, the typical family's increase was yet smaller.[39] And then even this modest advance collapsed into the seemingly bottomless decline of the depression.

The country had barely finished celebrating the Armistice ending World War I when a series of labor strikes began. By the end of 1919 these work stoppages had involved one out of every five American workers. At the same time, a wave of bombings, apparently carried out by political anarchists, hit many of the nation's cities. Recalling the successful Bolshevik revolution in Russia just two years earlier, and wary of the newly formed American Communist Party, both government officials and the general public feared that America too now faced a coordinated threat.

In the resulting "Red Scare" all labor agitation, including straightforward attempts to win wage increases to compensate for wartime price inflation, seemed potentially subversive. So too did ordinary expressions of political dissent. The government's response was some thousands of prosecutions and deportations ordered in January 1920 by Attorney General A. Mitchell Palmer, who proclaimed the urgent need to combat "a blaze of revolution." As Palmer testified before the House Judiciary Committee, "There is a condition of revolutionary intent in the country of sufficiently widespread a character . . . to destroy or overthrow the government of the United States by physical force."[40]

The "Palmer raids" blatantly violated their targets' constitutional protection—and, significantly, did so during peacetime—but the public at large registered little opposition. Instead, new private organizations like the National Security League and the National Civic Federation formed to offer support. In the end, the public hysteria and willingness to persecute anyone who expressed minority views rivaled the McCarthy episode that erupted more than thirty years later.[41]

The same spirit infected the nationally followed trial of Nicola Sacco and Bartolomeo Vanzetti, Italian immigrants and self-professed anarchists accused of murder during a 1920 Boston robbery. The trial that convicted the two men focused more on their political beliefs and activities than on the murder charge per se, and the presiding judge, Webster Thayer, displayed obvious bias. The case attracted so much national attention that in 1927 Massachusetts governor Alvan Fuller appointed a three-member commission, chaired by Harvard president Abbott Lawrence Lowell, to review the matter. But Lowell showed signs of prejudice as well—some years earlier he had tried, unsuccessfully, to impose a strict quota limiting the number of Jews in each Harvard class—and the commission supported the guilty verdict. Sacco and Vanzetti were executed in 1927. (The latest review of the evidence suggests that Sacco was guilty but Vanzetti innocent.)[42]

The Palmer raids and the prosecution of Sacco and Vanzetti foreshadowed much of the ugliness of the new postwar era, but they were idiosyncratic events nonetheless. Moreover, both occurred too early for most Americans to have realized that they now faced a new period of systematically slower economic growth. A more representative reflection of the public's reaction to the disappearance of robust income growth was the rise of the second Ku Klux Klan. Established (or reestablished) in 1915, largely at the instigation of Georgia's Tom Watson, writing in his newspaper, *The Jeffersonian*, the new Klan organization had remained insignificant in the face of rising incomes and the patriotic emotion inspired by the war effort. But once the war ended and large groups across American society began to face hard times, the Klan flourished. Its violent agenda recalled the populists of the previous century at their worst: anti-Catholic, anti-black, anti-Semitic, anti-immigrant.

The standard contemporary estimate of 4 million enrolled Klan members—or about one out of every six of the country's adult white Protestant males—was probably an exaggeration, but official Klan membership in the early 1920s certainly exceeded 2 million. (By contrast, the Southern Poverty Law Center has estimated Klan membership in the mid-1920s to have been 5 million.)[43] Moreover, the Klan of this era was neither exclusively southern nor, as many early analyses suggested, active only in small towns and rural areas. The four states with the largest known membership were Indiana, Ohio, Texas, and Pennsylvania, and approximately one-third of all Klan members apparently lived in cities of 100,000 or more. Chicago alone had 50,000 Klansmen, Indianapolis 38,000, and Detroit and Philadelphia 35,000 each. On a percentage basis, the most active Klan centers were Dayton; Portland, Oregon; Youngstown; and Denver.[44] Even so, it was in the South that the Klan's influence was most pervasive. In both Texas and Oklahoma, for example, the state governments were, for a while, almost completely under Klan domination.[45]

In the words of Stanley Frost, the journalist who wrote most comprehensively about the Klan at the time, at its height the Klan of the 1920s was "the most vigorous, active, and effective force in American life, outside business."[46] Under the burden of disappointing economic growth, the progressive, reformist coalition that had been so influential before World War I mostly collapsed. The Klan was emblematic of what replaced it.

It would be wrong to portray the rise of the second Ku Klux Klan as a purely economic phenomenon. Anti-Catholic, anti-Jewish, and anti-immigrant sentiment was a mainstay of native Protestant groups who saw their historical dominance over American society waning. The limited entry of blacks into the urban labor force during the war, and then the visible presence of blacks in uniform at home once the war ended, aroused overt racism that had not been all that latent to begin with. Perversely, the increased activism of the NAACP, which proclaimed the emergence of "a new Negro," also provoked a reaction in some quarters.[47]

Rising divorce rates, the wartime movement of women into previously all male jobs, and the spread of Jazz Age social habits like women's smoking and drinking (Prohibition notwithstanding), also seemed to threaten traditional ideas of hierarchy, place, and morality. Farms and small towns were rapidly losing both population and influence to urban areas. In northern cities, the migration of native white American Protestants from rural areas now collided not only with the arrival of immigrants from abroad, as had long been the case, but also with the new migration of blacks from the rural South. Although the two races rarely lived in close proximity, merely having significant numbers of blacks in the same city was a new experience for many northerners.[48]

But the rise of the Ku Klux Klan in the 1920s was also a response to the disappearance of sustained economic growth, and with it any practical hope of material advancement for large parts of the American public. Although the Klan's most spectacular social success was the induction of President Warren Harding, in a formal ceremony in the Green Room of the White House (with the president on his knees, taking the membership oath on the White House Bible),[49] Klansmen were rarely among the highly affluent. But nor were they often at the bottom of the economic scale. Instead they were farmers, skilled craftsmen, small business proprietors, blue-collar workers at large factories, and low-end white-collar workers of all kinds.[50] Hiram Wesley Evans, the Dallas dentist who served as the Klan's imperial wizard and emperor from 1920 to 1939, declared, "We are a movement of the plain people."[51]

The postwar hard times had made their aspirations no longer realistic. As historian Kenneth Jackson wrote in his classic study of the Klan in urban areas, the typical Klansman "had obviously been left at the post in an economic race he perhaps only inadequately understood. . . . Having fought his way above the lowest rung of the financial ladder, the potential Klansman remained something less than a success. . . . Moreover, he was faced with increasing competition from Catholics and from a new kind of Negro, who seemed anxious to take his job and live in his neighborhood."[52] As historian Nancy MacLean has more recently argued, "By and large, these were men who had climbed the economic ladder, if only by a rung or two. . . . Then, suddenly, just when their prospects had appeared most promising, they confronted unforeseen obstacles—if not disaster. Being on the edge to begin with, they reeled under the wave of the hard times that washed across the land."[53] Indeed, "a crucial factor in the Klan's appeal was the economic crisis of the twenties. It cut short the climb of men on the make and defied their dreams of being their own bosses. . . . Class standing and economic insecurity created a potential among white men for openness to the Klan's message."[54]

As Evans himself put it, writing in 1926, "The assurance for the future of our children dwindled. We found our great cities and the control of much of our industry and commerce taken over by strangers."[55] Those who joined the Ku Klux Klan clearly differed from their fellow citizens in choosing a self-consciously bigoted vehicle to voice their anger and seek redress. But they were hardly alone in their sense of disappointed prospects and frustrated hopes.

The same disappointment and frustration also permeated other dimensions of America's public culture. By highlighting the sordid backdrop to

Jazz Age glitter, F. Scott Fitzgerald's novels—especially *The Great Gatsby*, published in 1925—expressed a profound disillusionment with the classic American success ethic itself. In contrast to the appealing notion, grounded in traditional Calvinist thinking and articulated by spokesmen like Horatio Alger and Russell Conwell, that those who have great wealth have earned it, or at least possess moral qualities such that they deserve it, most of the rich in Fitzgerald's stories either inherit their money or acquire it by illicit means like bookmaking and bootlegging.

The particular focus of *Gatsby* was the casual cruelty of the very rich. As the story's more middle-class narrator finally concludes about his cousin and her fabulously rich husband, who between them have been directly responsible for a woman's death and indirectly for Gatsby's, "They were careless people, Tom and Daisy—they smashed things and creatures and then retreated back into their money or their vast carelessness, or whatever it was that kept them together, and let other people clean up the mess they had made."[56]

Other writers of the 1920s expressed a similar disillusionment, evident, for example, in Sinclair Lewis's *Main Street* and *Babbitt*, as well as in Dreiser's *An American Tragedy*. Lewis's Babbitt became a stock symbol for a coarse, vulgar materialism that many saw as emblematic of the American middle class in the new era. Similarly, in *An American Tragedy* the pursuit of material success takes the protagonist (no longer a hero) steadily away from his earlier dedication to religion and morality. Another Fitzgerald novel, *The Beautiful and Damned*, contrasted the moral outlook of a self-made millionaire, now retired, and his grandson who would not even consider working for a living. Instead of glorifying the desire to get ahead, Fitzgerald wrote of "that air of struggle, of greedy ambition, of hope more sordid than despair, of incessant passage up or down, which in every metropolis is most in evidence through the unstable middle class."[57]

The country had come a long way from Alger's can-do optimism, or even the let's-do reformism of Upton Sinclair. In a society where the average citizen no longer had a sense of getting ahead, the traditional value structure centered on achieving conventional success no longer provided a reliable mooring. Writers like Ernest Hemingway, in *The Sun Also Rises*, responded by dwelling on the search for something more sturdy, more physical, in which to believe. Others, like T. S. Eliot in *The Waste Land*, despaired altogether of achieving that goal and instead portrayed what they saw as the resulting emptiness of life.

. . .

As working- and even middle-class Americans confronted their stalled progress, one corner where they could not turn for help was their government. The progressive consensus of the pre–World War I era was simply gone. Tax legislation under the administrations of Warren Harding and Calvin Coolidge reduced rates on high-bracket taxpayers and high-wealth estates—the "surtax" rate applicable to incomes above $200,000 (approximately $2.2 million in today's dollars) was cut from 50 percent in 1923 to 20 percent beginning in 1925—and likewise favored corporations. But it did little for the average working taxpayer, or for small business.

In a far more dramatic display of the same spirit, when the great Mississippi River flood of 1927 killed hundreds and left nearly a million homeless, President Coolidge not only refused government help but publicly displayed a resolute indifference. Coolidge declined repeated pleas to visit the flood disaster, including a formal request made jointly by four governors and eight senators. The president likewise refused NBC's request to broadcast a nationwide appeal on radio, and even rejected Will Rogers's request for a telegram of sympathy to be read at a benefit for flood victims.[58]

The anti-monopoly fervor of the Progressive Era was also dead. The Interstate Commerce Commission, reinforced by the Hepburn Act under Theodore Roosevelt and reinvigorated by his support, now sought to *foster* railroad consolidations. The ICC also acted to suppress the new competition the railroads faced from the trucking industry, which was then just beginning to take advantage of the spread of paved road systems to enter the long-haul freight business. Even the Federal Trade Commission, established during the Wilson administration as a means of resisting business combinations, now became a vehicle for promoting them. The Sherman and Clayton Acts were both virtually suspended.

Despite the increased need, government efforts to assist or protect impoverished women and children also withered during the 1920s. True, the 1921 Sheppard-Towner Act "for the Protection of the Welfare and Hygiene of Maternity and Infancy" provided federal funding to subsidize the creation, by state governments, of clinics to provide both pre- and postnatal advice to expectant mothers. But Sheppard-Towner proved to be the last success achieved by the old coalition that had supported mothers' and children's welfare programs. Congress passed no further measures along such lines, and when funding for the clinics ran out in 1927 the most that supporters could get was a two-year extension. (The American Medical Association opposed Sheppard-Towner as "an imported socialist scheme"; despite the support of most women's organizations, conservative groups like the Woman Patriots opposed it as well.)[59] In 1929 the program died. In the meanwhile, in 1923 the Supreme Court ruled that the District of Columbia's minimum wage for women was unconstitutional, thereby also invalidating all state-level women's wage statutes.[60] The court also struck down state laws prohibiting employers from using injunctions against striking workers.[61]

The government also failed to protect America's black citizens from the renewed spread of both Jim Crow legislation and Klan-type violence. In 1922 Mississippi adopted legislation segregating taxicabs throughout the state. Elsewhere in the South cities adopted similar ordinances. As intercity buses began to provide a popular alternative to railroad travel, a new wave of Jim Crow laws segregated seating arrangements, waiting rooms, toilets, and other related facilities. In 1926 Atlanta passed an ordinance prohibiting Negro barbers from serving women and children.[62]

Most egregious, however, was the failure to stop, or even seriously oppose, lynching. Racial violence in America surged in the early 1920s, as it had in the 1880s and 1890s, including not only mass violence (the worst single episode was the 1921 Tulsa race riot, after which newspapers reported seventy-six dead; many accounts put the total far higher) but also the ritualized public murder of specific targeted individuals.[63] The NAACP during this period lobbied for numerous bills aimed at stanching the rise in lynching in particular, but none passed in Congress.[64] Part of the opposition was blatantly racist. Southern white supremacists like Mississippi senator William Van Amberg and Texas congressman James Buchanan echoed such earlier figures as Ben Tillman in openly hailing lynching as a legitimate instrument of social control—in this case supposedly necessary to protect white women from sexual assault by black men. Van Amberg publicly acknowledged having personally headed a lynch mob, saying "I led the mob . . . and am proud of it. I directed every movement of the mob and I did everything I could to see that he was lynched." Buchanan referred to blacks as the "race most addicted to the tragic infamy of rape."[65]

Others justified their opposition to anti-lynching legislation as a matter of federalism, expressing reluctance to enact federal legislation that would encroach on the states' police powers. As legal scholar Randall Kennedy has shown, however, the commitment to federalism that consistently prevailed over the supposed desire to protect black men proved less compelling when the focus of concern was some other objective. In 1910 Congress had passed the White Slave Traffic Act (the Mann Act), prohibiting the transportation of women and girls across state lines for prostitution "or any other immoral purpose." A statute passed in 1912 had similarly prohibited the interstate transportation of prizefight films. And the Harrison Act of 1914 was the nation's first federal narcotics law. Especially in the debate over the Mann Act, arguments based on federalism had figured prominently in opposition, but the legislation had passed anyway. Despite the rise in anti-black violence in the 1920s, none of the many anti-lynching bills became law.[66]

Not surprisingly, the 1920s also saw increasing rejection of American racial pluralism from within the black community. Marcus Garvey, a Jamaican immigrant who founded the Universal Negro Improvement Association in 1914, moved his organization to New York during World War I. Opposing the integrationist NAACP, Garvey's was a separatist movement raising the banner of black nationalism under the slogan "Back to Africa." By the early 1920s the UNIA had chapters in thirty American cities, and over 65,000 dues-paying members. The organization foundered soon thereafter, as Garvey was convicted of fraudulent commercial activities and went to jail in 1925. (Two years later he was released and deported to Jamaica.) But the Back to Africa movement spawned in the ugliness of the 1920s was a direct ancestor of the later Nation of Islam—Malcolm X's father was a Garvey organizer—and of the black nationalist movement alive in America today.

The chief way in which the government did rush to citizens' relief in the 1920s was to restrict immigration. The anti-immigrant sentiment of the populist era had long since brought about the exclusion of Chinese, Japanese, and Korean workers, and the long-standing effort to impose a literacy requirement had finally succeeded during World War I. But otherwise America's borders had remained open to newcomers. The flow of new immigrants had declined from over 1 million per year on average during 1905–14 to less than a quarter-million during the war years, but by 1921, even with a severe recession underway, immigration surged to 800,000. As before the war, most were from southern, central, and eastern Europe. (The new literacy requirement proved to be not much of a bar, since by this time the ability to read was already becoming fairly widespread in much of Europe. The test did not have to be in English.)

Resistance to immigration in America had traditionally combined economic motivations with racial and religious prejudice. With most Asians already excluded, anti-immigrant sentiment in the 1920s explicitly turned to arguments that non-Nordic whites were racially inferior to Nordics, so that continued large-scale immigration from areas other than northern and western Europe would weaken the genetic makeup of the population. In yet another echo from the 1880s, the eugenics movement—the attempt to improve the country's population by genetic selection—became a significant social force.[67] But the fact that immigrants from Europe were now likely to be Catholics, Jews, or Greek Orthodox only further compounded the issue for those, like the Klan's members, who still clung to the image of a Protestant America. (Although most Americans today associate the Ku Klux Klan primarily with bigotry against blacks, in the 1920s anti-Catholicism was the more important focus.) So too did the traditional association of Catholics, especially in the cities, with "wet" attitudes and behavior in a country that had just gone "dry" by constitutional amendment.

The drop in wages and increase in joblessness that followed World War I also helped attract to the anti-immigration effort constituencies who did not share these ethnic prejudices, or at least had been willing to put them aside during the earlier era of strong economic growth. Soon after the Armistice, once the implications of demobilization became clear, the American Federation of Labor petitioned Congress to halt immigration altogether for two years.[68] Although the cities where immigrants congregated and the occupations in which they worked tended to have higher than average wages, these patterns simply reflected the responsiveness of mobile, foreign-born workers to the lure of better paying jobs. More to the point of native workers' concerns, the impact of these immigrants on wage levels in the cities where they chose to go, and in the industries that they entered, was generally negative and often substantial. Not surprisingly, congressmen from areas where wages were stagnant or declining proved more likely to vote for restricting immigration than those whose working constituents enjoyed rising wages.[69]

In response to this complex mix of ethnically as well as economically motivated pressures, Congress not only ended the traditional policy of unlimited overall immigration but also imposed specific quotas that discriminated among Europeans. The Emergency Quota Act of 1921 limited annual immigration from each designated geographical region outside the Western Hemisphere to 3 percent of the number of people born in that region who were resident in the United States as of 1910. The resulting quota for all "Old World" areas other than northern and western Europe was a mere 158,000. (Before the war, immigration from those areas had averaged nearly 700,000 per year.) Then the National Origins Act of 1924 temporarily reduced the key percentage rate to just 2 percent and, in a further victory for advocates of discrimination, shifted the base for calculating the regional sub-quotas back to 1890. The resulting annual limit on immigrants from Old World areas other than northern and western Europe was now just 20,000. The 1924 legislation also established a new, permanent quota system, just as restrictive, that took effect in 1929.[70] The threat that Klansmen and their allies perceived from newly arriving Italians, Poles, and Russian Jews was over.

As in the populist era a third of a century before, anti-immigrant agitation was far from the only expression of the desire to barricade America from the rest of the world as the nation's postwar economy faltered. In 1920 President Wilson vetoed a proposed increase in tariffs, but his immediate successors had no such reservations. Despite America's growing net creditor position (which meant that foreigners could ultimately service their debts to the United States only if this country ran a trade deficit), Congress reinforced America's ongoing trade surplus by temporarily raising tariff rates to then record levels in 1921 and then regularizing these increases in the Fordney-McCumber Tariff Act the next year. The predictable result was to intensify both economic and financial pressures on the debtor countries abroad, including not only Germany, which owed reparations to the European victors, but also America's wartime allies, like Britain, which owed the United States more than $10 billion in war debts. In due course, only a series of additional, hastily arranged American loans avoided chaos in European financial arrangements.

The higher tariffs of the 1920s were only one concrete expression of the more general spirit of isolationism that had led America after World War I to reject the League of Nations as well as participation in the newly established World Court. Although the United States government increasingly took an interest in world affairs, the popular attitude of reckless disregard for the international consequences of American actions persisted. The decade ended with yet a further increase in tariffs, to all-time record levels, under the Smoot-Hawley Act.

As the 1920s went on, America's domestic politics, no less than the popular literature of the day, reflected the mood of disappointed expectations and rising tensions due in large part to the absence of any systematic improvement in living standards. The new tone of public cynicism, in contrast to the idealism of the Progressive Era, first became apparent as the financial scandals of Warren Harding's administration became public. Outside the usual muckraking circles, most pundits were more critical of the lesser figures who revealed the shady dealings of Teapot Dome and Elk Hills than they were of the higher-ups who perpetrated them. The 1924 Democratic convention split not only over the competition for the party's presidential nomination between New York Governor Al Smith (a Catholic) and William

Gibbs McAdoo, a prominent lawyer as well as Woodrow Wilson's secretary of the treasury (and son-in-law), but also over a proposal to denounce the Ku Klux Klan. In the end, John W. Davis—who thirty years later would act as the pro-segregation lawyer in the 1954 *Brown v. Board of Education* case— emerged as a compromise candidate on the 104th ballot. The anti-Klan proposal lost by 543 3/20 votes to 542 7/20.* Wisconsin's reform leader Robert La Follette left the Democratic Party to run for president as an independent candidate, attracting almost 5 million votes, or over 17 percent of all votes cast that year. Coolidge won reelection handily.

The Democrats did pick Smith in 1928, and that year's election sparked a renewed outpouring of anti-Catholic, anti-urban, anti-wet, and anti-foreign prejudice.[71] As Richard Hofstadter reflected many years afterward, "Although Hoover . . . would almost certainly have been elected in any case, the dimensions of his victory had a great deal to do with the personal snobbery and religious bigotry invoked against Smith. Not only did the election underline the fact that it was impossible for a Catholic to be elected president, but the underground campaign impugned the Americanism of Catholics and thus gave a blow to their efforts at assimilation and at the achievement of a full American identity."[72] It was not until thirty-two years later, and in a very different economic environment, that America again faced and finally resolved that nagging issue. In the meanwhile, the experience of the 1920s stands as another episode in the nation's history in which the tensions born of an absence of economic growth powerfully undermined the openness and tolerance of American society.

---

*The vote totals on the anti-Klan resolution do not add to an even integer because the Georgia delegation cast only 20 1/2 of that state's 28 votes.

Chapter 7

Great Depression, Great Exception

[C]hange is the order of the day. . . . [E]conomic problems, long
in the making, have brought crises of many kinds for which the
masters of old practice and theory were unprepared. . . . [S]ocial
justice, no longer a distant ideal, has become a definite goal.

FRANKLIN D. ROOSEVELT
1935 State of the Union Address[1]

The depression of the 1930s, the economic disaster that most Americans
now call the Great Depression, or more simply *the* depression, stands out as
exceptional in many ways. The business collapse was the most severe in
America's history, or at least that part of the nation's economic experience
for which sufficient information exists to make a judgment. It was also the
most subversive of belief in the free enterprise system and, more broadly, of
confidence in the durability of Americans' freedoms and even of the republic itself. As in other episodes of widespread economic disappointment and
distress like the mid-1890s and the early 1920s (and, as we shall see, in some
respects also the 1980s and early 1990s), the depression of the 1930s led to
efforts in some quarters to restrict American liberties and to close the society both externally and internally. But in the 1930s these movements were
not the dominant force of the time. Instead, the depression experience, on

balance, fostered a broader commitment to opportunity and mobility for all citizens.

The kind of bigotry on which many populists had thrived in the 1890s, and the Ku Klux Klan in the 1920s, also fed on the widespread economic hardship that so many ordinary Americans suffered in the 1930s. The Klan did not disappear. Outright racists like Mississippi senator Theodore Bilbo and Georgia governor Eugene Talmadge, with broad support from their constituents, continued to uphold the cause of white supremacy. Demagogues like Father Charles Coughlin and Gerald L. K. Smith exploited the new medium of radio to carry regular messages of racism and religious prejudice across the country; at its peak Father Coughlin's program drew 40 million listeners.[2] (In contrast to earlier eras, however, in the 1930s anti-black and anti-Jewish attitudes loomed larger than bias against Catholics; indeed, Father Coughlin was a Catholic priest.) Many of the witnesses at the 1939 Senate hearings to confirm Felix Frankfurter as a justice of the Supreme Court were openly anti-Semitic.

Especially after the violently anti-Semitic and internationally aggressive nature of the Nazi regime in Germany became fully apparent, the diplomatic and military isolationism championed by Charles Lindbergh and the America First movement likewise took on an overtone of prejudice that was at first implicit and later more blatant. The tight restrictions on immigration legislated in the 1920s remained in force, despite pleas to admit at least some additional refugees from Nazi persecution. (Opinion polls showed that two-thirds of Americans opposed a proposal, made in the wake of Kristallnacht—November 9, 1938—to admit 20,000 Jewish children.) At the same time, anti-democrats from the other end of the political spectrum looked to Stalin's Soviet Union as the model for the future, and some actively embraced communism. Yet others, including elected officials like Louisiana governor Huey Long, openly violated citizens' rights and in some cases partially undermined political democracy at the state level.

But troubling as they were, in the end these were not the dominant voices in American society of the era, and theirs were not the values that ultimately prevailed. The 1930s stand out as an exception—in many respects, *the* exception—to the more general tendency in the American experience for economic stagnation or decline to erode the society's tolerance, openness, and democracy. Instead, America during the Great Depression strengthened its commitment to these positive values and, moreover, did so in ways that proved lasting.

. . .

What caused the Great Depression has long been a subject of dispute.[3] The business expansion that began in late 1927—the American economy's fourth attempt to grow since World War I—lasted less than two years. Industrial production began to decline in July 1929, and nonfinancial activity overall peaked in August. The timing is significant because popular lore has often pointed to the following October's stock market crash as the origin of the depression. The crash was indeed part of the story of how what began as a fairly ordinary business cycle downturn became the Great Depression, but economic activity was already headed downward before the market plunged.

In an eerie reminder of the 1880s and early 1890s, prices were mostly falling throughout the latter half of the 1920s. American exports, after the sharp decline in the years immediately following World War I, had grown fairly steadily throughout the 1920s. But the pace of increase had slowed significantly by 1927, even after allowing for falling prices, and by 1929 American imports were rising more rapidly than exports (so that the net contribution of foreign trade to the overall demand for American-made products was shrinking). Business investment, especially the building of new factories, had peaked in 1926. Homebuilding had topped out the year before, and by 1929 the rate of new house construction was less than half that in 1925.

The government's economic policies were mostly contractionary too. Throughout the 1920s, Treasury Secretary Andrew Mellon had steered American fiscal policy along an orthodox conservative course, running a budget surplus year after year from 1920 onward in an effort to pay down the debt incurred during World War I. In the fiscal year ending in June 1929, the federal budget was in surplus by over $700 million, or nearly 1 percent of the nation's total income that year. At the same time, the Federal Reserve System had been raising interest rates, partly in order to neutralize the potentially inflationary consequences of gold inflows from abroad (the United States and other countries had gradually reestablished the international gold standard after the war) and partly in an unsuccessful attempt to squelch what monetary policymakers increasingly saw as harmful speculation on the stock market. During the course of the final pre-depression business expansion, the Federal Reserve had raised its discount rate in several steps from 3.5 percent at the end of 1927 to 5 percent by the summer of 1928 and then 6 percent in August 1929, *after* the business downturn had already begun. Short-term market interest rates had moved up roughly in line with the discount rate.[4]

With so many warning signs, the onset of yet another business recession in 1929 should not have been astonishing. The depression it turned into was. From a narrowly American perspective, the principal causes of the economic disaster were the stock market crash, repeated panics and crises in the banking system, and, most important of all, persistently perverse economic policy. At a deeper level, however, it is impossible to understand either the severity or the persistence of the depression without recognizing that what happened was a worldwide phenomenon.

The fall in stock prices—23 percent over the few days beginning on "Black Thursday" (October 24, 1929), 45 percent from the pre-crash peak in September 1929 to mid-November, and 86 percent from the peak to the market's ultimate bottom in June 1932—not only bankrupted tens of thousands of speculators who had bought on margin but also wiped out the wealth of ordinary Americans who simply owned stocks.[5] It also shattered the confidence of millions who did not. Predictably, household spending, including ordinary consumer demand as well as investment in homebuilding, dropped sharply in the year after the crash.[6] Even without the constricting effects of the resulting bankruptcies, or the loss of confidence, the disappearance of nearly $75 billion in household wealth (equivalent to 75 percent of America's total income in 1929) due to falling stock prices was by itself sufficient to explain one-third to one-half of the decline in Americans' overall consumer spending over the four years of the depression.[7]

When either individuals or businesses go bankrupt, they default on their debts and so whoever has lent to them may also incur financial difficulty. From late 1929 onward business borrowers, especially among the small- and medium-sized firms that accounted for half or more of American economic production, defaulted widely on bonds held by market investors (including individuals but also insurance companies, pension funds, and other institutions) as well as on loans from banks. Farmers, homeowners, and even state and local governments likewise defaulted on a widespread basis. By the time the depression hit bottom, more than half of all farm debt owed in the United States was in default. In some cities—Cleveland, Indianapolis, Birmingham—more than half of all mortgages were in default. Three states and more than thirty of the nation's 300 largest cities defaulted on their obligations.[8]

The proliferating defaults on bank loans and on bonds owned by banks were especially problematic because the banks that incurred the largest losses then became unable to meet the demands of their depositors and had to close their doors. As fear of losing their money spread, depositors in many cases staged runs even on banks that were otherwise sound. During three especially troubled periods—November and December 1930; March through July 1931; and January and February 1933—federal and state regulators had to put out of business banks with hundreds of millions of dollars in deposits outstanding, and the banking system as a whole took on a crisis atmosphere.[9] The blocking or out-and-out extinguishment of so many depositors' accounts spread the loss of liquidity and purchasing power that always accompanies a business downturn far more widely, and it further weakened the confidence of ordinary citizens as well as business and financial executives. By the time the depression hit bottom, more than 9,000 banks, or one out of every three in the entire country, had failed.

As the economy sank deeper into depression, government economic policy was at best irrelevant and more often a hindrance to any incipient forces for recovery. In early 1930 President Hoover requested modest funding for additional spending on government buildings and other public works (most memorably, damming the Colorado River upstream from Boulder Canyon, Colorado), but the federal budget surplus in the 1930 fiscal year was just as large as the year before. In 1931 declining tax receipts put the budget in deficit, but by less than $500 million. Only in 1932 did the government finally begin to run a more sizable deficit, and even then only because tax receipts were shrinking rapidly as incomes and profits plummeted.

At that point, however, Hoover reacted to the shock of a larger deficit by seeking both to raise taxes and to cut government spending. At the president's request, Congress increased tax rates by one-third in June 1932, just as business was nearing a state of total collapse. (The embrace of conservative fiscal orthodoxy was not a subject of partisan dispute. Franklin Roosevelt, campaigning for president that fall, criticized Hoover's policy as fiscally reckless and pledged to balance the federal budget.)

The Federal Reserve did act promptly after the stock market crash to reverse its tight monetary policy, and interest rates began to decline right away. But monetary policy simply failed to keep pace with the powerful contractionary force of repeated banking crises and spreading bank failures. As the banking system staggered through its spasmodic collapse, the nation's supplies of money and credit continually shrank. The Federal Reserve experimented with a more expansionary monetary policy in the spring of 1932, buying government securities on a scale nearly three times that of any comparable operation over the previous decade, but by summer it had abandoned the program.[10] Interest rates eventually declined to near zero (for technical reasons, rates on some debt instruments even went below zero at times), but with prices rapidly falling even a zero posted interest rate represented a high cost of borrowing in real terms.

In retrospect, the failure of American monetary policy to respond appropriately to the downturn, and especially to the financial disruptions the downturn produced, was probably the greatest single factor that turned the decline into a depression. One reason for this failure was simply that monetary policymakers did not yet understand how the central bank's actions affected the private banking system and, through the banking system, the nonfinancial economy. (The Federal Reserve System was only fifteen years old in 1929.) Later on, after Britain abandoned the gold standard in September 1931, another reason for the restrained monetary policy response was the perceived need to prevent gold outflows that might force America to do likewise. In retrospect it seems clear that lack of understanding of how policy worked, and bad choices within the limits of what policymakers understood, lay behind the consistent perversity of both fiscal and monetary policies throughout the depression years.

At a deeper level, economic policy was not just wrong but wrongheaded. Hoover's stance during the depression was oddly at variance with his experience before becoming president, which had shown him to be a concerned, active leader in times of public crisis. As a private citizen living in London in 1914, Hoover organized and led the effort to assist American citizens to return home when war broke out in Europe. He then chaired another private organization, the Commission for Relief in Belgium, which over the next several years provided nearly $1 billion in war relief. After the United States entered the war, President Wilson appointed Hoover as U.S. food administrator, and in that role he organized massive supply efforts both for America and for the nation's allies, including delivery to Europe of more than 18 million tons of food—three times the normal export volume—during the crucial period from mid-1918 to 1919. He also established a special relief program to assist 10 million homeless and undernourished European children. Later, as secretary of commerce during the 1927 Mississippi flood disaster, Hoover raised millions in charitable donations and directed the removal from danger areas of over 1 million citizens, despite President Coolidge's show of indifference.

Having spent his early career as an administrative engineer on numerous industrial projects around the world, Hoover was also hardly averse to public construction. One of the many commissions he chaired during the early 1920s led eventually to the building of Boulder Dam (subsequently renamed Hoover Dam), another to the St. Lawrence Seaway. Even at the outset of his presidency, Hoover showed every intention of being an activist. Soon after taking office, for example, he established a Research Committee on Social Trends to assemble a factual basis for understanding just what the "New Era" meant for how Americans now lived. The openly acknowledged intent was to provide the basis for new directions in U.S. social policies.[11]

But once the economic crisis struck, Hoover's public attitude changed. The president continually downplayed the severity of the nation's economic distress, always promising that prosperity was "just around the corner" and offering the comforting but under the circumstances false reassurance that "no one is actually starving."[12] He was even reported to have reacted to increasingly widespread unemployment by observing that "many persons [had] left their jobs for the more profitable one of selling apples."[13] When drought devastated the nation's southwestern farm areas, Hoover approved federal provision of livestock feed and new seed for planting but opposed any relief for the farmers and their families. When some 20,000 unemployed World War I veterans marched on Washington to seek prompt payment of the service bonus they were owed under the 1931 Bonus Act, which Congress had passed over his veto, Hoover sent army troops (commanded by General Douglas MacArthur) to break up their camp and disperse the petitioners. Under Coolidge, the resistance on principle to come to the aid of distressed citizens had appeared coldhearted in some situations, but it did not bear large-scale economic consequences. Under Hoover the same attitude not only left millions of Americans to suffer severe hardships but also prevented the government from taking steps that might have cushioned the economic decline.

The gross failure of monetary policy during the depression likewise reflected in part an explicitly moral disapproval of the rampant stock market speculation that had gone before, and a conviction that under the circumstances there was no way for the American economy as a whole to avoid paying for the sins of the speculators. Treasury Secretary Mellon's attitude, as Hoover later described it, was that "when the people get an inflation brainstorm, the only way to get it out of their blood is to let it collapse." In Hoover's words, Mellon's solution was to "Liquidate labor, liquidate stocks, liquidate the farmers, liquidate real estate." Even a panic "would purge the rottenness out of the system."[14] Especially during the first year of the decline, the concern that an easier monetary policy might rekindle "speculative excesses in the stock market" was a recurrent consideration deterring Federal Reserve policymakers from acting vigorously to oppose the downturn.[15]

The isolationist attitude of the 1920s likewise fostered poor economic policy decisions. In June 1930, Congress passed the Smoot-Hawley Act, which raised import duties significantly, especially for agricultural products. Under Smoot-Hawley the average tariff on goods brought into the United States rose to just over 50 percent, nearly double what it had been under the already record-level Fordney-McCumber tariff. Countries abroad began almost immediately to respond with an assortment of tariff increases, import quotas, and other restrictions on the flow of goods across their own borders.

The result was a collapse of world trade that spread the economic downturn to yet more countries and worsened matters in those where the downturn had already begun. In the twelve months before Congress passed Smoot-Hawley, the total volume of international trade among the seventy-five countries regularly surveyed by the League of Nations (including the League's member countries as well as nonmembers like the United States) had averaged $2.7 billion per month. A year later monthly trade volume was only $1.7 billion, and after another year just $1.1 billion.[16] America's exports shrank in real terms by almost one-half between 1929 and 1932.[17]

As industrial economies around the world began to contract, what might have been an ordinary business downturn in just a few countries turned into a worldwide depression. The global character of the collapse was important not only for how it affected international relations in the crucial years between the two wars but also because, as economic historian Barry Eichengreen has forcefully demonstrated, "the Great Depression was so severe precisely because so many countries were affected simultaneously."[18] Shrinking world trade was an obvious drain, but international financial markets also helped spread the decline. The collapse in May 1931 of Kreditanstalt, Austria's foremost financial institution, set off what amounted to an international bank run, spreading first to Germany, then other continental countries, then Britain—all while the United States was in the midst of its second major banking crisis within less than a year.[19] The Kreditanstalt failure, however, and the fragile European financial environment in which it occurred, were themselves partly due to repercussions from what was already happening in the United States.

In addition, the attempt to maintain the international gold standard prevented not just the Federal Reserve System but central banks around the world from adopting monetary policies that might more effectively have resisted the banking crisis, and with it the economic downturn. It was not a coincidence that Britain and those other countries that abandoned the gold standard earliest achieved the earliest economic recoveries, while those like France that held on to gold the longest (until October 1936 in France's case) stayed in depression the longest.[20] The United States suspended gold payments on March 6, 1933, two days after Franklin Roosevelt's inauguration as president. Standard business cycle analysis dates the beginning of this country's recovery to that same month.[21]

By 1933, however, nearly 13 million Americans, more than one-fourth of the country's entire labor force, were out of work. Among nonfarm workers, unemployment was more than 37 percent. Business activity overall had shrunk by almost one-third, and industrial production by more than one-half, even after allowing for declining prices. Between 1929 and 1933 prices had fallen by an average of 24 percent at the retail level and 32 percent at wholesale. Prices of farm products had fallen on average by 52 percent, and the average net income of American farmers had declined from $960 to $280. A quarter of a million farmers lost their land in 1932 alone, as banks foreclosed on unpaid mortgages. In the cities and suburbs, apartment dwellers faced eviction when they failed to keep up their rent payments, and by 1933 home mortgage foreclosures were running at the rate of 1,000 a day. Soup lines downtown and "Hoovervilles" in the parks and on the outskirts had become all too familiar scenes throughout urban America.

At the same time, investment—what the economy plows back to provide for its future—had disappeared almost entirely. Despite some decline during the latter half of the 1920s, investment of all kinds in the United States (including new factories, machinery, houses, and business inventories) totaled $16 billion in 1929. By 1933 total investment was barely $1 billion. Steel production fell from 62 million tons to 15 million, extraction of iron ore from 74 million tons to 10 million. In 1929 American factories had made 2,300 railroad cars, including both passenger and freight (already down from 2,900 three years earlier). The industry's entire production in 1933 consisted of seven passenger cars and two freight cars. Families too cut back especially sharply on expenditures that constituted household investments. Purchases of new automobiles, for example, fell from 4.5 million to 1.1 million.

In 1933—after the suspension of gold, after the "bank holiday," and after the introduction of the first New Deal initiatives under Roosevelt—

business finally began to recover. Prices started rising again. In 1934 overall economic activity expanded by almost 8 percent after allowance for the higher prices, and real gains of another 8 percent and then 14 percent followed in the next two years. By early 1937 overall business activity had almost regained its 1929 level, and industrial production had modestly surpassed the pre-depression peak. Even so, unemployment remained extraordinarily high. Nearly 8 million would-be workers, or more than 14 percent of the American labor force (and 21 percent of those off the farm), were still without jobs.

But 1937 turned out to be the economy's high point until after the onset of war in Europe began to spur demand for American-made goods, and then America's own entry into the war finally absorbed the country's remaining unemployed workers into either the armed services or war production industries. Another downturn, brought about in large part by cuts in government spending and a shift toward tight monetary policy by the Federal Reserve, began in the spring of 1937. (Neither Roosevelt nor the Congress was yet convinced of the merit of deficit spending for purposes of stimulating the economy.) Business did not start to rebound from this new setback until more than a year later. Unemployment once again rose above 10 million, or nearly 20 percent of the workforce. In the nonagricultural sector unemployment reached 27 percent. But despite fears that the new downturn might turn into renewed depression, the recovery that began in the summer of 1938 proved lasting. Even so, not until 1941 would fewer Americans be jobless than in 1937, and not until 1943 would there be fewer unemployed than in 1929.

It is difficult today, accustomed as we are to realizing at least some advance over time in our standard of living, and presuming as we do that any outright decline in this regard will prove short-lived, to comprehend the combined effect of the depth and duration of the 1930s depression, especially since the depression itself struck in the wake of only fitful growth in the decade following World War I. At the bottom, in 1933, Americans' per capita real income was not only smaller (by 25 percent) than it had been ten years earlier, but also smaller than *twenty* years earlier and even smaller than *thirty* years earlier. Americans were, in effect, back to where they had been at the turn of the century.

Even by 1938, the last full year before war broke out in Europe, real income per capita in the United States was below what it had been not just ten years before but twenty. Renewed business recovery in 1939 did finally boost the nation's per capita income above the level of 1918, but still not back where it had been in any year in the latter half of the 1920s (hence the largely inaccurate recollection, which still persists, of the late 1920s as a time of widespread prosperity). Only in 1940, as war production increased, did Americans on average finally regain the real income level they had first reached in 1929.

By the end of the 1930s, Americans had not only suffered through the most severe economic deprivation in their nation's history but also, over two decades, failed to mark any forward progress whatever in the economic condition of the average citizen. For many, the resulting hardships were extreme. On the basis of prior (and subsequent) experience, it would not have been surprising if the public commitment to a free society had therefore weakened. But in this instance the response to economic adversity was mostly different.

If the prevailing spirit that the progressives had brought to American politics and society in the years before World War I was a "can-do" attitude born of confidence nurtured by the nation's economic success, Americans in the New Deal era reflected a spirit of "must do" after four years of watching their economy sink to previously unimaginable depths with no assurance of a firm bottom. For the first time, an American president accepted national-level responsibility to deal with what had evolved into a national economy with national-level problems. As Roosevelt stated in his first inaugural address, "This Nation asks for action, and action now."[22] But because it was far from obvious just what action to take under such extraordinary circumstances, what "must do" really meant in practice was "must try."

Especially during the years when Roosevelt's large congressional majorities gave him a fairly free hand—that is, until after the 1938 midterm elections—what stood out was not just the number of new initiatives but the variety. Standard criticism of Roosevelt's economic program has emphasized its incoherence, including not only conflicting strains of thought within the administration but actual legislation and policy programs that at times ran at cross-purposes. But if there was a coherent theme, it was pragmatic experimentation. Since no one knew exactly what to do—Roosevelt himself clearly did not—trying whatever ideas offered a chance of working seemed preferable to focusing narrowly on the lines of action implied by just one or two consistent principles.

Even if there was no coherent policy, there was in fact an underlying predisposition: to broaden the society's conception of economic democracy, to reinforce existing notions of social fairness, and, most significantly, to make collective action via government at least partly responsible for achieving these ends. Like the progressives a quarter-century earlier, the New Dealers envisioned a larger democracy and sought, through many actions in diverse spheres, to make that vision a reality. By embracing new political voices and previously excluded pools of talent and ideas—Catholics like Jim Farley and Tommy Corcoran, Jewish lawyers like Ben Cohen and Sam Rosenman, southern and western entrepreneurs like Jesse Jones, and the new political coalition that brought organized labor, new immigrants, and the poor into the Democratic Party's traditional alliance of old-school southern whites and the Irish in the urban North—they expanded the frontiers of American pluralism.[23] Moreover, because of the contrast to the seemingly unbiquitous advance of Nazis, fascists, and communists under similar economic circumstances elsewhere, their doing so assumed yet further significance.[24]

In contrast to the attitudes of Coolidge and Hoover, there was no reluctance to involve the government in providing humane assistance. At the outset, many of the new administration's initiatives took the form of temporary measures to relieve the most acute distress of individuals and families, and, if possible, help turn business around. Key actions taken in Roosevelt's famous first "Hundred Days" included creation of the Civilian Conservation Corps to provide jobs, the Federal Emergency Relief Administration to provide urban income support, and the Agricultural Adjustment Administration to provide farm price supports and mortgage refinancing. Congress also appropriated more than $3 billion for new public works, and the administration implemented a variety of further measures to shield both farmers and urban homeowners from mortgage foreclosures.

These were not token efforts. The CCC initially employed 300,000 men and boys, and in time it provided jobs for more like 3 million. The AAA, replaced by a new program in 1938 after the Supreme Court ruled the first one unconstitutional, included in its programs 6 million farmers, working three-fourths of America's crop lands. The Farm Credit Administration refinanced one-fifth of all farm mortgages in America, and the Homeowners Loan Corporation refinanced a comparable fraction of home mortgages. Public works programs took a series of forms, culminating in 1935 in the Works Progress Administration, which over time provided jobs for 8 million people at surfacing roads; building schools, post offices, and urban swimming pools; writing guidebooks; staging theater productions and painting murals. At the greatest single point, 7 million American individuals or families were simultaneously on the rolls of one or another federal jobs or relief program. During the 1930s overall, one American in five received some form of federal assistance. (And, of course, their families benefited as well. In part because of government relief payments, infant mortality *declined* in the 1930s, despite all the joblessness and privation.)[25]

Other measures, some taken during the Hundred Days and some later on, likewise had the goal of advancing the business recovery while protecting individuals and families whose recent experience had all too forcefully demonstrated their vulnerability to the vicissitudes of an economy gone out of control. The Emergency Banking Act, passed on the first day of the special session of Congress that Roosevelt called after his inauguration, reopened the banks and also provided for new federal inspectors to ensure their soundness. The Glass-Steagall Act, passed that June, further strengthened the safety regulation of banks and created the Federal Deposit Insurance Corporation to guarantee individual accounts for up to $5,000 each (equivalent to about $73,000 in today's dollars). The Federal Securities (Truth in Securities) Act established disclosure requirements for sales of stock to investors. Subsequent legislation strengthened regulation of the stock market and created the Securities and Exchange Commission to enforce it. The Tennessee Valley Authority Act resolved a long-standing dispute over what to do with a nitrate plant, constructed at Muscle Shoals in the Tennessee River at government expense during World War I, by creating a new facility to control flooding and bring affordable electricity to rural homes throughout a region including part or all of seven states. The new U.S. Housing Authority, established in 1937, was charged with providing safe and sanitary housing for low-income families, and given substantial borrowing authority with which to do so. In response to the deaths of over one hundred people who had taken a new medicine called Elixir Sulfanilamide, Congress in 1938 passed the Food, Drug and Cosmetic Act, which effectively introduced modern drug regulation.[26]

Numerous spokesmen of the time, including Roosevelt himself, not only emphasized the need to take active measures in defense of otherwise helpless citizens but also drew a direct connection between relieving economic distress and preserving liberty and democracy. In his State of the Union address to Congress in January 1935, Roosevelt explicitly stated that the long-term goal of the New Deal was a greater measure of "social justice," a notion that he went on, much later in his presidency, to articulate as an "Economic Bill of Rights."[27] After years of depression, it had become clear that economic deprivation, no less than the traditionally feared excesses of big government or big business, constituted a significant threat to Americans' freedoms. The New Deal's answer was to take risks with both

big government and big business in order to defend against the more imminent threat from extraordinary and enduring economic hardship. As Roosevelt put it in his second inaugural address, in January 1937, "We . . .
sensed the truth that democratic government has innate capacity to protect
its people against disasters once considered inevitable, to solve problems
once considered insolvable. . . . We refused to leave the problems of our
common welfare to be solved by the winds of chance and the hurricanes of
disaster."[28]

It is easy to imagine how this desire to assure social justice to the
powerless could have developed into either a new antitrust effort aimed
at breaking up large corporations or a sustained regulatory program
designed to harness them. In fact, the Roosevelt administration tried both
and succeeded at neither. Early efforts to pursue an anti-monopoly program
along the lines of a quarter-century before—even arguing, in the spirit
of Brandeis's *Other People's Money*, that bigness per se constituted a threat
to democracy regardless of whether that bigness was abused—generated
high-sounding rhetoric but few visible results. A later attempt to revive
the anti-monopoly approach, through the vehicle of widely publicized
hearings before the Temporary National Economic Committee, likewise
came to more or less nothing. In the opposite direction, the National
Recovery Administration, originally considered the capstone achievement
of the Hundred Days, amounted in effect to tolerating, even encouraging,
anticompetitive business practices under the authority of government-
supervised regulatory codes. But the NRA proved such a failure that even
Roosevelt himself was silently relieved when the Supreme Court ruled it
unconstitutional in 1935.[29]

Instead, especially after the first few years of business recovery under
the New Deal had failed to restore full employment, the main focus of this
new willingness to intervene in the economy to achieve greater social justice
turned to the labor market. From the very beginning of the Roosevelt
administration, federal jobs programs and provision of relief payments
to those still out of work had already constituted fairly dramatic intervention in labor markets. But these programs were presumed to be temporary.
In 1935 Roosevelt began to implement a new agenda for this purpose,
intended to improve working conditions and ease the plight of the unemployed on an ongoing basis.

The Social Security Act, passed in the summer of 1935, established not
only the old-age pension system that still goes by that name but also unemployment insurance—before becoming president, Roosevelt had been the

first governor to advocate unemployment insurance during the depression—
as well as special aid programs for dependent children and the blind and
disabled.³⁰ (Interestingly, the federal government retained administrative
control only over the old-age and disability programs, leaving to the states
the administration of unemployment insurance, aid to families with dependent children, and extra payments to the "destitute aged," while still funding
these programs with federal money.)³¹ The Wagner Act, passed the same
year partly in response to the disappearance of the NRA's labor codes when
the Supreme Court declared the NRA as a whole unconstitutional, reaffirmed workers' freedom to organize into unions and to bargain collectively. The act also strengthened the bargaining role of unions once they did
exist and set up the National Labor Relations Board, with powers to enforce
these arrangements via "cease and desist" orders against employers. The
result was a large increase in union membership.

In 1938 the Fair Labor Standards Act finally succeeded in an area where
the progressives had tried but failed. Congress had passed the Keating-
Owen Child Labor Law in 1916, but the Supreme Court had invalidated it
soon thereafter, and in 1923 the Court had also thrown out state-level
efforts to limit women's hours.³² The new legislation set a forty-hour maximum on the regular workweek for all employees, provided time-and-a-half
for overtime, prohibited "oppressive child labor," and established a minimum wage of 25 cents per hour, rising to 40 cents (equivalent to about $5.50
today) in 1940. In the resolution of the inevitable legal challenge, in 1941,
the Supreme Court bluntly reversed its earlier position and allowed the Fair
Labor Standards Act to stand.³³

In short, the New Deal was exceptional as a response to economic adversity.
The concerns voiced over the plight of ordinary Americans, helpless against
the onslaught of forces that they neither recognized nor understood, were
familiar enough. Roosevelt and other prominent New Dealers like Harold
Ickes and Robert Jackson forcefully articulated those anxieties and fears, as
did spokesmen for anti-democratic brands of social protest like Father
Coughlin and Huey Long.³⁴ And in some respects the expression of those
concerns emanating from either source resonated with the statements made
by leaders of still uglier movements in earlier eras. Hiram Wesley Evans, the
Ku Klux Klan leader since the 1920s, or any of the populist spokesmen
of the 1890s, would surely have applauded when Roosevelt spoke of problems that "arise out of the concentration of economic control to the detri-

ment of the body politic—control of other people's money, other people's labor, other people's lives."[35]

But the New Deal's response to these concerns was different. To the extent that anything in this chaos of experimentation was systematic, it was the attempt to mobilize the effective energy of government to spread economic opportunity as widely as possible—to include those whom birth and the tide of events had left out of the distribution of America's economic dividend. Rather than seeking scapegoats to exclude for others' economic benefit, or even mere vengeful satisfaction, the route America took in the 1930s was deliberately pluralist and inclusive, seeking input and participation from a more diverse collection of constituencies than ever before. And the intent of all this political activism was not just restored economic prosperity but more equal economic opportunity.

While the progressive spirit of a generation before had been notable for its sympathy toward the less fortunate, Roosevelt's New Deal went further, not only coming to distressed citizens' relief in the midst of crisis but creating permanent institutions to advance their well-being. As historian David Kennedy has argued, beginning in the 1930s "Americans assumed that the federal government had not merely a role, but a major responsibility, in ensuring the health of the economy *and* the welfare of citizens. That simple but momentous shift in perception was the newest thing in all the New Deal, and the most consequential too."[36] Another historian, Alan Brinkley, could well have been describing the New Deal as a whole when he wrote of a report produced by one of its myriad agencies, "Even sixty years later, its proposals are striking for their sweep—and for the generosity of spirit . . . that surrounded them."[37] The same could not have been said of the program Hiram Wesley Evans championed as the Klan's imperial wizard.

Even the one blatant departure from open opportunity that proved most resistant to change, the systematic exclusion of blacks especially in the South, nonetheless reflected some glimmer of progress during the depression period. Although there was little movement in Congress to push for civil rights legislation, the federal agencies created by the New Deal opened some new opportunities in education, health care, employment, and housing.[38] For the first time since the Fifteenth Amendment had given blacks the right to vote, in the 1930s a majority of blacks as well as whites joined the same political party. And although southern senators continued to thwart any push for anti-lynching laws, by the end of the decade racial violence, including lynching in particular, declined markedly.[39]

A similar contrast that likewise highlights what made the 1930s in

America exceptional is that between the New Dealer Henry Wallace and the Georgia populist (and sometime congressman and senator) Tom Watson. Like Watson before him, Wallace was an agrarian (he was from Iowa) and a newspaper editor. Also like Watson, Wallace was keenly sensitive to the plight of farmers beset by falling crop prices, declining incomes, threatening creditors, and a pervasive sense of diminished respect in a society that was becoming more industrial, more urban, and more sophisticated. But where Watson had ultimately devoted his talents, his newspaper, and later his Senate seat to fostering bigotry and inciting racial and religious violence, Wallace used his position as secretary of agriculture (in Roosevelt's first two terms) and then vice president (in his third) to continue to advocate reformist policies aimed at constructively aiding the rural poor. And where Watson had trumpeted the nativist and isolationist themes of the populist era, Wallace was a firm supporter of Roosevelt's internationalism.

In the case of the New Deal no less than with respect to the political movements of earlier times, it would be foolish to pretend that all Americans unanimously endorsed either the government policies or the social attitudes that ultimately prevailed. Although Roosevelt drew nearly 61 percent of the popular vote in 1936, up from 57 percent four years earlier, the Democratic majority in both houses of Congress steadily shrank beginning in 1938. Specific elements of the New Deal program attracted sharp opposition, as did Roosevelt's ongoing attempt to lead America away from isolationism. Nor were the voices of opposition limited to fringe groups devoid of political credibility. The national chairman of the Republican Party, John Hamilton, openly labeled the New Deal "communist."[40] But societies do not require unanimity to move ahead (or back). The more important point is that in the 1930s, as in the Progressive Era—but unlike in the 1920s, or before the turn of the century when the populists flourished—a sufficient majority of the nation's citizens supported the pluralist, democratic spirit that the New Deal embodied to allow this program to move forward and this ethos to shape American society.

The same contrast to the 1920s, and the same parallel to the Progressive Era, were also evident in what Americans wrote and read. In their 1932 book, *The Modern Corporation and Private Property*, economists Adolf Berle and Gardiner Means not only reprised the earlier theme of "bigness" but broke new conceptual ground by pointing out the separation between ownership and control that had become increasingly prevalent in American business. Berle and Means's argument was that although the stockholders (perhaps including the firm's founder and his family) nominally owned a corporation, the managers who ran it were often different, not to mention distant. Historian Matthew Josephson's 1934 classic, *The Robber Barons*, recalled the efforts of the muckraker journalists of the early part of the century, using a narrative style to focus attention on the contributions—but in many cases also the misdeeds—of the titans who had built America's great railroads and financial houses.

The public literature of the 1930s likewise reflected the themes of a nation rejecting parts of its past while struggling to reclaim a future out of acute distress. F. Scott Fitzgerald's *Tender Is the Night* was a frightening story of spiritual bankruptcy and character disintegration at the individual level. The decade's major literary work, John Dos Passos's *U.S.A.* trilogy (with successive volumes published in 1930, 1932, and 1936), resembled Dreiser's novels of more than a decade earlier in its portrayal of a ruthless and self-centered search for gratification among the wealthy. It also portrayed the despair of the nonwealthy who became caught up in the quest that the American economy and the social structure that it fostered effectively forced on them. Among the major characters in *The Big Money*, the third novel in the series, a businessman loses his roots as a mechanic, loses his money in stock market speculation, and ultimately breaks down altogether. Another character in the same story, an aspiring actress, fails to become a star and fails also to find happiness.

Dos Passos extended this sense of despair to the country as a whole, which was, as critic Malcolm Cowley later argued, the story's real hero. More so than in either Dreiser or Fitzgerald, however, the sharpness and passion of Dos Passos's critique amounted to a call to collective action, an urgent plea to overcome individual despair through social reform.[41] *U.S.A.* was also free of the expressions of prejudice that had earlier characterized so much of the fiction of the populist period, as well as books like Fitzgerald's from the 1920s. Thomas Wolfe's *Look Homeward, Angel* likewise reflected a deep sensitivity to the pain brought by major transitions in society, yet combined that awareness with a commitment to the ultimate promise that America held forth. Even in the depression, the country had remained true to its democratic ideals and addressed its economic problems in a democratic way.

But the book from the 1930s that best reflected the spirit of cooperation and "must do" in the face of extreme economic adversity was *The Grapes of Wrath*. Published at the end of the decade, John Steinbeck's novel gave an emotionally sympathetic portrayal of the Joad family, dirt farmers driven from the Oklahoma Dust Bowl, moving from camp to camp on the way to the promise of work in California: traveling as well as living in makeshift jalopies, struggling for bare physical survival, and, for some family members, tragically losing that struggle.

Although Steinbeck's story focused on the hardships of a single family, in contrast to the sweep of Dos Passos's deliberate attempt to encompass an entire nation, *The Grapes of Wrath* nonetheless succeeded in capturing enduring themes of both economics and politics. What drove the Joads off their land was not just an accident of nature but the action of unrelenting and sometimes unscrupulous lenders, and, in an echo of even older battles, the introduction of new technology (in this case the tractor, which enabled far fewer hands to work the same acreage). The difficulty that the Joads and other migrants faced in finding work after they arrived in California was a nightmarish reminder of Frederick Jackson Turner's warning, forty years earlier, that the disappearance of a frontier offering free land to those willing to work it would fundamentally change the American experience. Discrimination against the "Okies" by the native Californians with whom they competed for what jobs there were, including police brutality and organized vigilante raids on the migrants' camps, mirrored the familiar clash between immigrants and natives that arises whenever jobs become scarce.[42]

More broadly, the Joad family's physical movement across America's geography, with deaths and deprivations along the way and the inevitable lost ties, abandoned friendships, and broken families all portrayed in terms of raw human emotion, served as a metaphor for a society in upheaval more generally: "The Western States are nervous under the beginning change. Need is the stimulus to concept, concept to action. A half-million people moving over the country; a million more restive, ready to move; ten million more feeling the first nervousness."[43] The Okies' loss of their sense of self-worth, and even of hope, was metaphoric too. The import throughout was that the economic system was failing to give citizens a reason to believe in American democracy.

Moreover, in Steinbeck's book not just economic forces but economic *institutions*—man-made social artifacts that it was within men's power to change if the society acted as a unified political force—were at the heart of the matter: "It's the monster. The bank isn't like a man. . . . It happens that every man in a bank hates what the bank does, and yet the bank does it. The bank is something more than men, I tell you. It's the monster. Man made it, but they can't control it."[44] In an echo of views like William Dean Howells's from the 1880s, Steinbeck also questioned whether business and personal morality were compatible: "Fella in business got to lie, an' cheat, but he calls it somepin else. . . . They call that sound business."[45] But despite the massive injustice perpetrated by lenders, landowners, car salesmen, even gas station operators on their travels, the Joads receive no help from government nor from anyone else in authority, only the occasional kindness of downtrodden people like themselves.

Yet in the end Steinbeck's real message was one of optimism, of transcendent hope, the assurance that something could be done and faith that ultimately it would be. *The Grapes of Wrath* dramatized, in an almost evangelical way, the generosity of spirit and the characteristic sympathy with the underdog that marked American society at the depth of its economic ordeal.[46]

The simplest—and most romantic—way to explain why the 1930s were such an exception in American experience is to point to Roosevelt's personal qualities: the vigor and vitality that he projected to the public at large (despite being crippled by polio), the energy and pragmatism he brought to the task of government, his willingness to experiment in a situation in which no one knew just what to do, and above all his personal commitment to "economic justice" at a time when so many Americans felt they were suffering injustice and the nation's most immediate problem was so plainly economic.[47] As the British philosopher Isaiah Berlin later wrote, looking back on the early 1930s, "The most insistent propaganda in those days declared that humanitarianism and liberalism and democratic forces were played out, and that the choice now lay between two bleak extremes, Communism and Fascism—the red or the black. To those who were not carried away by this patter the only light that was left in the darkness was the administration of Roosevelt and the New Deal in the United States."[48] Especially in comparison to Germany (America and Germany were the two countries hardest hit by the depression), the expanded pluralism that Roosevelt made central to his governance was also an important element in the story.

Further, while many New Deal initiatives made clear the responsibility of government to relieve individuals' distress and restore the economy as a whole to normal function, Roosevelt consistently heralded the *moral* value of work, addressing the most acute problem of the day in a way that resonated with traditional themes from Calvin to Cotton Mather to Horatio Alger. In a "Fireside Chat" broadcast in 1934, for example, Roosevelt declared that "no country, however rich, can afford the waste of its human resources. Demoralization caused by vast unemployment is our greatest extravagance. Morally, it is the greatest menace to our social order."[49] In his next State of the Union address, even while hailing the relief programs that were now rescuing so many Americans from destitution, he further elaborated this theme, arguing that "continued dependence on relief induces a spiritual and moral disintegration fundamentally destructive to the national fibre. To dole out relief in this way is to administer a narcotic, a subtle destroyer of the human spirit. . . . It is in violation of the traditions of America." The proper objective, he stated, was to "preserve not only the bodies of the unemployed from destitution but also their self-respect, their self-reliance and courage and determination."[50]

No doubt Roosevelt's persona was part of the story. But a second part of the explanation was, in all likelihood, the extraordinarily widespread impact of the economic disaster. This was not a situation in which farmers or industrial workers or small business operators were uniquely unfortunate while the rest of the nation went about its affairs as usual. When one-fourth of the entire country's labor force is unemployed at once, and a much larger fraction suffers joblessness at one time or another during the course of the crisis, people have a tendency to think that, whatever is happening, they are in it together. Nor, in this case, were the effects of the crisis limited to the working and middle-income strata of the population. Bankers too were losing their place, and stockbrokers were jumping from skyscraper windows. Economic hardship normally fosters conflict among different groups in a society, but feelings of greater loyalty and solidarity within groups. In the depression of the 1930s, enough Americans from different walks of life saw one another in distress that they may well have felt as if they were now, for practical purposes, part of one larger community.

Perhaps the best explanation, though, is that the socially corrosive power of more ordinary economic distress is overwhelmed by still stronger forces of a different kind if the distress is so great as to constitute an out-and-out crisis, which the Great Depression certainly was. Most people understandably exhibit generosity when they are doing well and defensiveness when they are doing badly. But they nonetheless pull together when they see their very lives threatened and the entire social and political structure in which they live thrown into imminent danger.

In the depression, many Americans' lives were acutely vulnerable. Many fell ill, and some died, from malnutrition or exposure. Many more simply gave up on living. At the same time, the constitutional basis of the republic faced threats from extremists on both the left and the right, threats that political upheavals abroad made credible as never before. Under such circumstances, ordinary citizens' reactions might understandably be different than in a more limited downturn where the distress is simply economic.

But regardless of just why, it is clear that America's experience in the

1930s does not conform to the general pattern that connects prosperity to advancing openness and tolerance and democracy, and adversity to rigidity, prejudice, and ungenerosity. Such a departure, even of this magnitude, does not mean that this more general historical pattern does not exist. As Alexander Gerschenkron observed, "Historical hypotheses are not . . . universal propositions. They cannot be falsified by a single exception. Testing them largely means trying to discover the boundaries of the area within which they seem reasonably valid."[51] America's response to the Great Depression stands in this context as the exception, and as such it informs us about the boundaries of what is clearly the more prevalent social and political response to economic stagnation.

Chapter 8

America in the Postwar Era

We believe that all men are entitled to the blessings of liberty.
Yet millions are being deprived of those blessings—not because
of their own failures, but because of the color of their skin. . . .
[T]his . . . cannot continue. Our constitution, the foundation of
our Republic, forbids it. The principles of our freedom forbid
it. And the law I will sign tonight forbids it.

LYNDON B. JOHNSON
Remarks on signing the 1964 Civil Rights Bill[1]

In this present crisis, government is not the solution to our
problem; government is the problem.

RONALD REAGAN
1981 Inaugural Address[2]

World War II ended America's economic depression. It also put on hold self-conscious social and economic reform. What movement toward a more open, mobile society did occur during the war years—for example, the dramatic opening of new employment opportunities to women and, to a lesser extent, blacks—was mostly a by-product of wartime strains on available manpower. Moreover, as is often the case under conditions of military threat, highly visible actions like the internment of immigrants as well as native-born Americans because they were of Japanese descent blatantly violated peacetime notions of citizens' freedoms. But the most direct domestic consequence of America's entry into the war was simply to put the country back to work.

By 1943 more than 9 million Americans were on active duty in the armed forces. The military's needs for goods, ranging from large-scale hardware—airplanes, ships, tanks, trucks, weapons—down to blankets and canned rations, took over whole industries, simultaneously expanding and converting their production. Steel output rose from 53 million tons in 1939 to a record 86 million by 1942 and stayed high for the remainder of the war, while the manufacture of ordinary automobiles for civilian use fell from 3.8 million in 1941 to fewer than 100 in 1943 and stayed low until the war ended. Direct spending by the federal government rose from $9 billion in the 1940 fiscal year to $91 billion, or 45 percent of the year's entire national income, in 1944. In many industries the distinction between private management of business and nationalized management by government officials simply dissolved, as the Roosevelt administration set up a series of bodies to oversee and coordinate war production, and they in turn appointed corporate executives (often at a salary of $1 a year) to manage their usual businesses.

Despite the drain of so many working-age Americans into the armed services, the number of people on the job in civilian clothes rose from 36 million in 1939 to 45 million in 1944. Part of this huge surge in employment came from a sharp (and temporary) increase in the fraction of Americans of working age who entered the workforce. Labor force participation among Americans age fourteen or older, which had fluctuated narrowly between 55 percent and 58 percent since before the turn of the century, quickly rose above 63 percent as increasing numbers of women took jobs instead of staying at home, and young men entered the military instead of attending school. To a much greater extent, however, the nation achieved its huge wartime growth of employment by putting the unemployed to work. In 1939 there were still 9.4 million would-be workers without jobs. By 1944 there were just 670,000. The 55 percent of 1944 production *not* commandeered by the government was alone greater than the economy's entire annual output in any year before the war.

If it had taken a full-scale war to restore full employment, what would happen, many people wondered, once peace broke out? Concerns that America might have exhausted the potential for vigorous economic expansion had ample historical precedent. The extended agricultural depression that culminated in the mid-1890s, for example, had fostered Turner's hypothesis that with the closing of the frontier the nation's opportunity for further economic growth was limited. The depression of the 1930s had led to similar ideas in an industrial setting. Prominent economists like Alvin Hansen and Lauchlin Currie foresaw what they called a "secular stagnation," arguing that America had become a "mature economy" no longer capable of achieving sustained expansion.3 Although Hansen in particular pushed the secular stagnation theme not as ground for passive despair but as motivation for adopting a new approach that would stimulate continued growth through activist government policy (after initially resisting the ideas of British economist John Maynard Keynes for using fiscal policy to stimulate the economy, Hansen had become America's foremost early enthusiast for Keynesian economics), fears of renewed depression once the war ended were widespread.

In addition to these fundamental questions about the shifting engines of America's long-run economic growth, by late in the war the imminent prospect of demobilization was a more tangible source of concern. Of the $93 billion the government spent in its fiscal year ending in June 1945, the military budget accounted for $83 billion. Recollections of the abrupt economic decline in the aftermath of the post–World War I demobilization—and that at a time when military spending had been far smaller, both absolutely and as a share of national income—gave these concerns particular credibility. Once the problem of wartime production had been mostly solved, therefore, how to maintain postwar full employment became the chief economic issue under discussion even during the war years themselves. After much debate, in February 1946, Congress finally passed the Employment Act (albeit not the *Full* Employment Act, as originally proposed), formally recognizing for the first time that it was "the continuing policy and responsibility of the federal Government . . . to foster and promote . . . conditions under which there will be afforded useful employment opportunities . . . for those able, willing, and seeking to work, and to promote maximum employment, production, and purchasing power."4

In the event, whether as the result of active policy or by mere force of circumstance, America in the quarter-century following World War II achieved these objectives to a greater extent than had ever seemed likely. Despite the reduction in armed forces personnel from over 12 million in 1945 to less than 1.5 million by 1948, and the parallel drop in the government's military spending from $83 billion to just $9 billion, the recession that ensued was brief and unemployment remained below 5 million. Three further recessions followed during the presidency of Dwight Eisenhower, but none of them was long-lasting, and only once, and briefly, did unemployment reach as much as 8 percent of the labor force. After the third of these recessions bottomed, in February 1961, output grew steadily and unemployment remained continuously low for almost nine years—at the time, the longest unbroken American economic expansion on record. From 1946 through 1973, when a quadrupling of the international price of oil by the OPEC cartel finally triggered a sharp recession, unemployment averaged 4.8 percent. After allowing for what had now become a persistent inflation of prices, the economy grew on average by 3.8 percent per annum.[5]

As in economically dynamic periods in the past, the strong growth that followed World War II was not merely a matter of more of the same. The postwar surge in births, after a decade and a half of record low birthrates during the depression and the war years, created massive demands for new housing. Especially for veterans with the financing of the G.I. Bill behind them, but for millions of other families as well, home ownership became an affordable option. The fraction of American families living in their own houses rose from less than 44 percent in 1940 to 55 percent in 1950 to nearly 62 percent by 1960. The increasingly pervasive organization of American life around the automobile, reinforced by the construction of the Interstate Highway System beginning in 1955, located many of those new houses in the suburbs. (The fraction of American families owning automobiles rose from 54 percent in 1948 to 82 percent by 1970.) The development of suburban shopping centers, and later malls, followed naturally. Between 1940 and 1970 the fraction of America's population living in the suburbs doubled, from 19 percent to 38 percent. The decline in the fraction living in small towns and rural areas exactly mirrored this increase.

The postwar baby boom reshaped the American economy in other ways too. Communities everywhere needed to build new schools, new hospitals, and new recreation facilities. The number of teachers in American elementary and secondary schools rose from 980,000 in 1940 to 2.3 million in 1970, and higher education became one of the nation's leading growth industries. So did the production of children's consumer products of all kinds, including clothing, toys, sports equipment, books, and entertainment.

New technologies and new products—in many cases, actually the full commercial development of what had existed on a limited basis before the war—added further to the sense of an economy and society moving forward. The spreading technology that directly affected the most people's lives was television. At the end of World War II, only nine TV stations were broadcasting in America, and fewer than .1 percent of families owned receivers. As early as 1950, however, the country was producing 7 million TV sets per year. By 1970 there were almost 900 stations, and 95 percent of American families had a TV in their homes.

New technologies affected people's lives in more fundamental ways as well. New medical advances gave ordinary citizens an especially keen sense of progress in the classic sense. Penicillin became widely available to treat what had earlier been often fatal infections, including pneumonia, spinal meningitis, and diphtheria, as well as age-old problems like syphilis and gonorrhea. The first decade after the war also saw the introduction of antibiotics (Aureomycin, streptomycin, and erythromycin) to treat penicillin-resistant bacteria, long-term dialysis for kidney patients, use of cortisone to treat arthritis, Pap smears and other tests for cancer, steroids, antihistamines, drugs to treat malaria and tuberculosis, and a vaccine for measles. The most dramatic single advance was Dr. Jonas Salk's development of a polio vaccine in 1952. By 1954 the Salk vaccine was already widely used. Major developments over the next fifteen years included mammography, the first kidney dialysis machine, and vaccines for rubella and meningitis.

The way people moved about the country also changed. Commercial air travel, which had been in its infancy before the war, now came into its own, especially with the introduction of the jet engine beginning with the Boeing 707 in 1958. Americans had first flown 1 million passenger miles on airplanes in 1940. The main means of intercity transportation then were railroads and bus lines. By 1970 commercial airlines were flying over 100 million passenger miles per year, more than three times the volume of passenger business done by railroads and buses combined.

Many of these changes in how Americans lived and what products they consumed went along with changes in how they worked. With the steady advance of farm mechanization and productivity, the share of American workers employed on the farm, including farm owners, had already declined from 38 percent in 1900 to 17 percent in 1940. By 1970 it was less than 3 percent. Unlike earlier in the century, however, during the postwar years the share of the labor force working at traditional blue-collar jobs also dipped modestly, with the largest decline occurring among unskilled laborers. By contrast, the growth of white-collar employment far outpaced growth of the labor force overall, rising from 31 percent of all jobs in 1940 to 47 percent in 1970.

This large increase in white-collar employment was a part of the broader transformation of postwar America into an advanced service economy. Before the war, the production and sale of goods had outpaced services by more than three to two. By 1970 the two sectors were almost equal. Between 1947 and 1970 health care expanded ninefold, banking sevenfold, and general business services—including advertising, consulting, and equipment rental—thirteenfold, versus a fourfold increase (in current dollars) for the economy as a whole.

These widespread changes in Americans' life and work proved especially important in shaping public attitudes. As we have seen, people's perceptions of whether or not they are getting ahead often depend on more than just the rise in their incomes. Once prior experience has made owning a single-family house a symbol of middle-class status, moving to the suburbs enables a family to think of its fortunes as rising even if so many other families are also buying suburban homes that their own position in the economic scale in fact remains unchanged. Similarly, when white-collar jobs carry the connotation of higher status, the fact that sons of farmhands and unskilled manual laborers are becoming salesmen and office workers encourages their families to see themselves as gaining in status even if most other comparable families are simultaneously enjoying the same experience.

These positive forces were broadly at work in post–World War II America. And, of course, they were stronger because incomes were rapidly rising. Americans' average income per capita in 1970 was more than double what it had been in 1940, even after allowance for higher prices. In the quarter-century between 1948 and 1973 (to take two years that were each business cycle peaks), real per capita income grew on average by 2.4 percent per annum. Moreover, America's economic growth was gaining momentum as the postwar period advanced. Between 1959 and 1973 (again, two business cycle peaks), real per capita income rose on average by 2.9 percent per annum.[6]

These population-wide gains were all the more impressive in that, because of the baby boom, for the first time on record the share of the American population not yet old enough to work was steadily increasing. Further, because the distribution of incomes was mostly becoming more equal during these years, gains enjoyed by the majority of Americans were even stronger than the growth of per capita income. Over the quarter-century spanning 1948–73, the real income of the median family rose on average by 3 percent per annum, from $20,600 to more than $43,200 in today's dollars.[7]

As had happened after World War I, America in the first few postwar years gave little sign of renewed commitment to an open and more democratic society. Euphoria from the victory over Germany and Japan soon gave way not only to fears of renewed economic stagnation but also to concerns about new international threats, and these in turn soured the country's political and social relations. By the end of the 1940s, the Soviet grip on eastern Europe was absolute, Mao Zedong's communists had driven Chiang Kai-shek's nationalists from the Chinese mainland, and the United States no longer enjoyed sole possession of atomic weapons. Many Americans feared that the nation was more vulnerable now than at the time of Pearl Harbor.[8]

The ensuing public recriminations over whether Roosevelt had yielded too much to Soviet premier Josef Stalin at Yalta, finger-pointing over "who lost China," organized witch hunts for spies and traitors at home, and a general paranoia over communists and communist sympathizers were all strongly reminiscent of the Red Scare that had followed World War I. The McCarran Act, passed by Congress over President Harry Truman's veto in 1950—"an act to protect the United States against certain un-American and subversive activities"—required members of the Communist Party to register with the government and subjected them to penalties such as denial of passports.[9] The House Committee on Un-American Activities (HUAC) blatantly violated traditional American notions of individual freedoms, as did Senator Joseph McCarthy's still more reckless investigations.[10] Even the Marshall Plan, hailed at the time as a humanitarian response (which in part it was) to the continued economic deprivation in western European countries that had not yet recovered from the damage and dislocation of the war, was in large part motivated by the perceived need to shore up the western barrier blocking the advance of communism.

Over time, however, attitudes changed. Fears that demobilization would lead to renewed depression faded with continuing evidence that the postwar prosperity was lasting. Frustration over the inability to win back China, or even eastern Europe, gave way to the realization that the advance of communism had at least been "contained." HUAC and McCarthy claimed some victims, but in time each overreached and each was destroyed. In the subsequent revulsion against their excesses, both became generic terms of opprobrium. In the meanwhile, the country moved on to other business.

The most dramatic dimension of the new agenda taken up during the first quarter-century or so following World War II was the effort to extend American democracy, both political and economic, to nonwhites. Although some New Dealers like Harold Ickes and Harry Hopkins, and especially Eleanor Roosevelt, had strongly advocated measures to combat racial discrimination and inequality, Franklin Roosevelt had never made redressing racial injustices a priority. Dependent on southern Democrats to advance his legislative aims, the president had even refused to support proposed legislation that would have made lynching a federal crime. The Roosevelt administration's one significant measure promoting racial equality, the creation of a Fair Employment Practices Committee to expand opportunities for blacks in war industries, had been initiated in large part to prevent a threatened march on Washington.[11]

Progress began—slowly—after the war. President Truman extended the life of the Fair Employment Practices Committee into peacetime, and in 1946 he appointed the first federal Civil Rights Commission. Among other recommendations, the commission called for an end to racial segregation in public schools (a plea echoed by the Commission on Higher Education, also appointed by Truman the same year), but no action to implement this radical idea followed. In 1948 Truman proposed a series of measures including federal protection against lynching, protection of voting rights, prohibition of discrimination in interstate transportation facilities, and creation of a new agency to prevent job discrimination. Congress accepted none of these ideas. Popular attitudes had not yet changed sufficiently to create adequate public support for major new steps toward openness and tolerance.

One tangible contribution to achieving racial equality that Truman was able to implement without congressional approval was his executive order in 1948 eliminating segregation in the armed services. Probably not coincidentally, Truman issued his order the year after Dodgers second baseman Jackie Robinson had successfully broken the race barrier in major league baseball. Also in 1948, the Supreme Court first signaled the role the federal judiciary would play in broadening the racial dimensions of American democracy by holding invalid the restrictive covenants that private homeowners often wrote into deeds and other sales agreements in order to maintain racial and religious segregation in housing.[12] (Truman later said it was at his request that the solicitor general argued the case before the Supreme Court.)[13] In 1953 the Court also ruled unconstitutional the practice, common in southern states, of white-only voting in party primaries.[14]

The real momentum of the postwar civil rights movement began in 1954, when the Supreme Court elevated to constitutional status the position on school desegregation advocated by the Civil Rights Commission seven years before. Squarely rejecting its predecessors' decision in *Plessy v. Ferguson* a half-century earlier, the Court concluded, in *Brown v. Board of Education*, "that in the field of public education the doctrine of 'separate but equal' has no place. Separate education facilities are inherently unequal."[15] Many school districts around the country delayed in implementing the Court's decision, and so the process of achieving actual desegregation dragged on into the 1970s. In other places, however—for example, Louisville, Baltimore, St. Louis, and Kansas City—local authorities complied promptly and willingly. President Eisenhower likewise ordered schools in Washington, D.C., desegregated immediately after the *Brown* decision. Although many whites throughout the South resisted, in some cases violently, both the Southern Presbyterian Church and the Southern Baptist Convention quickly adopted pro-integration resolutions.[16] Especially after Eisenhower sent troops to Little Rock in 1957 to enforce the Court's decision over open opposition by Arkansas governor Orval Faubus, it became clear that America had embarked on a new course in at least one major dimension of everyday life, education, that plainly affected most families.

The push for racial equality soon spread to other aspects of economic and political life as well. In response to agitation like the Montgomery bus boycott, Congress finally joined the effort by passing the Civil Rights Act of 1957—the first American civil rights legislation since Reconstruction—which made interfering with a citizen's right to vote a federal crime and established a new division of the Department of Justice, headed by an assistant attorney general, to enforce this and other related laws. By the time of President Kennedy's assassination six years later, public opinion surveys showed that a majority of Americans considered racial issues the lead item on the nation's public policy agenda.[17] Before he died, Kennedy had issued an executive order banning discrimination in public housing and had also proposed major new civil rights legislation.

The Civil Rights Act of 1964, pushed through Congress by President Johnson the next July, prohibited racial discrimination in hotels and other public accommodations, in education, and in employment. The act also authorized the Justice Department to bring suit to enforce desegregation and established the Equal Employment Opportunity Commission to prevent discrimination—not just based on race, but also religion, sex, and national origin—in hiring or promotion.[18] The Twenty-fourth Amendment, abolishing the use of poll taxes to prevent blacks (or, for that matter, anyone else) from voting in either primary or general elections for federal office, became part of the Constitution the same year. In 1965 Congress passed the Voting Rights Act, which outlawed literacy tests and other restrictions on eligibility traditionally used to bar nonwhites from exercising their electoral rights. The Civil Rights Act of 1968, the Fair Housing

Act passed the same year, the Equal Employment Opportunity Act of 1972, and the Equal Credit Opportunity Act of 1974 further consolidated these advances. Nor was activity in these areas limited to the federal level. The Fair Housing Act, for example, followed numerous efforts by individual states to bar discrimination in home sales, rentals, or financing.[19]

Some salient gains took place outside the sphere of either federal or state legislation. By the mid-1950s the NAACP was welcoming the "virtual disappearance" of lynching.[20] Some southern states adopted laws limiting or even prohibiting typical Ku Klux Klan activities like wearing masks and burning crosses. Some private universities in the South had begun to admit black students, and some southern cities had stopped segregating public facilities like parks and museums, in each case well before the new civil rights laws required these steps.

Such significant movement, compressed into so short a time, ignited elements of resistance and even backlash. Champions of segregation like Faubus, as well as governors George Wallace in Alabama and Ross Barnett in Mississippi, made their public stands and attracted temporary support. In 1968 Wallace ran for president as an independent candidate, carrying four southern states and winning 13 percent of the popular vote nationwide. Nor was resistance limited to the South. Some white neighborhoods in Boston, for example, reacted with violence to a federal judge's 1974 order that cross-district busing be used to eliminate what had merely been de facto, rather than formal, school segregation.

But the progress made in opening up American society to a sizable group who for a century had been second-class citizens was undeniable. More equal access to the education system delivered more equal education. In 1950 only 24 percent of young black adults had graduated from high school, compared to 56 percent among whites. By 1980, a quarter-century after the desegregation decision, the black graduation rate had risen to 77 percent (and the white rate to 89 percent). There are no consistent test data that would permit direct comparisons of educational achievement before desegregation and after, but the evidence that is available from the 1970s onward likewise shows a clear narrowing of black-white differences. In 1971, the average reading proficiency score of black seventeen-year-olds was 82 percent of the average score for whites of the same age. By 1988 the black-white ratio had risen to 93 percent. The same narrowing of the performance gap occurred over this period for younger children, and there is no reason to believe it was not already well in progress before 1971.[21]

Nor were blacks the only group to benefit from the advance of tolerance in the quarter-century following World War II. As Oscar and Lilian

Handlin later wrote, "Between 1950 and 1972 a striking diminution in discrimination dramatically improved relationships among most American ethnic groups. Prejudices persisted, in some respects deeper than earlier, but the form and context changed. Efforts to revive the Klan came to nothing, and the anti-Catholic and anti-Semitic movements of the 1930s and 1940s faded away."[22] Attempts by prewar bigots like Gerald L. K. Smith to attack Eisenhower for being too close to Jewish interests likewise got nowhere. And in 1960 Americans elected a Catholic as president.

The same increased openness to traditionally subordinated groups within America's own population also brought a new attitude toward immigration. Once the 1924 National Origins Act took full effect, in 1929, immigration into the United States had declined to barely 50,000 per year on average during the 1930s, and in the war years still fewer. After the war, immigration gradually rose to almost a quarter-million a year by 1950. In 1952 Congress voted to increase the overall limits, as well as to remove the bar against Asians, and total immigration rose to nearly 300,000 on average in the 1950s and early 1960s. Even so, the quota system put in place in the 1920s continued to reserve most of the visas available to immigrants from outside the Western Hemisphere for northern and western Europeans.

In 1965, in the full flush of demolishing old barriers confronting American blacks, Congress also passed a new Immigration Act that increased the annual limit and, more significantly, abolished the old system of quotas by national origin based on the historical composition of the country's population. In its place the new legislation set overall annual limits of 170,000 for immigrants from the Eastern Hemisphere and 120,000 from the Western. Within those limits, it gave priority to relatives of American citizens or resi-dents and, secondarily, to applicants possessing certain job skills. The new law also created exemptions whereby sufficiently close relatives (parents, spouses, minor children) of citizens or residents, and political refugees seeking asylum in the United States, did not count against these numerical quotas.

As a result of these new rules, total legal immigration into the United States rose to nearly 400,000 per year on average in the latter half of the 1960s and 450,000 per year in the 1970s—still only half as many as in the peak period before World War I, even in absolute numbers, but nonetheless a major change from the virtually closed-door period of the 1930s and 1940s. As had been the case before World War I, America also again welcomed a diverse mix of new arrivals. By the 1970s, two-fifths of all arriving immigrants were Latin American and one-third were Asian. In all, 94 percent were from countries other than northern and western Europe.[23]

This broader receptivity to immigration was also consonant with America's active engagement in world affairs. Unlike after World War I, when the United States played a leading role in creating the League of Nations but then refused to join, American wartime participation in creating the United Nations, the World Bank, and the International Monetary Fund led seamlessly to ongoing American involvement and leadership in these institutions. The United States also took the lead in institutionalizing ongoing mechanisms for negotiating lower tariffs and eliminating other barriers to free trade.

Similarly, far from retreating into a new isolationism, President Truman took an early and active role in resisting communist expansion into Turkey and Greece, gave western Europe $12 billion of assistance (equivalent to more than $500 billion today, in relation to U.S. national income) under the Marshall Plan, placed permanent American air and naval bases around the world, and established the North Atlantic Treaty Organization as the central mechanism for containing communism militarily within existing borders in Europe. When North Korea invaded South Korea in June 1950, the United States went back to war, this time under the United Nations umbrella.[24] Dwight Eisenhower as president negotiated a truce in Korea but then applied these same internationalist ideas even more broadly than Truman, adding to NATO a series of other regional alliances like SEATO (the Southeast Asia Treaty Organization) and CENTO (the Central Treaty Organization in the Middle East). John F. Kennedy, vowing in his inaugural address to "pay any price, bear any burden" to defend the cause of freedom not just at home but abroad, emphasized renewed military preparedness. He also created the Peace Corps as a vehicle for engaging young Americans in civilian efforts to promote development and democracy around the world.

America's more active engagement in foreign affairs in the first three decades or so of the postwar period hardly proved an unqualified success. Direct military action in Korea preserved the south of the country as an independent, non-communist and eventually prosperous nation, but the effort to do the same in Vietnam a decade later failed and, in so doing, disrupted and sharply divided American society. Intervention in Iran managed to maintain a pro-Western regime, but not indefinitely and not obviously to the country's longer-run benefit. Comparable interventions in Latin America succeeded in some cases, failed in others.

But the chief common thread throughout was the active engagement itself. There was no significant movement to turn inward, or tend only to America's internal affairs. Perhaps the most compelling symbols of how widely accepted that ongoing engagement had become in these years were the recognition of "Red" China in 1972 (complete with presidential visit) and the subsequent negotiation of "détente" with the Soviet Union—in both cases by Richard Nixon, who in the early postwar days had built his political career on a style of anti-communism reminiscent of the early 1920s.

The spirit of political inclusiveness and openness that flourished once Americans gained a secure sense of getting ahead in the postwar economy also fostered a willingness to include citizens more broadly in the benefits of rising prosperity. While incomes for most families were increasing at near-record rates by historical standards, there were still Americans whom the advancing prosperity was plainly passing by. In time it became clear that, Kennedy's catchy phrase notwithstanding, in fact a rising tide did not neces-sarily lift *all* boats.[25] In retrospect one of the most striking features of this era in the development of American society was the active effort to share the perceived prosperity with those who were being left behind.

In part this effort had its roots in Depression-era programs ranging from local relief to federal job creation and Social Security. But the pressing need then had been to blunt the force of outright deprivation for the one-third of the normal labor force who were out of work. In the postwar period, with unemployment less than 5 percent on average over a quarter of a century, the perceived challenge was different: first, to increase opportuni-ties for those who, with proper training or other assistance, could make themselves and their families economically viable; and second, to ameliorate poverty on an ongoing basis for others who, because of age, disability, or other impediments, were unable to succeed economically on their own.

The "Fair Deal" program that Truman proposed in his first State of the Union address after winning his own term as president included such mea-sures as extended unemployment insurance coverage (and an increase in the minimum payment to $25 per week), mandatory disability insurance cover-age, expanded Social Security coverage (and relaxation of the limits on what beneficiaries could earn), redirection of farm subsidies toward small family farms rather than large commercial concerns, expanded funds for elemen-tary and secondary education, hospital construction in rural and under-served areas, funds for vaccinations and treatment of easily spread diseases, and even universal prepaid medical coverage. None of these proposals survived opposition in Congress. The new prosperity appeared too fragile, and in any case had not yet made a sufficient impression on public attitudes. The Housing Act of 1949, which provided funding to build 3 million new homes and specifically financed renewal of urban slums and other inner-city areas, was the only significant element of Truman's Fair Deal to become law.

When Eisenhower took office, many opponents of the New Deal hoped he would undo what they saw as Roosevelt's mischief. But by then attitudes had begun to change. Not only had the permanent New Deal programs built up constituencies of their own, but with almost a decade of solid income gains already in hand the American public firmly supported them. As Eisenhower himself stated in 1954, "Should any political party attempt to abolish Social Security and eliminate labor laws and farm programs, you would not hear of that party again in our political history."[26] Instead, Eisenhower supported the expansion of Social Security to include previously uncovered workers and an increase in benefits, agreed to an increase in the minimum wage from 75 cents an hour to $1 (equivalent to $7 today), and created a new cabinet-level Department of Health, Education and Welfare to expand and administer the growing activity of federal social programs.

The principal expansion of such programs came during the Kennedy-Johnson era. The extension of Aid to Families with Dependent Children (AFDC) to two-parent families in which the primary income earner was unemployed, in 1961, was the first significant change in American welfare programs since Congress created AFDC in 1935.[27] The most sweeping changes, however, occurred only after the 1964 election gave Johnson large majorities in both houses of Congress and also boosted his personal standing with the biggest percentage of the popular vote ever recorded in an American presidential election.[28]

In his 1964 State of the Union message, just two months after assuming the presidency on Kennedy's death, Johnson had boldly called for new civil rights legislation: "As far as the writ of federal law will run, we must abolish not some, but all racial discrimination. . . . [T]his is not merely an economic issue, or a social, political, or international issue. It is a moral issue." But Johnson chose to focus on economic issues as well, and in the same address he "declare[d] unconditional war on poverty in America." The "chief weapons" in that war, Johnson proclaimed, would be "better schools, and better health, and better homes, and better training, and better job opportunities to help more Americans, especially young Americans, escape from squalor and misery and unemployment."[29]

To this end, Johnson proposed a broad array of specific new programs aimed at addressing the plight of the poor. Congress enacted much of this legislation beginning in 1965. Initiatives from this agenda that remain major federal government programs today include Medicare and Medicaid, providing health insurance for the elderly and the indigent, respectively; the Elementary and Secondary Education Act, which provides financial assistance to local school authorities in areas with high concentrations of low-income families; the Job Corps (which subsequently evolved into a series of federal job training and placement programs); food stamps; and a new cabinet-level Department of Housing and Urban Development.

Momentum slowed after Johnson left office, both because President Nixon was less committed to such initiatives and because by then most Americans considered enough programs to be in place. Like Eisenhower, however, Nixon did not retreat from the institutions so recently established but instead sought ways to rationalize and even broaden them. For example, picking up on an idea then under discussion in Congress, Nixon proposed automatic cost-of-living adjustments to ensure that inflation did not erode the real value of Social Security benefits. Congress amended the Social Security Act accordingly in 1972.[30] Nixon also presided over a large expansion of federal programs to benefit the disadvantaged, including not only universal entitlements like Social Security and Medicare but also straightforward welfare programs like AFDC.[31]

The administrations of both Nixon and Gerald Ford innovated in the federal social policy sphere, albeit less boldly and dramatically than under Johnson. In 1969 and again in 1971, the Nixon administration proposed a "negative income tax," which would have substantially broadened the existing welfare system (for example, by including individuals and couples with no children), but support for such a radical idea was limited and Congress never took action on it. In 1975, however, President Ford proposed a one-time direct payment to low-income adults, which Congress then converted into a form of permanent negative income tax—the Earned Income Tax Credit.* Nixon's first term also saw a new level of recognition of the federal government's responsibility to protect the interests of both citizens and the environment. Congress had passed the initial Clean Air Act under Kennedy and the Clean Water Act under Johnson, but it was Nixon, in 1970, who signed the legislation that created the Environmental Protection Agency (EPA) and the Occupational Safety and Health Administration (OSHA).

In the meanwhile, a series of Supreme Court decisions in the late 1950s

---

*The EITC is a refundable tax credit designed to lessen the often severe disincentive that the combination of income taxes, payroll taxes, and the loss of welfare benefits typically creates for a welfare recipient deciding whether to take a low-paying job or remain unemployed.

and throughout the 1960s had expanded the working conception of individuals' rights in a free society, in areas often far removed from economic activity. Some of these actions, like the 1967 ruling that state laws prohibiting interracial marriage were unconstitutional, were straightforward extensions of the Court's leadership role in advancing the nation's civil rights agenda.[32] (In light of the backlash then building over racial integration more generally, one notable aspect of this decision was the absence of negative public reaction.) Other key Supreme Court decisions of this period, however, had little to do with race relations.

In 1958, for example, the Court struck down a California requirement, imposed during the McCarthy period, that eligible state residents sign a loyalty oath on their tax forms in order to receive a veteran's exemption on their property taxes.[33] Similarly, in a series of decisions between 1963 and 1967, the Court progressively ruled unconstitutional elements of the 1950 McCarran Act.[34] In its most sweeping defense of free speech, the Supreme Court in 1969 struck down laws prohibiting "criminal syndicalism"—in other words, speech advocating violent overthrow of the state—which had been permitted ever since the Court's *Whitney v. California* decision in 1927.[35] The Court flatly declared that its decisions in *Whitney* and other related cases had been "thoroughly discredited," and it now took up as a new standard the free speech doctrine expressed by Oliver Wendell Holmes and Louis Brandeis in their dissents to the *Whitney* decision.

The Court also extended the boundaries of free speech on matters that did not bear on national security. In one widely publicized case, the Montgomery, Alabama, commissioner of public affairs had sued the *New York Times* for printing a paid advertisement describing the city's mistreatment of black students who protested against segregation. The trial court and the Alabama Supreme Court had found the ad libelous and ordered the *Times* to pay $500,000 in damages. In 1964, however, the Supreme Court ruled that the Alabama statute under which the *Times* had been found at fault was constitutionally deficient in that it failed to provide adequate safeguards for freedom of speech in the criticism of the official conduct of a public officeholder.[36] In a different area of free speech, several Court rulings led the film industry (specifically, the Motion Picture Producers and Distributors of America) to conclude that the Hays Code, under which it had strictly censored the content of films since the early 1930s, would not pass constitutional scrutiny.[37] The industry revised the censorship code in 1966, and two years later abandoned it altogether in favor of a system of ratings.

In yet another series of related opinions, the Supreme Court concluded that most of the individual freedoms established in the Bill of Rights (the first ten amendments to the Constitution) applied to citizens' dealings with state governments as well. A 1961 ruling, for example, precluded the states from using criminal evidence obtained by illegal search and seizure (the Fourth Amendment).[38] Analogous decisions over the next seven years successively confirmed—at the state level—protection against cruel and unusual punishment (the Eighth Amendment), the right to counsel (the Sixth Amendment), protection against self-incrimination (the Fifth Amendment), and the right to a speedy trial, to confront opposing witnesses, and to a trial by jury (all again the Sixth Amendment).[39]

Taken together with several other key cases—most famously the 1966 decision in *Miranda v. Arizona*, requiring that police officers inform suspects of their rights when making an arrest—these decisions amounted to a revolution in American criminal procedure. Further, although the rights being guaranteed apply to all Americans, it was clear at the time that they would most benefit those with lower incomes, and nonwhites more generally. (The majority opinion in the *Miranda* case stated that "were we to limit these constitutional rights to those who can retain an attorney, our decisions today would be of little significance.")[40] In this sense the Supreme Court's civil liberties decisions were of a piece with its active role in the civil rights movement, as well as with the more general climate of concern for citizens whom the strongly advancing economy of the day was still leaving behind.[41]

In sum, by the early 1970s America had become a much different society than it had been in the late depression years or, even more so, the 1920s. Blacks had rights, enforced by federal law, that may have been implicit in the constitutional amendments adopted after the Civil War but in practice had been unexercisable for a hundred years since. Individual citizens' freedoms were stronger, and more sharply defined, than ever before. Women composed a large and growing share of the labor force, with rapidly expanding access to many previously all-male professions.[42] Immigrants were welcome, not just from northern and western Europe, and domestic prejudice against Americans other than white Protestants was in retreat. The United States was an active participant, both institutionally and in numerous informal ways, in global affairs. At home Americans accepted new responsibilities to share the nation's material success with their less fortunate fellow citizens. Widely read books on what America as a nation was all about, such as historian Henry Steele Commager's *The American Mind,* or sociologist Seymour Martin Lipset's *The First New Nation,* displayed both an inclusiveness and a confidence in that inclusiveness that were reminiscent of what Americans had written and read a hundred years before.[43]

It would be wrong to attribute all of these changes, or perhaps even the entirety of any one, to the rising incomes and general prosperity of the time. But to suppose that the appearance of such a multidimensional movement toward tolerance and generosity was merely a coincidence, bearing no connection to the economic setting in which it took place, would surely be wrong as well.

The strong rise in incomes that marked America's first quarter-century following World War II did not continue into the second. Nor did the movement toward a more progressive society.

Although the single event that most visibly heralded the new era of sluggish growth was the price increase and (temporary) embargo imposed in 1973 by OPEC, it is clear in retrospect that changes in energy costs were not the fundamental force slowing America's economic progress. Indeed, despite voluminous economic research over the years, the causes of the post-1973 slowdown remain something of a puzzle. The oil price increase plainly helped trigger the severe recession that began shortly thereafter, but later on the timing of changes in energy prices did not correspond closely to economic developments in the United States.[44]

Other commonly suggested explanations for the slower average rate of expansion after the early 1970s—the burdens of business regulation, reduced spending on research and development, shrunken investment in new factories and machinery once the government began to run large budget deficits, reduced investment in infrastructure such as highways and airports, increased competition from foreign producers, and the failure of America's schools to prepare the nation's young men and women for the modern workplace—likewise either occurred at the wrong time to have caused the initial slowdown or failed later on to jibe with the revival of growth in the 1990s. Moreover, because most other industrial economies also suffered an economic slowdown dating from sometime in the 1970s, explanations focused narrowly on the American situation can at best have accounted for only part of the problem.[45]

Puzzle or no, the post-1973 slowdown was real enough. Growth of productivity—the increase in output for a fixed amount of labor input, which is ultimately the basis of rising living standards—slowed from the 2.9 percent per annum average pace that America had maintained from 1948 to 1973 to just 1.4 percent over the next twenty years.[46] Even the one major sector of the economy in which productivity growth more or less kept up, manufacturing, proved of little comfort. Manufacturers achieved much of their productivity gains during this period by substituting machinery for labor. Rather than redeploy the released workers in other jobs, firms often simply discharged them to go into other, less productive industries. Although the output produced in manufacturing increased by 51 percent between 1973 and 1993, the number of workers on manufacturing payrolls shrank from nearly 19 million to fewer than 17 million.[47]

With slower productivity gains, the growth of Americans' per capita real income likewise slowed, from the 2.4 percent per annum advance realized between 1948 and 1973 (and 2.9 percent between 1959 and 1973) to 1.7 percent on average over the next two decades. Further, because the distribution of incomes was becoming progressively more *un*equal beginning in the early 1970s, and especially from 1980 on, for most families the slowdown was far more abrupt.[48] After allowance for inflation, the income of a family at the midpoint of the income distribution was only 7 percent greater in 1993 than it was in 1973, representing an average gain of only .3 percent per annum over the twenty years. By contrast, the median family income in 1973 was more than double what it had been in real terms in 1948.

Moreover, the stagnation of most Americans' incomes seemed all the more frustrating because of the growing sense that people were working harder just to keep in place. While the share of the American population that is of normal working age fell from 59 percent in 1945 to 51 percent in 1965, mostly because of the postwar baby boom, by the mid-1980s it had regained the 1945 level. And as women increasingly sought and found work outside their homes, the share of the adult population actually in the job force steadily rose as well. By 1990, overall labor force participation stood at 67 percent, and nearly 63 percent of the population over age fifteen had jobs in the formal workforce—new record highs, above even the peak rates reached during the period of maximum effort (including the armed forces) at the height of World War II.[49]

Behind the continued albeit slower growth in real per capita incomes in the economy as a whole, and the flat trend in the median family's income, from the early 1970s to the early 1990s the majority of working Americans saw their own pay stagnate or even decline. In 1973 the average nonmanagement worker in American business made $631 per week in today's dollars. By 1993 the average paycheck was down to $491. Wage increases had outpaced inflation in only six years out of twenty, and even then by only paltry amounts.[50] After allowance for rising prices, by 1993 the median income of all American men working full-time throughout the year—even including lawyers and doctors, business managers, and other professionals—was 5 percent *less* than it was in 1973. The comparable average income for women rose over these twenty years, but by barely .5 percent per annum.[51]

As would be expected, the stagnation of incomes in turn affected how people lived. Home ownership rates, for example, declined throughout the 1980s. Especially among lower-paid workers, fewer received benefits like retirement plans or health care. For the first time since the 1930s, most Americans were losing ground.[52]

The brunt of this stagnation fell on younger workers and those just entering the labor force. Twenty years before, in 1953, a thirty-year-old male American who earned the median wage for his age group had made $22,200 in today's dollars. By 1973, as a fifty-year-old, if he was still at the median for his age group he was making $43,000 (again in today's dollars). His income had almost doubled over his prime working years, even after allowing for inflation. Perhaps more importantly for purposes of shaping citizens' attitudes about where their country is headed economically, if the same man in 1973 had a thirty-year-old son who likewise earned the median wage for his own age group, the son was making $37,100 in today's dollars: two-thirds more than his father had made starting out.[53]

Beginning in the early 1970s such comparisons were starkly different. If the son in this example remained at the median for his age group, by 1993, as a fifty-year-old, he was making $42,700. Over the two prime decades of his working life, his income had risen just 15 percent beyond inflation. And if he in turn had his own son, age thirty in 1993 and at the median for his age group, that son's wage was only $28,200, nearly one-fourth *less* than the father had made starting out two decades earlier.

In place of the steady advances that the previous generation had reaped over the course of a working lifetime, therefore, working Americans who were young in the early 1970s saw little real change in their incomes over the next two decades of their careers. And by the early 1990s their children were having to start off, on average, far behind where they had started. Not surprisingly, popular discussion of the country's economic prospects repeatedly pointed to the likelihood that a new generation of Americans would live less well than their parents.[54]

The impact of this economic stagnation on Americans' attitudes, and the consequences for American society, were strikingly similar to the changes that had taken place during the prolonged agricultural depression of the 1880s and early 1890s, and again during the stop-and-go decade that followed World War I. Movement toward opening American society, either domestically or with respect to outsiders, mostly slowed or ceased.[55] Institutional gains in this direction achieved during the preceding period of rising incomes increasingly came under attack. Attitudes among average citizens, now forced to question the security of their own economic position and made even more anxious for their children's, became less generous and less tolerant. And all too familiar tendencies, that in more prosperous times have constituted the radical fringe of intolerance and even opposition to the American republic itself, increasingly seized attention and in some quarters began to compete effectively for public understanding if not sympathy.

In contrast to the great volume of legislation, executive orders, and judicial opinions from the mid-1950s through the 1970s that consistently expanded the opportunities of nonwhites and sought to redress long-standing inequalities, by the mid-1980s the question on America's racial agenda had become where, and by how much, to roll back these efforts. As if to mirror the momentum of those earlier decades, the dimensions of American life that became the particular focus of this change in attitude were education, employment, and the electoral process.

Beginning in the late 1970s, successive state and federal court opinions increasingly challenged the affirmative action programs by which selective colleges and graduate professional schools gave preference, in one way or another, to nonwhite candidates for admission.[56] In time the public spoke directly as well. California's Proposition 209, passed by a clear majority of the state's voters in 1996, barred state and local government institutions, including public colleges and universities, from giving "preferential treatment" to any group on account of race or similar characteristics. Admission of blacks and Hispanics to the University of California's Berkeley campus dropped by more than half once new procedures consistent with Proposition 209 were in place.[57] In a widely discussed case based on admission practices at the University of Texas Law School, also concluded in 1996, the Fifth Circuit Court of Appeals ruled that public universities could not use race as a factor in admitting students.[58] Admission of blacks and Hispanics at the school promptly fell by 88 percent and 64 percent, respectively.[59]

In a parallel series of cases, the Supreme Court similarly restricted the use of affirmative action programs put in place by state and local governments to increase either direct or indirect employment of minority group members. A 1986 decision invalidated the Jackson (Mississippi) Board of Education's system that gave preference to black over white teachers.[60] In a 1989 case involving Richmond, Virginia's system giving preference to minority-owned contractors in awarding city-funded construction contracts, the court held that cities implementing such a system must show that they had historically engaged in discrimination, and that the remedy is narrowly tailored to rectify the resulting inequities.[61] A further decision reaffirmed this trend of restrictive opinions and extended it to the federal government.[62]

The Supreme Court also ruled unconstitutional states' drawing of electoral districts so as to increase the likelihood that their congressional delegations would include members of minority groups. Earlier, during the civil rights era of the 1960s, the Court had acted decisively in favor of the interests of urban blacks by ruling that voting for state legislatures must correspond to equal votes for equal population, not equal geographical area.[63] As late as 1986 the Court had been reluctant to interfere in cases of political gerrymandering.[64] In two cases in the early 1990s, however, the Court held that "benign discrimination" via racially motivated gerrymandering was unconstitutional.[65]

The point at issue here is not whether any of these specific policies and practices that came under challenge is consistent with correct constitutional interpretation, nor even whether they were wise policies in themselves, but rather that public attitudes toward such policies changed and as a result the society's inclusiveness with respect to nonwhite minority citizens began to erode. When incomes were rising for most Americans, ways of making the society more inclusive had enjoyed broad appeal. Once incomes stagnated, that appeal weakened.

Americans' attitudes toward immigration likewise began to take on a flavor reminiscent of the 1880s and the 1920s. In several states, again most prominently California and Texas, anti-immigrant groups pushed to bar immigrants, or their children, from receiving publicly provided benefits like education and vaccination against basic communicable diseases. While the most aggressive of these efforts were directed at illegal immigrants—for example, a 1975 Texas law that the Supreme Court struck down in 1982, and California's Proposition 187, which likewise failed to withstand court challenges—some proposals along these lines called for residency requirements that would limit legal arrivals' access as well.

The new federal welfare legislation passed in 1996 initially barred *legal* immigrants from receiving such benefits as food stamps, medical care, and child support until they had been in the United States for five years (after which they normally become eligible for citizenship). In the first year after the bill took effect, 770,000 legal immigrants were removed from the food stamp rolls.[66] President Bill Clinton, in signing the bill, deplored this feature in particular, and further legislation over the next few years restored some benefits taken away from legal immigrants who were already in the country when the bill was passed. During the welfare debate in 1996, some members of Congress had further proposed to hold back federal assistance and social services even from citizens, if they were foreign-born, but in the end there was little support for this idea. In areas apart from public assistance and publicly provided benefits, there were also calls to deny citizenship to children born to noncitizens living in the United States on temporary visas, and to bar government employees from using any language but English in dealings with members of the general public.[67]

For the first time in many years, the allowed quota of legal immigrants also became a hot-button political issue, attracting widespread attention and debate and even fostering large-scale violence. In April 1992 blacks living in South-Central Los Angeles, adjacent to the nation's largest Korean-American community, rioted against Korean-owned businesses, smashing windows, looting, and burning stores, and in all damaging some 600 Korean-owned retail outlets there and another 200 in nearby Koreatown.[68] By this time nearly two-thirds of all Americans (including those born abroad and their children) favored a reduction in legal immigration, compared to only one-third who wanted immigration cut in the early 1960s. In a 1993 poll, 76 percent of Americans thought immigration should be cut back or even stopped altogether until an improvement in the economy made jobs more plentiful.[69]

In 1995 the Commission on Immigration Reform appointed by President Clinton and chaired by former Texas congresswoman Barbara Jordan recommended cutting legal immigration from the recent 830,000 per year to 550,000. Such an action would have been the first reduction in the number of legal immigrants to America since 1924. The commission also recommended reducing the number of political refugees given asylum in the United States, eliminating the preference given to close relatives of American citizens, and reducing the number of visas awarded on the basis of skills to potential workers designated by American businesses. Various proposals in Congress called for each of these steps, and with greater severity than in the commission's recommendations.[70]

As in earlier periods of anti-immigrant agitation, much of the public discussion favoring these restrictions focused on the concern that immigrants were taking jobs away from native citizens and otherwise bidding down wages by working for less than prevailing rates. Concerns over the direct costs that immigrants imposed on taxpayers figured prominently in the discussion as well.[71] But the new immigration debate also revealed the familiar underlying strains of racial and ethnic prejudice. During the 1996 presidential primaries, Republican candidate Pat Buchanan echoed the open bias of the 1920s in stating straight out that immigrants from England were preferable to those from Africa.

With the income of average citizens no longer rising in real terms, American taxpayers also became less generous toward the nation's own economically disadvantaged. One sign was the sharp erosion in the minimum wage. Increases of 25 percent under Ford and another 15 percent under Jimmy Carter had helped to prevent the minimum wage from falling too far behind inflation. But there was no further action until 1989. By that time the real value of the minimum wage had fallen to the lowest level since 1949. Even after the 27 percent increase voted in 1989 took effect, the minimum wage was still at the early 1950s level in real terms. And even with the next increase, under Clinton in 1996, the real level remained well below where it had been throughout Eisenhower's second term.

The change in attitudes toward those who had no job at all was even more evident. Bill Clinton's pledge to "end welfare as we know it" became one of the most widely applauded promises of the 1992 presidential campaign. In contrast to the continuing strong support for Social Security and Medicare, from which virtually all elderly Americans draw benefits regardless of their incomes or assets, support for programs targeted for the indigent—Medicaid, food stamps, Aid to Families with Dependent Children, even free school lunches—had eroded sharply.

By the mid-1990s, even with the economy no longer in recession, 5 million families (including dependents, more than 5 percent of the American population) were receiving assistance under AFDC.[72] Worse yet, nearly half of all AFDC recipients had been on the rolls (although not always continuously) for at least five years.[73] The 1996 welfare bill, somewhat tendentiously titled the Personal Responsibility and Work Opportunity Reconciliation Act, formally ended the AFDC guarantee of cash assistance to the needy, a commitment the government had first assumed in 1935. Instead, the government adopted a new program of Temporary Assistance for Needy Families (TANF), under which the head of every family on welfare must return to work—and give up benefits—within two years. The new system further imposed a *lifetime* limit of five years of benefits for any recipient. As we have seen, the bill was particularly harsh on immigrants. The new system also provided money to the states in the form of lump-sum "block grants," rather than matching grants as under AFDC, thereby reducing the incentive for states to devote their own resources to the program.[74]

Some part of this increasing opposition to welfare programs was simply a reflection of resurgent bias against immigrants and native nonwhites, since these groups (in the case of immigrants, especially during the first few years after arriving) make up a disproportionately large share of America's welfare beneficiary population.[75] Some part, too, reflected a recognition that parts of the existing welfare system created perverse incentives that kept some recipients dependent on public assistance by discouraging them from seeking paying jobs in order to live on their own.[76] But changing attitudes toward the government's "safety net" also clearly reflected a broader reluctance of citizens who could support themselves, but now found it harder to do so, to come to the aid of those who could not.

Wholly apart from support for the welfare population, or even the wages of the working poor, the federal government's role as an active force promoting economy-wide growth and employment, and stabilizing insofar as is possible the fluctuations in both—a role that the government first took on in a major way in the 1930s, and that the Employment Act of 1946 then institutionalized as national policy—also increasingly came into question after the early 1970s. In response to large federal deficits that drained much of the country's private saving, beginning in the 1980s, some Republicans and also some Democrats proposed constitutional amendments to require the government to balance its budget not just on average over time but year-by-year.[77] Such a requirement would not only rule out deliberate fiscal actions aimed at damping the business cycle (the efficacy of which is dubious anyway) but also, and more importantly, shut off the "automatic stabilizers" that cushion the effects of economic fluctuations by allowing tax revenues to fall without requiring dollar-for-dollar cuts in spending when the economy is weak and incomes decline.

Several conceptually analogous proposals put before Congress would likewise have limited the Federal Reserve System, in its conduct of monetary policy, to pursuing the single objective of avoiding inflation, irrespective of whether the economy was strong or weak and whether unemployment was low or high.[78] Just as a year-by-year balanced budget requirement would eliminate the use of either discretionary or automatic *fiscal* policy to combat economic downturns, these proposals would have prohibited *monetary* policy from doing so. Either change would have represented a distinct rejection of the broader responsibility for achieving macroeconomic objectives that had been widely accepted throughout the post–World War II era.

What made these parallel proposals to limit the use of the government's fiscal and monetary policies particularly noteworthy was that by the mid-1990s the specific problem to which each was supposedly addressed had already become less pressing. Beginning in 1993, the federal budget deficit declined sharply, both in absolute dollars and in relation to national income. (By 1998 the budget was in surplus.) And in contrast to the rapid inflation of the 1970s and early 1980s, by the early 1990s the increase in consumers' cost of living had declined to less than 3 percent per annum.

This diminished sense of public responsibility for the nation's affairs also extended to the realm of education. Federal spending on primary and secondary education, while always small compared to state and local funding, had increased fivefold as a share of national income between the early 1950s and the early 1970s. Even after allowance for rising prices, federal spending per pupil had increased still more. But between the early 1970s and the late 1980s, real per-pupil spending *declined* modestly, while the share of national income channeled to schools via the federal government fell by nearly half. Parallel, though more muted, changes took place in the trend of education spending at the state and local level.[79]

The reduced commitment to America's public education was particularly striking in that it occurred despite a growing sense that the nation's schools were failing to do their job. As productivity growth slowed from the early 1970s on, and especially as many of the nation's manufacturing industries fell behind in international competition during the 1980s, a frequently suggested explanation was that American schools were not adequately preparing the country's youth for what was visibly becoming an ever more sophisticated workplace. Falling test scores and widespread reports of high school graduates whom employers found unable to read only strengthened these concerns.

To be sure, few people believed that simply spending more money, in the absence of substantive changes in curriculum or teaching methods, was the whole answer. But most such changes are costly to implement, and even basic remedies like adding teachers so as to reduce the number of pupils in each classroom obviously cost money too. Yet in the new climate of stagnating incomes for the average American family, these initiatives could not attract public support.

As in the 1880s and again in the 1920s—in a pattern familiar by now—public expression of racial, ethnic, and religious intolerance increased sharply over the two decades of stagnant incomes following 1973. The Ku Klux Klan did not achieve a major revival comparable to that of the 1920s,[80] but related white supremacist organizations like the Aryan Nations, National Alliance, White Aryan Resistance, Posse Comitatus, and Church of the Creator, as well as less formal organizations of "skinheads," gained in visibility and in membership. In 1990 David Duke, an acknowledged former

Klan leader and outspoken white supremacist, ran for the U.S. Senate in Louisiana and received 44 percent of the vote.[81]

In an ironic contrast to the typical stance of such groups in the past, which had self-consciously identified with American military victories, many of the new fringe groups turned back to World War II but expressed admiration for America's enemies. The Aryan Nations, founded in the 1970s by white supremacist Richard Butler, displayed swastikas, pictures of Adolf Hitler, and other Nazi memorabilia on the office walls of its Idaho compound. In the chapel was another portrait of Hitler, bearing the caption "When I Come Back, No More Mr. Nice Guy."[82]

Similarly, the new movement's literature featured not only the usual bias against Jews and foreigners, as in *Caesar's Column* and other tracts of the 1880s, but now an explicit view of the American government as the enemy to be defeated by military action. William Pierce's 1978 novel, *The Turner Diaries*, which depicted a bloody war against the government and nonwhite American citizens, attracted a huge following over the next decade.[83] The Order, the terrorist group at the center of the book's story, became the model for an actual group of the same name founded by prominent white supremacist and anti-Semite Robert Mathews. During the 1980s the real Order financed itself by counterfeiting money and carrying out a series of armed bank robberies. In 1984 members murdered Alan Berg, the Jewish host of a Denver radio talk show. Picking up another name coined in *The Turner Diaries*, many elements of the new anti-government movement in the 1980s began to refer to the United States government as the "Zionist Occupation Government" (acronym: ZOG).

Beginning in 1990, an arson wave across nine southern states, striking in more than five dozen mostly small towns, saw more than sixty churches with black congregations burned to the ground. Hate crimes other than murders also increased. As was true in the 1920s, the spread of white supremacist activity was not limited to the South. By 1994 the Aryan Nations had chapters in eighteen states, with the largest chapters located in California, Illinois, and Pennsylvania.[84]

The 1980s and early 1990s also saw the rise to prominence of the "militia" and "patriot" movements, including many new groups inspired by *The Turner Diaries*. In some states self-styled militias, many of which explicitly avow white supremacist beliefs and subscribe to the kind of paranoid conspiracy theories that are familiar from America's past, acquired large supplies of weapons and began training members for anti-government terrorist action.[85] In Montana, for example, a group calling itself the "Freemen" sought to set up its own government, denying the validity of either federal or Montana laws and attempting to finance itself by issuing and depositing phony bank "liens." The group's leader finally surrendered to government law enforcement officials only after an armed standoff that lasted eighty-one days.[86] In another echo of the past, the rise of these militia and patriot groups in some areas appeared to take particular impetus from the distress of farm debtors, and especially the wave of farm foreclosures in the 1980s. And, once again, those who were attracted to the movement were *not* disproportionately from families with below-average income or education.[87]

Some of these new groups not only advocated violence to promote their objectives but engaged in actual criminal terrorism. Members of such groups and individuals closely aligned with them carried out terrorist acts like the 1995 bombing of the Murrah federal office building in Oklahoma City, in which 168 people died; the derailment of an Amtrak train in Arizona, which killed one person and injured seventy-seven; and numerous death threats (though no actual murders) of judges, justices of the peace, and other citizens in Montana. Timothy McVeigh, who had close ties to the Arizona Patriots, carried out the Oklahoma City bombing using the same explosive—a mixture of heating oil and ammonium nitrate fertilizer—with which members of the fictional Order attacked a federal building in *The Turner Diaries*.[88]

In short, an ugly strain of attitudes and activism that earlier had remained mostly if not entirely out of the public view, and that appeared to be atrophying during the first quarter-century following World War II, sprang forward with renewed force to demand a place in America's public consciousness after the country entered a new era of economic stagnation. Just as striking, many of the nation's leading political figures (in both major parties) were reluctant to criticize the militia movement other than to condemn specific criminal acts, like the Oklahoma City bombing, after they occurred. The new bigotry and paranoid incitement to anti-government violence that so many of these groups propagated mostly passed without direct criticism.

A parallel development took place in the nation's public discourse. Beginning in the 1980s, talk shows that prominently feature outspoken racial bigotry became a regular staple of commercial radio in the United States. Similar shows—for example, *Race and Reason*, produced by the White Aryan Resistance—began to appear on cable television. Skinhead groups developed their own style of rock music, characterized by racist and neo-Nazi lyrics. (One recording and promotion agency, Resistance Records, specializes in skinhead records.)

Similar sentiments, though muted, also became more prevalent within the political establishment. Pat Buchanan's presidential campaigns, in 1992 and 1996, exhibited not only open nativist bias but also only thinly veiled anti-black, anti-Hispanic, and anti-Semitic prejudice. In 1991 the Reverend Pat Robertson, founder of the Christian Coalition, published *The New World Order*, a work strongly reminiscent of the literature of the late 1880s and early 1890s.[89] In it Robertson prominently reintroduced traditional conspiracy theories (some dating back more than two centuries), reproduced the arguments of long out-of-date anti-Semitic tracts, and warned of the excessive influence of "international bankers" in present-day America.[90] The book sold over a half-million copies.[91] Nor was resurgence of prejudice limited to whites. In the 1990s Louis Farrakhan, leader of the black Nation of Islam, emerged as a forceful and articulate voice of the most explicit anti-Semitism to emerge in the United States since the 1930s.

Yet another echo of the past was the renewed vigor of the anti-evolution movement in public education. The Scopes trial at which William Jennings Bryan had made his final public appearance took place in 1925, when the Ku Klux Klan revival was near its height and growing economic frustration was fostering threats to American liberties more broadly. The Tennessee statute under which John Scopes was convicted remained in force until 1968, when, at a time of rapidly rising incomes and a broadening of political as well as economic opportunities for many Americans, the Supreme Court firmly ruled such laws unconstitutional.[92] In 1996, however, the Tennessee legislature took up a new bill to bar teachers in the state's public schools from including the theory of evolution in their class curriculum unless they also offered a parallel presentation of the biblical account of creation, and to fire any teacher who tells Tennessee students that the theory of evolution is valid.[93] Kansas and Nebraska, both states in the 1890s populist heartland, as well as Alabama and New Mexico, likewise enacted such laws.[94]

In all these ways—from the agenda of public policy to the attitudes of private citizens, from broad social trends to individual incidents, from the books people read to the daily offerings of the airwaves—America during this latest period of economic stagnation from the early 1970s to the early 1990s increasingly came to resemble America in earlier eras when living standards also failed to rise. The story is not one of continuity of social forces but of their episodic reappearance whenever the sustained disappointment of hopes and expectations for rising incomes creates the right environment.

The populists of the late nineteenth century felt, all too concretely, the pain of being dispossessed both economically and culturally. They saw conspiracies among bankers, foreigners, Jews, railroads, anyone not belonging to their own part of America, and especially anyone who appeared to be succeeding as their circumstances deteriorated. The Klansmen of the 1920s reacted in a similar way. The reaction spawned by the more recent period of economic stagnation found new villains at whom to point—Hollywood, the World Bank, the United Nations, even the U.S. government—but the pattern was much the same. In each case large numbers of people have come to believe that some hidden, purposeful cabal must be at fault, and only its defeat can restore the America they love and of which they feel a part. And in each case as they have sought that end, the openness and tolerance of our society, and our commitment to our democratic ideals, have suffered.

The stagnation that so many ordinary Americans experienced in their personal economic situations, and even more so in their sense of their future prospects, abated sometime in the middle of the 1990s. From 1993 to the end of the decade, per capita income rose on average by a robust 2.6 percent per annum, well above the average gain during the prior two decades. More important, by the mid-1990s this stronger economic growth had begun to bring rising incomes to more than just those already at the upper end of the scale. After twenty years of little movement, the median family income rose, in today's dollars, from $46,300 in 1993 to $54,200 in 2000. What had been a slow increase in the incomes of working women became more rapid and, from 1995 on, even working men's incomes—including those of young men—began to rise again in real terms. In contrast to the 24 percent decline during the previous decades, the median wage for thirty-year-old men rose 19 percent, beyond inflation, by the end of the decade. Not surprisingly, the change attracted widespread attention in the popular media.[95]

At the same time, jobs became increasingly plentiful. Despite a continuing rise in the share of the population that is of working age, as well as in the percentage of the adult population actively in the workforce, unemployment rolls shrank. By the end of the 1990s fewer than 6 million would-be workers were jobless (in a labor force of 143 million), and the unemployment rate had dropped to a thirty-year low. Moreover, with inflation mostly low and stable, there was little indication that either the more favorable job market or the accompanying higher pay for the majority of workers was merely the product of an overheated economy, due to disappear with the next imminent turn of the business cycle. Especially in the latter half of the decade, rising incomes mostly reflected faster productivity gains, not a wage inflation that squeezed business profits. After a brief recession in 2001, those rapid productivity gains resumed.[96]

What lies behind the American economy's newly revitalized productivity growth remains a matter of ongoing debate. The surge of new investment in the latter half of the decade—net investment in new factories and machinery averaged 4 percent of national income in 1998–2000, a higher rate than in any three-year period since the beginning of the 1980s—was clearly a significant factor.[97] Within this overall investment boom, the increasingly pervasive use of desktop computers throughout the business world, together with rapidly spreading communication via the Internet, is especially noteworthy.[98] Other factors that plausibly may have contributed include changing patterns of business organization, retraining of labor, and general cost-cutting pressures associated with increasing global competition in the markets for many of the goods and even services that the American economy produces. The answer to the puzzle of what has accounted for America's faster productivity growth, and in particular the role played by computers—in short, does the computer represent a fundamental advance analogous to the steam engine, for example, or to electric power, or the internal combustion engine?—also carries strong implications for how durable the newly reestablished rise in incomes will prove to be.[99]

These questions notwithstanding, rising incomes after the early 1990s clearly affected public attitudes toward the nation's economy—although, as we have seen, doubts about America's long-run economic future, and especially about individual citizens' ability to attain "the American dream," persisted. By the end of the decade a poll conducted by the *Los Angeles Times* found that nearly 60 percent of the respondents who classified themselves as "lower or working class" thought their prospects for moving up were good, and a majority of all people surveyed agreed with the idea that anyone who works hard can get ahead.[100] By 2000 measured consumer confidence was at a record high.[101] Investors' enthusiasm likewise propelled the stock market to record highs. The resulting enormous returns on investment led ever more Americans—49 percent by 1998—to put at least some part of their savings into the stock market.[102] In contrast to 1992, when economic discontent was so widespread that the mantra of Bill Clinton's successful campaign for president was "It's the economy, stupid," in the 2000 election the chief economic issue was how much credit Clinton, and by association presidental contender Vice President Al Gore, were entitled to claim for America's strong performance.

As we have seen, a transition from economic stagnation to rising incomes does not immediately produce new social attitudes, nor, even more so, new public policy. Only with time do individuals realize that a lasting improvement has occurred, and it takes more time still for their renewed sense of security and eased frustration to shape popular views on social relations and national objectives. The shifting influence within political coalitions that produces new legislation typically follows yet later. Especially since in this instance it is difficult to date just when renewed expansion took hold, it is not surprising that many elements of the response to the two decades of stagnation that ended sometime around 1993—antipathy toward immigrants, ungenerosity toward the disadvantaged, resistance to affirmative action programs, growth of skinhead and militia groups, even violent acts like the Oklahoma City bombing—continued on for several years. By the end of the 1990s, however, signs of a different social and political climate had definitely appeared.

The area in which the most visible change occurred soonest was America's attitude toward receiving immigrants at home and engaging with the world abroad. In 1993, 64 percent of Americans polled said that immigrants mostly hurt the economy, while only 26 percent said they mostly helped. By 2000, a 44–40 majority held the opposite view.[103] Similarly, in 1993, 65 percent of Americans polled said they wanted immigration decreased, but by 1999 a 51–44 majority preferred keeping immigration at current levels or even increasing it.[104] Further, by the late 1990s opinion surveys showed that fewer than 10 percent considered immigration, either legal or illegal, a "major concern."[105] As events showed, a swing of this magnitude was sufficient—enough people had changed their minds, and among those who had not, the intensity of their feeling on this issue had softened enough—to make a difference politically.

As unemployment fell over these years, proposals to reduce the flow of legal immigrants mostly disappeared from the active political agenda. Indeed, by the end of the decade a coalition combining both conservative and liberal political groups (and co-chaired by a Republican former vice presidential candidate and a Democratic former cabinet secretary) had formed to campaign for an *easing* of immigration laws, including not just an expanded quota for workers with high-tech skills but also broader eligibility of refugees from wars and political chaos in other countries, and even legal status for many previous immigrants who had been living in the United States illegally.[106] New legislation passed in 2000 more than doubled the number of special skills visas, but omitted the other two proposals.[107]

In the same vein, under conditions of low unemployment and rapidly rising incomes the widening excess of imports over exports in the latter half of the 1990s triggered relatively little outcry for protectionism, and almost no action. By 2000 America's trade deficit in all goods had reached a record $452 billion, or 4.6 percent of national income (also a record).[108] Fully $84 billion of this deficit was from trade with China.[109] Yet Congress agreed to make permanent China's Most Favored Nation trade status with the United States, and to accept China as a member of the World Trade Organization. The one major national politician to place protectionist policies at the center of his proposed agenda was Pat Buchanan, whose widely publicized 1998 book, *The Great Betrayal,* called for high tariffs and other trade barriers to shield domestic American companies and American jobs from foreign competition. Despite the record-high trade deficit, Buchanan attracted so little support in his campaign for the 2000 Republican presidential nomination that he left the party altogether and ran instead on the Reform Party ticket. His showing in the national election was negligible. With profits high and unemployment low, protectionism had little popular appeal.

Increasingly in the 1990s, the United States, now the only remaining global superpower, also chose engagement over isolation in military and diplomatic dealings with the world at large, even in matters where (unlike the brief 1991 war against Iraq) few direct American interests were at stake. Although active interventions in conflicts abroad were initially hesitant and highly limited—for example, in Somalia and then in Bosnia—by 1999 America led the allied military effort to reverse Serbia's expulsion of 2 million ethnic Albanians from Kosovo. When a rolling series of currency and debt crises brought financial collapse to a series of Asian economies in 1997 and 1998, the U.S. Treasury, in cooperation with the International Monetary Fund, took a highly visible leadership role in restoring stability and pushing (in the view of some critics, far too hard and sometimes in the wrong direction) for policy reforms.[110] By the end of the decade Congress finally appropriated $926 million to pay the arrears on U.S. dues owed to the United Nations. On each of these fronts the connection to economics is far less direct than in the case of immigration and trade policies. Yet it is hardly a coincidence that these broader aspects of international engagement likewise flourished in the environment of renewed American economic prosperity.

At home, the ever expanding demand for labor broke down other barriers. Even young black men with a high school education or less, normally the group least likely to find and keep jobs, began to work in far greater numbers than ever before. Not surprisingly, the improvement was greatest in cities where overall unemployment was lowest. In areas where the local unemployment rate was consistently below 4 percent—Omaha, Des Moines, Raleigh-Durham, Madison (Wisconsin), Rochester (Minnesota), among others—the fraction of young, non-college-educated black men at work rose from barely one-half to nearly two-thirds. At the same time, these workers' pay drew closer to that of their white counterparts.[111] Nor were young men the only beneficiaries. Among single mothers with low job skills, nearly half were working by 1998 compared with fewer than one-third as of 1993.[112] Correspondingly, the early experience in moving long-term recipients off of the welfare rolls, now that TANF (Temporary Assistance for Needy Families) had replaced AFDC, went far more smoothly than many critics of the new program had anticipated.[113]

The end of the 1990s also saw an effective compromise on racial admissions programs in the public universities of those states that not long before had been the major battlegrounds over affirmative action. California, Florida, and Texas adopted new systems that guaranteed admission to those students placing in the top portion of their class (the top 4 percent in California, the top 10 percent in Texas, the top 20 percent in Florida) at *every* high school in the state.[114] Although none of these programs explicitly used race as an admissions criterion, because of continuing de facto segregation of so many high schools in these states the result was much the same. Non-white admissions to the state university systems in each of these states soon recovered to about the levels that had prevailed under explicit affirmative action.[115]

Finally, although there was little to show in actual legislation, the disposition of America's public discussion toward a variety of domestic policy issues also shifted during the 1990s. In place of earlier calls by prominent Republicans to abolish the Department of Education—for example, in Bob Dole's 1996 presidential campaign—in the 2000 campaign George W. Bush not only rejected any such intention but offered a variety of proposals to *increase* federal spending on education. The No Child Left Behind Act, passed in 2002, gave the federal government a more active role than ever before in primary and secondary education (although with little new funding behind it). Running for reelection in 2004, President Bush highlighted the new law as the flagship domestic accomplishment of his first term in office. Also missing from both the 2000 and 2004 Republican campaigns (except from Buchanan in 2000 before he dropped out) was much of the earlier rhetoric widely perceived as hostile to nonnatives, nonwhites, and non-Christians. Although reported instances of hate crimes continued to rise, by the end of the 1990s the broad public attention given just a few years earlier to the militia movement and groups like the Aryan Nations had dropped significantly. After peaking at 858 in 1996 the number of such organized groups fell to only 194 by 2000.[116]

Just as it is too soon to know whether the new era of widely distributed rising incomes that began in the early 1990s will prove durable, it is, even more so, too soon to judge with confidence whether rising incomes once again have brought, or will bring, an identifiable and durable redirection of American social attitudes and public policies. The 2001 business recession was not severe by postwar standards, but especially in the labor market the recovery to date has been disappointing. The quick return to rapid productivity growth, however, gives ground for optimism that in time incomes, and not just for those at the top, will likewise resume a robust increase.[117] If so, and if the renewed sense of getting ahead once again leads America's citizens toward a greater emphasis on opportunity and tolerance, that outcome will be consistent with the nation's prior experience.

Figure 8.1 gives an overview of the American experience in this regard from the end of the Civil War to the present. Over this time America's social and political system, and with it our sense of moral purpose as a people, have thrived when, and because, in historian David Potter's memorable phrase, "an economic surplus was available to pay democracy's promissory notes."[118] Sustained economic growth, grounded in rising productivity and resulting in rising incomes, has been the source of that surplus.

	Responses to *Growth*	Responses to *Stagnation*
Movements *toward* openness, tolerance, mobility, fairness, democracy	✓ Horatio Alger era (1865–80) ✓ Progressive era (1895–1919) ✓ Civil Rights era (1945–73) ✓ New beginnings ? (1993–)	✗ New Deal era (1929–39)
Movement *away from* openness, tolerance, mobility, fairness, democracy		✓ Populist era (1880–95) ✓ Klan era (1920–29) ✓ Backlash era (1973–93)

FIGURE 8.1

Consequences of Economic Growth Versus Stagnation:
America Since the Civil War

It would be foolish to pretend that whether or not citizens' incomes are rising is the sole determinant of how any nation's society evolves. Independent political forces both at home and abroad (including wars and, more recently, attacks by terrorists); the impact of new technologies; the pressures and opportunities presented by new ways of living and of making a living; such fundamentals as changing demographic trends: all are at work in shaping how people regard one another, collectively as well as individually. But the American experience suggests that widely shared economic growth or stagnation is also a powerful force in just this regard. As we have seen, there are cogent reasons why a society would respond to economic growth or its absence in the way that America's has. Further, at least in this respect America has not been unique.

PART III

OTHER TIMES, OTHER PLACES: THE EUROPEAN DEMOCRACIES

Chapter 9

Britain

What, then, is the overall strategic concept which we shall
inscribe today? It is nothing less than the safety and welfare, the
freedom and progress, of all the homes and families of all the
men and women in all the lands. . . . I have not spoken yet of
poverty and privation, which are in many cases the prevailing
anxiety. But if the dangers of war and tyranny are removed,
there is no doubt that science and cooperation can bring . . . an
expansion of national well-being beyond anything that has yet
occurred in human experience.

WINSTON CHURCHILL
Speech at Westminster College, March 1946[1]

The systematic influence of economic growth on the moral character of
society would be of substantial interest even if it were a feature of the
American experience only. But when we assess to what extent we should
take this relationship into account in how we regard economic growth, and
especially in how we evaluate policies that either facilitate or retard our
growth, it is also important to know whether the direction of social and
political change elsewhere has systematically reflected the improvement or
stagnation in living standards as well.

The United States is not the only country to have experienced a strong record of economic growth over the past two centuries and more, nor is it alone among today's high-income countries in having undergone periods of stagnation sufficient to cause many citizens to lose confidence in the future progress of their standard of living. In many western European economies, over the last quarter-century, wages have risen faster than in the United States for those who have had jobs but unemployment has been much more pervasive and persistent—in some countries typically 10 percent of the labor force or more, even in "good" times. Beginning in the mid-1990s most western European economies began to enjoy more vigorous growth than they saw in the 1980s and the post-OPEC-crisis 1970s, but the pace of expansion was both modest and irregular compared to that in the United States, and in the new decade growth has slowed once again. Especially in the larger continental countries, including France, Germany, Italy, and Spain, unemployment has remained stubbornly high. In the last few years of the 1990s job growth strengthened, and unemployment fell; but most recently the jobless rolls have been increasing, in some countries back to the levels of the early 1990s.[2]

Would a return to Europe's particular brand of stagnation present the same threat to the character of European societies that faltering incomes have often created in America? Attempting to answer such a question on the basis of the American experience alone would be foolhardy. So would trying to say whether any of the low-income and mostly nondemocratic countries in the developing world that have achieved especially rapid economic growth in recent years, like China, are likely to reform their political systems anytime soon. Or predicting what will happen if growth lapses once again in the East Asian economies, like Indonesia and South Korea, that stumbled in the region-wide financial turmoil of the late 1990s. Whether for purposes of policy guidance or merely as a matter of anticipating future developments, knowing whether the relationship between income growth and moral progress that we have seen in America's past is particular to just one country or applicable more broadly is essential to judging what implications to draw from it.

Knowing how widely applicable this link is can also provide important clues to how and why such a connection arises in the first place. Does the explanation lie in features that are unique to the American experience? Or in more universal aspects of human behavior, like the tendency we have seen for people to compare how they are living today not just to how they and their families lived in the past but also to how people around them live, and the much greater concern most people attach to losing ground compared to making gains? Such questions are unanswerable on the basis of examining the experience of the United States alone. We must look elsewhere as well.

Like the United States, the traditional European democracies now mostly have highly advanced industrial and even postindustrial economies. Their societies are, for the most part, relatively open, mobile, and tolerant. After allowing for differences in the cost of living, per capita income in most of the larger western European countries is now about 75 percent of that in the United States.³ Until fairly recently, Europe—although not just those countries that make up today's advanced industrial democracies—was the origin of most American immigrants.

And most of the countries for which reliable information about per capita incomes extends back more than a few decades are, indeed, the European democracies.⁴ As in America, the measured experience on average has been one of rising living standards for well over a century. Between 1869 and 2001, per capita income rose in real terms by 1.8 percent per annum in both France and Germany, identical to the growth rate in the United States, and by 1.4 percent per annum in Britain.⁵ But also as in America, growth in these countries has not been smooth, and at times incomes have fallen.⁶ Examining how the major political and social developments within these countries have corresponded to their respective experiences of increase or stagnation provides another valuable window on the consequences of economic growth.

Britain is the world's longest-standing democracy. But as we have seen from the American experience, what constituted a democracy in earlier times differs in important respects from what most people understand to be a genuine democracy today. Because in Britain a significant part of the evolution to a fuller democracy has occurred within roughly the past century and a half—the period for which reliable information about fluctuations in living standards is available—it is possible to situate most of the major steps along the way in the context of the economic setting of their time. As was true in the United States, the changes that have taken place in British society over these years have not uniformly or continuously taken a positive direction from the perspective of Enlightenment notions of the moral society. Identifying the economic background to the most important of the turns that Britain has taken in these dimensions can therefore shed light on how growth versus stagnation affects a society's moral progress.

Four specific acts of legislation over not quite a century, between the Napoleonic Wars and World War I, largely created today's modern British democracy. The early-nineteenth-century machinery for electing members to the House of Commons was at best chaotic and, in many respects, clearly at odds with representative democracy. A minority of members—80 out of 658, as of 1831—represented England's forty counties, and a smaller number represented counties in Wales, Scotland, and Ireland.[7] The electorate for purposes of these two-member county constituencies (one member per county in Wales and Scotland) consisted of adult males who owned at least a specified amount of real property. The remaining roughly 500 MPs represented the 314 one- or two-member "boroughs" to which British monarchs, over the centuries, had also granted parliamentary representation. Some of these boroughs, like the city of London and the nearby borough of Westminster, or other large cities like Liverpool and Bristol, or even towns like Preston and Coventry, clearly made sense as parliamentary constituencies. Many clearly did not.

The chief problem was the small number of eligible voters in many of the designated boroughs. With only a small and in many cases arbitrarily designated electorate responsible for choosing many MPs, the character of Parliament as a representative body was subject to serious question. Moreover, in an era when voting was open (secret ballots did not come into use in Britain until 1872) and bribery largely uncontrolled, the small number of voters in many boroughs rendered the election of MPs vulnerable to influence and corruption of a plainly nondemocratic nature.

In "rotten" boroughs, as they were commonly called, the electorate was sufficiently small that the local property magnate could effectively regard the associated seat in the Commons as his private property, and some seats actually traded as such. The borough of Camelford, for example, had just nine eligible voters in 1831. Gatton had only one. Dunwich, once a town on the Suffolk coast, had suffered so much coastline erosion that by 1832 its two MPs represented nothing more than a tiny bit of the North Sea. "Pocket" boroughs were somewhat larger than rotten boroughs, but still small enough that a patron capable of sufficient bribery or intimidation could consider the seat "in his pocket." In all, nearly 300 members of the Parliaments elected in the late 1820s and in 1830 represented either rotten or pocket boroughs.[8]

The Reform Act of 1832, often called the Great Reform Act, was the first significant step toward rationalizing this haphazard system. In large part because of the high political drama surrounding its passage, it has always held an aura of mystique in the history of British politics. The act abolished fifty-six rotten or pocket boroughs that had accounted for 111 members.[9] (Lord Grey, the prime minister, believed that the act's greatest weakness was its failure to eliminate them entirely.)[10] The act also nearly doubled the electorate, from less than half a million to over 800,000, largely by extending the franchise for the county constituencies to include men who rented property, or held property through long-term leases.[11] As a result, Britain's industrial, commercial, and professional upper-income classes gained the vote. In more abstract terms, the new property-based qualification was also significant in that it represented a universalistic criterion—to which, in principle, anyone might aspire—in place of the old system based either on family background or capricious holdovers from long before.[12]

Expanding the electorate was not the Reform Act's primary objective, however—abolishing the corrupt small-electorate boroughs was—and in some ways the act left the franchise even more restricted than before. For example, along with rotten and pocket boroughs the act abolished the privilege, previously granted from time to time by royal dispensation, that had allowed adult males in a designated borough to vote without having to meet any property qualification. In any case, an electorate of 800,000 out of a total population of 24 million hardly made Britain a democracy in the modern sense.[13]

Establishing the economic conditions in Britain leading up to the Reform Act is less straightforward than understanding what the act itself did and did not accomplish. A good part of the push for reform came from poorer people who hoped that electoral change would somehow increase their prosperity, but it is not certain how widespread this belief was. The limited data that exist for the period suggest that the country underwent a sharp depression in the years following the conclusion of the Napoleonic Wars in 1815, then a period of prosperity in the 1820s (interrupted for a while by the effects of a banking crisis in 1825), and then renewed depression and deflation in the early 1830s.[14] Occasional poor harvests, in what was still a predominantly agricultural economy, added further instability. As a result of the large and erratic fluctuations that ensued—together with the absence of modern record-keeping—it is simply not clear whether British subjects, during the agitation that surrounded the reform debate in 1831–32, thought they were getting ahead or falling behind. Even the timing of the renewed recession in the early 1830s is not known with certainty today.[15]

Whether the example of the Great Reform Act supports or contradicts the idea that economic growth fosters expanded democracy is therefore impossible to say. But for the three measures that followed over the next nine decades, which together had a far greater practical effect than the 1832 act, the economic background is clearer.

The Second Reform Act, passed in 1867, focused squarely on expansion of the electorate. The Liberals and the Conservatives, by then Britain's two major political parties, differed over by how much and in just what ways to achieve this objective, but the significant point is that each party sought at least the appearance of favoring a broader extension of the franchise. In the end, a combination of changes increased the electorate from 1.4 million to 2.5 million, in a population that by then still numbered only 25 million.[16] Within the borough constituencies, the new act came close to establishing universal adult male suffrage, limited primarily by a one-year residence requirement.

The Second Reform Act also heralded a significant change in how the British conducted politics. In the first subsequent election, in 1868, the Conservatives lost their parliamentary majority. Benjamin Disraeli, the prime minister, set an important precedent by resigning at once rather than waiting for the newly elected Parliament to meet and formally express its preference for the Liberals. Disraeli's action, which almost all subsequent prime ministers who lose elections have followed, was widely seen at the time as an acknowledgment that in the new postreform era it was the electorate, not the assembled MPs, who dismissed governments. A subsequent public indication of this new, more popular orientation of British politics, likewise widely perceived as such at the time—and today often considered the first modern political campaign—was the series of speeches on foreign policy that William Gladstone, who succeeded Disraeli (but then gave way to him once again in 1874), delivered to the general public in his "Midlothian campaign" preceding the election in 1880.*

Although the debate over the Second Reform Act occurred in the immediate context of a mild business recession, by the mid- to late 1860s British subjects could look back on a generation of mostly sustained economic expansion, primarily associated with advancing industrialization.[17] Between 1843 and 1865 growth of income in Britain had exceeded population growth in every year but four, and those exceptions were widely scattered over time. The average growth of real per capita income in the decade ending in 1865 was 1.4 percent per annum—a substantial achievement compared to the dismal overall record during much of the first half of the

---

*The 1867 reform debate had marked the beginning of the famous rivalry between Gladstone and Disraeli that was to dominate British politics for the next decade and a half.

nineteenth century. The astonishing pace of innovation not only boosted productivity but captured the public imagination. As we have seen, the Crystal Palace exhibition, which opened in London in 1851 in large part as a showcase for the application of new inventions to economic use, was a huge popular success. (The Dover–Calais undersea telegraph cable, which dramatically enhanced communications with Europe, was laid in the same year.) Even in 1867, at the bottom of a two-year recession, British income per capita was nearly 36 percent above what it had been a quarter-century earlier in real terms.[18]

In 1884 and 1885, in the course of the sustained period of economic weakness that by then affected both the United States and Europe, Parliament passed two measures that took the reform process substantially further. The Third Reform Act, energetically championed by the then Liberal MP and cabinet minister Joseph Chamberlain, and pushed through Parliament by Gladstone (once again the Liberal prime minister), extended to the county constituencies the broad male suffrage that the 1867 act had granted to the boroughs. The Redistribution Act, passed the next year at the insistence of the House of Lords—it was, in effect, the Lords' condition for approving the Third Reform Act—merged some of the smaller remaining boroughs, took seats away from others, and in their place created nearly 200 new one-member constituencies.[19] As a result of these two acts, the electorate increased from 3.2 million to 5.7 million (the population was now 31 million), and Britain's electoral map began to resemble its modern form. Of 670 constituencies, 647 now returned just one MP, and most were of a respectable size.[20]

The electoral reforms of the mid-1880s clearly stand as an exception to the idea that economic stagnation is an impediment to the strengthening of democracy. Britain did not enjoy a significant period of renewed expansion after the downturn at the beginning of the 1870s. In the decade and a half from 1871 through 1885, real income per capita in Britain advanced in only five years and fell in the other ten. The average growth rate was not even .2 percent per annum.[21]

The fourth and final major step in establishing modern British democracy—the Representation of the People Act, sometimes known informally as the Fourth Reform Act—was taken in 1918, at a time of substantial prosperity and growth. Spurred by wartime pressures not unlike those that led the next year to the Nineteenth Amendment in the United States, the act extended the franchise to the majority of adult British women.[22] The act also eased the residence requirement and other remaining restrictions on male voting. In all, the British electorate jumped from roughly 8 million before the war to 21.4 million (in a population of just under 39 million) who registered to vote in the election of 1918. Over 8 million of the new voters were women.[23]

Britain had enjoyed irregular but substantial economic growth in the years leading up to World War I, much of it based on expanding foreign trade. Over the ten years ending in 1918, British income per capita rose in every year but one (1912), and growth was especially strong at the outset of the war. Even after allowing for higher wartime prices, the average gain in income per capita over those ten years was an astonishing 3.1 percent per annum. By 1918 per capita income in Britain stood 36 percent above what it had been a decade earlier, and fully 56 percent above a quarter-century earlier.[24] The wartime prosperity had been especially beneficial to lower-income groups.[25] At the time of the Fourth Reform Act, therefore, the sense that people in Britain were getting ahead economically was widespread.

Because some of the landmark pieces of British social legislation in the nineteenth century became law in the immediate aftermath of the Great Reform Act, the economic conditions underlying these actions too remain as obscure as those behind the electoral reform itself. For example, although Britain had outlawed the slave *trade* in 1807, slavery continued to be legal in Britain's colonies and the plantation economy in the West Indies continued to rely on it. The suppression of legal importation of slaves resulted in a lively smuggling traffic, in which blacks were often transported across the Atlantic under conditions worse than those imposed by previously legal slave traders. The abolition movement led by William Wilberforce gained momentum throughout the 1820s, and one of the first major acts of the new Parliament that met in 1833 was to vote for an emancipation plan, with all slaves to be freed within twelve months (and £20,000 appropriated to compensate their owners).

Chattel slavery was not the only form of labor that attracted the attention of British reformers during this period. By the early nineteenth century the rapid advance of industrialization, especially in the north of England, had produced factories where working conditions were appalling. Angered especially by the plight of children, who worked up to sixteen hours at a time, often in shifts that went through the night, in 1830 an evangelical minister named Richard Oastler began a campaign for regulation of factory hours by publishing a widely read letter on "child slavery." Some members of Parliament then began to push for a "Ten Hours Bill" that would have limited children under eighteen to working no more than ten hours a day, and not at all at night. Because of the way in which most textile factories of the time combined adult and child labor, however, the bill would implicitly have limited most adults to a ten-hour day as well.

The Factory Act of 1833 did not go as far as the Ten Hours Bill, but it nonetheless marked Britain's first decisive movement toward the use of government authority to limit the direct hardships of working conditions in the new industrial economy. The legislation, which applied to virtually all textile factories, restricted children under eighteen to a twelve-hour day and those under thirteen to nine hours, all to fall between 5:30 a.m. and 8:30 p.m. Children under nine were barred from factory work altogether. The Factory Act also established boards of inspectors specifically charged to see to its enforcement, and it therefore proved effective where previous, more limited efforts at labor regulation had failed.

In contrast to the concern for both slave and free labor shown in these two landmark actions in 1833, the 1834 amendments to Britain's Poor Laws gave expression to a new lack of generosity—indeed, a harshness—toward both the working and nonworking poor. In place of the existing system that provided the poor with cash payments based on the size of their families, the 1834 amendments sought to end most "outdoor relief" and instead established "workhouses" designed to be so unpleasant that only those in dire straits would go there: separation of married couples, and of parents from their children; hard work for all residents older than seven; little exercise; few if any visitors. The motivating spirit was that the poor (or at least those among them deemed "able-bodied") were poor because of their own failings. Dickens's *A Christmas Carol*, published in 1843, was in part a commentary on the demoralizing effects of the new poor law system, especially after the economic downturn of 1837 left many of the working poor jobless and depressed the wages of those who still had work. (In the end, the new system failed; it proved so harsh that local governments had no choice but to provide outdoor relief in many cases.)

Because the economic data are unclear, establishing whether these significant steps in British social policy taken in 1833 and 1834 reflected the influence of economic growth or stagnation is impossible.[26] The debate over repeal of the Corn Laws, from the late 1830s through the mid-1840s, was a different matter, however. By then the British economy had clearly stagnated, and conditions for much of the working population had worsened. Britain suffered a financial crisis and, with it, a sharp economic decline in 1837. After a brief respite, income per capita fell during three successive years beginning in 1840. By 1842 the average real income was nearly back to the level of a decade earlier. Especially for low-income families, whose budgets were largely spent on food, poor harvests made matters even worse.[27]

The Corn Laws debate was not directly about social reform but rather protectionism: the Corn Laws imposed import restrictions on grain. But because the effect of these restrictions was to increase the price of bread, the issue became not just a theoretical debate over free trade but also a matter of distributive justice between mostly wealthy agricultural landlords and often poor consumers. Accordingly, the Anti–Corn Law League, led by Richard Cobden and John Bright, advanced arguments that were both economic and explicitly moral—repeatedly emphasizing (critics would say exaggerating) the outright hunger of working mothers and children. Parliament scaled back the grain import restrictions in 1842 and then repealed them altogether four years later. The effect was both to reduce rents on grain-producing land and to raise the standard of living of ordinary working families.[28] A system under which the poor paid to subsidize the rich had ended.[29]

The British economy was hardly doing well during the Corn Laws debate, so that on balance it is fair to consider their repeal more a response to stagnation than to growth. Even so, the matter is not as clear-cut as traditional British historiography implies. As one later historian argued, "The 1840s have always had a bad name, due partly to the writings of the Anti–Corn Law League, and partly to Engels' book *[The Condition of the Working Class in England in 1844]*. In fact, neither of these is a very reliable guide, since each was a form of propaganda. The phrase 'the hungry 'forties' does not seem to have been current at that time at all and was first widely in use at the beginning of the twentieth century, when the Free Traders saw the likelihood of a return to Protection."[30] The economy was advancing especially rapidly in the years immediately leading up to full repeal. Real income per capita grew by 4.7 percent per annum on average from 1843 to 1846, by which time it reached a level nearly 20 percent above that of the early 1830s.[31]

The latter half of the nineteenth century saw a variety of further efforts in such areas as labor regulation, education, criminal law, and provision for the poor. The most significant, from the perspective of creating a society more consistent with Enlightenment principles, was a series of administrative reforms and parliamentary actions that opened whole new areas of British life to those who had previously been either formally or implicitly excluded. In 1870 the civil service, until then largely a patronage preserve for candidates with family connections, was opened to entrance by competitive examination. Parallel reforms of the army and navy abolished the system whereby officers purchased their commissions.

Meanwhile, although parliamentary acts of 1854 and 1856 (by which time the British economy had nicely recovered from the previous hard times) had abolished religious restrictions for *students* at Oxford and Cambridge, only Anglicans could teach at Britain's "ancient universities." In 1871 Parliament passed the University Tests Act, which opened these posts to men of any religious belief. In the words of the English intellectual historian Noel Annan, these reforms—in university teaching, the civil service, and the military officer corps—collectively constituted a new "Glorious Revolution" for the descendants of those who had pushed for slavery abolition and the other major advances achieved nearly a half-century before.[32] The reforms of 1870 and 1871 followed a long period of robust economic growth. There had been only one brief economic downturn in the 1860s, and by 1870 British per capita income stood 20 percent above the level of a decade earlier and 35 percent above where it had been in 1850.[33]

Among the major British social reform movements in the twentieth century, the outstanding exception to the tendency for movement toward a more open society to occur when living standards are rising was the wide-ranging set of measures carried out under Prime Minister Herbert Henry Asquith between 1908 and 1911.[34] In 1906 the Liberals, under Sir Henry Campbell-Bannerman, won one of the largest electoral landslides in British history. Two years later Campbell-Bannerman died, and Asquith became prime minister until 1916.

The Liberal government, especially during the first years of Asquith's leadership, transformed British society. The "new Liberalism"—as David Lloyd George, one of its leading figures, labeled it in an electrifying speech in Swansea in October 1908—redefined the concept of citizenship to encompass new responsibilities of the society to the individual. Echoing Samuel Johnson a century and a half earlier, Lloyd George referred dramatically to "the sick, the infirm, the unemployed, the widows and the orphans" and went on to state, "No country can lay a real claim to civilization that allows them to starve."[35] In effect, Britain launched its New Deal a quarter-century before America.

The first step was a national old-age pension, proposed by Asquith himself just after he became prime minister. The pension was modest in amount, and available only at age seventy (in an era when life expectancy was much shorter than today). But recipients were not required to make a direct contribution in order to receive it, and its significance was great both practically and symbolically. In the end Lloyd George, who succeeded Asquith as chancellor of the exchequer, received most of the credit, and the pension was popularly known among grateful recipients as "the Lloyd George."

Three years later Parliament passed an even broader measure, which presaged two additional elements of the "social safety net" now in place in almost all modern democracies. The 1911 Insurance Act, also sponsored by Lloyd George as chancellor, provided "sick pay" (disability insurance in today's language) for all workers, as well as short-term unemployment insurance (up to fifteen weeks) for workers in designated industries, including textiles, shipbuilding, steelmaking, and construction, considered to be particularly vulnerable to large fluctuations in employment. The unemployment insurance measure in particular was a reflection of the economic experience of the first decade of the new century, when most workers had little or no savings and Britain suffered especially wide cyclical swings. Both insurance schemes were contributory—in effect, the idea was to force workers collectively to save for themselves—but on highly favorable terms. (Lloyd George's slogan was "ninepence for fourpence.") Like the old-age pension, both schemes were also highly significant in their immediate practical effect as well as in the path they set for the future, in Britain and elsewhere.

Perhaps the best-known reform of this remarkable period under Asquith was not economic but political: the Parliament Act of 1911, which limited the House of Lords to at most delaying, not permanently vetoing, legislation passed by the Commons, and, further, took away the Lords' authority over "money bills" entirely.[36] The trigger for these changes was the need to pay for the Liberals' new social programs. In 1909 the Lords had vetoed the additional taxes that Lloyd George included in his "People's Budget" to meet the increase in spending made necessary by the new pension system and also Britain's ambitious program of battleship construction in the recently accelerated arms race against Germany. After two parliamentary elections fought over the issue in 1910, and facing the prospect of the king's creating hundreds of new peers so as to overwhelm the traditional Conservative majority in the House of Lords, in 1911 the Lords acceded to the Parliament Act. Their power has remained diminished ever since.

Old age pensions, disability insurance, unemployment insurance, and a diminution of the hereditary component of British government held over from feudal times—not to mention some subsequent measures like partial disestablishment of the Church of England and elimination of plural voting for the privileged few—marked the first half of Asquith's premiership as one of the major eras of social reform in Britain in the twentieth century. But none of this was a response to strong economic growth. Beginning in 1900, a series of financial panics and business downturns had wracked the British economy. Growth in per capita income averaged less than .5 percent per annum over the next ten years.[37] In 1908, when Parliament voted "the Lloyd George," income per capita was within 1 percent of what it had been a decade earlier. Despite a solid recovery during the next few years, by 1911 income per capita was within .4 percent of a decade before. Like the New Deal in the United States, the Asquith reforms stand out as a striking exception.[38]

The two other periods of major social reform in Britain during the twentieth century occurred against the backdrop of powerfully rising incomes. Like the reforms of the Asquith era, the set of measures put in place after World War II focused primarily on social insurance. First outlined during the war in the widely heralded report drafted for the Churchill government by economist William Beveridge, this wave of changes fell to Clement Attlee's postwar Labour government to implement.[39] But in fact both parties endorsed the Beveridge program, during the war as well as during the 1945 election. As early as 1943, Churchill had delivered one of his famous radio broadcasts, committing his government to "national compulsory insurance for all classes for all purposes from the cradle to the grave."[40] At the same time, he established a new Ministry of Reconstruction, and then the even more important cabinet-level Reconstruction Committee, to plan for Britain's postwar society. In 1944 this powerful committee issued three key policy statements: on social insurance, health, and employment. (The White Paper on employment, which committed the government to seek to maintain "a high and stable level of employment after the war," presaged America's 1946 Employment Act.)[41] By 1945 the stage was set for a host of new social programs, regardless of who won the July election.[42]

The best-known element of the Beveridge program was national health insurance, which Parliament approved in 1946 and which went into effect two years later.[43] The National Insurance Act, also passed in 1946, consolidated and extended Britain's existing disability and unemployment insurance, even setting the old age pension at "full subsistence level" (contrary to the less generous recommendation of the Beveridge Report). The consensus favoring these steps continued to be bipartisan. When the Conservatives returned to power in 1951, again under Churchill, the only noteworthy measure that they undid was the Labour government's nationalization of the iron and steel industry.

Both in 1942 when Churchill's wartime government released the Beveridge Report, and later in the decade when Attlee acted on it, the British economy was growing solidly. Britain had begun to recover from the Great Depression before the United States, and British business had enjoyed an uninterrupted robust expansion from 1934 on. By 1942 income per capita was 45 percent above the pre-depression peak in 1929. Despite the predictable contraction due to postwar demobilization, in 1948 per capita income was still 11 percent above the final prewar year a decade earlier, and 26 percent above the pre-depression peak.[44] No doubt the extraordinary feelings of national camaraderie created by the shared dangers and hardships of the war, not just among the men fighting abroad but on the home front too, played a major role in motivating the Beveridge reforms. But rising incomes contributed as well.[45] Indeed, as robust economic growth continued into the 1950s (by 1960 per capita income was another 33 percent higher than in 1948), further changes made most of these programs more generous.

Two decades later, during the vigorous economic expansion of the 1960s, Parliament again undertook a series of significant moves toward a more open, in this instance tolerant, society. While the measures enacted lacked the dramatic scale and scope of the two earlier waves of twentieth-century domestic reform, taken together they nonetheless amounted to a noteworthy period in British social policymaking. Harold Wilson was prime minister at the time, but the major impetus for most of these measures came from Roy Jenkins.[46]

Two separate acts addressing race relations, an increasingly sore aspect of British society once postwar immigration reached large volume, stood at the center of the reforms. The Race Relations Act of 1965, passed just before Jenkins became home secretary, banned racial discrimination in public places as well as racial restrictions on the transfer of property. Jenkins then instigated the Race Relations Act of 1968—which Parliament passed shortly after he had left the Home Office to become chancellor of the exchequer—banning discrimination in housing, employment, and commercial services like insurance, as well as discriminatory advertising. Jenkins also abolished theater censorship (which had become an archaic relic, still the responsibility of the lord chamberlain), decriminalized private homosexuality among consenting adults, and eased restrictions on divorce.

The 1960s stand out in Britain as the years of the strongest sustained economic growth in the twentieth century. Income per capita rose in every year but one between 1959 and 1973, increasing on average by 2.9 percent per annum after allowing for higher prices. In 1968, when Parliament passed the second Race Relations Act, per capita income was 33 percent above the decade earlier level, and 66 percent above two decades earlier. Just as the American civil rights movement and Lyndon Johnson's Great Society initiatives in the 1960s had drawn strength from the nation's robust growth of that era, so too did the Jenkins reforms grow out of Britain's economic prosperity.

As with the American experience, for purposes of understanding the effects of economic growth or stagnation on social progress, what does *not* happen is sometimes just as significant as what does. In Britain the contrast between the far-reaching reforms promised by Churchill during World War II and implemented by Attlee immediately after the war, and the unfulfilled promises made by Lloyd George during World War I, is an especially useful case in point.

Lloyd George replaced Asquith as prime minister in 1916 and soon began planning for the country's postwar needs. The government Reconstruction Committee, previously established by Asquith, was upgraded to the status of a ministry. During the next election campaign, in 1918, Lloyd George pledged to create a postwar Britain "fit for heroes," including health services, public transportation, and jobs for "demobbed" veterans. The centerpiece of the program was housing. The Reconstruction Ministry estimated that as a result of population growth and the wartime halt in construction, Britain would need 800,000 new housing units soon after the war ended.[47]

Lloyd George continued as prime minister for another four years, during which Britain fell on hard economic times. A sharp and prolonged decline from 1919 until 1922 depressed income per capita by nearly one-third, and it was not until the mid-1930s that incomes recovered to the level they had reached on the eve of the war.* Unemployment rose to nearly

---

*The post–World War I economic decline was in many respects an international phenomenon, as was intermittent weakness during much of the 1920s. But Britain's problem in this regard became greater than elsewhere after 1925, when the country returned to the gold standard at the prewar parity. Moreover, the fact that prices were falling in many other countries during the 1920s (especially, as we have seen, in the United States) made Britain's need for deflation in order to make the gold parity sustainable all the more severe.

15 percent in 1921. One consequence of the resulting economic distress was periodic social unrest, highlighted later on by a nine-day general strike in May 1926.[48] The more immediate result was that Lloyd George's attempts to implement his economic and social program failed.

Several acts passed shortly after the war provided Lloyd George's intended subsidies for homebuilding (by both private companies and local authorities), and a 1920 act expanded the coverage of unemployment insurance. But the tide of government action soon turned. In 1921 a committee under the leadership of Sir Eric Geddes, head of the recently created Ministry of Transport, recommended a major scaling back of government spending. The "Geddes Axe" cut back government efforts on education, rail transportation, housing—only 200,000 of the planned 800,000 units were built—and even war pensions.[49] At the same time, the Safeguarding of Industries Act imposed high tariffs on imports of glass, chemicals, and electrical instruments, thus placing Britain firmly on the path to protectionism.

The fiscal retrenchment begun in 1921 probably exacerbated the economic downturn then in progress. More to the point, Lloyd George's "land fit for heroes" remained just a wartime dream. Ironically, a quarter-century later continuing bitterness over Lloyd George's failure, especially among families of working-class veterans, may have helped defeat Churchill in the 1945 election and also helped ensure that Attlee's post–World War II government would indeed implement the Beveridge Report. British voters may have been reluctant to trust yet another great wartime prime minister to fulfill his promises for postwar domestic programs, and politicians of all parties feared the consequences of attempting to wield another Geddes Axe after the sacrifices required to defeat Hitler. As one World War I veteran put it, "We had been promised a land fit for heroes; it took a hero to live in it. I'd never fight for my country again."[50]

There were also earlier examples of proposed reform thwarted at least in part by an environment of economic stagnation. Building on the momentum generated by the Reform Act of 1832 and the Factory Act of 1833, a variety of new reformist movements flourished in 1830s Britain. Some, like Robert Owen's Grand National Consolidated Trades Union, were plainly socialist in their aims and had little prospect of attracting meaningful support from the middle class. Others focused on narrower issues, including the movement that developed into the Anti–Corn Law League at the end of the decade. The one that attracted the most attention and support before the Corn Laws debate erupted in full in the 1840s was the Chartist movement, so called because of the "People's Charter" that a group called the

London Working Men's Association published in 1838 and first presented to Parliament, as a petition, the next year.

The charter presented six demands for further electoral reform, of which the two that resonate most strongly today were universal male suffrage and voting by secret ballot. (The others were equal-size electoral districts, annual Parliaments, an end to the requirement that members of Parliament own property, and salaries for MPs.) Parliament's refusal to discuss the Chartist petition led to rioting in some cities and a show of force by the army designed to discourage more disturbances. A second petition in 1842, this time centered on universal male suffrage and reform of the now-hated Poor Laws, led to the same result.[51]

In time, every Chartist demand except annual Parliaments became a reality in Britain. But in the late 1830s and the 1840s, the movement got nowhere. As always, the reasons lay partly in the politics of the movement itself. Like the American populists of a half-century later, who failed to make the alliance they sought with urban workers and therefore achieved little of their agenda (including many reforms that came about later), the Chartists failed to attract support from Britain's middle classes. But the economic climate of the time—the aftermath of the 1837 decline, and then the especially sharp drop of 1840–42—was not conducive to middle-class sympathy for the working class, nor to political support for working-class aims.[52]

Not all aspects of Britain's social and political development over the last two centuries have represented moral progress, of course, and examining some of the leading episodes that took British society in different directions sheds further light on how the difference between economic growth and stagnation affects a society's moral character. In the aftermath of the Napoleonic Wars, widespread economic hardship led in Britain to a series of "radical" (as they were perceived at the time) calls for economic relief, as well as for improved representation in national politics for the new industrial towns. Driven by recollections of the French Revolution, however, the Tory government under Lord Liverpool responded mostly with spies, soldiers, and repressive legislation. The resulting social tension reached its height on August 16, 1819, when the Manchester Radical Union sponsored an outdoor open meeting at nearby St. Peter's Fields. A crowd of some 60,000 turned out to hear the famed radical speaker Henry "Orator" Hunt. When the local magistrates decided to arrest Hunt rather than allow him to speak, the volunteer yeomen assigned to make the arrest became swallowed up in the crowd, and a professional cavalry troop armed with sabers had to take over. In the resulting confusion the cavalry charged the crowd, killing eleven and wounding several hundred.[53]

In a satirical reference to Britain's great victory over Napoleon just four years earlier—the regiment of hussars sent to St. Peter's Fields had also fought at Waterloo—the British press promptly labeled the tragedy "the Peterloo massacre." The opposition Whigs demanded a parliamentary inquiry, but the Tories not only held firm but went on to pass the notorious "Six Acts," which restricted civil liberties in ways rarely even contemplated in peacetime Britain in the nearly two centuries since. The new laws increased the state's powers of search, prohibited unauthorized meetings, imposed stamp taxes intended to make even cheap newspapers too expensive for popular readership, empowered the courts to order destruction of publications deemed seditious or blasphemous, and provided for accelerated trials of individuals charged with sedition.[54] (No doubt part of the motivation underlying the government's forceful and unyielding response was the lesson, from France, that once popular agitation got out of hand the result might be outright revolution.) This unfortunate episode, the last such wholesale assault on British civil liberties, clearly occurred during a time of widespread economic distress.[55]

A similarly distinctive wave of repression occurred nearly a century later, under Asquith. This time the focus was the suffragette campaign for women's right to vote. That Asquith opposed female suffrage with such intensity seems somehow out of character. As we have seen, despite a stagnant economy throughout the first decade of the century, he led the way to a series of reforms that transformed British society. Moreover, a majority of his party's MPs supported women's suffrage. But Asquith was personally opposed, and his government reacted fiercely to those who agitated for it.

Beginning in 1906, militant organizations like Emmeline Pankhurst's Women's Social and Political Union had engaged in a variety of tactics that covered the spectrum from the mildly annoying to the severely disruptive.[56] WSPU activists interrupted political speeches, invaded the House of Commons, chained themselves to railings outside the Houses of Parliament, broke windows, and even placed bombs in mailboxes.[57] The government responded by arresting the protesters, often with substantial violence on the part of the police. Once in jail, some of the women staged hunger strikes. The government resorted to forced feedings, which required having a guard forcibly insert a tube into a woman's throat while others held her down. (The analogy to rape was not lost on the British press.) Public revulsion at these practices led to passage of the Prisoners Temporary Discharge for Ill-Health Act—popularly called the "Cat and Mouse Act"—which enabled the prison authorities to release a hunger striker from jail but rearrest her as soon as she had recovered. Mrs. Pankhurst herself went to prison several times, and in 1913 she was sentenced to a three-year term. When war broke out the next year, however, she called off the WSPU campaign and the government released all suffragette prisoners.

What is astonishing about the government's actions is not so much Asquith's opposition to giving women the vote—others were opposed too, although the tide in favor of women's suffrage did become overwhelming a decade later—but the extraordinary means to which his government went to stifle the pro-suffrage agitation. Britain had not experienced this degree of personal repression for decades, nor would it again. Especially in the period through 1912, the government's reaction against the suffragettes clearly fit the economically stagnant climate of the time.

In much the same way that repression of the suffragettes stood at variance with the more general evolution of domestic policy in Britain during the Asquith period, the social reformist years of the 1960s had their exception too: immigration policy. Significant immigration of nonwhites to Britain had begun in the 1950s. In 1962, when incomes were already rising solidly (and had done so for nearly fifteen years), Parliament under Harold Macmillan's Conservative government passed the Commonwealth Immigrants Act, which for the first time restricted the entry into Britain of citizens from the Commonwealth countries. The motivation behind the bill was openly racial. Moreover, the prejudice was bipartisan. Frank Soskice, the home secretary in the new Labour government that took office in 1964, publicly opined that "If we do not have strict immigration rules, our people will soon be coffee-coloured."[58]

After Britain granted independence to Kenya in 1963, Kenyans of Indian descent sought to escape persecution by emigrating to Britain. Over the next few years the inflow steadily increased. The Labour government declared the situation an emergency and responded with a second Commonwealth Immigrants Act, passed in 1968. Under the new act, possession of a British passport did not grant automatic right of entry to the United Kingdom: the prospective immigrant had to have, in addition, a parent or grandparent who had been born in the U.K. As was intended, the act heavily restricted immigration of nonwhites from Africa and Asia, while leaving the door substantially more open to Canadians, Australians, and New Zealanders. At just the time when Britain was bolstering its native citizens' civil liberties, therefore—including taking action to bar domestic racial discrimination—British immigration policy became not just more restrictive but deliberately discriminatory on racial lines.

Finally, much of what determines the moral character of any society takes place apart from the world of government action and party politics. Popular feelings—expressed in the press, in the literature of the time, and sometimes even in public mass actions—can often tell as much about what is going on in a country as any review of elections won and legislation passed. Attitudes toward religious minorities are a useful case in point.

Benjamin Disraeli, the Conservative who first became prime minister in 1868, just after passage of the Second Reform Act, was the first and only Jew to hold that office in Britain and one of the few to achieve the top political post in any modern democracy then or since. Although Disraeli had been baptized in the Church of England as a child, British society clearly regarded him as a Jew. It was also clear, from both his actions and his writings—especially his romantic portrayal of the fictional character Sidonia in his novel *Coningsby*, together with the broader historical theme he developed in *Tancred*—that he not only regarded himself as a Jew but took substantial pride in his family background.[59]

Over time, following the Napoleonic Wars, Britain had removed the formal restrictions barring Jews from participating in politics and other aspects of public life. Beginning in 1826 Jews could be naturalized as British subjects. In 1858 it became possible for practicing Jews to become members of Parliament—the first Jewish MP was Lionel Rothschild, who had been elected several times previously but had been barred from taking his seat—and after 1866 it became possible for a practicing Jewish peer to sit in the House of Lords. (The first to do so, albeit not until some years later, was Nathan Rothschild, Lionel's son.) In 1871, just at the end of the period of strong economic growth that lasted from the mid-1850s through the 1860s, the Promissory Oaths Act finally removed the last formal disqualification of Jews from British public life.[60]

The British economy turned in the 1870s, however, and so in time did public opinion about religious diversity. The specific development that attracted attention to the issue and also created an excuse in some eyes was the seemingly callous lack of concern exhibited by Disraeli toward the brutality with which the Ottoman empire put down a rebellion among its Christian subjects in Bulgaria in 1876. Disraeli may or may not have been right that the realpolitik of Britain's need to defend Turkey against Russia should outweigh popular revulsion over the "Bulgarian Horrors." But his dismissive response to questions on the subject in the House of Commons—made all the worse by an attempt to be witty in answering—did nothing to attract sympathy to his position, or to him personally.*

Gladstone, and Disraeli's other political opponents, seized the opportunity to introduce anti-Semitism as a political weapon, arguing that Jews in general, Disraeli included, were pro-Turkish because Jews typically received much better treatment in Turkey than in Russia or elsewhere in eastern Europe. As the decade went on, these attacks appeared in the Liberal press and even in scholarly journals allied with Liberal party causes. Much of this discussion, reexamining whether Jews were fit to participate in Britain's (or any other country's) politics, took on a pseudoscientific gloss of a now recognizably nineteenth-century flavor in which racism dressed up as biology increasingly reinforced the more traditional religious prejudice. New extremist journals, including Henry Labouchere's *Truth*, emerged to exploit the fever. As would happen in America beginning a decade or so later, the popular fiction of the day featured obviously Jewish characters portrayed in ways ranging from merely unflattering to far worse. (Baron Glumthal, the mighty German banker in Charles Lever's *Davenport Dunn*, was an obvious Rothschild caricature. The uncouth Melmotte in Trollope's *The Way We Live Now*, is another example, although here—and the contrast may have been part of Trollope's intended point—the morally upstanding Brehgart is Jewish as well.) To be sure, anti-Semitic prejudice had long been a staple of British popular opinion and had confronted Disraeli throughout his career. But this kind of organized anti-Semitism, especially in politics, was new.

While the immediate cause of this efflorescence of British anti-Semitism stemmed from Turkey's Bulgarian atrocities and Disraeli's apparently casual dismissal, the economic stagnation of the late 1870s into the 1880s clearly created a climate in which this movement rose and spread. After 1871 per capita income in Britain declined in five of the next six years, and then in five of the next seven years after that. Throughout the early 1880s, average real income was little changed from a decade earlier. In short, living standards stagnated and tolerance eroded.

---

*In one exchange, Disraeli retorted, "I cannot doubt that atrocities have been committed in Bulgaria; but that girls were sold into slavery, or that more than 10,000 persons have been imprisoned, I doubt. In fact, I doubt whether there is prison accommodation for so many, or that torture has been practiced on a great scale among an Oriental people who seldom, I believe, resort to torture, but generally terminate their connection with culprits in a more expeditious manner." William Flavelle Monypenny and George Earle Buckle, *The Life of Benjamin Disraeli, Earl of Beaconsfield*, Vol. 2 (London: John Murray, 1929), p. 915.

The two major eruptions of organized anti-Semitism in Britain in the century and more since Disraeli's day have likewise occurred at times of economic hardship. Although South Wales had experienced scattered anti-Semitic violence in 1911, the most visible impact at the national level occurred the next year. The triggering event this time was the revelation that two members of Asquith's cabinet—Attorney General Rufus Isaacs, and Lloyd George, then chancellor of the exchequer—had invested in the American Marconi Radio Company at the same time that the British government was contracting with British Marconi, the American company's parent, to establish a chain of radio stations around the world to enable the Admiralty to improve its communications with Royal Navy ships. Godfrey Isaacs, Rufus's brother and the managing director of British Marconi, bought shares as well. Although it was public knowledge that the negotiations were in progress, the purchases took place before the contract was publicly announced, and so the men's actions drew widespread accusations of what amounted to insider trading (though both Rufus Isaacs and Lloyd George lost money on their investment).

After an embarrassing report by a select committee, Parliament soon lost interest in the matter. But the fact that the Isaacs brothers were Jewish—as was Herbert Samuel, the postmaster general who gave final approval to the contract on the government's behalf—proved irresistible to anti-Semites, who used newspapers like the *National Review* and *Eye Witness* not only to keep the scandal alive but to allege a variety of ever wider conspiracies.[61] In this instance the economic background of the time was certainly conducive to the public outbreak of prejudice that occurred. Fairly sharp economic downturns had occurred in both 1902–1903 and 1906–1908, and by 1911 real income per capita was little greater than it had been a decade earlier.

The riots that occurred a quarter-century later in London's East End, marking Britain's first experience in modern times with mass political violence motivated in significant part by religious or racial prejudice, grew out of the economic and political frustrations of the 1930s. The British suffered less than did Americans during the depression, and, as we have seen, their economy began to recover somewhat earlier. But unemployment remained high, reaching over 21 percent in 1931, and few people saw themselves getting ahead. In 1936, when the riots occurred, average incomes had been rising for three years. Even so, per capita income in real terms was still where it had been in the distressed year of 1911 (which in turn was about the same as in 1901).

In 1932 a prominent former MP and cabinet official considered by some to be a potential future prime minister, Oswald Mosley, had become inspired by a visit to Mussolini's Italy and founded the British Union of Fascists. Soon afterward, Lord Rothermere's press empire, centered on the *Daily Mail* newspaper, began forcefully promoting fascism as the only alternative to socialism, with articles by Rothermere himself carrying titles like "Hurrah for Blackshirts."[62] Beginning in 1934, as Hitler replaced Mussolini as the object of Mosley's admiration, the BUF became openly anti-Semitic and began to focus its operations on the East End of London, an extremely poor section where half of Britain's Jewish population lived. By 1935 the press began to report an increasing volume of fascist attacks in the area, mostly involving broken windows and personal assaults.

On October 4, 1936 (a Sunday), the BUF attempted to stage a march of some 3,000 uniformed members through a succession of East End neighborhoods, with a speech by Mosley at each stop. Anti-fascists erected barricades to stop them. Despite police intervention, the outcome was a large-scale melee (prompted dubbed the "Battle of Cable Street"), in which both fascists and anti-fascists were injured. Shock over the mass violence prompted the government to pass the Public Order Act, which struck at the BUF in several key ways, including banning private quasi-military organizations and forbidding the wearing of uniforms for political activity.[63] But the BUF—renamed the British Union of Fascists and National Socialists, to highlight its affinity to Germany's Nazi Party—continued its activities until it was outlawed (and Mosley himself interned) in 1940. Although the fascists' influence on formal British politics was small, their ready ability to incite popular violence reflected attitudes that are familiar from episodes of economic stagnation not just in Britain but elsewhere.

Britain's most significant modern encounter with racially motivated mass violence was both longer lasting and far more devastating, but in this case the role of economic forces is less straightforward. In April 1980, a confrontation between police officers and suspected drug dealers in the largely working-class city of Bristol erupted into a fierce battle between more than fifty officers and some 2,000 mostly black local residents. In the end twenty-two of the police officers had to be hospitalized, and most of the rest suffered lesser injuries.[64] Just a year later, a similar outbreak occurred in the heavily black London suburb of Brixton. This time the rioting lasted for several days, and the injured included 279 police officers and forty-five local residents.[65] In July 1981, the rioting spread to Liverpool and Manchester, and further riots took place in the London suburb of Toxteth. Several weeks later, Toxteth erupted yet again.

The riots of 1980–81 were clearly an expression of frustration among mostly nonwhite urban populations whose economic situation and prospects were dismal. Moreover, Britain, like much of the industrialized world, was suffering a significant recession in 1980–81 in the wake of the OPEC cartel's recent quadrupling of oil prices. In 1979 conventional political opinion had been that the existing unemployment, then in excess of 1 million, virtually guaranteed the Labour government's loss in that year's election. By 1981 Britain had 3 million unemployed. Unemployment was especially concentrated among nonwhites in just the kind of urban areas where the rioting occurred.

Even so, economic growth in Britain overall had been strong for much of the decade and more leading up to the rioting. Despite the recession, nationwide income per capita in 1981 stood 15 percent above the level of a decade earlier, and 46 percent above what it had been a decade before that. The specific economic distress of those who rioted no doubt contributed to their frustration, and the astonishingly high nationwide unemployment meant that looking for a job offered them little prospect for improvement. But Britain's economic situation at the time of the 1980–81 riots included elements of strong growth too, so that framing what happened as a specific response to one kind of economic backdrop or another is impossible.

Figure 9.1 summarizes the relationship connecting major movements in the tenor of British society, and in the development of Britain's democracy, to economic growth or stagnation. (It omits the landmark legislation of the early 1830s—the first Reform Act, the Factory Act, and the Poor Law amendments—as well as the 1980–81 race riots, because of the difficulty in each case of judging the underlying economic conditions.)

The relationship is not exact—nor should it be—since economic growth or its absence is hardly the only influence affecting social and political development. Among the exceptions, the most important, and the most clear-cut, is the set of sweeping reforms carried out by the Asquith government during 1908–11. But on the whole, the British experience, like that of the United States, indicates that a society is more likely to achieve moral progress when its citizens' standard of living is rising, and to move in the opposite direction when living standards stagnate.

	Responses to *Growth*	Responses to *Stagnation*
Movement *toward* openness, tolerance, mobility, fairness, democracy	✓ Second Reform Act (1867) ✓ Civil Service and Army-Navy reforms (1870) ✓ University Tests Act (1871) ✓ Promissory Oaths Act (1871) ✓ Women's suffrage (1918) ✓ Beveridge reforms (1942–48) ✓ Jenkins reforms (1965–67)	✗ Corn Law Repeal (1842, 1846) ✗ Third Reform Act (1884) ✗ Asquith Reforms (1908–11)
Movement *away from* openness, tolerance, mobility, fairness, democracy	✗ Immigration Acts (1962, 1968)	✓ Peterloo repressions (1819) ✓ Failure of Chartism (1839–42) ✓ Organized anti-Semitism (1876, 1912) ✓ Repression of suffragettes (1906–14) ✓ Geddes Axe to Lloyd George programs (1921–22) ✓ East End riots (1936)

FIGURE 9.1

Consequences of Economic Growth Versus Stagnation:
Britain Since the Napoleonic Wars

Chapter 10

France

[E]verything is connected in the misfortunes of a nation. . . . .
We have to bring about, despite great difficulties, a drastic
reconstruction that will make it possible for each man and
woman to lead a life of greater ease, security, and happiness, and
that ought to increase our numbers and make us more powerful
and united. We must preserve the freedom that we have
safeguarded with so much effort.

CHARLES DE GAULLE
Speech at Bayeux, June, 1946[1]

The French experience is less straightforward than that of either the
United States or Britain, for several reasons. France in the modern era has
undergone far sharper discontinuities, especially in political structure. Over
the last two centuries or so, the French have lived under five distinct
republics and two empires, not to mention a variety of other shorter-lived
arrangements. Some of the more dramatic of these discontinuities have
occurred in the wake of either wars or organized domestic violence of a kind
not seen in Britain in modern times (the last English civil war was in the
1640s) nor in post-revolutionary America except for the Civil War. In addition to the Revolution of 1789, France also had lesser revolutions in 1830

and 1848, and the events surrounding the Paris Commune in 1871 amounted to a small-scale civil war as well. Again unlike Britain and the United States, France has repeatedly experienced military defeat, occupation of its territory by foreign troops, and, in some cases, the need to accede to terms laid down by foreign powers. It would be astonishing if the social and political reverberations from these extreme traumas did not overwhelm the influence of rising or falling living standards at several important junctures.

A more serious impediment is the profound ambiguity that surrounds many of the landmark developments in French domestic society and politics. For example, the Dreyfus Affair, which dominated French politics for half a decade beginning in 1894, still stands out, after more than a century, as one of the most significant events in the country's modern political and social history. But was the main import of this episode the pervasive climate of anti-Semitism surrounding it, and the suppression of individual rights represented in Captain Dreyfus's false conviction for treason and his imprisonment on Devil's Island? Or was the more important development the reaction of a French society that, energized by Georges Clemenceau's political agitation and by Émile Zola's startling open letter "J'Accuse," refused to let the matter rest until Dreyfus was exonerated and both the plot against him and the subsequent cover-up were fully revealed?[2] The French at the time vigorously—indeed, violently—debated just this question.

Among French historians, that debate continues today. Many now agree that "L'Affaire" strengthened the French republic in the years immediately afterward: in one view, the Dreyfus Affair "ultimately served the cause of the Republic, strengthened parliamentary democracy, ensured the defeat of the forces of reaction, and ruined the hope for a restoration of the old order."[3] But there is little question that it also inspired a profusion of reactionary sentiment that would haunt the Third Republic for decades afterward, reaching its apex in the right-wing triumph at Vichy in 1940.[4]

But these ambiguities notwithstanding, enough of the major events of France's recent history do lend themselves to less controversial interpretation to make it instructive to place them systematically into their economic context.

France's longest-lived governmental regime since 1789 was the Third Republic. Established by civilian politicians in September 1870, within days of the humiliating French defeat in the first significant battle of the Franco-Prussian War—a battle that culminated in a surrender in which the Germans took more than 100,000 French prisoners, including the emperor

Napoleon III—the Third Republic survived until July 1940, when the Germans again overran France at the beginning of World War II. Initially proclaimed by Jules Favre and Léon Gambetta, the Third Republic over the years had among its leaders such outstanding figures as Clemenceau, Aristide Briand, and Raymond Poincaré.

Not all of the Third Republic's leaders were so distinguished, however, nor were its politics always stable. Over the not quite seventy years of its existence, there were ninety-nine successive governments. But from its inception the new regime was fairly democratic, especially by European standards of the time. The new constitution adopted in 1875 placed power in the hands of the Chamber of Deputies, elected by universal male suffrage. In the next year's election more than 7 million Frenchmen, out of a population of 36 million, cast their ballots.[5]

Although the early years of the Third Republic had their bad moments, by the late 1870s France had embarked on a domestic program that did much to consolidate the new republic and lay the basis for its survival as a democratic regime. The Freycinet Plan of 1878 (named for the minister of public works, Charles de Freycinet) launched a massive endeavor to build a French national rail system covering 16,000 kilometers of track, at a cost of 9 billion francs. The goal was to make French infrastructure competitive with that of such other powers as Britain, Germany, and Sweden. In addition, 50,000 Frenchmen were put to work in the process.[6] At the same time, the leaders of the new republic deliberately moved to foster social unity through a series of mostly symbolic acts. In 1880 the government, led by Freycinet as prime minister, established July 14, the anniversary of the storming of the Bastille in 1789, as France's official national holiday. And on the eve of the first Bastille Day celebration, the government extended amnesty to all prisoners and exiles still serving sentences resulting from their participation in the bloody 1871 insurrection of the Paris Commune.

The government under Freycinet and his immediate successors also took several concrete steps to expand French civil liberties. An act passed in 1881 abolished the long-standing requirement that public meetings have prior government approval. A new press law, passed that same year, not only abolished a requirement that newspapers have government approval but also eliminated press censorship, thereby promoting more widespread and unhindered political debate. An 1882 law gave all municipal councils the right to elect their mayors, and abolished the old system (inherited from the days of limited franchise under the monarchy) whereby citizens who paid the most in taxes automatically became council members for purposes of certain votes. In 1884 a new law legalized divorce. Another act that year made trade unions legal, in the expectation (which in time proved correct) that providing workers a legitimate vehicle for pursuing their objectives would help prevent large-scale violent uprisings like those of 1848 and 1871. In the meanwhile, legislation passed in 1874 had cut back the abuse of child labor, limiting the workday to twelve hours, forbidding night work for boys under sixteen or girls under eighteen, and outlawing the employment of children under twelve.

The greatest achievement of the early years of the Third Republic, however, was the reform of French education. Under the leadership of Jules Ferry, who served as minister of education for five years beginning in 1879 (and, twice during these years, as prime minister), France finally achieved what had been a key aspiration since the Revolution: providing public primary education for all citizens. Ferry's three key aims were that primary education be compulsory (for ages six through thirteen), free, and secular. Acts passed in 1881 and 1882 accomplished the first two. Laicization of primary school teaching staffs followed in 1886, shortly after Ferry left office. In the realm of secondary education, Ferry's chief innovation was the creation of lycées and colleges for girls. He also shifted the secondary school curriculum, which had traditionally given primacy to the classical humanities, to allow a somewhat greater role for science and modern languages. Finally, Ferry also initiated the process that led to both expansion and reform of French higher education, including the creation of new faculties and chairs at existing institutions and the establishment of autonomous universities.[7]

Although French economic performance in the early Third Republic years was far from smooth, on average, incomes were advancing at a satisfactory pace. Economic growth in the 1860s, under the empire, had also been vigorous.[8] In part, this success was a reflection of the more general, worldwide expansion that we have already seen at work in both America and Britain. The robust growth in France revolved in part around railway building, but also manufacturing (mostly in and around Paris), coal (mostly in the north of the country), and metals and textiles (both centered in the region near Lyon). Financing this activity also led to a profusion of new banking and credit institutions, famously including Crédit Mobilier, which enjoyed a spectacular success from its founding in 1852 to its equally spectacular failure in 1867.[9]

As a result, by the mid-1870s the French economy had more than fully recovered from the trauma of the Franco-Prussian War and the Paris Commune. In what would represent a sharp contrast to the plight of Germany's Weimar Republic a half-century later, the strong economy allowed France to pay—ahead of schedule—the war reparations that Prussia had imposed, thus ending the military occupation of French territory.[10] By 1875 French citizens' real income per capita was 23 percent above the decade-earlier level, and 53 percent above that of the mid-1850s. After several weak years in the late 1870s, growth resumed, due in part to the expansionary effect of the Freycinet Plan. Per capita income hit a peak in 1882, just as the governments led by Freycinet, Gambetta, and Ferry were accomplishing their most far-reaching reforms.[11]

Beyond the rise in incomes, the economic transformation then underway in France gave many citizens an even greater sense of making progress. The emerging industrial economy required more bank clerks, accountants, and office workers, not just absolutely but in proportion to the total job force. In time the government's reforms opened the way for more schoolteachers, post office workers, and junior-level civil servants. Although these new positions were often less well paid than work in agriculture or mining, or the new jobs in industry, those who held them dressed differently (the "white collar") and lived in different kinds of houses, their incomes were more stable, and they often received pensions. As historians Jean-Marie Mayeur and Madeleine Rebérioux later observed, "It was the good fortune of the Republic, and one of the reasons why it took root, to have thus offered numerous jobs to a social stratum anxious to rise in the world."[12]

The rising tide of this new lower middle class was part of the broader set of changes that led historian Daniel Halévy to label the early years of the Third Republic "the end of the notables."[13] As early as 1872 Gambetta had hailed a "new social stratum" ("nouvelle couche sociale"), whose advent he saw as crucial to the success of the new republic. Over the next decade that success drew on an effective alliance that embraced this "new stratum," the working people in the towns and countryside, and a portion of the existing upper middle class. The benefits of a quarter-century of economic growth were part of what enabled such a coalition to form and, for a while, survive the ordinary strains of political division.[14]

Similar widespread political and social reform in a setting of rapid postwar growth followed World War II. The war's economic impact was of course devastating. By 1944 French per capita income had fallen to just half of the pre-occupation peak in 1939.[15] Not until March 1945, after the Battle of the Bulge, did the last German soldiers leave French soil.

The French economy soon stabilized and then began a thirty-year postwar expansion—"les trentes glorieuses," in Jean Fourastié's famous phrase.[16]

By 1949 income per capita had surpassed the prewar peak.[17] But even before incomes had fully recovered, the pace of advance was visibly rapid, and people who looked forward with confidence to a rising standard of living far beyond anything they had known before the war were proved right.

Although economic policy after the war protected the interests of French agriculture, including the place of small-scale independent proprietors, the engines of the postwar economic growth were more modern: new power stations, up-to-date factories to take the place of old industrial facilities damaged during the war, electrified railways, new roads, and rebuilt bridges. Production and foreign trade surged. By 1955 per capita income was not only more than double the level at the end of the war but nearly one-third above the prewar peak. And despite rapid population growth, per capita income achieved at least some rise in every year from 1945 through 1974.

Moreover, the qualitative transformation of the French economy during the *"trentes glorieuses"* was even more profound than what had occurred in the 1860s and 1870s. More so than the other large western European countries, France had remained a heavily agricultural economy with a population based in rural areas and small towns. The postwar modernization greatly expanded job opportunities in industry, as well as in the long undernourished service sector. It also fostered urbanization. To a greater extent than ever in the past, the sons of French peasants were likely to become pharmacists or municipal workers. And even for those who lived where they always had, and who worked as they always had, the newly widespread availability of high-visibility consumer goods made life very different. Before the war, as well as in the early postwar years, owning an automobile was unusual for French workers. By the late 1960s half owned one. Before the war, for most people making a telephone call required going to the post office or to a café. Soon many people had telephones in their homes.[18]

The change in French politics after the war was virtually immediate. A provisional government set up and headed by Charles de Gaulle, leader of the Free French army during the war, laid the groundwork for what became the Fourth Republic. The new republic had a decidedly democratic character, both in formal structure and in political tone. In the initial postwar elections in October 1945, French women for the first time voted on the same basis as men. A new movement in French politics, the Mouvement Républicain Populaire, for the first time combined Christian faith with democratic principles and nonmonarchist sympathies in an electoral context, thereby ending a century and a half of antipathy at the political level between these powerful forces in France's social fabric.

Such immediate postwar changes as universal women's suffrage came too early to be a reflection of the return to rising living standards. (Public euphoria over the liberation drove events at first.) But as the postwar growth continued, so too did progressive changes in government and in popular political attitudes. Once in civilian office, de Gaulle acted quickly to reunify the country physically, rebuilding roads and bridges and restoring railroad and other transportation services. He also reformed the civil service and nationalized basic service industries like electricity and insurance, as well as major companies like Renault (in 1945) and Air France (in 1948).[19] De Gaulle also established the Commissariat-General of the Modernization and Investment Plan to map a strategy for the reconstruction of the French economy. To run the new Commissariat du Plan, he appointed Jean Monnet, who had served as deputy secretary-general of the League of Nations before the war, and had then headed France's wartime purchasing mission in Washington.

After de Gaulle resigned in early 1946, successive governments reached an agreement with France's labor unions to raise wages, embarked on a massive building program (funded in part by Marshall Plan aid) to renew the country's dated industrial facilities and transportation infrastructure, and followed through on what became known as the Monnet Plan for modernizing basic French industries like coal, steel, and agriculture. The economic planning and coordination process *("concentration")*, which became a widely remarked feature of French government and private sector interaction during the first postwar decades, clearly aimed not just at smoothing the wheels of change but also achieving a fairer distribution of the fruits of economic growth than France had known historically. Taken together, the broad array of measures put in place during these years constituted a decisive break with what historian Stanley Hoffmann has called the "stalemate society" of the latter decades under the Third Republic.[20]

At the same time, French foreign policy in the late 1940s and early 1950s displayed an unprecedented degree of cooperation with both allies and former enemies, in military as well as economic affairs. In June 1948, France agreed to unify its zone of military occupation in Germany with the previously unified British and American zones. The next April the three Allies agreed on the creation of the Federal Republic of Germany (commonly known as "West Germany" until its unification with the German Democratic Republic in October 1990). In July 1949, France joined NATO. In a triumph for the European unification effort led by Monnet, France became a founding member of the European Coal and Steel Community (in 1950) and then, in 1957, one of the original six countries to sign the Treaty of Rome, which created the "common market" that in time evolved into today's European Community.[21]

As was true for the domestic reforms carried out during that first post-war decade, the experience of defeat, rescue, and ultimate victory in World War II did much to shape French actions in the international political and economic sphere. But the confidence born of the country's strong and sustained economic growth during these years no doubt played a significant positive role as well.

Although the connection is less obvious, it is also likely that the same climate of steadily rising living standards enhanced France's ability to resolve the crisis over Algerian independence, which led to the creation of the Fifth Republic in 1958 (by which time income per capita had risen to 46 percent above the prewar peak level reached in 1939).[22] The political crisis, and even more so the divisions in French society that lay behind it, were not unlike the strains that in the past had led to civil violence and worse. But in this case the country achieved a peaceful resolution.

The greatest tensions under the Fourth Republic were generated by the piece-by-piece abandonment of the French presence abroad, in Indochina and especially in North Africa. With difficulty, the French government in 1955 managed to adopt a policy favoring independence for Tunisia and Morocco, and independence for both countries followed successfully the next year. But in Algeria an indigenous independence movement, increasingly popular among the Arab population, faced vigorous opposition from a French settler community that by the mid-twentieth century was deeply rooted. Intervention by the French army, beginning in 1954, not only failed to resolve the conflict but instead split French society between those who sought to retain control over Algeria at all costs and those who regarded the mounting intervention—by then there were nearly half a million French troops in Algeria—as brutal, costly, and ultimately doomed to failure.

In 1956, Prime Minister Guy Mollet in effect ceded control over the fighting to a coalition of settlers and army leaders "on the spot" in Algeria. Continuing divisions over this policy, however, brought down not only Mollet's government but the two that followed. In two of these transitions there was no prime minister for a month or more at a time because of the difficulty of forming a government under such trying circumstances. Finally, in May 1958, Pierre Pflimlin, a politician widely known to doubt the long-term viability of France's presence in Algeria, took over as prime minister. French colonists immediately seized control of the government in

Algeria, and the French army there offered no opposition. Within days French soldiers sympathetic to the settlers flew from Algeria to Corsica and took over the French administration there. Many thought civil war was imminent. Pfimlin's government resigned after only fifteen days in office.

At this point de Gaulle, out of office since resigning as prime minister twelve years before, announced his willingness to return to power. The French president, René Coty, promptly invited de Gaulle not only to form a government but to restructure the constitution as well. De Gaulle sought unity by putting together a cabinet representing all parties except the Communists and extreme right-wing Poujadistes, and including his predecessors Mollet and Pfimlin. By September he submitted to popular vote a new constitution, which greatly strengthened the role of the president of the republic. Turnout was overwhelming, 79 percent voted yes, and the Fifth Republic was born.[23]

De Gaulle's reentry into French politics and the creation of the Fifth Republic were especially significant for their strengthening of civilian government. From the outset, de Gaulle insisted that he would take power by constitutional means only, and once in office he quickly submitted to the electorate the important constitutional changes he sought. Few members of his original cabinet were his avowed supporters. He assumed the newly powerful post of president only after running for the office in the first election held under the new constitution.

And throughout, de Gaulle kept the army firmly subordinate to civilian authority. Within a few years he presided over Algerian independence and French withdrawal from North Africa more generally, acting decisively to put down expressions of opposition within the army.[24] France has experienced no such dangerous episodes in the more than four decades since, and the country has continued to govern itself under the Fifth Republic.[25]

The favorable developments that accompanied France's sustained economic growth after World War II presented a sharp contrast with the years following World War I. Although much of the fighting in the first war also took place in France, the constricting wartime impact on French economic activity was less pronounced, and recovery began promptly once the Armistice was signed. But like both the United States and Britain, France underwent a recession at the outset of the 1920s, then irregular growth for the remainder of the decade, and then the depression of the 1930s. Especially during the first half of the 1920s, wide fluctuations in the foreign exchange value of France's currency gave economic matters an even more chaotic feel. Initially pegged at 18.5 U.S. cents at the Armistice in 1919, the franc had fallen to just 2 cents by 1926.

At some times through these years French citizens could look back on progress in their living standard since prewar days. As in other countries, matters from this perspective were far better in the latter part of the 1920s and again in the latter part of the 1930s than in the early years of either decade. But there was little in France's economic experience during the interwar period to give the average citizen either a sense of sustained progress in hand or much confidence in prospects for the future. The result was a series of generally regressive social and political movements, punctuated by a dramatic attempt at liberalization that just as dramatically failed, and in the end the disaster of the pro-Nazi Vichy regime.

The first sign of the trends that would dominate France's interwar years was the increasing visibility of the Action Française, beginning in the early 1920s. Initially founded by right-wing literary figures in 1899, in reaction to the pro-Dreyfus turn of both events and public opinion after evidence emerged showing the perjury and subsequent cover-up by ranking Defense Ministry officials, Action Française was the most prominent organized anti-democratic and anti-Semitic movement in France under the Third Republic. Its program centered on submission to traditional authority, including restoration of the monarchy and deference to the Roman Catholic Church, and it embraced street violence aimed at overthrowing the republic. The organization's newspaper, also called *Action Française*, was for years a major organ of extreme-right-wing opinion in France.

Although it had been in existence since before the turn of the century, Action Française, like the Ku Klux Klan in the United States, enjoyed its greatest efflorescence in the early 1920s. By 1926 its daily newspaper had a circulation of 120,000.[26] In December of that year, however, Pope Pius XI publicly condemned Action Française for subordinating Christian doctrine to nationalist goals. As a result, many of the group's members withdrew their support and the newspaper's circulation quickly declined by one-half. Even so, Action Française continued as an influence in French politics, promoting its anti-republican, anti-democratic, and anti-Semitic agenda throughout the remainder of the 1920s and the 1930s, and on into the wartime Vichy years. It finally collapsed, and its newspaper ceased publication, only when the Allies began the liberation of France in the summer of 1944.

Several years of strong economic growth in the late 1920s perhaps helped to dampen the kind of public sentiment that Action Française represented, but by 1930 French incomes were falling again as what became the

Great Depression began to take hold on both sides of the Atlantic. Per capita income in France reached bottom in 1932, and improvement during the next few years was negligible. Only after 1936, when France finally abandoned the gold standard, did a significant recovery begin.[27]

One of the first reactions to renewed economic distress was anti-immigrant agitation. France had long welcomed immigrants, and by the early 1930s approximately 7 percent of all French residents were foreign-born (a slightly higher percentage than in the United States at the time).[28] Soon after unemployment began to rise, however, *"La France aux Français"*—"France for the French"—became an increasingly popular slogan even in the writings of columnists and intellectuals who usually represented an internationalist point of view. French businesses began to fire foreign-born workers, and the government rapidly shifted from encouraging immigrants to expelling them. Formal immigration quotas followed in 1932, and a series of regulations adopted in 1934 and 1935 effectively barred foreigners from such professions as law, medicine, and dentistry.[29]

At the same time, organized political violence became an ever more familiar aspect of right-wing agitation. Years earlier, Action Française had formed the Camelots du Roi (Hawkers of the King) as a private paramilitary organization. A similar group founded in 1924, the Jeunesses Patriotes (Patriotic Youth), had 300,000 members by the end of the decade.[30] Both gained new momentum beginning in 1930. The Croix de Feu (Cross of Fire), which drew most of its members from discontented World War I veterans and had strong militaristic overtones, had also been founded earlier but became far more politically active from 1931 on. By 1937 it had nearly 1 million members.

Like fascist-oriented groups elsewhere in Europe, these organizations encouraged bands of mostly young, virulently right-wing activists who engaged in repeated street violence that often grew out of belligerent political demonstrations openly intended to provoke such disturbances. The most dramatic such episode occurred in February 1934, when a demonstration held outside the Chamber of Deputies in Paris by several fascist-oriented groups (including Action Française, Jeunesses Patriotes, and Croix de Feu, together with Solidarité Française and the Fascistes, both of which had just been founded the year before), in conjunction with France's largest veterans organization, exploded into an anti-government—and, more fundamentally, anti-republican and anti-democratic—riot that left fourteen people dead and hundreds wounded. (Just two days earlier the veterans group, the Union Nationale des Combattants, had published a cartoon on the front page of its newspaper picturing the Chamber of Deputies in flames and some of its members hanging by their necks from nearby lampposts.)[31] The next day Prime Minister Edouard Daladier, who had assumed office just eleven days earlier, resigned in favor of the conservatives.

While the left-versus-right tensions of party politics clearly played a role in the rise of French fascism, in France as elsewhere the spreading unemployment and even more general loss of confidence in the nation's economic future that came with the onset of the depression was a powerful force as well. As historian Robert Soucy has argued, "The resurgence of fascism in France in the early 1930s and its eventual decline in the late 1930s cannot be understood in the absence of some account of the larger historical context in which it operated, particularly the political consequences of the Depression in France. Although France suffered less from the Depression than Germany, the effects were still grim."[32] As was true elsewhere, the 1930s depression was the longest and most severe economic downturn France had experienced in more than a century. And in part because France stayed on the gold standard longer than other countries, recovery there came later and even then it was slower. The American correspondent William Shirer, who witnessed the riot in front of the Chamber of Deputies in February 1934, wrote that "It was the bloodiest encounter in the streets of Paris since the Commune of 1871."[33] It was not coincidental that it occurred during the worst economic crisis of modern times.

Even the heightened left-right tensions that underlay the rise of French fascism and fascist violence in the 1930s were themselves in part due to the economic crisis. Germany was an example to be feared (or, by some, admired), as was Russia. The continually shifting alliances among French political parties sometimes brought to power coalitions that included the Socialists, the Radicals, and even the Communists. Many supporters of France's new fascist movement saw their country's democracy threatened not from the right but from the left. That threat too grew out of the country's economic collapse.

Political reaction to the wave of fascistlike violence in the mid-1930s eventually helped mobilize support for France's one real effort between the two world wars to achieve what many conceived as a fairer, more democratic society. The Popular Front, an anti-fascist coalition of mostly left-wing parties led by socialist Léon Blum, achieved a decisive majority in the elections held in the spring of 1936. Taking office in June, Blum moved quickly to address the mounting concerns expressed through a series of major strikes, some involving workers' occupation of factories. In his first month as premier, he successfully negotiated with France's principal labor federation and with representatives of major employers what became known as the

Matignon Accords (after the name of the French prime minister's official residence), which put in place a broad array of measures aimed at improving the lot of ordinary French workers. Key elements in this agreement included wage increases, paid vacations, a forty-hour workweek, and creation of authorized workers' delegations to deal with management in labor disputes. Other initiatives undertaken by the Popular Front included more extensive unemployment relief and old-age pensions, expanded public works, nationalization of the munitions industry, and achieving at least some degree of government influence over the monetary policy decisions of France's still private central bank.34

It is doubtful that the Matignon program constituted sound economic policy. Some elements of the accords, such as paid vacations and the forty-hour workweek, anticipated the development of Western industrialized economies more generally, and proved lasting. But the wage increases and public works spending failed to produce the hoped-for economic recovery. (Much of their force was dissipated by Blum's delaying the inevitable devaluation of the franc, which, when it finally came, was the only French devaluation during the interwar period to prove a failure.)35 The significance of Matignon for our present purposes lies instead in the attempt that it represented to achieve a fairer society in the industrial age, embracing not only the traditional dimension of how a country's economic product is distributed—the wage question—but also basic work arrangements and the economic security of those who were retired or unemployed. In those respects, at least, Blum's program attempted to replicate in France parts of what Roosevelt's New Deal was then bringing to America.

The Popular Front was a short-lived anomaly, however, in part simply because it ran against the grain of its time. In contrast to the waves of reform in the Third Republic's early years, and also following World War II, during the interwar period the national climate was just not receptive. Blum soon became the focus of continuous personal attacks from the right, for his policies and because he was Jewish. In early 1937 he had to call for a "pause" in reforms, and he resigned a year after concluding the Matignon Accords. (In the political merry-go-round that followed, Blum briefly returned to power a year later.)

The Popular Front then dissolved into its constituent parties, none of which had the support to present a successful bulwark against the generally anti-democratic public sentiment of the time. In addition, developments nearby—the Nazis in Germany, the Fascists in Italy, civil war in Spain, and then the onset of war when Germany invaded Poland in September 1939—heightened tensions in France as well. As a result, the domestic reform effort mounted by the Popular Front halted altogether. Although the main elements of the Matignon program remained in place, from then until the occupation one ineffective government after another stumbled into office and then out.

France's surprisingly quick and crushing defeat by German forces thrust the domestic political turmoil aside. In June 1940, Paul Reynaud, the last prewar prime minister, resigned in favor of Marshal Philippe Pétain, a hero of the French army in World War I. Pétain immediately sought and obtained an armistice, which in effect surrendered the northern half of the country to the Germans while retaining nominal French control over the southern half. The National Assembly—relocated from Paris, which was under German occupation, to the resort town of Vichy near the country's geographical center—voted overwhelmingly to authorize Pétain to revise the constitution. Rather than do so, Pétain simply suspended it and governed for four years without one. The Third Republic was dead.

The Vichy regime was no mere puppet installed by foreign forces of occupation but rather an embodiment of much of the openly reactionary sentiment that had dominated domestic French politics throughout the interwar period: authoritarian, conservative, ruralist, anchored in traditional provincial prejudices, firmly opposed to all things associated with modern urban society. It was of course anti-socialist and anti-Semitic. Its sympathies for the Nazis were hardly the usual feelings of a defeated, occupied people toward their conquerors. Although the obfuscations of the early postwar era tended for a time to shroud the Vichy regime's role in often deliberate ambiguities, historical research in the last two to three decades has made clear that many Vichy leaders and other government officials went far beyond merely collaborating with the Germans when pressed to do so, instead eagerly seeking ways to ingratiate themselves with Hitler and other Nazi representatives.[36]

The Vichy regime's active effort to align itself with the Nazis' program began almost immediately, long before the German army completed its occupation of France in November 1942, and it lasted until the liberation. Just after assuming power, the government issued a decree declaring that all French citizens who had become refugees after the beginning of the German offensive (obviously including many Jews) had "removed themselves from the reponsibilities and duties of members of the national community," so that their property could be confiscated.[37] The government adopted its first explicitly anti-Semitic laws in October 1940, and the next year the government seized all remaining Jewish-owned businesses. The Protocols of Paris, signed in May 1941, gave the Germans military use of French bases and ports abroad, especially in the Middle East.[38] In the summer of 1942, foreign-born Jews living in the *unoccupied* zone were arrested and delivered to German custody.[39] In late 1942 the Vichy government even offered to form a new French army and join the war on Germany's side.[40] The effort to make Vichy France the partner of Nazi Germany ended only in August 1944, when the retreating German forces took Pétain and "chief of government" Pierre Laval to Germany with them, just ahead of the advancing Allies.

The contrast between the abrupt halt in the Matignon reform program and the far greater durability of both the early Third Republic reforms and those of the early post–World War II period graphically shows the difference between movements that draw support from their underlying economic context and others that run counter to it. Two far lesser episodes in modern French history further illustrate the contrast. In the mid-1880s Georges Boulanger was a highly popular French general and minister of war. His resolute (indeed, bellicose) reaction in the wake of a French-German border dispute in 1887 appealed to a public that still felt humiliated by France's overwhelming defeat in the Franco-Prussian War. The prime minister who formed a new cabinet later that year deemed Boulanger's actions impudent, however, and excluded him from the cabinet. Boulanger's ambitious political maneuvering soon led to his dismissal from the army as well, but his increasing public demagoguery only heightened his popular appeal.

Out of office, Boulanger formed a new political movement based on fierce nationalism, xenophobia (including, but not limited to, the usual anti-Semitism), and militarism, as well as a less articulately expressed but nonetheless forceful opposition to domestic elites and political corruption.[41] In 1889, after a series of successes by his followers in by-elections for seats in the Chamber of Deputies, Boulanger himself ran for a Paris seat and won a huge victory from an electorate of over half a million. Many expected him to take over the government by force.

Boulanger chose not to stage a coup, and his movement soon disappeared as an organized political effort. (Threatened with arrest, Boulanger fled the country later that year; two years afterward, distraught over the death of his mistress, he committed suicide.) But the themes that Boulanger emphasized—nationalism, militarism, xenophobia, opposition to corruption together with an assumption that corruption is endemic to the democratic process—persisted as a powerful force in French politics and society more generally. The anti-Semitism that Boulanger consciously used as a strategy for attracting supporters whose interests did not otherwise lie with traditional conservatism did much to create the public atmosphere surrounding the beginning of the Dreyfus Affair five years later. In short, Boulangism survived although Boulanger did not.

Another movement, seven decades later, also achieved a resounding electoral success with a similar program. In the early 1950s Pierre Poujade, a bookstore owner from the town of St. Céré, founded the ambitiously named Union for the Defense of Shopkeepers and Artisans. Like Boulangism, Poujade's movement adopted a stance of extreme right-wing nationalism combined with populism. It also drew on France's republican traditions. The union organized protests against mass production as well as the centralizing tendencies of twentieth-century economic and political forces more generally. It was also openly opposed to the independence movements then gaining momentum in various French colonies, and it had a mostly unstated undercurrent of anti-Semitism. Although Poujade sought to defend the interests of the urban lower middle class, most of his support came from the small-town lower middle class, as well as from agricultural workers in France's still very large rural economy, groups that, despite the country's more general prosperity, were not getting ahead.

The Poujadistes enjoyed their greatest political success in the elections held in January 1956, gathering over 13 percent of the popular vote and winning 55 seats (out of 596) in the National Assembly.[42] But the movement found few allies among the more established parties, and the return of de Gaulle two years later dissolved most of its support. In the elections of November 1958, Poujadiste candidates won less than 3 percent of the vote.[43] The Union for the Defense of Shopkeepers and Artisans survived and in time evolved through a series of different names and forms, but after the mid-1950s it had little or no serious impact.

Why did Poujadism vanish almost without a trace, while Boulangism, which was about equally short-lived as a formal political movement, helped shape public attitudes for well over a decade? The political specifics of the two movements account for part of the story, together with the personalities of their respective leaders.[44] But the larger part of the explanation lies in the fact that the two otherwise similar movements occurred against different economic backgrounds.

After a reasonable (though not outstanding) growth performance in the first decade or so under the Third Republic, the mid- to late 1880s were a stagnant period in France, with literally no growth in per capita incomes for six years running.[45] By then agricultural depression and deflation were in full force, as in much of the rest of the Western world, and France's economy was highly centered on agriculture and the population largely in rural areas and in small towns. The railway-building boom of the late Second Empire and early Third Republic years had paused, and the growth of the new industrial economy had also (temporarily) lost momentum. By contrast, as we have seen, economic growth in France in the 1950s was strong and sustained. It is not surprising that nationalist movements with anti-democratic and anti-modern agendas would thrive in the former period but sputter in the latter.

Two further episodes in French history present a similarly instructive contrast. In the wake of France's stunning capitulation at Sedan in September 1870, the German army subjected Paris to a four-month siege in which food supplies as well as conditions of everyday life like sanitation deteriorated to horrible lows. The resulting hardships, together with a widespread feeling that conservative leaders and their followers from the provinces had not put much effort into the war against the Germans, aroused revolutionary passions among ordinary citizens of Paris. In particular, the Parisians had no affection for the new provisional government led by longtime politician Adolphe Thiers, which based itself some fifteen miles away in Versailles.

Thiers only made matters worse in March 1871 by sending troops in broad daylight to remove all cannon from Paris so as to render the city defenseless. A mob gathered, some of the government's soldiers went over to the civilians, and the crowd proceeded to execute two generals. Barely a week later, municipal elections in Paris produced a new city government dominated by extreme leftists bitterly opposed to Thiers's government. Within two days the new government proclaimed Paris an independent commune.[46]

The Paris Commune reflected reformist aspirations, to be sure, but its basic ethos was revolutionary, anticlerical in the extreme—the archbishop of Paris was taken hostage and executed on flimsy legal grounds—and unconcerned with individual rights in the face of any conflict with the perceived needs of the collective. Despite myriad proposals intended to improve workers' lives, there was little actual legislation. (Some debts were canceled, and night shifts in bakeries were outlawed.) The communal government instead dissipated its energies in endless fractious debates, reminiscent of the worst days of the Revolution, on matters of procedure. Also as in the Revolution, the commune promptly adopted its infamous Law of Hostages, under which it publicly executed perceived enemies. The commune, both officially and in the spontaneous acts of its citizens, exhibited a spirit of cruelty and intolerance that reflected the deep enmity still separating opposing political allegiances in a defeated and humiliated nation.

Thiers's government matched that cruelty, and more, in putting down the commune. After concluding a peace treaty with Germany on May 10, under which France surrendered the eastern provinces of Alsace and Lorraine and also agreed to pay the Germans 5 billion francs, the government turned its attention to Paris. Thiers displayed no interest in negotiating. During the "Bloody Week" of May 21–27, government troops and Parisian citizens fought a small-scale civil war in the city's streets. The fighting and the retributions that followed left 20,000 communards dead. The commune collapsed and the Versailles government restored order, sentencing over 5,000 Parisians to either prison or hard labor and sending some 7,000 more into exile.

Neither the commune nor the actions of Thiers's government in violently suppressing it advanced the cause of democracy and freedom in France.[47] But the legacy of the harsh forces at work on both sides did not long dominate the new Third Republic either. As we have seen, later in the decade France embarked on a broad program of political, social, and educational reforms that consolidated the new republic and enabled it to survive for more than another half-century.

Part of the reason France was able to move on in such a positive way was the sense of economic progress that citizens of the time were experiencing. For the decade and a half before the Franco-Prussian War, and then for more than a decade afterward, French standards of living were generally improving. The rise of Gambetta's "new social stratum" added to the sense of getting ahead, even for many whose incomes remained low. As a result, over the decade following the commune the Third Republic coalition was able to focus its energies on reform rather than recrimination.

Another uprising in Paris, nearly a hundred years later, is also instructive. The events of May 1968 began with a mounting series of disturbances staged by students discontented with the overcrowded French university system and also eager to protest against the Vietnam War. The police responded on May 10 with mass beatings of the demonstrators, and arrests by the hundreds. At the same time, workers in Paris and elsewhere went on strike, some in sympathy with the students but mostly on account of specific grievances of their own. Hundreds of thousands of workers marched with students in a demonstration in Paris on May 13, and across the country some 10 million workers went on strike and in some cases occupied shop floors. De Gaulle's government seemed in danger of imminent collapse.

The government proved resilient, however, promptly entering into negotiations with the major French labor organizations. The Grenelle Accord that ensued (named for the street in Paris where the Labor Ministry building stands) provided for a staggered series of wage increases as well as greater worker representation on committees authorized to resolve industrial disputes. Although the government clearly took the workers more seriously than the students, it also at least gave the impression of addressing student concerns by reducing overcrowding and bureaucratic interference in the universities. A year later de Gaulle resigned, turning over the presidency of the republic to his former premier Georges Pompidou.

But the result of May 1968 was more than just a wage increase and a few more classrooms. Over the next several years French society underwent a significant modernization and liberalization. Pompidou's prime minister, Jacques Chaban-Delmas, and his advisor Jacques Delors (subsequently the author of the report that paved the way for the European common currency), set the national tone by calling for a "Nouvelle Société." One sign of the new social attitudes was the introduction of coeducation and relaxed dress codes in public schools. Even French language usage changed, with the familiar second-person *"tu"* increasingly replacing the more formal *"vous"* in many more contexts of everyday conversation. Although Valéry Giscard d'Estaing, the new president elected in 1973, was from the conservative political party, his policies—for example, liberalizing restrictions on abortion and lowering the voting age from twenty-one to eighteen—were hardly representative of France's traditional rightist authoritarianism. In a symbolic break with the past, Giscard even declined to pose for the traditional French president's photograph in morning coat and tails.

Although here too many forces were no doubt at work, part of what fostered the French response to May 1968 was the rising tide of strong economic growth. More than two decades into *les trentes glorieuses,* French citizens had good reason to take satisfaction in their economic progress and to have confidence in their prospects. As we have seen, by 1968 real per capita income in France had risen every year since 1945, and it continued to do so until 1975. Moreover, the increase in living standards was especially rapid in the 1960s. By 1969 income per capita was 56 percent above what it had been at the end of the 1950s, and well over double what it had been at the end of the 1940s (by which time it had already surpassed the peak prewar level). While the origins of the May 1968 disturbances were mostly unrelated to economic causes, against this strong economic background the resulting opening of French society had lasting effects.

The French economy has continued to grow since the mid-1970s but, as in most of the industrial world, at a much reduced rate. In the twenty years ending in 1973, real per capita income rose on average by 4.6 percent per annum. Since then annual growth has averaged just 1.7 percent. (The phrase *les trentes glorieuses* came into use only after the period of rapid growth had ended; it was, in effect, an expression of nostalgia.)[48] More important, France, like most countries in Europe, has experienced chronic high unemployment.

As in the United States, the tight monetary policy of the 1980s that overcame the surge in inflation following the first OPEC price increase initially triggered recession and consequent unemployment in Europe. In the United States, as we have seen, the result was also a significant decline, over more than a decade, in the average real wage of workers who kept their jobs. European countries, where the labor force is more highly unionized and centralized negotiations play a much larger role in setting pay, blunted the wage decline but did so at the expense of continuing high unemployment. In contrast to America's fluid labor market practices, government restrictions on hiring and firing further added to the persistence of unemployment in many European countries.[49] In 1973 less than 3 percent of the French labor force was unemployed, compared with 5 percent in the United States. Fifteen years later unemployment was more than 10 percent in France, but not quite 7 percent in the United States. And by 1997 unemployment in America was back down to 5 percent, while French unemployment had risen above 12 percent—the highest since 1945. After a welcome decline, to 8.5 percent in 2001, unemployment in France began to rise again, reaching nearly 10 percent in early 2005.[50]

The new political phenomenon spawned by this slower growth and chronic high unemployment was the rise to prominence of the National Front, initially founded in 1972 by attorney and onetime army officer (in Indonesia and Algeria) Jean-Marie Le Pen, who had first entered politics as a Poujadiste elected to the National Assembly in 1956.[51] Le Pen's National Front recalls not just the Poujadistes but many earlier movements in French politics. It is nationalist, xenophobic, anti-Semitic, and openly racist. (In 1996 Le Pen publicly declared, "Some races are more equal than others.")[52] Le Pen has also made provocative remarks about the Nazis, including the statement that the Holocaust was a "mere detail in the history of the Second World War," and in 1997 a French court found him guilty of a criminal offense on these grounds.[53]

Although in its early days the National Front appealed mainly to a small and aging constituency nostalgic for Vichy, in time its strength came more from its appeal to young workers confronting the challenge of chronically high unemployment. The party's rhetoric focuses mostly on France's rising numbers of immigrants, many from North Africa, accusing them of stealing jobs from native French citizens. In the wake of the attacks on New York and Washington on September 11, 2001, and the Madrid train bombing of March 11, 2004, it also emphasizes these immigrants' Muslim religion, warning of a threat to French culture and society. The party's program proposes to address these problems both by limiting new immigration and by refusing to renew the work permits and visas of those already in France. The National Front also opposes French participation in most aspects of European unification, although it maintains informal alliances with far-right parties in Austria, Serbia, and other countries.

Although immigration in France since the mid-1970s has actually been smaller than during the first three-quarters of the twentieth century, the National Front's electoral presence gained strength as France's economy faltered, and that strength has persisted. In the 1981 elections the party received less than 1 percent of the vote. In 1988, however, Le Pen ran for president and drew 4.4 million votes, or nearly 15 percent of all ballots cast. Running again in 1995, he again drew 15 percent. In 2002, Le Pen drew 17 percent on the first round, edging out the Socialist candidate, Lionel Jospin, to become incumbent president Jacques Chirac's only opponent in the final round (where Chirac won handily, despite having gotten not even 20 percent on the first round). Nor is the National Front's success merely a matter of Le Pen's personal appeal as a candidate. In the 1997 legislative elections, for example, National Front candidates got nearly 1.5 million votes (although the party wound up with only a single seat in the National Assembly). In the 2004 nationwide election for regional councils, the party once again drew 15 percent of the vote.

The conventional image of the National Front's support is that it comes primarily from southern French cities like Nice, Toulon, and Marseille with large populations of nonwhite immigrants, and there is some truth to this view. In Marseille, for example—France's second-largest city—Le Pen received over 28 percent of the vote in 1988. As Stanley Hoffmann has pointed out, however, "a map showing the concentration of the Le Pen votes is not the same as one showing the centers of the North African immigration; it conforms much more closely to a map showing where unemployment is high."[54] It is difficult to avoid the conclusion that, as is so often the case with political and social movements drawing heavily on racial or religious prejudice, support for the National Front's anti-immigrant policies was (and remains) in large part a response of people who realize that they are currently not getting ahead *economically*, and who fear that their future economic prospects, and their children's, are doubtful as well.

Figure 10.1 summarizes the relationship that political and social movements in France have borne to the underlying background of economic growth versus stagnation over the last century and a quarter.

	Responses to *Growth*	Responses to *Stagnation*
Movement *toward* openness, tolerance, mobility, fairness, democracy	✓ Third Republic reforms (1878–84) ✓ Postwar reforms (1945–50) ✓ Fifth Republic (1958) ✓ May 1968 and after (1968–71)	✗ Matignon Accords (1936)
Movement *away from* openness, tolerance, mobility, fairness, democracy	✗ Paris Commune (1871) ✗ Poujadism (1956–58)	✓ Boulangism (1889) ✓ Action Française (1921–26) ✓ Anti-immigrant agitation and fascist violence (1932–36) ✓ Vichy (1940) ✓ National Front (1988–95)

FIGURE 10.1

Consequences of Economic Growth Versus Stagnation:
France Since the Founding of the Third Republic

It is especially interesting to note how short-lived the three major episodes that represent exceptions to the more familiar consequences of economic growth proved to be in France. Although neither the actions of the Paris Commune nor its brutal suppression by the Thiers government sprang in any meaningful sense from the country's economic growth at that time—the trigger was the disastrous loss of a war with Germany—what matters here is that they occurred in the middle of an era of sustained and mostly robust economic advance. That said, however, what seems equally important is that the country soon moved on from that experience to under-take the early Third Republic reforms, which did prove lasting. Similarly, the Poujadiste movement was not a response to the economic growth of the 1950s so much as a reaction by those whom that growth had left behind, but the fact remains that it occurred squarely in the middle of *les trentes glo-rieuses*. It too rose and then faded quickly. By contrast, the Popular Front program was clearly an attempt to respond to the economic crisis of the 1930s. While some of its measures lasted (the forty-hour workweek, for example), much of the program was likewise very short-lived.

For the most part, the French experience largely supports the view that periods when living standards are rising mostly tend to foster positive movements in society, while times of stagnation are much more likely to support efforts to retreat and retrench.

Chapter 11

Germany

Dare more democracy.

WILLY BRANDT
Inauguration Address to the Bundestag, October 1969[1]

To a far greater extent than in most other countries, and certainly more so than is the case in America, Britain, or France, a single terrible episode has dominated the history of Germany in the modern era. The military aggression and civilian atrocities committed by Germany during the Nazi period require no elaboration. But examining in some detail the economic setting in which Adolf Hitler and the Nazi Party came to power is very much to the point.

Germany and the United States were the two countries hit hardest by the depression of the 1930s.[2] From 1930 to 1938, on average nearly 22 percent of German workers were unemployed, 26 percent in America.[3] In both countries, beginning in 1933 the government took an increasingly activist, interventionist approach to the economic crisis, adopting policy measures aimed directly at reviving and even restructuring economic activity.[4]

As we have seen, however, the outstanding anomaly of the American experience in this respect is that the nation's people responded to the hardships of the depression by embracing a broader conception of personal freedom that led to a more open and democratic society. In Germany the opposite response emerged. What was, and remains, remarkable is not the direction of that response but the extraordinary degree to which Nazi Germany crushed individual freedoms, demolished democratic institutions, and imposed its deadly vision on citizens of other countries.

It would be foolish to seek the origins of the Nazi ascendancy narrowly in the events of the early 1930s, or even in economic influences alone over a longer period of time. The roots of Nazism lay partly in aspects of the German experience extending back at least to the nineteenth century.[5] Germany's defeat in World War I, and the nation's diminished status in postwar Europe, were important as well.[6] But the fact remains that the particular manifestation of these tendencies that actually came to rule the German state, and that willfully inflicted so much harm elsewhere, was a phenomenon of the interwar period, incubated in the chaos of the 1920s and reaching full fruition only after first a hyperinflation and then the depression had severely dislocated German economic life.

World War I seemed to many Germans to have ended with surprising abruptness. In 1917 the German army under General Erich Ludendorff had blocked the Allied offensive on the western front. The prolonged campaign on the eastern front contributed to the collapse of the czarist regime in Russia, and in March 1918, the new Bolshevik government signed the Treaty of Brest-Litovsk, withdrawing Russia from the war on terms that appeared to represent a victory for Germany. That same month Ludendorff launched a new offensive in France. The German push initially went well, with major victories against the British at Ypres in April and against the French on the Aisne in May. But suddenly the full weight of American forces arrived at the front, the French struck back at the Marne in July, and the British and Canadians achieved a dramatic breakthrough at Amiens in August. By the end of September, even though German troops still occupied large stretches of foreign territory on both fronts, Ludendorff concluded that the war was lost and sought an immediate end to the fighting. The Armistice was signed less than six weeks later.

The German empire immediately collapsed. The kaiser abdicated and fled the country, a republic was proclaimed, and the Social Democrats in the Reichstag were left in charge of the government. In the ensuing political chaos a Soviet-style social revolution began, the far-left Spartacists staged an additional uprising, and a variety of groups on the far right made attempts to restore the kaiser. For the next two months the various parties that had comprised the empire's political opposition engaged in intense backroom maneuvering accompanied by mass demonstrations and frequent street violence. By late January, however, after the communist leaders Karl Liebknecht and Rosa Luxemburg had been murdered, democratic forces emerged in sufficient control to hold elections for a new national assembly. This body met at Weimar, a small eastern city mostly known as a cultural center, and began to draft a new constitution. This governing structure for the new German republic, democratic but not explicitly socialist (though the Social Democrats had the largest role in the post-election coalition), took effect in August 1919, barely a year since the German empire had seemed on the verge of a two-front victory in the field.[7]

That spring the assembly meeting at Weimar had accepted, as it had to, the hard terms laid down by the victorious Allies at the conclusion of the Paris Peace Conference. Under the terms of the treaty signed at Versailles, Germany returned Alsace-Lorraine to France (thereby reversing the main territorial conquest of the Franco-Prussian War) and surrendered other previously German territory to Poland, Denmark, Belgium, and even Lithuania—in all, territories with a population of over 7 million.[8] Allied troops were to occupy the left (west) bank of the Rhine, and the right bank was set aside as a demilitarized zone. The German army was limited to 100,000 officers and men, without the right to conscript troops or to operate military aircraft. The navy was similarly limited in size, as was the merchant fleet. German financial holdings abroad were confiscated. The arrangements for war reparations, not finalized until 1921, were that Germany should pay 132 billion gold marks (worth about $2.1 billion at 1921 exchange rates), primarily to France, Britain, and Belgium.[9]

None of these developments constituted a favorable beginning for the new German republic. Army officers, and conservatives more generally, exploited the suddenness of the military defeat to claim that Germany had been "stabbed in the back" by democrats and socialists who threw away a hard-won military victory. Even the Social Democratic leader, Friedrich Ebert, had welcomed the returning troops home saying "No enemy has overcome you."[10] (Several years later, Ludendorff, invited to contribute to a current-events book sponsored by the *Encyclopaedia Britannica*, titled his article "Germany Never Defeated!" and attributed Germany's loss in World War I to "the betrayal of the fatherland—brought about by the disintegrating influence of enemy propaganda, by revolutionary agitation, and finally by the outbreak of the Revolution itself," all of which were "acting in accordance with that damnable precept of German democracy . . . that Germany shall lower her banner once for all, without even bringing it home victorious for the last time.")[11]

The political revolution that took place from November 1918 to January 1919 also left a legacy of multiparty chaos. Its democratic orientation notwithstanding, the Social Democratic Party at the head of the Weimar coalition relied on the Freikorps—street gangs made up mostly of right-wing, anti-Semitic former soldiers together with young students who had "missed out" on the war, almost all of whom felt loyal not to the new republic but to the old monarchy—to crush its further-left opponents. Political assassinations continued into the early 1920s, with prominent victims including Matthias Erzberger, the moderate conservative leader of the Catholic Center Party who was serving as Germany's finance minister; Kurt Eisner, the Bavarian leader of the Independent Socialists; and most famously Walther Rathenau, a prominent industrialist and a founder of the middle-class Democratic Party (also a Jew), who at the time was Germany's foreign minister.

Other factors were unfavorable as well. The Weimar constitution itself had flaws, most notably Article 48, which authorized the president to govern through emergency powers "should public order and safety be seriously disturbed or threatened."[12] The conditions imposed at Versailles were not only harsh but humiliating, all the more so in that the Allies had simply presented them without negotiation. The specified reparations represented a huge burden for the German economy, as John Maynard Keynes pointed out at the time, although in the end Germany refused to pay most of the amount due anyway.[13] Which among these significantly contributed to the weakness and ultimate disaster of the Weimar Republic has been a topic of robust debate ever since.[14]

Even during the war, economic conditions had been difficult for Germans on the home front. A wave of workers' strikes in early 1918 had far more to do with wages and working conditions than with any broader political concerns. By 1919 income per capita was 29 percent below the level in the year before the war started.[15] Peacetime expansion, financed in large part by foreign borrowing, began the next year and continued irregularly through the 1920s. Still, it was not until 1927 that Germans on average regained the incomes they had enjoyed in 1913.[16] Moreover, the recovery was far from complete. Unemployment averaged over 9 percent during the years 1921 to 1929.[17] As in other countries, so high a level of joblessness, sustained year after year, was a new phenomenon.[18]

For Germany in the early 1920s, however, merely noting aggregate-

level trends in incomes and unemployment fails to capture the economic
chaos and uncertainty of the times. Much of German industry, converted to
munitions during the war, was now shut down. Wholly apart from the
transfer to other countries of territory containing a tenth of its prewar population, Germany lost 15 percent of its arable land, 26 percent of its coal
resources, 38 percent of its steel-producing capacity, and 75 percent of its
iron ore deposits.[19] The resulting need for imports led to a trade deficit,
but the confiscation of Germany's foreign holdings eliminated receipts of
interest and dividends from abroad that could have helped to finance the
imbalance. Reparations, which Germany did pay at first, widened both
the international payments deficit and the new government's budget deficit.
In the government's 1921–22 fiscal year, reparations payments constituted
5.1 billion marks out of total expenditures of just under 12 billion.[20]

Faced with a widening gap between its expenditures and its tax revenues, the government called on the Reichsbank, the German central bank,
to finance its ongoing operations by increasing the number of marks in
circulation—in other words, by printing money. The bank approximately
doubled the volume of mark notes during the course of 1921, and then doubled it again by August of the next year. Not surprisingly, the mark's worth
rapidly deteriorated compared to other countries' currencies and also to
goods at home. The mark went from 62 per dollar in January 1921, to 188
in December, to 312 in June 1922. Wholesale prices in Germany went up
142 percent in 1921 and another 101 percent in the first half of 1922.[21]

By this point most Germans understood that holding marks was a way
to lose money. Ordinary wage earners spent their pay as quickly as possible.
People with assets increasingly transferred what they had into accounts
abroad, to be held in other currencies. The value of the mark therefore
began to fall even more rapidly. The decline only led the Reichsbank to
print new marks still faster.

The result was hyperinflation. Prices rose twenty-one-fold in the second half of 1922, then another thirteenfold in the first half of 1923. In June
1923 alone, prices more than doubled. Prices then rose almost fourfold in
July, twelvefold in August, twenty-five-fold in September, and nearly three-
hundred-fold in October. In international exchange, the mark declined to
4.2 *trillion* to the dollar. At this point the Reichsbank introduced a new currency, with one new "Rentenmark" equal to 1 trillion old marks. Only after
a government decree placed firm limits on how many notes could be issued
did the inflation finally stop.

Everyday economic activity had become chaotic. In place of the old
monthly paydays, firms now paid wages twice a week, if not daily. Wage

earners literally ran to spend their marks, and images of citizens going off to buy groceries with sacks (in some cases wheelbarrows) full of almost worthless paper money became permanently fixed in the nation's collective memory. Barter transactions increasingly replaced ordinary commercial dealings. Shortages led to food riots and other disturbances.[22]

On average, real incomes declined in 1923 by 17 percent from the previous year's "high," but the inflation created both winners and losers.[23] Many middle-class families saw their savings entirely wiped out, and people living on fixed pensions became destitute. At the same time, debtors— including farmers with mortgages, businessmen who had financed their activities by borrowing, and speculators of all kinds—profited enormously. (The lesson that debt in large amounts was good for profits came back to haunt a number of major industrialists later in the decade, after prices stabilized.)[24]

By late 1923, after French troops had occupied the German Ruhr—as the Versailles treaty had specified in the event of German nonpayment of reparations—the British and French agreed to reschedule Germany's financial obligations. The ensuing Dawes Plan, named for the American official who chaired the commission charged with resolving the problem, not only rescheduled the payments but enabled Germany to borrow the needed funds in New York. Beginning in 1924, Germany also borrowed large amounts from abroad to finance its continuing current account deficit. Ironically, the huge inflation had essentially wiped out all German debts. As a result, after 1922 reparations payments were really not a burden to Germany, although Germans then and afterward continued to point to the onerous obligations imposed by the victorious Allies as a key source of the country's economic problems.[25]

Living standards in Germany improved in 1924 and mostly continued to do so for the remainder of the decade. An especially good year in 1927 finally boosted per capita income past the prewar peak. Despite increasingly tight monetary policy, and a crash in the German stock market in May of that year, the expansion continued at a modest pace through 1929. But then the depression arrived, and by 1932 German income per capita was back to the level of the first few years of the twentieth century.

The response of German economic policy initially made the downturn worse. Fearful of renewed inflation, and anxious to stem the outflow of gold, the Reichsbank kept its discount rate well above the prevailing rates in New York and London.[26] Beginning in 1930 the government also turned toward fiscal austerity in an attempt to balance its budget in the face of shrinking tax revenues. The deficit did narrow, as transfer payments and other spending declined faster than tax payments, but the effect was to depress economic activity even further. In 1931 the government imposed wage reductions, which further compounded the decline.[27]

Between 1929 and 1932 German industrial production fell by 42 percent, more than in any country except the United States.[28] Businesses failed across the country. In 1931 the large Darmstadt and National Bank closed its doors. Unemployment, which was already fairly high in Germany in the late 1920s—nearly 9 percent even in 1928, the last "golden year"—rose to 34 percent.[29] The interlude of economic success in the latter half of the 1920s had disappeared.

It was against this background of more than a decade of economic disappointments and crises that the Nazi Party rose from nothing to assume absolute power in Germany. In 1919 Adolf Hitler, an Austrian who had served in World War I as a corporal in the army of the king of Bavaria, became only the thirtieth member of an obscure group called the German Worker's Party. The next year he pushed aside the group's founder (a nonentity named Anton Drexler) and assumed the leadership himself. Renamed the National Socialist German Workers Party in 1920, the party combined in concept the respective right- and left-wing strands of German nationalism and proletarian socialism. Its application of these principles, however, was extremist. While many of the party's positions on the issues of the day resembled the stance of the more traditionally conservative Nationalist Party—both parties, for example, detested the Versailles treaty as well as the new German republic—the "Nazis" (from the first two syllables of "National" in the German pronunciation) also displayed from the outset a proclivity for violence, directed against not only Jews and political opponents but also those within the party whom one faction or another wanted to purge.

In its early years the Nazi Party was one of a number of paramilitary groups operating at the fringe of German politics, maintaining contacts with one another, with war veterans who provided them with arms, and with former army officers who saw them as a kind of reserve to be called on when the time was ripe to avenge the "stab in the back" of 1918. In November 1923, with French troops in the Ruhr and the German economy wracked by the previous year's hyperinflation, Hitler's small group joined forces with former general Ludendorff in an attempt to overthrow the German republic. (The episode became known as the "Beer Hall Putsch.")[30] The coup failed, and Hitler spent several months in the Bavarian state prison, where he wrote *Mein Kampf* (My Struggle).

Once out of prison, Hitler not only resumed the Nazis' usual street activities, together with his own role as a beer hall orator, but also began to take part in regularly organized politics.[31] In the Reichstag election of May 1924, with German unemployment up to 13 percent and other dislocations due to the previous year's hyperinflation still lingering, Nazi candidates drew 7 percent of the vote. The party's total dropped to just 3 percent in the subsequent election held that December (by which time unemployment was on the way down).

In the election of May 1928, after the German stock market crash but with the hyperinflation of 1922–23 now a receding memory, and still well before the full economic decline of the depression set in (in the spring of 1928 the unemployment rate was still below 9 percent), the Nazi Party again drew only 2.8 percent of the vote. The Nazis *were* a visible presence in Germany, active in propaganda and occasional street violence, and like other such groups they had their core of fanatical supporters. But until the mass unemployment of the depression years, they were only one among several such groups. In the 1928 election seven other political parties got more votes, ranging from the Nationalists on the right (14 percent) to the Communists on the left (11 percent).

That changed once the depression arrived. In 1929, the Nazis began to attract more support in state-level elections. In the national election for the Reichstag in September 1930, with unemployment now nearly 23 percent, Nazi candidates drew 18.3 percent of the votes, second only to the Social Democrats, and wound up holding 107 of the 491 seats.[32] Hitler had become a major figure on the German political scene, and the Nazi Party a serious force.

Even apart from any role played by Hitler and the Nazis, by this time parliamentary democracy in Germany had largely ceased to function. Effective coalitions in the multiparty Reichstag proved impossible to assemble. Successive chancellors instead governed mostly by having the republic's president, the World War I Field Marshal Paul von Hindenburg, now quite old and never a great advocate of democracy anyway, sign decrees under the Weimar constitution's emergency powers clause. But the government's economic policy was counterproductive anyway, and the depression in Germany continued to worsen. As it did, the Nazis continued to gain strength.

In early 1932, with unemployment now above 6 million (an astonishing

44 percent), Hindenburg's term as president was nearing an end. Hitler ran against him and, in the final runoff, polled 13.4 million votes against Hindenburg's 19.4 million. Then, in Reichstag elections in July, the Nazis polled a stunning 37.3 percent of the vote to emerge as Germany's top political party, with 230 seats. The Social Democrats had fallen to a distant second, with 133 seats on 21.6 percent of the vote.[33]

As Nazi supporters waited eagerly for their leader to join the government, Hitler steadfastly refused to accept any office but chancellor. But although the small group of aristocrats surrounding Hindenburg was glad to use the Nazis as an authoritarian bulwark against the Communists (who had also gained strength during the 1920s, and had come out of the July 1932 election with the third-largest number of Reichstag seats), making an Austrian ex-corporal the new chancellor of Germany remained highly unpalatable. The standoff continued until September, when Hitler managed to force Franz von Papen, who was then chancellor, to dissolve the Reichstag and call yet another round of elections for November.

The Nazis' share of the vote fell to 33.1 percent, versus 20.4 percent for the Social Democrats and 16.6 percent for the Communists, and Nazi-held seats in the Reichstag dropped from 230 to 196. Part of the erosion presumably reflected the frustration of Nazi supporters impatient at Hitler's seeming reluctance to govern. Initial signs of economic recovery, including a short-lived increase in industrial output and a decline in unemployment, probably mattered as well.[34] A transit strike in Berlin had also made clear, at least to some German voters, the contradictions inherent in the Nazis' promising workers that they would crush the power of the large-scale industrialists while simultaneously promising businessmen that they would smash the trade unions. (In the end, however, Hitler made good on both promises.) But with the support of Papen, who was deposed as chancellor in December and who then agreed to serve as vice chancellor, Adolf Hitler finally became chancellor of Germany on January 30, 1933.[35]

"Who voted for Hitler?" is a question that historians and others have debated ever since,[36] but what is most noteworthy is the breadth of Nazi support by 1932 among different groups of Germans. Historian Richard Hamilton has highlighted the fact that "the vote for the National Socialists varied inversely with the size of the community," but even in cities of more than 100,000, the Nazis in July 1932 drew on average 32 percent of the vote (compared to 41 percent in cities of less than 25,000).[37] Especially in Berlin and other urban areas, the Nazis seem to have drawn support disproportionately from the middle and in particular the lower middle class, while urban working-class voters instead preferred either the Socialists or the Communists. But the Nazis attracted substantial support from working-class voters too, especially among the young and the unemployed.[38] Finally, as historian Thomas Childers has documented, the Nazis also developed "a surprisingly large following in more established social circles," including mostly upper-middle-class university students, civil servants even in the middle and upper grades, and voters residing in the affluent districts of Berlin, Hamburg, and other cities. Among these "established elites of German society," motivations for supporting the Nazis included "fear of the Marxist left, frustrated career ambitions, and resentment at the erosion of social prestige and professional security."[39]

Once in office Hitler moved rapidly to consolidate his power. He promptly called new elections for March 5. Conveniently, on the night of February 27–28 the Reichstag building burned to the ground.[40] Citing the supposed threat to public security, Hitler persuaded Hindenburg to sign an emergency decree that abolished freedom of the press and the right of public assembly. The Socialists and the Communists, the second- and third-largest parties after the Nazis in the November elections, were unable to campaign. To make matters worse, the SA, the Nazis' private army commonly known as the Brownshirts, now openly harassed the opposition and its supporters.

Even under these conditions the Nazis won only 43.9 percent of the March 5 vote, but that proved enough. Meeting in the Berlin Opera House on March 23, with the Communist deputies either under arrest or otherwise forcibly prevented from attending, with the middle-class parties intimidated by chanting storm troopers, and with only the Socialists openly opposed, the Reichstag gave the required two-thirds majority to the all-important Enabling Act that permitted Hitler, as chancellor, to govern without either the legislature or the president.[41] The German republic gave way to the Third Reich.

Governing under the March 1933 Enabling Act, Hitler soon removed all obstacles to his and the Nazis' absolute power. In early May the SA occupied the offices of every German trade union, and a week later all unions were merged into a new government-sponsored German Labor Front. By the end of the month a new law made clear that the front's purpose was not representation of workers but regimentation, and state compulsion replaced free bargaining over wages. No independent trade unions were allowed. In July the Law Against the Formation of Political Parties did just what its name implied, banning all parties other than the Nazis.[42]

A year later, in the bloody purge popularly called the "Night of the Long Knives," Hitler's personal followers murdered the ambitious SA leader Ernst Röhm, a potential rival, and other members of the radical wing of the Nazi movement, along with some non-Nazis (like Hitler's immediate predecessor as chancellor, General Kurt von Schleicher) who still opposed Nazi rule. Hitler now formed an alliance with Heinrich Himmler's black-shirted SS troops and with the leadership of the German army. When President Hindenburg died in August 1934, Hitler added the title "führer" (leader) to that of chancellor—44 million Germans voted in a referendum held to confirm this new office, and 88 percent voted yes—and from then on all German soldiers had to swear an oath of loyalty to him personally rather than to the government or the nation.

Within days, the ordinary rule of law started to atrophy.[43] During the first nine months, more than 100,000 people, mostly German citizens with left-wing political sympathies, were sent to newly built concentration camps.[44] In July, Hitler negotiated the "super concordat" with the Vatican, paving the way for the liquidation of the Catholic Center Party and the destruction of German Catholicism as an independent political force.[45] (Hitler's electoral support had been disproportionately Protestant.) A wave of anti-Semitic violence had already accompanied Hitler's appointment as chancellor in January 1933. In April, within a month of the passage of the Enabling Law, a Law for the Restitution of the Professional Civil Service barred anyone of "non-Aryan descent" from civil service employment. The Nuremberg Laws, the chief weapon in the Nazi campaign against the Jews in Germany, followed in 1935. That same year Germany launched a massive program of rearmament.

In March 1938, Hitler sent troops to occupy Austria rather than permit a plebiscite on whether the country should join the Reich. Germany seized the Sudetenland region of Czechoslovakia later that year, and in March 1939 took the rest of that country. In the meanwhile, on November 9, 1938, Kristallnacht, the "Night of Broken Glass," made clear the Nazis' intentions toward the Jews. On September 1, 1939, Germany invaded Poland and World War II began. In January 1942, meeting at Wannsee, just outside Berlin, the Nazi leadership agreed on the "Final Solution" to the "Jewish Question."

. . .

The change of regime in Germany in 1933 also led to new economic policies that fostered a recovery from the depression. Most significant for political purposes, German unemployment dropped from 44 percent in 1932 to 16 percent in 1935, to only 3 percent in 1938.[46] Government spending, initially for housing, roads, and automobiles, and later (only after 1936) for military matériel, boosted the demand for labor.[47] In contrast to Roosevelt's program in the United States, however, which allowed American wages to recover strongly at the cost of a slower decline in unemployment, Hitler used the state's new control over wage bargaining to hold most wages down. (In the five years following the low in 1932, weekly earnings in manufacturing rose by 34 percent in real terms in America compared with 16 percent in Germany.)[48] In 1935 the Nazis introduced compulsory labor service. Additional measures, like tax incentives and propaganda designed to induce women to leave the workforce, also helped to reduce unemployment.[49]

As a result of these internal forces, together with the more general economic recovery that by then was slowly gaining momentum worldwide, overall economic activity in Germany expanded extremely rapidly in the early years under the Nazis. By 1938 per capita income had risen fully 87 percent from the low in 1932 (versus only a 32 percent rise over the same years in the United States).[50] Spurred in part by preparations for war, industrial production more than doubled.[51] Because of the Nazi low-wage policy, however, as well as a rising tax burden imposed on wage earners, the advance in most workers' living standards was more modest. Even so, production of consumer goods in 1938 was back above what it had been in 1929, and 38 percent above 1932.[52]

Whether the post-depression return of economic growth and prosperity would in time have prevented Germany's disastrous course had the country retained a democracy will forever remain a hypothetical question. But adoption of Nazi rule, and with it the Nazis' program, was a one-way street. As Alexander Gerschenkron put the matter in his 1943 book, *Bread and Democracy in Germany*, "The decisive lesson taught by the history of the German Republic after 1918 is that, under certain conditions, a well-established democracy may choose to destroy itself." Gerschenkron went on, "The causes may be temporary, but the effects are not. Rejection of democracy may be the result of a temporary combination of special circumstances that produce an antidemocratic psychosis among the populace. The popular mood may pass rapidly, along with the conditions that have occasioned it. But the profound political change which it has caused remains, and remains permanently unless, indeed, it is reversed by the immense effort of global war."[53]

. . .

The Nazis' rise to power and the events that followed under their rule constitute the most dramatic episode in the modern history of the West demonstrating a connection between economic distress and perverse social and political development. More clearly than in any other Western country, the most severe economic decline in a nation's history powerfully contributed to the total, indeed catastrophic, collapse of democracy and of any pretense of tolerance. Other parts of the modern German experience, however, are also instructive in showing the effects of economic growth or stagnation.

To begin, it was not until 1870, with the diplomacy of the Prussian minister president Otto von Bismarck, that Germany existed as a national entity. Instead, two of Europe's great powers, the kingdom of Prussia and the Austrian Habsburg empire, loosely presided over a variety of small states, petty dukedoms, and free cities. The Austro-Prussian War, which concluded with Austria's defeat at the battle of Königgrätz in 1866, finally determined which of the two would take the lead in assembling a larger Germany. Bismarck adeptly exploited his opportunities to do so, and in January 1871, with the Prussian army still laying siege to Paris, Wilhelm I of Prussia was proclaimed emperor of Germany. Bismarck became the united Germany's first chancellor.[54]

Although German unification was a top-down project, far from the "We the People" spirit that had created the United States out of thirteen former colonies,* it was nonetheless a product of the "liberal era" in Prussian-German politics.[55] To be sure, the new German constitution left most fundamental rights unspecified, and it also made no provision for a responsible executive. But to Europeans familiar with Britain's tradition of a wholly unwritten constitution, these omissions were not necessarily problematic.[56] The new constitution did establish a parliament, the Reichstag, to be elected by all male citizens over age twenty-five (a far broader franchise than existed in Britain at the time). As was appropriate in light of the

---

*The song "Deutschland, Deutschland Uber Alles" (Germany, Germany Above All) was originally popularized during this period as a way of promoting feelings of attachment to the unified German empire, rather than to Prussia, Saxony, or any of the other component elements that had previously claimed citizens' allegiance, and that had often opposed one another in the past. As recently as 1866, for example, Saxony and Bavaria had fought on the Austrian side in the Austro-Prussian War. (The song's title later took on different overtones, and the words were legally banned in Germany after World War II even though the music remained the national anthem.) Even in the American context, as the Civil War had demonstrated, achieving popular identification with the nation in preference to one's home state could prove difficult.

empire's federal structure, with many powers left to the member states, the Reichstag's powers were limited. But importantly in the German setting, it had the right to approve or reject the military budget.

Bismarck's main vehicle of parliamentary governance for almost a decade after the empire's founding was the National Liberal Party, which won 155 of 397 seats in the first Reichstag elections. With the cooperation of several smaller parties, the Liberals in these early years proceeded to pass a series of important legislative acts that modernized and secularized the German government as well as German society. Key innovations during this period included uniform codes of law, a new commercial code, the development of free markets internally and promotion of freer trade across Germany's borders, and establishment of a central bank (the Reichsbank) and a uniform coinage (the mark). As the decade went on, the Reichstag developed new judiciary and bankruptcy codes, extended the federal government's jurisdiction in both civil and criminal law, and established the Imperial Supreme Court.[57]

Because German unification was also bound up in German nationalism, and also because the strong role of the chancellor under Bismarck meant that the new empire fell well short of a true parliamentary democracy, historians have sometimes disparaged the extent of the liberal reforms that followed. But in the context of the time, when monarchs still not only reigned but ruled throughout most of Europe, the direction of change was clear. Moreover, beyond the realm of actual legislation, the newly unified Germany seemed to embrace an ethos of greater openness in many other dimensions. The last remaining legal restrictions on the rights of Jews, for example, were removed in the early 1870s, thereby completing the process of emancipation that had been underway for much of the nineteenth century (especially since 1848). As historian Geoff Eley has described the thrust of the new Germany more broadly, "unification brought the cultural ascendancy of a distinctive set of values, stressing merit, competition, secularism, law and order, hostility to hereditary privilege, ideas of personal dignity and independence, and generalized belief in the modern morality of progress."[58]

Although German economic performance was mixed in the years leading up to unification, the period following the middle of the nineteenth century was a time of rapid industrialization in most of the German states and on average living standards rose solidly. The overseas aspects of Germany's new imperialism provided a further boost, as colonies abroad provided cheap goods for German consumers. In 1871 German income per capita stood 24 percent above the level of a decade earlier, and 43 percent above that of two decades before.[59] The initial few years following unification turned out to be a period of especially rapid expansion, so much so that later on the label *"Gründerzeit"* (founders' time) conventionally called to mind a booming economy, marked by widespread industrial as well as residential investment. (Houses dating to that era are still called *"Gründerzeit* houses.") Entrepreneurs founded new companies in rapid order, and the volume of private finance surged in the newly integrated German capital market with centers in Frankfurt, Berlin, and Hamburg. Spurred by a stock market boom as well as reparations being received from the French, German per capita income rose at an average rate of over 6 percent per annum from 1871 through 1874.[60] Along with Prussia's military successes and Bismarck's adroitness, the strong sense of economic progress helped shape the direction that the new empire took in its early years.

Eighteen seventy-five marked a change in the current of economic affairs in Germany (although the first warning was a financial crisis in the summer of 1873). Per capita income declined in seven of the next eight years, and despite a modest recovery after 1882, by 1884 the average living standard stood below what it had been at the peak ten years before.[61] It was not until the end of the decade that backward-looking comparisons once again showed any noticeable progress for the average citizen.

With the onset of economic stagnation, the political stance of the newly unified Germany changed as well. In what is often called the "second founding" (or the "conservative refounding") of the German empire, at the end of the 1870s, Bismarck abandoned his alliance with the National Liberals and instead began to govern primarily with the support of the Catholic Center Party. The result was a distinct shift in policy.

One immediate change was a turn from free trade to protectionism. As late as 1877, Germany was still abolishing the last of the customs duties inherited from the old Zollverein (literally, "toll union"). But in 1879 Bismarck introduced a new tariff on iron and grain—meant to gain support from the Rhine industrialists and East Prussian Junkers, respectively— together with indirect taxes on tobacco, salt, and coffee. The new tariff rates were low, but what is significant in the prevailing climate of free trade is that Germany adopted them at all. New tariffs were, in effect, a symbolic rejection of the economics of liberalization of the 1870s.[62]

The National Liberals opposed the measure and broke into two separate groups over the issue. But the Center Party supported the tariff in exchange for Bismarck's agreeing that the federal government would share the proceeds with the states. The result was not only to make Germany a protectionist country once again but also to strengthen the more conservative forces in the state governments. At the same time, Bismarck ended the "*Kulturkampf*" campaign aimed at weakening the position of the Catholic Church in Germany.

Another sign of the new times was Bismarck's exploitation of two assassination attempts on the kaiser in 1878 to outlaw the Social Democratic Party. Although there was no evidence of the party's involvement in either incident, Bismarck proclaimed a "social peril" and immediately called for new elections. The Social Democrats, the National Liberals, and the Progressives all lost seats, while most of the conservative parties gained. Bismarck then got the new Reichstag to approve legislation that declared the Social Democratic Party illegal, shut down its press, forbade its meetings, and authorized the government to expel presumed agitators from their homes.[63] The party as an organization virtually closed down, and its newspapers now had to be smuggled into the country from Switzerland. By 1890 some 1,500 people had been imprisoned and another 900 expelled from their homes under the 1878 law, for such violations as holding meetings, distributing newspapers, and otherwise "subverting the social order" by promoting the party's views.[64]

Another turn toward social and political reaction at the end of the 1870s was a new defensive alliance with the conservative Austro-Hungarian empire. Although the treaty was, in historian A. J. P. Taylor's words, "the first permanent arrangement in peace time between two Great Powers since the end of the *ancien régime*," it was seen as an outward symbol of Bismarck's return to unambiguous conservatism and support for monarchism after his nearly decade-long collaboration with the German liberals.[65] By the last quarter of the nineteenth century, the Habsburg empire was already a sinking ship (although no one could have known at the time that binding Germany to come to the defense of Austria-Hungary would create the basis for what became Germany's disastrous participation in World War I).

The late 1870s and early 1880s also marked what historian Thomas Nipperdey has called the first "boom" in modern German anti-Semitism.[66] In 1878 the Berlin preacher Adolf Stoecker founded the Christian Socials, a movement intended to wean the working classes away from the Social Democrats and win their allegiance for the monarchy. Stoecker's opportunistic approach incorporated both anti-capitalism and anti-Semitism, and in its early years the movement drew widespread support. Soon thereafter, men including Wilhelm Marr, Ernst Henrici, and Bernhard Förster began forming new parliamentary parties and other formal organizations expounding "scientific" anti-Semitism. Later in the 1880s, German anti-Semitism increased further with the efforts of agrarian activist Otto Böckel (the "Hessian peasant-king") and then such nationalist groups as the Pan-German League and the Navy League.[67] All of this bigotry was in part motivated by economic concerns. One of its staples, for example, was opposition to "Jewish department stores" that competed with independent craftsmen and tradesmen.

Although the political parties that took the explicit label "Anti-Semites" achieved only limited electoral success—their share of the national vote peaked at 3.8 percent in the 1890s—like many new parties they achieved far greater impact by pushing the established parties to adopt what amounted to their program.[68] The far larger German Conservative Party, for example, adopted much of the anti-Semites' agenda as part of the "Tivoli Program," its official 1892 policy platform. Clearly the perceived electoral threat these small parties represented went well beyond their recorded vote totals.[69]

Although Germany after 1878 or 1879, during a period of economic struggles, adopted a nonprogressive and even anti-progressive stance in many respects, there was an important exception. Between 1883 and 1889, Bismarck put in place a remarkable series of genuinely innovative social programs that in time served as explicit models for many other countries, including the United States during the New Deal and Britain during the reforms led by Asquith and Lloyd George as well as during the later reforms that followed the Beveridge Report. In 1881 Bismarck proposed a compulsory system of worker's accident insurance, to be paid not only out of employers' contributions but also from a direct government subsidy. After much debate, the Reichstag approved the measure in 1884 (but with the full cost paid by employers).[70]

Bismarck meanwhile had proposed a form of compulsory national health insurance ("sickness insurance"), and in 1883 this scheme had taken effect, with the costs split between employers and employees. And in 1889, again at Bismarck's urging, the Reichstag adopted a system of "old age and disability insurance" to be financed in part by employers' and employees' contributions but also subsidized directly by the government. (The label "Old Age, Survivors, and Disability Insurance," used from its inception by America's Social Security System, was taken directly from Bismarck's pension program, as was the choice of sixty-five as the eligible retirement age.)

Bismarck's objective in all this was not social reform for its own sake but rather to undermine workers' interest in socialism and, more broadly, to foster their allegiance to a German empire conceived along paternalist lines.[71] (In his memoirs, published privately in 1893 and then for the public in 1898, Bismarck failed even to mention these innovations.)[72] But regardless of the motivation, in so doing he wound up pioneering the modern "social safety net" and even paving the way for other aspects of the modern welfare state.

As dark as Germany's crisis was between the two world wars, in many respects the first four or even five decades after World War II virtually constitute one long period of movement toward enhanced democracy. At the same time, German standards of living were rising dramatically and almost continuously. Several distinct sets of events during this period stand out.

First, the founding and consolidation of the new West German republic out of the wreckage of war laid a basis for Germany's subsequent democracy that remains strong today. By the spring of 1949, the United States, Britain, and France had successfully created new governments in the states within their respective zones of military occupation, unified the three separate zones, established both an economic council and a parliamentary council (elected by the state legislatures), and introduced a new uniform currency. The Soviet attempt to blockade and thereby isolate West Berlin, which the western Allies had overcome only with a massive airlift the year before, had made clear that further unification, to include the eastern zone still under Soviet occupation, was impossible on any reasonable terms. The Allies therefore convened a special conference—not an elected assembly, but including representatives of the revived non-Nazi parties—to create the governing basis for a new republic.[73]

The proposed new *Grundgesetz*, or Basic Law—called that to emphasize that it was not yet a constitution *(Verfassung)*—was an obvious effort to avoid the flaws in the Weimar constitution.[74] In contrast to the old presidential authority to rule by decree in time of threat to public order and safety, the Basic Law made the president of the new republic a mostly ceremonial figure. In contrast to the instability of the old chancellor's hold on office—between 1919 and Hitler's assumption of power in 1933 the Weimar Republic had twenty-one governments—the Basic Law provided for a "constructive" vote of no confidence, under which any parliamentary motion to overturn the existing government had to specify who the new chancellor would be. In contrast to the confusion of the old parliament with its numerous splinter parties, the Basic Law required that a party receive at least 5 percent of the total popular vote, or elect a minimum of three deputies, in order to achieve representation in the new parliament (the Bundestag).

The new Basic Law also sought to guarantee the essential civil liberties that the Nazi regime had brutally suppressed. Its first section, with articles bearing such titles as "Protection of Human Dignity," "Rights of Liberty," and "Freedom of Faith, Conscience and Creed," guaranteed freedom of speech, freedom of religion, the right to assembly, the right to move from place to place, and freedom of the press, to all citizens *except*—in order to prevent any repetition of the Nazi experience—those who advocate over-throwing the republic. Women's rights, including the right to vote, were explicitly made identical to men's. The Basic Law also returned to Germany some of the federal structure of Bismarck's empire, requiring that new legis-lation also be approved by the council of *Länder* (states), and restoring to the *Länder* substantial jurisdiction over such matters as health, education, and criminal justice.[75]

By early May the conferees had finished drafting the Basic Law. In rapid succession the parliamentary council, the committee of allied military gov-ernors, and the legislatures of all the states except Bavaria (which held out for a more decentralized structure, but declared the Basic Law valid any-way) approved it. On May 23, 1949, the Federal Republic of Germany came into being.

The new republic's first election, in August, delivered roughly one-third of the seats in the new Bundestag to the Christian Democrats, another one-third to the Social Democrats, and the rest to other parties. In an alliance with the Free Democrats, the largest of the smaller parties, the Christian Democrats formed a government with their leader Konrad Ade-nauer as chancellor. Almost immediately, the new government proceeded to launch a comprehensive wave of domestic reforms affecting virtually all aspects of government. It also quickly embraced moves toward freer trade as well as European unification, thereby setting the path that led to Germany's key role in the European Coal and Steel Community and, in due course, the Treaty of Rome and the European Common Market.

Further measures—for example, a new antitrust policy, the use of pub-lic funds to alleviate the continuing housing shortage, and a 60 to 75 percent increase in the generosity of pensions—followed in the 1950s.[76] By the time Adenauer left office, fourteen years later, the modern West Germany was firmly established.[77] Although later on many feared that the still new democ-racy might succumb to the student violence of 1968, which hit Germany no less than other European countries, or to the terrorist assassinations subsequently carried out by the Baader-Meinhof Gang and the Red Army Faction, the West German state, and its democracy, continued to thrive.

Whatever sense of economic progress German citizens perceived by the end of the 1940s had to be mostly forward-looking. Postwar reconstruction was only just getting underway in many areas, smaller towns still faced great deprivations, and beginning in the summer of 1948 the Berlin Blockade created new dislocations. But by 1949 the pace of recovery was rapid, and apart from the lingering Soviet threat, the economic future looked clear. Steel production doubled in 1948 alone, and industrial production overall almost doubled in just the second half of the year. Although income per capita in 1949 was already up by 48 percent from the postwar low three years earlier, it was still nearly one-third below what it had been in 1937, the last year before Germany's external military operations began.[78] (This difference probably overstates the effective gap in living standards, however, because so much of Germany's income in the mid- to late 1930s was diverted into paying for rearmament.)

Those who had looked ahead optimistically proved correct. Spurred in part by American aid under the Marshall Plan, economic activity expanded rapidly. By 1953 per capita income was well above that of 1937 (even including all the military spending), and by 1958 it was already more than double the level of 1949.[79] The German "economic miracle" would continue uninterrupted until after the OPEC crisis of the early 1970s. Indeed, by the 1960s German economic expansion was sufficiently vigorous to draw in large numbers of foreign "guest workers," thereby helping to reduce unemployment (and provide additional income from wage remittances) in other parts of Europe as well.

The disaster of the war and the will of the occupying powers were clearly significant forces behind the creation of the new West Germany. But the character of the new regime, as laid down in the Basic Law with its strong commitment to democracy and civil rights, was very much a German undertaking, and in this regard the strong sense of renewed economic growth, both in hand and sure to come, also contributed to public acceptance of the new republic.[80] Over the next decade the awareness of rising living standards further helped to create a climate in which the new German state under Adenauer charted its early course: continued protection of civil liberties and democratic government, a commitment to the Western alliance as the centerpiece of foreign policy, and, under economics minister Ludwig Erhard, a strategy of free markets at home and progressively free trade abroad.

.   .   .

The election of Willy Brandt as chancellor in 1969 marked a renewal and extension of West German democracy. After twenty years under Adenauer, then Erhard, and then Kurt Georg Kiesinger, all Christian Democrats, the country was reaffirming the principle of competitive party politics by turning for the first time to a Social Democrat as chancellor. The fact that Brandt had fought in the German resistance during World War II, while his immediate predecessor, Kiesinger, was a former Nazi functionary who had been interned by the Allies for two years after the war, only made the change more palpable.

In contrast to the Christian Democratic slogan of "No Experiments," Brandt in his first formal statement as chancellor appealed to Germans to "Dare more democracy."[81] In practice this meant new reform initiatives in a variety of areas, including labor relations, education, old-age pensions, and criminal law. As part of an overall emphasis on broadening participation in German democracy, the Brandt government also lowered the voting age to eighteen.

Brandt's first major success was the 1971 Works Organization Law, which strengthened the long-standing work councils that provided forums for German labor and management to resolve issues that arose in business operations. The Federal Education Promotion Law, also passed in 1971, guaranteed all students the right to secondary education of their choice. Although a more radical effort to restructure Germany's traditionally hierarchical primary and secondary education systems failed after meeting opposition from conservative state governments, a set of reforms of German universities went through after several years of debate. The 1972 Pension Reform Law made German government pensions independent of beneficiaries' previous contributions. A 1974 bill reformed several aspects of Germany's criminal code, including making abortion legal (though still subject to restrictions).

Over subsequent years several key aspects of the domestic reforms instituted in Germany under Brandt's leadership proved counterproductive. For example, the cost and difficulty of discharging or even reassigning German workers, much of which dates to this period, was (and continues to be) an important reason why the high unemployment that resulted from the tight monetary policy Germany used in the 1970s to reduce its post-OPEC-crisis inflation proved lasting. German consumer prices rose by 7 percent in 1973 and again in 1974, and by 6 percent in 1975. Not until 1984 did inflation fall below 3 percent on a sustained basis. By then, however, unemployment had risen from less than 1 percent (before 1973) to more than 9 percent.[82] Many people also believed, with reason, that elements of the Brandt education reforms impaired the quality and functioning of Germany's universities.

But as in the case of the Matignon program carried out under Léon Blum's Popular Front in France (and, to some extent, the Beveridge reforms in Britain and even parts of the New Deal in America), whether each of these measures ultimately represented optimal policy is not the issue here. Along with other actions of the period that proved not just well-intentioned but also efficacious, they are significant because they reflected the political desire to achieve both a fairer and a more democratic society, a goal that in Germany at that time attracted unusually widespread public support.

In addition to these domestic initiatives, the Brandt government adopted a new foreign policy that contributed not only to German reunification two decades later but also to the broader rapprochement between the West and the Soviet Union. Although Brandt did not abandon the long-standing West German position that the Federal Republic was Germany's sole legitimate government, in 1970 he held two official meetings with the head of East Germany's Council of Ministers. Also in 1970, Germany under Brandt signed a treaty with the Soviet Union acknowledging the inviolability of the post–World War II border between East Germany and Poland (the Oder-Neisse Line), thereby paving the way for reconciliation between West Germany and Poland later that year. (In Warsaw, for the signing of the treaty with Poland, Brandt visited the memorial to those killed in the April 1943 uprising of the Warsaw Ghetto, poignantly bowing his head and dropping to his knees on the monument's steps.) In recognition of these accomplishments, Brandt received the Nobel Peace Prize in 1971.

When Brandt took office in 1969, West Germany had enjoyed unbroken economic growth since 1947. Real income per capita was more than triple what it had been at the founding of the republic twenty years earlier. Price inflation, a special concern in Germany after the hyperinflation of the Weimar days, had averaged just 2 percent per annum over these years. Unemployment had declined steadily throughout the 1950s, and in most years of the 1960s fewer than 1 percent of German workers were without jobs.[83]

Moreover, this strong economic performance continued through the Brandt government's early years, with per capita income rising on average by nearly 4 percent per annum for 1969 through 1973. Brandt was therefore able to undertake both his domestic reforms and his diplomatic initiatives at a time when West German citizens saw the world through the lens of remarkably robust and sustained economic progress.[84]

Finally, the reunification of West and East Germany—the realization of German hopes (as well as Allied objectives) dating from the earliest post-war days, as well as of the aspirations that had motivated Brandt's foreign policy—also occurred at a time of substantial prosperity in West Germany. Although growth had slowed after the OPEC oil price rise (Germany imports almost all of the oil it uses, and more than three-fourths of its natural gas), and again when the United States underwent back-to-back recessions in 1980 and 1981–82, in the latter half of the 1970s and throughout much of the 1980s Germany continued to enjoy rapidly rising standards of living despite the high unemployment. By 1989 real income per capita was more than half again higher than when Brandt became chancellor twenty years before. And in 1989 unemployment fell below 8 percent for the first time since the early years of the decade.

Unification with East Germany stood as a goal quite independent of economic considerations, and the specific catalyst at work in bringing it about was the collapse of the Soviet empire and, shortly thereafter, of the Soviet Union itself. But West Germany's strong economic performance in the years (and decades) leading up to 1989 was important because it enabled chancellor Helmut Kohl's government to commit to the financial burdens of unification in sufficient measure to allow the entire endeavor to proceed. By 1989 East Germany was clearly crumbling, both economically and politically. East Germans by the thousands were fleeing to the West, first through Hungary, then via Czechoslovakia and Poland. By early November crowds in the hundreds of thousands were gathering in Leipzig and East Berlin to demand an end to travel restrictions altogether, and to protest the regime more generally. In Berlin some demonstrators even began to dismantle sections of the city's infamous wall. The Soviet Union under Mikhail Gorbachev no longer had the means or the will to support continued repression. On November 9, East German border guards opened the wall and throngs of jubilant East Berliners streamed into the long-forbidden western sector of the city.

Opening the Berlin Wall only increased the westward flow of East Germans. In just the first three months of 1990, more than 150,000 came to the West. This mass immigration began to place substantial strains on West Germany's social services, so much so that the government urgently needed to find a way to persuade the remaining East Germans to stay home. Meeting with Hans Modrow, the new head of the East German Council of Ministers, Kohl had already begun to make long-range plans for unification.

In February Kohl took what proved to be the crucial step by proposing an economic union, in which the West German mark would become the currency for both Germanys. One month later he announced that West Germany would exchange most individual East Germans' holdings of increasingly devalued "East marks"—in the end, up to 6,000 marks per adult and 2,000 per child—for West German marks at a one-for-one ratio, and any excess East marks at two for one. The announcement created an immediate euphoria that enabled the new parties in East Germany that were most strongly committed to unification, including the new eastern division of Kohl's Christian Democrats, to draw the largest share of the vote in the next month's elections.

Within a month of the election, the new East German government announced it would proceed not only with currency union but also full political reunification. The currency union took effect on July 1. The formal unification treaty between East and West Germany was signed by the end of August. In September the United States, Britain, France, and the Soviet Union gave their approval and renounced all of their remaining rights as occupying powers. Formal reunification took place on October 3, 1990. For the 16 million citizens of the former East Germany, the expansion of democracy and enhancement of fundamental freedoms was as sweeping as it was sudden.

The return of democracy and personal freedoms to the one-fifth of the nation's combined population that had known neither since 1933 was clearly one of the major events in modern German history. Freedom of expression also includes the freedom to express anti-democratic sentiments, however. Germany's experience in the decade and a half since unification has not only demonstrated once again the universal nature of this truth but has shown that the prevalence and intensity of such tendencies hinge in part on whether ordinary citizens have a sense of getting ahead economically. As has often been the case elsewhere, the specific focus of such sentiment in post-unification Germany has been the presence and status of foreign immigrants.

As in France, where Le Pen's National Front has enjoyed success mostly in centers of high unemployment, the return of anti-immigrant poli-

tics and even deadly violence in Germany has mostly appeared in what used
to be East Germany, where large numbers of inefficient Soviet-era enterprises have closed and many of these firms' former workers have yet to find
new jobs. Within two years of unification, 3.4 million East Germans had
lost their jobs and unemployment in the region was estimated to be 30 percent.[85] As of 2000, even before the economic slowdown that began the new
decade, average unemployment remained 17.4 percent in areas of the former East Germany, as opposed to 7.8 percent in the former West.[86] In a survey taken at the time of reunification, in 1989, 94 percent of young East
Germans said they were optimistic about their futures. Ten years later, only
15 percent of young people in what had been East Germany looked forward
optimistically.[87]

At the same time, significant numbers of foreigners, many from Turkey,
continued to work in Germany, as they had since the 1960s. Beginning in
the 1980s, Germany also accepted a smaller but still noticeable number of
refugees seeking asylum from political repression and civil war in the
Balkans. By the 1990s, with the collapse of the Soviet Union and the widespread political and economic chaos in many parts of Eastern Europe, the
inflow became far greater. Far-right, nationalist, and even neo-Nazi political parties sought (and are seeking) to capitalize on the resulting frustrations
of many German voters.

Especially in light of Germany's past, whether these reactionary parties
will in time pose a serious electoral threat at the national level has been a
much debated question. The Republican Party, which is overtly neo-Nazi,
has had the greatest national presence, but its impact in national elections
has remained limited. In the former East, however, where unemployment is
especially high and where the public had little exposure to foreign residents
during the decades under Soviet rule, the Republicans and other far-right
parties have sometimes done well in state-level elections.[88] In 1998, for
example, the German People's Union, a previously small and unsuccessful
group with a program mostly based on extreme German nationalism and
open hatred of foreigners, captured 12 percent of the vote in statewide elections in Saxony-Anhalt, where unemployment was over 20 percent. More
telling, the party drew one-fourth of the votes cast by citizens under age
thirty, and fully one-third of the votes cast by those without jobs.[89] The next
year the German People's Union took 5.3 percent of the vote in Brandenburg, where unemployment was also 20 percent, a smaller electoral success
than in Saxony-Anhalt but still above the 5 percent threshold necessary to
gain representation in the state's legislature.[90]

Beyond electoral politics, Germany in recent years has experienced a wave of political violence mostly directed at foreigners. In the first year following unification, Germany received more than 250,000 refugees, some from the former Soviet Union and elsewhere in Eastern Europe, many from as far away as Vietnam and Mozambique. A series of physical attacks on these refugees peaked on a weekend in September 1991 when local youths attacked buildings where large numbers of foreigners lived in twenty towns across what had been East Germany. In Hoyerswerda, an economically depressed town between Berlin and Dresden, gangs besieged two apartment complexes for an entire week, despite more than eighty arrests by the police. Finally, in the middle of the night police placed 230 foreigners, including Vietnamese and Africans, on buses and took them to safety at a nearby army base. Jubilant local residents later appeared on national television to proclaim Hoyerswerda "foreigner-free."[91]

In 1992, as Germany's inflow of immigrants swelled to more than a half-million, the number of violent attacks on foreigners or on their homes rose to 2,000.[92] In the most massive of these incidents, which occurred after a week of anti-immigrant rioting, a crowd of more than 1,000 neo-Nazi youths firebombed a ten-story refugee hostel in the Lichtenhagen section of Rostock, an industrial seaport where unemployment had reached nearly 40 percent. Once again, police had to evacuate several hundred foreigners, this time Romanian Gypsies, to a local army base. Once again, local residents appeared on national television to offer support for the rioters, chanting "foreigners out" and "Germany for the Germans."[93]

Other episodes proved more deadly. Later the same year, in Mohlin, not far from Hamburg, a twenty-five-year-old neo-Nazi firebombed two multifamily houses where ethnic Turks were living. An adult woman who had lived in Germany for many years and two girls, aged ten and fourteen, died. Moments after the bombs hit, anonymous callers telephoned the local police and fire departments to take responsibility, offering the "Heil Hitler" salutation.[94] The next spring five members of a Turkish family burned to death—two young women and three girls—in a neo-Nazi arson attack on their house in Solingen, near Cologne, where the total population of 180,000 included 7,000 Turks. The victims' family had settled in Solingen more than twenty years earlier.[95]

A further disturbing aspect of many of these episodes was the initially passive response of both the police and Helmut Kohl's government. Indeed, almost simultaneously with the Solingen attack, the Bundestag moved to tighten the liberal asylum laws specified in Germany's constitution. Opponents of the action denounced it, to no avail, as a surrender to right-wing violence.[96] The latter years of Kohl's record-long chancellor-ship were marked more generally by political stagnation, often called the *"Reformstau"* (reform congestion), in which he lacked the energy or the nec-essary majority in the *Länder* council to take decisive action on practically any front.

Although incidents of political violence in Germany abated after 1993, they nonetheless continued through the decade at a level three to four times that of the pre-unification period.[97] The greater frequency of such acts in the former East, with its far higher unemployment, also persisted. In 1999 the frequency of reported "extreme-right violent acts" there ranged between 2 and 3 per 100,000 inhabitants, depending on the state. Among the nine former West German states, where unemployment was lower, the greatest incidence of such acts was 1.4 per 100,000 inhabitants in Hamburg, and in each of the others it was 1 or below (and in most cases well below).[98]

Analysis of Germans' attitudes based on opinion surveys has shown that the prospect of unemployment—actually, the fear of becoming unem-ployed, more than the fact of unemployment—significantly increased any given individual's likelihood of exhibiting, or at least expressing, bias against foreigners.[99] By contrast, having a favorable perception of either one's own or the nation's future economic prospects reduced the likelihood of bias, as did having more education and being employed in a professional career, as well as belonging to a labor union (presumably because German unions provide at least limited employment protection for their members).[100] One largely unexpected finding has been that skilled workers in Germany were more likely to exhibit anti-foreigner bias than unskilled workers, perhaps because skilled workers felt they had more to lose, and perhaps because they felt especially at risk if their skills were of use primarily to their current employer (so that losing their current job would effectively mean dropping from the skilled to the unskilled labor force).[101]

Overall, the survey evidence makes clear the role that feelings of eco-nomic insecurity play in accounting for German resistance to immigration—and, by extension, related expressions of xenophobia including political activity and even criminal violence. In this respect post-unification Ger-many has proved no different from other countries, both today and in the past.

Figure 11.1 summarizes the relationship between economic growth or stag-nation, and the direction of political and social movement, in Germany since the early 1870s.

	Responses to *Growth*	Responses to *Stagnation*
Movement *toward* openness, tolerance, mobility, fairness, democracy	✓ Unification and the early empire (1871–75) ✓ Federal Republic (1949) ✓ Brandt reforms (1969–74) ✓ Reunification (1989–90)	✗ Bismarck social reforms (1883–89)
Movement *away* from openness, tolerance, mobility, fairness, democracy		✓ Conservative refounding (1878–79) ✓ Nazi rise to power (1930–33) ✓ *Reformstau* (1993–98) ✓ Anti-immigrant agitation and violence (1991–99)

FIGURE 11.1

Consequences of Economic Growth Versus Stagnation:
Germany Since Creation of the Modern State

The Nazis' rise to power, beginning in the economic and political chaos of the Weimar years but then especially during Germany's decline into the Great Depression—surely the most significant single episode in German experience during this entire period—is squarely consistent with the notion of a correspondence between stagnating (in this case, declining) living standards and a movement away from openness, tolerance, and democracy. So are other significant unfortunate episodes. Conversely, the major episodes representing the opening of German society and the extension of German democracy have mostly occurred against the background of rising incomes.

PART IV

DEVELOPMENT, EQUALITY, GLOBALIZATION, AND THE ENVIRONMENT

Chapter 12

Economics and Politics in the Developing World

[M]odernity breeds stability, but modernization breeds
instability. . . . It is not the absence of modernity but the efforts
to achieve it which produce political disorder.

SAMUEL P. HUNTINGTON
Political Order in Changing Societies[1]

It is today difficult to understand how Marxism was so long so
successful in presenting social conflict, impressively dressed
up as . . . "class struggle," as the principal, ultimate, and most
irreconcilable type of conflict of modern society,
when it is in fact the conflict that lends itself most readily
to the arts of compromise.

ALBERT O. HIRSCHMAN
Social Conflicts as Pillars of Democratic Market Society[2]

The attraction of economic growth in the developing world, where incomes
are mostly very low compared to Western industrial standards, is in many
ways straightforward. In more than three-fourths of the world's countries,
encompassing roughly 5 billion of the world's 6 billion inhabitants, if per

capita incomes are higher, people can expect to live longer. Fewer of their children die in infancy. Both children and adults suffer less from malnutrition and disease. They are more likely to have clean water and basic sanitation, and they have better access to medical care. They are more likely to be able to read and write, and they enjoy greater access to education in general. When incomes and living standards are low to begin with, what economic growth means before anything else is enhancement of the most basic dimensions of human life.[3]

Even so, whether rising incomes lead to a more democratic society is, if anything, a question of even greater importance for the economically developing world than among industrialized countries. It is also a harder question to resolve. The issue is so important because what is at stake in many developing countries is not marginal improvement or erosion of established institutions but, all too often, whether basic human freedoms will prevail over political and personal repression, including in some cases outright persecution and even genocide.[4] The question is complex not only because the range of social and political conditions is so broad in the developing world, and hence the potential for change is so great, but also because economic growth normally means something different when it occurs in a preindustrial economy.

In settings where economic growth is also economic *development*, structural change, often involving sharp discontinuities, is central to the process by which incomes increase and living standards improve. New industries—manufacturing, assembling goods from parts made elsewhere, or today even computer programming and staffing service-call centers—draw labor away from agriculture. The new factories and offices require different sets of skills, and a different work discipline, from what farm labor entails. Working in a factory or taking an office job often means moving, sometimes far from home and typically into a much more urban setting. Even farm work becomes more mechanized, as tractors, reapers, and threshers take the place of hand labor. Newly available goods—household appliances, different clothing, cars for the lucky few, above all television sets—change the daily content of ordinary citizens' lives away from work.

And the same possibility for radical change also exists for many developing countries' political institutions and social relations. In contrast to the United States at the time of the Civil War, for example, where a firmly established albeit limited democracy had already been in place for nearly a century (the election of 1860 marked the nineteenth quadrennial vote for president in unbroken succession, and even during the war the 1864 election proceeded on schedule), in many parts of the developing world the challenge has been to create whole new democratic institutions where none existed before.[5]

The possibility of far-reaching change in both the economic and the political and social spheres together is not coincidental. As Daniel Bell has forcefully argued, "structural changes . . . set the contexts of economic opportunity, occupational advancement, and social mobility that give people the resources to sustain or challenge their attitudes."[6] Economic development is precisely such a structural change. And because it fosters the creation of new attitudes, while at the same time providing new resources, economic development often leads to political and social change. The important question is what kind of change.

Two basic facts describing the range of economic conditions across the world at the outset of the twenty-first century frame any effort to address such a question. Even after allowing for differences in the cost of living, the range spanned by the average income in different countries is astonishingly wide: from $54,000 per person in Luxembourg to just $530 in Sierra Leone.[7] And across roughly the lower half of this range, country-to-country differences in the most basic indicators of human well-being or deprivation make unmistakably clear that richer is better.

Indeed, the very breadth of the differences in incomes and in basic living standards across the world today immediately flags the enormous variety of human experience that complicates any attempt to assess the impact of economic growth outside the industrialized world. In South Korea, for example—a developing country until only recently—life expectancy is now seventy-two years for men and seventy-nine for women. In Uganda and Ethiopia life expectancy is below fifty for both men and women, and in AIDS-stricken Malawi and Zimbabwe neither men nor women can expect to live to forty. In Sierra Leone more than 28 percent of all children die before reaching their fifth birthday; in Sri Lanka fewer than 2 percent. In India nearly half of all children are malnourished; in China one in nine is, and in Jamaica one in sixteen. In Bangladesh barely half of the adult men and fewer than one-third of adult women can read; in Thailand only 5 percent of men and 9 percent of women are illiterate.[8]

To be sure, each of these comparisons contrasts countries occupying very different places on the income scale. But that is just the point. Raising people's incomes and living standards is precisely what economic growth does, and the consequent improvement in lifespan, health, and literacy is the foundation of why higher incomes matter so greatly for citizens of a developing country. What is less obvious, but what is at issue here, is what happens more broadly to a developing country's society along the way.

The fact that different countries today enjoy such widely disparate average incomes means that in the past they have experienced different trajectories of economic growth. Because any country's growth rate can change over time, however, international differentials in economic well-being are not constant. A century ago, Britain enjoyed the highest per capita income in the world, while southern European countries like Italy and Spain were far behind, as were distant parts of Britain's own empire like Canada and Australia. Today Britain ranks eighteenth in the world in this regard, with income per capita not quite three-quarters what it is in the United States after allowing for differences in the cost of living. Canada and Australia now have higher average income than in Britain (as does Ireland). So do most countries in northwest Europe. Italy's average income is almost the same as Britain's, and even Spain's is nearly four-fifths of Britain's.[9]

The same is true among many of today's developing countries. In the mid-1970s India's per capita income was nearly twice China's. But China began to grow rapidly once Deng Xiaoping's economic reforms took hold, and by 1991 it had moved ahead. Today the average income in China is 73 percent higher than in India (after allowing for differences in living costs). Since 1975 India's growth pace has been a respectable 3.2 percent per annum. But China has grown at 7.7 percent.

Too often, however, the relevant comparison in the developing world is not between rapid growth and slower growth but between growth and no growth. At the middle of the twentieth century, the average per capita income throughout Africa was 25 percent greater than that in Asia (again, allowing for differences in the cost of living). But most Asian economies grew more rapidly, so that by 1975 the income differential was 25 percent in the opposite direction. Worse yet, per capita income in Africa as a whole stopped growing after 1980. By century's end Asian incomes were, on average, more than two and a half times Africa's.[10] Today nearly one African in two lives on the equivalent of less than $2 per day. (In sub-Saharan Africa nearly 60 percent do.) And although Africa represents only one-seventh of the world's population, the continent now accounts for almost half of those living in such dire poverty.[11]

Country-by-country comparisons make the difference between growth and stagnation all the more evident. Twenty-five years ago the per capita income in Thailand and Ghana was virtually identical, in each case not quite one-tenth that of the United States after allowing for the higher American cost of living. But since then the two countries' economic paths have diverged sharply. Thailand has successfully pursued a classic East Asian development pattern, interrupted only by the region's 1997–98 financial crisis (from which it subsequently made a substantial recovery). By now only 10 percent of the Thai economy is still agricultural; 40 percent is industrialized, and half is in the service sector. Thailand's overall economic growth since 1975, net of both inflation and population growth, has averaged 4.9 percent per annum.

By contrast, Ghana has faltered both economically and politically. In 1957 Ghana became the first country in sub-Saharan Africa to gain independence during the modern postcolonial period. At the time, the country enjoyed the highest average income of any West African country, and one of the highest anywhere on the continent. The economy was heavily dependent on exports of cocoa, however, and in the mid-1960s the world cocoa price fell sharply. Over the next decade the country's cocoa output fell by half, and its production of minerals, another key economic sector, fell by one-third. Even so, for political reasons the government under Kwame Nkrumah resisted domestic entrepreneurship and creation of new businesses. The coup that overthrew Nkrumah in 1966 turned out to be only the first in a series that brought the country five successive military governments over the next fifteen years. (Ghana's first democratic transfer of power did not take place until 2000.) All the while, endemic corruption, periodic bouts of price inflation (sometimes greater than 100 percent per annum), and the burden of accumulating foreign debt continually thwarted attempts to advance economically. Today more than one-third of Ghana's economic output is still agricultural. Although the economy overall has grown over the past quarter-century, the population has grown nearly as fast. Income per capita has risen at only .4 percent per annum since 1975.

The difference between a 4.5 percent growth rate and .4 percent, cumulated over two and a half decades, matters enormously. Today per capita income in Thailand is $7,500. In Ghana the average income is only $2,200. Life expectancy in Ghana is shorter than in Thailand by nine years for men and by fourteen years for women. Infant mortality in Ghana is more than double that in Thailand. In Ghana only 64 percent of the country's children receive even a primary education. In Thailand 90 percent do.[12]

Jamaica and South Korea present a similar contrast. A quarter-century ago both countries had average incomes about 20 percent of the level in the United States, after allowing for cost-of-living differences, with a slight advantage to Jamaica. But since then, on average, Korea's economy has outpaced the country's population growth by fully 5.5 percent per annum while in Jamaica per capita income has grown by only .4 percent. By now South

Korea ranks among the world's highest-income countries, with income per capita (again, adjusted to reflect cost-of-living differences) of nearly $18,000—nearly half what Americans have and almost as high as in some western European countries like Greece and Portugal. In Jamaica the average income is less than $3,800. Not surprisingly, life expectancy is longer in Korea, infant mortality is less, and school enrollment (especially at the secondary level) is greater. Indeed, on most such measures South Korea has approximately reached American levels. Jamaica certainly has not. Here too, the difference between rapid economic growth and very slow growth, cumulated over more than a generation, powerfully affects how people live.*

Ghana and Jamaica are hardly the only examples of countries where living standards have stagnated or even fallen over time. Most of the new nations created out of the former Soviet Union experienced declining per capita income on average during the 1990s, but there much of the shrinkage reflected the discontinuity of these economies' abrupt transition to independence, including in particular the need to shut down inefficient and heavily subsidized state-owned enterprises. More disturbing, most countries in Africa south of the Saharan desert have suffered declining per capita incomes during the last few decades. In Sierra Leone and the Democratic Republic of Congo, both beset by civil wars, economic output has shrunk absolutely. In most of the region production has expanded, but not by enough to keep up with the growing population. In the Americas over the last decade, not just Jamaica but also Haiti, Venezuela, and Bolivia have seen their living standards decline.[13] In all too many countries around the world, the chief problem so-called developing economies face is that, in fact, they are *not* developing.

But just as average incomes and economic growth rates change over time, so also do many countries' political institutions and social conditions. Today's roster of nations includes functioning democracies, military dictatorships, religious theocracies, and countries where conditions are so chaotic, and government so corrupt and ineffective, that no standard label would suffice. Countries like South Korea, Taiwan, Brazil, and some pieces of what used to be the Soviet Union have experienced rapid movement toward political democracy and civil freedoms. Others, like Burma (Myanmar), have moved in the opposite direction. In a few countries the

---

*An even starker contrast is between North and South Korea. At the time they separated, following the South Korean elections in 1948, the two halves of what had been one country had approximately the same standard of living (with perhaps some advantage to North Korea).

movement has come full circle. In Chile, for example, a military coup in 1973 overthrew the established democratic government, but the regime headed by General Augusto Pinochet then ceded power in several stages so that by the 1990s the country once again became a viable democracy.

Moreover, as we have seen from examining the experience of America and the large European democracies, having a democratically elected government hardly guarantees a country's consistent commitment to democratic values. As political theorists from Aristotle to James Madison plainly understood, *any* form of government is potentially subject to the exploitation of specific groups, or to the repression of individuals' freedoms however defined. Western thinkers since the Enlightenment have looked to democracy as the form of government least prone to such abuses, but they have also repeatedly emphasized the dangers that even democratically constituted systems face.

The creation or destruction of democratic political institutions, and within functioning democracies the advance or retreat of citizens' rights, have therefore emerged as matters of paramount importance throughout today's developing world.[14] At the center of one public policy debate after another—the costs versus benefits of globalization; whether industrial countries should seek to impose Western labor or environmental standards on goods imported from developing economies; on what terms the United States should trade with China; whether to trade with Cuba at all—the question at issue is not just what economic benefit will ensue, but also what broader political and social consequences might follow.

One of the most welcome developments of the closing decades of the twentieth century, at least from a Western perspective, was the spread of democratic political institutions and the fundamental rights of free citizens. The collapse of the Soviet Union and its eastern European sphere of influence was a major element of this story, but there was much more besides. In 1950, only twenty-two among the world's 154 independent nation-states and colonial units had some form of functioning electoral democracy. As recently as the early 1980s, there were sixty. By the beginning of the 1990s, seventy-six countries had some form of democracy, and by the opening of the new century, 120 of the world's 192 independent countries were electoral democracies. The spread of political rights and civil liberties defined more broadly has been similar.[15]

But what influence has *economic growth* exerted on this process? Has the fact that some countries have enjoyed rapidly rising incomes, while others have stagnated or suffered declines, had much to do with which countries have become democracies and which have not? How should we expect the experience of rising or falling incomes in the coming decades to affect the attitudes of citizens of developing countries in particular toward such aspects of their society as openness, mobility, tolerance, and democracy?

The answer is not automatically to connect rising incomes to the advance of democracy and vice versa. As we have seen from the American experience, as well as that of Britain, France, and Germany, even in a mature democracy economic growth often creates social and political conflicts. In many circumstances, however, growth also provides the means for resolving conflicts. The outcome of the ensuing tug-of-war often shapes just those attitudes and events that determine whether a society becomes tolerant and democratic or not.

One immediate reason why economic development in particular may generate pressures leading to social conflict is that development typically shifts a country away from the traditional organization of not just its economy, but the broader society too, centered on agriculture. In most developing countries the source of much of the initial acceleration of productivity, and hence of the faster rise in average incomes, has been industrialization. This was certainly the pattern in nineteenth-century America, and it is so among most developing countries today. When protesters in Seattle and Genoa and Davos rally to voice their objections to globalization, part of what they have in mind is the spread of industrialization to areas of the world that have thus far remained largely preindustrial.

Industrialization disrupts previously existing social arrangements. It brings together workers, who had been widely dispersed in agricultural activities, to work in factories and live in more centralized locations. In the not infrequent case when farmworkers have been less than fully employed, industrialization also imposes a more rigorous work regimen. Even for those who had been fully engaged in farm labor, factory work typically imposes a more regimented discipline. And because the creation of new factories, and even more so the pioneering of whole new industries, requires entrepreneurship and the accumulation of capital, the early stages of industrialization typically vault some individuals into positions of wealth and power far beyond the experience or even the imagination of their fellow citizens. Each of these changes is practically a recipe for the kind of resentment voiced in America's past by Mary Elizabeth Lease, Tom Watson, Hiram Wesley Evans, and Charles Coughlin, and in more recent times by Pat Buchanan. If these resentments remain unchecked, they contain the makings of social conflict and even violence.

In other respects, what creates political alienation and conflict as societies develop economically is not industrialization per se but the broader process of modernization, of which economic development is a part and to which development also contributes. Urban life differs from life in farm communities, and for those who are new to it, it brings unfamiliar strains. Industrialization, participation in international trade (which draws both workers and entrepreneurs to a country's coastal areas), and, in some countries, immigration are all familiar forces leading to urbanization.[16]

Similarly, the increasing literacy and wider exposure to communications that are characteristic of modern societies are also, in part, a direct consequence of economic development. The differences in this regard between rich countries and poor ones are plain enough. But today governments in many low-income countries also promote basic education (often with international assistance) as a way of promoting economic development. Moreover, enhanced literacy and communications also typically go along with urbanization in developing countries, and newspapers, films, radio, television, and even the Internet are increasingly ubiquitous in urban areas.

Even if they are not employed in high-productivity industrial enterprises, therefore, citizens of countries that are beginning to develop economically are more likely to live away from the extended family networks that characterize traditional rural life, they are more likely to read newspapers describing the doings of their countries' business and government elites, and they are more likely to watch television programming that illustrates (and often idealizes) higher-income lifestyles abroad.[17] Many of the social and political tensions that inevitably result are simply the product of the general pattern of modernization that today increasingly characterizes the world as a whole.[18]

When these aspects of modernization erode a society's traditional institutions and loyalties, like those within the extended family, the consequences depend crucially on what emerges to take their place. Forty years ago, as these modernizing forces first began to take hold in many parts of Africa, Asia, and Latin America, political scientist Samuel Huntington pointed out that the new allegiances that emerge often direct people's energies not just outside the family but also outside the established political order, and that in so doing they sometimes threaten the stability of the society in the most fundamental terms.[19] In many cases, Huntington argued, these new loyalties also leave people more intensely identified by region, or race, or ethnicity, and they therefore render the society as a whole more vulnerable to fracturing along those lines. Experience since then—in Indonesia, in Sri Lanka, in Kosovo, in Rwanda—has sadly confirmed these insights. An all too familiar form of group consciousness is group prejudice, and the outcome is often group conflict.

The problem that Huntington identified is not limited to extreme cases of racial and ethnic armed conflict, however. For example, early in the twentieth century Argentina was widely considered one of the world's most promising economies. The country had a highly developed agricultural sector, ample resources for industrialization, and a well-educated population by the standards of the time. Its per capita income exceeded Canada's. But industrialization led to urbanization, as Argentinians in increasing numbers moved to Buenos Aires and Córdoba, and the emerging urban workforce became progressively more volatile politically. The result was at first political chaos, then a quarter-century of domination by Juan Perón and the Perónista political movement, and then a further quarter-century marked by successive military coups and political repression, including waves of government-sponsored kidnappings and assassinations. Along the way, under Perón as well as the military, the damage to the country's economic prospects was enormous. By century's end Argentina had returned to democracy, albeit a shaky one that was still sorting out the political debris left by decades of military misrule. Its economy has still not found a secure footing. Even before the country's most recent economic crisis, Argentina's per capita income was less than half of Canada's (and also well below South Korea's).

As we have seen from the experience of America and other industrialized countries, however, to the extent that the conflicts that emerge from modernization are over questions of "who gets what?"—in other words, to the extent that they are inherently subject to compromise, so that opposing interests can each come away with something positive in hand—the material gains that economic growth brings can help to resolve them. In doing so, growth not only relieves such tensions but also helps bind a society's competing groups together by fostering the sense that cooperation and compromise gain results.[20]

Not all conflicts are readily subject to compromise in this way, and so countries can (and some do) tear themselves apart with intractable disputes over what religion to practice, or what language to speak, or whether to permit abortion or divorce.[21] But where people are in conflict over issues like who gets better jobs, or which neighborhoods will receive roads, sewers, and hospitals, or whose children will become educated and have a chance to make something more of themselves, what is significant about economic growth is that it creates more good jobs, it generates the resources to build more roads and hospitals, and it provides more opportunities for personal advancement. By providing the wherewithal, economic growth makes it easier to find compromises in which competing interests see that they are each getting ahead.

Further, once a society becomes accustomed to achieving satisfactory compromises on issues like jobs, hospitals, and schools, chances are it will be less vulnerable to strains over its lingering inability to resolve potentially more dangerous differences. In time, the institutional mechanisms and the networks of political communication that have developed in the process of regularly reaching agreement on "divisible" issues may carry over to make even such "either-or" matters as language or abortion seem potentially subject to compromise. Indeed, the development of tolerance, of individual rights, and of democracy itself has historically evolved out of just this kind of give-and-take, in which different groups vie with one another to advance their interests yet ultimately recognize either that they cannot achieve total victory or that they are better off not to do so.[22]

This process of building a functioning democratic society through the resolution of conflicts is especially important in the developing world, precisely because so many developing countries are newly building not only a modern economy but, at the same time, a modern society. Even some of the very aspects of modernization that, as Huntington argued years ago, lead to discontent, frustration, social division, and conflict—urbanization, education and literacy, more efficient communications—also provide the eventual basis for an effective civil society.[23]

The increasing economic diversity that accompanies economic growth is a further asset to a country newly creating a democracy. What matters for this purpose is not just the size and vitality of the growing middle class but that its members be distributed widely throughout the society: not only businesspeople but doctors, lawyers, teachers, bureaucrats, and others as well whose professional outlook is compatible with democratic values and whose economic success gives them a sense that they have a stake in helping to promote a stable, modern society.

And economic growth also helps this process by fostering the kind of interpersonal trust that is a prerequisite for any democracy, either new or old. As political scientist Edward Banfield pointed out long ago, some minimum degree of trust between individuals who are not related by blood or marriage is an essential underpinning to many everyday arrangements—political, commercial, social—in which people must act on the assumption that others will reciprocate.[24] This trust becomes especially important during economic development and modernization, when large numbers of people physically move away from the family- and clan-oriented social networks that often underpin traditional societies. It is important in particular to the functioning of democratic political institutions, under which governing parties that lose elections willingly surrender power because they assume that in the future their successors will do the same.[25] Romantic notions of life in primitive societies to the contrary, surveys have repeatedly shown that the prevailing level of interpersonal trust is greater in countries where incomes on average are higher.[26]

Here too how people's perceptions evolve over time is important. A familiar aspect of modernization, regardless of whether it involves industrialization (or even of whether the economy develops), is that most people's aspirations for themselves and their children rise. With greater literacy and ready access to newspapers and especially television, people no longer compare themselves only to their immediate neighbors. They become aware of contrasts—often to their own disadvantage—between their standard of living and how their country's political leaders and successful entrepreneurs live. Often, they learn about the gap between living standards in their country and abroad. Moreover, because modernization erodes traditional social ties, both the perception and the reality of these inequalities are likely to be increasing just when the social institutions that might otherwise render them legitimate in people's eyes are atrophying.*

But how people react to this increasing awareness of inequality depends on their circumstances. If a country is experiencing broadly based economic growth—if productivity and therefore average incomes and living standards are rising and, importantly, if these gains are accruing to the benefit of more than just a narrow group—then people are more likely to accept the differential between their own and others' living standards, and, for a while, even acquiesce if the gap widens further. As occurs in the developed democracies, for those whose incomes are already rising the improvement in hand outweighs the sense that others are getting ahead still faster. But even people who have not participated in the general rise of living standards are more

---

*Although the claim would be hard to prove, it is frequently argued that the collapse of the Soviet Union became inevitable once a large fraction of the population, including virtually all members of the country's important decision-making groups, became aware not only that the gap between Soviet living standards and those in the West was vast but also that the gap was not shrinking. Especially when modernization occurs in the context of industrialization, people can readily observe that others' incomes are rising while their own is not.

likely to believe, if the improvement is sufficiently widespread, that in time they, or at least their children, will enjoy the benefits of growth that they already see working to others' advantage. Under circumstances of economic growth and of confidence in its pervasiveness and durability, other people's success can inspire not just envy but hope. Indeed, as we have repeatedly seen, these are precisely the circumstances under which upward mobility is likely to be admired rather than resented.

Patience has a limit, however. It is important that growth not falter, and that the rise in incomes spread sufficiently widely across a country's population. As we shall see, inequalities sometimes worsen in the early stages of industrialization. What then matters is that those people who have not yet benefited from this growth have a reasonable expectation that their turn will come.

In a classic analogy, political economist Albert Hirschman once likened attitudes toward widening income inequalities in the beginnings of economic development to the response of drivers stuck in a traffic jam. After a lengthy period in which all cars are stopped, one lane typically begins to move forward. When it does, even those drivers who are still stuck in the other lanes are usually relieved. They infer that whatever obstruction was blocking the road ahead has dissipated, and they assume that soon their lane too will begin to move forward. But if time passes and they remain stuck, while those in the one lane keep moving ahead, their newly found optimism eventually gives way to yet greater frustration that is all the more intense if there is no practical way to change lanes.[27]

Indeed, a situation in which living standards begin to rise but then falter often proves more frustrating than continuing stagnation. Many of modern history's best-known political revolutions—in America and France in the eighteenth century, in Germany in the nineteenth century, in Mexico and Russia (and, ironically, later on in the Soviet Union) in the twentieth century—have occurred under just such circumstances.[28] As Tocqueville observed, referring to his own country's experience on the eve of its revolution, "it was precisely in those parts of France where there had been *most* improvement that popular discontent ran highest. . . . Patiently endured so long as it seemed beyond redress, a grievance comes to appear intolerable once the possibility of removing it crosses men's minds."[29] More than 200 years later, in a world of modern communications, the possibility of alleviating poverty, ill health, and blocked opportunity is inevitably on people's minds. Once modernization is underway, raising economic aspirations but simultaneously creating social tensions, whether economic growth is durable and its benefits widespread becomes all the more important.

Fairness matters too. If economic growth is to shape people's hopes for their own or their children's future well-being so that they will tolerate the widening inequalities that economic development initially brings, it is important that the distribution of the rewards of that growth appear fair, in the sense that those who get ahead deserve their good fortune—or if not fair, then at least random, so that anyone has an equal chance to be lucky. For just this reason, the tolerance for inequality is typically greater in countries with market-oriented economies than in socialist countries. Market economies, at least in principle, distribute success in response to individuals' talents, efforts, and luck. Societies with more centralized economic systems, in which the bureaucracy assigns everyone's position, almost invariably espouse a more rigid egalitarianism, and most socialist countries go to some lengths to hide from public view whatever inequalities they allow in practice.

Even in market economies, however, tolerance for inequality is likely to be greater when people see fewer arbitrary distinctions limiting who gets ahead—for example, if the population is racially or ethnically more homogeneous, or, where people do differ by race, or religion, or language, if they nonetheless see little bar to economic success on that account. By contrast, where most of the visibly successful entrepreneurs belong to a distinct ethnic minority (for example, the overseas Chinese in many Asian countries), people who are left behind in the initial stages of economic development are less prepared to believe that in time they too will benefit.[30] South Koreans, for example, a mostly homogeneous population, accepted sharp inequalities during the rapid growth that initially brought the average citizen from severe poverty to near-Western prosperity. But in Sri Lanka, which forty years ago was about on Korea's economic level, the Tamil minority who originally migrated from India have long believed that their opportunity to advance is blocked by discrimination by the native Sinhalese population. The result has been decades of ethnic violence, including bombings and suicide attacks, and consequent political instability. In part for this reason, Sri Lankans now have a standard of living only one-fifth what South Koreans enjoy. "Equality of condition," the feature of early America that Tocqueville found so remarkable, is important for successful economic development as well.

What is the balance of these often opposing forces? The only way to judge the resulting overall effect of economic growth on the character of developing societies is to examine actual experience across as broad a group of countries as is possible. Moreover, the experience that matters for this purpose encompasses not just the formalities of electoral democracy but intangible aspects of how people live, both individually and collectively: Do a country's citizens enjoy at least rough "equality of condition," in the sense of absence of distinctions based on birth, or is there legal or other effective discrimination against some racial or ethnic groups? Do citizens have the ability to influence their government and, if they choose, a genuine opportunity to change it? Do they have ready access to information about what is happening in their country, as well as abroad? If so, are they free to say what they think about what they learn? Each of these aspects of individual and public life is relevant to the question of how the experience of economic growth affects a society's moral character.

In recent years several researchers have constructed summary measures that embrace, in a compact way, many of these diverse questions about politics and society in different countries. One of the most widely used measures devised for this purpose is an evaluation of individual countries' political rights and civil liberties that Freedom House, a private research institution based in the United States, has carried out on an annual basis since the early 1970s.[31] Each year the survey rates the extent to which both "political rights" and "civil liberties" exist *in practice* in each of nearly 200 countries. Key issues that determine the Freedom House rating for political rights include whether those government officials who wield actual power are elected through open and fair elections, whether people have the right to organize political parties, whether the governing institutions include a role for a functioning opposition, and if so whether that opposition can compete for power through the electoral process. Major elements reflected in the separate rating for civil liberties include free and independent media, freedom of discussion and assembly, citizens' equality under law and access to an independent judiciary, religious freedom, and freedom of movement.[32] (The two ratings for any given country in any one year are usually close if not identical.)

Most of the large Western democracies have the top possible Freedom House rating for both political rights and civil liberties. So do some smaller countries such as Andorra, Barbados, and San Marino. At the other end of the scale, the most recent survey lists just eight countries—Burma, Cuba, Libya, North Korea, Saudi Arabia, Sudan, Syria, and Turkmenistan—with the lowest possible ratings for both political rights and civil liberties.[33] Other oppressive regimes, like China, Somalia, and Uzbekistan, rate almost as low. In the middle, again usually on both scales together, are countries like Venezuela, Bangladesh, Tanzania, and Indonesia, along with many of the newly independent countries that have emerged out of the former Soviet Union.

It is not hard to guess that citizens of higher-income countries tend to enjoy more comprehensive political rights and civil liberties, and indeed this is true.[34] But as Figure 12.1 shows, the positive relationship between higher per capita incomes and these fundamental ingredients of an open and democratic society is more than just a reflection of the handful of Western democracies with high standing both economically and politically.[35]

The line running through the scatter of individual countries in the figure traces the average relationship between a country's political rights and civil liberties and its per capita income that most closely mirrors the experience of all countries in the Freedom House survey for which there are usable data on per capita incomes (adjusted for cost-of-living differences). The relationship is far from exact, indicating that a country's average income is hardly the sole influence determining its commitment to citizens' freedoms. Indeed, it would be astonishing if it were. Culture, religion, influences exerted by neighboring countries, and the impact of specific historical events and even individual national leaders can all be important in just this context.* It is presumably not an accident that the first group of countries to adopt democratic principles of government and civil society in modern times were all either located in northwest Europe or settled by northwest Europeans, or that among countries elsewhere there is a strong relationship between being a democracy and having once been a British colony.[36] The fact that the victors in World War II consigned much of central and eastern Europe to decades of Soviet domination was of crucial importance in limiting the freedom of citizens throughout the region, and the consequences of that historic compromise have only recently begun to be reversed. Individ-

---

*Moreover, especially in the developing world, measured per capita income may fail to represent even key aspects of material well-being. In many low-income countries a significant part of economic activity takes place in informal settings far removed from the visible market economy, and black markets are significant as well. For just these reasons, some thoughtful observers have questioned how much there is to learn from this kind of cross-country statistical analysis, either in the very simple form shown here or in the more complex forms found in the existing literature, which is voluminous. T. N. Srinivasan and Jagdish Bhagwati, for example—two distinguished scholars of the economics of trade and development—have rejected such methodologies in favor of country-specific analyses that admit far greater nuance. Nuanced country-specific analysis is precisely what Chapters 5 through 11 above seek to do for America and the other three large established Western democracies.

Figure 12.1: Relationship Between Rights/Liberties and Average Income

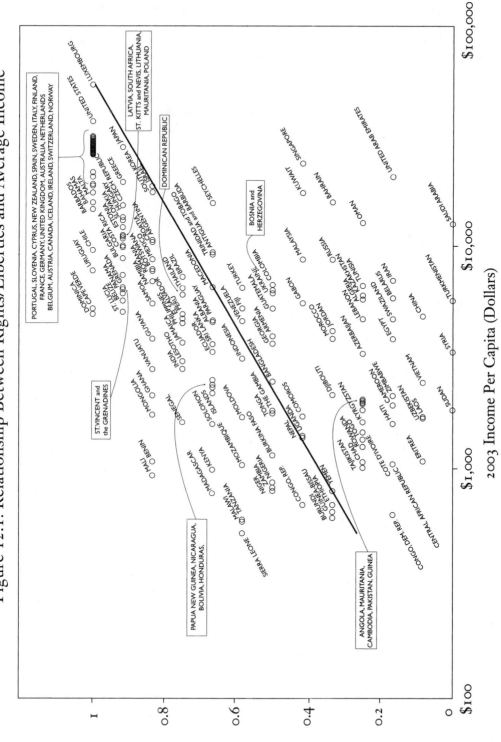

2003 Income Per Capita (Dollars)

2004 Average Rights and Liberties Rating

ual leaders like Lenin, Stalin, Franco, Mao, Perón, Nehru, Adenauer, and de Gaulle each exerted an influence over their respective countries that lasted for decades.[37]

Indeed, the relationship between different countries' average income levels and the extent to which their respective citizens today enjoy the freedoms of a modern liberal democracy exhibits some striking exceptions. In a few countries—Kuwait, Singapore, and the United Arab Emirates, for example—people on average have a high standard of living but only modest political rights or civil liberties. In Saudi Arabia the average income is almost as high, but Saudi citizens' rights and liberties rank at the very bottom of the scale. On the other hand, the citizens of a few smaller countries such as Mali and Benin enjoy fairly robust freedoms despite incomes that are far below the world average.

But these exceptions notwithstanding, there is no doubt that more extensive political rights and civil liberties generally accompany higher living standards. Across the entire range of the world's countries, each doubling of per capita income—roughly the step-up between Armenia and Bulgaria, or between Brazil and Portugal—improves a country's average rights and liberties rating by about one-sixth of the total distance between the absolute bottom of the Freedom House scale and the absolute top.[38]

That there is usually more freedom in countries with higher per capita incomes does not by itself reveal whether having a high income leads a society to value and therefore provide these freedoms, or whether having widespread rights and liberties enables a country to achieve a higher level of income—in other words, whether a high material standard of living fosters freedom, or freedom facilitates economic success.[39] As we shall see, both are often true. A country can therefore get stuck, either in a favorable situation in which a high income level promotes a democratic society and vice versa, or in a vicious circle in which poverty and the absence of basic freedoms mutually reinforce each other.

More to the immediate point, however, enjoying a high standard of living is not the same as undergoing rapid or sustained income *growth*. Per capita incomes in China, Thailand, and Malaysia, for example, have grown rapidly in recent decades. But because that growth began from such a low level, each of these countries has an average standard of living today that is still only a small fraction of that in the highly developed Western democracies. (Thailand's per capita income is less than one-fifth the level in the United States; Malaysia's is nearly one-fourth; China's is slightly more than one-eighth.) At the same time, some of the world's highest-income countries—most dramatically Japan, but also many European countries—have recently experienced only sluggish growth.

What makes this distinction complex is that the *level* of a country's income and its income *growth* are obviously related. Any country that enjoys a high standard of living today must have undergone fairly robust growth over some substantial period in the past. Conversely, any country that grows fast enough, and for long enough, will eventually achieve a high living standard too. (If China can maintain the 8.1 percent per annum growth pace it has achieved over the past quarter-century, after another sixteen years its average income will be up to today's level in South Korea or Portugal, and another nine years will take it to where America stands today.) Hence merely observing that countries where freedoms are more widespread today tend also to have higher average incomes does not by itself say much about the consequences of economic growth.

The distinction is important because some of the most significant implications of a connection relating economic growth to the political and moral improvement of a society would not follow merely from a relationship to a high living standard. If what mattered were only a country's current level of income, there would be no cause for concern in this regard when a country like the United States begins to stagnate economically. Similarly, if the current income level were all that mattered, there would be less ground for optimism that a country like China, where per capita income is still low but growth is rapid, might become more open and democratic anytime soon.

As Figure 12.2 shows, however, there is also a positive relationship between the political rights and civil liberties that different countries' citizens enjoy today and the prior quarter-century's *growth* of per capita income.[40] Here too the relationship is far from exact—the outstanding exception in the world today is China—but the positive connection to prior income growth is apparent nonetheless. (If China alone were omitted, the line showing the average relationship would be much steeper.) On the whole, in faster-growing countries citizens enjoy greater freedoms than on average across the world. Conversely, in countries where incomes have risen little, or even declined, more often than not basic freedoms are curtailed.[41]

There are clear exceptions to the relationship between economic growth and the depth and breadth of citizens' freedoms, and each has an interesting story behind it. China, for example, has experienced the fastest economic growth in the world over the past quarter-century, but it still ranks at the bottom of the scale on political rights and next to the bottom on

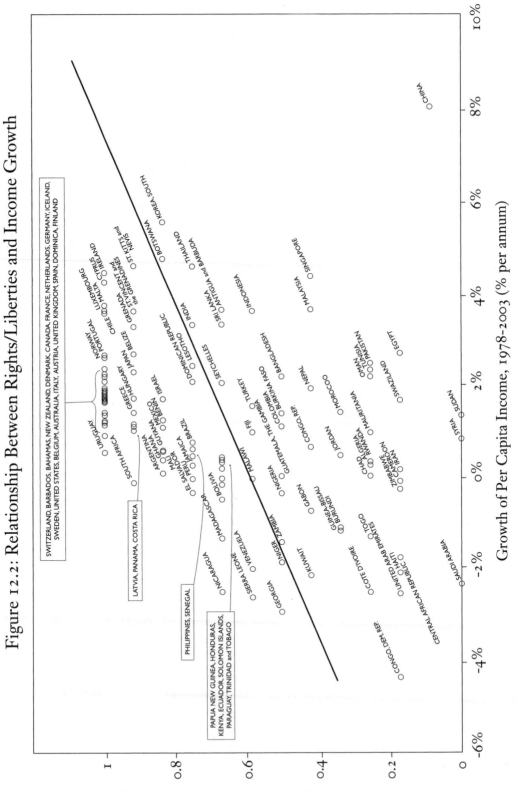

Figure 12.2: Relationship Between Rights/Liberties and Income Growth

civil liberties. Singapore and Malaysia likewise have only limited freedoms despite fairly rapid income growth. There are also countries where income growth has been slow, or even where living standards have shrunk, but citizens today enjoy fairly robust freedoms anyway. Prominent examples include South Africa, Argentina, and El Salvador. America, Britain, and most of the other Western democracies have somewhat more comprehensive rights and liberties than their income growth alone would suggest.

One important question that these departures from the average relationship raise (especially the unfavorable ones) is the matter of timing. No society undergoes fundamental institutional change each time a turn in the business cycle either spurs or retards the growth of its citizens' incomes for a year or two. As we have seen from the experience of America and the large western European democracies, it normally takes time for the experience of growth or stagnation to affect people's perceptions, then more time for these changed perceptions to influence prevalent social attitudes, and then still more time for a country's political institutions to respond even to widespread changes in popular thinking. Many of the countries where citizens enjoy substantial freedoms today—for example, South Korea, Taiwan, Argentina, Chile, and South Africa—were much different twenty, or in some cases just ten, years ago. Figure 12.2 relates each country's average income growth over a quarter of a century to the status of its citizens' freedoms *at the end* of that span. One interpretation of the atypical posture of countries like China and Singapore, therefore, might be that under some conditions even twenty-five years is insufficient for the influence of economic growth to manifest itself in a society's political institutions.[42] (Further, the form in which economic growth occurs matters as well: as ever more Chinese citizens have access to the Internet, and with increasingly efficient operating systems, will the government continue to succeed in blocking access to overseas sites, or even internal communications, that it considers threatening?)

That the positive effect of rising living standards on citizens' freedoms typically emerges only with the passage of time also helps to resolve the important question of what is causing what. When we observe, in Figure 12.1, that the extent to which citizens enjoy political rights and civil liberties in different countries is positively related to those countries' respective living standards measured at about the same time (actually, a year earlier because of the delay in tabulating data on per capita incomes), we simply do not know whether higher incomes have fostered more extensive freedoms or more open societies are able to achieve higher incomes, or perhaps both. But when we observe that freedom in different countries is positively related to their respective economic growth over the preceding quarter-century, we can be more confident that a rising standard of living contributes to the advance of democracy.

Because political and social institutions change over time—indeed, that is what makes the difference between economic growth and stagnation so important—it is also useful to ask not only about the political rights and civil liberties that currently exist in different countries but also about how these freedoms have either advanced or retreated. Does the development of more extensive rights and liberties typically follow a period of rising incomes? Does deterioration occur primarily where living standards have stagnated?

The most important single impetus to the advance of democracy and freedom in recent decades has been the demise of the Union of Soviet Socialist Republics. Since 1991 the fifteen "republics" that composed that union have become independent nation-states, with the opportunity to develop their own separate governments and political institutions. Similarly, eleven countries in eastern and central Europe that used to be under nearly complete Soviet domination (including the newly independent states that used to be parts of Yugoslavia or Czechoslovakia) have at last been able to seek their own paths. Before the Soviet regime collapsed, citizens of the fifteen USSR republics enjoyed few political rights or civil liberties, and citizens of the European satellite countries were in many cases only marginally better off in this regard. In at least some of these newly independent countries, the situation today is far different. Nor is this process yet complete. Popular uprisings swept away the remnants of Soviet-era regimes, and brought more democratic parties to office, in Georgia in 2003 and in Ukraine in 2004.

The experience of these former Soviet republics and satellites further illustrates how the economic setting affects the emergence of basic freedoms. In 1991, the Soviet Union's final year of existence, the country ranked below the middle of the Freedom House scale for political rights and just in the middle for civil liberties. Today the former Soviet republics span almost the entire scale, from the three Baltic states with top ratings on political rights and next-to-top on civil liberties (identical to Greece, for example, or South Africa) to Turkmenistan with ratings at the very bottom in both categories.

These differences are not entirely random. As always, there are exceptions, but across the entire range—from Tajikistan, where the average income is now the second-lowest in the world outside of Africa (the lowest is in Yemen), to Estonia where per capita income is above that in Mexico and Chile—the former Soviet republics that enjoy higher average living standards have also granted their citizens more extensive political rights and civil liberties. Because the average income has fallen since 1990 in most of these countries, those where living standards are higher today are also typically those where economic growth has been the least negative. (In Moldova per capita income has shrunk by an astonishing 6.1 percent per annum on average since the Soviet Union collapsed, so that the standard of living is now less than half what it was then.)

A similar relationship between higher incomes and more extensive freedoms is also apparent among the Soviet Union's former European satellites. Slovenia, the country in the group where living standards are highest (per capita income of $19,200), has a top rating for both political rights and civil liberties. Bulgaria, the Czech Republic, Hungary, Poland, and Slovakia, all with high average incomes by eastern European standards (between $7,000 and $16,000), have top ratings for political rights and next-to-top for civil liberties. By contrast, lower-income Albania ($4,700) is only in the middle of the scale (though it nonetheless ranks above all of the former Soviet republics except the three Baltic states). Macedonia, where living standards have declined on average since 1990 (although the standard of living remains well above that in Albania), is likewise only in the middle of the Freedom House scale.

Many countries outside the former Soviet sphere have also expanded citizens' freedoms in recent years. A handful of others have moved in the opposite direction. With the end of apartheid and white minority rule, and the election of Nelson Mandela as president of a newly constituted government in 1994, South Africa improved its average rights and liberties rating from well below the midpoint of the Freedom House scale in the mid-1980s to nearly the top by the mid-1990s. In Chile, the piecemeal replacement of General Augusto Pinochet's military junta by a working democracy gradually boosted the country's ratings, so that by 2004 they finally reached the top level on both political rights and civil liberties. South Korea, which started out at roughly the middle of the scale in the 1980s, has risen sharply as well. In several of the smaller African countries—Benin, where a new democratic constitution was adopted following elections in 1990 and 1991; Mali, where a multiparty system was established after a 1991 coup overthrew the government of President Moussa Traoré (who had been in power since 1968); Malawi, where a new constitution and consequent elections in 1994 finally ended the thirty-year rule of Dr. Hastings Kamuzu Banda (a process speeded by the Catholic bishops' criticism of Malawi's human rights record); Cape Verde, where in 1991 the one-party government of President Aristide Pereira finally held democratic elections—the improvement over the last decade has been even greater.

By contrast, over the same years Egypt's freedoms have deteriorated from the middle of the scale to very near the bottom, as the ruling National Democratic Party enacted broad emergency laws, in part to combat terrorism by the Muslim Brotherhood and other terrorist groups, and the "emergency" has gone on for decades. Venezuela has fallen from near the top of the scale to the middle (with the erosion of civil liberties particularly severe), especially since the constitutional changes put in place by President Hugo Chávez following his election in 1998. Other countries where the recent deterioration in political rights and civil liberties has been significant include Colombia, Peru (which has now partly restored its democracy), The Gambia, and Liberia.

These countries' experiences have been more idiosyncratic, lacking the central driving event that has dominated the recent evolution of what used to be the Soviet Union and its European satellites. But here as well, the general pattern across these diverse countries suggests that a rising standard of living helps to foster political rights and civil liberties, while stagnating or declining living standards instead subvert those freedoms.

It is tempting to suppose that the way in which economic growth brings about the advance of freedom, especially in the more extreme cases in which a democracy replaces a patently nondemocratic regime, is by greasing the wheels for just such a transition. At least over significant spans of time, this seems to be so. But the role that economic growth plays along the way is more complex, indeed paradoxical. Over shorter periods, a rising standard of living acts as a stabilizing force in most societies, making more secure whatever political structure a country has in place, be it democratic or not. Conversely, in the short run stagnation or outright economic decline generates opposition to a country's existing political system, regardless of how open or democratic it may be.[43]

The paradox stems from the fact that economic growth, as a source of short-run stability, does not discriminate between democratic and repressive regimes. Although improving living standards ultimately generate pressures for greater openness, even the most dictatorial government has a better chance of surviving, for a while, if it can provide its citizens with the material benefits of a rising average income. For just the same reason, in electoral democracies an incumbent government typically faces a better prospect of reelection if its economy is thriving. (In the United States, the pace of economic growth over even just the few immediately preceding months usually has a pronounced effect on the outcome of presidential elections, and some influence on off-year congressional elections as well.)[44]

By contrast, when people's incomes shrink they are likely to be discontented with whatever government they have, and often they will seek to change it. In well-functioning democracies, that discontent normally results in a change of government—in the sense of replacing the party in power, or perhaps merely the individual officeholders—without any threat to the underlying institutional structure. If the discontent is sufficiently intense and widespread, however, the political system itself may also be vulnerable. After all, from time to time democracies are overthrown. Where the government operates as a dictatorship to begin with, changing the government is often tantamount to changing the institutional structure as well.

As the experience not just of the Soviet Union and its dependencies but of many countries in Latin America, Asia, and even Africa indicates, the path from dictatorship to democracy is only sometimes smooth. Chile, Mexico, Taiwan, and South Korea managed, for the most part, to achieve this transition gradually, with dictatorial regimes surrendering their powers step by step and eventually giving way to elected replacements. (Not coincidentally, each of these countries was also an economic success story.) In far more countries, what marked the beginning of democracy—whether it proved durable or not—was the sudden collapse of the prior nondemocratic regime.[45]

Just as the experience of countries across the world confirms the longer-run relationship between economic growth and the advance of freedom, experience also shows that over shorter periods the effect of rising incomes is to foster political stability, while economic stagnation more often precipitates change, sometimes including radical change. Political scientist Adam Przeworski examined the experience of 139 countries over the four decades preceding the democratization wave of the 1990s and identified ninety instances of radical political transition—from dictatorship to democracy in fifty cases, and from democracy to dictatorship in forty.[46] Some of the familiar instances of a transformation to democracy during this period include South Korea in 1960, Greece in 1973, Spain in 1977, Argentina in 1983, and both Nicaragua and Grenada (after an invasion by American armed forces) in 1984. Transitions to dictatorship during these years include Argentina in 1955 (and again in 1976), Greece in 1967, Chile in 1973, Pakistan in 1977, and Iran in 1984.[47]

The occurrence of so few major transitions in the form of government over so many years means that the probability of radical political change in any particular country in any one year is small. But comparing the countries where such changes have taken place to other countries, and to themselves in other years, clearly shows that a radical change in regime—in either direction—is more likely when a country's standard of living is falling than when it is rising. Moreover, democracies appear to be especially vulnerable to political instability due to declining incomes. For the forty years examined by Przeworski, the probability that any individual democracy would be overthrown by a dictatorial regime was nearly four times as great if the country's per capita income was falling than if its income was rising. The probability that a dictatorship would be replaced by a democracy was barely one and a quarter times as great when the country's income was falling as when it was rising.[48]

This vulnerability of democracies, especially new ones, to economic downturns—and, conversely, the role of vigorous and broadly distributed economic growth in shoring up a new democracy—is not surprising in light of historical experience. New democracies are often overthrown: France on several occasions following the French Revolution of 1789, numerous European countries that tried some form of electoral democracy after the widespread local revolutions of 1848, other European countries following World War I (more than half of Europe's parliamentary democracies in 1920 were no longer in existence by 1938), and many countries in Africa and Latin America in the post–World War II period. Democracies that emerge "ahead of their time" from an economic perspective are especially fragile.[49]

The reasons are not hard to fathom. Any new system of government, whether democratic or not, faces the need to establish legitimacy in the eyes of its citizenry. Delivering a rising standard of living to the majority of those citizens is, under many circumstances, the most reliable way to do so. Conversely, falling incomes undermine the legitimacy that new political structures so badly need.[50] Indeed, public opinion surveys taken in a large number of democratic countries show that the durability of democratic institutions over time is related more to how satisfied people say they are with their lives in general (which in turn depends heavily on what is happening to their standard of living) than to the satisfaction they express specifically with their respective countries' political institutions. By contrast, the support that people in such surveys express for revolutionary action to change their countries' political systems is systematically smaller when living standards are higher.[51]

Focusing in particular on military coups—one all too familiar form of radical political transition—likewise reveals the same short-run relationship between falling incomes and political instability. Because sometimes one dictatorial regime overthrows another, and sometimes a coup can even be the mechanism for creating a democracy, the number of successful military coups that have occurred in recent decades is much greater than the small number of cases (just forty during 1950–90 in Przeworski's study) in which a dictatorship has replaced a democracy.[52] These abrupt changes in government have taken place not only against the background of different regions and different cultures but also under widely varying political circumstances. Some still stand out, many years later, as significant events in the political history of the postwar era: Gamel Abdel Nasser's coup against the government of King Farouk in Egypt in 1954, the overthrow of Syngman Rhee in South Korea in 1960, the colonels' coup in Greece in 1967, the overthrow of the Allende government in Chile by Pinochet in 1973, the Sandinista revolution against the Somoza regime in Nicaragua in 1979, and the assassination of President Park Chung Hee in South Korea that same year. Many others received widespread attention at the time but by now have largely faded from memory, at least outside the countries where they took place.

Military analysts have often surmised that a poor economy is one of the essential ingredients for a successful coup, and the record of the postwar era proves them right.[53] Despite the enormous variety of specific circumstances in different countries, and of their individual histories of stability or instability, a systematic overview shows that the probability of any country's undergoing a coup depends on both the level and the recent growth of its average income. One classic study found that each doubling of per capita income reduces the probability of a country's experiencing a successful coup by between 40 percent and 70 percent, depending on the region of the world.[54] In light of this strong relationship—together with the parallel tendency for political instability to depress economic growth—the authors suggested that unfortunate countries may fall into a "coup trap," in which poverty fosters political coups, which in turn foster more poverty, and hence more coups. Other forms of extreme political instability, such as attempted coups that do not succeed (in practice less than half do), or political assassinations and executions, likewise occur far more frequently in countries with low per capita incomes.

But even apart from a low average level of income, the absence of economic *growth* is also a key ingredient for a successful coup. From the 1960s through the early 1980s, for example, there were 121 military coups or other comparable irregular political changes in conventionally recognized countries. On average, per capita income in those that experienced these coups was falling (by 1.4 percent) in the years in which the coups occurred. But incomes in these and other countries rose on average (coincidentally, also by 1.4 percent) in years when their governments underwent major changes but by legitimate means, and rose even faster (2.7 percent) in years when these countries experienced no major change in government.55 As is the case for the "coup trap" based on a low level of income, the connection between successful coups and negative income growth is consistent both with the idea that falling incomes create a fertile environment for coups and with the idea that political instability leads to poor economic performance. As we shall see, in all likelihood both forces are at work.

Here, too, the connection between political instability and either poverty or falling incomes is not merely a reflection of events in just a few countries that are all in the same region, or that are highly similar in some other way. The same patterns appear among developing countries as well as industrialized countries, and likewise in different parts of the world. In either Africa or Latin America, where countries have been the most prone to coups in recent decades, doubling the level of per capita income has, on average, cut the probability of experiencing a coup by 40 percent to 55 percent.56 Among African countries, those that experienced coups also saw their per capita income decline, by an average 2.6 percent, in the years when the coups happened. African countries' incomes declined by only .8 percent on average in years when governments underwent legitimate major changes, and rose by 1.9 percent in years when there were no major changes. In Latin America, incomes in countries where coups occurred experienced an average decline of .6 percent in those years, an increase of 1 percent in years of legitimate major changes in governments, and an increase of 2.5 percent in years of no major change.57

Even in Asia, where incomes rarely fall and coups are more unusual (probably for just that reason)—among the few examples are Burma in 1962, Thailand in 1971, and South Korea in 1979—political instability is again systematically related to both a low standard of living and weaker than normal economic growth. The average growth of per capita income in the Asian countries that have experienced coups, in the years in which the coups occurred, was 1 percent—far superior to the situation during coup years in Africa and Latin America, but still disappointing by the standards of much of Asia during the post–World War II period. By contrast, Asian countries' average incomes rose by slightly more (1.4 percent) in years when major government changes occurred in legitimate ways, and by 3.5 percent in years when governments did not change.58 Similarly, among Asian countries, doubling the level of per capita income cut the probability of a successful coup by more than 50 percent.[59]

But just as having a high average income, or a rapid increase in average income, is not always sufficient to deliver the usual benefits of economic growth, the level and growth rate of *average* income are not all that matters in fostering political stability. In the developing world no less than in America and other industrialized democracies, how incomes are distributed matters too. As we shall see, for a given average living standard and a given growth rate, the incidence of nearly all forms of political instability—coups, political assassinations, domestic mass violence—is systematically lower in countries with more even income distributions.[60] In particular, the probability that an already democratic country will succumb to a dictatorship is likewise reduced as its incomes are more evenly distributed.[61]

One of the fortunate aspects of the latest "wave" of democratization in Africa and Latin America, as well as in what used to be the Soviet Union and its sphere of close influence, is that—at least so far—only a few of these new democracies have reverted to outright dictatorship. But it is still much too soon to assess this record. Historical experience strongly suggests that among these new democracies the ones that succeed in achieving a rising standard of living for the broad majority of their citizens will be those most likely to survive.

Fifty years ago, W. Arthur Lewis, at the time one of America's most prominent development economists, wrote that "The advantage of economic growth is not that wealth increases happiness, but that it increases the range of human choice. . . . The case for economic growth is that it gives man greater control over his environment, and thereby increases his freedom."[62]

Lewis wrote in the early flush of optimism about prospects for the developing world that accompanied both the end of colonialism and the increasingly widespread awareness that the world as a whole, or at least the part of it not under communism, had entered a postwar era of robust economic growth: Europe was largely rebuilt. Germany and Japan had become democracies. International trade was expanding rapidly, and the demand for products from countries that had not yet industrialized was surging. Throughout the countries that either had been or still were colonies of the great European empires, the expectation of the departing powers was that the newly installed democratic institutions and forms they were leaving behind would follow the path of the Western democracies. As they did, these new governments would be welcome members of the international community, including in particular the United Nations. Further alliances, like the myriad regional pacts established during the Eisenhower-Dulles era (SEATO and CENTO, for example), would further help steer these newly independent countries' economic and political development on an advancing course.

Many developing countries went on to realize these expectations, but many did not. A quarter-century ago, and a quarter-century after Lewis articulated the hope of his day that the spread of economic growth would foster the spread of human freedom, prospects looked much grimmer. Many countries had failed to advance economically, and many of those that had succeeded economically were, in effect, dictatorships of either the communist or the authoritarian variety. Democracy appeared to be a relic, confined to the handful of mostly European and European-settled countries that had industrialized early and had become democracies when the idea still seemed new.

The most recent quarter-century has brought a more mixed record. Some developing economies have succeeded to such an extent that the label no longer suits. By century's end, both South Korea and Mexico had become members of the OECD (the Organization for Economic Cooperation and Development), long regarded as a "rich countries' club." In other countries the label does not fit because they have not developed and are not developing. Democracy, though, is clearly on the rise, and especially so among the former group. As a result, Lewis's optimistic view looks better today than at any time since he wrote.

And, with the progress of the last two decades, uneven as it has been in both the economic and the political dimensions, the idea of economic growth as a force for human freedom has gained renewed force. Economist and philosopher Amartya Sen, in his 1999 book aptly titled *Development As Freedom*, called for a more expansive conception of "development" to incorporate not only economic development, in the conventional sense of a rising standard of living brought about by the modernization of economic activity, but also the expansion of human freedoms that Lewis and others of his generation looked to economic growth to bring forth.[63] Because *economic* development is not, of itself, sufficient to bring forth human freedoms in all settings, Sen's call for explicit attention to those freedoms, and for conscious efforts directed toward establishing and sustaining them, is apt. But at the outset of the twenty-first century the record of experience is more supportive of the belief that economic development fosters the freedoms that are integral to such a broader conception of "development" than has been the case for a long time.

Chapter 13

Virtuous Circles, Vicious Circles

Where there is no bread, there is no Law; where there is no
Law, there is no bread.

RABBI ELEZAR BEN AZARIAH
Chapters of the Fathers[1]

The idea that a society's moral well-being depends on its economic well-being, *and* vice versa, also has a long-standing pedigree. We have seen that a rising standard of living fosters openness, tolerance, and democracy. Do these in turn help boost living standards?

Most people everywhere would like to know how to earn more and live better, and so any insight into what might improve a country's economic performance is certainly interesting enough in its own right. But the possibility that an open society and democratic political institutions could foster rising living standards is especially important because it raises the prospect that social and political influences may reinforce existing economic trends, either spurring growth in economies that are already advancing or holding back those that are currently sluggish or stagnant. Indeed, if this kind of mutually reinforcing interaction becomes sufficiently powerful, after some time a society might get stuck—either in a "virtuous circle" in which vigorous economic growth, democratic politics, and open social institutions continually strengthen one another, or in far less fortunate circumstances, a "vicious circle" combining economic stagnation, repressive government, and limited civil or political freedoms.

The debate over how to break out of such a vicious circle inevitably revolves around questions of what to do first: whether to take whatever steps are necessary to promote rising incomes, in the hope that political and social reforms will then follow in due course, or instead to give first priority to key elements of political and social liberalization on the grounds that progress in those dimensions is a precondition for successful economic growth. If the two-way reinforcement between the character of a society and the performance of its economy is sufficiently strong, however, this familiar discussion of the proper sequencing for political and economic reform misses the point. Jump-starting economic growth in a closed, repressive society is then just as problematic as implanting the outward forms of democracy where incomes are stagnant.[2] Either endeavor is then difficult at best, and neither on its own is likely to prove lasting.

But do social openness and democratic political institutions actually play a significant role in either fostering or impeding economic growth?[3]

What makes incomes rise has been a central focus of economic inquiry ever since people became aware that economic growth was a possibility in the first place (in the modern era, roughly since the Industrial Revolution). And to the extent that some of the ingredients of economic growth turn out to be conditions that governments can either create or suppress, the subject has a direct link to practical issues of public policy. The issue then is not just why some countries succeed economically while others do not, but what kinds of institutions, and what potential policy interventions, might help or hurt.

One universally recognized factor that determines any society's economic potential is the amount and kind of productive resources it can put to work. An industrial economy that has twice as many factories as another, or more up-to-date machinery, has an obvious advantage. So does an economy with more trained engineers and technicians, or simply a labor force that is better able to read and write, comprehend instruction manuals, and perform basic business computations. Airports, highways, telecommunications systems, and other forms of infrastructure also matter. So do natural resources like fertile land, mineral deposits, and coastal harbors.

A traditionally important line of thinking about economic growth, both in advanced industrial economies and in the developing world, has therefore focused on the accumulation of productive resources. More resources mean greater potential output. Investment in new physical capital, or enhanced education of the labor force, means that resources—and therefore potential output, and therefore the achievable standard of living—are increasing. On close inspection, much of the widely celebrated "miracle" of economic growth in East Asia in the latter part of the twentieth century turns out to be a matter of these countries' intensive devotion to saving and education, and therefore their especially rapid accumulation of both physical capital and skilled labor.[4]

The usual question addressed in this line of inquiry is what role specific public policies can play in spurring a country's pace of overall resource creation, or in guiding its choice of what kinds of resources to create. But such characteristics of a society as openness of opportunity and social mobility also clearly affect the pace and composition of its resource creation. There are reasons for believing that the presence or absence of democratic political institutions, together with other basic freedoms, does as well.

As examples like Congo (formerly Zaire) and Argentina quickly show, however, an ample resource base is not all there is to achieving a high level of income. Similarly, enjoying a sustained increase in living standards over time is more than just a matter of investing in ever more human and capital resources. A large part of the ongoing debate over why some countries are so much richer than others, and why some succeed in realizing economic growth while others do not, has therefore turned on the role of resource accumulation versus the way in which a society uses what resources it has.[5] And, especially following the contributions of economic historian Douglass North, in recent years much of the effort to understand differences in how countries put their economic resources to work has focused on the role of legal, political, and social institutions—what North called "the rules of the game in a society . . . the humanly devised constraints that shape human interaction."[6]

Making the best use of the resources an economy has in place is partly a matter of efficiency, but also of motivation. As we shall see, many aspects of democratic government bear on economic efficiency, and in this area the balance between positive and negative forces is far from obvious. What seems to matter most is the general "rule of law"—maintaining law and order, avoiding corruption, and protecting property rights—and democracies do not always have the better record in this regard. By contrast, the positive influence of the greater motivation for economic effort that an open, mobile society fosters is straightforward. The greater the opportunity to distinguish oneself among one's fellow citizens, and the fewer the impediments to advancement based on arbitrary distinctions like birth and family connections, the more most people will exert themselves—even to the point of the "restlessness of temper" and "feverish ardor" that Tocqueville observed in America when it was a developing economy—in many dimensions of human endeavor, economic activity included.

The willingness to think and act in new ways—to adapt, to innovate, to create—also matters for economic growth. Especially in advanced economies, further growth requires the creation of new technologies and new forms of organization that extend the frontier of what is possible. But even for economies that currently trail behind, growth depends on the ability to acquire and deploy the superior technology and organization already in use elsewhere. In either setting, an open, mobile society and a democratic government can make a difference.

The potential consequences for economic growth of just these kinds of social and political characteristics have long been debated. One traditional view, especially in Western societies, has been that personal freedom and political democracy are conducive to economic growth, and that the capitalist market institutions that freedom and democracy can foster are particularly important in this regard.[7] Others have rejected the idea that "all good things go together" in this way.[8] Some students of economic development have even suggested that there is a "cruel dilemma" between a country's desire for rising incomes and its aspirations for freedom and democracy.[9]

The immediate context of this debate, and the specific examples most frequently introduced, have changed in recent years. The collapse of the Soviet Union and the associated communist regimes in central and eastern Europe has resolved at least one incarnation of this long-standing argument. Comparisons of the respective economic success of East and West Germany, or North and South Korea, or even the Soviet Union and the United States, no longer pose unanswered questions in this context. But the comparison of India and China—a large, mostly low-income democracy with relatively well-established civil liberties and political rights (notwithstanding the erosion in the early 1990s, which proved temporary), and a large, mostly low-income communist state lacking in either, but both of which have recently been growing at an impressive pace—remains as apt as it has been for decades. The similarly impressive economic success of Singapore, a city-state which its longtime leader, Lee Kuan Yew, holds out in contrast to the "indiscipline and disorderly conduct" of Western democracies, has highlighted precisely the same tension in yet another guise.[10]

The fact that practical questions of such major significance remain unsettled despite so many years of intense scrutiny immediately suggests that the ways in which a country's social and political institutions affect its economic growth prospects are varied and conflicting. The mix of ingredients that promotes the most rapid accumulation of productive resources need not be the same as what encourages the most efficient allocation of those resources once they are in place, and neither may be best for fostering creativity and innovation. Government interventions that help at one stage of the economic growth process may get in the way in another.

But another important reason for the continuing lack of clear answers is that few if any countries develop all aspects of an open society and a functioning political democracy precisely in parallel. In the United States, for example, far-reaching civil and political freedoms for white male citizens coexisted with chattel slavery for nearly a century, and thereafter the rights of both blacks and women, as well as the society's openness to foreigners and its attitudes toward citizens who were Catholics or Jews, evolved irregularly over the course of the next century. Most countries, at most times, have likewise been more democratic in some respects than in others. In examining how these characteristics of a society bear on economic growth, therefore, it is necessary to distinguish them, rather than consider them together as if they evolved in lockstep.

It seems unambiguous that openness and tolerance enhance an economy's ability to use productively its existing human resources, as well as to augment its productive labor force over time. Even in advanced industrial economies, two-thirds of total output typically reflects the contribution of human input.[11] And as more economies progress to ever higher post-industrial technologies based primarily on processing information, the share of output attributable to human input may well increase further. Deploy-ing existing human resources efficiently, and developing greater human resources, is therefore a major key to economic growth in the modern world.

The apparent paradox of labor's accounting for so great a share of total output even in industrial economies with large amounts of sophisticated factories and machinery reflects the simple fact that there is more to human effort than mere man-hours. A computer programmer, a skilled mechanic, a trained electrician, an experienced banker, and a research scientist each bring something more to bear on the productive process. Even apart from their education and training, some people have natural talents that make them surer with their hands and therefore better surgeons, or more expressive with words and therefore better newspaper editors, or quicker with complex analytical processes and therefore better physicists. Some people are naturally more energetic than others, or more disciplined, or more adept at interpersonal dealings, or more able to organize endeavors that involve many individuals' efforts.

Using human resources effectively is therefore in large part a matter of putting the right people in the right places so that the economy gets the most advantage from what each individual can contribute to the productive process. Barriers that keep people from doing the work through which they could otherwise make that maximum contribution directly impair the economy's productive potential. So do arbitrary preferments—based on race, religion, gender, family connections—that boost people into positions for which they are mostly unsuited, or in which they are simply less productive than somebody else would be in their place.

An obvious advantage that more open, meritocratic societies enjoy, therefore, is the ability to make the most of their human resources. In America careers in university teaching, medicine, law, and banking have opened to groups like women and blacks only within living memory. Wholly apart from their moral value, these changes have proved highly beneficial even in a narrow economic sense.

Outright discrimination is the most clear-cut way in which intolerant societies fail to allocate their existing human resources to best effect, but social hierarchies act in an analogous way. Parents who are well educated and economically comfortable, or who themselves occupy highly productive positions, can help their children become more productive economically, while children of the uneducated (and often unemployed) poor often do without such advantages. Once these children mature, with their different levels of knowledge and education, there is no loss of productive potential if the economy sorts out their respective positions in the workforce accordingly. (The resulting reduction in economic and social mobility across generations is clearly undesirable, but not because it impairs the economy's growth.) Often, however, the preferment given to people from economically or socially privileged backgrounds is unwarranted by any differences in their acquired productive capacities, and the outcome is undesirable on both moral and economic grounds. But the greater problem is that too few children, and in many instances the wrong children, are getting educated in the first place.

Openness and tolerance not only enhance a society's ability to use its existing human resources efficiently but also foster the development of greater human resources over time. Having an opportunity to get ahead creates the motivation—under the right circumstances, even the sense of obligation—to do so, and in most modern societies education has been one of the primary vehicles for achieving upward mobility. In the United States of not so long ago, barring blacks from most public schools and universities, or women from medical schools, law schools, and business schools, artificially limited the pool of potentially qualified candidates for a broad range of positions throughout the economy. Removing these restrictions has allowed American society to increase sharply its average level of education. So has the increased availability of both private and government-funded scholarships, as well as loans, which enable students from lower- and middle-income families to go on to college.[12] At the opposite end of the economic development spectrum, in many lower-income countries numerous forms of oppression based on gender or ethnicity depress school enrollments and more generally retard the building of human resources.[13]

Because education and training are so important to people's economic productivity (all the more so in advanced economies), and because individuals differ in their natural aptitudes and energies, which people receive which kinds of education also matters for an economy's growth. In a more open society the specific individuals who become doctors, or engineers, or teachers, or business executives are more likely to be those who are best suited for those positions in the first place, rather than simply whoever happens to enjoy the benefit of one or another kind of preference. Removing arbitrary bars and providing scholarships and loans for children of lower-income parents has not only raised America's overall level of education but also enabled the society to allocate that education more efficiently.

Insofar as education is concerned, democratic political institutions are likewise a positive force for economic growth.[14] Democracies tend to foster education systems that are both more extensive and more meritocratic. Political democracy therefore reinforces the development and efficient use of human resources that follow from social openness and mobility at the individual level.

Totalitarian regimes have historically viewed the written word—over which the government seeks to exercise the maximum possible control—as a key means of directing mass opinion. (Countries like China, Saudi Arabia, and Singapore not only tightly regulate what is printed and broadcast but even block their citizens' access to certain sites on the World Wide Web.)[15] As a result, nondemocratic governments often bring their populations to high levels of literacy. A striking feature of many of the former Soviet republics, for example, is that they have effectively universal adult literacy despite their low incomes. Tajikistan, for example, has an income per capita barely half that of nearby Pakistan ($1,040 per year versus $2,060), and more on a par with some African countries like Chad and Eritrea (both $1,100). Yet while adult literacy in Tajikistan is nearly universal, in Eritrea only 57 percent can read, in Chad 46 percent, and in Pakistan just 42 percent. Similarly, in China adult literacy is now 91 percent, while in India it is just 61 percent.[16]

Education is more than just a matter of basic literacy, however, and here democracies clearly have the advantage. Totalitarian regimes, the Soviet Union again a prime example, typically train small elites to high levels of proficiency, especially in subjects like physics and mathematics that can potentially further their military ambitions. Democracies are more likely to extend a greater degree of economically productive education across a wider share of the population, thereby developing a broader base of productively educated human resources.[17]

The interaction of public support for education and meritocratic selection of who gets educated is often crucial in this respect. Even in high-income countries, only a small percentage of families can afford to pay for their children's postsecondary education. For the rest, even though educating their children may represent a better investment than stocks or bank certificates, or whatever other investments they might hold, this is often irrelevant because families have only small amounts of such assets anyway.[18] Moreover, few private lenders are willing to advance funds to pay for education expenses without some kind of guarantee. Hence in the absence of scholarships or loans, or perhaps government loan guarantees, a country will systematically under-invest in higher education.[19]

In the developing world the issue is most often secondary or even primary schooling, although the fundamental problems are much the same. In many countries in Africa, only one-half to two-thirds of children complete a primary education, and in a few countries only one child in three does.[20] Even where enough schools are available (in many developing countries they are not), so that in principle all children have the opportunity to attend, many stop their education prematurely because their families need the extra income they can earn. In light of the very low wages usually paid to child labor, the investment represented by leaving these children in school would pay a handsome rate of return through the increased earning power that these children would have when they entered the workforce, with greater skills, some years later.[21] But their families cannot afford that investment. The advantage of government enabling them to remain in school is clear.[22]

Some nondemocratic governments do that too, but democracies have a better record in this regard. Countries where political democracy prevails typically attain greater overall levels of education. Because the more democratic countries are also richer on average, part of the reason is simply that they can afford to provide more education for their citizens. And a more educated citizenry presumably seeks, and in time achieves, more democratic political institutions. But even after allowing for countries' different income levels, and for the effect of education in promoting democracy, it is clear that democratic institutions lead to greater educational attainment.[23] In light of the central role that human resources play in advancing economic growth, the favorable implications for education may well constitute the most powerful single way in which democracy per se helps to promote a rising standard of living.

Apart from the positive influence that works through education, however, whether democratic political institutions systematically improve a country's economic growth prospects is unclear. Some forms of government initiative or intervention—especially maintaining the "rule of law"—normally promote economic growth. Others are just as clearly harmful. In many cases it is far from obvious whether having a democratic or an undemocratic political system makes governments more inclined to pursue those policies that enhance economic growth and to avoid those that create impediments.

For example, health matters as well as education—not just for its own sake but also because, whatever their knowledge and training, healthier workers are likely to be absent fewer days as well as more productive when they are on the job. Moreover, because investors know this, developing countries where workers are healthier are better able to attract foreign capital.[24] There is some evidence that democracies tend to have better health outcomes—lower child mortality, for example—even after allowing for the effect of higher or lower overall living standards (and surprisingly, in the case of child mortality, even after allowing for the average education level of the female population).[25] But these relationships are hardly unambiguous, and some nondemocratic countries, like China and Cuba, have far superior health outcomes than democracies with comparable income levels.

Like the creation of human resources through education and training, under most circumstances accumulating physical capital through investment in factories, machinery, and infrastructure is essential to achieving rapid growth in any modern economy.[26] Investment, in turn, requires saving. But it is not clear whether democracies or dictatorships are better able to maintain high rates of saving, and therefore high investment rates, over extended periods of time. In some cases, like the Soviet Union under Stalin and China under Mao, repressive governments have managed to hold down workers' pay and limit the availability of consumer goods, and have thereby generated high levels of "forced saving" over several decades. China today still has one of the world's highest saving rates—43 percent of national income—and the few countries where the rate is higher also have minimal political democracy.[27]

In many other cases, however, authoritarian or totalitarian regimes have been unable to match the saving rates achieved in democratic countries, where political and economic freedoms leave greater room for private incentive and initiative. In Haiti, Burundi, Lebanon, Jordan, and Moldova—all countries where political democracy is not well developed—domestic saving is practically nonexistent.[28] At the same time, some Asian countries that are substantially more democratic than China have saving rates that, while not as high as China's, are ample nonetheless: for example, South Korea (32 percent) and Thailand (29 percent). And although America and Britain each save only a paltry 14 percent of their national income, most of the western European democracies maintain saving rates in the 20 to 25 percent range. In a few, like Norway (33 percent), saving is even greater.

A country that fails to generate adequate saving domestically can go ahead and invest anyway if it can finance that investment from abroad. But here too there seems to be little if any systematic influence of political institutions on most countries' ability to finance investment in their economies by borrowing from abroad or attracting foreign equity capital. China, Indonesia, and Nigeria all have nondemocratic governments, yet each has been an attractive target for international investors. Many other nondemocratic regimes have also succeeded in attracting substantial foreign capital. Indeed, some investors seem to find it more convenient to settle business matters quickly and quietly with a dictatorial regime than to cope with the apparent "chaos" of democracy.

One potential advantage democracy offers is that it may allow a country to focus its resources on productive economic activity that raises living standards, while autocratic rulers, who feel less responsibility for the welfare of the citizenry at large than if their hold on power depended on popular voting, may instead dissipate their countries' resources on various forms of self-aggrandizement.[29] Massive unproductive public works, oversized defense establishments, and military adventurism are all familiar features of dictatorships, often where it is obvious that the country should be devoting its scarce saving to productive investment. In some cases—Ferdinand Marcos in the Philippines and Idi Amin in Uganda come to mind—dictators manage to appropriate to themselves personally (and to their close associates) amounts that are large enough to impair their countries' overall growth prospects.

But democracies too have their limitations in this respect. "Crony capitalism" can occur almost anywhere. Having a democratic political system does not always, and certainly does not immediately, lead to a transparent financial system. Even in Western democracies, costly business and financial scandals are all too familiar.[30] The cost of cleaning up the American savings and loan industry in the late 1980s and early 1990s, mostly borne by the taxpayers, was $155 billion—more than the annual income of all but about two dozen of the world's 200-odd countries at the time.[31] Just in the past few years, bankruptcies of American corporations involved in questionable accounting or other fraudulent practices—Enron, Tyco, WorldCom, and other onetime highfliers that turned out to be scams—triggered far greater losses, including defaulted debt obligations as well as the collapse of these firms' equity values. Vanishing balance sheets and losses, whether borne by taxpayers or by lenders and investors, normally mean that economic resources have been wasted or stolen.

Another important area in which it is not clear whether democracies have the advantage in promoting economic growth is tax policy. In any political system based on popular voting, the upper-income elite is bound to comprise an electoral minority. If the distribution of income is sharply skewed, as it often is in the early stages of economic development, that minority will be a very small one. A potential risk to a country's growth prospects in a democratic system is that the lower-income majority will seek to use the government's tax and spending authority to create jobs on unproductive public works projects (too many and too elaborate government office buildings), pad the employment rolls in government-run companies (too many train and bus conductors, too many workers in nationalized industries that always lose money), and provide overly generous outright welfare programs—in each case using resources that could otherwise go into productive investment.

Whether these familiar tendencies of modern democracies outweigh the squandering of dictators is impossible to judge. Moreover, such redistributive policies are hardly limited to democracies. Dictatorships too can face pressures for fiscal redistributions from a mostly impoverished population.[32] Apart from the obvious tendency of dictatorships to spend more on the military, on balance there is little systematic difference between democratic and nondemocratic governments in their pattern of either taxing or spending.[33]

Respect for basic safety of person and property, together with other aspects of the "rule of law," clearly makes capital investment, as well as productive economic activity in general, both more feasible and more attractive.[34] People who fear for their lives, or who face the risk of losing, through theft or force, or expropriation, whatever valuable assets they might accumulate, are unlikely to undertake significant economic initiatives. Government corruption and lack of legal and financial transparency likewise act as disincentives to investment (including much-needed investment from abroad) and other forms of productive economic activity.[35] But in neither case is there ground to say whether democracies or autocratic regimes systematically enjoy the advantage.[36]

Business executives in democracies often complain about the depressing effects of costly litigation, or of excessive regulation intended to ensure the safety of either workers or consumers or to protect the environment. These impediments to investment and growth occur in both advanced and developing economies, and their costs are borne by ordinary workers as well as investors and business owners. In India, for example, there is evidence that some regulation intended to help workers has impeded economic growth and therefore resulted in even more poverty.[37]

But here too it is not obvious that in practice these impediments to investment and growth are more severe than those stemming from the tendency of many dictatorships to restrict important economic opportunities to a politically favored few, who in many cases also receive what amount to monopoly rights that shield their operations from market competition. In Indonesia during the Suharto regime, Hutomo Mandala Putra—Tommy Suharto, the president's son—was given an exclusive exemption from luxury sales taxes and import tariffs on car components to enable him to create what amounted to a near monopoly on the production and sale of automobiles.[38] Suharto's other children likewise enjoyed extraordinary treatment in their business ventures, and as a result of their and Suharto's own activities the family amassed a fortune variously estimated at between $16 billion and $35 billion.[39] The even more blatant patronage systems run by Idi Amin in Uganda, Teodoro Nguema in Equatorial Guinea, and Jean-Bédel Bokassa in the Central African Republic plainly retarded their countries' growth as well. (Amin also expelled Uganda's entire Asian minority, which was small in number but had accounted for nearly three-fourths of the country's wholesale trade.)[40]

It is also unclear whether democratic political institutions enjoy an advantage in controlling population growth. Especially for economies that are newly industrializing, limiting the natural growth of population is often crucial to bringing a country's demand for food within the limits of its domestically produced supply. With slower population growth, a low-income country can therefore use more of its scarce foreign exchange earnings to finance imports of the capital goods it needs to industrialize, rather than having to buy foodstuffs. Limiting population growth is also often crucial to increasing literacy, improving health standards, and extending life expectancy.

As countries begin to modernize, however—as we have seen, a process that is not identical to industrialization but that typically occurs alongside it—death rates usually fall with the introduction of sanitation, medical care, and improved nutrition.[41] Unless the birthrate also falls, population growth will accelerate. Hence reducing fertility (the number of births per woman of childbearing age) is essential to limiting population growth, which in turn is often central to allowing economic growth to continue.[42]

Because democracies foster more widespread education, and because fertility typically declines as education (especially of the female population) advances, countries with democratic governments have at least one clear advantage in this respect. But nondemocratic countries sometimes find other ways to restrain population growth, including methods that would be simply unacceptable in a free society. For example, China's notorious one-child-per-family policy—often enforced by intrusive inspections and, when necessary, forced abortions—reduced the number of expected births over the average woman's childbearing years from 5.8 in 1970 to 2 by the early 1990s. India, with its more democratic institutions, also managed to reduce its fertility rate over this period, but much less dramatically (from 5.5 to 3.7).[43] As a result, during the 1990s China's population grew by only 1.2 percent per annum, while India's grew at 2 percent.[44]

There is also little certainty about what kinds of political institutions best foster social and political stability. Riots, assassinations, military coups, and other such changes in government plainly deter investment, and the climate of tension surrounding these disorders probably hinders an economy's growth in other ways as well.[45] But it is far from clear whether democratic or undemocratic regimes foster greater political stability. The older Western democracies obviously have long records of government stability, with relatively little politically motivated violence, but that stability may simply be a consequence of these countries' high average income. As we have seen, governments in democracies are not systematically more stable than in dictatorships, and fledgling democracies in low-income countries are especially vulnerable to being overthrown.

The distribution of income and wealth can also influence a country's economic growth, but in this case not only is the role of political institutions unclear but even the more fundamental question of how equality versus inequality affects growth in the first place is a matter of great uncertainty. As we shall see, incomes sometimes become more unequal in the early stages of industrialization and then narrow once again as economic development advances, but the influence that the income distribution in turn exerts on the pace of economic growth is not clear. More to the point, how democratic versus nondemocratic institutions bear on income distribution is unclear as well.

Much of the ambiguity stems from the extremely wide range of experience in this regard among the world's *non*democratic regimes. Some, especially in Africa, have income distributions that are significantly more unequal than in the United States (which has by far the greatest inequality among the industrialized countries).* Other countries with nondemocratic governments, particularly in East Asia, have surprisingly equal income distributions, especially in light of their current low levels of per capita income. In China the top 10 percent of the population accounts for 33 percent of all consumer spending, not that different from the comparable American share (30 percent), despite the fact that the two countries stand at the opposite ends of any scale measuring democratic freedoms, and despite China's having a per capita income only one-eighth that in the United States.[46]

Finally, what about the "chaos of democracy"? Is Lee Kuan Yew right that a more "disciplined" approach—to the Western mind, he means a totalitarian or authoritarian government—is necessary to accumulate physical capital, train human resources, and harness both effectively so as to achieve rising incomes? And are "orderly" (in other words, nondemocratic or even anti-democratic) political institutions the necessary underpinning of such a pro-growth regime?

Many of the shortcomings of democracy do seem counterproductive in just this context. Squabbling politicians, obstructive partisanship, periodic labor unrest, and a sometimes vitriolic press are all standard features of modern political democracy. All too often, narrowly based but well-organized and well-financed groups protecting one economic interest or another—labor unions, manufacturers, electric utility operators, radio and television broadcasters, mining companies, dairy farmers, sugarcane

---

*Income inequality on the whole is greater in Latin America than in Africa, but the Latin American countries are in most cases more democratic.

growers—manage in effect to capture control over the politics of whatever aspect of economic activity most directly concerns them. The result is a vast network of price supports, sweetheart regulations, explicit or implicit government subsidies, tariffs and quotas that keep out competitive foreign goods, and barriers that block potential domestic competitors. Once these subsidies or tariffs or favorable regulations are in place, and both businesses and individuals have relied on them in making investments, their continuing force often takes on the character of an entitlement. An analogous situation sometimes applies to environmental and other advocacy groups in the nonprofit sector.

The democratic political process favors such outcomes because the interest of each particular group in matters affecting its specific aspect of economic activity is typically intense while the interest of the broader public in resisting such special pleading is both weak and widely dispersed.[47] It is easy to see why dairy farmers, for example, care strongly enough about raising milk prices to make it worth their while to organize, lobby, and make political contributions in order to achieve their goal. The number of citizens who would prefer lower milk prices is far larger, but cheaper milk is not a strong enough priority for them to mount an effective opposition.

The combined effect of these market distortions and impediments to competition and efficient resource allocation can be large. Worse yet, as political economist Mancur Olson argued, over time democracies typically accumulate more and more of them. Indeed, Olson suggested that a major factor contributing to the "economic miracle" that both Japan and West Germany enjoyed in the early decades following World War II may, ironically, have been these countries' total defeat—which allowed their postwar political regimes to sweep away their accumulated underbrush of economically counterproductive impedimenta.[48] In effect, the "creative destruction" that Joseph Schumpeter had earlier identified as the crucial by-product of economic depressions occurred in these countries instead as a consequence of military defeat.[49]

Many critics of economic and social policy in countries with democratic governments have likewise argued that these societies experience great difficulty—much more so than in authoritarian or totalitarian states—in responding to adverse situations that nonetheless lack the urgency of an outright crisis. Chronic problems like malnutrition, illiteracy, or inadequate health care can fester for decades (as they have in India) without being addressed in a satisfactory way. Countries like China, or even Cuba, have sometimes made greater progress in bringing their populations up to some minimum standard in these respects than have democracies with far higher average incomes.[50] Especially in the case of matters that affect long-term economic growth, like education and capital investment, the difference between a slow growth rate and a more rapid one simply does not have the immediacy of more visible issues like drug abuse or street crime, or especially terrorism, and therefore does not arrest public attention to the extent required to call forth corrective action through democratic politics.[51]

A feature of democracy that contributes to the ongoing failure to resolve such endemic problems is the system of checks and balances, both formal and informal, that makes democracies what they are. In a democracy the right of different constituencies to be heard is itself a form of entitlement. (As Churchill once complained in a wartime telegram to Roosevelt, "Action is paralyzed if everybody is to consult everybody else about everything before it is taken.")[52] The democratic process therefore makes it difficult to override the objection of intensely focused interests. As a result, at least on questions of a magnitude not sufficient to engage the broad public, those interests hold what amounts to veto power.

When the problem at hand *is* an out-and-out crisis, however, democratic governments often have a much better record of implementing solutions. Here again, the contrast between China and India is instructive. China has achieved greater literacy than India, a higher saving rate, and slower population growth. Life expectancy is also greater in China than in India (seventy-one years versus sixty-four).[53] But the experience of the two countries in dealing with acute crises—in particular, widespread famine and starvation—tells a different story.

In China, deaths from hunger during the period from 1958 to 1961, mostly as a result of the restructuring of agricultural production under Mao's ill-conceived "Great Leap Forward," numbered somewhere between 15 million and 30 million. India, during the country's colonial period, also suffered numerous famines—most recently in the Great Bengal Famine of 1943, when some 3 million people died. But India has not suffered a single famine since gaining independence in 1947. There is chronic hunger and malnutrition, to be sure, and the country has also experienced occasional more acute food shortages, typically as a result of crop failures. But in each instance the government has implemented sufficient measures, including food redistribution, to avert significant human crisis.[54]

Amartya Sen's explanation for this puzzling contrast is the positive interaction, in times of crisis, between two essential institutions of any working political democracy: the press and a partisan opposition. These, of course, are two of the features to which critics like Lee Kuan Yew point as the origin of much of the "noisy chaos" that democracy entails. But as Sen explains, "a free press and an active political opposition constitute the best 'early warning system' that a country threatened by famine can possess." Indeed, "no substantial famine has ever occurred in a country with a democratic form of government and a relatively free press."[55] Instead, famines have occurred in Mao's China, and more recently in Sudan, Chad, Uganda, and North Korea, where governments are free to persist in their disastrously failed policies. One economist (Jagdish Bhagwati) stated the point clearly: What is often "mistaken for crippling chaos . . . is merely the robust noise of a functioning democracy." It is "a safety valve that strengthens, instead of undermining, the state and provides the ultimate stability that is conducive to development."[56]

With so many crosscurrents through which personal freedoms and political institutions affect a country's prospects for economic growth, it is hardly surprising that no consensus exists about whether, on balance, democracy (and all that it entails) nurtures or hinders economic growth.[57] We also therefore do not know in general whether the favorable effect of economic growth on a country's freedoms is part of a two-way interaction that opens the way for countries to fall into either virtuous circles or vicious ones.

In two closely related contexts, however, openness and democracy do appear on balance to spur economic growth, so that the prospect of virtuous or vicious circles—especially the latter—is real. First, the reason many studies of this question fail to find a positive influence of political democracy on economic growth is that they account separately for the very ingredients of growth that open societies and democratic governments help create.[58] Asking whether the economy in a democracy will grow faster than that under a dictatorship if both are assumed to have identically educated populations is not the same as simply asking whether an economy in a democracy will grow faster than one under a dictatorship. A major part of the difference is that the two will probably *not* have identical education systems, nor will they be identical in other respects that could well affect their growth prospects. (As development economist Dani Rodrik suggested, "We can think of democracy as a meta-institution for building good institutions.")[59]

The distinction between these two ways of posing the question takes on particular force in the case of lower-income countries, where the education system is still not yet fully developed. As we have seen, under those circumstances a more open society and more democratic political institutions presumably would advance education and the development of human resources.[60] (And, as we shall see, there is also ground to think that an open society and political democracy would help make incomes more equal as well.) Conversely, a low-income country could fall into a situation in which its closed society and undemocratic government block the development of widespread education and other forces that otherwise would enable its citizens' incomes to rise, while at the same time the economic stagnation retards any nascent progress toward openness and democracy. Hence a vicious circle.

Virtuous circles seem less likely. Once a country has already developed many of the fundamental ingredients needed for growth, the relevant question then does become whether an open society and democratic political institutions *by themselves* provide any additional impetus to the growth process. The experience of today's advanced democracies provides no clear answer. Just as a country's high income is no guarantee of its openness and democracy if its economic growth should stagnate, the personal freedoms and democratic institutions that such a country's citizens enjoy will not in themselves maintain their country's economic growth.

The conclusion that vicious circles are more likely than virtuous circles in this setting also draws support from the findings of economist Robert Barro, who has argued that even apart from the positive effect of democracy on education and other aspects of the growth process, up to some point—roughly corresponding to the middle of the Freedom House measure of political rights—more democratic political institutions per se do help spur economic growth, mostly by helping to boost the country's investment rate. After that point, however, democratic institutions per se seem to hold back investment and growth (although their overall role, including their effect via education, may of course still be positive).[61] Barro's suggested explanation is that for countries with few freedoms the most powerful way in which democratization affects the economy may be by curtailing the arbitrary exercise of dictatorial powers. Once a country's political institutions are already moderately democratic, however, further gains along these lines are outweighed by the increased prospect of redistributive policies involving higher tax rates.[62] As we have seen, both of these developments are familiar consequences of democratic political systems, and both affect a country's economic growth.

The point is not that there is no value to further democratization once some middling level has been achieved. We value democracy both instrumentally and intrinsically—not just for the practical benefits it can bring but for its own sake as well. But it is also important not to expect democracy to deliver benefits that it will not bring, and especially so not to rely complacently on supposed advantages that are not forthcoming without independent efforts and correct choice of government policies.

A generation ago, Daniel Bell, in his classic book *The Cultural Contradictions of Capitalism*, anticipated an analogous kind of changing relationship—in this case between economic growth and capitalist market institutions.[63] The fundamental contradiction Bell saw was that while capitalist market systems foster economic growth, and therefore enable living standards to rise, with higher standards of living people in time seek entitlements and other redistributive arrangements, as well as various forms of protective regulation, that impair the functioning of capitalist markets and, ultimately, undermine them. Moreover, the depressing effect of high taxes that dull incentives, or of regulations that strangle economic initiative, is likely to be especially damaging to growth in already advanced economies that must rely heavily on innovation and creativity for further growth. Barro's suggestion about the relationship between economic growth and democracy, at advanced levels of democracy, is therefore much like Bell's view of the relationship between capitalism and incomes at high levels of income.

Whatever the exact relationship between democratization and economic growth, the risk of a country's falling into a vicious circle combining economic stagnation and political dictatorship means that the favorable consequences of economic growth for openness, tolerance, and democracy among countries that are just beginning to advance in these ways is all the more compelling. At the same time, the unlikelihood of self-sustaining virtuous circles carries a warning to high-income countries, where personal freedoms and political institutions are already well developed, that these precious features of their society are at risk if their economies falter and their citizens' incomes stagnate.

Chapter 14

Growth and Equality

It is therefore the greatest of blessings for a state that its
members should possess a moderate and adequate property. Where
some have great possessions, and others have nothing at all, the
result is either an extreme democracy or an unmixed oligarchy; or it
may even be—indirectly, and as a reaction against both of these
extremes—a tyranny. . . . Where democracies have no middle class,
and the poor are greatly superior in number, trouble ensues,
and they are speedily ruined.

ARISTOTLE
The Politics[1]

The natural human tendency to compare ourselves to others—in terms of
our athletic prowess, or good looks, or professional achievements, or our
possessions and standard of living—is no less important in accounting for
how people think and behave in the developing world than it is in today's
already industrialized societies. Like any shakeup in who stands where, economic development heightens people's awareness of comparisons concerning income and wealth. Further, the more sweeping modernization of
which economic development is a part usually expands communications in

ways that broaden the range of the comparisons most people can make. The resulting tensions surrounding income inequality affect political stability in developing countries as well as in new democracies more generally.

But how does economic development affect the distribution of incomes in the first place? Is it inevitable that economic rewards become more unequal when an economy begins to grow? Does a country's continued development into an industrial or even postindustrial economy then cause inequalities to narrow once again? Does today's setting of advancing globalization change how all this happens?

What most citizens of a developing country see when they compare themselves to one another differs sharply from what they would find if they were to compare their own standard of living to how people live in a typical industrialized economy. As we have seen, evidence from surveys suggests that once television became widely available throughout the industrialized world, the weight people placed on *cross*-country comparisons increased. The distinction is important because economic development, including in particular the development fostered by globalization, does not affect inequality within each country and inequality across countries in the same way.

Nearly everyone says that a more equal distribution of income and wealth is better, all else aside. But in explaining why they dislike inequality, many people offer an asymmetrical rationale. What troubles them is that some of their fellow human beings should live too far below what they take to be the appropriate norm for their society. Whether some others live far above that standard is of less concern. But is inequality then what actually matters? Or is it poverty? This distinction is important too, especially in the developing world, because experience shows that the effects of economic development on inequality and on poverty are not the same.

The traditional view of the connection between growth and distribution formulated by economist and demographer Simon Kuznets a half-century ago is that the tug-of-war between forces that either widen or narrow income inequalities has historically shifted in a systematic way as economic development proceeds.[2] At the outset of industrialization, the movement of a significant part of the working population from low-wage agricultural employment to higher-wage jobs in factories and related services is sufficient to widen inequality. Wages also typically vary more in industry than in agriculture. Moreover, the initial rise in living standards reduces death rates fairly promptly, while birthrates come down only after some delay.

The result is rapid population growth, which further depresses low-end industrial and urban wages especially in the early stages of economic development.

The beginning of industrialization, by its very nature, also involves the introduction of new technologies and new ways of organizing an economy's production. (In today's increasingly global economy, many of these new technologies and business approaches come from abroad.) Some of these activities, precisely because they are new, require skills that few workers have: the ability to operate complex machinery, or in some settings even just to read and write. The few who have these skills can command much higher wages, thereby making inequalities even greater.

Other new aspects of economic activity require initiative and entrepreneurship, in which inevitably only a few people will succeed and some will succeed more dramatically than others. Moreover, the process is cumulative. Those who do succeed find it easier to get loans to enable them to try again on a larger scale. Then, once incomes have begun to rise unequally, families with higher incomes normally do a disproportionate share of an economy's saving, and so they go on to accumulate a disproportionate share of its newly created wealth. The gap between their incomes and those of families who do little or no saving therefore becomes all the wider.

The shift in the composition of a country's wealth as it develops economically, from land to assets that are easier to buy and sell, provides yet further opportunities for some individuals to run up significant gains. Sadly, the growth of trading and commerce also brings increased opportunities for corruption, especially when democratic political institutions are weak or nonexistent, and neither law enforcement nor government economic regulation is effective. All too often, top government officials and their families and supporters manage to appropriate for themselves truly astonishing sums.

Kuznets also emphasized, however, that as development proceeds many of the forces that cause greater inequality weaken while new forces emerge that work to reduce inequality. After some time, birthrates typically decline as incomes on average advance, and so population growth slows. The tendency of the poorest and least-educated workers to flock to the cities, and thereby depress low-end urban wages, also ebbs. As incomes in general continue to rise, families other than those with the very highest incomes are able to save and accumulate assets. A rising standard of living also enables a country to devote more resources to law enforcement—just as improved communications increases the awareness of what corrupt politicians and business executives are doing, and therefore leads to popular demands for a more honest system—and hence helps to reduce the corruption that enables some individuals to garner enormous wealth dishonestly.

The internal dynamic of the growth process itself also operates so as to reverse the widening inequality that the initial stages of industrialization have created. More workers acquire the skills that earn the highest wages. At the same time, firms introduce new technologies to economize on the skilled labor that is now so expensive. For both reasons, pay differences become smaller.

Changing technologies and enhanced market competition matter too, in many cases including competition from abroad as a developing country becomes better integrated into world markets. New industries continually move to the forefront, creating fresh opportunities for different groups of workers to gain employment at higher wages, as well as outlets for new entrepreneurial energies. Economic growth typically brings new financial institutions, and better functioning credit markets, so that more people with ideas and aspirations can borrow to start a new business. At the same time, advancing technology diminishes the value of the productive assets already in place, which are typically owned by whichever groups had benefited most during the earlier stages of industrialization.

The result of this shifting interplay of opposing forces, Kuznets suggested, is that income inequality typically widens at first, then levels off, and in time narrows, as an economy develops.[3] As we have seen, the wider inequality that accompanies the initial stages of industrialization adds importantly to the strains that economic growth places on a country's political and social fabric. It also retards the tendency of a rising average standard of living to foster openness and tolerance.[4] But if a country's economic growth follows the course Kuznets outlined, incomes will again become more equal. In time the initially severe inequality will become a historical artifact. (Kuznets argued, for example, that Karl Marx's claim that capitalism inevitably leads to ever increasing misery of the working classes, and hence to an explosive polarization of society, resulted from Marx's myopic extrapolation of the widening inequality that accompanied England's economic growth in the first half of the nineteenth century.[5] In fact, inequality in Britain leveled off not long after Marx wrote and began to narrow well before the nineteenth century ended.)

The accumulation of evidence in the decades since Kuznets suggested this pattern of widening and then narrowing inequality has provided somewhat more support for the second half of his hypothesis than the first.[6] The earliest examples of economic development appear to fit the Kuznets pattern best. In England's industrial revolution incomes became more unequal from about the middle of the eighteenth century to about the middle of the nineteenth. A similar widening of inequality occurred in America during much of the nineteenth century and perhaps even into the first few years of the twentieth.

Other countries that have industrialized more recently have done so from very different starting points, however, and under highly diverse circumstances: some under democratic governments and some under dictatorships, some in the wake of wartime destruction and some under more peaceful conditions, some with broad education systems and some with education targeted toward narrow elites, some with the benefit of massive foreign aid and some more nearly on their own. As a result, the record of income inequality during the early stages of economic development looks more mixed today. For example, inequality remained quite limited in the early postwar growth of many East Asian countries, which surely rank among the most dramatic cases of recent economic development.[7] (The reason was probably these countries' commitment to broadly based education.)[8]

The tendency for incomes to become more equal as a country's average per capita income advances beyond some moderate level has more solid support. Although there are some notable exceptions—for example, the combination of high average income and extreme *in*equality in the oil-producing Middle East—on the whole, countries with higher average incomes do tend to have more equality than low-income countries. An apparent exception is the United States, where inequality is the greatest in the industrialized world, though still less than in most developing countries. But until the final quarter of the twentieth century, when inequality began to increase again—as it did in many other industrialized countries—inequality among Americans had been mostly narrowing for some decades.

The recent increase in inequality in America and other high-income countries suggests that the interaction between technological change and the effect of education in reshaping the labor force is especially important to how a society's degree of inequality changes over time. Although industrialization initially raises the value placed on skills that few workers have, and therefore initially widens wage differentials between skilled and unskilled labor, in time it is *un*skilled workers who become increasingly scarce as education becomes more broadly available and practically all young workers receive the training that higher-wage employers require. Similarly, once these skill-based differentials in wages become large enough, businesses have an incentive to develop new technologies that economize on skilled labor—for example, robots to replace assembly line workers and even laboratory technicians, just as bulldozers earlier replaced strong bodies wielding picks and shovels.

But if yet newer technologies appear later on, and again change the mix of workers' skills that are most essential, skill-based wage differentials can widen once again, at least for a while, even at much later stages of economic development. Hence the tendency of incomes to become more equal as development advances may be interrupted, from time to time, by new waves of technological advance. The increasing inequality in the United States and in many western European countries since the mid-1970s in part reflects just such a renewed widening of pay differentials, as the shift from industrial production to information-based services accelerated while many workers initially lacked the new computer skills rewarded in the labor market. To the extent that this kind of skill imbalance is what lies behind the recent worsening in these countries' income distributions, however, historical patterns suggest that in time the spread of education imparting these skills (together with the introduction of yet newer technologies that will economize on the labor that has these skills and therefore commands such high premiums today) is likely to reverse it. A large part of what allows so many more people to acquire these skills is publicly provided education, and a rising standard of living not only renders a society better able to afford that education but also makes its citizens more inclined to support the effort.

Further, rising incomes on average also increase the willingness of those who can afford it to assist their less fortunate fellow citizens in more direct ways, ranging from public welfare to private charity. As a result, in most higher-income countries the inequality of *living standards* is distinctly less than the inequality of *incomes*. Part of this difference, to be sure, is that people with higher incomes save more, while those at the bottom of the scale need to spend all they earn. But an important part too is that in practically all medium- and higher-income countries, the people who earn more also pay more in taxes, and some of what they pay goes to support the living standard of those who earn only a little.

But is inequality really what matters? Human privation is a tragedy regardless of whether only some people live in poverty or everyone does. For most people, in most societies, poverty means not only being poor now but having little prospect of not being poor in the future. In most cases it also means seeing one's children have only limited chances of escaping poverty themselves. And even more so than inequality, a poor standard of living, for much of a society's citizenry, blocks the formation of democratic institutions and then threatens the survival of whatever democracies do manage to emerge. As Samuel Huntington has argued, "Poverty is a principal—probably *the* principal—obstacle to democratic development."9

The evidence is clear that regardless of whether economic growth in time reduces inequality, it surely reduces poverty. Many observers of the early Industrial Revolution, especially in Britain but soon thereafter in America too, were appalled by the conditions in which urban factory workers and their families lived. Blake's poetic allusion to "dark Satanic mills," and Dickens's gritty portrayals of small-town factory work in *Hard Times* and of London's seamy underbelly in *Oliver Twist*, reflected a commonplace view, in the mid-nineteenth century, that industrialization—and, by extension, economic and technological advance in general—created only misery for most of those whom it touched. Other contemporary assessments, like Elizabeth Gaskell's *North and South* and Disraeli's *Sybil* (subtitled "The Two Nations") dwelled at length on the contrast between the old, agrarian way of English life and the rising new industrial economy, and they left no doubt that these authors thought the comparison favored preindustrial ways.

Agrarian resistance to the pressures brought by industrialization and urbanization dominated American politics during the latter decades of the nineteenth century, as we have seen, and again for a while in the years between the two world wars. Some early postwar economists, extending these ideas to what was then the newly developing world, likewise took up Marx's conception of economic growth as "immiserating."10 The concerns increasingly expressed about "sweatshop labor" in today's developing countries continue this same line of thinking.

But if "misery" in the economic context corresponds to what most people understand as poverty, the weight of experience since World War II has mostly demonstrated the opposite. Repeated studies have shown that as average incomes rise in developing countries, the incomes of the poor rise in pace. Whatever widening of inequality takes place typically occurs as those at the top pull ahead even faster, not because those at the bottom see their incomes stagnate or decline.

For example, among the sixty countries for which data on income distribution currently exist for two or more periods at least ten years apart, so that direct comparisons across time are possible within each country, in only three (none a developing country) did the average income of the poorest one-fifth of the population decline while the average income in the country as a whole was rising. Overall, the income of the poorest fifth rose more rapidly than that of the population as a whole in just as many cases as it failed to keep pace. And in countries where the poorest fifth of the population started off with the smallest share of total income—in other words, in countries where the inequality was widest—the poorest fifth typically enjoyed *faster* income growth than did the population as a whole, so that the poor were, in effect, catching up.[11] On balance, the evidence for today's developing economies suggests about a one-to-one relationship between a country's average income growth and the gains achieved by its lowest-income groups.[12]

Recent investigations into what has happened to poverty on a world scale lead to a similar conclusion. A familiar measure of poverty in the developing world, endorsed and widely publicized by the World Bank, is the share of a country's population who live on as little as $1 a day, or perhaps $2 a day.[13] It is shocking to most residents of any Western industrialized country to learn that in both Mali and Nigeria more than 90 percent of the population live on $2 a day or less, and more than 70 percent live on $1 or less. Many other African countries are nearly as poor. But poverty is not limited to Africa, and it extends to the very largest countries as well. In India 80 percent of the population live on $2 a day or less. In China 47 percent do.[14]

For purposes of assessing whether someone is well-off or miserable, however, what matters is not how many dollars that person's income could buy in the foreign exchange market but what standard of living it can support in the place where he or she lives. Because currency values established in foreign exchange markets often depart from levels that reflect equivalent purchasing power, and official exchange rates set by governments for currencies that do not trade in markets are also often far from that mark, the difference is sometimes large. In India, for example, the average person's income in rupees in 2003 (the latest year for which figures are available) translated into just $530 per year at the prevailing market exchange rate of nearly 47 rupees for $1. But because food, clothing, housing, and other consumer necessities are much cheaper in India than in the United States, the same amount of rupees was equivalent to an American income of nearly $2,900—extremely low by Western standards, to be sure, but more than five times what the simple translation at market exchange rates would suggest. Similarly, the average Chinese income in 2003 was $1,400 at the official yuan-dollar exchange rate, but almost $5,000 on a purchasing-power-equivalent basis.[15]

Even calculated on a basis that allows for differences in the cost of living between one country and another, the number of people around the world who live on $1 or $2 a day is still depressingly large. According to one estimate, as of 1998 nearly 300 million people—more than the entire population of the United States—lived on $1 a day or less. Another 680 million lived on incomes of more than $1 a day but less than $2.[16] Together, not quite 1 *billion* people, or nearly 19 percent of the world's population, were in dire poverty by this standard.

Poverty on this scale is unimaginable to most citizens of the developed world. But for purposes of understanding the consequences of economic development, the key question is whether poverty has become more or less widespread as individual countries' economies, and the world economy more generally, have grown. And here the answer seems clear. A quarter-century earlier, even after adjustment for price inflation, the number of people living on less than $1 a day was not 300 million but nearly 700 million. Those living on less than $2 totaled nearly 1.5 billion.[17]

Further, this decline in the number of people facing dire poverty has occurred despite an increase from 4 billion to nearly 6 billion in the world's population over this period.[18] The *fraction* of people around the world living in poverty has therefore declined even more rapidly. Thirty years ago more than 44 percent of the world's inhabitants lived on less than $2 a day. By 1998 fewer than 19 percent did. The share of the world's population living on less than $1 a day has declined from 20 percent to somewhat over 5 percent.

Because China and India are so large (their combined population is now more than 2.3 billion), and because most Chinese and Indians still have low incomes by world standards, the strong economic performance in these two countries has accounted for a large part of the overall decline in world poverty. Since the late 1970s, China's increase in per capita income has been the fastest in the world. India's growth has also stepped up considerably since the early 1990s.[19]

And while *inequality* has increased in both countries—the gap between rural and urban living standards in particular has widened—*poverty* has clearly abated. In India, for example, much of the recent political debate has focused on whether the growth prompted by the country's 1991 economic reforms has left the poor behind. There surely remains room for improvement, and continuing low literacy (still just 61 percent for adults) is a major impediment to furthering many poor people's economic prospects. But the evidence is clear that the incidence of poverty has continued to decline since 1991, as India's growth has become more rapid as well as more unbalanced.[20]

At the other end of the scale of economic growth performance, however, most African countries, especially south of the Saharan desert, have done poorly. To make matters worse, as living standards on average have either stagnated or declined, the distribution of incomes there has become more unequal.[21] The result has been many more people living below any plausible poverty benchmark. On the same $1-a-day standard for which world poverty has declined from 20 percent three decades ago to just 5 percent, in sub-Saharan Africa the poverty rate has risen from 48 percent to 60 percent.

As most Asian countries have achieved economic success over this period, while most African countries have not, extreme poverty has correspondingly shifted from being a mostly Asian to a largely African phenomenon. Africa as a whole represents one-sixth of the world's population, but today nearly half of the world's poor are African.[22] The consequences of failing to grow can be severe.

The changes that have taken place in worldwide living standards are not mere statistical abstractions. They represent concrete differences in the conditions under which the great majority of people in developing countries live. Thirty years ago more than one child in five in India died before reaching age five. Now fewer than one in ten do—still a horror, but a welcome improvement nonetheless. (In high-income industrial countries it is usually below 1 percent.) In China the death rate for children under five has fallen from more than one in ten to under 4 percent. Under-five mortality has also fallen from 14 percent to less than 3 percent in Ecuador, and from nearly 18 percent to less than 4 percent in Peru.

Even some of the hardest-pressed African countries, where AIDS is at its worst and child mortality for other causes too remains shockingly high, have seen some improvement: from 29 percent to less than 21 percent in Burkina Faso, for example, and from 24 percent to just over 17 percent in Ethiopia. Nor are these isolated cases. Even in the fifty countries that have the world's lowest per capita incomes, the average child mortality rate has fallen from 24 percent thirty years ago to 12 percent today.[23]

Other tangible aspects of what it means to live in poverty have followed a similar pattern. In 1990, 74 percent of the population of the Philippines had access to adequate sanitation. By 2000, 83 percent did. The parallel improvement has been from 61 percent to 72 percent in Ghana, and from 52 percent to 70 percent in Bolivia.[24] The fraction of children immunized against measles has gone from 16 percent to 81 percent in Ghana, from 21 percent to 89 percent in Belize, and from 56 percent to 93 percent in Brazil.[25] Since 1980 the fraction of the population that is undernourished—adults as well as children—has fallen from 38 percent to 21 percent in India, from 22 percent to 13 percent in Colombia, and from 64 percent to 17 percent in Burkina Faso.[26]

Aspects of how people live that bear important implications for how their economy and their society will fare in the future likewise convey the strong message that a higher average standard of living not only can but in fact does remove some of the most important barriers that living in poverty normally creates. Among the fifty countries with the world's highest per capita incomes today, the average fraction of the school-age population enrolled in education at all levels is 87 percent. For the fifty countries in the middle of the world's income distribution, the average enrollment rate is 71 percent. For the fifty lowest-income countries it is just 49 percent.[27]

But changes over time are what economic development is all about, and in this respect as well the low-income countries that have growing economies are catching up, rapidly expanding and improving their educational systems. In China the overall enrollment rate has risen from 44 percent to 56 percent over the last thirty years, and for primary and secondary school ages it is now 87 percent. In India enrollment has risen from 38 percent to 52 percent (72 percent for primary and secondary school). By making it possible for a country to broaden and deepen the education its citizens receive, economic growth not only alleviates a crucial aspect of poverty but also breaks the cycle through which poverty perpetuates itself by preventing large numbers of the next generation from receiving the education that would enable them to become economically productive.

Rapid population growth is another way poverty breeds more poverty. A high birthrate means more children to educate, greater need for food, housing, and medical care, and greater strain on a country's limited government infrastructure. But poor countries, where both economic and political resources are most limited, usually have the most rapid population growth. Some part of this difference simply reflects the fact that low-income countries have typically had rapid population growth in the past, and in most the life expectancy is short, so that women of childbearing age represent a larger share of the total population than in high-income countries. But in most low-income countries the number of births per woman of childbearing age is also much greater.

Slowing a country's population growth is normally an essential underpinning of a successful economic development strategy. But it is also clear that a high average living standard helps to lower fertility and thereby to slow population growth. The fifty countries with the world's lowest incomes average 4.7 births per woman. Among the middle fifty countries the average fertility is 2.6. In the fifty highest-income countries it is just 1.8.[28]

In all of these respects, therefore—and many more—it is clear that over time economic growth, in the familiar sense of a rising per capita income, enables ever more citizens of a developing country to escape the sorry conditions that make up the everyday burdens and genuine miseries of poverty. And, conversely, in the countries that the world labels as "developing" but that in fact are failing to do so, the rise out of poverty is slower and in some cases nonexistent.

Among the fifty countries that had the world's lowest per capita incomes in 1990, the average growth rate over the next ten years, corrected for both inflation and population increase, ranged from *minus* 9 percent per annum (in war-ravaged Sierra Leone) to an astonishing 16 percent (in Equatorial Guinea). For the twenty-four of these countries where incomes fell, the cumulative decline during the 1990s averaged 21 percent. Among the twenty-six where incomes rose, the average gain was 30 percent. In 1990 the average income was nearly the same in these two groups. By the end of the decade, citizens of the countries that grew enjoyed far higher living standards than citizens of those that did not.

This difference in economic growth rates, sustained over a decade, mattered for more than just measured incomes. True, both groups of countries scored gains on a few important dimensions such as fertility rates and infant mortality, mostly as a result of the worldwide advance of medical technologies together with the efforts of international health agencies and private charities funded from abroad. But in some of the most basic aspects of what it means to live, and to be poor, those that experienced positive economic growth made gains while those that shrank economically lost ground. Life expectancy increased on average in the countries that grew and declined in those that shrank. Malnutrition became less prevalent in countries that grew economically, more so in those that shrank.

As we have seen, in one setting after another, most people do care about how they are getting along compared to what they see when they look around them. They care because observing how others live gives them an idea of what is customary, what to expect, in whatever contexts they take to be relevant, and it further gives those with imagination some sense of what is possible. Most people also care because of the natural human desire to stand up well among one's friends and neighbors and fellow citizens. It is hardly surprising that especially wide inequalities of income and wealth tend to foster political instability and sometimes help to undermine new, vulnerable democracies. Inequality clearly matters.

But, to repeat, it is important to distinguish between inequality and poverty, and especially so in assessing the implications of economic development. The record is mixed on whether the early stages of economic growth lead to greater inequality. Some successful development paths apparently create large inequalities, others do not. But it is clear that economic growth leads to less poverty.

Just as there are numerous ways in which economic growth can widen or narrow the inequalities among a nation's citizens, the extent of inequality can in turn affect a country's prospects for achieving economic growth. But is more or less equality better for growth? Assessing the balance of the evidence is important because so much of the debate about inequality usually revolves around balancing egalitarian social goals against the incentives that inequality creates to undertake productive economic activity.[29] If inequality impedes growth, however, weighing that balance becomes irrelevant.

A view first advanced by Adam Smith and other observers of the beginnings of the Industrial Revolution emphasized the role of high-income groups in providing the saving that is necessary to finance accumulation of physical capital, such as factories and machines, and thereby facilitate more advanced division of labor.[30] (At the same time, Smith also believed too much inequality retarded economic growth; he thought excessive wealth, relative to the standard of the day, reduced the incentive to save and invest carefully.)[31] Especially at the outset of economic development, a country's per capita income is so low that only people earning well above the average can afford to save significantly. But many potentially productive investment projects are viable only on a scale that exceeds some minimum threshold. An unequal income distribution, which gives even a small minority at the top the wherewithal to save in meaningful quantities, therefore allows the necessary accumulation to begin.[32]

Today economists are increasingly skeptical that this remains a good description of the development process. Many low-income countries turn out to have extremely high saving rates, and in much of the developing world inflows of saving from abroad have financed large amounts of investment. Indeed, the most recent evidence even casts doubt on whether inequality helped generate saving and investment in the early industrialization in Britain that Smith and others had in mind.[33]

A similar idea is that inequality enables at least some children in a poor country to receive more than a minimal education. In light of the key role that more comprehensive secondary schooling regularly plays in promoting rapid economic growth, the implication is again that greater inequality may be good for growth.[34] But the evidence shows instead that in the developing world a more equal distribution of incomes apparently facilitates greater enrollment in secondary school, especially among girls.[35]

This positive effect of income equality in facilitating female education is especially important because of the crucial role of slower population growth. More widespread female education leads to fewer births per woman, not only because more educated women normally have more information about birth control but also because education creates alternative opportunities that are often more attractive than immediate childbearing. The resulting lower fertility apparently constitutes one of the principal ways in which the distribution of income and wealth affects economic growth in low-income countries.[36]

Recent thinking has also identified ways in which equality helps promote growth by increasing saving and investment. The social and political instability that large income disparities create are of concern in their own right,[37] but they also discourage investment. Faced with instability or even violence, and the prospect that a country's government may give way to a dictatorship, citizens with high incomes may choose to put their savings into foreign bank accounts rather than business ventures in their own country, and potential foreign investors will likewise shy away. Because of just this kind of favorable effect on stability, the land reforms carried out in many East Asian countries after World War II, which dramatically reduced inequalities of wealth and income, probably helped foster these countries' postwar growth.[38] By contrast, the record of the postwar period also shows that countries with more *un*equal income distributions tend to have more politically motivated assassinations, more people killed as a result of domestic mass violence, and more political coups as well as more unsuccessful coup attempts. It is no surprise that the share of the economy's income devoted to new investment is systematically smaller where such events occur more frequently.[39]

Large income disparities also create pressures for redistributive spending policies that require high rates of taxation. Nondemocratic regimes that are doing badly at achieving economic growth often turn to radical redistribution policies as a way to quell popular discontent, and newly established democracies sometimes take the same route in an effort to buy legitimacy among a broader public. But high tax rates, or even merely the fear of high tax rates—not to mention outright expropriations—likewise depress incentives to invest in the local economy and to undertake other initiatives that promote a country's economic development.[40]

In the setting of a low-income economy, a more even distribution of incomes also helps promote economic growth by broadening consumer markets. With broader markets it becomes profitable for domestic industries to develop and, in time, take the place of imports (especially of manufactured products) that would otherwise drain the country's scarce supply of foreign exchange.[41] Some economists have also suggested that because the majority of individuals can expect to live longer when incomes are more equally distributed, greater equality helps to encourage better work habits, increased willingness to acquire economically productive skills, and more careful attention to saving and investment plans.[42] Greater equality also promotes interpersonal trust and fosters other forms of "social capital" conducive to economic growth.[43]

The question of what balance between equality and inequality is best for economic growth is difficult to answer in part because there are so many possible influences at work and also because some of these influences act in opposing directions. In addition, however, just as the effect of democracy on economic growth appears to be different in high-income and low-income countries, many of the effects of equality or inequality are likely to have more force under some circumstances than under others. When a country's saving rate is already high, or when ample foreign capital is available, whether inequality facilitates or inhibits saving matters little. Similarly, once most of a country's children (including girls) are already finishing high school, the effect of equality in boosting enrollments, and thereby reducing fertility and slowing population growth, is small at best. Fears that excessive inequalities will lead to coups, assassinations, or other forms of political instability may loom large in new democracies, and in the low-income developing world more generally, but this prospect is less of a threat in the well-established industrialized democracies. Concerns that inequality may create pressures for redistributive tax and spending policies are normally more relevant in democracies than in dictatorships.

Especially in low-income countries in the developing world—that is, countries where school enrollment is low and fertility high, and where political instability and even violence are concrete facts of national existence—the available evidence suggests on balance that countries where incomes are more *equal* achieve somewhat superior economic growth. Although the net effect is not large, the income range across which greater equality influences economic growth positively appears to encompass much of the developing world: in one estimate, up to a per capita income (on a purchasing power basis) of approximately $3,000, or not quite the income of either Ecuador or Indonesia today.⁴⁴ Not counting countries that are so poor or where conditions are so chaotic that no reliable income data exist, like Afghanistan and North Korea, more than fifty countries fall within this range.⁴⁵ For a significant portion of today's developing world, therefore— including almost all of sub-Saharan Africa, but also countries in Asia, in both Central and South America, in the Caribbean, and in the parts of Europe that used to be within the Soviet Union; in all, countries with a total population of 2.4 billion—the route to an improved standard of living lies, at least in part, through greater equality.⁴⁶

Few economic phenomena have been as easily visible during the past half-century as the enormous expansion of international trade and investment flows—globalization. Continual advances in the technology of transportation and communications have dramatically reduced the cost of moving goods and people from one country to another, as well as of gathering information on what is happening elsewhere. The free trade policies implemented by most industrialized countries since World War II, both in bilateral settings and in successive rounds of negotiation under the General Agreement on Tariffs and Trade, have further lowered barriers to the cross-border flows of goods and of investment capital (though not of people, at least not those seeking immigration).

At the same time, few economic phenomena seem to provoke such angry protest. To be sure, few people have objected to the advances in transportation and communications technology that have made so much of today's international economic activity possible. The focus is instead on government policies, including in particular the undertakings of such multinational institutions as the World Bank, the International Monetary Fund, and the new World Trade Organization (since 1995 the successor to the GATT). The heart of the protest movement, not just in the streets but in a burgeoning volume of books and articles, is the claim that the consequence of these institutions' pro-globalization agenda, perhaps inadvertent but maybe deliberate, is to widen the already enormous inequalities between rich countries and poor countries as well as between the upper-income elites and the working poor within each.⁴⁷

As we have seen, the gap between the world's richer and poorer countries *is* huge, whether measured by incomes or by the most basic elements of human living conditions. The gap has also widened over time although it may have narrowed more recently.⁴⁸ But is globalization the cause of this greater inequality? And even if it is, is the answer to slow or perhaps reverse the ongoing integration of world markets, as much of the protest movement urges?

Economic globalization is not a new phenomenon. The technology of transportation and communication has been improving almost since the beginning of recorded history, and each notch along the way has typically marked some further increase in cross-border economic activity as well. This process gained particular momentum early in the nineteenth century, as first the steamship and then railroads came into common use. Development of the telegraph, followed by the laying of undersea cables, advanced communications along with transportation.

Free trade policies, the other key underpinning of economic globalization, do not have such early roots. But by the second half of the eighteenth century, David Hume and Adam Smith, as well as French "physiocrats" like Quesnay and Mirabeau, were voicing reasoned opposition to Europe's mercantilist legacy. By early in the nineteenth century, almost all prominent British economists favored free (or at least freer) trade, and by mid-century Britain, then the world's leading economic power, had adopted a mostly free trade orientation.[49] (The decisive step was repeal of the Corn Laws in 1846.) An increasing number of countries followed suit.

As a result, the hundred years from the end of the Napoleonic Wars to the beginning of World War I saw an expansion of international economic activity to levels that in many dimensions matched, and in a few exceeded, what occurred at the end of the twentieth century.[50] By 1913 cross-border trade in goods was as large a share of the world's total economic production as it is today. Cross-border investment flows, which in those days mostly went from Europe to the Americas, were more important then than now on a net basis.[51] The pricing of financial assets in the major markets around the world was similarly more integrated than is the case today.[52] In what amounted to an era of mostly unrestricted mass immigration, the cross-border flow of labor—again mostly from Europe to the United States and other land- and resource-rich New World countries like Argentina—far exceeded today's labor flows. (Whether cross-border transfers of productive technology were as important then as now is harder to judge.)

Although technology does not run backward, government policy sometimes does. The period between the two world wars brought an abrupt retreat from international economic integration, almost entirely as a result of newly autarkic policies including restrictive immigration quotas in countries that had previously been recipients of large labor inflows, as well as prohibitive tariffs almost everywhere. In many respects, therefore, the advance of economic globalization in the latter half of the twentieth century did no more than recoup the ground lost earlier. Tariffs, for example, are lower now than they were in 1913, but today there are far more nontariff barriers to trade, including not only outright quotas but also "voluntary" export restraints and technological requirements that many producers find impossible to satisfy.

But if globalization has been underway for a long time, the gap between the world's rich and poor countries has been widening even longer—since at least the beginning of the seventeenth century.[53] It is always possible that economic globalization has accounted for this divergence since the Napoleonic Wars, while other forces, which have since dissipated, were largely responsible earlier on. At the least, however, the fact that the cross-country divergence in average incomes predates the acceleration of cross-border economic activity by at least two centuries indicates that other influences were, and may still be, at work.

It is not even obvious that international flows of goods, capital, labor, or technology necessarily worsen cross-country inequality in the first place. To take the kind of example that attracts the most attention today, when an American manufacturing firm that sells its products mostly to domestic consumers closes a plant in the United States and builds a replacement in India—or in Mexico, Indonesia, or any of the other typical recipients of American investment flows—American workers lose their jobs while Indian workers get new jobs. The move presumably saves money for the firm (why else would it have relocated its plant?), and so profits and therefore the incomes of the firm's owners will increase. Many of its former employees will have to take jobs elsewhere at lower wages, however, and probably some will not find jobs at all. On the reasonable assumption that the owners' incomes are already higher than the employees', the result is to widen inequality *within* America.

At the same time, while the hourly wage rate that the firm is now paying its new Indian employees is well below what it was paying in the United States, that rate is probably far above the average wage in India. (It is not uncommon for a foreign firm to open a factory in a developing country and have thousands of people line up to apply for a few hundred jobs.) Hence the result is to widen inequality within India as well.

But on a *cross-country* basis the result is to narrow inequality. Income that used to go to American workers now goes to their Indian counterparts. After all, that is why this kind of shift in production facilities to another country usually attracts so much opposition at home, especially from organized labor. Since India's average income is far below America's, the same relocation of production that widens inequality within the United States as well as within India therefore *narrows* the gap *between* the two countries' average incomes.*

Not all elements of economic globalization take this particular form, and the consequences for inequality differ from one situation to another. But as the logic of this one typical example shows, globalization certainly need not increase inequality across countries. Indeed, it need not increase within-country inequality either. As we have seen, Corn Laws repeal in nineteenth-century Britain lowered the incomes of British landowners. It also raised the living standard of British workers, by making bread cheaper. The move to freer trade therefore reduced inequality within Britain.54

As the factory relocation example also importantly shows, the effect of globalization on inequality across countries and inequality within countries need not be in the same direction. The possibility that cross-country inequality and within-country inequality may not move together raises yet again the question of just what comparisons, and therefore what concepts of inequality, people take to be relevant. If India's average income draws closer to America's, but in the process some Indians—in this example, the lucky workers who get the new factory jobs—pull ahead of their neighbors, is the net outcome a victory or a defeat for the cause of equality? As is often the case, inquiry into whether globalization widens or narrows "inequality" requires a more discriminating analysis.

Over the nearly 200 years since economic globalization began in earnest, then, has the effect been to narrow or widen the world's economic inequalities?

From the middle of the nineteenth century until World War I, both average wages and average living standards mostly became more equal across the increasingly interconnected group of countries that in time became today's industrialized world.55 A major reason was globalization—in particular, large-scale migration. The working poor from Italy, Ireland, and other countries where land and other resources were limited moved in vast numbers to America and other Western Hemisphere countries that needed labor. The effect was to raise wage levels in the countries where these work-

---

*If the new plant is more efficient than the old one, and enough of the gains from this enhanced efficiency accrue to the firm's owners, America's *total* income could rise, perhaps even more than that in India. But this gain would be a consequence of building a more efficient plant, not specifically of locating it abroad.

ers came from and to reduce wages (in other words, to retard the rate of increase) in the countries to which they went. In the meanwhile, because it was mostly poor workers who emigrated, incomes within the countries they left therefore tended to become more equal. At the same time, because their arrival held down wages (and consequently benefited landowners, who were mostly better-off), the result was to make incomes more unequal within the countries where they immigrated.

On a broader world scale, including the countries that did not participate in these large-scale labor movements and that were also less integrated into the international flow of goods and investment capital, cross-country inequality widened during this earlier era of economic globalization.[56] For the most part, however, this widening was not the consequence of globalization, at least not in any direct way. As economic historians Peter Lindert and Jeffrey Williamson have forcefully argued, other forces were at work: Some countries, especially America, made large investments in educating their populations, while others did not. Some developed secure property rights, governments relatively free of stifling corruption, and other public and private institutions that provided an environment conducive to productive economic activity; others did not. Some countries participated eagerly in the burgeoning international economy. Others, either landlocked or simply located too far away given the limitations of that era's transportation possibilities, could not. Still others, like Spain and Portugal, could have joined the international economy but chose not to.[57]

As we have seen, income inequality within Britain widened during the first half of the nineteenth century but then narrowed thereafter, while inequality within America continued to widen through the end of the century. Elsewhere the pattern was more mixed, with emigration mostly narrowing inequality in the poor, land-scarce European countries that were the origin of so much of the era's mass movement of labor. Overall, within-country inequality showed little change during the first great period of globalization.[58]

Between World War I and World War II, within-country inequalities mostly narrowed in much of what is now the industrialized world. By contrast, the inequality in average incomes across countries increased even more rapidly than before. But in neither case could globalization have played much of a role. The interwar period was, in effect, a time of anti-globalization, in which the worldwide retreat into autarky, abetted twice by disruption due to world-scale warfare, unraveled much of the international economic network built up over the previous century.

Since World War II the record has also been mixed. Among the industrialized countries, for which data on income distributions are more readily available, within-country inequality typically narrowed during the first quarter-century after the war but widened thereafter. As we have seen, however, the most likely explanation was the introduction of new computer-based technology, not the continuing expansion of international trade and investment. At the same time, some developing countries, though hardly all, have experienced greater within-country inequality, perhaps because they were riding up the first part of the "Kuznets curve" (if that part of the relation that Kuznets posited is indeed valid) as their economies developed and their average incomes rose. Most studies have concluded that whatever effect globalization has had on within-country inequality has been small.[59]

What is most interesting about the postwar period in this context is that as economic globalization has again gained momentum, the centuries-long widening of cross-country inequality has, at the very least, slowed significantly, and it may even have reversed.[60] Further, a large part of this change reflects a development that is explicitly part of globalization: the increasing share of manufactured goods in not just the total output *but also the exports* of the typical developing country. According to U.N. estimates, thirty years ago manufactured goods constituted 17 percent of all exports originating from developing countries. By the mid-1990s the manufacturing share was 64 percent.[61] The image of the typical developing country participating in international trade mostly by selling agricultural commodities and extracted minerals in order to pay for the manufactured goods that it exclusively buys from abroad is long out-of-date.

But perhaps these gains may come at some other cost.[62] One especially sensitive issue in today's globalization debate is whether the industrialization that many developing countries have achieved in recent years is built on child labor, as was much of the initial Industrial Revolution in Britain and continental Europe two centuries ago. Child labor is a serious problem in many parts of today's developing world, not least because it takes children away from the schooling that otherwise would make them more productive later on (and, for girls, help reduce fertility). But the available evidence suggests that child labor is more of a problem in the "nondeveloping" world than among the low-income countries that are actually achieving economic progress. The evidence also shows that most child labor in these countries is used not in manufacturing but in agriculture, where the work is harder and the opportunities for schooling are even more limited.[63] (As one observer concluded, barring child labor in low-income countries' export manufacturing sectors would probably have the effect of sending the children not to school but back into agricultural work.)[64]

Even within low-income countries' agricultural sectors, there is some evidence that the globalization of trade may reduce, rather than increase, the use of child labor. As is so often the case, the question is more subtle than may first appear because two influences are potentially at work, acting in opposite directions. Allowing a country's agricultural products to be sold abroad typically increases the price that growers receive and therefore raises farm wages. With higher wages, poor families find it all the more enticing to send their children to work. At the same time, with higher agricultural wages fewer families are poor, and so more can afford the "luxury" of letting their children attend school instead of working.

The evidence shows that on balance the effect of international trade in lifting families out of poverty, and thereby enabling them to leave their children in school, is more powerful. Countries that trade more tend to have less child labor. What matters is not any direct effect of trade activity per se, however, but the resulting alleviation of poverty in general.[65]

Vietnam for example—a very poor country where the economy is largely agricultural—began to participate in the global economic community only recently. The rising prices due to the country's entry into foreign trade have clearly helped reduce the use of child labor. In 1993, more than one-fourth of all Vietnamese children six through fifteen worked in agriculture.[66] Between 1993 and 1998, as the country's self-imposed quota on rice exports gradually loosened and then became nonbinding, rice exports doubled and the price of rice rose by 29 percent compared to the country's consumer price level. At the same time, the use of child labor dropped by 28 percent. School enrollment and attendance also rose, with the largest increase among girls of secondary school age. Although in principle these national-level events could have occurred together by coincidence, a detailed analysis on a commune-by-commune basis suggests that almost half of the decline in child labor was due to the higher price of rice. Four-fifths of the decline was due to the improvement in poor households' living standards. Participation in trade reduced poverty, and as poverty abated so too did child labor.[67]

The evidence overall suggests that economic globalization was a major engine underlying widening world inequalities neither in the century preceding World War I nor in the half-century following World War II. Some countries obviously achieved far faster growth than others during these two eras of globalization. But other forces—countries' differing institutions, endowments, and policies, and perhaps even their different "cultures"—accounted for who succeeded and who did not.[68]

Perhaps the greatest impact of globalization in the cross-country divergence of average incomes and living standards has simply been to create opportunities that different nations have exploited in a variety of ways. Most countries have increasingly engaged in the exchange of goods, in either exporting or importing investment capital, and in either sending their citizens abroad or receiving immigrants. But some, for one reason or another, have stood back.

Here, too, the contrast between China and India is instructive, although neither represents the extreme in this regard. Beginning with Deng Xiaoping's reforms in the late 1970s, China has energetically embraced international trade and the influx of foreign investment. The Chinese record of economic growth since then is foremost in the world. India has opened its economy more slowly, with major changes coming only since the early 1990s. As a result, according to development economist T. N. Srinivasan (himself an Indian), Indians lament "the costs of our hesitant and reluctant globalization in terms of foregone growth, the avoidable delay in the eradication of poverty and our falling behind our competitors such as China."[69]

The lesson from this experience, not just in China and India but throughout the world, is that the countries that chose to engage with the global economy did better than those that chose not to. The contribution of globalization to inequality, such as it was, came as those countries that did not participate fell behind those that did.[70] As Lindert and Williamson concluded, "these facts do not show that globalization favors rich participants. Rather, globalization favors all participants who liberalize, especially those who are newly industrializing, and penalizes those who choose not to liberalize, leaving them behind."[71]

This conclusion carries a sharp warning for any country thinking of holding itself apart from the global economy. On the record to date, China's strategy of engagement is a long-term winner. Myanmar's economic isolation is a long-term loser. As Lindert and Williamson went on to say, in the modern era of globalization, participation in international trade has unambiguously helped most developing economies: "[T]here are no anti-global victories to report for the postwar third world."[72]

Chapter 15

Growth and the Environment

Humanity has the ability to make development sustainable—
to ensure that it meets the needs of the present without
compromising the ability of future generations to
meet their own needs.

BRUNDTLAND COMMISSION
Our Common Future[1]

It is surprising to recall how early, in the post–World War II era that was widely thought to be "the American century," concerns about limited resources and collateral damage to the environment began to figure prominently in both popular discussion and public affairs in the United States.[2] In January 1951, President Truman constituted the Commission on Materials Policy to study what he described as "one of the crucial problems facing the nation" and to recommend appropriate policy actions. Part of the motivation for launching the inquiry was an awareness, heightened by the recent war effort, that adequate supplies of specific materials were essential to military preparedness. But Truman also charged the commission "to study the broader and longer range aspects of the nation's materials problem as distinct from the immediate defense needs." His instructions referred directly to the needs created by "the continued economic growth of the United

States," and he went on, "We cannot allow shortages of materials to jeopardize our national security nor to become a bottleneck to our economic expansion."3

The commission's report, filed the next year, was comprehensive. It examined many of the key aspects of resource availability that emerged as important issues over the course of the next quarter-century: extractable minerals, timber and other forest products, land for agricultural use, ocean resources, and water (among others). An extended discussion of energy needs addressed oil, natural gas, and coal, as well as the question of how much electricity the United States would need and how to generate it. The potential role of technology and of new policies to shape technology was a particular focus of attention, and here too the commission anticipated major themes of later years. There were sections on "Broader Recycling," "More Use of Renewable Resources," and "Stretching Supply by Effective Use." An entire separate volume discussed "The Promise of Technology," including a chapter on "The Possibilities of Solar Energy."4

A decade later, an entirely different dimension of concern about the environment captured wide attention among the American public. Rachel Carson's 1962 bestseller *Silent Spring*, which grew out of a series of articles she had written for *The New Yorker*, both shocked and frightened readers with accounts of the consequences of America's increasing reliance on pesticides and other toxic chemicals. These contaminants did not disappear on application, Carson wrote, but instead lingered to pollute our air, soil, and water. The end result, she argued, was death: in the first instance to birds (hence the book's title) and fish, but ultimately to humans as well. Beyond the physical risks, Carson framed the issue in explicit moral terms. What she was describing was a "chain of evil."5

Carson further highlighted the dangers posed by indiscriminate use of toxic chemicals by drawing an analogy to the risks of nuclear weapons and nuclear radiation, including the possibility of human genetic mutation, all of which loomed large in the minds of many Americans in the early postwar period: "Along with the possibility of the extinction of mankind by nuclear war, the central problem of our age has therefore become the contamination of man's total environment with such substances of incredible potential for harm—substances that accumulate in the tissues of plants and animals and even penetrate the germ cells to shatter or alter the very material of heredity upon which the shape of the future depends."6

The concerns galvanized by *Silent Spring* soon began to affect American public policy. Congress passed the Clean Air Act in 1963 and the Clean Water Act in 1972. The National Environmental Policy Act, passed in

1969, created the advisory Council on Environmental Quality and formally declared that "it is the continuing policy of the Federal Government . . . to create and maintain conditions under which man and nature can exist in productive harmony."[7]

April 22, 1970, marked the first "Earth Day," a nationwide event organized by Wisconsin senator Gaylord Nelson that drew an estimated 20 million participants to rallies, teach-ins, and other activities in thousands of cities and towns across the country. Later that year Congress amended the Clean Air Act to require reduced automobile emissions (among other changes) and also established the Environmental Protection Agency. A flurry of further legislation and rule-making followed during the next few years.

In the meanwhile, other countries—most prominently Japan (where the country's postwar industrial development, especially in heavily polluting chemical industries, had led to dramatic increases in sulfur dioxide and nitrogen dioxide) and Sweden, but others too, especially in Europe—were conducting similar debates and adopting parallel policies. West Germany enacted the Waste Disposal Act in 1972 and an Emission Control Act in 1974. Taiwan passed the Water Pollution Control Act in 1974 and the Air Pollution Control Act in 1975. In 1974 seven nations bordering the Baltic Sea—Denmark, Finland, East and West Germany, Poland, Sweden, and the Soviet Union—signed the Helsinki Convention to protect the sea's water and fishery reserves.[8] By the mid-1970s, the place of environmental concerns, both on the American public policy agenda and, increasingly, elsewhere in the world as well, was clearly established.

What remained unclear was the connection of these new concerns to economic growth. Many of the air and water contaminants at the heart of popular anxieties were of course a consequence of the transition over time to an industrial economy and the mode of living to which industrialization gave rise (the automobile, for example), and ever greater production meant more contamination. But the primary focus of *Silent Spring* had been insecticides, which farmers as well as ordinary suburbanites who disliked mosquitoes were free to use or avoid. Further, as the numerous acts passed by Congress and regulations adopted by the EPA repeatedly demonstrated, manufacturing, electricity generation, automotive transportation, and myriad other activities could, at some cost, be rendered less polluting.

In contrast, by the early 1970s a growing body of opinion had concluded that limited resource availability, into which the Truman commission had inquired twenty years earlier, would in all likelihood impede future economic expansion. In 1972 a team of little-known researchers from the Massachusetts Institute of Technology published a small book bearing the ominous title *The Limits to Growth*, and further identified as "A Report for the Club of Rome's Project on the Predicament of Mankind."[9] (Who or what, people wondered, was the Club of Rome?)* *The Limits to Growth*, purportedly based on scientific analysis, offered a stark conclusion: "If the present growth trends in world population, industrialization, pollution, food production, and resource depletion continue unchanged, the limits to growth on this planet will be reached sometime within the next one hundred years. The most probable result will be a rather sudden and uncontrollable decline in both population and industrial capacity."[10]

Actually, the book argued the impact would be felt much sooner than a hundred years. One chapter began, "What will be needed to sustain world economic and population growth until, and perhaps even beyond, the year 2000?" A few pages later, after reviewing recent trends in food production, the authors asked, "Do these rather dismal statistics mean that the limits of food production on the earth have already been reached?" They also wrote, "The answers we obtain will give us some estimate of the upper limits to population and . . . growth, but no guarantee that growth will actually proceed that far."[11]

The confluence of political and economic events soon placed the ideas advanced in *The Limits to Growth* at the center of public attention and, further, seemed to validate their credibility. In 1973 the member countries of the Organization of Petroleum Exporting Countries (OPEC) agreed to limit oil production, thereby raising the market price of crude oil as well as derivative products like gasoline and fuel oil. Soon afterward, the Arab countries' embargo of oil sales to the United States, motivated by the latest round of politics and warfare in the Middle East, temporarily created lengthy lines at the gas pump for many Americans. By year's end further cuts in OPEC production had more than tripled the price of crude oil compared to just a few months before. Suddenly the relationship between oil

*The Club of Rome began in 1967 as an informal group assembled by Italian industrialist Aurelio Peccei and British chemist Alex King, concerned with what its members saw as the unsustainability of current patterns of economic growth, including environmental degradation, overconsumption of finite resources, and high rates of population increase in already crowded areas. The group formally incorporated in 1970. At its first meeting, held that year, the new organization decided to produce the report that appeared two years later as *The Limits to Growth*.

reserves in the ground and annual production became a staple of everyday conversation: how many years of oil did we have left? But that was precisely the question posed, across a broad range of resources, by the Club of Rome report.

Also in 1973, another book, *Small Is Beautiful* by British economist E. F. Schumacher (who had spent the previous two decades as head of planning at the British Coal Board), drew a connection of a different kind between environmental concerns and economic growth.[12] Far more so than either Rachel Carson or the Club of Rome team, Schumacher linked concerns over pollution and resource availability with the more general process of modernization that, as Samuel Huntington had argued a half-decade earlier, economic development normally entails. But while Huntington mostly accepted economic development as a given, and sought to understand the political consequences of the associated societal transitions, Schumacher framed the pace and, even more so, the *scale* of economic activity as matters subject to choice. His title made plain which choices he advocated.

In addition, much more so than the Club of Rome report, Schumacher's treatment of resource availability highlighted the disparities between the industrialized West and the developing world. Because the resources in question increasingly traded in world markets, scarcities resulted from excessive consumption relative to supply on a global basis. Schumacher emphasized that a small minority of the world's population was systematically doing the majority—often the great majority—of the world's consuming. But what distinguished industrialized countries from developing countries was mostly the gap in living standards, which had resulted from the industrial countries' past economic growth, and which was continuing to widen as those countries achieved ongoing superior growth. Hence economic growth per se was an important part of the problem.

In subsequent years, two further dimensions of environmental concern came to prominence in public discussion and policymaking, and here too the tensions with economic growth were explicit. First, during the 1980s scientists increasingly became aware of the increased concentration of carbon dioxide (CO_2) in the earth's atmosphere and, in parallel, a slight rise in global average temperatures.[13] These findings were soon reported in the popular press. A front-page story in the *New York Times* in 1981 started off, "A team of Federal scientists says it has detected an overall warming trend in the earth's atmosphere extending back to the year 1880. They regard this as evidence of the validity of the 'greenhouse effect.' "[14] (The story was headlined "Study Finds Warming Trend That Could Raise Sea Levels.")

Another front-page story two years later began, "The Environmental Protection Agency warned in a report made available today that the warming of the earth known as the 'greenhouse effect' will begin in the 1990s."[15]

Further research (largely based on examining layers of ice deeply buried in Greenland and Antarctica, among other places) revealed that over hundreds of thousands of years, eras of above-average carbon dioxide concentration roughly corresponded to eras of above-average temperatures. Excess CO_2 in the atmosphere, reflecting radiated heat back down onto the earth rather than allowing it to escape into space, provided a ready explanation. What was new in all this was the hypothesis that the current period of increasing CO_2 concentration, and hence rising temperatures, was not a random occurrence that would reverse itself in time but a consequence of the human use of coal, oil, and other carbon-based fuels, which in the future was only likely to increase.

In time, the issue of "global warming"—together with other aspects of global climate change like the dissipation of protective atmospheric ozone, apparently due to the release of chlorofluorocarbons from common aerosol sprays—assumed first-rank importance on the environmental agenda. Because hydrocarbon fuels are essential to powering not only much of the world's industry but also most forms of transportation (airplanes, trains, trucks, automobiles) as well as a large share of electricity generation, the connection between advancing economic growth and rising concentrations of carbon dioxide and other greenhouse gases is direct. And although the entire planet is affected, at least for now the overwhelming majority of the greenhouse gas emissions comes from the industrial world and from those countries that are rapidly industrializing. (Five countries—the United States, China, Russia, Japan, and India—account for more than half of all CO_2 emissions, and just a dozen countries account for more than two-thirds.)[16] Bringing the developing world closer to the living standard of the Western world, presumably in large part through industrialization, would only exacerbate the problem.

A still more recent dimension of environmental concern is the link between economic growth and the extinction of living species through the elimination of these species' habitats. In industrialized countries, this is mostly a matter of isolated cases arising from logging operations (for example, spotted owls in Oregon), damming rivers (snail darters in Tennessee), or land development. In the developing world what is at issue is the large-scale conversion of primal forest and other natural areas to agricultural use, human settlement, or industrial facilities. As of 1990 the Amazon rain forest in Brazil, for example, was shrinking by 12,000 square miles each year. As a result, Brazil's total forest area was 23 percent smaller than it had been two decades earlier. Over the same period Thailand's rain forests had shrunk by 70 percent.[17] Deforestation has slowed since then in most countries, but it is still continuing. During the 1990s Brazil's forest area shrank on average by just over 9,000 square miles each year.[18]

The desire to protect natural environments was not a new, late-twentieth-century phenomenon. In the nineteenth century the Romantic movement in Europe prompted not just the attempt to create the urban illusion of nature—"English gardens" scattered across the continent were one manifestation—but the desire to preserve natural landscapes like Germany's Rhineland.[19] In the United States conservationists like John Muir and Theodore Roosevelt led the campaign that eventually resulted in the creation of America's national parks. But the motivation behind these movements was mostly aesthetic (or, as in the case of German interest in the Rhineland, nationalistic). The issue today is also preservation of the species that live in these habitats.

This concern is in part a matter of self-interest. No one knows which as yet undiscovered form of plant or animal life may contain within its chemical or genetic makeup the key to some new drug, cosmetic, or fragrance. But there is also a moral dimension: whether one species—humanity—has the right to extinguish another. (In fact, species are always disappearing, in the ongoing Darwinian struggle. The moral issue is human intervention.)[20]

While protecting spotted owls and snail darters may be only a trivial impediment in the context of America's economic growth, declaring large sections of the Amazon in Brazil and the Songkhla region of Thailand off limits would potentially affect these countries' development in far more extensive ways. After all, most of North America was natural forest and grassland just a few hundred years ago, and further back so was much of Europe. Today's highly advanced industrial economies achieved that status in part by what amounted to large-scale habitat destruction (although few participants in the process thought of it this way at the time), with significant extinction of plant and animal species. Now that a large and growing segment of world opinion does think of the matter in this way, the question is whether today's economically developing countries will follow the same path. And if not, what are the consequences for these countries' economic growth?

In the years since environmental concerns first gained momentum in the Western democracies, many people (especially economists) have come to view questions of resource availability as distinct from issues like pollution, global climate change, or species extinction. When markets for resources are allowed to function normally, so that increasing demand relative to supply creates higher prices, the result is not only to signal the resulting scarcity but to trigger actions that can, and more often than not do, work to alleviate it. In the first instance, higher prices discourage individuals from consuming whatever is scarce and likewise discourage businesses from using it in production. When oil prices rose in the 1970s, many home-owners turned their thermostats down and car owners drove less. Some people insulated their houses more effectively, and others bought more fuel-efficient cars. At the same time, companies across a broad range of industries looked for more energy-efficient ways of making their products and delivering their services.

While the United States uses more energy today than it did then, energy consumption has fallen sharply compared to economic output and has even declined on a per capita basis despite the continued advance in American living standards. Since 1973 the energy used to produce each dollar of America's gross national product (adjusted for inflation) has fallen by nearly one-half. As of 1973, the nation's total energy consumption per capita had risen during the postwar period by an average of 2 percent per annum, but since then per capita energy consumption has declined slightly.[21]

But the price mechanism does more than discourage people from using whatever is scarce. Higher prices also stimulate additional supply. A large part of the discussion spurred by the OPEC price hike in 1973 centered on comparing the then current annual world consumption of 20 billion barrels of oil to the existing "proved reserves" of 611 billion barrels. Contrary to what many of the more naive participants in that discussion suggested, the world has not run out of oil after thirty years. Instead, reserves of extractable petroleum today total more than 1.2 trillion barrels, despite the fact that nearly 750 billion barrels have been consumed since 1973. And annual consumption of oil is now up to 29 billion barrels. Moreover, even with the recent increase to more than $50 per barrel, the price of oil remains well below the levels of the late 1970s and early 1980s after allowing for overall inflation since then.[22]

There are certainly nonrenewable resources for which the ability to produce new supplies is subject to sharper limits, and supplies of many potentially renewable resources like forest timber and ocean fish can be made to expand only so fast, virtually regardless of price. If the world still relied on whale oil for lighting, it is hard to imagine supplies having kept pace with the increased demand after the middle of the nineteenth century (moral concerns about the slaughter of whales aside). But higher prices spur the development of new technology that enables users of what is scarce (and therefore expensive) to use it more efficiently, that enables suppliers to find or make more of it, and that leads to new substitutes. In fact, the world prices of most of the foodstuffs and industrial commodities that the Club of Rome report identified as potential bottlenecks to growth have *fallen* over the more than three decades since the book initially appeared, and not because population and economic output have declined as the authors warned might happen.

The *Limits of Growth* authors made such faulty predictions because they underestimated the power of technological advance, and ignored altogether the role of initially higher prices both in encouraging substitution by users and in stimulating new supplies.[23] The conceptual framework they took as their model was essentially that of Malthus, who nearly two centuries before, living in what was still a predominantly agricultural economy, had focused on the tension between the arithmetic increase of food production and exponential population growth. (The first two chapters of *The Limits to Growth* were titled "The Nature of Exponential Growth" and "The Limits to Exponential Growth.") But Malthus had failed to see the implications of the technological revolution that was beginning to take place around him, including advances in agricultural methods as well as new modes of transportation that opened the way to grow food on land previously too far away to be useful.* On the evidence of the three decades since the Club of Rome report appeared, its authors similarly failed to anticipate the power of new technology, or to understand the functioning of the price mechanism.

The unaided functioning of the price mechanism is impotent, however, to solve problems like pollution, or global climate change, or species extinction, all classic examples of market failures caused by externalities—that is, by social consequences of private actions. When a utility company saves money by burning cheaper coal with a high sulfur content, the reduction in its costs either boosts its profits or allows it to cut the price of electricity, or perhaps both. At most, its shareholders and its customers benefit. But the sulfur dioxide it releases into the air affects whoever lives downwind of the plant, even hundreds of miles away. (Hence eastern states' continual com-

---

*In the later editions of his book, Malthus backed away from this position; but his renown today is due to the ideas set forth in the first edition.

plaints, and lawsuits, directed at plants in America's Midwest.) There is nothing in the ordinary market mechanism to induce the company to take these costs into account, and no incentive for it to pay for a stack scrubber or switch to more expensive low-sulfur fuel.

The externality problem is even more pronounced in the case of global climate change and species extinction. In the absence of some nonmarket incentives or restrictions, the shareholders, workers, and customers of even the largest firm bear only a tiny fraction of the cost of whatever damage may result from their company's choices. But these three constituencies together, in some combination, retain 100 percent of the savings from doing business more cheaply; put another way, together they would bear 100 percent of any expenses involved in limiting greenhouse gases or protecting species habitats.

Concern over public externalities like pollution (including waste disposal), and the realization that purely private decision making cannot be expected to solve such problems, has a very long standing. The Bible contains detailed instructions about which activities could and could not take place within the Israelites' camp in the desert. Greek city-states had regulations governing where in the city operations like tanning hides and slaughtering animals could locate. So did medieval European towns. As early as 1285 the city of London established a commission to look into the air pollution caused by extensive burning of coal, and for much of the next two centuries the use of coal for fuel was prohibited in England.[24]

In these areas of concern, both the scale and the form of economic activity matter. As economist Jeffrey Frankel has pointed out, if the human species still consisted of a few million hunter-gatherers there would be little man-made pollution and almost no greenhouse gas emissions.[25] With a world population in excess of 6 billion, of whom some 1 billion live in highly developed industrial economies and more than another 3 billion in countries including China, India, and Brazil that are now rapidly industrializing, the situation is different. Moreover, the effects of CO_2 emissions on climate are global.

Growing awareness in recent years of the nature of this entire class of problems—and of the fact that the market mechanism left to itself cannot be expected to solve them—has spawned a profusion of governmental actions, and far more proposals for action, at all levels: within countries, between countries on a bilateral basis, and multinationally, depending in large part on the geographical scope of the externality being addressed. Understandably, the landmark international agreements have attracted the greatest public attention. The United Nations Law of the Sea, negotiated between 1973 and 1982, deals with matters such as conservation of marine resources and protection of the ocean environment (in addition to specifying nations' territorial sea limits, navigational rights, and marine jurisdiction). The Basel Convention on Hazardous Wastes (1989) created an international mechanism to monitor and control the movement of waste products, such as dyes and organic solvents, across national borders, and in particular to limit industrial countries' sending such products to developing countries where disposal costs are lower. The Convention on International Trade in Endangered Species (1973) imposes restrictions on buying and selling designated plant and animal species, including live animals, exotic leather goods, certain wood timbers, and some medicinal plants. The Montreal Protocol on Substances That Deplete the Ozone Layer (1987) imposed restrictions that have greatly reduced the use of most chlorofluorocarbons. (It is especially instructive that while most of the Montreal Protocol's success has been due to the availability of ready substitutes for chlorofluorocarbons, the fact that these substitutes existed was not known when the protocol was negotiated.)[26]

Most recently, the Kyoto Protocol to the U.N. Framework Convention on Climate Change, negotiated in 1997, represents an attempt to limit the industrial nations' greenhouse gas emissions. The United States has declined to ratify this agreement (America *signed* the agreement in 1998, but this action has no legal force unless the Senate ratifies it).[27] By 2004, however, 126 of the 136 countries that are parties to the process had formally accepted the final agreement—including, as required, countries accounting for at least 55 percent of industrial countries' emissions of six designated gases—and the treaty went into effect in February 2005.[28] In principle, the Kyoto Protocol (as amended) requires thirty-eight industrialized countries to reduce their CO_2 emissions at least 1.8 percent by 2012. Although there is doubt about whether the participating countries will actually meet this target, together with continuing debate over whether the Kyoto agreement constitutes the right approach to addressing this problem, the broader point is that the great majority of nations around the world have recognized that a problem exists and have begun a cooperative effort to address it.[29]

The Law of the Sea, the Basel Convention, the Endangered Species Convention, the Montreal Protocol, and most recently the Kyoto Protocol have all achieved high visibility on the world stage. Beyond these major international milestones, however, a multitude of laws and regulations at the national and subnational level now exist as well, addressing pollution, waste disposal, and even species extinction in settings where the geographical range of the underlying externality is more limited.

. . .

The key unresolved question, in light of this burst of environmental policy-making during the last quarter-century, is what role economic growth plays in environmental problems and in whatever solutions can be found. Does continually advancing industrialization simply bring more pollution and ever greater exhaustion of resources as living standards rise? Or do changes in what economies produce, and in how they produce it, negate the effects of ever greater scale? What role does—and should—public policy play? And to what extent is the response of policy itself an aspect of the systematic consequences of sustained economic growth?

The least polluted areas of the globe are, of course, those where there is no industrial activity and little or no human settlement. Pristine lakes and air that admits unlimited visibility are easier to find in national parks, or in the little-inhabited regions of Finland, Nepal, and New Zealand, than in the metropolitan or suburban parts of the industrialized world. Mostly agricultural areas, where human density is low and most economic activity consists of cultivating crops, typically stand somewhere in between.

But it does not take much traveling around the world to discover that the places where pollution is greatest and environmental blight is most readily visible are *not* those with the highest living standards. Whether the issue is smoke in the air or germs in the water, or even just the discarded clutter and refuse accumulated from ongoing human habitation, countries, regions, and even individual cities where living standards are high in other respects rarely have the most pollution or present the worst eyesores. Within Europe, one of the greatest shocks to many people after the collapse of the Soviet Union was the stark gap in environmental standards between the former Soviet satellites and their higher-income neighbors just to the west, with whom the newly independent countries now sought to affiliate themselves economically and politically. Not until 1990 did the first eastern European country—the Czech Republic—introduce unleaded gasoline. Four years later it became the first to require catalytic converters on new automobiles.[30]

In short, scale is not all that matters. As an economy develops, and the living standard of its people rises, the composition of economic activity typically changes as well. When an agricultural economy first develops a significant manufacturing capacity, many familiar kinds of pollution, especially those that result from burning coal and oil, increase. (Agricultural expansion often brings its own forms of pollution, however, especially from burning in order to clear land or from applying fertilizers to the soil.) But the service industries that normally emerge as incomes rise yet further mostly involve less pollution than does manufacturing. In the forty-two countries where per capita income today is below $2,000 (after allowing for international differences in purchasing power), on average only 43 percent of the economy's production is in services. Where per capita income is between $2,000 and $8,000, the service sector share averages 54 percent. In the $8,000 to $20,000 range, it is 60 percent, and in the countries where per capita income is above $20,000 (there are twenty-three of them), the service sector on average accounts for 69 percent of total output.[31]

This shift into services as incomes rise is not just a matter of moving manufacturing facilities "offshore." If the composition of what a society consumes remained unchanged as living standards improved, and richer countries simply shifted their manufacturing operations to distant locations and correspondingly increased their reliance on imports, their doing so might help to contain their own pollution problem but it would make no difference on a global basis. Many services are not readily transportable, however, at least not across international lines. The service sector's share of what the United States produces, for example, is nearly identical to the share of services in what the country consumes. Moreover, the shift in American production toward "cleaner" industries in recent decades, with the advance of free trade and the tightening of anti-pollution laws, has been matched by a shift to cleaner industries in what the United States imports.[32] Throughout the world, the increase in the share of services in overall economic activity as living standards rise mostly represents a change not just in what people make but also in what they consume.

Rising living standards also influence the technology by which economies produce. For example, roughly four-fifths of the world population's total exposure to particulates in the air takes the form of smoke from indoor cooking fires, typically fueled by wood or coal or peat.[33] For the most part, this form of pollution does not result from any externality. The families that cook their food on these indoor fires expose *themselves* to smoke inhalation, but typically not others. Most of them have low incomes, and live in low-income countries. If their income were greater, they could afford to cook their food using some other technology.

The same influence of rising living standards on people's choice of technology also applies, however, in settings in which externalities are the crux of the issue, so that the choices involved are matters of collective decision making—in other words, public policy: whether to allow the use of (cheaper) leaded gasoline, whether to require cars to carry (expensive) catalytic converters, whether to ban (cheaper) high-sulfur coal, whether to require (expensive) stack scrubbers for factories and utility plants. In each case, altering individuals' or firms' behavior in ways that reduce pollution imposes a cost. Just as families who have sufficient incomes typically choose not to live with the smoke created by cooking indoors over an open fire, *societies* where living standards are high can afford to bear some cost for limiting pollution, and most choose to do so. As a result, their incomes as conventionally measured are usually smaller than would otherwise be the case. But because they also care about the air they breathe and the water they drink, and perhaps also about the global climate and the preservation of species, they are nonetheless better-off.*

The relationship between economic development and environmental degradation may therefore follow a pattern analogous to what Simon Kuznets years ago posited as the relationship between development and inequality: In the initial stages of development, the transition from traditional agriculture to manufacturing increases pollution and greenhouse gas emissions. But in time further shifts in the composition of economic activity (mostly toward a larger service sector), the evolution of new technology, and both private and public choices that higher incomes make possible, all lead instead to an improvement. Just as Kuznets hypothesized that economic development at first involves more inequality but that this greater inequality will prove temporary, the dynamic interaction among these opposing effects presumably exacerbates environmental problems for a while along the economic growth process, but may then limit and even reverse the environmental damage as living standards rise yet further.[34]

Empirical investigation into this kind of "environmental Kuznets curve," since the idea first drew attention in the early 1990s, has mostly supported the conclusion that the consequences of economic development for many of the most familiar forms of air and water pollution are indeed negative up to levels of per capita income of between $2,000 and $8,000, but then become positive—and not just in terms of pollution per capita, or per unit of the country's economic output, but absolutely. In cross-country comparisons, sulfur dioxide, nitrous oxide, carbon monoxide, smoke, and lead from automotive emissions all show increasing atmospheric concentra-

---

*Because of the role of changing technology, however, imposing environmental restrictions does not always cause even conventionally measured income to be less than it would have been. Business strategist Michael Porter has suggested that the additional research that firms have to do in order to comply with environmental restrictions also serves to make them more productive in other ways, thereby *increasing* their overall profitability (Michael E. Porter, "America's Green Strategy," *Scientific American* 264 [April 1991]: 168).

tion up to some income level, but a decreasing concentration thereafter.[35] A similar pattern obtains for fecal contamination in rivers, as well as contamination by heavy metals such as lead, arsenic, cadmium, mercury, and nickel, all of which carry well-established health risks. Conversely, the level of dissolved oxygen in rivers (a key sign of biological vitality) appears to decrease at first with economic development and then increase.[36] Deforestation at first increases with economic development (how could it not?), but there is even some evidence that it too reverses as living standards rise further.[37]

As always, it is important to be cautious in using comparisons across different countries, at different income levels, to infer what will happen over time in any single country as its average income rises. But the limited evidence that is available suggests that, at least for many familiar pollutants, initial environmental deterioration is indeed followed by improvement as incomes rise. In the United States, ambient sulfur dioxide in the air is down by 54 percent since two decades ago (even more since the early 1970s), while carbon monoxide levels are down by 65 percent and lead by 94 percent.[38] Measures of water quality, like siltation and bacterial content, have shown similar though less dramatic improvements. The area covered by forests is increasing once again, and total forest area in the United States is only 1 percent smaller than it was fifty years ago (or, for that matter, a hundred years ago). Further, the total volume of wood grown has steadily exceeded the total amount cleared, so that America's forests now contain nearly 40 percent more wood than they did fifty years ago.[39]

It would be a mistake, however, to conclude from this rise-and-fall pattern that environmental concerns somehow "take care of themselves" as part of the economic growth process, leaving no need for public policy. The reversal in so many elements of environmental degradation as living standards rise beyond some level is due in part to changes in the composition of economic activity and in part to changes in technology. But these changes are themselves often the outcome of active public policy decisions.

Environmental policies have been crucial to bringing about at least part of the turnaround that comes with higher incomes, because of the familiar role of externalities in so many basic elements of everyday pollution. The impressive improvement in America's air quality in recent decades is hardly likely to have happened if automobile drivers had been left to decide *individually* whether to use leaded or unleaded gas, or if coal-burning utility plants had faced no legal or regulatory incentive to switch to lower-sulfur fuel. The original 1963 Clean Air Act, and the amendments to that law in 1970 and again in 1990, largely account for why Americans fuel their cars and their factories differently, and generate their electricity differently, than they did forty years ago. The result has been less-polluted air, reduced disease, and fewer associated deaths (especially among infants).[40]

In much the same way, even though water in most American cities was already provided either directly by public facilities or by privately owned but publicly chartered utilities, the series of federal water pollution laws that began with the 1972 Clean Water Act—including the Water Pollution Control Act (also in 1972), the Safe Drinking Water Act (1974), and further amendments to these laws in 1977, 1986, 1992, and 1996—was clearly effective in stopping industrial firms from dumping pollutants into rivers and lakes, as well as in getting local water companies, including those owned and operated by local governments, to purify water to a higher standard. The role of public policy is even more obvious in programs like the "Superfund" (established in 1980) that provide federal funds to clean up existing toxic waste sites.

None of these environmental improvements could have taken place in the absence of the enabling technology. But the mere existence of a technology does not guarantee its use—people knew about unleaded gasoline and catalytic converters long before the 1963 Clean Air Act—and in most familiar cases the technology that has reduced air pollution or produced cleaner water is (or at least was at the outset) more expensive than what was previously in use. Even where the technology already exists, the role played by public policy is to induce ordinary individuals and firms to use it despite the availability of a cheaper but more polluting alternative.

Moreover, in many cases environmental rules or legislation prompts the development of new technology. In recent decades the automobile industry has made impressive advances both in increasing fuel efficiency and in reducing emissions. No doubt the industry would have developed some of this new technology anyway, even without the numerous restrictions and requirements put in place by the United States and many other countries (although the automakers' fierce opposition to these requirements suggests that such independent progress would have been far more limited). In the event, much of the industry's progress in producing fuel-efficient, low-emission cars has been a response to the carrots and sticks provided by governmental policies.[41]

Two further aspects of recent experience also support the idea that public policy, responding to changes in popular preferences as incomes rise, accounts for much of the improvement in so many elements of the environment. First, not only do many forms of pollution begin to abate when incomes on average rise above some level, but environmental regulation also increases.[42] As the experience of Russia and the former Soviet satellites in Europe suggests, however, these improvements are also linked to whether a country has a democratic government.[43] The effect of rising living standards on popular preferences, operating through the political process, therefore appears to be an essential part of the story. Democracies translate the increasing value that the public attaches to the environment, as its living standard rises, into public policies that reduce pollution and otherwise cause the environment to improve. If the only influence that led a country's environment to improve as it moved beyond a certain income level were its enhanced ability to afford pollution-reducing technologies, there would be no reason to expect the nature of its political system to matter one way or the other.

Second, the one major environmental contaminant for which no study has ever found any indication of improvement as living standards rise is carbon dioxide. Carbon dioxide emissions vary in relation to economic output from one country to another, depending on a host of often idiosyncratic factors. Countries that are major producers of oil and gas naturally have very large emissions (for example, more than 1,200 tons of CO_2 for every $1 million of total output in Kuwait, and more than 1,500 tons in Saudi Arabia). It is also no surprise that Russia (nearly 1,400 tons per $1 million of total output) and other parts of the former Soviet Union have very large emissions. The extent to which a country uses nuclear or hydroelectric power also matters, and so does the extent to which a country's citizens rely on automobiles (if they are rich) or on wood fires (if they are poor). But there is no evidence of any systematic downward tendency as average incomes rise beyond some point. The United States, with CO_2 emissions of 572 tons per $1 million of total output, is modestly above the world average.[44]

The reason is clear. In the absence of some global agreement like the Kyoto Protocol, which has only just gone into effect, single countries acting on their own, whether high-income or not, have had little incentive to take steps—especially expensive ones, which most proposals in this area turn out to be—to limit how much CO_2 they generate. Carbon dioxide is harmless locally; the concentration in the earth's atmosphere as a whole is what matters. Because the externality operates at the global level, there is no reason to expect any individual country to restrict its CO_2 emissions just because it is better able to afford the cost of doing so. Public policy is central to the dynamic that makes a country's environment improve after its living standard reaches some level, but no country brings policy to bear unless it anticipates some benefit. In the case of CO_2 emissions, that benefit would only come with participation in a global-scale effort.

Environmental concerns have also become an important dimension of today's fractious debate over globalization. The questions at issue are in part about the effects of economic growth per se, but also more specifically about growth that takes place in the context of developing countries' increasing economic engagement with the world at large. As we have seen, the historical record makes clear that countries that have participated in the ongoing worldwide integration of economic activity have enjoyed, on average, a distinctly faster rise in living standards than those that have stood apart. What this difference means for any country's environment, however, is less apparent.

The beginnings of economic development clearly worsen many forms of pollution. Depending on the specific form of pollution in question (and also on details that differ from one study to another), the situation begins to turn around when a country reaches a per capita income somewhere between $2,000 and $8,000. Today 108 countries, with a combined population of 4.6 billion, have per capita incomes less than $8,000. If historical patterns hold true, then in much of the developing world the more rapid economic growth spurred by globalization will make pollution worse for quite some time before yet further growth begins to foster an improvement.

Past patterns may not repeat themselves, however. As we have seen, in many areas of economic and social activity in which technology is crucial, countries that lie behind the frontier enjoy the considerable advantage of being able to exploit knowledge that already exists, rather than having to create it on their own. For example, China today has an average life expectancy of seventy-one years, despite its per capita income of not quite $5,000. The United States, where per capita income is $37,500, has life expectancy of seventy-seven years. But in 1880, when Americans' average income first reached what China's is today, their life expectancy was only forty-one years. Similarly, in the 1850s, when America first reached the $2,900 average income level that India has now, the life expectancy was only thirty-nine years, compared to sixty-four in India today. Indeed, not until 1940 did Americans have a life expectancy as high as what Indians have now.[45]

The reason for these historical differences is plain enough. Much of the medical expertise, equipment, and drugs that have enabled Americans to live longer—and that are also widely available today in both China and

India despite those countries' far lower general standards of living—were simply unknown a century ago. It is no accident that many of the medical problems that remain most acute in the developing world today are tropical diseases like malaria and schistosomiasis. The countries that have achieved industrialized standards of living mostly enjoy more temperate climates in which these diseases rarely occur, and so they have had little reason to develop cheap, effective treatments.[46] As a result, apart from efforts coordinated by international agencies, the developing countries that confront these problems have had to do so mostly on their own.

The same kinds of historical differences are even more immediately apparent in the widespread availability of consumer technology in much of today's developing world: telephones, televisions, buses and automobiles, and increasingly even computers. Daily life in China and India—as in Guatemala, Egypt, Paraguay, Indonesia, or even Zimbabwe (all likewise countries with per capita income above $2,000 but less than $5,000)—differs enormously from what American life was like in the late nineteenth century. The overall standard of living may be on a par with how Americans lived then, but in key respects the technology is more like that of the United States today.

But technology for reducing many aspects of pollution also now exists. China, India, and other countries in that income range do not have to invent catalytic converters, unleaded gasoline, or modern water purification systems. (Nor do they have to invent stoves and other alternatives to cooking over open fires.) Just as important, their people and their governments are aware of the dangers of air and water pollution, and of the sources of pollution, in ways that Americans a hundred years ago were not. The key question is whether, at their standard of living, they feel able to afford the costs of doing something about it.

It is too early to judge whether these countries and others now on a path of rapid economic growth will wait until their incomes reach the levels found in most studies of the "environmental Kuznets curve" before limiting their pollution sufficiently to allow improvement. Some signs—the air pollution that has accompanied the explosive growth in the number of cars on the streets in Beijing, Shanghai, Delhi, and Mumbai (Bombay), for example, or the yellowish cloud, easily visible from tens of miles away, that hangs over the dense concentration of factories surrounding Guangzhou—suggest that they may. But beginning in 1984, and even more so since 1996, China has invested vast sums in its effort to provide cleaner water for everyday consumption. And since 1992 India has not only built a series of sewage treatment plants along the Ganges River but has also forced most of the industries that had been polluting the river to install their own effluent treatment plants (or, in a few cases, go out of business).[47]

Other prominent examples of pollution abatement initiatives at the national level in the developing world have occurred in Korea, Indonesia, and Venezuela. As early as 1981, Brazil adopted a National Environmental Protection Act closely based on America's 1969 legislation bearing the same name. Some countries with far lower average incomes (for example, Kenya, in 1994) have followed suit.[48] If past patterns prevail, future economic growth in the developing world will entail a great deal of pollution. But awareness of the problem and the availability of the technology needed to address it provide ground for hope that improvements will come much faster than in the past.

The prospect that much of the developing world's economic growth will take place in the context of globalization renders the question complex in other ways as well. One of the strongest fears that critics of globalization have voiced is that individual developing countries may compete with one another by offering potential investors and trading partners ever greater freedom from restrictions governing pollution and waste disposal, thereby creating an environmental "race to the bottom."[49] Rules, intended to force new plants built in any one country to limit the pollution they generate, may instead result in investors' going elsewhere. If so, what may ultimately be eliminated is not pollution, but anti-pollution restrictions.

These concerns about what may happen when individual countries compete for foreign investment take on even more force because of how they intersect with the issue of free trade. Successive rounds of multilateral negotiations extending over much of the postwar period (the "Kennedy Round," the "Tokyo Round," and their successors) have either reduced tariffs to modest rates or eliminated them altogether for a wide array of goods that make up the great bulk of international trade. As a result, most of the effective government-imposed impediments to trade today are nontariff measures, in some cases including outright quotas but more often consisting of more specific regulations setting standards that goods brought into a country for sale must meet: rules about what those goods contain, or how they are packaged and labeled, or how they are produced.

No one questions a country's right to impose restrictions on how goods are made, packaged, or labeled within its own borders. But when such rules apply to goods imported from abroad, they become a form of nontariff barrier to trade. Indeed, in some cases it appears that their chief purpose is precisely to exclude certain foreign products so as to shield domestically produced alternatives from competition (or so it seems, at any rate, to the makers of the excluded goods).

Environmental restrictions are hardly the most troublesome cases of this kind of conflict between domestic regulation and free trade. Examples like the European prohibition of "genetically modified organisms" (which mostly keeps out American-grown corn and beef) and America's prohibition of goods made with prison labor (which mostly keeps out Chinese-made clothing) are both more visible and more controversial. Even so, many countries have imposed import restrictions on environmental grounds— for example, Canada's prohibition of certain electronic products made using polychlorinated biphenyls (PCBs)—and when they do, the structure of the debate is analogous. Those who favor such restrictions on environmental grounds often find themselves in league with domestic producers who may care little about the environment but simply seek protection from foreign competition. Conversely, they are often at odds with defenders of free trade.

The evidence is mixed on whether in practice environmental regulations have had a significant impact on most countries' trade flows, although what effects do occur tend to be stronger for trade between industrialized countries and developing countries. The relocation of "dirty" industries like industrial chemicals and pulp and paper production to developing countries seems mostly to have taken place only partly because of differences in environmental regulation.[50] One reason the effects of regulation are not larger is that, for most industries, the cost of pollution abatement is only a small component of total production costs. Moreover, industries where pollution abatement costs are largest also tend to be the least geographically mobile. Even so, these concerns remain significant especially for countries seeking to advance their economic development through industrialization.

The forces specific to globalization are not wholly unfavorable to environmental concerns, however. Indeed, some aspects of globalization are clearly conducive to the ability of individual countries, and the world at large, to address these issues. As we have seen, globalization has historically involved more than just trade and investment. Political and cultural exchange are significant as well. As a result, developing countries not only have access to the pollution abatement technology that the industrialized world has developed, but they are also exposed to environmental concerns and values emanating from the industrialized world. When the United States had the same per capita income that Brazil has today, Americans were still chopping down the nation's forests with abandon. Not long before, they were still clearing land for agricultural production. What Brazilians hear today, from countless organizations based in America as well as other high-income countries, is the urgent plea that they preserve the Amazon.

The cooperation that advancing globalization fosters in so many economic and political discussions also provides a vehicle for dealing with environmental problems that require multinational (or even supranational) solutions because the scope of the underlying externality is itself broader than just one country. The most obvious example is again greenhouse gas emissions. Until recently, there has been no multinational agreement and therefore no mechanism in place for limiting the generation of carbon dioxide and similarly harmful gases. Whether the Kyoto Protocol (with or without America's participation) will prove effective remains to be seen. But it is clear that without some form of multinational agreement there is no real prospect for limiting these emissions. If globalization were still in the same infant state that prevailed fifty years ago, there would be little chance of a productive discussion of the subject even taking place. It is also hard to imagine achievements like the Montreal Protocol and the Basel Convention apart from advancing globalization.

It is even possible that in time globalization will provide both the motivation and the mechanism to address problems like habitat preservation. The planet's biodiversity is not a local matter; people everywhere have an interest in species preservation, wherever it occurs. But if what gives Americans and Europeans standing to say what should happen to the Amazon, for example, is their own interest in the practical and moral benefits of species preservation, then this implies that they too—not just the Brazilians—bear responsibility for the associated costs.

The implications of globalization for the environment, and specifically for the way in which economic growth will affect the environment, are therefore less straightforward than much of the popular discussion today suggests. But whatever the strength of the competing forces at work, the net outcome will probably hinge to a large extent on the role played by policy. Even when economic growth fostered by globalization causes living standards to rise, the environment will not simply take care of itself.

In 1983 the U.N. General Assembly established the World Commission on Environment and Development, chaired by Norwegian prime minister and former environment minister Gro Harlem Brundtland. The commission's task was to formulate "a global agenda for change," specifically including "long-term environmental strategies for achieving sustainable development."51 The intention, in part, was to elevate environmental concerns to a place on the international agenda comparable to what the 1972 U.N. Conference on the Human Environment had achieved in the area of human rights.

The commission's report, published in 1987, highlighted what it called "critical survival issues" stemming from development, poverty, and population growth that "place unprecedented pressures on the planet's lands, waters, forests, and other national resources, not least in the developing countries." The report hailed "the possibility for a new era of economic growth, one that must be based on policies that sustain and expand the environmental resource base." Brundtland made the argument even more explicit in her introductory comments: "What is needed now is a new era of economic growth—growth that is forceful and at the same time socially and environmentally sustainable."52

The concept of "sustainable development," which the Brundtland Commission introduced, has since figured prominently in the ongoing public discussion of environmental issues at both the global and national levels. The central idea is intergenerational equity and continuity: in the commission's words, meeting "the needs of the present without compromising the ability of future generations to meet their own needs."53

And what would achieving sustainable development require? "The concept of sustainable development does imply limits—not absolute limits but limitations imposed by the present state of technology and social organization on environmental resources and by the ability of the biosphere to absorb the effects of human activities." In the commission's view the need for change in these dimensions applied both to the high-income industrialized countries and, implicitly, to the low-income developing world: "Sustainable global development requires that those who are more affluent adopt life-styles within the planet's ecological means—in their use of energy, for example. Further, rapidly growing populations can increase the pressure on resources and slow any rise in living standards; thus sustainable development can only be pursued if population size and growth are in harmony with the changing productive potential of the ecosystem."54

The call for reduced population growth is the part of the Brundtland Commission's argument for sustainable development that was most straightforward, at least on economic grounds. Environmental issues, whether the subject is resource depletion, pollution, waste disposal, climate change, or species extinction, are almost always about *total* economic activity. The aspects of economic activity that bear most directly on human well-being are *per capita* living standards. In principle, any rate of improvement in per capita living standards can be rendered consistent with some different rate of expansion of total production and consumption, as long as the associated population growth rate is right.

As we have seen, today rapid population growth is almost entirely a problem of the developing world. The industrialized countries have mostly stopped growing, apart from immigration. What little national population growth there is in the industrialized world is mostly a product of past growth patterns that have, for the present, left a disproportionately large percentage of women of childbearing age. Among the thirty countries with the world's highest incomes, the average population growth net of immigration is just .3 percent per annum. The average fertility rate is 1.7 births per woman, well below the population replacement rate. Even in the United States, where population growth is normally greater, the increase, apart from immigration, has recently been only .5 percent per annum, and the fertility rate is down to 2.1.[55]

Despite the progress made in recent years by China and quite a few other low- to middle-income countries, the developing world is still experiencing distinctly more rapid population growth stemming from fertility well above the replacement rate. The forty-two countries where per capita income is below $2,000—nearly a billion people—have average population growth of 2.2 percent per annum. Their average fertility is 4.9 births per woman. In the thirty-eight countries with per capita income in the $2,000 to $5,000 range, population growth averages 1.4 percent per annum, and the average fertility rate is 3. (Because China and India together account for more than three-quarters of the people living in these countries, however, the situation from a world perspective is actually somewhat better. China's latest population growth is just .7 percent per annum, and the Chinese fertility rate is 1.9. In India population growth has been 1.6 percent and fertility 2.9.)[56]

As we have also seen, the low-income developing countries have ample incentive to slow their population growth for reasons wholly apart from environmental concerns. In countries where population is increasing rapidly, living standards are improving only slowly or, in all too many cases, eroding. It is clear that limiting fertility, and therefore the increase in its population, is one of the most effective ways for a country with a low-income developing economy to spur the rise in its living standards.[57]

In 1968 biologist Garrett Hardin ended his pathbreaking article "The Tragedy of the Commons," which first clarified for a broad public the character of pollution and other environmental problems as classic externalities, by saying, "The only way we can preserve and nurture other and more precious freedoms is by relinquishing the freedom to breed, and that very soon."[58] More than three decades later, the world's high-income countries have achieved Hardin's objective—sharply reduced population growth—without abridging family freedoms in this regard. Among what were then the low-income countries, China has achieved this objective but in the more coercive way that Hardin envisioned. It remains to be seen whether, and if so how, many of the other low- and middle-income countries today will slow the growth of their populations.

The Brundtland Commission's call for changes in "life-styles" in the affluent countries may also be conceptually straightforward, but it leaves open the question of what balance is needed between policy intervention and market forces. To the extent that sustainable economic growth means growth with limited pollution and with appropriate protection against species extinction and global climate change, the argument is clearly about environmental policy. These are externalities, and no ordinary market forces will induce individuals deciding what and how much to consume, or firms deciding on production, to take them into account.

By contrast, inasmuch as sustainable growth means not running out of essential resources, as the commission's example of energy use suggests, the higher prices resulting from increasing scarcity can presumably carry much of the burden.* The sharp break in the relationship between the industrial countries' total economic output and their total energy consumption that occurred in the mid-1970s was still a relatively new phenomenon when the commission began its work just ten years later. Today it is well established. And although worldwide economic output has more than doubled since 1973, the prices of most forms of energy are no higher now after allowance for overall inflation. Even oil, at the recent (2005) price of more than $50 per barrel, is not much more expensive in inflation-adjusted dollars than the average price in 1974, following the first OPEC increase, and far cheaper than during 1979–82, after OPEC raised prices for the second time.

The greatest challenge of all for "sustainable development" is likely to result from bringing ever larger segments of the world community up to living standards more nearly comparable to what citizens of the industrialized countries already enjoy. The average per capita income in the thirty richest

---

*Energy use affects more than just scarcity of hydrocarbon fuels. Burning these fuels creates pollution, importantly including CO_2 emissions; exploring for new supplies, and then either mining the coal or pumping the oil and gas, is destructive of local environments; and transporting oil from where it is pumped to where it is refined is prone to environmentally noxious accidents. But these considerations are, again, clear externalities.

countries is seven times the average income in the other 134 (again counting only the countries for which reasonably reliable data exist).59 Even without any allowance for population growth, bringing the rest of the world up to the standard of living that prevails *today* in Portugal, the last country on the list of the richest thirty, would more than double total world output. If that project were to take fifty years, and if the combined population of all the countries that are poorer than Portugal today continued to grow on average at the recent rate of 1.3 percent per annum, the required increase would more than quadruple world economic output. And even these enormous increases exclude whatever ongoing rise occurs in the living standards of the richest countries.

The resulting challenge, from the perspective of resource availability as well as pollution and other externalities, is significant. Moreover, the concept of sustainable development means, or should mean, more than simply making it through the next fifty or one hundred years without encountering growth-stopping scarcities, or irrevocably fouling the air and the water: The world's inhabitants of that future time should likewise be able to look ahead to further growth over what will be, in *their* eyes, the coming fifty or one hundred years. Bequeathing future generations a better state of life than our own—including not just their material standard of living but also the physical environment in which they live and the societal institutions under which they go about their daily lives—is central to what sustainable development means.

Assessing the prospects for such sustainability is difficult in part because, as has been true in the past, new technology will shape future developments in vital but unpredictable ways. To what extent agricultural productivity continues to increase, or new energy sources emerge, or human economic activity becomes less damaging to the environment, will depend on knowledge not yet in hand—for example, when and by how much the technologically achievable relationship between greenhouse gas emissions and economic growth will improve. But past experience suggests that such improvements will occur sooner, and will bear more directly on the problem at hand, when either market forces or policy interventions aimed at specific externalities create strong incentives to undertake the necessary research and innovation.

In thinking about the challenge that sustainable development presents, in a world in which the majority of the total population justly aspires to standards more like those of the industrialized countries while those countries' citizens also rightly expect ongoing improvement in their own living standards, it is important to keep in mind the central principle that sustainability is ultimately about fairness across generations. As economist Robert Solow has argued, the obligation to leave future generations the ability to be at least as well off as we are does not imply an obligation to leave them the world exactly as we found it. Rather, what matters is the balance between "the resources we use up and the resources we leave behind, but also the sort of environment we leave behind including the built environment," which importantly includes productive capacity as well as technical knowledge.[60] And, we can add, it also includes social and political institutions.

Depleting any one specific resource, or converting any particular area of land or water from a natural to a developed state, is therefore not the issue. In Solow's example, "There is no reason for us to feel guilty about using up aluminum as long as we leave behind a capacity to perform the same or analogous functions using other kinds of materials."[61]

As a practical matter, sustainability as a dimension of integenerational fairness points instead toward investment: not just investment in physical productive capacity and in a more productive labor force, but more specifically investment in the existing environment and in research to generate the technology that will enable key relationships bearing on resource use and on the environment to be different in the future from what they are today. Here as well, market forces will do part of the job. But it bears repeating that where externalities are central, so too is the role for public policy.

PART V

LOOKING FORWARD

Chapter 16

Economic Policy and
Economic Growth in America

[A] slow and gradual rise of wages is one of the general laws of
democratic communities. In proportion as social conditions
became more equal, wages rise; and as wages are higher, social
conditions become more equal.

ALEXIS DE TOCQUEVILLE
Democracy in America[1]

Countries where living standards improve over sustained periods of time
are more likely to seek and preserve an open, tolerant society, and to
broaden and strengthen their democratic institutions. But where most citizens sense that they are not getting ahead, society instead becomes rigid and
democracy weakens. What implications follow? Who should therefore act
differently? And what should they do?

The positive influence of rising living standards on the public character
of the society makes economic growth itself the source of an externality.
Enhanced mobility and greater tolerance do not appear on any company's
balance sheet, nor does a stronger democracy enter directly into any firm's
income statement. As we have seen, a more open society and enhanced
democracy may well help an economy to grow, and its businesses to prosper.
But that is not the same as giving any particular firm cause to promote

openness or democracy. A business deciding whether to modernize a factory, or a bank evaluating whether to finance a construction project, or an individual considering starting a new business, has no direct incentive to take into account the advantage to the society as a whole that might follow from any of these actions.

Externalities create a vacuum in the functioning of the market system, and therefore a role for public policy. Today it is generally accepted that market-driven private economic initiative systematically produces more pollution, congestion, and litigation than we want, while producing too little of beneficial activities like on-the-job training (because businesses rightly worry that other firms will hire away the workers they train). In just the same way, the market mechanism left to itself will deliver too little economic growth. Because of this externality, the familiar injunction that government actions not stand in the way of an economy's achieving the growth that unfettered private initiative would produce fails to recognize the proper role for public policy. Because economic growth positively affects the character of the society as a whole—and, crucially, because neither openness nor tolerance, nor democracy, is a good that private markets trade and price—there is a consequent role for policy measures to seek growth beyond what the market would provide on its own.

And public policy does matter for economic growth. Even in a market system like America's, in which the decisions that set economic activity in motion are mostly private undertakings, businesses and individuals take those decisions within a setting shaped by what government is or is not doing. Only the government can provide the safety from external attack, and the internal rule of law, that make most forms of economic initiative worth pursuing in the first place. As the experience of all too many countries makes evident—and in America the attacks of September 11, 2001—the effects of armed conflict on a society's ability to carry out ordinary economic activity can be devastating. The experience of a broad range of countries around the world likewise demonstrates the *economic* importance of generally respected property rights and freedom of personal movement, and the *economically* depressing effects of crime and government corruption.

Public policy affects the growth of living standards in ways that bear more concrete connections to economic activity as well. Companies may have the capacity to produce goods, but without an adequate infrastructure for transportation there is no way to make those goods available to potential buyers, and so why produce them? Individuals may save, and corporations may seek to borrow that saving to build new offices and equip new factories, but if the government is absorbing most of what people save, then the high cost or limited availability of credit to private borrowers will discourage investment. Firms may seek to expand, but if workers with the required skills or training—or even just the ability to read and write, and to understand basic arithmetic—are in short supply, then one company can grow only by hiring labor away from another. Policies that encourage saving, however, or produce an educated and skilled workforce, instead enhance economic growth.

The point, however, is not merely that governments *can* take steps to foster the long-term advance of their citizens' living standards, but that they *should*. The prospects for achieving economic growth are now in question in much of the world. Growth in the core European countries has been disappointing for the past two decades. Japan's economy has only just begun to grow again after a decade of stagnation. Elsewhere in Asia, some of the previously fast-growing countries like Korea and Malaysia have mounted full recoveries from the regional financial crisis of the late 1990s, but others (for example, Indonesia) have not. Political turmoil has destabilized previously prosperous economies in Argentina and Venezuela, and many other Latin American countries face uncertain economic prospects as well. The majority of countries in Africa, especially south of the Sahara, remain desperately poor with little likelihood of imminent improvement.

America too is at an economic crossroads. As we have seen, living standards for the majority of citizens grew little from the early 1970s to the early 1990s, and along the way inequality widened significantly. The economic surge that followed, in which incomes rose across the spectrum and inequality began to narrow, proved all too brief. By 2000 growth had again slowed, and inequality was once more increasing. The recovery since then has been halting, with less-than-normal job creation, and especially few "good" jobs paying high wages and offering workers the prospect of training and advancement. After a welcome increase averaging more than 1 percent per annum in the latter half of the 1990s, the average weekly pay of most workers in American businesses has once again stagnated since 2000, and the median family income has again been falling in real terms. Moreover, because the economy's growth in the new century has relied so heavily on imported goods, in future years the increase in production will have to outpace the increase in domestic consumption (plus investment) in order to close the resulting record-large international imbalance. Adopting government policies that will foster economic growth—that will enable the living standard of the average American to rise once again, as it did in the first half of the postwar period (and, for that matter, during most of the nation's experience before that)—is no less important in the United States than elsewhere, and no less important today than in the past.

At the same time, to the extent that the rationale for seeking to encourage economic growth reflects not only the attraction of rising living standards for their own sake but also the social and political externalities that follow from them, the question is not just what measures can stimulate growth but also which among them are broadly consistent with achieving a more open and democratic society. It makes no sense to seek economic growth beyond what the market on its own would deliver, on the ground that rising living standards lead to a stronger democracy, but then attempt to spur growth through policy measures that undermine just that objective. The challenge is to seek growth-promoting policies that are consistent with a fairer, more open society, and, where possible, that further these ends as well.

Any economy has three basic ways of enhancing its ability to produce goods and services, and hence of delivering a higher standard of living to the society of which it is a part: create and deploy more resources, devise new technologies for using those resources in production, and use existing resources and technology more efficiently.

Government at the national level can take some steps to encourage the pace of technological advance—patent protection, tax credits for business-financed research, seed money for those research initiatives that are likely to benefit an entire industry rather than just one firm—but in free societies the development of new knowledge is mostly independent of direct public policy actions.[2] Similarly, while there are plenty of ways in which governments at all levels could enable businesses to function more efficiently, primarily by easing regulation in any of a wide variety of areas, most forms of regulation are intended to achieve some independent public purpose. Besides, most such actions represent opportunities for one-time gains in the economy's efficiency, not for ongoing economic growth.

The principal focus of public policy to foster growth in living standards is therefore the economy's productive resources, both physical resources and human. Apart from the ups and downs of the business cycle, most factories in the United States that are economically productive are already in use, and most Americans who want to work (and are capable of doing so) are already in the labor force. While adding hours to what is already a long work-week by international standards would of course increase measured output, longer hours would not necessarily enhance people's economic well-being. The key to people's having a sense of getting ahead is making the hours they put in more productive. That means increased capital formation—again, both physical and human.

The importance of physical capital accumulation in raising the economic productivity of an individual industry, or even an entire nation, has been recognized at least since the beginning of the Industrial Revolution.[3] It is not difficult to grasp the fundamental concept that giving people more or better tools enables them to do the job better. People dig more efficiently with a shovel than with their hands, and bulldozers are a big improvement on shovels. The same principle seems all the more apt now that physical capital increasingly means sophisticated equipment for telecommunications, data manipulation, and automated production.

At least at a broad-brush level, the evidence confirms that more and better capital makes an economy more productive. The quarter-century of especially rapid productivity growth that followed World War II— 2.8 percent per annum average growth in output per hour in all of American nonfarm business, between 1948 and 1973—was a time of especially rapid increase (2.2 percent per annum on average) in the amount of plant and equipment per employed worker. Over the next two decades, following OPEC's oil price increases, productivity growth slowed to an average 1.5 percent per annum, while the increase in the capital-labor ratio also slowed to 1.5 percent. From the mid-1990s through 2003, an investment boom restored the growth of the capital-labor ratio to an average 2 percent per annum, despite unusually rapid job growth during these years, and productivity growth surged to 3 percent. Moreover, a sector-by-sector breakdown of the sources of those productivity gains makes clear the key role played by the American economy's massive investment in new technologies in the latter half of the 1990s.[4] The investment boom has since ended, however, and prospects for further gains in both capital intensity and productivity are unclear.[5]

Comparisons across different countries further reinforce the idea that physical capital formation, especially in business equipment, fosters productivity growth.[6] The Asian countries that have devoted especially large shares of their national income to investment in business equipment, including China and Singapore, and earlier on Japan, also achieved especially rapid gains in output per worker. At the other end of the scale, countries that have invested only small shares of their respective national incomes (for example, Pakistan, Sweden, and Britain) have experienced only modest productivity growth. Germany, Brazil, Korea, Israel, and many other countries are in the middle range on both dimensions.[7] (The United States tends to enjoy a somewhat better performance than would be expected purely on the basis of the country's investment rate.)[8]

Not all productive capital is physical capital, of course, and in a world economy that increasingly requires specialized skills as well as general literacy and numeracy, *human* capital formation plays an especially important role in generating productivity and economic growth. Indeed, as we have seen, one of the chief reasons for believing that more open societies will enjoy superior economic growth is their tendency to provide more extensive education. In a cross-country context, the link between economic growth and formal education (which is only one aspect of human capital formation, but by far the most straightforward to observe and measure) is systematic and strong. More education on average for a country's citizens means faster economic growth.[9] Direct measures of how well educated different countries' workforces are, based not on how much schooling they have had but on how well they perform on cognitive achievement tests, show a similarly strong and positive effect on countries' respective rates of economic growth.[10]

Within any single country, including the United States, the evidence demonstrating the link between education and productivity comes mostly from the relationship between different individuals' education and their respective job responsibilities and pay rates. Workers with more education systematically occupy more responsible positions and also earn more.[11] Moreover, in most industrialized countries pay differentials connected to differences in education have widened sharply in recent years, indicating that the connection between human capital and productivity has been growing in importance, and that employers in many industries are less able to substitute unskilled workers for those who can bring more to the job.[12] In the United States, in 1980 men who had graduated from college earned 39 percent more than workers with only high school educations, and women college graduates earned 35 percent more than their high school–educated counterparts. By 2003 the differential in favor of college graduates was 77 percent for men, and 70 percent for women.[13]

While physical and human capital both clearly raise an economy's productivity, it is difficult to be precise about the contribution of either one. Both quality and quantity matter in each case, but quality is especially hard to measure. Different machines embody different technologies, and having the wrong kind of capital can be just as damaging as having too little. The benefits of an extra year of education likewise depend on what a person

studies, and where. On-the-job training, family education, and other informal ways by which most people acquire knowledge, all of which are typically much harder to observe than their schooling, are also important
elements of human capital formation. And when a high investment rate and
rapid growth, or widespread education and rapid growth, occur together, it
is sometimes hard to determine what is causing what.[14]

But the broader point remains that both physical and human capital
formation contribute to an economy's productivity and thereby foster its
long-term growth. And it is in large part up to public policy to determine
how much investment in these resources an economy undertakes, as well as
what kind.

In America the last quarter of the twentieth century was mostly a period of
unusually low investment and therefore unusually slow growth in the
nation's physical capital, especially compared to the growth in the American
workforce. In contrast to the 4.2 percent of the country's national income
that American business devoted to investment in new factories and machinery (after allowance for depreciation) on average during the 1960s and
1970s, the net business investment rate since 1980 has averaged only 3.2
percent. During the latter half of the 1980s and the first half of the 1990s,
net investment as a share of national income averaged just 2.7 percent. Even
during the investment boom of the late 1990s, net investment never
regained the average rate of the 1960s and 1970s. (The peak was 4.1 percent
in 2000.)[15]

With weak investment, growth in the stock of capital at the disposal of
firms in the economy's nonfarm business sector has slowed from 4 percent
per annum on average during the 1960s and 1970s (even including the
depressed post-OPEC-crisis years) to just 3.1 percent since then (including
the late 1990s investment boom). And with slower growth of the capital
stock, the amount of capital per worker has also risen more slowly, despite
the fact that labor force growth slowed after the 1960s and 1970s, when
most of the baby boom generation was coming of age. In 1960 there were
46 million Americans at work in nonfarm businesses, with an average of
$51,000 in capital (at today's prices) behind each one. By 1980, 74 million
were at work—an increase of 62 percent in just twenty years—with an average $76,000 of capital for each one. The American economy's supply of
capital *per worker* had increased by 2.1 percent per annum. In 2003, 108 million Americans worked in nonfarm businesses, with an average of $105,000

in capital behind each one. From 1980 on, capital per worker rose by only 1.4 percent per annum. Apart from the high-investment years of the late 1990s, the increase was even less.

Investing too little in any one year, or even for a few consecutive years as sometimes happens during a prolonged business recession, has little impact on an economy's long-term growth. But maintained over longer periods, subpar capital formation makes a large difference. Even without allowing for the effect of higher output due to additional job creation along the way, simply maintaining the pre-1980s net investment rate of 4.2 percent would have given the American economy 16 percent more in plant and equipment by 2003 than it actually had. The capital behind each worker in nonfarm businesses would have been $122,000 instead of just $105,000.

These large differences in capital formation, in turn, matter for productivity and ultimately for the growth of living standards. The reduced rate of increase in capital per worker after 1980 contributed to the economy's weak productivity growth, and therefore to the stagnation of incomes for much of the American working population. On average during the 1960s and 1970s, output per hour in nonfarm business rose by 2.2 percent per annum, and employees' per-hour compensation rose at a rate 1.7 percent faster than inflation. In the 1980s and 1990s productivity rose by 1.8 percent per annum and real hourly pay by 1.1 percent—roughly a half-point slowing on each measure. (Until the high-investment years of the late 1990s, real pay had risen at just .7 percent per annum.)[16] Clearly, productivity matters for pay, and capital formation matters for productivity. The 16 percent in additional plant and equipment that America would have had by 2003, if the country had maintained its pre-1980 net investment rate, would have resulted in an overall national income nearly 5 percent larger.

The slow pace of business investment in America during most of the past three decades has not been the result of any absence of investment opportunities. New technologies with commercially practical applications have evolved rapidly throughout this period, and some industries—most obviously, telecommunications and computer software—have mounted especially robust capital spending (in retrospect, some might argue overly robust) despite the sluggish overall trend. The period since 1980 has also mostly been one of reduced business regulation, unlike the 1960s and 1970s, and this too should have spurred the pace of new investment.

In addition, the tax rates applicable to income earned from capital invested in the United States have declined sharply over this period, on both the individual and corporate levels, thereby making new investments all the more attractive on an after-tax basis. In 1980 the maximum federal tax rate on individual income earned from interest and dividends was 70 percent. Since 1984 it has been successively 28 percent, 39 percent, 38.6 percent, and now 35 percent for interest and only 15 percent for most dividends. Similarly, in 1980 the standard federal tax rate on corporate profits was 46 percent. From 1986 on it has been either 34 percent or (since 1993) 35 percent. Because profits earned by corporations and paid out in dividends to shareholders were fully taxed at both levels until 2003, the consequence of these paired changes is that the maximum combined federal tax rate on taxable income from capital invested in the corporate sector, where most U.S. business investment takes place, fell from nearly 84 percent in 1980 to under 45 percent. The tax rate on individual income from capital gains has come down as well, and so the story is much the same for income that corporations earn but do not distribute directly to shareholders.

The weakness of business investment during this period has instead resulted from two quite different problems. First, Americans have been spending more of their incomes on current consumption and, correspondingly, saving less. And second, during much of the last quarter-century, large-scale government borrowing has absorbed the lion's share of what little Americans do save.

The decline in private saving in the United States is a new phenomenon. For many decades, until fairly recently, American families and American businesses combined regularly put aside some 16 to18 percent, or even 19 percent, of the total national income.[17] After allowing for the saving that they had to reinvest merely to replace the factories and machinery that wore out or became obsolete, and to repair their houses, the corresponding net saving rate typically averaged around 9 percent. From the 1960s through the first half of the 1980s, the average was 9.9 percent.

Since then the decline in private saving has been sharp and persistent. In the latter half of the 1980s the U.S. economy's net private saving rate averaged 7.9 percent, and in the first half of the 1990s it was 7 percent. Since 1995 it has been just 4.8 percent. To make matters worse, the modest surpluses that many state and local governments used to run (primarily to fund the pensions of the 19 million teachers, firemen, policemen, and other employees who work for government at this level), have mostly disappeared. Net saving including both the private sector and state and local governments has therefore declined even further.

During much of this period the federal government has run large budget deficits, at times absorbing the majority of the nation's net saving.

Before the 1980s the government typically came fairly close to balancing its spending and its revenues except during wartime or periods of high unemployment. The budget deficit averaged just .3 percent of the national income in the 1950s and .8 percent in the 1960s. In the 1970s the average deficit rose to 2.4 percent of national income, in part because of high unemployment and reduced incomes and profits in the post-OPEC-crisis years. In the 1980s, however, the combination of large tax cuts and accelerated military spending increased the deficit to 4.1 percent of national income on average. In 1992 the deficit reached what was then an all-time record high in dollar terms, $290 billion, corresponding to 4.5 percent of national income.[18] (According to the Congressional Budget Office, even if the economy had been at full employment in 1992 the deficit would still have been $229 billion.)[19]

Deficits of this magnitude, even at times of nearly full employment, matter because they absorb so much of the economy's available saving. When the government spends more than it takes in from taxes, the Treasury has to borrow in the financial markets to cover the overage. People who put their savings into banks or mutual funds do not ordinarily think of themselves as financing the government's deficit, but when these institutions use the deposited funds to buy Treasury securities that is exactly what they are doing. The government's borrowing therefore absorbs private saving that otherwise would have been available to finance investment in new factories, equipment, or research.

In an era of global capital markets, it is always possible for a country like the United States to turn to foreign lenders to fund investment that it cannot finance from its own saving, and increasingly America has been borrowing from abroad. But this is no solution either. Debts owed abroad must be serviced, and eventually repaid, requiring Americans in the future to give up part of what they will earn in order to meet their overseas obligations. The borrowing America has done just within the last twenty years has already transformed this country from the world's largest creditor nation to its largest debtor.

If America had a saving rate like China's or Korea's, or even like that of many other industrial countries around the world, having the government absorb an amount of saving equal to a few percentage points of the national income would be of little concern. But even before the recent decline, Americans had always maintained a lower saving rate than in most other countries. As a result, the average federal deficit in the 1980s amounted to not quite half of the net saving done in that decade by the economy's private sector plus the aggregate surplus of state and local governments. In the early

1990s it was more than half. (By contrast, in the 1960s and 1970s the federal deficit averaged just one-sixth of net private saving alone, and state and local governments were collectively running a healthy surplus.)

It is a simple matter of accounting arithmetic that what a country saves, less whatever part of that saving its government absorbs to finance any budget deficit, must equal what the country invests (including any net investment abroad). But in the absence of further evidence, the fact that investment is small whenever the available saving is small says nothing about what is causing what. The limited available saving may be preventing business from investing more, but it is also possible that businesses' limited desire to invest may be depressing economic activity and thereby limiting what the country is able to save.

One indication that the reduced availability of saving in the 1980s and early 1990s was restraining America's investment, rather than vice versa, is that the emergence of new technologies was creating a multitude of investment opportunities—opportunities made all the more attractive by the new lower tax rates. An even more straightforward way to judge whether low saving was causing low investment or vice versa, however, is to look at the behavior of interest rates, preferably after allowance for both inflation and taxes.

A central part of the market mechanism that renders saving equal to investment is the role of higher or lower interest rates in making it either expensive or cheap for businesses to build factories and buy machines, and for families to buy houses. If too little saving is available to finance all of the investment that firms and families want to do, the heightened competition for funds causes interest rates to rise and the higher cost of financing discourages some of them from going ahead. But if there is ample saving that nobody wants to use for investment, interest rates decline. (This is why during recessions interest rates are usually low compared to inflation, despite the government's running a deficit. In a recession fewer firms seek to undertake new investments, and fewer families want to build new houses.)

Real interest rates in the United States were at record highs in the 1980s and the early 1990s, and because of both lower inflation rates and lower tax rates they were even more so on an after-tax basis. Real interest rates were unusually high not just during 1981 and 1982, when the Federal Reserve System under Paul Volcker was imposing extremely tight monetary policy in order to combat price inflation, but over more than a decade. On average during the 1960s and 1970s, the interest rate on short-term business borrowing in the United States was just 1.4 percent above the inflation rate. During the 1980s the real interest rate measured in this way averaged

4.6 percent. Even after the period of especially tight monetary policy ended, in 1982, the average for the remainder of the decade was still 4.4 percent, far above the levels that had prevailed since World War II.

The decline in tax rates further magnified these differences. For a corporation taxed at 46 percent, the average pretax real interest rate of 1.4 percent before the 1980s corresponded to a real after-tax *subsidy* (that is, a *negative* cost of borrowing) of 1.5 percent. Corporate borrowers could deduct against their profits the full nominal interest rate, in this case 6.3 percent on average during the 1960s and 1970s, and then repay their loans in cheaper dollars, thereby getting an added after-tax advantage from greater inflation at a given real interest rate. The cost of funds was clearly no impediment to investment in these years.

In the 1980s, however, with pretax real interest rates up, the tax rate on profits down, and inflation down as well, borrowing became a cost. For a corporation taxed at 34 percent, the real after-tax cost of funds based on the average interest rate and inflation rates prevailing during the 1980s (even excluding 1981 and 1982) was 1.7 percent—not huge, but a far cry from the negative cost of the previous two decades. As a result, it is not surprising that during the 1980s and early 1990s net business investment declined to what was then a postwar record low as a share of U.S. national income (nor is it surprising that America had to turn to foreign borrowing merely to sustain even that shrunken investment rate).

Matters changed in the 1990s, both for the government's budget and for the nation's investment. In 1990 President George H. W. Bush and the Democratic majority in Congress agreed on a budget package combining slower growth of government spending (mostly for defense but also on Medicare payments), a large increase in the ceiling on earnings subject to the Medicare payroll tax, and increased tax rates on upper-level incomes. (This out-and-out violation of the pledge on which Bush had campaigned for president two years earlier—"Read My Lips: No New Taxes"—no doubt played a significant role in his losing the next election.) Once the 1990–91 recession had ended, the combined result of the 1990 tax increase and the slower trajectory of federal spending was to reduce the deficit substantially compared to what it otherwise would have been.

In 1993 the newly elected President Clinton persuaded Congress to approve a budget package including yet further reductions in the growth of spending (again mostly for defense) together with an extra 5 cents per gallon federal tax on gasoline at the pump, a further increase in the tax rate on individual incomes above $250,000 per family, and elimination entirely of the Medicare payroll tax ceiling. This action carried substantial political risk as well. It was, and remains, the only piece of major policy legislation to be passed in recent memory without a single vote in favor from the opposition party in one or another house of Congress. All forty-one Republican senators were opposed.

Critics of the 1993 budget package warned that increased tax rates would cause higher-income citizens, and especially those contemplating investments, to "go on strike" economically. Others predicted that higher taxes would squelch the still-fragile recovery from the 1990–91 business recession. On both counts, opponents claimed, the additional tax revenues and therefore the deficit reduction that the Clinton administration held out in support of its proposals would fail to materialize.[20]

The critics were wrong. After 1993 the business expansion gained momentum, incomes and profits surged ahead, and the resulting increase in tax revenues contributed enormously to reducing the deficit over the next few years and then eliminating it altogether. Instead of faltering, business investment proved to be the single strongest force in the expansion, increasing over the remainder of the decade by 10 percent per annum in real terms compared to 3.9 percent for economic activity overall.

Public reaction to Clinton's tax increase clearly played a role in the Democrats' loss of their congressional majority the next year. The new Republican majority tightened restraints on federal spending, especially on entitlements and other domestic programs. With the strong economy, revenues bolstered by the 1993 tax increase, and a conservative approach to both defense and domestic programs, the deficit shrank to just $22 billion in 1997 and the next year the government ran a surplus. By 2000 the surplus had grown to $236 billion, or 2.5 percent of the national income. Not surprisingly, with the government now adding to the saving available to finance investment rather than absorbing saving done by the private sector, America's net investment rate rose sharply, nearly reaching the levels that the nation had maintained before 1980, when the private savings rate was significantly greater.

Alas, these hard-won successes proved all too fragile. One terrorist attack, two wars, and three tax cuts later—most important among them the 2001 tax cut, which President George W. Bush hailed as the largest in American history—the government was again solidly in deficit. In 2004 the deficit reached $412 billion, a new record in dollar terms and the largest as a share of the national income (3.6 percent) since 1993. In January 2001 the Congressional Budget Office was projecting, on the basis of the tax and spending policies then in place, that over the coming ten years (2002–11) the government would run a cumulative surplus of $5.6 trillion. By January 2005 the CBO projection for the same ten-year span was a cumulative *deficit* of $2.6 trillion—a swing representing, on average, 6.5 percent of the national income over this period—even without including funding for the ongoing military effort in Iraq and Afghanistan.[21] Nearly two-thirds of this swing represents the lower expected trajectory for revenues.

As of February 2005, when the president submitted his budget proposals for fiscal 2006, the government officially anticipated further deficits averaging 2 percent of national income over the remainder of this decade, even with a presumed return to full employment, and with only minimal funding for Iraq and Afghanistan after 2005.[22] If the administration's estimates of the cost and duration of American engagement in Iraq continue to turn out to be too low, or if further tax reductions are enacted—for example, changes to prevent the huge expected increase in the number of taxpayers subject to the Alternative Minimum Tax—the deficit will be just that much larger. (One set of more realistic assumptions about taxes and spending, though still with no more funding for Iraq or Afghanistan, would add another .7 of national income to the deficit on average over these five years.)[23] Then, beginning in 2010 the oldest members of the baby boom generation will become eligible for Medicare insurance, and for full retirement benefits under Social Security in 2011.

Social Security and Medicare are already large programs, and even before the echo of the post–World War II jump in the birthrate arrives they are growing rapidly. In 2004 the two together accounted for 34 percent of federal spending.[24] (Including retirement benefits for federal civilian and military employees, plus costs for nursing home care paid by Medicare, the total for direct support of the retired elderly was 43 percent.) Over the last decade Social Security benefits have increased by 4.5 percent per annum, and Medicare payments by 6.7 percent, versus only a 3.9 percent per annum increase in the rest of the federal budget—all compared to an average 1.8 percent rise in prices.

This growth is modest compared to what the retirement of the baby boomers will bring, however. The problem from a fiscal perspective, and therefore also from the perspective of maintaining the availability of adequate saving to finance capital formation, is that even without the recent tax cuts, under current law spending on these two programs would have outstripped any plausible growth in the government's revenues. Reducing taxes only made an already difficult situation worse.

There are now 39 million Americans receiving Social Security retirement or survivors' benefits, plus another 7 million on disability, or in total about one beneficiary for every 3.3 workers who contribute to the system via the payroll tax. By 2010 there will still be nearly 3.2 contributors for every beneficiary. In the twenty years following 2010, however, the beneficiary group will expand by another 60 percent. As a result, under the program's existing structure the increase in Social Security spending will exceed inflation by an average 3.6 percent per annum (compared to 2.7 percent during the last ten years). Meanwhile, the number of covered workers will expand by only 8 percent, thereby reducing the beneficiary-to-contributor ratio to just 2.2.[25]

With the rising costs of medical care, the problem confronting Medicare is more severe. Even with all of the recently legislated savings in place—but also with the new prescription drug benefit that Congress added in 2003—the cost of providing medical care to each beneficiary is likely to rise more than 2 percent faster than inflation. With the increase in the number of beneficiaries, as the country's population ages, the program's total cost will increase at 5.3 percent beyond inflation.[26] As a result, the long-term gap between likely expenditures and currently legislated revenues in the Medicare program is more than five times that in Social Security.[27]

President Bush and other supporters of the tax cuts legislated since 2001 have argued that some of the accompanying changes in the structure of the tax system (for example, the reduced tax on corporate dividends legislated in 2003) will help promote investment and growth. That might be true, if everything else remained the same.[28] But in this case not everything else will be the same. In large part because of the tax cuts, the government will already be running a sizable deficit even before the population bulge hits retirement age. And once that happens, the tax cuts will result in even larger deficits in the years when the federal budget would have been under enormous pressure anyway. In the end the depressing effect on America's investment due to chronic large deficits will probably outweigh any spur that might otherwise come from changes to the tax structure.

A low private saving rate, a chronic government deficit even at full employment and even before the baby boomers turn sixty-five, and then the added drain of meeting society's promises to today's working citizens once they retire—no nation can maintain adequate investment under such circumstances. And without adequate capital formation, the prospects for maintaining a vigorous trend of increasing productivity and a consequent improvement in American standards of living are dubious at best.

The vital need is to restore the government to a position in which, at the least, it will not be draining the nation's scarce saving. Achieving that goal will require forceful, even radical action.

In principle, four different approaches to solving this problem are possible: (1) Economize on government spending apart from programs for the retired elderly. (2) Raise taxes. (3) Restructure Social Security and Medicare. (4) Increase what America saves, so that the country can finance both adequate capital formation and a chronic government deficit.

In fact, several of these routes are unpromising, at least on the scale required to address the problem that now exists. For example, while it goes without saying that maintaining restraint on federal spending in areas unrelated to the retired elderly will be both necessary and important, Americans are unlikely to sacrifice progressively more of all the rest that the government does—defense, highways, space exploration, crime prevention, border patrols, disease control, disaster relief, education assistance, food stamps, medical care for the indigent—in order to devote an even greater share of federal revenues to Social Security and Medicare. A nation's government is more than a mechanism for transferring resources to its elderly citizens. Especially after the September 11 attacks, maintaining the nation's defenses is a top priority for most citizens. And federal spending for all domestic purposes other than support of the retired elderly is already smaller, compared to America's national income, than it was in 1940.

Raising America's private saving rate is likewise a dubious prospect, in this case because no one knows how to do so. Throughout much of the postwar period, but especially since the federal deficit ballooned in the 1980s, there have been numerous proposals for using the tax code to encourage private saving. Some of these ideas—Individual Retirement Accounts, Keogh Accounts, and 401(k) plans, all of which enable taxpayers to set aside pretax income to accumulate returns on a tax-deferred basis—have become standard features of American family finance. More far-reaching tax reforms, advanced in part to spur saving but never adopted, involve replacing the individual income tax (which accounts for more than two-fifths of all federal revenues) by a consumption tax, a national sales tax, or a European-style value-added tax.

The crucial assumption underlying each of these ideas is that if people can earn a higher return on what they save, after paying whatever tax they owe, they will save more. This may be true, but the opposite response is also possible. For people who save primarily to fund their future retirement, for example, earning a higher after-tax return on their IRA or 401(k) account enables them to put aside *less* of their current income and still enjoy a given standard of living later on. For the public as a whole, greater after-tax returns might induce people to save more, or save less.

The evidence suggests that on balance whatever effect higher after-tax returns have in either encouraging or discouraging saving is probably small. In the United States the experience since the 1980s has been particularly disappointing in this regard. Real after-tax returns in American financial markets rose dramatically in the 1980s as a result of higher pretax real interest rates (due in part to large government deficits), slower inflation, and reduced tax rates. Expanded IRA and Keogh account provisions made the effective increase in after-tax returns still greater for many taxpayers. Yet despite these supposedly favorable developments, Americans on average saved *less* of their incomes during the 1980s than in the 1960s and 1970s, when real after-tax returns were much lower.[29] And, as we have seen, the reduced levels of saving compared to income have persisted since then.

There is also no lack of proposals to amend either Social Security or Medicare to ease the fiscal strains that will result from the baby boomers' retirement. The age for retirement with full Social Security benefits, originally set by Congress at sixty-five (apparently copying Bismarck's original retirement program in Germany), began rising in 2000 and under current law will gradually climb to sixty-seven by 2027. Americans who are sixty-five today enjoy far better health and much longer life expectancy than did their forebears of 1935, when Social Security began (and even more so compared to Germans in the 1880s).[30] Many Americans in their sixties not only want to continue working but actively resist pressures to retire. Merely moving forward to 2011 the increase in retirement age that is already legislated would reduce each year's Social Security spending, between then and 2027, by an amount beginning at $10 billion.[31]

A host of other familiar proposals would narrow the long-term gap between Social Security spending and revenues by either trimming benefits or raising taxes, or both.[32] Frequently suggested forms of benefit reductions range from outright cuts to changing the formula by which benefits rise with inflation, to making benefits depend on family income to a greater extent than they implicitly do already via the tax system. Proposed tax increases mostly involve either a higher payroll tax rate or (in a departure from the practice since Social Security's inception) use of the government's general revenues to supplement payroll tax receipts. Privatizing Social Security by substituting individualized savings accounts for part of workers' coverage—a far more fundamental change, but one proposed by President Bush—would only make the funding gap larger in the short and even medium run, but might (that is, under the right circumstances) sufficiently stimulate private saving to ease the problem over longer horizons.[33]

There are also numerous proposals aimed at achieving long-run savings in Medicare. Most focus on the program's widely recognized incentives for overuse of medical services.[34] The Medicare savings legislated in recent years, though, have mostly stemmed from simply reducing the rate at which the government reimburses hospitals and doctors for providing their services.* In the long run major savings can only come from restructuring the program so that beneficiaries will not have an incentive to seek services and drugs they do not need and doctors will not have an incentive to provide them. The key to changing these perverse incentives is to broaden Medicare to allow elderly Americans to choose among different medical insurance plans, presumably with differing extent of coverage and probably with differing prices.

In recent years both Republicans and Democrats have offered proposals to provide, within Medicare, different insurance plans for beneficiaries who do or do not want to assume the burden of larger co-payments and deductibles, who do or do not want to limit their choice among doctors and hospitals or the range of covered services, and who do or do not want to use their private funds to supplement whatever basic plan their Medicare benefits would cover in full (or, under some proposals, who want to accept cheaper insurance than the basic plan, and take the difference in cash).[35] Various proposals differ, most importantly in how they would provide coverage for those elderly citizens who already have, or who develop, medical conditions that make them unattractive prospects for most private insurance programs. But the basic idea all share is to let elderly individuals choose (at different prices) the plans that best meet their needs, to force both doctors and hospitals to compete for Medicare patients just as they increasingly have to compete for nonelderly patients, and to create incentives for cost-saving technical change in medical care.[36]

But no one expects such changes, in either Social Security or Medicare, to achieve sufficient economies to overcome altogether the fiscal implications

---

*These actions are not always effective. When the government reduces payment rates to providers of medical services, some providers respond by performing more tests and other services so as to make up the lost revenue.

of America's aging population. In 2000, one American in eight was sixty-five or older. By 2025 it will be more than one in six.37

Both Social Security and Medicare are among the most remarkable successes in the history of federal government programs. Forty years ago, well after the creation of Social Security but before the major postwar growth in benefit levels, and also before the creation of Medicare, elderly Americans suffered poverty at approximately double the rate of the working-age population. In 1960, more than one out of three Americans over sixty-five lived on an income deemed insufficient to support a minimal acceptable living standard.38 Today in the United States the elderly are *less* likely to live in poverty than are their children and grandchildren.39 Forty years ago elderly Americans systematically had less access to medical care than did other citizens—44 percent had no health insurance at all—and that too is no longer so.40 As a result today's elderly are healthier, and they also live longer. In contrast to forty years ago, surveys no longer show that the elderly are on average less happy with their lives than younger Americans.41 Gutting Social Security, or Medicare, is surely not in the nation's interest.

Nor would doing so be consistent with the idea that a major reason for seeking to enhance the economy's long-term growth is to foster a fairer and more open society. Almost two-thirds of America's retired elderly get at least half of their income from their Social Security checks, and for nearly one in three Social Security comprises at least nine-tenths of their income.42 Roughly the same fraction of the elderly population would be unable to afford medical insurance were it not for their coverage under Medicare. In one very important dimension along which any society naturally divides— citizens of working age versus those who once worked but are now too old to do so—cutting monthly payments to retirees and eliminating their medical coverage would undermine many Americans' conception of what a fair society is all about.

The same shortcoming attaches to many attempts to use the tax system to increase what Americans save, even assuming such devices lead to that result. Most of the private saving in America is done by families with higher incomes, both because they have more income to begin with and because they save a greater fraction of what they earn. Whether or not it adds to saving, broadening the existing array of deductions, exclusions, credits, and other tax incentives to savers would benefit in the first instance those who are already high up in the income scale.

Seeking to overcome this drawback by targeting saving incentives at lower-income taxpayers (as, for example, with IRA contributions, which are deductible only if a family's income is below $75,000) would be unlikely to generate enough additional saving to improve the nation's saving-investment balance very much. One reason is, again, simply that lower-income families account for so little of America's total saving. In addition, because low-income families also have low marginal tax rates, proportional tax incentives have less room to work. For a family with income over $326,000, and therefore in the 35 percent tax bracket, making only half of its ordinary investment income taxable would boost its after-tax return by 27 percent. On a bond or savings account paying 5 percent, for example, it would now net 4.13 percent after taxes instead of just 3.25 percent—perhaps enough of a difference to matter for its decisions on how much to save. But a family earning $50,000, after all of its exemptions and deductions, is in the 15 percent bracket. The same tax break would increase its after-tax return by only 9 percent: from 4.25 percent to 4.63 percent on the same 5 percent bond. Such a small improvement is hardly likely to generate a significant boost even in the family's own saving, much less in the economy-wide total.

By contrast, undoing much of the tax reduction that Congress has enacted since 2001 offers the prospect not only of making a large contribution to addressing America's saving-investment problems but also of doing so in a way that does not further skew the distribution of benefits toward the already advantaged. The effect of these tax cuts on federal revenues is sizable. Even if all of the provisions in the 2001, 2002, and 2003 tax bills that the legislation specified as temporary actually disappear on schedule, by 2014 the likely total reduction in revenues will be about $260 billion *per year*, or well over 1 percent of national income at that time. More likely—and nearly everyone understood at the time that this was really what Congress intended—the legislated cuts will be extended. In addition, Congress will almost surely liberalize the income exemption from the Alternative Minimum Tax, and probably allow deductions for dependents, in order to stem the rapid growth in the number of taxpayers subject to the AMT. Under these more likely assumptions, the revenue loss by 2014 will be over $400 billion per year, or more than 2 percent of national income.[43] Compared to the recent net private saving rate of only 4.8 percent (even less since the beginning of this decade), eliminating government *dis*saving on this scale would make an important contribution to America's ability to undertake continuing investment.

The majority of these tax cuts have accrued to the benefit of those with the highest incomes, or the greatest wealth, or both. By far the largest element in the 2001 legislation was to lower marginal tax rates, including bringing the rate on the highest incomes down from 39.6 percent to 35 percent. The centerpiece of the 2003 legislation was to cut the tax rate on income earned from dividends and capital gains. Not only do lower- and middle-income families own much less corporate equity than richer families, but what stocks they do own are mostly held in IRAs, 401(k) accounts, or other exempt vehicles, so that the dividends they receive were already free of tax.

A further element of the 2001 legislation was the elimination of the estate tax, again helpful only to families of wealth.[44] Under existing law, only estates valued at above $1 million (scheduled to rise to $3 million), and only those left to someone other than a surviving wife or husband—in a typical year about two estates out of every one hundred deaths—are subject to any tax at all. Moreover, because a few estates are so large while most are fairly small, only 7 percent of those (corresponding to just .14 percent of all deaths) account for more than half of all the tax paid.[45] The total revenue received from the estate tax is not so large in economic terms ($22 billion in 2004, including gift taxes),[46] but the role of estate taxation in limiting the establishment of permanent dynasties of wealth—the "class of rich men" that Tocqueville emphasized did not exist in the America he visited—is an important element in maintaining an open, mobile society.

In all, three-quarters of the total tax reduction enacted since 2001 benefited families in the top fifth of the income distribution, all of whom have incomes (after all deductions and exemptions) above $80,000, and nearly 60 percent of the total tax reduction went to the top tenth of families, all with incomes above $120,000.[47] Undoing the 60 percent or 75 percent of the tax cuts that benefits families at the top of the scale would substantially shrink the government's ongoing deficit, and doing so would also contribute to achieving a fairer, more open society. Together with reforms of Social Security and Medicare (which also make sense on other grounds), as well as ongoing restraint in what the government spends apart from these two huge and rapidly growing programs, these measures would go a long way toward enabling America to finance an adequate rate of physical investment, and thereby to enjoy rising productivity and a rising standard of living, in the first quarter of this century.

Resolving the even larger fiscal imbalance that America is likely to face thereafter will be harder. Under current projections for Social Security and Medicare, and on the assumption that per capita federal spending for all purposes other than entitlements (including defense as well as domestic programs) remains constant after allowing for inflation, the average gap between spending and revenues from now until 2080 is 4.6 percent of national income.[48] After 2080 it is even larger. (The recently enacted Medicare prescription drug benefit—the first major entitlement ever established

by Congress with no provision whatever for funding it—added about
$10 trillion to the cumulative imbalance from now to 2080.)

Looking forward over so long a period naturally opens up a wider range
of possibilities for favorable developments that might ease, or even resolve
the problem: for example, new technologies that would permit faster than
expected growth (based perhaps on energy from nuclear fusion), much
larger immigration (to provide additional working-age taxpayers), or cost-
saving innovations in medical technology. Of course the longer horizon
opens the way for unfavorable developments as well. But while they are
unlikely to eliminate in full the nation's longer-term fiscal imbalance, the
same set of changes that should be adequate for the next quarter-century—
rolling back high-income tax cuts, implementing Medicare and Social Security reforms, braking increases in other government spending—nonetheless
represent a strong start. And maintaining strong economic growth between
now and then will likewise make the task easier.

Human capital formation in America has also been inadequate during the
last quarter-century. In contrast to the large gains in educational attainment
made by earlier generations, since 1980 the American labor force has, in
economist David Ellwood's apt phrase, "sputtered."[49] Despite the dramatic
widening of wage differentials favoring workers with more education—
indeed, to historic highs—the percentage of young Americans who complete high school has stagnated at about 90 percent, as has the percentage of
those who go on to college (about 60 percent) and also of those who eventually earn a four-year degree (about 28 percent). Among those who are in
school, academic performance on most objective measures has deteriorated.
Although American schools spend more per pupil than schools anywhere
else, American students rank poorly compared to students in other industrialized countries. Certainly no western European country has anything like
the mass of unskilled and even illiterate youth that America has.[50]

These shortcomings have also contributed to America's disappointing
productivity gains over this period. Modern technology requires trained
workers no less than sophisticated machines. As economist James Heckman
has bluntly put it, "The problem is clear. The supply of skilled workers is
not keeping pace with demand."[51] The need for more and better education,
to enable the economy to deliver long-term gains in living standards, is clear
as well.

At the same time, America has distinct advantages on which to build.
The nation's top-level universities are widely regarded as the world's finest

institutions of higher learning and research. At the secondary level too, technologically driven changes in the economy's occupational structure have made the American emphasis on general cognitive skills, especially verbal and mathematical reasoning, all the more valuable compared to the kind of more specific vocational skills that many European countries emphasize. Indeed, there is reason to believe that this difference in the orientation of education has helped account for the faster growth of productivity in America than in Europe during the past two decades.[52]

Enhancing the development of America's human capital presents a different set of opportunities and challenges from what building physical capital formation entails. Unlike investment in factories and machinery, most education in America is not only publicly funded but publicly provided. Close to 90 percent of American children in the first through twelfth grades attend public schools. Even in higher education, 95 percent of all students attending two-year colleges, and almost two-thirds of all students at four-year colleges and universities, attend public institutions.[53]

In America primary and secondary education is overwhelmingly the responsibility of government at the state and local level and, below that, of the nearly 15,000 independent school districts all across the country.* Despite a series of attempts over many years to expand federal influence in this sphere, including most recently the No Child Left Behind Act, the federal government's role in shaping education policy remains both limited and contested. Local and state governments together provide twelve times as much funding as the federal government does for primary and secondary education, and more than twice as much for higher education.[54]

In the public consciousness, education has always resonated strongly with traditional values and aspirations that have seemed particularly American. Education epitomizes the ideals of individual striving and individual opportunity that from the beginning figured centrally in why many of America's immigrants chose to come here. In the early colonial days education was also key to advancing the program of many of America's founding religious groups. In time, self-improvement through education became a kind of secular extension of personal salvation, with many of the same connotations albeit not the explicitly religious rationale. Americans have also

---

*In 1892 the National Education Association established the Committee of Ten (headed by Charles William Eliot, then president of Harvard) to look into a variety of questions including the potential creation of a national education system. The commission firmly recommended against any such plan. As a result, America has no federally sponsored schools, colleges, or universities other than the national service academies.

traditionally emphasized the benefits education imparts to the strength of democracy by creating a more engaged, better informed citizenry. At a more practical level, education also reduces crime.[55]

Today education in America retains much of this aura and many of the same emotive overtones. Especially in an era when the gap is widening not just between rich and poor but between the middle class and either rich or poor, the connection between education and the creation of individual opportunity readily lends itself to fostering the ideals of equality and mobility in ways that differ sharply from the circumstances surrounding the accumulation of physical capital. While saving and investment are inevitably activities carried out disproportionately by upper-income groups, so that most incentive-based measures designed to increase either one tend in the first instance to render incomes and wealth less equal, many of the most effective measures aimed at enhancing the society's human capital formation through education clearly make opportunities *more* equal. The greatest opportunities for expanding the education of America's population today are mostly found lower on the income scale.

It is not just that workers with little education earn ever less compared to those who are better educated; they are less likely to work at all. The problem is especially acute among women. Among American women who fail to complete high school, fewer than half hold jobs. Merely finishing high school boosts the probability of working to more than two-thirds, and finishing college raises it above four-fifths. Moreover, these differences in labor force participation have been increasing since the 1970s—the same period during which education-based wage differentials have widened so rapidly.[56]

Worse yet, lack of education limits mobility across generations as well. In America today, one of the strongest influences governing how much education children receive is their parents' education.[57] And this is not only a question of who goes to college. Even the difference of an extra year of high school, and even for only one parent, makes a child more likely to finish high school, and less likely to repeat a grade along the way.[58] It is not surprising that American public opinion strongly and consistently supports education as the best way to help the nation's disadvantaged.[59]

Education—human capital formation—is about more than helping the disadvantaged, however. It is also an investment, and the evidence makes clear that the return, in terms of added productivity for the economy as a whole, can be large. Repeated studies of Americans' education and subsequent work experience suggest that each additional year of schooling increases a person's lifetime earnings by 7 to 8 percent, mostly by increasing hourly wage rates.[60] More educated workers earn more, not just because they work more hours but because they are also more productive. And, not surprisingly in light of the spread of new technologies in American business in recent decades, there is evidence that the returns to education are higher in the United States than in other industrialized countries, and higher now than they were earlier on.[61]

A 7 to 8 percent increase in lifetime earnings is substantial, especially in a country where working lives are long and wage levels are already relatively high. In 2003 the median income earned by American men who worked full-time throughout the year was $41,500. An extra 7 percent would mean $2,900 *per year* in additional earnings. Even after allowance for the time value of money at a real interest rate of 5 percent (which is fairly high), an extra $2,900 in earnings each year over a work span from, say, age twenty-one to sixty-five represents added value of more than $54,000. Given that it costs American taxpayers roughly $6,500 on average to provide a year of high school education for each student, a gain of this magnitude is unquestionably a good investment. Similarly, most estimates of the rate of return on education calculated on an investment basis exceed 10 percent, and some are as high as 17 to 20 percent.[62] (Over long periods of time the after-inflation rate of return on investing in the stock market is about 6 percent.)

The economic value of providing more education is not simply a matter of making sure that young people graduate from high school. In 2003 the average hourly wage of Americans who had graduated from high school (but not gone on to college) was 34 percent above what people made who had not finished high school. But college graduates made 73 percent more than high school graduates, and those with advanced degrees made another 26 percent beyond that.[63] Across a surprisingly broad range of grade levels—according to some estimates, all the way from third grade through the junior year of college—the cumulative effect of each additional year's schooling in increasing a person's subsequent lifetime earnings is approximately the same, and the effect of completing a four-year college degree or a more advanced professional degree is even larger.[64] All across the educational spectrum, students have a clear economic incentive to get more schooling.

Because education in America is free through high school (though some parents choose private schools), the challenge at this level is to persuade more youngsters to take advantage of what society already offers. Simply raising the compulsory schooling age, perhaps to eighteen, would be one obvious answer. But most states have been reluctant to do so out of concern that people of that age, compelled to be in school against their will, not only would learn little but might be sufficiently disruptive to impede other students' learning as well.[65] The challenge is to keep them in school voluntarily.

Experience shows, however, that some approaches to doing so are more effective than others. Mere exhortation has little effect; either do counseling sessions that take place only as students near their sixteenth birthday. What works instead is intervention, in a broad-based and intensive way, over much longer spans of time, in the educational experience of students who stand at significant risk of not staying in school. And the earlier that intervention begins, the better.

For example, whether early-intervention programs like Project Head Start have a lasting impact on students' academic performance remains subject to substantial controversy.[66] But students who have been in Head Start—and, even more so, those who have been in more intensive early-intervention programs like the Syracuse Preschool Program and the Perry Preschool Program—do tend to stay in school longer than students from comparably disadvantaged family backgrounds who have not participated in these programs. While in school, they are less likely to have to repeat a grade, and less likely to require "special education." (They also have much lower crime rates in their teenage years, and girls have lower rates of teenage pregnancy.) As James Heckman has often argued, learning begets learning, and skill begets skill.[67]

Early childhood intervention is not all that matters, of course. But experience with efforts directed at older children is in many ways similar to that of Head Start. Students who participate in programs designed in part to encourage high school completion, such as the nationwide Big Brothers/Big Sisters program and the Philadelphia Futures Sponsor-A-Scholar program, are more likely to finish high school and, if they do, more likely to go to college.[68] (These programs also result in lower crime rates and reduced frequency of other social pathologies.) The programs that succeed are the ones that begin early, that provide intensive mentoring and tutoring, and that target those students who are at greatest risk of dropping out.

Getting more young Americans to go to college—and among those who do, getting more to finish—presents a different set of issues. College is not free. High school students from middle-income families often find it a struggle to go to the best institutions willing to accept them. Students from lower-income backgrounds find it difficult to go to any college at all without a scholarship.

Just how important financial considerations are in preventing talented students from attending college is subject to debate. The fact that children from lower-income families have increased their rates of college attendance only slightly as the wage premium for college graduates has grown suggests that financing is a serious problem. Other evidence, however, indicates that much of the difference across income groups in this regard instead reflects the fact that by the time these students near college age their academic skills have fallen far behind those of their middle- and upper-income counterparts.[69] A conservative estimate is that, even with the array of scholarship and loan programs that are in place, today about 8 percent of young Americans are financially constrained from getting the college education they should have.[70] With just 28 percent of America's student-age population currently finishing four-year degrees, finding ways to enable that additional 8 percent to join them would significantly upgrade the educational attainment of the nation's workforce.

To achieve this end, financial resources need to target that part of the potential student population that is financially constrained. American colleges and universities, allocating their own scholarship funds, are reasonably successful at doing just that. The government has a more mixed record. Pell Grants, for example, which the federal government has provided since 1973 to low-income students seeking to attend either two- or four-year colleges, have proven to be an especially effective mechanism for this purpose, and there is a clear case for expanding this program well beyond the $12 billion per year (for 5 million students) that now supports it.[71] By contrast over 90 percent of the funds provided under the government's HOPE Scholarship program, aimed at middle-income families, went to students who would have attended college anyway.[72] At the state level, California's Cal Grant program has had a sizable impact (3 to 4 percentage points) on the number of financial aid applicants who attend college, and especially large effects on the choice of private four-year colleges within the state.[73]

At both the high school and the college levels, targeted programs designed to keep young Americans in school therefore represent a twofold opportunity. By increasing the average education level of the American workforce, they further the economy's overall productivity growth. And by helping to overcome the disadvantages of family backgrounds that often lead children to become high school dropouts, and the lack of financial resources that stand in the way of many going to college, they make opportunity more equal and American society more mobile. On both counts they represent a worthwhile investment. Even programs directed at the very youngest school-age and preschool children, like Head Start, offer some of the same advantages by keeping students in school (and out of trouble) later on.

While there is widespread agreement that increasing the *quantity* of schooling that the average American receives represents a good use of the nation's resources, there is no consensus on how to improve the *quality* of education in America. There is even debate over whether devoting additional resources to America's schools would make them more effective.

It may seem almost self-evident that what most schools could have with additional financial resources—smaller classes, better-trained teachers, more computers, superior physical facilities like science labs, larger libraries, more up-to-date textbooks—would improve the quality of the education they provide. Surprisingly, experience provides at best only weak support for this presumption. Three decades ago the Coleman Report shocked both education experts and the general public by showing that measurable aspects of schooling like class size or physical facilities, or even the content of the curriculum, bore little or no systematic connection to students' performance as measured by scores on nationally standardized cognitive tests. Since then an enormous volume of educational research has mostly come to the same conclusion.[74]

Some studies have found beneficial effects of additional school resources, however, especially for children from low-income families and for non-whites more generally.[75] The most promising example to date has been a Tennessee experiment—Project STAR, for Student/Teacher Achievement Ratio—in which, beginning in 1986, school districts randomly assigned more than 11,000 students from seventy-nine elementary schools to classes with different sizes.[76] Students in the smaller classes (thirteen to seventeen students) showed more improvement in their cognitive test scores. Later on, they were also more likely to take college entrance exams, less likely to have been arrested, and less likely to have become teenage parents.[77] Resources also appear to matter for preschool programs like Head Start. In areas where Head Start spends more per pupil, or where pupil-teacher ratios are smaller, those who participate go on to have higher reading scores and they are less likely to have to repeat a grade.[78]

What stands out most prominently after more than three decades of voluminous research inspired by the Coleman Report, however, is not how many such examples there are but how few. It therefore remains unclear whether the gains that do appear to follow from smaller class size, for example, are sufficiently widespread and sufficiently lasting to offer a serious prospect of boosting America's economic growth.[79] Initiatives that improve the chances of disadvantaged youth to do well in school and to succeed in the labor market later on are, of course, meritorious on that account. So are any programs that succeed in reducing crime and teenage pregnancies. But this is not the same as making the country's labor force as a whole more productive.

In the end, the best case to be made for smaller class sizes as a policy for spurring economic growth is as part of a broader strategy of getting students to stay in school. Experience shows that students who have had the advantage of smaller-size classes tend to do exactly that, and on this account alone they would be likely to be more productive and to earn more. One study of more than 150 school districts in Illinois found that a 10 percent reduction in a high school's student-to-teacher ratio corresponded on average to about a 1.5 percent increase in its graduation rate.[80] Other studies, using information from a number of states, show that a lower average student-teacher ratio not only increases the fraction of a state's students who graduate from high school but increases even more the fraction who go on to graduate from college.[81] Adding to school resources in this way may therefore be less a matter of improving the quality of students' education than an additional means of increasing the quantity of schooling that the average student receives.

The troublesome fact is that spending on education in America has already been rising steadily over a long period of time with little measurable impact. After allowing for inflation, spending per student in public primary and secondary schools has increased at an average rate of 3.4 percent per annum throughout the last century (although the increase has slowed since the 1990s).[82] The average cost of four years in an American public high school is now $26,000. In many respects, what is remarkable is not how little is being spent but how much.[83]

Because of this increased spending, average class sizes have fallen as the student-teacher ratio in the public schools has declined from 26-to-1 in 1960 to 16-to-1 today.[84] In recent years most schools have made far more provision for small-group instruction, and even individualized attention to students' needs. Most schools' physical facilities are also greatly superior to what they were not many years ago.[85] Yet students' average test scores stopped rising more than thirty years ago.*

---

*One reason that scores on college entrance tests like the SAT have not improved, however, is actually good news: larger numbers of students who are not at the very top of the scale in America's high schools are now applying to selective colleges and universities, and therefore need to take these tests.

As a result, attention has recently begun to focus less on the amount of financial resources available than on how they are used: specifically, on the absence of systematic incentives for students, teachers, and administrators to make the most of the resources that schools already have.[86] For students who do not plan to attend college, for example, there is no external incentive to improve their academic performance beyond the minimum necessary to graduate from high school. Employers almost never ask to see prospective employees' high school records (in part because they sense that grades for students who do not go on to college contain little useful information, and in part because they fear the charge that standardized tests may be discriminatory along racial or gender lines). As a result, many community colleges now amount to an expensive screening mechanism to enable employers to distinguish among potential employees in the absence of hard information from the high schools.

The absence of incentives is more profound at the level of teachers and administrators. Teachers who perform well—as reflected, for example, by the improvement over the year in their students' performance—normally do not receive more pay, or better working conditions, or more rapid career advancement, than those whose students make little progress.[87] Even when school systems do seek to recognize and reward teachers who perform well, the difficulty of assessing individual teachers' contributions is a major stumbling block.

Similarly, principals whose schools perform well by one or another educational measure are rarely rewarded. Nor do schools whose students perform well normally benefit by receiving additional resources. Only among district-level school administrators do promotion and career incentives become a significant factor, and even then the aspects of performance that bear on these incentives mostly address financial management and efficient administration, not educational outcomes for students.

In this crucial respect, therefore, American education resembles American health care. Each serves a purpose that is crucial to the life of the great majority of the nation's citizens. The financial resources that the country devotes to each purpose are large, and in each case those resources have been growing not just absolutely but in relation to the number of people being served. In each case indefinite further growth in resources used, as a share of the national income, is clearly impossible. But at the same time, no one wants to sacrifice the basic purpose being achieved. And in each case the existing structure of the industry that provides this basic service offers the mostly competent and well-intentioned people working within it little incentive, apart from personal satisfaction, to deliver superior performance.

Just as thinking about health care has increasingly focused on creating such incentives by giving patients and their employers a wider range of choices among different insurance arrangements and different providers of medical services, thinking about primary and secondary education has increasingly focused on creating incentives to superior performance by giving students and their families more choice among different schools and, where possible, even among different kinds of schools. In each case the motivation for change springs from disappointment with what the application of ever greater resources has delivered. And it reflects a recognition that no amount of resources will lead to improved outcomes unless both the people who provide these services and the people who use them have an incentive to do so effectively.

In its more extreme forms, the idea of restructuring primary and secondary education along choice-based lines could threaten the very existence of America's traditional system of public schools, and for this reason many so-called voucher plans—which give the parents of school-age children a fixed sum (typically $1,500 to $2,000) to be used exclusively for tuition payments at either public or private schools—have attracted intense criticism. Such plans are currently in effect on a limited basis in some American cities and a few states, mostly with severe eligibility restrictions to ensure that funds go only to families who could not afford private school tuition on their own. Proposals for nationwide, federally funded voucher programs, operating through either cash payments or tax credits, have also appeared in Congress.

One common objection to voucher plans is that, eligibility restrictions notwithstanding, some of the money will inevitably go to families who would have used their own funds to pay for private school tuition, so that the expenditure of public funds in this way does not lead to any different educational outcome. A more fundamental objection stems from the fact that for many families the preferred alternative to public education would be a parochial school. Whether and under what circumstances the Constitution permits using government funds to support religious activities, in this case by paying tuition to a religious educational institution, is a controversial matter to say the least.[88] Just as fundamentally, many people have traditionally viewed reliance on public schools as an important underpinning of American democracy, and they therefore regard with suspicion proposals that might threaten the health, or perhaps even the survival, of the public school system.[89]

But the goal of introducing greater choice and more competition so as to create incentives for superior educational performance is achievable *within* the public school system as well. Some limited elements of choice have always been at work within the American public school system, along with the long-standing competition between public schools and both private and parochial schools. The experience of *public* school systems shows that introducing greater choice often leads to improved school performance and superior educational outcomes. Many cities and towns not only have multiple schools for each age but multiple school districts (some metropolitan areas in the United States have more than 200 independent school districts) with differing levels of taxpayer support; differing emphasis on core academic subjects, special "enrichment" programs, athletics, and other extracurricular activities; and differing levels of overall commitment to quality education. Schooling is often a dominant influence governing where families with children choose to live.[90]

Some school districts have also introduced elements of choice independent of family decisions about where to live. In Cambridge, Massachusetts, and District 4 (East Harlem) in New York City, students are free to attend any school within the entire district, with a lottery used to ration places when especially popular schools are oversubscribed. Many more school districts have designated specific "magnet" schools that any student in the district can choose to attend, again with a lottery in case of oversubscription. "Charter" schools are much like magnet schools, though in most districts charter schools also have significantly more freedom to adopt an innovative or otherwise unconventional curriculum.[91] In areas with multiple school districts, some communities allow children living in one district to attend a school in another. In Minnesota, for example, children at all ages are now free to attend any public school they choose, anywhere in the state. One aim of the federal government's 2001 No Child Left Behind legislation is to enable all students enrolled in schools deemed underperforming (on the basis of standardized test scores) to choose a different public school.

Each of these forms of school choice results in competition among school districts, and increasingly among schools within a single district, thereby creating incentives for schools to do better. Further, the 2001 federal legislation requires that schools test all children in grades three through eight on a standardized basis, in both reading and math, and that these test results be made public. At least in principle, therefore, the competition can take place with greater information than was available just a few years ago. (Whether the rating system established under the 2001 law is effective or not remains an open question.)[92]

Nobody likes losing a popularity contest. But in the case of school choice, the incentives created are far more direct. Most public schools receive their financing on a direct dollars-per-student basis, and so losing students means losing money—money that schools would otherwise spend not only to employ more staff to teach the additional students but also in countless other ways that improve the everyday experience of students, teachers, and administrators. In some cases, even a school's continued existence depends on whether enough students choose to go there. The choices made by students and their parents also give district-level officials a way to distinguish successful from unsuccessful schools and therefore to reward principals and teachers for their performance.

When all schools in a district where there are opportunities for choice confront these incentives, the benefits are not limited to just those students who decide to change schools. In practice, even when they are allowed to choose, far more students attend their own neighborhood school than switch to some alternative. But the point is that some do switch, and many more would do so if their neighborhood school fell too far behind the next most convenient alternative.

The measure of success of allowing choice in a public school system, therefore, is not how many students change schools but how much all the schools improve, and how much better all the students do, regardless of which school they choose. (An ideal result might well be that all schools in the area improve to the point that no student sees any need to make a switch.) This is why expanding school choice also constitutes a policy for spurring economic growth. If the students who changed schools were the only ones to get a better education, the benefit to them would be valuable but it would hardly affect the American labor force as a whole. The goal, however, is to improve the education provided by all schools to all students, thereby enhancing the nation's human capital formation.

The experience to date suggests that allowing choice in public schools leads to improved results in several important ways. Introducing greater choice not only leads to improved student achievement and to more students completing high school, but does so at reduced cost to taxpayers. In the Milwaukee voucher experiment, for example, the public schools that faced the greatest competition from private schools achieved dramatically improved student performance in tests administered under the National Assessment of Educational Progress, while spending no more than other schools.[93] There is also evidence that having a choice among public schools reduces many families' desire to have their children attend private schools.[94]

These gains apparently stem from incentives that affect the behavior of schools as well as students and their families. Schools in areas where there are more independent school districts tend on average to offer more high-powered courses, and to impose more academic requirements as well as stronger discipline. Parents of students living in areas where there is more choice among public schools tend to discuss school curriculum matters with their children more often, and also visit their children's schools more often. Students living in these areas on average report doing more hours of homework each week.* In high school they also take more advanced-placement courses, presumably as a result not only of their own motivation but also greater encouragement by their schools.[95]

Because the experience to date of increasing the range of choice either within school districts or across districts in a particular area is limited, much of this evidence comes from long-standing differences between communities with either many or few independent school districts. But the evidence from both sources suggests that increasing choice among schools creates incentives that influence the behavior of schools, of parents, and of students, and that the result is often superior education, often at lower cost. Together with policies that increase the amount of schooling young Americans receive, this kind of structural shift, implemented on a far wider basis, offers the prospect of improving the effectiveness of American education and thereby enhancing the nation's investment in its human capital and, in turn, its productivity and economic growth.

Finally, formal schooling is not the only vehicle for investing in a nation's human capital. Many of the skills that bear most directly on how well workers do their jobs, and even much of the knowledge they bring to bear, comes instead from the training and experience they receive in the course of their working careers. Many employers, especially larger firms, offer or even require structured training programs for their employees. Both job experience and on-the-job training are widely known to be important factors contributing to workers' productivity.[96] Whether there is an appropriate role for public policy in providing workers with either training or experience is more complicated, however.

Encouraging private firms to provide more on-the-job training is, in principle, sound policy. Because individual firms have no way to prevent the workers they train from leaving for a new job, they are likely to provide too

---

*Self-reported homework estimates are notoriously unreliable, but in this case the self-reported differences gain credibility because they correspond to differences in objectively measured student performance.

little training. The case for some kind of public subsidy therefore seems clear. The problem is that much of the training employers give their workers is difficult to measure in any concrete way. In addition, firms are always happy to receive a subsidy for doing what they would do on their own anyway. As a result, tax incentives have mostly been ineffective in increasing the amount of on-the-job training activity actually undertaken at private companies.[97]

A further problem is that private sector training often excludes workers with the lowest skills, yet they are precisely the ones most in need of training.[98] The federal government and most states have therefore devised many programs over the years to provide that training themselves: at the federal level, the Civilian Conservation Corps and the Works Progress Administration during the depression, and in the postwar era such landmark programs as the Area Redevelopment Act (1958), the Manpower Development and Training Act (1962), the Job Corps program (1964), the Comprehensive Employment and Training Act (1973), and the Job Training Partnership Act (1982).[99] The federal government currently provides training and other employment services to about 1 million people each year, most of whom are economically disadvantaged. The largest single element in most of this effort is direct classroom training in job skills. Many states have additional programs along similar lines.

The consensus is that government-provided training does have some positive effect on workers' productivity, but that in most cases these gains are limited. In contrast to private firms, which understandably seek to train the most able individuals they can find, government programs not only take all comers but seek out low-ability participants. And the programs that seem to deliver long-lasting increases in workers' subsequent earnings, and presumably in their productivity on the job, are those that are the most expensive.[100]

For example, the Job Corps, which currently serves more than 60,000 disadvantaged high school dropouts each year—the average participant reads at the eighth-grade level and one-third have previously been arrested—does tend to raise participants' subsequent earnings relative to what otherwise comparable young people who have not been in the program earn.[101] (It also reduces their probability of being arrested, and of serving time in jail, as well as their rate of welfare dependence.) But how large these earnings gains are, and how long they last, remains subject to debate.[102] Moreover, with most of the participants living on dedicated residential campuses, the program is expensive: $20,000 per participant per year, or roughly three times the average cost of one year of high school.

(The average cost of a year in prison is about \$25,000, however, and so even the Job Corps may be cost-effective depending on what the young people it serves would be doing otherwise.)

But whether or not these government training programs are worth what they cost to help rectify society's inequities, they are unlikely to make a sufficient contribution to the nation's human capital formation to represent a way of spurring aggregate economic growth. Indeed, from a broader perspective the strongest argument in favor of government-sponsored training and even government-subsidized job creation programs is simply that they put people to work and, in so doing, have a positive effect on the *children* of those participants who go on to become regular workers.

Work, even subsidized work, enables people to provide for themselves and their families, and thereby to gain a sense of dignity and self-worth.[103] But whether people hold a regular job of some kind (even a subsidized job) or simply live on welfare—or, worse yet, crime—also makes a large difference for whether their children stay in school, how those children perform in school, and how much they earn when they in turn enter the workforce later on.[104] Simply being on the job helps form traits like discipline, promptness, and the ability to work with other people, and the evidence is clear that parents pass these basic ethics along to their children. There is also evidence that parents' incomes affect their children's health, including their vulnerability to chronic health problems that can impair their earning ability (not to mention require expensive medical care) in their adult lives.[105] Here, as elsewhere, one generation may be too narrow a perspective for judging what constitutes good economic policy.

Limiting government spending, undoing tax cuts, accelerating the increase in the Social Security retirement age, reshaping Medicare on choice-based lines, providing intensive early-intervention programs for the youngest schoolchildren, encouraging more students to finish high school and enabling more to attend and finish college, restructuring primary and secondary public education to provide more choice among schools—these are all hard choices for public policy, and in some cases they are radical choices. But the stakes are high, and the consequences far-reaching.

What is at issue in the first instance is whether, and if so by how much, the American economy will deliver an improving standard of living, for most of the people who draw their daily livelihood from it, over the first quarter or perhaps even the first half of the twenty-first century. The central question is not the poverty of the most disadvantaged, nor the success of the most privileged. It is the economic well-being of the broad majority of the nation's citizenry.

But it is more than an issue of advance or stagnation in strictly material terms, and it is certainly not a question of material gain at the expense of moral, social, or political improvement. Broadly distributed economic growth creates the private attitudes and public institutions that foster, not undermine, a society's moral qualities.

The historical experience of the United States has reflected the strength or weakness of the nation's economic advance in the changing course of its prevailing political directions and social behavior. The experience of other industrialized (and, in many respects, postindustrial) Western democracies has as well. So too, albeit in different ways, do developments today in many countries around the world that are moving toward industrialization but still have far lower average living standards. Any nation, even one with incomes as high as America's, will find the basic character of its society at risk if it allows its citizens' living standards to stagnate.

In 1938, after the deepest crisis of the depression had passed but while unemployment stubbornly remained far above acceptable levels, Congress convened the Temporary National Economic Committee to propose solutions for the nation's lingering problems. Nothing important came of it. As *Time* magazine put it when TNEC (as it was universally called) finished its work three years later, "With all the ammunition the committee had stored up, a terrific broadside might have been expected. Instead, the committee rolled a rusty BB gun into place and pinged away at the nation's economic problems."[106] It remained for World War II to restore full employment.

At the outset of the twenty-first century, America's problem is not unemployment. It is the slow pace of advance in the living standards of the majority of the nation's citizens. The twenty years from the early 1970s through the early 1990s saw the income of the average American family stagnate, and the earnings of the average American worker sharply decline. Some improvement returned in the latter half of the 1990s, but it was modest and it did not persist. For the majority of American families, the pace of their advance remains much too slow, and the economic growth fueling that advance remains fragile. The widespread sense that our standard of living has stagnated over the last generation does not stem from the public's study of national income statistics, but from average Americans' awareness of what they have personally experienced.

Broad-based economic growth in America was not a myth. Nor is it true that the growth Americans enjoyed in the early postwar decades was merely an aberration to which we nonetheless became accustomed. The pace of increase in living standards in those years was little more than what the nation had experienced on average during the previous century and a half. It is instead our own era, dating from the early 1970s, that stands out as exceptional. A rising standard of living for the great majority of our citizens has in fact been the American norm, and it is we, today, who are failing to achieve it.

America's greatest need today is to restore the reality, and thereby over time the confident perception, that our people are moving ahead. If doing so will require public policy choices that are hard, so be it. Only with sustained economic growth, and the sense of confident progress that follows from the advance of living standards for most of its citizens, can even a great nation find the energy, the wherewithal, and most importantly the human attitudes that together sustain an open, tolerant, and democratic society.

Notes

CHAPTER 1
What Growth Is, What Growth Does

1. Daniel Bell, *The Cultural Contradictions of Capitalism* (New York: Basic Books, 1976), p. 237.
2. Alexander Gerschenkron, *Bread and Democracy in Germany* (Berkeley: University of California Press, 1943), p. 5.
3. Wage data are from the Bureau of Labor Statistics.
4. Median family income data are from the Census Bureau.
5. Data on median wages (for twenty-five- to thirty-five-year-old men) are from the Census Bureau.
6. *Time*, Cable News Network, Yankelovich Partners Poll, January 1998; CBS News, New York Times Poll, August 7, 1996. Data are from the Roper Center for Public Opinion Research.
7. See, for example, Robert D. Putnam, *Bowling Alone: The Collapse and Revival of American Community* (New York: Simon & Schuster, 2000).
8. Data on political rights and civil liberties are from Freedom House.
9. Data on per capita income in China are from the World Bank's online *World Development Indicators*.

CHAPTER 2
Perspectives from the Enlightenment and Its Roots

1. Adam Smith, *Lectures on Jurisprudence*, edited by R. L. Meek, D. D. Raphael, and P. G. Stein (Oxford: Clarendon Press, 1978), pp. 14, 16.
2. Montesquieu (Charles de Secondat, Baron de), *The Spirit of the Laws*, translated and edited by Anne M. Cohler, Basi Carolyn Miller, and Harold Samuel Stone (Cambridge: Cambridge University Press, 1989), pp. 48, 338.

3. See Asa Briggs, *The Age of Improvement* (New York: David McKay, 1962), and Patrick Beaver, *The Crystal Palace, 1851–1936: A Portrait of Victorian Enterprise* (London: Hugh Evelyn, 1970).

4. Robert Muccigrosso, *Celebrating the New World: Chicago's Columbian Exposition of 1893* (Chicago: Ivan R. Dee, 1993).

5. Henry Adams, *The Education of Henry Adams: An Autobiography* (New York: Modern Library, 1996), p. 380.

6. See, for example, the surveys in John Bagnell Bury, *The Idea of Progress: An Inquiry into Its Origins and Growth* (London: Macmillan, 1920), and Robert A. Nisbet, *History of the Idea of Progress* (New York: Basic Books, 1980).

7. David S. Landes, *The Wealth and Poverty of Nations: Why Some Are So Rich and Some So Poor* (New York: Norton, 1999), p. xvii.

8. See Ludwig Edelstein, *The Idea of Progress in Classical Antiquity* (Baltimore: Johns Hopkins University Press, 1967).

9. See, for example, Sidney Pollard, *The Idea of Progress: History and Society* (New York: Basic Books, 1968). Also see again Bury, *The Idea of Progress*, and Nisbet, *History of the Idea of Progress*.

10. The Botanic Gardens at Kew, established in 1759 to showcase foreign as well as domestic plants, developed into a symbol of the relation between science and commerce analogous to what the Crystal Palace would become a century later. The gardens were also greatly expanded in the nineteenth century.

11. See the discussion in Ronald L. Meek, *Social Science and the Ignoble Savage* (Cambridge: Cambridge University Press, 1976).

12. See again ibid.; also John Huxtable Elliott, *The Old World and the New, 1492–1650* (Cambridge: Cambridge University Press, 1970).

13. John Locke, *Two Treatises of Government*, edited by Peter Laslett (Cambridge: Cambridge University Press, 1988), p. 301, italics in original. The idea that in some respects the native Americans' culture might be as advanced as Europe's, or even more so, did not occur to them.

14. Ibid., p. 339, italics in original.

15. Turgot (later France's finance minister under Louis XVI, and also the originator of the term "laissez-faire") lectured at the Sorbonne in 1750. His initial written contribution on this subject, in *Plan of Two Discourses on Universal History*, dates to either 1750 or 1751. This work was not published until the nineteenth century, however, and Turgot's first published exposition of the idea appeared in 1770, in his *Reflexions*. Smith's parallel contribution to this line of thought, contained in his *Lectures on Jurisprudence*, is harder to date because he never published these lectures; they exist today only in the form of edited notes taken by two students who heard him deliver them in 1762–63 and 1763–64, respectively. But Smith began lecturing on this subject at Glasgow in 1751, and there is reason to think that his formulation of the specific ideas may have long predated the first

set of student notes (and may even have appeared in his public lectures at Edinburgh, before he began teaching at the University of Glasgow). The first published appearance of the idea was due to neither Turgot nor Smith, but rather Sir John Dalrymple (in his *Essay Towards a General History of Feudal Property*, 1757) and then Lord Kames (in his *Historical Law Tracts*, 1758). By the 1760s and 1770s the idea had become almost commonplace. See the historical account in Meek, *Social Science and the Ignoble Savage*, especially Chapters 3 and 4, and Ronald L. Meek, *Smith, Marx and After: Ten Essays in the Development of Economic Thought* (London: Chapman & Hall, 1977), Chapter 1.

16. Smith referred to these stages of economic development as "stages of subsistence." The idea clearly anticipated (though in a much different context) what Marx, a century later, more famously called "stages of production." Although the specific application to *economic* development was new, the more general notion of human development proceeding through successive distinct stages was long familiar. Hesiod, a Greek of the eighth century before the common era, related a myth of successive "ages" identified by metals: golden, silver, bronze, and finally iron. (He also included an "age of heroes" between the bronze and iron ages.) But both the Egyptians and the Babylonians had also had a notion of successive ages long before Hesiod. For a useful account, see Nisbet, *History of the Idea of Progress*, Chapter 1.

17. Smith, *Lectures on Jurisprudence*, p. 16.

18. Malthus's *Essay on the Principle of Population* first appeared in 1798.

19. In this regard Smith and Turgot were following John Locke, who argued that what leads men to create laws and governing institutions is the desire to "seek *the preservation of their property*." Locke, *Second Treatise of Government*, p. 352, italics in original. Or, as Harvey Mansfield has nicely put it, in Locke "government is formed to preserve property rather than *vice versa*." Harvey C. Mansfield, "On the Political Character of Property in Locke," in Alkis Kontos (ed.), *Powers, Possessions and Freedom: Essays in Honor of C. B. Macpherson* (Toronto: University of Toronto Press, 1979), p. 29.

20. Montesquieu's *Spirit of the Laws* was the first explicit statement of the general method of explaining the evolution of social institutions in terms of the "condition of mankind."

21. Modern echoes of Rousseau appear in the fictionalized treatment of the supposed gentleness of contemporary pre-modern peoples like the !Kung in the Kalahari Desert—who, on closer inspection, turn out to have very high rates of murder and other forms of intracommunity violence. See Richard Lee, *The Dobe !Kung* (New York: Holt, Rinehart & Winston, 1984).

22. Jean-Jacques Rousseau, *The Social Contract and Discourses*, translated by G. D. H. Cole (London: J. M. Dent; Rutland, Vt.: C. E. Tuttle, 1993), pp. 91–92, 96–97, 99.

23. Auguste Comte, *The Positive Philosophy*, translated by Harriet Martineau, Vol. 2 (London: George Bell & Sons, 1896), p. 98.

24. The key prophecies are in Revelation, Chapter 20, and Daniel, Chapter 2.

25. On many readings, the "beast" in Revelation is the Roman empire (on other readings, the emperor Nero, or even Nero revived), and much of the book's symbolism likewise refers to real individuals and events in the contemporary Roman world; see Ernest Lee Tuveson, *Millennium and Utopia: A Study in the Background of the Idea of Progress* (New York: Harper & Row, 1964). Similarly, the last of the four earthly kingdoms whose downfall is prophesied in Daniel is usually taken to be Rome.

26. See again Tuveson, *Millennium and Utopia*, and also *Redeemer Nation: The Idea of America's Millennial Role* (Chicago: University of Chicago Press, 1968).

27. The most prominent exception during this long period was Joachim of Fiore, a late-twelfth-century monk who offered a new interpretation of the apocalypse and millennium that, as in pre-Augustinian thinking, did refer to the temporal world. Subsequently Joachim had his followers, and others too offered their own views along these lines, although none achieved Joachim's prominence. See Bernard McGinn, *Visions of the End: Apocalyptic Traditions in the Middle Ages* (New York: Columbia University Press, 1976).

28. Among Christian thinkers, the idea of progressive decline followed in large part from St. Cyprian, who in the third century envisioned the earth as experiencing what amounted to a kind of exhaustion from old age (there are some resonances to today's environmental concerns about irreversible pollution, global warming, depletion of nonrenewable resources, and the like, although damage attributable to human activity is not what Cyprian had in mind), and also extended this notion to a decline of the moral order.

29. Tuveson, *Millennium and Utopia*, p. 25.

30. See again ibid. and Tuveson, *Redeemer Nation*.

31. James H. Moorhead, *World Without End: Mainstream American Protestant Visions of the Last Things, 1880–1925* (Bloomington: Indiana University Press, 1999), p. 44.

32. Tuveson, *Redeemer Nation*, p. 33.

33. As Hans Frei pointed out, during approximately the same period a change also took place in how people understood the Bible as a frame of reference for thinking about the temporal world: "the earlier situation was now exactly reversed. Then, historical judgment had been no more than a function of the literal (or sometimes figurative) sense of a narrative passage; now, on the contrary, the sense of such a passage came to depend on the estimate of its historical claims, character, and origin. . . . In its own right and by itself the biblical story began to fade." Hans W. Frei, *The Eclipse of Biblical Narrative: A Study in Eighteenth and Nineteenth Century Hermeneutics* (New Haven: Yale University Press, 1974), pp. 41, 50.

34. See George M. Marsden, *Jonathan Edwards: A Life* (New Haven: Yale University Press, 2003), Chapters 3 and 4, especially pp. 48, 70.

35. Tuveson, *Millennium and Utopia*, especially p. 132. See also the discussion of Edwards's works, especially *The History of the Work of Redemption* and his later *An Humble Attempt to Promote an Explicit Agreement and Visible Union of God's People thro' the World, in Extraordinary Prayer for the Revival of Religion, and the Advancement of Christ's Kingdom on Earth, Pursuant to Scripture Promise and Prophecies Concerning the Last Time*, in Marsden, *Jonathan Edwards*.

36. Moorhead, *World Without End*, p. 2.

37. See, for example, Clarendon's 1674 essay "Of the Reverence Due to Antiquity," cited in Tuveson, *Millennium and Utopia*, pp. 108–9.

38. Moorhead, *World Without End*, p. 8. For discussions of millennialism more generally, including in particular the distinction between premillennialism and postmillennialism, see also William R. Hutchison, "Review" of Moorhead, *World Without End*, *Church History* 70 (June 2001): 389–90; and Charles H. Lippy, "Millennialism and Adventism," in Charles H. Lippy and Peter W. Williams (eds.), *Encyclopedia of the American Religious Experience: Studies of Traditions and Movements*, Vol. 2 (New York: Scribner, 1988).

39. See Marsden, *Jonathan Edwards*, especially Chapter 20; quotation from p. 69.

40. Tuveson, *Millennium and Utopia*, p. x.

41. Richard Baxter, *A Holy Commonwealth* (1674), cited in Tuveson, *Redeemer Nation*, pp. 35–37.

42. Edwards, *History of the Work of Redemption*, cited in Tuveson, *Redeemer Nation*, p. 54.

43. Charles Webster, *The Great Instauration: Science, Medicine and Reform, 1626–1660* (London: Duckworth, 1975), p. xiii.

44. Robert King Merton, *Science, Technology and Society in Seventeenth Century England* (New York: H. Fertig, 1970). In America, where the Puritan clergy were typically the most educated citizens, the local minister was often the interpreter of new scientific developments to the community; see Marsden, *Jonathan Edwards*, Chapter 4.

45. Nisbet, *History of the Idea of Progress*, Chapter 5.

46. Ibid., p. 67.

47. Tuveson, *Redeemer Nation*, p. 39.

48. It was especially so to those like Adam Smith and David Hume, who, following Locke, thought of property ownership as essential to what makes a complete human being.

49. Whether productivity and living standards would continue to rise without limit was another matter. See, for example, Robert L. Heilbroner, "The Paradox of Progress: Decline and Decay in *The Wealth of Nations*," in Andrew S. Skinner and Thomas Wilson (eds.), *Essays on Adam Smith* (Oxford: Clarendon Press, 1975).

50. Jerry Z. Muller, *Adam Smith in His Time and Ours: Designing the Decent Society* (New York: Free Press, 1993), especially p. 164.

51. See, for example, the account in Liah Greenfeld, *The Spirit of Capitalism: Nationalism and Economic Growth* (Cambridge: Harvard University Press, 2001), Chapter 1. As Istvon Hont and Michael Ignatieff have further pointed out, the argument for commerce advanced by Smith and his contemporaries was therefore also a defense of what amounted to modernity against the Christian ideal of communal goods, as well as the classical humanist ideal in which slaves did all the work; see the introductory essay in Istvan Hont and Michael Ignatieff (eds.), *Wealth and Virtue: The Shaping of Political Economy in the Scottish Enlightenment* (Cambridge: Cambridge University Press, 1983). The emphasis on the advent of commerce as the dividing line between the premodern and the modern first gained currency in the writings of Dugald Stewart, who lectured on Smith's *Wealth of Nations* in Edinburgh beginning in the 1790s.

52. See Muller, *Adam Smith in His Time and Ours*, for an extended discussion of the connection between *The Wealth of Nations* and *The Theory of Moral Sentiments*. Also see Emma Rothschild, *Economic Sentiments: Adam Smith, Condorcet, and the Enlightenment* (Cambridge: Harvard University Press, 2001), Chapter 1, and, again, Meek, *Social Science and the Ignoble Savage*.

53. See Albert O. Hirschman's classic discussion of these intellectual developments in *The Passions and the Interests: Political Arguments for Capitalism Before Its Triumph* (Princeton: Princeton University Press, 1977).

54. William Letwin, *The Origins of Scientific Economics: English Economic Thought, 1660–1776* (London: Methuen, 1963), p. 93.

55. Christopher Lasch, *The True and Only Heaven: Progress and Its Critics* (New York: Norton, 1991), p. 52.

56. See the account in Albert O. Hirschman, "Rival Interpretations of Market Society: Civilizing, Destructive, or Feeble?," *Journal of Economic Literature* 20 (December 1982): 1463–84.

57. Montesquieu, *Spirit of the Laws*, p. 338.

58. Cited in Nisbet, *History of the Idea of Progress*, p. 177.

59. Cited in Arthur Herman, *How the Scots Invented the Modern World: The True Story of How Western Europe's Poorest Nation Created Our World and Everything in It* (New York: Crown, 2001), p. 99.

60. Thomas Paine, *The Rights of Man* (New York: Dutton, 1951), p. 215.

61. This idea too stems from Locke. In Mansfield's trenchant summary, under commerce "The 'quarrelsome and contentious' are diverted from politics to the making of money, where much of their political ambition can be satisfied. This is good for them and others. . . . Let the contentious engage in the bloodless killing of commerce." Harvey C. Mansfield, Jr., *The Spirit of Liberalism* (Cambridge: Harvard University Press, 1978), p. 10.

62. See Daniel Yergin, *The Prize: The Epic Quest for Oil, Money and Power* (New York: Simon & Schuster, 1991), for a comprehensive account of the pivotal

role that the desire to control oil resources has played in international conflict since the nineteenth century.

63. Thomas Friedman, for example, has advanced the theory that two countries will not go to war with each other if each has at least one McDonald's restaurant; Thomas L. Friedman, *The Lexus and the Olive Tree* (New York: Farrar, Straus & Giroux, 1999).

64. See again Hirschman, "Rival Interpretations of Market Society."

65. Antoine Barnave, *Power, Property, and History: Barnave's Introduction to the French Revolution and Other Writings*, translated by Emanuel Chill (New York: Harper & Row, 1971), p. 80; also cited in Meek, *Social Science and the Ignoble Savage*, p. 228.

66. See Meek, *Smith, Marx and After*, for a further elaboration of this argument.

67. Max Weber, *The Protestant Ethic and the Spirit of Capitalism*, translated by Talcott Parsons (London: George Allen & Unwin, 1930), and Michael Walzer, *Revolution of the Saints: A Study in the Origins of Radical Politics* (Cambridge: Harvard University Press, 1965). Weber's claims have generated heated controversy virtually from the time they were published. For a sample of differing views on the "Protestant ethic controversy," see, for example, Richard H. Tawney, *Religion and the Rise of Capitalism: A Historical Study* (New York: Harcourt Brace, 1926); Hugh R. Trevor-Roper, *Religion, the Reformation and Social Change, and Other Essays* (London: Bowes & Bowes, 1963); S. N. Eisenstadt (ed.), *The Protestant Ethic and Modernization: A Comparative View* (New York: Basic Books, 1968); Kurt Samuelsson, *Religion and Economic Action*, translated by E. Geoffrey French (New York: Basic Books, 1961); Daniel Bell, *The Cultural Contradictions of Capitalism* (New York: Basic Books, 1976); Greenfeld, *The Spirit of Capitalism*; and Philip S. Gorski, *The Disciplinary Revolution: Calvinism and the Rise of the State in Early Modern Europe* (Chicago: University of Chicago Press, 2003). Examples of more empirically oriented recent work on this set of questions are Philip S. Gorski, "The Little Divergence," in William H. Swatos, Jr., and Lutz Kaelber (eds.), *The Protestant Ethic Turns 100* (Boulder: Paradigm, 2005), and especially Robert Barro and Rachel M. McCleary, "Religion and Economic Growth Across Countries," *American Sociological Review* 68 (October 2003): 760–81.

68. In contrast to the later image created by Puritan preachers (among others), however, Calvin meant the doctrine of predestination to be comforting, not exhortatory, and he was concerned that "double predestination" (the determination not just of who is saved but also who is condemned to eternal damnation) *not* be proclaimed from the pulpit as a way of frightening people. The point was grace, not condemnation. He also chided his readers not to speculate on who is among the elect and who is not. See John T. McNeill (ed.), *Calvin: Institutes of the Christian Religion*, translated by Ford Lewis Battles (Philadelphia: Westminster Press, 1960), Chapters XXI–XXIV,

especially pp. 922–23, 926–29. See also William James Bouwsma, *John Calvin: A Sixteenth Century Portrait* (New York: Oxford University Press, 1988), especially pp. 36, 173.

69. *The Westminster Confession of Faith*, Great Commission Publication, 1997, p. 6 (also cited in Weber, *The Protestant Ethic*, p. 100).

70. John Calvin, *Commentary on Exodus*, 11:2, translated in Bouwsma, *John Calvin*, p. 196.

71. John Calvin, *Commentary on Genesis*, 39:1, translated in Bouwsma, *John Calvin*, p. 96.

72. They also continue to distinguish Americans' opinions from how others view the world. For example, data from the World Values Survey show that 60 percent of Americans, but only 26 percent of Europeans, think "the poor are lazy." Conversely, 54 percent of Europeans, but only 30 percent of Americans, believe "luck determines income." Alberto Alesina, Edward Glaeser, and Bruce Sacerdote, "Why Doesn't the United States Have a European-Style Welfare State?," *Brookings Papers on Economic Activity* (No. 2, 2001), Table 13, p. 243.

73. In Daniel Bell's apt phrase, a calling is "a moral obligation that projects religious behavior onto the everyday world." Bell, *Cultural Contradictions of Capitalism*, p. 288.

74. Weber, *The Protestant Ethic*, p. 80.

75. Cotton Mather, *A Christian at His Calling* (1701), cited by Greenfeld, *The Spirit of Capitalism*, p. 375.

76. See David Walker Howe, *The Making of the American Self: Jonathan Edwards to Abraham Lincoln* (Cambridge: Harvard University Press, 1997).

77. Walzer, *Revolution of the Saints*, p. 10, italics in original.

78. Ibid., Chapter 1.

79. See, for example, E. Digby Baltzell, *Puritan Boston and Quaker Philadelphia: Two Protestant Ethics and the Spirit of Class Authority and Leadership* (New York: Free Press, 1979), p. 44, italics in original.

80. Quoted in John E. Adair, *Founding Fathers: The Puritans in England and America* (London: J. M. Dent, 1982), p. 266.

81. See Walzer, *Revolution of the Saints*, Chapter 4; see also Perry Miller, "The Puritan Way of Life," in Perry Miller and Thomas H. Johnson, *The Puritans* (New York: American Book Company, 1938).

82. Samuel Eliot Morison, *The Founding of Harvard College* (Cambridge: Harvard University Press, 1935).

83. John Adams, "Dissertation on the Canon and the Feudal Law" (1765), in *The Works of John Adams* (Boston: Charles C. Little and James Brown, 1851), Vol. III, p. 448; also cited in Tuveson, *Redeemer Nation*, p. 21.

84. Samuel Hopkins, *A Treatise on the Millennium* (1793), p. 40; cited in Tuveson, *Redeemer Nation*, p. 60. Also see Marsden, *Jonathan Edwards*.

85. John Calvin, *Commentary on Matthew*, 25:20, translated in Bouwsma, *John Calvin*, pp. 197–98.

86. John Calvin, *Commentary on Genesis*, 23:16, translated in Bouwsma, *John Calvin*, p. 197.

87. Tawney, *Religion and the Rise of Capitalism*, p. 105.

88. See, for example, Joyce O. Appleby, *Economic Thought and Ideology in Seventeenth-Century England* (Princeton: Princeton University Press, 1978), Chapter 7. Interestingly, Appleby places this development in the context of "a new argument for economic freedom." Another example is Liah Greenfeld, who does not push the awareness of growth as far back as Appleby but nonetheless argues that "when the Industrial Revolution began, the British economy was already consciously oriented to . . . sustained growth"; Greenfeld, *The Spirit of Capitalism*, p. 58.

89. See again Heilbroner, "The Paradox of Progress," and several of the other essays in Skinner and Wilson (eds.), *Essays on Adam Smith*. As David Landes has argued more recently, only with the Industrial Revolution "for the first time in history, both the economy and knowledge were growing fast enough to generate a continuing flow of improvements"; Landes, *The Wealth and Poverty of Nations*, p. 187. Even Malthus, who lived until 1834, was unable to distinguish whether the increase he saw over his lifetime was the beginning of sustained growth or merely another "long cycle."

90. John Millar, *The Origin of Ranks* (1771), cited in Meek, *Social Science and the Ignoble Savage*, p. 163.

91. Adam Smith, *The Theory of Moral Sentiments*, edited by D. D. Raphael and A. L. MacFie (Oxford: Oxford University Press, 1976), p. 205.

92. Alexis de Tocqueville, *Democracy in America*, translated by Henry Reeve, Vol. 2 (New York: Vintage, 1990), p. 106.

93. James S. Coleman, *Foundations of Social Theory* (Cambridge: Harvard University Press, 1990); Robert D. Putnam, Robert Leonardi, and Raffaella Y. Nanetti, *Making Democracy Work: Civic Traditions in Modern Italy* (Princeton: Princeton University Press, 1993); and Robert D. Putnam, *Bowling Alone: The Collapse and Revival of American Community* (New York: Simon & Schuster, 2000).

94. Putnam's preferred explanation is the advent of television; see Putnam, *Bowling Alone*.

CHAPTER 3
Crosscurrents: The Age of Improvement and Beyond

1. Thomas Babington Macaulay, *The History of England: From the Accession of James the Second* (London: Macmillan, 1913), Vol. 1, p.2.

2. "Smith . . . attempted to subsume technological change under the rubric of of the extension of the division of labor"; Peter McNamara, *Political Economy and Statesmanship: Smith, Hamilton, and the Foundations of the Commercial Republic* (DeKalb: Northern Illinois University Press, 1998), p. 131. By

contrast, Alexander Hamilton apparently did understand the notion of economic growth in something approximately like the modern sense, including the important role of technology. See Liah Greenfeld, *The Spirit of Capitalism: Nationalism and Economic Growth* (Cambridge: Harvard University Press, 2001), especially p. 395, as well as Ron Chernow, *Alexander Hamilton* (New York: Penguin, 2004).

3. Adam Smith, *An Inquiry into the Nature and Causes of the Wealth of Nations*, edited by Edwin Cannan (New York: Modern Library, 1937), pp. 4–5.

4. David S. Landes, *The Wealth and Poverty of Nations: Why Some Are So Rich and Some So Poor* (New York: Norton, 1999), p. 188.

5. Data on textile production are from Phyllis Deane and W. A. Cole, *British Economic Growth, 1688–1959, Trends and Structures* (Cambridge: Cambridge University Press, 1962), p. 213, Table 53.

6. Data on pig iron production are from B. R. Mitchell, *Abstract of British Historical Statistics* (Cambridge: Cambridge University Press, 1962), p. 131, Table 2-A.

7. Data on London's population are from Ben Weinreb and Christopher Hibbert, *The London Encyclopedia* (London: Macmillan, 1983), p. 614.

8. Peter Laslett, *The World We Have Lost* (London: Methuen, 1965).

9. Smith, *The Wealth of Nations*, pp. 734–35.

10. Ibid., p. 735.

11. Ibid., pp. 735, 738, 740.

12. In fact, Scotland had long had something very much like the school system Smith described. (The pre-union Scottish parliament passed its first statute creating a national system of education in 1640, and in 1696 the famous Act for Setting Schools went on to establish a school in every parish in Scotland that did not yet have one.) England did not. At the time Smith wrote, literacy in England lagged far behind that in Scotland. In some respects, therefore, Smith's recommendation was simply an extension of what he had known as a boy growing up in Kirkcaldy, across the Firth of Forth from Edinburgh.

13. See, for example, the discussion in Michael J. Sandel, *Democracy's Discontents: America in Search of a Public Philosophy* (Cambridge: Harvard University Press, 1996), Chapter 6.

14. Frederick Jackson Turner, "The Significance of the Frontier in American History," in *Annual Report of the American Historical Association*, 1893.

15. Abraham Lincoln, "Speech at Kalamazoo, Michigan," cited by Sandel, *Democracy's Discontents*, p. 182.

16. Smith, *The Wealth of Nations*, p. 822; Lincoln, "Speech at New Haven, Connecticut," cited in Sandel, *Democracy's Discontents*, p. 182.

17. See the account of Turgot's writings in Sidney Pollard, *The Idea of Progress: History and Society* (New York: Basic Books, 1968), pp. 76–77.

18. Helvetius, *On the Law* (1758), cited in Ronald L. Meek, *Social Science*

and the Ignoble Savage (Cambridge: Cambridge University Press, 1976), pp. 92–93; italics in original.

19. Asa Briggs, *The Age of Improvement* (New York: David McKay, 1962), pp. 395–96.

20. The supporters of America's new manufacturing industries—Hamilton early on, and then the Whigs, who likewise favored canals, turnpikes, and other "internal improvements" that made manufacturing more economic—instead saw these new industries as a vehicle for upward mobility. See again Chernow, *Hamilton*, and Greenfeld, *The Spirit of Capitalism.* See also David Herbert Donald, *Lincoln* (New York: Simon & Schuster, 1995), especially p. 76.

21. Tocqueville, *Democracy in America,* translated by Henry Reeve (New York: Vintage, 1990), Vol. 2, p. 158.

22. Ibid., p. 159. In modern times, economic historian Douglass North has likewise argued that economic specialization and division of labor create divergent perceptions of reality and thereby weaken a society's commitment to common ideologies and social norms; see, for example, Douglass C. North, "Institutions, Transaction Costs and Economic Growth," *Economic Inquiry* 25 (July 1987): 419–28.

23. Tocqueville, *Democracy in America*, Vol. 2, pp. 160–61.

24. The International Labor Organization's convention on child care is the most rapidly expanding ILO convention. Even so, there remains much room for improvement. See the 2002 ILO report, *A Future Without Child Labor: Global Report Under the Follow-up to the ILO Declaration on Fundamental Principles and Rights at Work.* Also see the surveys of the recent literature on child labor by Kaushik Basu, "Child Labor: Causes, Consequences and Cures, with Remarks on International Labor Standards," *Journal of Economic Literature* 37 (September 1999): 1083–1119, and Drusilla Brown, Alan V. Deardorff, and Robert M. Stern, "Child Labor: Theory, Evidence, and Policy," in Kaushik Basu et al. (eds.), *International Labor Standards: History, Theory and Policy Options* (Malden, Mass.: Blackwell, 2003).

25. Laslett, *The World We Have Lost.*

26. Charles Dickens, *Hard Times* (London: Methuen, 1987), p. 280.

27. John Ruskin, *Modern Painters* (1846), cited in Robert W. Hill, Jr., *Tennyson's Poetry: Authoritative Texts, Contexts, Criticism,* 2nd ed. (New York: Norton, 1999), p. 199.

28. John Stuart Mill, *Principles of Political Economy: With Some of Their Applications to Social Philosophy* (Fairfield, Conn.: Augustus M. Kelley, 1976), p. 748.

29. See Christopher Lasch, *The True and Only Heaven: Progress and Its Critics* (New York: Norton, 1991), Chapter 3.

30. Pollard, *The Idea of Progress*, provides numerous examples.

31. Karl Marx and Friedrich Engels, *Communist Manifesto* (London: Junius, 1996), p. 16.

32. Karl Marx, *Critique of the Gotha Programme* (New York: International Publishers, 1938), pp. 10, 3.

33. As Tuveson has pointed out, "It was no accident, perhaps, that Marx was writing when millennialism was particularly strong in both Britain and the United States." Ernest Lee Tuveson, *Redeemer Nation: The Idea of America's Millennial Role* (Chicago: University of Chicago Press, 1968), p. 51.

34. Macaulay, *History of England*, Vol. 1, p. 2.

35. Ibid., p. 420.

36. Lord Macaulay, "Sir James Mackintosh," in *Critical, Historical, and Miscellaneous Essays* (New York: Hurd and Houghton, 1878), Vol. 3, p. 272; also cited in Jerome Buckley, *The Triumph of Time: A Study of the Victorian Concepts of Time, History, Progress and Decadence* (Cambridge: Harvard University Press, 1966), p. 39 (emphasis added).

37. Macaulay, "Southey's Colloquies on Society," in *Essays*, Vol. 2, p. 183; cited in Buckley, *The Triumph of Time*, p. 35.

38. George Bancroft, *History of the United States: From the Discovery of the Continent* (New York: Appleton, 1882), Vol. 1, pp. 1–3.

39. Ibid., p. 3.

40. Alfred Marshall, *Principles of Economics*, 9th ed. (London: Macmillan, 1961), pp. 3–4.

41. *Presbyterian Quarterly Review* 2 (1853): 417–18; cited in Tuveson, *Redeemer Nation*, pp. 75–76.

42. Samuel Hopkins, *A Treatise on the Millennium* (1793), cited in James H. Moorhead, *World Without End: Mainstream American Protestant Visions of the Last Things, 1880–1925* (Bloomington: Indiana University Press, 1999), p. 9. Also see George M. Marsden, *Jonathan Edwards: A Life* (New Haven: Yale University Press, 2003).

43. See Tuveson, *Redeemer Nation*, Chapter 3.

44. Moorhead, *World Without End*, p. 9.

45. Charles H. Lippy, "Millennialism and Adventism," in Charles H. Lippy and Peter W. Williams (eds.), *Encyclopedia of the American Religious Experience: Studies of Traditions and Movements*, Vol. 2 (New York: Scribner, 1988), especially p. 832.

46. See, for example, the discussion of this idea in Joseph Ellis, *Founding Brothers: The Revolutionary Generations* (New York: Knopf, 2001), especially p. 134.

47. See again Michael Walzer, *Revolution of the Saints: A Study in the Origin of Radical Politics* (Cambridge: Harvard University Press, 1965).

48. See, for example, Oscar Handlin and Mary Handlin, *The Dimensions of Liberty* (Cambridge: Harvard University Press, 1961), and the "Afterword" to Daniel Bell, *The Cultural Contradictions of Capitalism* (New York: Basic Books, 1996).

49. Walzer, *Revolution of the Saints*, p. 279.

50. Jonathan Edwards, *Some Thoughts Concerning the Present Revival of Religion* (1743). *Works of Jonathan Edwards*, Vol. 4, p. 353; cited in Marsden, *Jonathan Edwards*, p. 264. See also Marsden, *Jonathan Edwards*, pp. 197, 266, 316.

51. "If the American Revolution followed by constitution making was an Enlightenment project, the building of the new nation was a surprisingly evangelical project. . . . [T]he history of the early republic—its political divisions, moral crusades and economic development—is indissolubly linked with the spread of populist forms of evangelical religion." David Hempton, "Alternative Metaphors: Religion in Europe and America Since 1750," in Peter van Rooden, *New Perspectives on Secularization* (Amsterdam: University of Amsterdam Press, forthcoming), quotation from pp. 19, 27 in prepublication version.

52. See Albert K. Weinberg, *Manifest Destiny: A Study of Nationalist Expansionism in American History* (Baltimore: Johns Hopkins University Press, 1935), for a traditional account of the religious connotations of American Manifest Destiny.

53. Tuveson, *Redeemer Nation*, p. 46.

54. Herman Melville, *White-Jacket* (1850), cited in Tuveson, *Redeemer Nation*, pp. 156–57 (italics in original).

55. Oliver Wendell Holmes, Jr., serving as a young officer in the 20th Massachusetts Volunteer Regiment, wrote of the war as "the Christian Crusade of the 19th century. If one didn't believe that this was such a crusade . . . it would be hard to keep the hand to the sword." Letter to Charles Eliot Norton, April 17, 1864, in Marc De Wolfe Howe (ed.), *Touched with Fire: Civil War Letters and Diary of Oliver Wendell Holmes, Jr.* (New York: Fordham University Press, 2000), p. 122.

56. Proverbs 13:18.

57. Russell H. Conwell, *Acres of Diamonds* (New York: Harper, 1915), p. 21.

58. William Lawrence, "The Relation of Wealth to Morals," *The World's Work* 1 (January 1901): 287.

59. Conwell, *Acres of Diamonds*, p. 17.

60. Ibid., p. 18.

61. Ibid., p. 19.

62. In the meanwhile, throughout the nineteenth century premillennialism had retained its appeal in more populist evangelical circles, occasionally giving rise to spectacular prophecies and mass popular responses like the Millerite movement of 1843–44. Groups like the Mormons, the Seventh-day Adventists, the Sabbatarians, and the Jehovah's Witnesses all grew out of this premillennialist fervor. See Lippy, "Millennialism and Adventism."

63. Tuveson, *Redeemer Nation*, p. 136.

64. T. H. Huxley, "Evolution and Ethics," in T. H. Huxley and Julian Huxley,

Evolution and Ethics (London: Pilot Press, 1947), pp. 79–80; also cited in Buckley, *The Triumph of Time*, p. 56.

65. Norman Angell, *The Great Illusion: A Study of the Relation of Military Power in Nations to Their Economic and Social Advantage* (New York: G. P. Putnam's Sons, 1911), p. vii.

66. Ibid., p. ix.

67. Paul Fussell, *The Great War and Modern Memory* (New York: Oxford University Press, 1975), pp. 8, 169.

68. Alvin H. Hansen, "Economic Progress and Declining Population," *American Economic Review* 29 (March 1939), pp. 1–15. An analysis by the National Resources Committee, *The Problems of a Changing Population* (Washington, D.C.: Government Printing Office, 1938), put forth the same theme.

69. Edward Gibbon, *The History of the Decline and Fall of the Roman Empire* (New York: Modern Library, 1932), Vol. 2, p. 1440.

70. See, for example, Walter Lippmann, *Essays in the Public Philosophy* (Boston: Little, Brown, 1955); see also David M. Potter, *People of Plenty: Economic Abundance and the American Character* (Chicago: University of Chicago Press, 1954).

71. Daniel Bell, *The Cultural Contradictions of Capitalism* (New York: Basic Books, 1976), pp. 237–38.

72. That message is unmistakable, for example, in the 1960s television series *Star Trek*.

73. Bell, *The Cultural Contradictions of Capitalism*.

74. Gabriel Almond et al. (eds.), *Prosperity and Its Discontents* (Berkeley: University of California Press, 1982), p. ix.

75. See, for example, Gertrude Himmelfarb, *The De-Moralization of Society: From Victorian Virtues to Modern Values* (New York: Knopf, 1995). Similar themes are evident in works of fiction like Tom Wolfe, *The Bonfire of the Vanities* (New York: Farrar, Straus & Giroux, 1987).

CHAPTER 4

Rising Incomes, Individual Attitudes, and the Politics of Social Change

1. Alfred Marshall, *Principles of Economics*, 9th ed. (London: Macmillan, 1961), Vol. 1, p. 135.

2. John Stuart Mill, "On Social Freedom," *Oxford and Cambridge Review* (June 1907): 69. Mill went on, "The avaricious or covetous man would find little or no satisfaction in the possession of any amount of wealth, if he were the *poorest* amongst all his neighbors or fellow-countrymen" (italics in the original).

3. Dirk Johnson, "Facing Shortage, Builders and Labor Court Workers," *New York Times*, March 13, 1999, p. A1.

4. See Daniel Kahneman and Dale T. Miller, "Norm Theory: Comparing Reality to Its Alternatives," *Psychological Review* 93 (April 1986): 136–53.

5. See, for example, the reviews of this survey evidence in Ruut Veenhoven et al., *World Database of Happiness: Correlates of Happiness* (Rotterdam: Erasmus University, 1994), and Michael Argyle, "Causes and Correlates of Happiness," in Daniel Kahneman, Edward Diener, and Norbert Schwartz (eds.), *Well-Being: The Foundations of Hedonic Psychology* (New York: Russell Sage Foundation, 1999), and the overview in Robert E. Lane, "Does Money Buy Happiness," *Public Interest* 113 (Fall 1993): 56–65. Also see Ruut Veenhoven, *Conditions of Happiness* (Boston: D. Reidel, 1984), and Tibor Scitovsky, *The Joyless Economy: An Inquiry into Human Satisfaction and Consumer Dissatisfaction* (New York: Oxford University Press, 1976).

6. See Norval D. Glenn and Charles N. Weaver, "A Multivariate, Multisurvey Study of Marital Happiness," *Journal of Marriage and the Family* 40 (May 1978): 269–82; Ronald Inglehart, *Culture Shift in Advanced Industrial Society* (Princeton: Princeton University Press, 1990); and again Argyle, "Causes and Correlates of Happiness."

7. See Michael Argyle and Luo Lu, "The Happiness of Extraverts," *Personality and Individual Differences* 11 (No. 10, 1990): 1011–17, and Ed Diener and Robert Lucas, "Personality and Subjective Well-Being," in Kahneman et al. (eds.), *Well-Being*.

8. See again Argyle, "Causes and Correlates of Happiness." Also see Edward L. Glaeser, David Laibson, and Bruce Sacerdote, "An Economic Approach to Social Capital," *Economic Journal* 112 (November 2002): F437–F458.

9. See the survey data reported, for example, in Richard A. Easterlin, "Does Economic Growth Improve the Human Lot? Some Empirical Evidence," in Paul A. David and Melvin W. Reder (eds.), *Nations and Households in Economic Growth: Essays in Honor of Moses Abramowitz* (New York: Academic Press, 1974); Ed Diener, Ed Sandvik, Larry Seidlitz, and Marissa Diener, "The Relationship Between Income and Subjective Well-Being: Relative or Absolute?," *Social Indicators Research* 28 (March 1993): 195–223; and Andrew J. Oswald and David Blanchflower, "Well-Being over Time in Britain and the USA" (National Bureau of Economic Research, Working Paper 7487, 2000). Also see the reviews of this literature in Veenhoven et al., *World Database of Happiness;* Argyle, "Causes and Correlates of Happiness"; and Bruno S. Frey and Alois Stutzer, "What Can Economists Learn from Happiness Research?," *Journal of Economic Literature* 40 (June 2002): 402–35.

10. See, for example, David T. Lykken and Auke Tellingen, "Happiness Is a Stochastic Phenomenon," *Psychological Science* 7 (May 1996): 186–89.

11. Ronald Inglehart, a political scientist who describes this phenomenon as "adjusting one's aspirations," provides some detailed evidence for it from public opinion surveys; see Inglehart, *Culture Shift in Advanced Industrial Society*, Chapter 7. Following James Duesenberry and George Constanti-

nides, most economists today simply call it "habit formation"; see James S. Duesenberry, *Income, Saving and the Theory of Consumer Behavior* (Cambridge: Harvard University Press, 1949), and George M. Constantinides, "Habit Formation: A Resolution of the Equity Premium Puzzle," *Journal of Political Economy* 98 (June 1990): 519–43. Also see evidence provided in numerous studies by Bernard Van Praag, most recently Bernard Van Praag and Ada Ferrer-i-Carbonell, *Happiness Quantified: A Satisfaction Calculus Approach* (Oxford: Oxford University Press, 2004). Also see the overview in Shane Frederick and George Loewenstein, "Hedonic Adaptation," in Kahneman et al. (eds.), *Well-Being*. Also see again Scitovsky, *The Joyless Economy.*

12. See David Herbert Donald, *Lincoln* (New York: Simon & Schuster, 1995), p. 547.

13. See Stephen Smith and Peter Razzell, *The Pools Winners* (London: Caliban, 1975); Philip Brickman, Dan Coates, and Ronnie Janoff-Bulman, "Lottery Winners and Accident Victims: Is Happiness Relative?," *Journal of Personality and Social Psychology* 36 (August 1978): 917–27; Jonathan Gardner and Andrew Oswald, "Does Money Buy Happiness? A Longitudinal Study Using Data on Windfalls" (unpublished paper, Warwick University, 2001); and Martin Seligman, *Authentic Happiness* (New York: Free Press, 2002).

14. Adam Smith, *An Inquiry into the Nature and Causes of the Wealth of Nations*, edited by Edwin Cannan (New York: Modern Library, 1937), p. 81.

15. Oliver Wendell Holmes, Jr., "The Path of the Law," *Harvard Law Review*, 10 (March 25, 1897): 457–78, quotation from p. 477.

16. Alexis de Tocqueville, *Democracy in America*, translated by Henry Reeve (New York: Vintage, 1990), Vol. 2, p. 155.

17. See Daniel Kahneman and Amos Tversky, "Prospect Theory: An Analysis of Decision Under Risk," *Econometrica* 47 (March 1979): 263–92; "Choices, Values, and Frames," *American Psychologist* 39 (April 1984): 341–50; and "Loss Aversion in Riskless Choice: A Reference-Dependent Model," *Quarterly Journal of Economics* 106 (November 1991): 1039–61.

18. This attitude has important implications for the relative returns on stocks and bonds, as well as for asset pricing in general. See Shlomo Benartzi and Richard H. Thaler, "Myopic Loss Aversion and the Equity Premium Puzzle," *Quarterly Journal of Economics* 110 (February 1995): 73–92, and the subsequent literature of asset pricing under loss aversion.

19. Kahneman and Tversky, "Prospect Theory."

20. See William Samuelson and Richard Zeckhauser, "Status Quo Bias in Decision Making," *Journal of Risk and Uncertainty* 1 (March 1988): 7–59.

21. A classic way to demonstrate this reaction to a roomful of people is to give half of them some small object, like a souvenir pen or coffee mug, and the other half an equivalent amount of money, and then hold an auction to establish the terms on which anyone who received the object can sell it to a

willing buyer from among those who initially received the cash. The surprising result—surprising not only because of the ready availability elsewhere of the object in question but also because of how short a time people have had it in their possession before being asked whether they are willing to sell it—is that few of the objects given out actually change hands in the auction. The reason is that the object has quickly become more valuable in the eyes of those who already have it than to those who are now contemplating buying it. See Richard H. Thaler, "Toward a Positive Theory of Consumer Choice," *Journal of Economic Behavior and Organization* 1 (March 1980): 39–60; Daniel Kahneman, Jack L. Knetsch, and Richard H. Thaler, "Experimental Tests of the Endowment Effect and Coase Theorem," *Journal of Political Economy* 98 (December 1990): 1325–48; and Richard H. Thaler, *The Winner's Curse: Paradoxes and Anomalies of Economic Life* (New York: Free Press, 1992), Chapter 6. A related phenomenon is that people who have won something in a lottery—Ronald Dworkin's example is tickets to the Wimbledon tennis championships—typically will not sell them, even for a price far above the level at which they would have been unwilling to buy them if they had not won them in the lottery; Ronald M. Dworkin, "Is Wealth a Value?," *Journal of Legal Studies* 9 (March 1980): 191–226. On the Woburn (Mass.) tragedy, see Jonathan Harr, *A Civil Action* (New York: Random House, 1995).

22. See Linda Babcock and George Lowenstein, "Explaining Bargaining Impasse: The Role of Self-Serving Biases," *Journal of Economic Perspective* 11 (Winter 1997): 106–26.

23. Voting patterns in U.S. elections, for example, reflect just this kind of asymmetry. Incumbent parties suffer during economic downturns to a far greater extent than they gain when business is strong. See, for example, Howard H. Bloom and Douglas Price, "Voter Response to Short Run Economic Conditions: The Asymmetric Effect of Prosperity and Recession," *American Political Science Review* 69 (December 1975): 1240–54.

24. For most people in the United States, the chief object of such comparisons is apparently not neighbors but co-workers. See Juliet B. Schor, *The Overspent American: Upscaling, Downshifting and the New Consumer* (New York: Basic Books, 1998).

25. This idea also is hardly new. In Marx's famous example, "A house may be large or small; as long as the surrounding houses are equally small it satisfies all social demands for a dwelling. But let a palace arise beside the little house, and it shrinks from a little house to a hut." Marx went on to generalize, "Our desires and pleasures spring from society; we measure them, therefore, by society and not by the objects which serve for their satisfaction. Because they are of a social nature, they are of a relative nature." Karl Marx, *Wage Labor and Capital*, in *Selected Writings* (New York: Oxford University Press, 1977), p. 259.

26. Poll data are reported in George H. Gallup, *The Gallup Poll: Public Opinion*,

1935–1971 (New York: Random House, 1972); George H. Gallup, *The Gallup Poll: Public Opinion, 1972–1977* (Wilmington, Del.: Scholarly Resources, 1978); and George Gallup, Jr., *The Gallup Poll: Public Opinion, 1986* (Wilmington: Scholarly Resources, 1987). Also see Robert H. Frank, *Choosing the Right Pond: Human Behavior and the Quest for Status* (New York: Oxford University Press, 1985), Table 2.3, p. 32.

27. Current data are from the Census Bureau; historical data are from Stanley Lebergott, *The American Economy: Income, Wealth and Want* (Princeton: Princeton University Press, 1976), p. 301.

28. The well-known failure of standard inflation indices to allow adequately for the introduction of new goods is yet another source of understatement; see, for example, Lebergott, *The American Economy*.

29. Amartya Sen, *Poverty and Famines: An Essay on Entitlement and Deprivation* (Oxford: Claredon Press, 1981), p. 12.

30. See, for example, Karl Marx, *Capital: A Critique of Political Economy*, translated by Ben Fowkes (London: Penguin, 1990), Vol. 1, p. 275.

31. See Constance F. Citro and Robert T. Michael (eds.), *Measuring Poverty: A New Approach* (Washington, D.C.: National Academy Press, 1995). See also A. B. Atkinson, "On the Measurement of Poverty," *Econometrica* 55 (July 1987): 749–64; Particia Ruggles, *Drawing the Line: Alternative Poverty Measures and their Implications for Public Policy* (Washington, D.C.: Urban Institute Press, 1990); and James E. Foster, "Absolute Versus Relative Poverty," *American Economic Review* 88 (May 1998): 335–41.

32. See Gordon M. Fisher, "Is There Such a Thing as an Absolute Poverty Line over Time? Evidence from the United States, Britain, Canada, and Australia on the Income Elasticity of the Poverty Line" (unpublished paper, U.S. Census Bureau, Poverty Measurement Working Papers Web site, 1995).

33. The poverty threshold (for 2004) is from the Census Bureau.

34. See Koji Taira, "Consumer Preferences, Poverty Norms and Extent of Poverty," *Quarterly Journal of Economics and Business* 9 (Summer 1969), Table 1, p. 37; also Scitovsky, *The Joyless Economy*, pp. 116–17.

35. David Landes cites numerous examples of the use of the word "decline" to describe this development; Landes, *The Wealth and Poverty of Nations: Why Some Are So Rich and Some So Poor* (New York: Norton, 1998), pp. 450–51.

36. In 1870, per capita income in the U.K. was nearly 3.7 times the world average at the time, compared to 2.8 times the world average in the United States and about 2.1 in both France and Germany. By the early 1970s, U.K. per capita income had "slipped" to 2.9 times the (now far greater) world average, the same as in Germany, while in the United States and France the ratio to the world average had risen to 4.1 and 3.2, respectively. Angus Maddison, *The World Economy: A Millennial Perspective* (Paris: OECD, 2001), Table B-21, p. 264.

37. A question that immediately arises in this kind of inquiry is whether the

concept of "happiness" translates well across different languages. Most researchers are satisfied that it does. See, for example, Alex Inkeles, "Industrial Man: The Relation of Status to Experience, Perception, and Value," *American Journal of Sociology* 66 (July 1960): 1-31, especially p. 15.

38. See Hadley Cantril, *The Pattern of Human Concerns* (New Brunswick, N.J.: Rutgers University Press, 1965), and Easterlin, "Does Economic Growth Improve the Human Lot," Table 6, p. 105.

39. Inglehart, *Culture Shift*, Figure 1-2, p. 32.

40. See Ruut Veenhoven, "Is Happiness Relative?," *Social Indicators Research* 24 (February 1991): 1–34; Ed Diener, Marissa Diener, and Carol Diener, "Factors Predicting the Subjective Well-Being of Nations," *Journal of Personality and Social Psychology* 69 (November 1995): 851–64; and Ronald Inglehart and Hans-Dieter Klingemann, "Genes, Culture, Democracy, and Happiness," in Ed Diener and Eunkook M. Suh (eds.) *Culture and Subjective Well-Being* (Cambridge: MIT Press, 2000). (These cross-country comparisons stand in contrast to the idea of local comparisons in Frank, *Choosing the Right Pond.*)

41. Support for the idea that the introduction of television is responsible for these changes also comes from the finding that, after controlling for such matters as income and health, the satisfaction with their lives reported by citizens of different developing countries is negatively related to the prevalence of TV, radio, and other communications devices. See Genevieve Wang, "Foreign Contact, Communication, and Exposure: A Study of Low Life Satisfaction in Developing Nations" (unpublished paper, Harvard University, 2003).

42. John Steinbeck, "Dreams Piped from Cannery Row," *New York Times*, November 27, 1955, section 2, p. 1.

43. Daniel Bell, "Models and Reality in Economic Discourse," in Daniel Bell and Irving Kristol (eds.), *The Crisis in Economic Theory* (New York: Basic Books, 1981). Moreover, according to Smith, man desires "not only praise, but praise-worthiness." See Adam Smith, *The Theory of Moral Sentiments*, edited by D. D. Raphael and A. L. MacFie (Oxford: Oxford University Press, 1976), pp. 113–34 (quotation from p. 114).

44. Thorstein Veblen, *The Theory of the Leisure Class* (New York: Penguin, 1994), p. 30; see also Duesenberry, *Income, Savings and the Theory of Consumer Behavior*, p. 28.

45. Veblen, *The Theory of the Leisure Class*, p. 102.

46. Smith, *The Wealth of Nations*, pp. 821–22.

47. Veblen, *The Theory of the Leisure Class*, p. 16.

48. Fred Hirsch, *Social Limits to Growth* (Cambridge: Harvard University Press, 1976). Smith too made much the same observation, at least with regard to the affluent. Referring to "the greater part of rich people," he noted that "In their eyes the merit of an object . . . is greatly enhanced by its scarcity. . . . Such objects they are willing to purchase at a higher price

than things much more beautiful and useful, but more common" (*The Wealth of Nations*, p. 172).

49. This idea bears a connection to the conceptual framework presented in Andrew B. Abel, "Asset Prices Under Habit Formation and Catching Up with the Joneses," *American Economic Review* 80 (May 1990): 38–42, but Abel does not apply it to this set of questions.

50. See, for example, Edward C. Banfield, *The Moral Basis of a Backward Society* (Glencoe, Ill.: Free Press, 1958); Gabriel A. Almond and Sidney Verba, *The Civic Culture: Political Attitudes and Democracy in Five Nations* (Princeton: Princeton University Press, 1963); and Robert D. Putnam, Robert Leonardi, and Raffaella Y. Nanetti, *Making Democracy Work: Civic Traditions in Modern Italy* (Princeton: Princeton University Press, 1993).

51. Decile values are calculated from Census Bureau data on the 2003 distribution of income by families.

52. See Peter Gottschalk, Robert Moffitt, Lawrence Katz, and William T. Dickens, "The Growth of Earning Instability in the US Labor Market," *Brookings Papers on Economic Activity* (No. 2, 1994), pp. 217–72, Table 1.

53. See again the studies reported in Diener et al., "The Relationship Between Income and Subjective Well-Being: Relative or Absolute?"; Easterlin, "Does Economy Growth Improve the Human Lot?"; and Lane, "Does Money Buy Happiness?"

54. See Samuel Stouffer, *The American Soldier* (Princeton: Princeton University Press, 1949); Robert K. Merton and Alice S. Rossi, "Contributions to the Theory of Reference Group Behavior," in Robert K. Merton, *Social Theory and Social Structure* (Glencoe, Ill.: Free Press, 1957); and the discussion of these findings in W. G. Runciman, *Relative Deprivation and Social Justice: A Study of Attitudes to Inequality in Twentieth-Century England* (London: Routledge & Kegan Paul, 1966).

55. William W. Freehling, *The Road to Disunion* (New York: Oxford University Press, 1990), p. 42.

56. Alexis de Tocqueville, *The Old Regime and the French Revolution*, translated by Stuart Gilbert (Garden City, N.Y.: Doubleday, 1955), pp. 88–89.

57. See Alberto Alesina, Rafael Di Tella, and Robert McCulloch, "Inequality and Happiness: Are Americans and Europeans Different?," *Journal of Public Economics* 88 (August 2004): 2009–42, and Alberto Alesina, Edward L. Glaeser, and Bruce Sacerdote, "Why Doesn't the United States Have a European-Style Welfare State?," *Brookings Papers on Economic Activity* (No. 2, 2001): 187–277, on differences between Americans and Europeans in this regard.

58. See, for example, Charles Murray, *Losing Ground: American Social Policy, 1950–1980* (New York: Basic Books, 1984).

59. John Kenneth Galbraith made a similar point in *The Affluent Society* (Boston: Houghton Mifflin, 1958), but here the focus is on growth, not the level of a society's living standard.

60. See again Putnam et al., *Making Democracy Work*, and Putnam, *Bowling Alone*, especially the emphasis on building what Putnam calls "norms and networks of social engagement."

61. See Kenneth A. Shepsle and Mark S. Boncheck, *Analyzing Politics: Rationality, Behavior, and Institutions* (New York: Norton, 1997), and Melvin J. Hinich and Michael C. Munger, *Analytical Politics* (Cambridge: Cambridge University Press, 1997).

62. See, for example, Frank R. Baumgartner and Beth L. Leech, *Basic Interests: The Importance of Groups in Politics and in Political Science* (Princeton: Princeton University Press, 1998).

63. See Benjamin Y. Page and Robert Y. Shapiro, *The Rational Public: Fifty Years of Trends in America's Policy Preferences* (Chicago: University of Chicago Press, 1992), and William G. Mayer, *The Changing American Mind: How and Why American Public Opinion Changed Between 1960 and 1988* (Ann Arbor: University of Michigan Press, 1992).

64. See Ronald Inglehart, "The Silent Revolution in Europe: Intergenerational Change in Post-Industrial Societies," *American Political Science Review* 65 (December 1971): 991–1017; Ronald Inglehart, *The Silent Revolution: Changing Values and Political Styles Among Western Publics* (Princeton: Princeton University Press, 1977); and Inglehart, *Culture Shift in Advanced Industrial Society*. Although the specifics have evolved over the years, the basic format of these surveys is to ask respondents to rank in importance a small number of suggested goals for their country. Some of these goals address concerns that are in the first instance matters of people's material well-being, while others refer to intangible concerns about the vitality of the society's democracy or the division of its resources between public and private uses. None of the listed goals is in itself controversial, and so most people will presumably be in favor of them all. The object of the survey is to see how people rank them against one another. See Inglehart, *Culture Shift in Advanced Industrial Society*, pp. 74–75, for the full list.

65. On the basis of this finding, Inglehart predicted that in time the rising percentage of European electorates consisting of voters born after the war would alter these countries' politics by enhancing the prominence attached to these "nonmaterialist" issues. Subsequent developments in many European countries—for example, the rise of Green parties in electoral politics—proved that prediction largely correct.

66. See Ingelhart, *Culture Shift in Advanced Industrial Society*, and Ronald Inglehart and Paul R. Abramson, "Economic Security and Value Change," *American Political Science Review* 88 (June 1994): 336–54. Also see Harry Eckstein, "A Culturalist Theory of Political Change," *American Political Science Review* 82 (September 1988): 789–804.

67. Ronald Inglehart, *Modernization and Postmodernization: Cultural, Economic and Political Change in 43 Societies* (Princeton: Princeton University Press, 1997), p. 31.

CHAPTER 5
From Horatio Alger to William Jennings Bryan

1. Alexis de Tocqueville, *Democracy in America*, translated by Henry Reeve (New York: Vintage, 1990), Vol. 2, pp. 129–30.
2. Ibid., pp. 136, 137, 153.
3. Data on hours worked in industrial countries are from the OECD (Organisation for Economic Cooperation and Development) and the International Labor Organization. Also see Juliet Schor, *The Overworked American: The Unexpected Decline of Leisure* (New York: Basic Books, 1991); Linda A. Bell and Richard B. Freeman, "The Incentive for Working Hard: Explaining Hours Worked Differences in the U.S. and Germany," *Labour Economics* 8 (May 2001): 181–202, and the sources on hours worked cited there; Robert H. Frank, *Microeconomics and Behavior* (Boston: McGraw-Hill, 2000), p. 49; and data from the Bureau of Labor Statistics.
4. See the evidence in Chinhui Juhn, Kevin M. Murphy, and Robert H. Topel, "Unemployment, Nonemployment and Wages: Why Has the Natural Rate Increased Through Time?," *Brookings Papers on Economic Activity* (No. 2, 1991), pp. 75–126; Chinhui Juhn, "The Decline in Male Labor Market Participation: The Role of Declining Market Opportunities," *Quarterly Journal of Economics* 107 (February 1992): 79–121; Dora L. Costa, "The Wage and the Length of the Work Day: From the 1890s to 1991," *Journal of Labor Economics* 18 (January 2000): 156–81; and John Pencavel, "A Cohort Analysis of the Association Between Work and Wages Among Men," *Journal of Human Resources* 37 (Spring 2002): 251–74. Costa shows that the wage rate–hours relationship has changed over time: a century ago the lowest-paid workers put in more hours than the highest-paid, but today the reverse is true.
5. Alexis de Tocqueville, *Democracy in America*, translated by Henry Reeve (New York: Vintage, 1945), Vol. 1, p. 3.
6. Daniel S. Landes, *The Wealth and Poverty of Nations: Why Some Are So Rich and Some So Poor* (New York: Basic Books, 1999), p. 296. (The visitor was Lord Adam Gordon.) Modern studies confirm that wealth-holding was much more equal in colonial America than in England and Wales at that time; see Alice Hanson Jones, *American Colonial Wealth: Documents and Methods* (New York: Arno, 1977); Alice Hanson Jones, *Wealth of a Nation to Be: The American Colonies on the Eve of the Revolution* (New York: Columbia University Press, 1980); and the discussion in Peter H. Lindert, "Three Centuries of Inequality in Britain and America," in A. B. Atkinson and Francois Bourguignon (eds.), *Handbook of Income Distribution*, Vol. 1 (Amsterdam: Elsevier Science, 2000).
7. David Herbert Donald, *Lincoln* (New York: Simon & Schuster, 1995), p. 202, citing Robert W. Johannsen (ed.), *The Lincoln-Douglas Debates of 1858* (New York: Oxford University Press, 1971).

8. See Jeffrey G. Williamson and Peter H. Lindert, *American Inequality: A Macroeconomic History* (New York: Academic Press, 1980), and the review of the evidence given in Peter Lindert, "Three Centuries of Inequality in Britain and America." For an earlier contrary view, however, see Lee C. Soltow, "Evidence on Income Inequality in the United States,1866–1965," *Journal of Economic History* 29 (June 1969): 279–86, and "Economic Inequality in the United States in the Period from 1790–1860," *Journal of Economic History* 31 (December 1971): 822–39.

9. See, for example, William W. Freehling, *The Road to Disunion* (New York: Oxford University Press, 1990), Chapter 12.

10. Gordon S. Wood, *The Radicalism of the American Revolution* (New York: Knopf, 1992), p. 234.

11. Tocqueville, *Democracy in America*, Vol. 2, p. 133.

12. Landes, *The Wealth and Poverty of Nations*, p. 297. Political scientist Liah Greenfeld further elaborated this view: "Equality became the standard for one's social position and aspirations. Theoretically, one was equal to all other members of society and measured oneself against them. In practice, this implied desire for parity only with those who were 'more equal' than the others and, as a result, a constant race, justified and spurred on by the supreme national ideal, for social superiority. . . . One was as good as anyone else, but there was always somebody who was doing better." Liah Greenfeld, *The Spirit of Capitalism: Nationalism and Economic Growth* (Cambridge: Harvard University Press, 2001), p. 366.

13. The Census Bureau publishes data on the foreign-born fraction of the United States population, including historical data back to 1850. For an investigation into data for earlier periods, see H. A. Gemery, "Immigration and Economic Growth in the Early National Period: Some Kuznets Questions" (unpublished paper, Colby College, 1990). In 2003, 11.7 percent of the American population was foreign-born.

14. Cited by Greenfeld, *The Spirit of Capitalism*, p. 376.

15. "Even the Puritans, dedicated as they were to the goal of exemplifying holiness on earth, early came to interpret prosperity as a measure of their ability to please God. Steps that added to the total store of goods were desirable as evidence of divine favor toward the community, just as the individual's acquisition of riches was a sign of his progress toward salvation." Oscar Handlin and Mary Handlin, *The Dimensions of Liberty* (Cambridge: Harvard University Press, 1961), p. 134. In a similar view, "From early on the proof of the Americans' election was seen in the material prosperity of the colonial society" (Greenfeld, *The Spirit of Capitalism*, p. 371).

16. See again Handlin and Handlin, *The Dimensions of Liberty*, p. 134.

17. See Ray C. Fair, "The Effect of Economic Events on the Vote for President," *Review of Economics and Statistics* 60 (May 1978): 159–73, together with Fair's series of quadrennial follow-up papers.

18. Robert Gallman and Thomas Berry have constructed estimates for U.S.

gross national product, in Gallman's case dating back to 1834 and in Berry's to 1789. Both series are generally regarded (and were regarded by their creators) as very rough, and neither has yet been published in the regular scholarly literature. See Robert E. Gallman, "Real GNP, Prices of 1860, 1834–1909" (unpublished paper, University of North Carolina), and Thomas Senior Berry, "Production and Population Since 1789: Revised GNP Series in Constant Dollars" (Bostwick Press, Bostwick Paper No. 6, 1988).

19. Income data are from Gallman, "Real GDP, Prices of 1860, 1834–1909"; Nathan S. Balke and Robert J. Gordon, "The Estimation of Prewar Gross Domestic Product: Methodology and New Evidence," *Journal of Political Economy* 97 (February 1989): 38–92; and the Bureau of Economic Analysis, National Income and Product Accounts. Population data are from Susan B. Carter et al. (eds.), *Historical Statistics of the United States* (Cambridge: Cambridge University Press, 1997), and the Census Bureau. Here and elsewhere "today's dollars" refers to 2004, the last year for which full-year data were available as of the time of writing.

20. Again see Williamson and Lindert, *American Inequality*, and Lindert, "Three Centuries of Inequality in Britain and America."

21. See Charles P. Kindleberger, *Manias, Panics and Crashes: A History of Financial Crisis* (New York: Basic Books, 1978), Chapter 14.

22. Data on U.S. real income during this period are Gallman's unpublished estimates. Data on U.S. population are from *Historical Statistics*. Using Balke and Gordon's estimates for real income instead of Gallman's makes the average 1869–80 increase 2.9 percent annum.

23. Both cited by Greenfeld, *The Spirit of Capitalism*, p. 428.

24. See Robert Muccigrosso, *Celebrating the New World: Chicago's Columbian Exhibition of 1893* (Chicago: Ivan R. Dee, 1993), Chapter 1; see also Robert W. Rydell and Nancy E. Gwinn (eds.), *Fair Representations: World's Fairs and the Modern World* (Amsterdam: VU University Press, 1994), and John Allwood, *The Great Exhibitions* (London: Studio Vista, 1977).

25. Horatio Alger, Jr., *Ragged Dick, or Street Life in New York with the Boot-blacks* (New York: Penguin, 1990), p. 77; Tocqueville, *Democracy in America*, Vol. 2, p. 152.

26. A further, more practical reason for the widespread appeal of Alger's stories is that in the 1870s New York City had thousands of homeless children, so that he was in fact addressing one of the central issues of the day. See George J. Lankevich and Howard B. Furer, *A Brief History of New York City* (Port Washington, N.Y.: Associated Faculty Press, 1984), p. 176.

27. Alger's title continued to resonate for many years, and not just in America. Anthony Burgess, in his 1962 novel, *The Wanting Seed*, referred to "the best of British luck and pluck." Anthony Burgess, *The Wanting Seed* (New York: Norton, 1962), p. 221.

28. See Theda Skocpol, *Protecting Soldiers and Mothers: The Political Origins of Social Policy in the United States* (Cambridge: Harvard University Press, 1992), Chapter 2, especially p. 118.

29. See Morton Keller, *Affairs of State: Public Life in Nineteenth Century America* (Cambridge: Harvard University Press, 1977), Chapters 4 and 5.

30. As a practical matter, post–Civil War civil rights legislation was also in part intended to prevent a large migration of freed blacks to the North, where they would compete for jobs against low-income whites. See Eric Foner, *Politics and Ideology in the Age of the Civil War* (New York: Oxford University Press, 1980), p. 97.

31. In addition to these achievements in national-level legislation, there was also some degree of black-white political cooperation, and even social cooperation, in the South. See C. Vann Woodward, *The Strange Career of Jim Crow* (New York: Oxford University Press, 1955), Chapter 1.

32. The underlying income data are again Gallman's. Using instead Balke and Gordon's estimates makes the average 1880–90 increase .6 percent per annum.

33. Most students of trends in income growth treat this period as one characterized by a series of severe business cycles, most prominently the downtown in 1893–95, rather than a break in the country's trend rate of growth. For our purposes, what matters is simply that most citizens saw little or no improvement over a decade and a half. Whether in retrospect their disappointment was due to a series of adverse cycles or a new, lower trend growth rate does not matter.

34. Sean Dennis Cashman, *America in the Gilded Age: From the Death of Lincoln to the Rise of Theodore Roosevelt* (New York: New York University Press, 1984), p. 274.

35. William Dean Howells, *The Rise of Silas Lapham* (Boston: Houghton Mifflin, 1957), p. 294.

36. William Dean Howells, *A Hazard of New Fortunes* (New York: Signet, 1965), p. 226.

37. Ibid., pp. 379–80.

38. Ibid., pp. 292–93.

39. Ibid., p. 151.

40. Edward Bellamy, *Looking Backward: 2000–1887* (Cambridge: Harvard University Press, 1967), p. 123.

41. See William Gillette, *Retreat from Reconstruction, 1869–1878* (Baton Rouge: Louisana State University Press, 1979), for an account of the erosion of northern white support for freed southern blacks. Also see again Foner, *Politics and Ideology in the Age of the Civil War.*

42. Woodward, *The Strange Career of Jim Crow*, p. 81.

43. Ibid., p. 85.

44. Ibid., p. 82.

45. *The Civil Rights Cases*, 109 U.S. 3 (1883).

46. *Louisville, New Orleans & Texas Railway v. Mississippi*, 103 U.S. 587 (1890); *Williams v. Mississippi*, 170 U.S. 213 (1898).

47. See, for example, Daniel T. Rodgers, *Atlantic Crossings: Social Politics in a Progressive Age* (Cambridge: Harvard University Press, 1998), for an account of the flow of ideas about social insurance between Europe and the United States, beginning in this period.

48. Bellamy, *Looking Backward*, p. 149.

49. See Skocpol, *Protecting Soldiers and Mothers*, Chapter 3.

50. William Graham Sumner, "Sociology," in *Collected Essays in Political and Social Science* (New York: Henry Holt, 1885), p. 91.

51. See Jeffry A. Frieden, "Monetary Populism in Nineteenth Century America: An Open Economy Interpretation," *Journal of Economic History* 57 (June 1997): 367–95.

52. Silver mining in the United States had taken off after the discovery of Nevada's Comstock Lode in 1859, and production increased especially rapidly beginning in the mid-1870s.

53. See Milton Friedman and Anna Jacobson Schwartz, *A Monetary History of the United States, 1867–1960* (Princeton: Princeton University Press, 1963), Chapter 3; Milton Friedman, "Bimetallism Revisited," *Journal of Economic Perspectives* 4 (Autumn 1990): 85–104; and Barry J. Eichengreen, *Golden Fetters: The Gold Standard and the Great Depression, 1919–1939* (New York: Oxford University Press, 1992), Chapter 2. For contemporary views of the free silver controversy, see J. Lawrence Loughlin, *The History of Bimetallism in the United States* (New York: D. Appleton, 1886); Robert Giffen, *The Case Against Bimetallism* (London: J. G. Bell & Sons, 1892); William Hope Harvey, *Coin's Financial School* (Chicago: Coin, 1894); William Arthur Shaw, *The History of Currency, 1252–1984* (New York: G. P. Putnam's Sons, 1895); and Leonard Darwin, *Bimetallism: A Summary and Examination of the Arguments for and Against a Bimetallic System of Currency* (New York: Appleton, 1898).

54. The standard form of the bimetallism proposal called for free coinage at the old ratio of 16 ounces of silver for 1 ounce of gold. By 1894 the prevailing market price ratio exceeded 30 to 1.

55. Again see Frieden, "Monetary Populism in Nineteenth Century America."

56. Keller, *Affairs of State*, p. 383.

57. See Robert W. Fogel, *Railroads and American Growth: Essays in Econometric History* (Baltimore: John Hopkins University Press, 1964); Robert A. McGuire, "Economic Causes of Late Nineteenth Century Agrarian Unrest: New Evidence," *Journal of Economic History* 41 (December 1981): 835–52; and Robert Higgs, "Railroad Rates and the Populist Uprising," *Agricultural History* 44 (July 1970): 291–97. See also the useful summary in Jeremy Atack and Peter Passell, *A New View of American History: From Colonial Times to 1940* (New York: Norton, 1994), Chapter 16.

58. "The ideal [Bryan] appealed to was equality, the emotion—envy." Green-feld, *The Spirit of Capitalism*, p. 447.

59. The People's Party, the populists' organized political vehicle, convened for the first time in 1892, and that year it nominated former Civil War general James Weaver for president. Weaver carried six western states. That same year the party's candidates were successful in three races for governor, five for the United States Senate, and ten for the House of Representatives. See Nell Irvin Painter, *Standing at Armageddon: United States, 1877–1919* (New York: Norton, 1987), especially p. 116. Also see, more generally, Richard Hofstadter, *The Age of Reform: From Bryan to F.D.R.* (New York: Knopf, 1955), Chapters 2 and 3; Lawrence Goodwyn, *Democratic Promise: The Populist Movement in America* (New York: Oxford University Press, 1976); John Donald Hicks, *The Populist Revolt: A History of the Farmer's Alliance and the People's Party* (Minneapolis: University of Minnesota Press, 1931); and Robert C. McMath, Jr., *American Populism: A Social History, 1877–1898* (New York: Hill & Wang, 1993).

60. Then too, however, economic conditions mattered. The recession of 1854–55, which temporarily halted railroad construction and thereby put immigrants in direct competition with native-born American labor, did much to energize the anti-foreigner movement and its nationally organized political manifestation, the American Party (the "Know-Nothings"). The Know-Nothings were in many ways forerunners of the populists who followed three decades later.

61. Cashman, *America in the Gilded Age*, p. 94.

62. See Ashley S. Timmer and Jeffrey G. Williamson, "Immigration Policy Prior to the 1930s: Labor Markets, Policy Interactions, and Globalization Backlash," *Population and Development Review* 24 (December 1998): 739–71; and Paul W. Gates, *History of Public Land Law Development* (Washington, D.C.: Government Printing Office, 1968), especially pp. 454, 461, 482–83.

63. Bellamy, *Looking Backward*, p. 270.

64. Though widely recognized as a populist in spirit and in his policies, Tillman, like Bryan, ran as a Democrat.

65. For a good account, see Stephen Kantrowitz, *Ben Tillman and the Reconstruction of White Supremacy* (Chapel Hill: University of North Carolina Press, 2000).

66. See Donald Louis Kinzer, *An Episode in Anti-Catholicism: The American Protective Association* (Seattle: University of Washington Press, 1964); see also Cashman, *America in the Gilded Age*, p. 98.

67. The previous year, after the Treasury arranged a loan from J. P. Morgan & Company to enable America to remain on the gold standard, Bryan had registered his protest on the floor of Congress by asking the clerk to read the speech from *The Merchant of Venice* stating Shylock's bond.

68. "It is not too much to say that the Greenback-Populist tradition activated much of what we have of popular anti-semitism in the United States." Hofstadter, *The Age of Reform*, p. 80.

69. Mary Elizabeth Lease, *The Problem of Civilization Solved*, pp. 319–20; cited in Hofstadter, *The Age of Reform*, p. 79.

70. An example is Gordon Clark, *Shylock: As Banker, Bondholder, Corruptionist, Conspirator* (1894). Clark alleged that America's adoption of the gold standard had stemmed from a conspiracy between Hugh McCulloch, Lincoln's and then Johnson's secretary of the treasury, and the Rothschilds. See Hofstadter, *The Age of Reform*, pp. 75–76; and Niall Ferguson, *House of Rothschild: The World's Banker* (New York: Viking, 1999), Vol. 2, p. 270.

71. The book also explicitly embraced the populist distaste for cities: "cities do not breed statesmen." Harvey, *Coin's Financial School*, pp. 116–17.

72. Early in his career Donnelly had been a Republican congressman (from Minnesota), but he migrated politically to the Populists. In 1892 he wrote the preamble to the party's Omaha platform, which declared that America was on "the verge of moral, political and material ruin." *Caesar's Column*, his only novel, appeared in 1891.

73. An insightful account is Richard Hofstadter, *The Paranoid Style in American Politics and Other Essays* (New York: Knopf, 1965), Chapter 1.

74. Keller, *Affairs of State*, p. 443.

75. Hofstadter, *The Age of Reform*, p. 66.

76. See Leonard Dinnerstein, *The Leo Frank Case* (New York: Columbia University Press, 1966); Philip Dray, *At the Hands of Persons Unknown: The Lynching of Black America* (New York: Random House, 2002); and Steve Olney, *And the Dead Shall Rise: The Murder of Mary Phagan and the Lynching of Leo Frank* (New York: Panther, 2003).

77. Bryan had traveled to Dayton especially for the trial. The jury deliberated for just nine minutes before convicting Scopes. For a recent account, see Edward J. Larson, *Summer for the Gods: The Scopes Trial and America's Continuing Debate over Science and Religion* (New York: Basic Books, 1997).

CHAPTER 6
From TR to FDR

1. Theodore Roosevelt, "Inaugural Address" (March 4, 1905), *Inaugural Addresses of the Presidents of the United States*, Vol. 2 (Bedford, Mass.: Applewood Books, 2001), p. 42.

2. See Milton Friedman and Anna Jacobson Schwartz, *A Monetary History of the United States, 1867–1960* (Princeton: Princeton University Press, 1963), p. 135. An early expression of the renewed economic confidence of the new era came from the chief statistician of the 1900 census: "The present census, when completed, will unquestionably show that the visible

material wealth in this country now has a value of ninety billion dollars. This is an addition since 1890 of twenty-five billion dollars. This is a saving greater than all the people of the Western Continent had been able to make from the discovery of Columbus to the breaking out of the Civil War" (cited in William Lawrence, "The Relation of Wealth to Morals," *The World's Work*, January 1901, p. 286).

3. Even in narrow terms, the return of economic growth helped defeat the populists in the 1896 election. The depression that began in 1893 had hit bottom by the end of 1895, and 1896 was mostly a good year for the American economy. William McKinley's victory over Bryan that fall was in part a direct consequence of the fortuitously timed business recovery, and in particular the especially large rise in farm prices beginning shortly before the election.

4. *The Cathedral of Commerce* (Baltimore: Munder-Thomsen, 1916), a booklet of photographs with text by Edwin A. Cochran, published in 1916 to celebrate New York's recently completed Woolworth Building, even hailed this new structure in religious terms.

5. Real income data to 1909 are from Robert E. Gallman, "Real GNP, Prices of 1860, 1834–1909" (unpublished paper, University of North Carolina, undated), and thereafter from Nathan S. Balke and Robert J. Gordon, "The Estimation of Prewar Gross National Product: Methodology and New Evidence," *Journal of Political Economy* 97 (February 1989): 38–92. On the basis of the Balke-Gordon data alone, the average 1896–1913 growth rate was 2.4 percent per annum.

6. Jean-Pierre Bardou and Patrick F. Chanaron, *The Automobile Revolution: The Impact of an Industry*, translated by James M. Laux (Chapel Hill: University of North Carolina Press, 1982).

7. Walter E. Weyl, *The New Democracy: An Essay on Certain Political and Economic Tendencies in the United States* (New York: Macmillan, 1912), p. 246; also cited in Richard Hofstadter, *The Age of Reform: From Bryan to F.D.R.* (New York: Vintage, 1955), pp. 147–48.

8. The period's focus on the nation's ills and what to do about them was not limited to muckraking, however. For example, between 1908 and 1914 the Russell Sage Foundation published a series of volumes with data documenting the cycle of urban poverty that trapped generations of families and showing that the children of paupers were likely to become paupers themselves because of deprivation, not heredity.

9. Sherwood Anderson, *Winesburg, Ohio* (New York: Viking, 1960), p. 71.

10. Ibid., p. 81.

11. Ibid., p. 120.

12. Ibid., pp. 246–47.

13. Edith Wharton, *The Age of Innocence* (New York: Scribner, 1968), p. 353.

14. Henry F. May, *Protestant Churches and Industrial America* (New York: Harper, 1949), p. 170.

15. Walter Rauschenbusch, *Christianizing the Social Order* (New York: Macmillan, 1912), p. 9; cited in May, *Protestant Churches and Industrial America*, p. 201.

16. See C. Vann Woodward, *The Strange Career of Jim Crow* (New York: Oxford University Press, 1955), p. 100.

17. *Buchan v. Warley*, 245 U.S. 60 (1917).

18. Additional legislation regulating the railroads during the Progressive Era included the Elkins Act (1903), which prohibited the railroads from granting rebates or other preferential rate reductions to large shippers, and the Mann-Elkins Act (1910), which empowered the Interstate Commerce Commission to suspend or fix railroad rates, in effect making it the most powerful government agency of the time.

19. *Muller v. Oregon*, 208 U.S. 412 (1908). Two years earlier, in another modest victory for civil rights, the Supreme Court ruled unconstitutional the "grandfather clauses" that some states (in this case Oklahoma) used to exempt citizens from literacy and other voter registration requirements if at least one direct-lineage ancestor had been eligible to vote at the time of the Civil War—in other words, before the Fifteenth Amendment enfranchised blacks.

20. See David Von Drehle, *Triangle: The Fire That Changed America* (New York: Atlantic Monthly Press, 2003), for an account of the fire and its subsequent impact.

21. See Theda Skocpol, *Protecting Soldiers and Mothers: The Political Origin of Social Policy in the United States* (Cambridge: Harvard University Press, 1992), Chapter 7.

22. In two key decisions in 1918 and 1922, however, the Supreme Court invalidated first the Keating-Owen Act and then a tax law aimed at eliminating child labor, arguing that Congress lacked the power to legislate in this area; *Hammer v. Dagenhart*, 247 U.S. 251 (1918), and *Baily v. Drexel Furniture Co.*, 259 U.S. 20 (1922). In 1923 the Court also ruled that the law setting minimum wages for women in the District of Columbia violated the Fifth Amendment protection of freedom of contract; *Adkins v. Children's Hospital*, 261 U.S. 525 (1923). Only in the 1930s and 1940s did the Court in effect reverse itself on these two issues.

23. See Skocpol, *Protecting Soldiers and Mothers*, especially p. 464.

24. A selection of Hine's photographs was published as recently as 2000; see Vicki Goldberg, *Lewis W. Hine: Children at Work* (Munich: Prestel Verlag, 1999). The National Child Labor Committee still exists and carries out an active program today.

25. Claudia Goldin, "America's Graduation from High School: The Evolution and Spread of Secondary Schooling in the Twentieth Century," *Journal of Economic History* 58 (June 1998): 345–74, especially Figure 1; and Thomas D. Snyder (ed.), *120 Years of American Education: A Statistical Portrait* (Washington, D.C.: U.S. Department of Education, Office of Educa-

tional Research and Improvement, National Center for Education Statistics, 1993), Tables 9 and 19.

26. See Claudia Goldin and Lawrence F. Katz, "Human Capital and Social Capital: The Rise of Secondary Schooling in America, 1910 to 1940," *Journal of Interdisciplinary History* 29 (Spring 1999): 683–723; R. Freeman Butts, *Public Education in the United States: From Revolution to Reform* (New York: Holt, Rinehart & Winston, 1978); and Linda E. Perle (ed.), *State Constitutional Provisions and Selected Legal Materials Relating to Public School Finance* (Washington, D.C.: U.S. Department of Health, Education, and Welfare, 1973).

27. Cited in Nathan Glazer, *We Are All Multiculturalists Now* (Cambridge: Harvard University Press, 1997), p. 86.

28. See Sandra Adickes, *To Be Young Was Very Heaven: Women in New York Before the First World War* (New York: St. Martin's, 1997), for an account of broader aspects of the political and practical emancipation of women in the Progressive Era.

29. See again Robert Putnam, *Bowling Alone: The Collapse and Revival of American Community* (New York: Simon & Schuster, 2000).

30. For accounts of the early years of the NAACP, see James M. MacPherson, *The Abolitionist Legacy: From Reconstruction to the NAACP* (Princeton: Princeton University Press, 1975), and Michael L. Levine, *African Americans and Civil Rights: From 1619 to the Present* (Phoenix, Ariz.: Oryx Press, 1996).

31. See, for example, James S. Coleman, *The Foundations of Social Theory* (Cambridge: Harvard University Press, 1990), and Putnam, *Bowling Alone.*

32. In 1894 Congress passed the populist-supported Wilson-Gorman Tariff Act, which also instituted a graduated income tax, but the Supreme Court ruled the measure unconstitutional before it took effect; *Pollock v. Farmer's Loan & Trust Co.,* 158 U.S. 601 (1895).

33. Hofstadter, *The Age of Reform,* pp. 243–44. White support for the NAACP, and the growing awareness of black America on the part of upper-income northern whites during this period, was another expression of the same kind of sympathies.

34. David Newton Lott (ed.), *The Inaugural Addresses of the American Presidents from Washington to Kennedy* (New York: Holt, Rinehart & Winston, 1961), p. 200.

35. Paul A. Samuelson and Everett E. Hagan, *After the War, 1918–1920* (Washington, D.C.: National Resource Planning Board, 1943).

36. See, for example, Theodore Saloutos and John Hicks, *Agricultural Discontent in the Middle West, 1900–39* (Madison: University of Wisconsin Press, 1951).

37. See Jeffrey G. Williamson and Peter H. Lindert, *American Inequality: A Macroeconomic History* (New York: Academic Press, 1980), especially pp. 174, 236.

38. Real income data to 1928 are from Balke and Gordon, "The Estimation of Prewar Gross National Product," and thereafter from the U.S. Department of Commerce, Bureau of Economic Analysis, National Income and Product Accounts. (On the basis of the Balke-Gordon data alone, the average 1918–29 growth rate was higher, 1.3 percent per annum, largely because of a one-year surge in 1929. For 1918–28 the Balke-Gordon data show average growth of .9 percent.)

39. Peter Lindert, "Three Centuries of Inequality in Britain and America," in A. B. Atkinson and François Bourguignon (eds.), *Handbook of Income Distribution*, Vol. 1 (Amsterdam: Elsevier Science, 2000).

40. Cited in James Chase, *Acheson: The Secretary of State Who Created the American World* (New York: Simon & Schuster, 1998), p. 48.

41. See ibid., especially p. 48.

42. See Francis Russell, *Sacco and Vanzetti: The Case Resolved* (New York: Harper & Row, 1986).

43. See Sara Bullard (ed.), *The Ku Klux Klan: A History of Racism and Violence*, 4th ed. (Montgomery, Ala.: Southern Poverty Law Center, 1991).

44. Kenneth T. Jackson, *The Ku Klux Klan in the City: 1915–1930* (New York: Oxford University Press,1967), pp. 236–37.

45. Woodward, *The Strange Career of Jim Crow*, pp. 115–16.

46. Stanley Frost, *The Challenge of the Klan* (Indianapolis, Ind.: Bobbs-Merrill, 1924), p. 1.

47. Nancy MacLean, *Behind the Mask of Chivalry: The Making of the Second Ku Klux Klan* (New York: Oxford University Press, 1994), p. 129.

48. See Nicholas Lemann, *The Promised Land: The Great Black Migration and How It Changed America* (New York: Knopf, 1991).

49. Wyn Craig Wade, *The Fiery Cross: The Ku Klux Klan in America* (New York: Simon & Schuster, 1987), p. 165.

50. Again see Jackson, *The Ku Klux Klan in the City.*

51. Cited by Hofstadter, *The Age of Reform*, p. 295.

52. Jackson, *The Ku Klux Klan in the City.* p. 245.

53. MacLean, *Behind the Mask of Chivalry*, p. 53.

54. Ibid., pp. 62–63.

55. Hiram Wesley Evans, "The Klan's Fight for Americanism," *North American Review* 213 (March–April–May 1926), pp. 33–63; also cited in Hofstadter, *The Age of Reform*, p. 295.

56. F. Scott Fitzgerald, *The Great Gatsby* (New York: Scribner, 1953), pp. 180–81.

57. F. Scott Fitzgerald, *The Beautiful and Damned* (New York: Scribner, 1950), p. 417. The contrast that Fitzgerald highlighted between Adam Patch and his grandson Anthony personified the debate over "producerism" versus "consumerism," which by the 1930s had developed into a major focus of debate about the evolution of the U.S. economy; see, for example, Alan

Brinkley, *The End of Reform: New Deal Liberalism in Recession and War* (New York: Knopf, 1995).

58. John M. Barry, *Rising Tide: The Great Mississippi Flood of 1927 and How It Changed America* (New York: Simon & Schuster, 1997), pp. 286–87.

59. Skocpol, *Protecting Soldiers and Mothers*, pp. 513, 518.

60. *Adkins v. Children's Hospital*, 261 U.S. 525 (1923).

61. *Duplex Printing Press Co. v. Deering*, 254 U.S. 443 (1921).

62. See Woodward, *The Strange Career of Jim Crow*.

63. See Tim Madigan, *The Burning: Massacre, Destruction and the Tulsa Race Riot of 1921* (New York: Thomas Dunne/St. Martin's, 2001), for a detailed account of the Tulsa incident. Whether the year-by-year frequency of individual lynchings was related to economic conditions has long been a controversial question. The classic early study by Arthur Raper, *The Tragedy of Lynching* (Chapel Hill: University of North Carolina Press, 1933), concluded that it was. Recent work has cast doubt on Raper's work on statistical grounds; see Donald P. Green, Jack Glaser, and Andrew Rich, "From Lynching to Gay-Bashing: The Elusive Connection Between Economic Conditions and Hate Crime," *Journal of Personality and Social Psychology* 75 (July 1998): 82–92. In addition, as we shall see, lynchings abated in the 1930s. (The period Raper examined ended just before the depression.)

64. See Robert L. Zangrando, *The NAACP's Crusade Against Lynching, 1909–1950* (Philadelphia: Temple University Press, 1980).

65. Randall Kennedy, *Race, Crime and the Law* (New York: Vintage, 1998), pp. 46, 55. Also see Philip Dray, *At the Hands of Persons Unknown: The Lynching of Black America* (New York: Random House, 2002).

66. Kennedy, *Race, Crime and the Law*, pp. 55–58.

67. See Edwin Black, *The War Against the Weak: Eugenics and America's Campaign to Create a Master Race* (New York: Four Walls Eight Windows, 2003). The eugenics movement, however, was directed as much against what were now domestic groups as foreigners. In a key case in 1927, for example, the Supreme Court validated Virginia's forced sterilization law; *Buck v. Bell*, 274 U.S. 200 (1927).

68. Even beforehand, during the years when the principal means that opponents of immigration sought to use to limit the inflow was a literary test, "almost all serious calls for the literacy test were preceded by economic downturns, some of major proportion, and few economic downturns of the era were not accompanied by a call for restriction in the halls of Congress." See Claudia Goldin, "The Political Economy of Immigration Restriction: The United States, 1890–1921," in Claudia Goldin and Gary D. Libecap (eds.), *The Regulated Economy: A Historical Approach to Political Economy* (Chicago: University of Chicago Press, 1994), especially p. 239.

69. Goldin, "The Political Economy of Immigration Restriction," especially Tables 7.8 and 7.9, pp. 251 and 254.

70. The 1929 national origins system limited total immigration from outside the Western Hemisphere to 150,000—the limit had been 165,000 under the temporary provisions of the 1924 act—with regional sub-quotas based on the proportions shown in the 1920 census.

71. Robert A. Slayton, *Empire Statesman: The Rise and Redemption of Al Smith* (New York: Free Press, 2001), provides a good account of the vitriolic nature of the anti-Smith campaign in 1928, including the active role of the Ku Klux Klan. See also Christopher M. Finan, *Alfred E. Smith: The Happy Warrior* (New York: Hill and Wang, 2002).

72. Hofstadter, *The Age of Reform*, p. 300.

CHAPTER 7
Great Depression, Great Exception

1. Franklin D. Roosevelt, "Annual Message to the Congress. January 4, 1935," *The Public Papers and Addresses of Franklin D. Roosevelt*, Vol. 4, *The Court Disapproves, 1935* (New York: Random House, 1938), p. 15.

2. John George and Laird Wilcox, *American Extremists: Militias, Suprema-cists, Klansmen, Communists and Others* (Amherst, N.Y.: Prometheus, 1996), p. 37.

3. The research literature addressing this question is voluminous. For just a few of the major highlights, presenting differing points of view, see Milton Friedman and Anna Jacobson Schwartz, *A Monetary History of the United States, 1867–1960* (Princeton: Princeton University Press, 1963), Chapter 7; Peter Temin, *Did Monetary Forces Cause the Great Depression?* (New York: Norton, 1976) and *Lessons from the Great Depression* (Cambridge: MIT Press, 1989); Barry J. Eichengreen, *Golden Fetters: The Gold Standard and the Great Depression, 1919–1939* (New York: Oxford University Press, 1992), especially Chapters 8–11; Ben S. Bernanke, *Essays on the Great Depression* (Princeton: Princeton University Press, 2000); and many of the essays in Michael D. Bordo, Claudia Goldin, and Eugene N. White (eds.), *The Defining Moment: The Great Depression and the American Economy in the Twentieth Century* (Chicago: University of Chicago Press, 1998).

4. See James D. Hamilton, "Monetary Factors in the Great Depression," *Journal of Monetary Economics* 19 (March 1987): 145–69, and Christina D. Romer, "The Nation in Depression," *Journal of Economic Perspectives* 7 (Spring 1993): 19–39, for evidence that the tighter monetary policy contributed to the initial economic downturn.

5. How many Americans owned stocks at the time is also a matter of dispute. According to one estimate, when the depression began about 15 million Americans (nearly one in eight) owned some stocks or corporate bonds; see Maury Klein, *Rainbow's End: The Crash of 1929* (New York: Oxford University Press, 2001), p. 126. The New York Stock Exchange claimed there

were 20 million. By contrast, other estimates put the number of Americans who owned stocks at 2 million or less, and the number who even had brokerage accounts at less than 3 million. See John Steele Gordon, *An Empire of Wealth: The Epic History of American Economic Power* (New York: Harper-Collins, 2004), p. 318.

6. By contrast, in the severe 1920–26 downturn household spending had held up fairly well; see Peter Temin, *Did Monetary Policy Cause the Great Depression?*

7. See Jeremy Atack and Peter Passell, *A New Economic View of American History: From Colonial Times to 1940* (New York: Norton, 1994), p. 595; also Temin, *Did Monetary Forces Cause the Great Depression?*

8. Albert Gailord Hart, *Debts and Recovery: A Study of Changes in the Internal Debt Structure from 1929 to 1937 and a Program for the Future* (New York: Twentieth Century Fund, 1938), pp. 134, 138, 225; also see Ben S. Bernanke, "Nonmonetary Effects of the Financial Crisis in the Propagation of the Great Depression," *American Economic Review* 73 (June 1983): 257–76.

9. Friedman and Schwartz, *A Monetary History of the United States*, p. 309.

10. See Chang-Tai Hsieh and Christina D. Romer, "Was the Federal Reserve Fettered? Devaluation Expectations in the 1932 Monetary Expansion" (National Bureau of Economic Research, Working Paper 8113, 2001), for a detailed analysis of this episode. Hsieh and Romer concluded that the best explanation for policymakers' actions was "a misguided model of the economy" (p. 3).

11. See David M. Kennedy, *Freedom from Fear: The American People in Depression and War, 1929–1945* (New York: Oxford University Press, 1999), pp. 11–13.

12. Richard Norton Smith, *An Uncommon Man: The Triumph of Herbert Hoover* (New York: Simon & Schuster, 1984), p. 130.

13. Stephan Thernstrom, *A History of the American People* (San Diego: Harcourt Brace Jovanovich, 1984), Vol. 2, p. 722.

14. Herbert Hoover, *The Memoirs of Herbert Hoover: The Great Depression, 1929–1941* (New York: Macmillan, 1952), p. 30.

15. Friedman and Schwartz, *A Monetary History of the United States*, p. 375, note 103.

16. See Charles P. Kindleberger, *The World in Depression, 1929–1939* (Berkeley: University of California Press, 1973), p. 172, and League of Nations, *Monthly Bulletin of Statistics* (February 1934), p. 51.

17. Some economists have argued, however, that Smoot-Hawley was not a significant part of what caused the depression; see for example, Temin, *Lessons from the Great Depression*, p. 46, and Douglas A. Irwin, "The Smoot-Hawley Tariff: A Quantitative Assessment," *Review of Economics and Statistics* 80 (May 1998): 326–34. Others have also argued that Smoot-Hawley did not provoke retaliation; see, for example, Alfred E. Eckes, Jr., *Opening*

America's Market: U.S. Foreign Trade Policy Since 1776 (Chapel Hill: University of North Carolina Press, 1995).

18. Eichengreen, *Golden Fetters*, p. 3.

19. See Charles P. Kindleberger, *Manias, Panics, and Crashes: A History of Financial Crises* (New York: Basic Books, 1978), Chapter 10.

20. See Ehsan U. Choudhri and Levis A. Kochin, "The Exchange Rate and the International Transmission of Business Cycle Disturbances: Some Evidence from the Great Depression," *Journal of Money, Credit and Banking* 12 (November 1980): 565–74; Barry Eichengreen and Jeffrey Sachs, "Exchange Rates and Economic Recovery in the 1930s," *Journal of Economic History* 45 (December 1985): 925–46; Eichengreen, *Golden Fetters*, Chapter 10; Ben S. Bernanke and Harold James, "The Gold Standard, Deflation, and Financial Crisis in the Great Depression: An International Comparison," in R. Glenn Hubbard (ed.), *Financial Markets and Financial Crises* (Chicago: University of Chicago Press, 1991); Ben S. Bernanke, "The Macroeconomics of the Great Depression: A Comparative Approach," *Journal of Money, Credit, and Banking* 27 (February 1995): 1–28; and Temin, *Lessons from the Great Depression*.

21. "Business Cycle Expansions and Contractions," National Bureau of Economic Research Web site. Also see again Temin, *Lessons from the Great Depression*.

22. Franklin D. Roosevelt, "Inaugural Address. March 4, 1933," *Public Papers and Addresses*, Vol. 2, *The Year of Crisis, 1933* (New York: Random House, 1950), p. 12.

23. See Jordan Schwartz, *The New Dealers: Power Politics in the Age of Roosevelt* (New York: Knopf, 1993).

24. See Richard Hofstadter, *The Age of Reform: From Bryan to F.D.R.* (New York: Vintage, 1955), especially pp. 302, 310; also see Morton Keller, *Regulating a New Economy: Public Policy and Economic Change in America, 1900–1933* (Cambridge: Harvard University Press, 1990).

25. Recent research has attributed nearly one-third of the 1930s decline in infant mortality to changes in relief spending. See Price V. Fishback, Michael R. Haines, and Shawn Kantor, "The Welfare of Children During the Great Depression" (National Bureau of Economic Research, Working Paper 8902, 2002).

26. Peter Temin, *Taking Your Medicine: Drug Regulation in the United States* (Cambridge: Harvard University Press, 1980), pp. 42–43.

27. Roosevelt, "Annual Message to the Congress. January 4, 1935," p. 15.

28. Franklin D. Roosevelt, "The Second Inaugural Address. January 20, 1937," *Public Papers and Addresses*, Vol. 6, *The Constitution Prevails, 1937*, p. 1.

29. See Ellis W. Hawley, *The New Deal and the Problem of Monopoly: A Study in Economic Ambivalence* (Princeton: Princeton University Press, 1966). See also Alan Brinkley, *The End of Reform: New Deal Liberalism in Recession*

and War (New York: Knopf, 1995), on the conflict within the New Deal program between traditional progressive anti-monopoly attitudes and "associational" cooperation of business under government oversight and regulation.

30. For the history of this central piece of New Deal legislation, and the program that resulted from it, see, for example, Carolyn L. Weaver, *The Crisis in Social Security: Economic and Political Origins* (Durham, N.C.: Duke University Press, 1982); Dora D. Costa, *The Evolution of Retirement: An American Economic History, 1880–1990* (Chicago: University of Chicago Press, 1998); and Jeffrey A. Miron and David N. Weil, "The Genesis and Evolution of Social Security," in Bordo et al. (eds.), *The Defining Moment.*

31. See Paul M. Romer, "Preferences, Promises, and the Politics of Entitlement," in Victor R. Fuchs (ed.), *Individual and Social Responsibility: Child Care, Education, Medical Care, and Long-Term Care in America* (Chicago: University of Chicago Press, 1995), and, again, Miron and Weil, "The Genesis and Evolution of Social Security." Prior to 1935, twenty-eight states had some form of old-age pension program, but not one was contributory; see David A. Moss, *When All Else Fails: Government as the Ultimate Risk Manager* (Cambridge: Harvard University Press, 2002).

32. The key cases were *Hammer v. Dagenhart*, 247 U.S. 251 (1918), and *Adkins v. Children's Hospital*, 261 U.S. 525 (1923).

33. *U.S. v. Darby Lumber Co.*, 312 U.S. 100 (1941).

34. See Alan Brinkley, *Voices of Protest: Huey Long, Father Coughlin, and the Great Depression* (New York: Knopf, 1982).

35. Franklin D. Roosevelt, "Annual Message to the Congress. January 3, 1938," *Public Papers and Addresses*, Vol. 7, *The Continuing Struggle for Liberalism, 1938*, p. 11.

36. Kennedy, *Freedom from Fear*, p. 377; emphasis added.

37. Brinkley, *The End of Reform*, p. 251; Brinkley is specifically referring here to "Security, Work, and Relief Policies," a report by the wartime National Resources Planning Board.

38. In addition, some positive developments occurred at the state level. For example, in a case that helped to create the climate for the Supreme Court's classic desegregation opinion nearly two decades later, in 1936 the Maryland Court of Appeals (the state's highest court) required that a black student be admitted to the University of Maryland Law School, on the grounds that Maryland had no other law school open to blacks; *Murray v. Pearson*, 169 Md. 479 (1936). Two years later the Supreme Court, citing the Maryland court's decision, ordered Missouri to grant a black student admission to that state's law school rather than pay to send him out of state for legal education; *Missouri ex rel. Gaines v. Canada*, 305 U.S. 337 (1938). Some recent historical opinion has also taken a more favorable view toward Roosevelt's own efforts to advance civil rights and improve the lives

of the nation's black citizens; see, for example, Kevin J. McMalin, *Reconsidering Roosevelt on Race: How the Presidency Paved the Road to Brown* (Chicago: University of Chicago Press, 2003).

39. C. Vann Woodward, *The Strange Career of Jim Crow* (New York: Oxford University Press, 1955), p. 118. After a brief decline in 1931 and 1932, lynchings of blacks rose in 1933 to the highest level since the mid-1920s. They then declined irregularly over the remainder of the decade, reaching a lower level than in any previously recorded year. See Donald P. Green, Jack Glaser, and Andrew Rich, "From Lynching to Gay-Bashing: The Elusive Connection Between Economic Conditions and Hate Crime," *Journal of Personality and Social Psychology* 75 (July 1998): 82–92.

40. James Chase, *Acheson: The Secretary of State Who Created the American World* (New York: Simon & Schuster, 1998), p. 74.

41. Dos Passos singled out architect Frank Lloyd Wright as an example of what the country could again become, describing Wright in tones that echoed Russell Conwell a generation and more before: "he preaches the horizons of his boyhood, a future that is not the rise of a few points in a hundred selected stocks . . . but a new and clean construction, from the ground up, based on uses and needs, towards the American future." John Dos Passos, *The Big Money*, in *U.S.A.* (New York: Modern Library, 1937), p. 431.

42. During the depression Steinbeck had worked as a farm laborer in California, and so he was able to give his account of this part of the Joads' experience a particular realism. For a fuller (but also contemporary) treatment of this aspect of California history, see, for example, Carey McWilliams, *Factories in the Field: The Story of Migratory Farm Labor in California* (Boston: Little, Brown, 1939).

43. John Steinbeck, *The Grapes of Wrath* (New York: Penguin, 1992), p. 207.

44. Ibid., p. 45.

45. Ibid., p. 164.

46. Brinkley, *The End of Reform*, p. 251; Hofstadter, *The Age of Reform*, p. 325.

47. See, for example, Arthur Meier Schlesinger, *The New Deal in Action, 1933–1938* (New York: Macmillan, 1939); James MacGregor Burns, *Roosevelt: The Lion and the Fox* (New York: Harcourt, Brace, 1956); Kennedy, *Freedom from Fear*; John Kenneth Galbraith, *Name-Dropping: From F.D.R. On* (Boston: Houghton Mifflin, 1991); and Robert H. Jackson, *That Man: An Insider's Portrait of Franklin D. Roosevelt*, edited by John Q. Barrett (New York: Oxford University Press, 2003).

48. Isaiah Berlin, "Roosevelt Through European Eyes," *Atlantic Monthly* 196 (July 1955): 67–71; also published as "President Franklin Delano Roosevelt," *Political Quarterly* 26 (October–December 1955): 336–44.

49. Franklin D. Roosevelt, "Fireside Chat," September 30, 1934, *Public Papers and Addresses*, Vol. 3, *The Advance of Recovery and Reform, 1934*, p. 420.

50. Roosevelt, "Annual Message to the Congress. January 4, 1935," pp. 19–20.

51. Alexander Gerschenkron, *Economic Backwardness in Historical Perspective: A Book of Essays* (Cambridge: Harvard University Press, 1962), p. 360.

CHAPTER 8
America in the Postwar Era

1. Lyndon B. Johnson, "Radio and Television Remarks upon Signing the Civil Rights Bill. July 2, 1964," *Public Papers of the Presidents of the United States: Lyndon B. Johnson, 1963–64* (Washington, D.C.: Government Printing Office, 1965), Book II, pp. 842–43.

2. Ronald Reagan, "Inaugural Address, January 20, 1981," *Public Papers of the Presidents of the United States: Ronald Reagan, 1981* (Washington, D.C.: Government Printing Office, 1982), p. 1.

3. See, for example, Alvin H. Hansen, *Full Recovery or Stagnation?* (New York: Norton, 1938), and "Economic Progress and Declining Population Growth," *American Economic Review* 29 (March 1939): 1–15.

4. Employment Act of 1946, 79th Congress, 2nd Session, Public Law 304, Section 2 (15 U.S.C. Sec. 1021, 1994 ed.).

5. Data on gross domestic product are from the Bureau of Economic Analysis, National Income and Product Accounts.

6. Data on gross national product are from the National Income and Product Accounts. Data on population are from the Census Bureau.

7. Data on median incomes are from the Census Bureau, stated in 2003 dollars.

8. James Chase, *Acheson: The Secretary of State Who Created the American World* (New York: Simon & Schuster, 1998), p. 225.

9. The McCarran Act (formally the Internal Security Act) also famously led to a variety of foreigners' being denied entry to the United States, often not because their visa applications were denied but because the necessary reviews were so cumbersome. Prominent examples included Australian physicist Marcus Oliphant, who had worked on the Manhattan Project during the war, British author Graham Greene, and Ernst Chain—also British, but born in Germany of Russian parents—who had shared the Nobel Prize in 1945 for his work developing penicillin.

10. Some contemporary observers placed an economic interpretation on McCarthyism. As Peter Viereck, a historian and Pulitzer Prize–winning poet argued, "McCarthyism is the revenge of the noses that for twenty years of fancy parties were pressed against the outside window pane." Peter Viereck, "The Revolt Against the Elite," in Daniel Bell (ed.), *The Radical Right: The New American Right* (Garden City, N.Y.: Doubleday, 1964), p. 163.

11. Alan Brinkley, *The End of Reform: New Deal Liberalism in Recession and War*

(New York: Knopf, 1995), p. 167. See again, however, the alternative view of Roosevelt in this context presented in Kevin J. McMahon, *Reconsidering Roosevelt on Race: How the Presidency Paved the Road to Brown* (Chicago: University of Chicago Press, 2003).

12. *Shelley v. Kraemer,* 334 U.S. 1 (1948).

13. *Public Papers of the Presidents of the United States: Harry S. Truman, 1952–53* (Washington, D.C.: Government Printing Office, 1966), item 290, p. 799.

14. *Terry v. Adams,* 345 U.S. 461 (1953).

15. *Brown v. Board of Education,* 348 U.S. 886 (1954), p. 495.

16. David L. Chappell, *A Stone of Hope: Prophetic Religion and the Death of Jim Crow* (Chapel Hill: University of North Carolina Press, 2004.)

17. George H. Gallup, *The Gallup Poll Public Opinion 1935–1971* (New York: Random House, 1972), Vol. 3, p. 1812.

18. The Equal Employment Opportunity Commission was given litigation authority in 1972, and it immediately became the most active government agency in bringing suit on behalf of not just blacks but also women; see Karen J. Maschke, *Litigation, Courts and Women Workers* (New York: Praeger, 1989).

19. In practice, however, these state-level efforts had limited effectiveness— hence the perceived need for federal legislation. See William J. Collins, "The Housing Market Impact of State-Level Anti-Discrimination Laws, 1960–1970" (National Bureau of Economic Research, Working Paper, 9562, 2003).

20. C. Vann Woodward, *The Strange Career of Jim Crow* (New York: Oxford University Press, 1955), p. 143.

21. Data on high school completion rates and reading proficiency scores are from Thomas D. Snyder, *Digest of Education Statistics 2002*, published by National Center for Education Statistics (Washington, D.C.: Government Printing Office, 2003), Tables 8 and 111, pp. 17 and 135.

22. Oscar Handlin and Lilian Handlin, *Liberty and Equality, 1920–1994* (New York: HarperCollins, 1994), p. 198.

23. See George J. Borjas, *Friends or Strangers: The Impact of Immigrants on the U.S. Economy* (New York: Basic Books, 1990), for a comprehensive account of the changes in American immigration during this period.

24. Truman's internationalism drew attacks from isolationists in both political parties—prominent examples included Senator Robert Taft, former ambassador Joseph Kennedy, and former president Hoover—but in the end Truman's policies prevailed; see Chase, *Acheson,* p. 327.

25. John F. Kennedy, "Remarks in Pueblo, Colorado, Following Approval of the Fryingpan-Arkansas Project. August 17, 1962," *Public Papers of the Presidents of the United States: John F. Kennedy, 1962* (Washington, D.C.: Government Printing Office, 1963), p. 626.

26. Stephan Thernstrom, *A History of the American People* (San Diego: Harcourt Brace Jovanovich, 1984), Vol. 2, p. 804.

27. See Robert A. Moffitt, "The Temporary Assistance for Needy Families Program," in Moffitt (ed.), *Means-Tested Transfer Programs in the United States* (Chicago: University of Chicago Press, 2003). By the end of the decade twenty-five states had elected to set up and administer expanded AFDC-UP programs (UP for "unemployed parent"), for which the federal government provided matching funds.

28. Johnson's 61.1 percent share of the popular vote narrowly exceeded Roosevelt's 60.8 percent in 1936, and it still stands as the all-time record. Richard Nixon received 60.7 percent in 1972, Ronald Reagan 59 percent in 1984.

29. Lyndon B. Johnson, "Annual Message to the Congress on the State of the Union. January 8, 1964," *Public Papers of the Presidents of the United States: Lyndon B. Johnson, 1963–64*, Book I, pp. 114, 116.

30. See Robert M. Ball, *Social Security, Today and Tomorrow* (New York: Columbia University Press, 1978). Because of a technical error in drafting the legislation, benefits were actually "over indexed," in other words, the mandated adjustment to inflation caused each beneficiary's payment to *increase* in real terms. Further legislation corrected this problem, but not until 1977. See C. Eugene Steuerle and Jon M. Bakija, *Retooling Social Security for the 21st Century: Right and Wrong Approaches to Reform* (Washington, D.C.: Urban Institute Press, 1994), and Robert J. Myers, "The Social Security Double-Indexing Myth," *Benefit Quarterly* 2 (Third Quarter, 1986): 21–25.

31. See Vincent J. Burke and Vee Burke, *Nixon's Good Deed: Welfare Reform* (New York: Columbia University Press, 1974); see also Maurice Isserman and Michael Kazin, *America Divided* (New York: Oxford University Press, 2000), Chapter 14.

32. The decision striking down state laws prohibiting interracial marriage was *Loving v. Virginia*, 388 U.S. 1 (1967).

33. *Speiser v. Randall*, 357 U.S. 513 (1958).

34. *Albertson v. Subversive Activities Control Board*, 382 U.S. 70 (1965); *Aptheker v. Secretary of State*, 378 U.S. 500 (1964); and *U.S. v. Robel*, 389 U.S. 258 (1967).

35. *Brandenburg v. Ohio*, 395 U.S. 444 (1969).

36. *New York Times v. Sullivan*, 376 U.S. 254 (1964).

37. *Burstyn v. Wilson*, 343 U.S. 495 (1952), and *Freedman v. Maryland*, 380 U.S. 51 (1965).

38. *Mapp v. Ohio*, 367 U.S. 643 (1961).

39. *Robinson v. California*, 370 U.S. 660 (1962); *Gideon v. Wainwright*, 372 U.S. 335 (1963); *Malloy v. Hogan*, 378 U.S. 1 (1964); *Klopfer v. North Carolina*, 386 U.S. 213 (1967); *Pointer v. Texas*, 380 U.S. 400 (1965); and *Duncan v. Louisiana*, 391 U.S. 145 (1968).

40. *Miranda v. Arizona*, 384 U.S. 436 (1966), p. 472.

41. In Morton Horwitz's summary, "The court initiated a revolution in race

relations; expanded the constitutional guarantee of 'equal protection of the laws'; drastically expanded the protection of freedom of speech and press; overturned unequally apportioned legislative districts; accorded defendants in criminal trials massively expanded constitutional protections; and recognized for the first time a constitutional right to privacy." Morton J. Horwitz, *The Warren Court and the Pursuit of Justice* (New York: Hill & Wang, 1998), p. 3.

42. The Harvard Law School, for example, first admitted women as LLB students in 1950, and the Harvard Business School first admitted women to its MBA program in 1963. The rate at which American women completed college remained approximately steady until the mid-1960s, but then it rose sharply. This cohort of women entered the labor force in much greater numbers than before; see Claudia Goldin, *Understanding the Gender Gap: An Economic History of American Women* (New York: Oxford University Press, 1990). Meanwhile, the 1963 Equal Pay Act prohibited outright wage discrimination against women in employment.

43. See also the examples given by Nathan Glazer, *We Are All Multiculturalists Now* (Cambridge: Harvard University Press, 1997), p. 152, and Glazer's accompanying discussion.

44. See, for example, Zvi Griliches, *Productivity Puzzles, R&D, Education and Productivity: A Retrospective* (Cambridge: Harvard University Press, 2000); William Nordhaus, "Retrospective on the 1970s Productivity Slowdown" (National Bureau of Economic Research, Working Paper 10950, 2004); and Robert Barsky and Fritz Kilian, "Oil and the Macroeconomy since the 1970s (National Bureau of Economic Research, Working Paper 10855, 2004). Also see the symposium on this question, "Symposium: The Slowdown in Productivity Growth," featuring papers by Zvi Griliches, Dale W. Jorgenson, Maureen Olson, and Michael J. Baskin (and an introductory essay by Stanley Fischer), *Journal of Economic Perspectives* 2 (Fall 1988): 3–71.

45. It is always possible, of course, that the decline in economic growth abroad could have occurred simultaneously with that in the United States yet resulted from different causes. For example, in many other countries growth was artificially rapid during the initial decades following World War II. Germany and Japan had obviously suffered the greatest wartime destruction, but war damage was also widespread in both Italy and France, and Britain too suffered serious losses. All grew more rapidly during the rebuilding phase.

46. Data on productivity growth, for the economy's nonfarm business sector, are from the Bureau of Labor Statistics.

47. Data on manufacturing output are from the Board of Governors of the Federal Reserve System; data on manufacturing employment are from the Bureau of Labor Statistics.

48. The Gini ratio (a standard measure of inequality) for American family

incomes rose from .349 in 1969 to .365 in 1980, and then to .429 in 1993; data are from the Census Bureau.

49. Data on labor force participation and employment are from the Bureau of Labor Statistics. There is also some evidence that the workweek is getting longer (in large part because of multiple jobs), with consequent sacrifice of families' leisure time; see Robert H. Frank, *Luxury Fever: Why Money Fails to Satisfy in an Era of Excess* (New York: Free Press, 1999), especially p. 49.

50. Data on weekly earnings are from the Bureau of Labor Statistics, in 2004 dollars.

51. Data on median annual incomes are from the Census Bureau.

52. Income and living standard measurements are inevitably subject to error, and there is room to question whether the erosion was greater or smaller than the standard figures indicate. See, for example, Daniel Slesnick, *Consumption and Social Welfare: Living Standards and Their Distribution in the United States* (Cambridge: Cambridge University Press, 2001). An important part of this issue is whether the measured price indexes used to adjust nominal incomes for inflation are accurate. A congressional commission, appointed in 1995, concluded that the U.S. Consumer Price Index, as conventionally measured, overstated inflation by approximately 1 percent per annum, by failing to take adequate account of the introduction of new products, the improved quality of existing products, shifts from more expensive to less expensive items within broad categories of goods, and shifts from more expensive to less expensive outlets for making purchases; see again Michael J. Boskin et al., "Consumer Prices, the Consumer Price Index, and the Cost of Living," *Journal of Economic Perspectives* 12 (Winter 1998): 3–26. What matters for purposes of the discussion here, however, is not whether the index has such a bias but whether the bias has increased over time, and there is little reason to believe that it has. (The commission did not report evidence of an increasing bias in recent decades.)

53. Data on median wages by age are from the Census Bureau, corrected to 2004 dollars.

54. The cover story in *BusinessWeek*'s issue for August 19, 1991, was titled "What Ever Happened to the American Dream?" and numerous other publications emphasized the same theme. For examples of books making the same point, see John E. Schwartz, *Illusions of Opportunity: The American Dream in Question* (New York: Norton, 1997), and Paul R. Krugman, *The Age of Diminished Expectations: U.S. Economic Policy in the 1990s* (Cambridge: MIT Press, 1990).

55. As Nathan Glazer later observed, "the mid-1970s now emerge as a turning point, in which progress, by various measures—such as percentages of blacks going on to college, percentage in poverty—slowed down or stopped." Glazer, *We Are All Multiculturalists Now*, p. 127.

56. The most prominent example at the Supreme Court level was *Regents of University of California v. Bakke*, 438 U.S. 265 (1978).

57. See Ethan Bronner, "Fewer Minorities Entering U. of California," *New York Times*, May 21, 1998, p. A28.

58. *Hopwood v. State of Texas*, 78 F. 3d 932 (5th Cir.), 518 U.S. 1033 (1996).

59. Ellis Cose, "The Color Bind," *Newsweek*, May 12, 1997, pp. 58–60.

60. *Wygant v. Jackson Board of Education*, 476 U.S. 267 (1986).

61. *City of Richmond v. J. A. Croson*, 488 U.S. 469 (1989).

62. *Adarand Constructors v. Pena*, 515 US 200 (1995).

63. *Reynolds v. Sims*, 377 U.S. 533 (1964).

64. *Davis v. Bandemer*, 478 U.S. 109 (1986).

65. *Shaw v. Reno*, 509 U.S. 630 (1993), and *Miller v. Johnson*, 515 U.S. 900 (1995).

66. See "Public Sector Tax Cheats," *New York Times*, December 8, 1997, p. A24.

67. The 1990s campaign against the use of Spanish in particular, especially in bilingual education programs, bore a striking resonance with the anti-German campaign of the late 1880s and early 1890s; see Glazer, *We Are All Multiculturalists Now*, pp. 85–87.

68. See Seth Mydans, "Riot in Los Angeles: Pocket of Tension," *New York Times*, May 3, 1992, p. A1. Although the overall effect of immigration on American natives' wages and ability to find jobs is small, these effects fall disproportionately on workers with less than a high school education; see James P. Smith and Barry Edmonston (eds.), *The New Americans: Economic, Demographic, and Fiscal Effects of Immigration* (Washington, D.C.: National Academy Press, 1997), and Steven A. Camarota, "Does Immigration Harm the Poor?" *Public Interest* (Fall 1998): 23–32. These effects also fall disproportionately on blacks, who remain one-third more likely than whites to drop out of high school.

69. George Gallup, Jr., *The Gallup Poll: Public Opinion 1993* (Wilmington, Del.: Scholarly Resources, 1994), p. 253.

70. Prominent examples included the legislation submitted in 1995 and 1996 by Senator Alan Simpson (104 S. 269), Senator Orrin Hatch (104 S. 1664), and Representative Lamar Smith (104 H.R. 2202).

71. Although the net fiscal burden imposed by immigrants (that is, the excess cost of public services that immigrant-headed households consume over the taxes that they pay) is small on a nationwide basis, it is significant in the handful of states, including California and Texas, that account for the bulk of the immigrant population. A 1997 study by the National Research Council of the National Academy of Sciences found that the average immigrant-headed household in California used $3,463 more in state and local public services than it paid in taxes. The resulting additional burden to the average native-headed California household was $1,178. See again Camarota, "Does Immigration Harm the Poor?"

72. Data on AFDC recipients are from *Statistical Abstract of the United States, 2000*, Table 625, p. 391.

73. U.S. House of Representatives, Committee on Ways and Means, *2000 Green Book: Background Material and Data on Programs Within the Jurisdiction of the Committee on Ways and Means* (Washington, D.C.: Government Printing Office, 2000), p. 447. Another study showed that as of 1995 over 76 percent had been on the rolls for five years or longer, with the mean duration thirteen years; see Ladonna Pavetti, "Helping the Hard-to-Employ," in Isabel V. Sawhill (ed.), *Welfare Reform: An Analysis of the Issues* (Washington, D.C.: Urban Institute, 1995).

74. To be eligible to receive federal funds under TANF, a state must maintain its own welfare spending at 80 percent or more of the 1994 level, including spending on AFDC and other programs. (This requirement falls to 75 percent if the state meets certain standards for engaging adult TANF recipients in work activities.)

75. In 1998, for example, 20 percent of immigrant households drew on some form of program welfare (cash assistance, food stamps, Medicaid, and others) versus 13 percent of native households; see George Borjas, "Welfare Reform and Immigrant Participation in Welfare Programs," *International Migration Review* 36 (Winter 2002), Table 2, p. 1101. In 2002, a recession year, use of welfare rose to 23 percent and 15 percent, respectively (unpublished estimates from George Borjas). See also George J. Borjas, *Heaven's Door: Immigration Policy and the American Economy* (Princeton: Princeton University Press, 1999), and David Reimers, *Unwelcome Strangers: American Identity and the Turn Against Immigration* (New York: Columbia University Press, 1998), for a more comprehensive treatment of this set of issues.

76. By 1995 forty states had already begun experimenting with various forms of welfare reform on their own; see again Moffit, "The Temporary Assistance for Needy Families Program."

77. See for example, the 1991 proposal by Texas representative Charles Stenholm (102 Congress, 1st Session, H.J. Res. 290); other prominent proposals along these times were those by Senator Paul Simon (1992) and Senate majority leader Bob Dole (1995).

78. See for example, the 1989 proposal by Congressman Stephen Neal (101 H.J. Res. 409) and the 1995 proposal by Senator Connie Mack (104 S. 1266).

79. Data on school expenditures, revenues and enrollments are from Snyder, *Digest of Education Statistics*, Tables 3, 29, 156, and 166.

80. Official Klan membership has fluctuated irregularly over the last quarter century; see, for example, Sara Bullard (ed.), *The Ku Klux Klan: A History of Racism and Violence*, 4th ed. (Montgomery, Ala.: Southern Poverty Law Center, 1991).

81. In 2002 Duke pled guilty to charges of tax and mail fraud, and subse-

quently served a year in a federal prison. See Ariel Hart, "Out of Prison and Back on the Job," *New York Times*, May 11, 2004, p. A16.

82. Kenneth S. Stern, *A Force Upon the Plain: The American Militia Movement and the Politics of Hate* (New York: Simon & Schuster, 1996), p. 20.

83. Andrew Macdonald, *The Turner Diaries* (New York: Barricade, 1996). "Andrew Macdonald" was a pseudonym used by Pierce.

84. "Aryan Nations Stages Alarming Comeback in 1994," in Southern Poverty Law Center, *Klanwatch Intelligence Report* (March 1995): 1, 5–7.

85. For accounts of the militia movement, see Richard Abanes, *American Militias: Rebellion, Racism and Religion* (Downers Grove, Ill.: InterVarsity, 1996); John George and Laird Wilcox, *American Extremists: Militias, Supremacists, Klansmen, Communists and Others* (Amherst, N.Y.: Prometheus, 1996); Michael Kazin, *The Populist Persuasion: An American History* (New York: Basic Books, 1995); Kathy Marks, *Faces of Right-Wing Extremism* (Boston: Branden, 1996); Daniel Levitas, *The Terrorist Next Door: The Militia Movement and the Radical Right* (New York: Thomas Dunne/St. Martin's, 2002); *False Patriots: The Threat of Antigovernment Extremists* (Montgomery, Ala.: Southern Poverty Law Center, 1996); and Kenneth Stern, *A Force Upon the Plain.*

86. Carey Goldberg, "The Freemen Sought Refuge in an Ideology That Kept the Law, and Reality, at Bay," *New York Times*, June 16, 1996, p. 14.

87. See James A. Aho, *The Politics of Righteousness: Idaho Christian Patriotism* (Seattle: University of Washington Press, 1990). It is not clear, however, that there is a connection to more general economic conditions across geographical areas. Philip Jefferson and Frederic L. Pryor, "On the Geography of Hate," *Economics Letters* 65 (December 1999): 389–95, showed that the existence of hate groups in individual counties in the United States in 1997 was not systematically related to the unemployment rate in that county. See also Alan B. Krueger and Jitka Maleckova, "Education, Poverty, Political Violence and Terrorism: Is There a Causal Connection?" *Journal of Economic Perspectives* 17 (Fall 2003): 119–44.

88. Macdonald, *The Turner Diaries*, p. 38. In addition, excerpts from the novel were subsequently found in McVeigh's getaway car; Jo Thomas, "Behind a Book That Inspired McVeigh," *New York Times*, June 9, 2001, p. A7.

89. Pat Robertson, *The New World Order* (Dallas: Word, 1991).

90. For an analysis of *The New World Order*, see Michael Lind, "Rev. Robertson's Grand International Conspiracy Theory," *New York Review of Books* 42 (February 2, 1995): 21–23, and "On Pat Robertson and His Defenders," *New York Review of Books* 42 (April 20, 1995): 67–68.

91. Abanes, *American Militas*, p. 195.

92. *Epperson v. Arkansas*, 393 U.S. 97 (1968).

93. Peter Applebome, "70 Years After Scopes Trial, Creation Debate Lives," *New York Times*, March 10, 1996, p. A1.

94. Pam Belluck, "Board for Kansas Deletes Evolution from Curriculum,"

New York Times, August 12, 1999, p. A1. In 2001, after a new school board election, Kansas reversed its anti-evolution rule; John W. Fountain, "Kansas Puts Evolution Back into Public Schools," *New York Times*, February 15, 2001, p. A12. The controversy, in various forms, continues to the present day in several states including Kansas, Georgia, and Pennsylvania. See James Dao, "Sleepy Election Is Jolted by Evolution," *New York Times*, May 17, 2005, p. A12.

95. In contrast to *BusinessWeek*'s 1991 cover story, for example, the magazine's issue for August 31, 1998, featured an article titled "A Rising Tide." The article's layout highlighted two statements: "It's no longer just the elite who are gaining from the innovation boom. Wages are growing across the board—and that's no surprise" (p. 72). "Far from being left behind, the working and middle classes are reacting to the high-tech boom by getting training so they can prosper in the years ahead" (p. 75).

96. As of the time of writing, the post-recession recovery in the labor market has lagged behind the rebound of production; unemployment, at 5.1 percent, remains modest by the standards of postwar American recession episodes, but well above the immediately prior pre-recession low. Productivity growth since the recession ended has averaged 3.8 percent per annum.

97. Data on net investment are from the National Income and Product Accounts.

98. One question that the early literature investigating the new acceleration in productivity emphasized was how much of this phenomenon reflects more than the remarkable technological gains of the computer-*producing* industry, which even including software still accounts for only 5 to 6 percent of U.S. nonfarm output; data are from an unpublished update to Stephen D. Oliver and Daniel E. Sichel, "Information Technology and Productivity: Where Are We Now and Where Are We Going?," Federal Reserve Bank of Atlanta, *Economic Review* 87 (Third Quarter 2002): 15–44. For two viewpoints on this issue, see Robert J. Gordon, "Does the 'New Economy' Measure Up to the Great Inventions of the Past?," *Journal of Economic Perspectives* 14 (Autumn 2000): 49–74, and Stephen D. Oliner and Daniel E. Sichel, "The Resurgence of Growth in the Late 1990s: Is Information Technology the Story?," *Journal of Economic Perspectives* 14 (Autumn 2000): 3–22.

99. The literature analyzing the post-1995 productivity acceleration is already extensive. See, for example, Dale W. Jorgenson and Kevin J. Stiroh, "Raising the Speed Limit: U.S. Economic Growth in the Information Age," *Brookings Papers on Economic Activity* (No. 1, 2000), pp. 125–235; Susanto Basu, John G. Fernald, and Matthew D. Shapiro, "Technology, Utilization, or Adjustment? Productivity Growth in the 1990s,"*Carnegie-Rochester Conference Series on Public Policy* 55 (December 2001), pp. 117–65; Erik Brynjolfson, Lorin M. Hitt, and Shinkyu Yang, "Intangible Assets: Com-

puters and Organizational Capital," *Brookings Papers on Economic Activity* (No. 1, 2002), pp. 137–98; Robert J. Gordon, "Exploding Productivity Growth: Context, Causes, and Implications," *Brookings Papers on Economic Activity* (No. 2, 2003), pp. 207–98; and Susanto Basu, John G. Fernald, Nicholas Oulton, and Sylaja Srinivasan, "The Case of the Missing Productivity Growth, or Does Information Technology Explain Why Productivity Accelerated in the United States but Not in the United Kingdom?," *NBER Macroeconomics Annual,* 2003, pp. 9–63.

100. Kathleen Decker, "7 in 10 Californians Support Higher Taxes to Help Schools," *Los Angeles Times,* June 18, 1999, p. A1; 30 percent of the poll's respondents called themselves "working-class," 5 percent "lower-class."

101. Data on consumer confidence are from the Conference Board.

102. See the 1998 Survey of Consumer Finances, as reported in Arthur B. Kennickell, Martha Starr-McCluer, and Brian J. Surette, "Recent Changes in U.S. Family Finances: Results from the 1998 Survey of Consumer Finances," *Federal Reserve Bulletin* 86 (January 2000): 1–29.

103. Gallup poll results, cited in Eric Schmitt, "Trapped; Americans (a) Love (b) Hate Immigrants," *New York Times,* January 14, 2001, p. D1.

104. George Gallup, Jr., *The Gallup Poll: Public Opinion 1999* (Wilmington, Del.: Scholarly Resources, 2000), p. 159. See also the poll results cited by John J. Miller, "The Politics of Permanent Immigration," *Reason* 30 (October 1998): 34–41.

105. Todd S. Purdum, "A Demographic Shift Alters California," *New York Times,* July 4, 2000, p. A12. An article in the *Times* a year later began, "Five years on, it takes some effort to recall the full fury of the anti-immigration hurricane that hit Washington in 1996"; Susan Sachs, "The Nation: Second Thoughts; Cracking the Door for Immigrants," *New York Times,* July 1, 2001, p. D3.

106. Steven Greenhouse, "Coalition Urges Easing of Immigration Laws," *New York Times,* May 16, 2000, p. A16.

107. Lizette Alvarez, "Congress Approves a Big Increase in Visas for Specialized Workers," *New York Times,* October 4, 2000, p. A1.

108. Trade balance data are from the Bureau of Economic Analysis.

109. Data are from the Census Bureau. Following the 2001 recession, the trade deficit with China increasingly became a significant political issue. By 2004 the deficit on trade with China alone had grown to $162 billion.

110. For a harsh critique of the IMF and its policies, see Joseph E. Stiglitz, *Globalization and Its Discontents* (New York: Norton, 2002). Also see *Report of the International Financial Institution Advisory Commission* (Washington, D.C.: International Financial Institution Advisory Commission, 2000).

111. Richard B. Freeman and William M. Rodgers III, "Area Economic Conditions and the Labor-Market Outcomes of Young Men in the 1990s Expansion," in Robert Cherry and William M. Rodgers III (eds.), *Prosperity for All? The Economic Boom and African Americans* (New York: Russell Sage

Foundation, 2000); see also Table A2, p. 16, in the prepublication version of the paper (omitted in the published version).

112. David T. Ellwood, "The Impact of the Earned Income Tax Credit and Social Policy Reforms on Work, Marriage, and Living Arrangements," *National Tax Journal* 53 (December 2000): 1063–1105; see especially Figure 2, p. 1079.

113. Those who "leave welfare" under TANF are still eligible to receive government assistance in other forms—food stamps, Medicaid, child support, housing subsidies—and most do so. See Andrea Williams, *Time Limited Welfare Recipients* (Denver: National Conference of State Legislatures, 2002).

114. In addition, the California program guaranteed admission to a community college, and then admission to the University of California after two years of satisfactory work, to all students not in the top 4 percent but in the top 12.5 percent.

115. Jodi Wilgoren, "New Law in Texas Preserves Racial Mix in State's Colleges," *New York Times*, November 24, 1999, p. A1, and "Deal Advances Education Bill," *New York Times*, April 5, 2001, p. A16; Rick Bragg, "Minority Enrollment Rises in Florida College System," *New York Times*, August 30, 2000, p. A18; and Diana Jean Schemt, "U.S. Schools Turn More Segregated, a Study Finds," *New York Times*, July 20, 2001, p. A14. Although the Texas program guaranteed top students admission to a campus of their choice, including the University of Texas in Austin, the California and Florida programs merely guaranteed admission to one of the state's university campuses. As a result, nonwhite admissions to some campuses—most notably the Berkeley and UCLA campuses of the University of California—remained well below what they had been under affirmative action.

116. Data are from the Southern Poverty Law Center, reported in Jo Thomas, "Behind a Book That Inspired McVeigh."

117. The median family income declined, after allowing for inflation, in each of 2001, 2002, and 2003. As of the time of writing, data on median incomes are not yet available for 2004.

118. David M. Potter, *People of Plenty: Economic Abundance and the American Character* (Chicago: University of Chicago Press, 1954), p. 93.

CHAPTER 9
Britain

1. Winston Churchill, Speech at Westminster College, Fulton, Missouri, March 5, 1946, in Robert Rhodes James (ed.), *Winston S. Churchill: His Complete Speeches 1897–1963*, Vol. VII: *1943–1949* (New York: Chelsea House, 1983), pp. 120, 122.

2. A typical assessment is that unemployment "appeared to turn around in the mid-1990s, but the decline is (temporarily?) on hold"; Olivier Blanchard, "Explaining European Unemployment," *NBER Reporter* (Summer 2004): 6. As of year-end 2004, unemployment was 9.7 percent in France, 9.5 percent in Germany, 8.0 percent in Italy, and 10.4 percent in Spain ("standardized unemployment rates" from the OECD). By contrast, in the U.K., unemployment was only 5 percent. For analyses of the continental countries' problems in this regard, including in particular the contribution of rigid labor market institutions, see, for example, Olivier Blanchard, "The Economics of Unemployment: Shocks, Institutions, and Interactions" (Lionel Robbins Lectures, unpublished manuscript, MIT, 2002); Olivier Blanchard and Justin Wolfers, "The Role of Shocks and Institutions in the Rise of European Unemployment: The Aggregate Evidence," *Economic Journal* 110 (March 2000): 1–34; and Steve Nickell, "Labor Market Institutions and Unemployment in OECD Countries," *CESifo DICE Report* 1 (Spring 2003): 13–16. On declining unemployment in the U.K., see, for example, David Card and Richard B. Freeman, "What Have Two Decades of British Economic Reform Delivered?" in Richard Blundell, David Card, and Richard Freeman (eds.), *Seeking a Premier Economy* (Chicago: University of Chicago Press, 2004).

3. Data on per capita incomes, measured on a purchasing power parity basis (for 2003), are from the World Bank, *World Development Report 2005: A Better Investment Climate for Everyone* (Washington, D.C.: World Bank, 2004), Table 1, pp. 256–57. Spain is exceptional among the larger western European countries in having an income level only 58 percent of that in the United States. A few of the smaller countries—Norway, for example—have per capita incomes greater than in the United States. (The exact comparison for any country depends on the method used to adjust for currency values and differences in price levels.)

4. Among the seventeen countries for which Angus Maddison's 1995 compendium of the most frequently used standard sources provided data on per capita incomes extending back into the nineteenth century, twelve were in western Europe. (The United States and three other former British colonies—Canada, Australia, and New Zealand—accounted for four of the remaining five; the other was Japan.) See Angus Maddison, *Monitoring the World Economy, 1820–1992* (Paris: OECD, 1995). Maddison's more recent collection of such data provides series going back to the nineteenth century for six additional countries, two more in western Europe plus four developing countries (Brazil, Uruguay, Indonesia, and Sri Lanka). See Angus Maddison, *The World Economy: Historical Statistics* (Paris: OECD, 2003).

5. Data on growth in per capita income are from Maddison, *The World Economy: Historical Statistics*, Table 1c, pp. 60–65.

6. Indeed, Europe and the United States have shared major periods of

strength or weakness: the agricultural depression of the 1880s and early 1890s, the irregular growth of the 1920s and then the Great Depression, the vigorous growth following World War II, and the stagnation that followed the first OPEC price increase. These were clearly international phenomena, although the intensity of each episode differed from one country to another, as did the specific beginning and ending dates.

7. Chris Cook and John Stevenson, *The Longman Handbook of Modern British History, 1714–1980* (London: Longman, 1983), and Norman Lowe, *Mastering Modern British History* (Basingstoke, U.K.: Macmillan, 1984).

8. Jonathan Philip Parry, *The Rise and Fall of Liberal Government in Victorian Britain* (New Haven: Yale University Press, 1993). It was presumably to avoid just such abuses that Article I, Section 2 of the Constitution of the United States provided that "Representatives . . . shall be apportioned among the several States which may be included within this Union, according to their respective numbers."

9. See Cook and Stevenson, *The Longman Handbook of Modern British History*.

10. Parry, *The Rise and Fall of Liberal Government*, p. 83.

11. Electorate data are from Anthony Wood, *Nineteenth Century Britain, 1815–1914* (New York: David McKay, 1960), pp. 449–53.

12. Albert O. Hirschman, *The Rhetoric of Reaction: Perversity, Futility, Jeopardy* (Cambridge, Mass.: Belknap Press, 1991), pp. 89–90. Even so, the idea of giving all male citizens the right to vote was still considered "radical" at the time. The role of a property qualification, which was widely accepted, was to restrict the franchise to men sufficiently independent economically to play an independent role in public affairs as well. The point is that by the 1830s, at least in principle, any man might at least aspire to do so.

13. As of 1830, only five of the twenty-four states in the United States still imposed explicit property qualifications for voting, although seven others required that voters be taxpayers. It is difficult to estimate how many Americans were therefore eligible to vote, but in the 1832 presidential election 1,150,000 actually voted, out of a population of not quite 14 million. See Erik W. Austin, *Political Facts of the United States Since 1789* (New York: Columbia University Press, 1986), Table 3.11; Stephen Thernstrom, *A History of the American People* (San Diego: Harcourt Brace Jovanovich, 1989), Vol. 2, p. A-22; and *Historical Statistics of the United States*, series A 6-8.

14. See Michael Brock, *The Great Reform Act* (London: Hutchinson, 1973). Charles Feinstein's estimates for "real earnings adjusted for unemployment (Great Britain)" show a peak in 1822; irregular fluctuation over the next ten years, with a sharp one-year low in 1830; and then sharp growth during 1833–35, which surpassed the previous (1822) peak; Charles Feinstein, "Pessimism Perpetuated," *Journal of Economic History* 58 (September 1998): 625–56.

15. For example, compare Feinstein, "Pessimism Perpetuated," to Jeffrey G.

Williamson and Peter H. Lindert, *American Inequality: A Macroeconomic History* (New York: Academic Press, 1980). Or compare Brian R. Mitchell, *International Historical Statistics: Europe, 1750–1988* (New York: Stockton, 1992), to Phyllis Deane and W. A. Cole, *British Economic Growth, 1688–1959: Trends and Structure* (Cambridge: Cambridge University Press, 1962).

16. Electorate data are from Wood, *Nineteenth Century Britain*, p. 453.

17. The interruption in British economic growth in 1866 looked more severe from the perspective of the financial markets. The failure of Overend, Gurney, a banking firm that had converted itself to a public company in the midst of a wave of speculation, broke the bubble and triggered a short-lived financial crisis. To the extent that the banking crisis had an economic origin, it was the return of normal conditions to the international cotton market following the end of the Civil War in the United States. See Charles P. Kindleberger, *Manias, Panics and Crashes: A History of Financial Crisis* (New York: Basic Books, 1978), p. 106, and Niall Ferguson, *House of Rothschild: The World's Banker, 1849–1999* (New York: Viking, 1999), p. 144.

18. Data on per capita income (here and elsewhere in this chapter, unless indicated otherwise) are from Mitchell, *International Historical Statistics*, Table J1, pp. 889–908. Mitchell's data for the U.K. are from C. H. Feinstein, *National Income, Expenditure and Output of the United Kingdom, 1885–1965* (Cambridge: Cambridge University Press, 1972), and then the official national accounts; see Mitchell, p. 909. According to the data in Maddison, *The World Economy: Historical Statistics*, the increase over this period was even greater (59 percent); see pp. 31–32, for a listing of underlying sources, including N. F. R. Crafts and C. K. Harley, "Output Growth and the British Industrial Revolution: A Restatement of the Crafts-Harley View," *Economic History Review* 45 (November 1920): 703–30; Phyllis Deane, "New Estimates of Gross National Product for the United Kingdom, 1930–1914," *Review of Income and Wealth* 14 (June 1968): 95–112; and Feinstein, *National Income, Expenditure and Output of the United Kingdom*.

19. Chris Cook and Brendan Keith, *British Historical Facts, 1830–1900* (London: Macmillan, 1975), pp. 114–15.

20. Lowe, *Mastering Modern British History*, p. 228. Andrew Jones, *The Politics of Reform, 1884* (Cambridge: Cambridge University Press, 1972), provides further detailed background to this episode.

21. The same general pattern appears in the Maddison data, although the average growth rate for the fifteen-year period is greater (.8 percent per annum).

22. The new voting qualifications for women were more restrictive than those for men, however; for example, the voting age for women was thirty, versus twenty-one for men, or nineteen if they had served in the armed forces. Further legislation a decade later abolished these differences.

23. Electoral data are from Martin Pugh, *Electoral Reform in War and Peace, 1906–18* (London: Routledge & Kegan Paul, 1978), p. 85.

24. In the Maddison data these increases are 23 percent and 43 percent, respectively.

25. J. M. Winter, *The Great War and the British People* (Basingstoke, U.K.: Macmillan, 1986).

26. The same is also true for Nonconformist Protestant and then Catholic emancipation—that is, the removal of restrictions on the right to sit in Parliament and hold government office (with a few exceptions still held out for Catholics)—in 1828 and 1829, respectively.

27. A further aspect of the economic background to the Corn Laws debate is that by this time the rise of city-based commerce had created other sources of tax revenues, thereby reducing the government's need to rely on tariff revenues. Britain was unique, however, at least within Europe, in turning toward free trade during this period; there was no corresponding movement on the continent. See Douglas A. Irwin, *Against the Tide: An Intellectual History of Free Trade* (Princeton: Princeton University Press, 1996).

28. See Jeffrey G. Williamson, "The Impact of the Corn Laws Just Prior to Repeal," *Explorations in Economic History* 27 (April 1990): 123–56, for estimates of the magnitude of these two effects.

29. Some historians argue that repeal of the Corn Laws in 1846, together with suspension of the Bank Charter Act in 1844, helped prevent the rash of revolutions that swept over continental Europe in 1848 from reaching Britain; see, for example, Niall Ferguson, *The House of Rothschild: Money's Prophets, 1798–1848* (New York: Viking, 1998).

30. Wood, *Nineteenth Century Britain*, p. 113.

31. In the Maddison data, the 1843–46 average growth rate is 5 percent per annum, and the total increase from the early 1830s is 23 percent. Feinstein's adjusted real earnings estimates show a ten-year low in 1841, followed by four years of growth at 4.3 percent per annum to a peak in 1845; Feinstein, "Pessimism Perpetuated."

32. Noel Annan, *The Dons: Mentors, Eccentrics and Geniuses* (Chicago: University of Chicago Press, 1999), p. 15. A further reform during this period, somewhat more closely related to the themes of the abolitionist movement, was ending the practice of sending convict ships abroad (in 1867).

33. In the Maddison data the 1860–70 increase is significantly more modest (13 percent), but the 1850–70 gain is slightly greater (37 percent).

34. Peter Rowland, *The Last Liberal Governments*, Vol. 1, *The Promised Land, 1905–10*, and Vol. 2, *Unfinished Business, 1911–14* (London: Barrie & Jenkins, 1968 and 1971), provides a comprehensive account of this period. The Asquith reforms clearly drew inspiration from Bismarck's program of thirty years before. As in the case of the United States, why Britain delayed for an entire generation before following suit is an interesting question. In Britain, as in America, part of the answer is probably the poor economic

environment of the post-Bismarck years. But the Asquith reforms of 1908–11 did not take place in a climate of economic growth either. As we shall see, the completion of this process after World War II did.

35. Bentley Brinkerhoff Gilbert, *David Lloyd George: A Political Life*, Vol. 1, *The Architect of Change, 1863–1912* (London: Batsford, 1987), pp. 355–56.

36. Roy Jenkins, *Asquith: Portrait of a Man and an Era* (London: Collins, 1965), provides an especially good account of the House of Lords crisis.

37. In the Maddison data the average 1900–1910 growth is even smaller: less than .3 percent per annum. The Aliens Act of 1905, passed the year before the Liberals' great election victory, was more in line with what the depressed economic conditions of that decade might have been expected to produce. Like the United States, Britain at that time was a magnet for immigrants fleeing persecution or economic hardship or both. Refugees from Czarist Russia, including Jews in particular, represented a large part of British immigration, spurring widespread popular opposition. The result was the 1905 Aliens Act, which for the first time explicitly regulated immigration to Britain. The act curtailed the inflow in part by restricting the admissible class of refugees, and it also allowed recent immigrants to be deported not just for criminal offenses but for vagrancy or poverty. See Bernard Gainer, *The Alien Invasion: The Origins of the Alien Act of 1905* (London: Heinemann, 1972), and James Stephen Goldman, "The Conservative Struggle over Immigration Restriction: The Significance of National Efficiency; A Reconsideration of the 1905 Aliens Act" (unpublished thesis, Harvard University, 1997).

38. One plausible explanation for how these reforms came to be is that the post-1906 Liberal program was a reflection of the expansion of the franchise in 1867 and especially in 1884–85, which had created a new incentive for competition for working-class votes. Even so, the question remains why all this happened during 1908–11, when the British economy was stagnant, rather than at a time of more robust economic growth either before or after. As with Roosevelt's New Deal, one potential explanation is leadership—in this case Asquith's and, even more so, Lloyd George's.

39. Great Britain, Inter-Departmental Committee on Social Insurance and Allied Services, *Social Insurance and Allied Services* (London: H.M. Stationery Office, 1942).

40. Paul Addison, *The Road to 1945: British Politics and the Second World War* (London: Pimlico, 1994), p. 265.

41. J. M. Lee, *The Churchill Coalition, 1940–1945* (Hamden, Conn.: Archon, 1980), p. 136.

42. Even so, one interpretation of Atlee's landslide victory in 1945 was that the British public saw Labour as more likely to follow through on the White Paper's promises. See Addison, *The Road to 1945*; Kenneth Morgan, *Labour in Power, 1945–1951* (New York: Oxford University Press, 1984); and Correlli Barnett, *The Audit of War: The Illusion and Reality of Britain as a Great*

Nation (London: Macmillan, 1986) and *The Lost Victory: British Dreams, British Realities, 1945–1950* (London: Macmillan, 1995), for differing interpretations of Britain's postwar political history, especially regarding implementation of the Beveridge program.

43. Although most workers already had access to doctors via their employment, the new system was far more comprehensive and it extended coverage to dependents and the unemployed, both of which groups had previously been excluded.

44. In the Maddison data per capita income in 1942 was 39 percent above the 1929 level, and the 1938–48 and 1929–48 gains were 8 percent and 23 percent, respectively.

45. It is interesting that the increase in per capita income in Britain's early postwar period did not carry over to an increase in per capita private consumption. Britain maintained its wartime austerity programs longer than did the United States, and instead devoted the increased income to investment and government programs.

46. Jenkins had outlined his plans for these and other reforms (for example, eliminating censorship and liberalizing British divorce procedures) in his 1959 book, *The Labour Case* (Harmondsworth, U.K.: Penguin, 1959). See also Jenkins's later account in his 1991 book, *A Life at the Center: Memoirs of a Radical Reformer* (New York: Random House, 1991). See also Clive Ponting, *Breach of Promise: Labour in Power, 1964–1970* (London: Hamish Hamilton, 1989), which portrays Jenkins's role favorably despite a negative view of the Labour government overall.

47. See Paul Barton Johnson, *Land Fit for Heroes: The Planning of British Reconstruction, 1916–1919* (Chicago: University of Chicago Press, 1968).

48. Labor union militancy per se was limited throughout this period, however. The coal miners' efforts to launch a general strike in 1921 failed to attract the support of other unions. When the coal miners again called for a general strike, in 1926, the other unions agreed but withdrew their support after only nine days. See D. E. Baines and R. Bean, "The General Strike on Merseyside, 1926," in J. R. Harris, *Liverpool and Merseyside: Essays in the Economic and Social History of the Port and Its Hinterland* (London: Frank Cass, 1969).

49. See Charles Loch Mowat, *Britain Between the Wars, 1918–1940* (London: Methuen, 1955).

50. Martin Middlebrook, *The First Day on the Somme, 1 July 1916* (Harmondsworth, U.K.: Penguin, 1984), p. 310. See also Ross McKibbin, "Class and Conventional Wisdom," in *The Ideologies of Class: Social Relations in Britain, 1880–1950* (Oxford: Clarendon Press,1990).

51. Yet a third attempt to present a Chartist petition occurred in 1848, at the time of the widespread revolutions on the continent. It attracted little support, and the ensuing public disturbances were mostly limited to London.

52. See Gareth Stedman Jones, "Rethinking Chartism," in *Languages of Class:*

Studies in English Working Class History, 1832–1982 (Cambridge: Cambridge University Press, 1983), for an analysis of Chartism. The question of why the Corn Laws repeal succeeded while Chartism failed is especially intriguing. One part of the answer is the role of arguments over matters of economic principle—free trade versus protectionism—in the Corn Laws debate. Another is that grain protection benefited upper-class landowners but not the middle class. Yet another is the divergence of interest, among upper-income groups, between landowners and manufacturers, and even between owners of grain-producing and other lands; see again Williamson, "The Impact of the Corn Laws." The 1832 Reform Bill had, in part, realigned voting strength in favor of the newly emerging industrial elite, and the 1846 Corn Laws repeal removed an important subsidy to the landed aristocracy; both measures were signs of the power shift that accompanied the Industrial Revolution. See, for example, David S. Landes, *The Wealth and Poverty of Nations: Why Some Are So Rich and Some So Poor* (New York: Norton, 1998). Finally, the religious motivation of the early-nineteenth-century English reformers was also probably a factor. Corn Laws repeal (like the Poor Laws amendments) enhanced the role of market competition as a way to reinforce Christian discipline and, in effect, force people to compete for their salvation. By contrast, Chartism (especially the demand for universal suffrage) sought to enfranchise an underclass that, in the eyes of the middle classes, had not proved its worth economically; see Boyd Hilton, *The Age of Atonement: The Influence of Evangelicalism on Social and Economic Thought, 1795–1865* (New York: Oxford University Press, 1988).

53. See Norman Gash, *Aristocracy and People: Britain, 1815–1865* (Cambridge: Harvard University Press, 1979). For a further account of the background to the massacre, see R. J. White, *Waterloo to Peterloo* (New York: Macmillan, 1957).

54. See J. E. Cookson, *Lord Liverpool's Administration: The Crucial Years, 1815–1822* (Hamden, Conn.: Archon, 1975), pp. 193–95.

55. Wage rates were falling throughout the 1810s; see Deane and Cole, *British Economic Growth*, p. 23.

56. See Andrew Rosen, *Rise Up, Women! The Militant Campaign of the Women's Social and Political Union, 1903–1914* (Boston: Routledge & Kegan Paul, 1974).

57. See George Dangerfield, *The Strange Death of Liberal England* (New York: H. Smith & R. Haas, 1935), for examples of the contemporary perception that the suffragettes were contributing to the erosion of civility in British society. (Whether that perception withstands scrutiny from the perspective of later generations is another matter.)

58. Ponting, *Breach of Promise*, p. 331.

59. See Robert Blake, *Disraeli* (London: Oxford University Press, 1969); also

Benjamin Hett, "Disraeli and the Problem of Anti-Semitism" (unpublished paper, Harvard University, 1997).

60. Jewish civil emancipation had also been a lively political issue in the 1840s, a time of economic stagnation overall, but the Tories in particular had opposed the idea and it failed to advance; Ferguson, *The House of Rothschild*, Vol. 1, p. 381.

61. See Colin Holmes, *Anti-Semitism in British Society, 1876–1939* (New York: Holmes & Meier, 1979), Chapter 5. Jenkins, *Asquith*, also provides a good account of this episode.

62. Robert Skidelsky, *Oswald Mosley* (New York: Holt, Rinehart & Winston, 1975), p. 322.

63. See again Holmes, *Anti-Semitism in British Society.*

64. Brian Spittles, *Britain Since 1960: An Introduction* (Basingstoke, U.K.: Macmillan, 1995), p. 85.

65. Alan Sked and Chris Cook, *Post-War Britain: A Political History*, 4th ed. (London: Penguin, 1993), p. 351.

CHAPTER 10
France

1. Charles de Gaulle, Speech at Bayeux, June 16, 1946, in Roy C. Macridis, *De Gaulle: Implacable Ally* (New York: Harper & Row, 1966), pp. 41–43.

2. Because it initially appeared in the popular press, "J'Accuse" had more than 200,000 copies in circulation on its first day in print. Paradoxically, Zola's novel *L'Argent* ("Money"), published three years before Dreyfus was first accused of treason, had plainly reflected the pervasive anti-Semitism of France at that time.

3. Jean-Denis Bredin, *The Affair: The Case of Alfred Dreyfus*, translated by Jeffrey Mehlman (New York: George Braziller, 1986), p. 520; see also Maurice Agulhon, *The French Republic, 1879–1992*, translated by Antonia Nevill (Oxford: Blackwell, 1993), p. 93.

4. See for example, Michael R. Marrus, "Popular Anti-Semitism," in Norman L. Kleeblatt (ed.), *The Dreyfus Affair: Art, Truth and Justice* (Berkeley: University of California Press, 1987); David L. Lewis, *Prisoners of Honor: The Dreyfus Affair* (New York: Morrow, 1973); and Robert L. Hoffman, *More than a Trial: The Struggle over Captain Dreyfus* (New York: Free Press, 1980). Also see again Bredin, *The Affair,* and Agulhon, *The French Republic.*

5. Peter Campbell, *French Electoral Systems and Elections Since 1789* (Hamden, Conn.: Archon Books, 1958), p. 73.

6. Eugen Weber, *Peasants into Frenchmen: The Modernization of Rural France, 1870–1914* (Stanford, Calif.: Stanford University Press, 1976), p. 210.

7. See Weber, *Peasants into Frenchmen*, and Jean-Marie Mayeur and Madeleine Rebérioux, *The Third Republic from Its Origins to the Great War, 1871–1914*, translated by J. R. Foster (New York: Cambridge University Press, 1984).

8. France in the latter half of Napoleon III's empire had likewise undergone a fair amount of political liberalization, and so including the 1860s would add another episode in which economic growth and democratization went together.

9. See Charles P. Kindleberger, *Manias, Panics, and Crashes: A History of Financial Crises* (New York: Basic Books, 1978), and Niall Ferguson, *The House of Rothschild: The World's Banker, 1849–1999* (New York: Viking, 1999). Other new banking institutions established during this period included the Crédit Industriel et Commercial (1859), the Société de Dépôts et Comptes Courants (1863), and Société Générale (1864). The Crédit Lyonnais first opened a Paris branch in 1865.

10. See Ferguson, *The House of Rothschild*, Vol. 2, pp. 204–5, for a broader discussion of the financial differences between France's successful Third Republic and Germany's failed Weimar Republic.

11. Data on per capita income, here and below unless stated otherwise, are from B. R. Mitchell, *International Historical Statistics: Europe, 1750–1988* (Basingstoke, U.K.: Macmillan, 1992), Table J1, pp. 889–908 (for total income), and Table A5, pp. 76–88 (for population). Using instead the per capita income data in Angus Maddison, *The World Economy: Historical Statistics* (Paris: OECD, 2003), Table 1c, pp. 58–65, gives an increase of only 15 percent for 1865–75 and 37 percent for 1855–75. The Maddison data also show strong growth at the beginning of the 1880s, with a peak in 1882.

12. Mayeur and Rebérioux, *The Third Republic*, p. 70.

13. Daniel Halévy, *La Fin des Notables* (Paris: B. Grasset, 1930–37).

14. See again Mayeur and Rebérioux, *The Third Republic*, Chapter 1.

15. This comparison relies on the Maddison data. Mitchell does not give income figures for France for 1939–48.

16. Jean Fourastié, *Les Trentes Glorieuses, ou, La Révolution Invisible de 1946 à 1975* (Paris: Fayard, 1979).

17. In the Mitchell data, real per capita income in 1949 was 10 percent above the 1938 level. In the Maddison data, 1949 was 3 percent above 1939 (and 11 percent above 1938).

18. David S. Landes, *The Wealth and Poverty of Nations: Why Some Are So Rich and Some So Poor* (New York: Norton, 1998), pp. 468–69.

19. The rationale for nationalizing Renault was in part economic but also partly in retribution for the pro-fascist activities of the firm's founder, Louis Renault, who went to prison just after the liberation.

20. See Stanley Hoffmann, *In Search of France* (Cambridge: Harvard University Press, 1963), and also "Protest in Modern France," in Morton A. Kaplan (ed.), *The Revolution in World Politics* (New York: Wiley, 1962),

p. 79; see also Michael Crozier, *La Société Bloquée* (Paris: Editions du Seuil, 1970), which took its title from Hoffmann. For more general accounts of French politics and government during this period, see Frank Giles, *The Locust Years: The Story of the Fourth French Republic, 1946–1958* (London: Secker & Warburg, 1991), and Jean-Pierre Rioux, *The Fourth Republic, 1944–1958*, translated by Godfrey Rogers (New York: Cambridge University Press, 1987).

21. The first formal step toward European economic integration had been the Committee of European Economic Coordination, founded at Paris in response to the Marshall Plan's requirement that the Europeans themselves agree on how to divide American aid funds. The committee completed its report in September 1947. The European Payments Union was established in 1949 under the sponsorship of the Marshall Plan's administrative arm, the Economic Cooperation Agency.

22. This comparison (of 1958 to 1939) is from the Maddison data. In the Mitchell data, real per capita income in 1958 was 54 percent above 1938.

23. Philip M. Williams, *French Politicians and Elections, 1951–1969* (London: Cambridge University Press, 1970), p. 124.

24. In 1960, when both the army and the settlers began openly to oppose de Gaulle's policy of self-determination for Algeria, he promptly dismissed the commanding general. The settlers in Algeria attempted a new revolt, but the army remained loyal and the uprising collapsed within ten days. See Alexander Harrison, *Challenging de Gaulle: The OAS and the Counter-revolution in Algeria, 1954–1962* (New York: Praeger, 1989).

25. Algeria's experience since independence has, alas, been less fortunate.

26. Eugen Joseph Weber, *Action Française: Royalism and Reaction in Twentieth Century France* (Stanford: Stanford University Press, 1962), p. 262.

27. See again Barry J. Eichengreen, *Golden Fetters: The Gold Standard and the Great Depression, 1919–1939* (New York: Oxford University Press, 1992), and Peter Temin, *Lessons from the Great Depression* (Cambridge: MIT Press, 1989).

28. Eugen Weber, *The Hollow Years: France in the 1930s* (New York: Norton, 1994), pp. 87–89.

29. Robert O. Paxton, *Vichy France: Old Guard and New Order, 1940–1944* (New York: Knopf, 1972), p. 169, and Weber, *The Hollow Years*, p. 92.

30. Philippe Bernard and Henri Dubief, *The Decline of the Third Republic, 1914–1938*, translated by Anthony Forster (Cambridge: Cambridge University Press, 1985), p. 160.

31. Robert Soucy, *French Fascism: The First Wave, 1924–1933* (New Haven: Yale University Press, 1986), p. 29.

32. Ibid., p. 26.

33. William L. Shirer, *The Collapse of the Third Republic: An Inquiry into the Fall of France in 1940* (New York: Simon & Schuster, 1969), p. 200; also cited in Soucy, *French Fascism*, p. 32.

34. Apart from the economic sphere, the Popular Front government also acted to dissolve some of France's fascist leagues. For good accounts of the Popular Front, see Julian Jackson, *The Popular Front in France: Defending Democracy, 1934–38* (New York: Cambridge University Press, 1988), and Weber, *The Hollow Years.*

35. Temin, *Lessons from the Great Depression*, pp. 124–25.

36. See Paxton, *Vichy France*, Chapter 1, and Michael R. Marrus and Robert O. Paxton, *Vichy France and the Jews* (New York: Basic Books, 1981), pp. 228–34. Not all of Vichy's leaders sought to become close to the Nazis, however. Robert Gildea, *Marianne in Chains: In Search of the German Occupation, 1940–1945* (London: Macmillan, 2002), emphasizes the disparities in how Vichy operated from region to region and even from village to village.

37. Ferguson, *The House of Rothschild*, Vol. 2, p. 475.

38. In the end, the Protocols proved symbolic only. They were never applied.

39. Vichy France was one of only two European countries—the other was Bulgaria—to turn over to the Nazis Jews from territory that the Germans did not occupy; see Adam Nossiter, *The Algeria Hotel: France, Memory, and the Second World War* (Boston: Houghton Mifflin, 2001).

40. Paxton, *Vichy France*, pp. 320–21.

41. See William D. Irvine, *The Boulanger Affair Reconsidered: Royalism, Boulangism, and the Origins of the Radical Right in France* (New York: Oxford University Press, 1989), and Frederic Seager, *The Boulanger Affair: Political Crossroads of France, 1886–1889* (Ithaca, N.Y.: Cornell University Press, 1969), for accounts of this episode. Agulhon, *The French Republic*, presents Boulanger in a more favorable light than either Irvine or Seager; see pp. 37–42.

42. See Philip M. Williams and Martin Harrison, *De Gaulle's Republic* (London: Longmans, 1960), pp. 108–9.

43. Roger Eatwell, "Poujadism and Neo-Poujadism: From Revolt to Reconciliation," in Philip G. Cerny (ed.), *Social Movements and Protest in France* (New York: St. Martin's, 1982), pp. 72, 77.

44. Although Boulanger was far more prominent than Poujade, he fled the country and died soon afterward. Poujade lived on for decades, dying only in 2003, and he continued to be active at the margins of French politics.

45. In both the Mitchell data and the Maddison data, per capita income in 1888 was below what it had been in 1883 in real terms.

46. For useful accounts of the Paris Commune, see Alistair Horne, *The Fall of Paris: The Siege and the Commune, 1870–1871* (New York: Penguin, 1981); Roger L. Williams, *The French Revolution of 1870–1871* (New York: Norton, 1969); and Stewart Edwards (ed.), *The Communards of Paris, 1871* (Ithaca, N.Y.: Cornell University Press, 1973), especially Edwards's "Introduction," pp. 9–42.

47. Thiers's actions did, however, persuade some doubters that a republican government was capable of maintaining public order.

48. Fourastié's book bearing that title appeared in 1979, and the phrase caught on rapidly thereafter.

49. See again Olivier Blanchard, "The Economics of Unemployment: Shocks, Institutions, and Interactions" (Lionel Robbins Lectures; unpublished manuscript, MIT, 2000), and Olivier Blanchard and Justin Wolfers, "The Role of Shocks and Institutions in the Rise of European Unemployment: The Aggregate Evidence," *Economic Journal* 110 (March 2000): 1–33.

50. Unemployment data are from the OECD and U.S. Bureau of Labor Statistics.

51. See Jonathan Marcus, *The National Front and French Politics: The Resistible Rise of Jean-Marie Le Pen* (New York: New York University Press, 1995); Harvey G. Simmons, *The French National Front: The Extremist Challenge to Democracy* (Boulder, Colo.: Westview, 1996); and Philip Gourevitch, "The Unthinkable," *The New Yorker*, April 28/May 5, 1997, p. 110, for useful early accounts of the National Front and the movement behind it.

52. Untitled article, *Le Monde*, September 17, 1996, p. 1 (the phrase is "certaines sont plus égales que d'autres"); another example appeared in Marlise Simons, "The French Far Right Thrives on Outrage," *New York Times*, October 2, 1996, p. A8.

53. Craig R. Whitney, "French Far-Right Leader Convicted of Slighting Holocaust," *New York Times*, December 27, 1997, p. A5, and "Le Pen May Be Charged for a Remark About the Holocaust," *New York Times*, October 7, 1998, p. A5.

54. Stanley Hoffmann, "The Big Muddle in France," *New York Review of Books* 35 (August 18, 1988), p. 56.

CHAPTER 11
Germany

1. Willy Brandt, Inauguration Address to the Bundestag, October 28, 1969, in Dennis L. Bark and David P. Gress, *A History of West Germany* (Oxford: Blackwell, 1989), Vol. 2, p. 157.

2. Peter Temin, *Lessons from the Great Depression* (Cambridge: MIT Press, 1989), p. 25.

3. Barry Eichengreen and Timothy Hatton (eds.), *Interwar Unemployment in International Perspective* (Boston: Kluwer Academic Publishers, 1988), Table 1.2. Here and below, the unemployment figures given for Germany in the first half of the twentieth century are Galenson and Zellner's annual estimates based on the industrial sector; see Walter Galenson and Arnold Zellner, "International Comparison of Unemployment Rates," in

Universities-National Bureau Committee for Economic Research, *The Measurement and Behavior of Unemployment* (Princeton: Princeton University Press, 1957), Tables 1 and F-1. By contrast, Maddison's annual figures are lower; see Angus Maddison, *Economic Growth in the West: Comparative Experience in Europe and North America* (New York: Twentieth Century Fund, 1964), Table E-1. Eichengreen and Hatton suggest that the "true" figures are probably somewhere in between. See also Dan P. Silverman, "National Socialist Economics: The *Wirtschaftswunder* Reconsidered," in Eichengreen and Hatton, *Interwar Unemployment in International Perspective.*

4. See again Temin, *Lessons from the Great Depression.* Also see Thomas Childers, *The Nazi Voter: The Social Foundations of Fascism in Germany, 1919–1933* (Chapel Hill: University of North Carolina Press, 1983), pp. 44–45.

5. See Fritz R. Stern, *The Politics of Cultural Despair: A Study in the Rise of Germanic Ideology* (Berkeley: University of California Press, 1961), and Ralf Dahrendorf, *Society and Democracy in Germany* (Garden City, N.Y.: Doubleday, 1967).

6. See Alan Bullock, *Hitler: A Study in Tyranny* (New York: Harper & Row, 1964); Dahrendorf, *Society and Democracy in Germany*; and Ian Kershaw, *The Nazi Dictatorship: Problems and Perspectives of Interpretation* (New York: Arnold, 1993). Also see Gerald D. Feldman, *The Great Disorder: Politics, Economics and Society in the German Inflation, 1914–1924* (New York: Oxford University Press, 1993).

7. In addition to the Social Democratic Party (SPD), the "Weimar Coalition" also included the Catholic Center Party and the left-liberal German Democratic Party. The much smaller Independent Social Democratic Party (the USPD), which had split off from the SPD during the war, and which stood to the left of the SPD, was not part of the governing coalition. In the early 1920s an element of the USPD became the German Communist Party and the remainder rejoined the SPD.

8. Karl Hardach, *The Political Economy of Germany in the Twentieth Century* (Berkeley: University of California Press, 1980), Figure 1, Appendix Table 1, and p. 17.

9. See the exchange rate data given in John Parke Young, *European Currency and Finance: Commission of Gold and Silver Inquiry of the United States Senate: Foreign Currency and Exchange Investigation* (Washington, D.C.: Government Printing Office, 1925), Vol. 1, p. 532, and also the details of reparations given in Mark Trachtenberg, *Reparation in World Politics: France and European Economic Diplomacy, 1916–1923* (New York: Columbia University Press, 1980), p. 71. In fact the reparations arrangements were never fully finalized. Negotiations went on through the 1920s, leading to the Dawes Plan (1924), the Young Plan (1929), the one-year moratorium declared by Hoover (1931), and the Lausanne Conference (1932), which reduced Ger-

many's obligation to a token sum (and in the end the new government under Hitler never ratified the Lausanne agreement anyway).

10. Richard J. Evans, *The Coming of the Third Reich* (New York: Penguin, 2004), p. 61.

11. Erich Ludendorff, "Germany Never Defeated!," in *These Eventful Years: The Twentieth Century in the Making, as Told by Many of Its Makers* (London: Encyclopaedia Britannica, 1924), Vol. 1, pp 269–83, quotation from p. 283.

12. Gordon A. Craig, *Germany, 1866–1945* (New York: Oxford University Press, 1978), p. 415.

13. See John Maynard Keynes, *The Economic Consequences of the Peace* (London: Macmillan, 1919); Charles P. Kindleberger, *The World in Depression, 1929–1939* (Berkeley: University of California Press, 1973); and again Temin, *Lessons from the Great Depression.*

14. See, for example, Eberhard Kolb, *The Weimar Republic,* translated by P. S. Falla (Boston: Unwin Hyman, 1988), and Detlev J. K. Peukert, *The Weimar Republic: The Crisis of Classical Modernity,* translated by Richard Deveson (New York: Hill & Wang, 1992). Also see again Dahrendorf, *Society and Democracy in Germany,* and Kershaw, *The Nazi Dictatorship.*

15. Data on per capita income are from Maddison, *The World Economy: Historical Statistics* (Paris: OECD, 2003), Table 1c, pp. 60–65. The estimates Maddison reports for Germany are largely based on Walther G. Hoffman, Franz Grumbach, and Helmut Hesse, *Das Wachstum der Deutschen Wirtschaft seit der Mitte des 19 Jahrhunderts* (Berlin: Springer-Verlag, 1965). The data in B. R. Mitchell, *International Historical Statistics: Europe, 1750–1988* (New York: Stockton, 1992), do not give figures for German gross national product (or gross domestic product) for 1914–24.

16. German income data for the 1920s are subject to great uncertainty, in part simply because of the economic chaos of the time but also because of government obfuscations related to the Versailles reparations. But for our purposes the general trend is what matters, and the available data on employment, which are probably more reliable, are consistent with this impression.

17. See again Eichengreen and Hatton, *Interwar Unemployment in International Perspective.*

18. Kindleberger, *The World in Depression,* p. 33.

19. Hardach, *The Political Economy of Germany,* pp. 17–18.

20. Young, *European Currency and Finance,* Vol. 2, p. 393.

21. Ibid., Vol. 1, pp. 530, 532.

22. See Gerald Feldman, *The Great Disorder,* and Stefan Zweig, *The World of Yesterday: An Autobiography* (New York: Viking, 1943), for accounts of the economic as well as political and social consequences of the German hyperinflation.

23. Data on per capita income are again from Maddison, *The World Economy.*

24. Gustav Stolper, *The German Economy, 1870–1940: Issues and Trends* (New York: Reynal & Hitchcock, 1940), p. 159.

25. Temin, *Lessons from the Great Depression*, pp. 23–30.

26. See Barry J. Eichengreen, *Golden Fetters: The Gold Standard and the Great Depression, 1919–1939* (New York: Oxford University Press, 1992).

27. See Kindleberger, *The World in Depression*, for an account of pre-Hitler German economic policy, including the politics of reparations payments and nonpayments.

28. Volker R. Berghahn, *Modern Germany: Society, Economy and Politics in the Twentieth Century* (Cambridge: Cambridge University Press, 1987), p. 226; also see R. J. Overy, *The Nazi Economic Recovery, 1932–1938* (London: Macmillan, 1982), Table IV, p. 14, and Claude W. Guillebaud, *The Economic Recovery of Germany from 1933 to the Incorporation of Austria in 1938* (London: Macmillan, 1939), p. 31.

29. The unemployment data cited are again from Eichengreen and Hatton, *Interwar Unemployment in International Perspective*. Hardach, *The Political Economy of Germany*, also highlights the high unemployment in the late 1920s, albeit using slightly different data.

30. The Beer Hall Putsch, like such earlier episodes of violence as the Spartacist uprising in Berlin and the "White Terror" in Bavaria, as well as the assassination by right-wingers of prominent politicians of the left and the center, is probably best seen as part of the aftermath of Germany's defeat in the war and the subsequent revolution that overthrew the empire, rather than as a direct response to economic decline and (by 1923) the hyperinflation. By contrast, the more systematic mass violence carried out by the Nazis and other far-right and far-left groups from 1930 to 1933 seems much more tied to that period's economic decline, and especially to the spreading unemployment.

31. See Ian Kershaw, *Hitler, 1889–1936: Nemesis* (New York: Norton, 1988), Chapter 5, for an account of Hitler's experience as a beer hall orator.

32. Berghahn, *Modern Germany*, pp. 113, 301.

33. Ibid., p. 301.

34. The number of unemployed listed by government labor offices declined from 6.1 million in February 1932 to 5.1 million in September and October (before rising back above 6 million in January 1933). By contrast, the monthly unemployment *rate*, in the series now published by Global Financial Data, Inc., shows no significant decline until mid-1933.

35. Both Papen and Hindenburg, along with many of Germany's major industrialists, apparently thought that once Hitler was chancellor they would be able to manipulate him to their own political ends. They underestimated him (as did British prime minister Neville Chamberlain in 1938). In the end, the only party in the Reichstag not to vote for Hitler as chancellor was the Social Democrats (SPD). See again Bullock, *Hitler*, and Kershaw, *The*

Nazi Dictatorship, for accounts of the political dealings that led to Hitler's assuming the chancellorship.

36. See Richard F. Hamilton, *Who Voted for Hitler?* (Princeton: Princeton University Press, 1982). Also see Thomas Childers, *The Nazi Voter* and *The Formation of the Nazi Constituency, 1918–1933* (London: Croom Helm, 1986). Bullock, *Hitler*; Dahrendorf, *Society and Democracy in Germany*; and Kershaw, *The Nazi Dictatorship*, all deal with this question also.

37. Hamilton, *Who Voted for Hitler?*, p. 37. The Nazi vote was also very disproportionately Protestant. District by district, the correlation between the Nazi share of the vote in July 1932 and the Catholic share of the population was not only negative but, depending on the section of the country, very strongly negative. In districts with significant numbers of Jewish voters, mostly in Berlin and Hamburg, the Nazis also had lower than average vote totals.

38. See ibid., especially Chapters 3 and 4.

39. Childers, *The Nazi Voter*, pp. 264–65.

40. For years historians debated whether the fire was set by a communist, as Hitler claimed, or by the Nazis themselves. Recent research appears to have exonerated the Nazis. See Kershaw, *Hitler*, Chapter 11.

41. In addition to giving the president authority to issue emergency decrees, the Weimar constitution had given the German parliament the ability, with a two-thirds majority, to vote the end of parliamentary rule.

42. See Norbert Frei, *National Socialist Rule in Germany: The Führer State, 1933–1945* (Oxford: Blackwell, 1993).

43. For a good account, see Karl A. Schleunes, *The Twisted Road to Auschwitz: Nazi Policy Towards German Jews, 1933–1939* (Urbana: University of Illinois Press, 1970).

44. See Michael Burleigh, *The Third Reich: A New History* (New York: Hill & Wang, 2000).

45. See John Cornwell, *Hitler's Pope: The Secret History of Pius XII* (New York: Viking, 1999).

46. As indicated before, German unemployment data for the interwar period are subject to great uncertainty on ordinary grounds, and in addition there is ground for concern that the Nazis may have manipulated these figures for their political advantage.

47. Germany did not experience a resurgence of *private* investment spending such as America enjoyed beginning in 1933.

48. Temin, *Lessons from the Great Depression*, Table 3.3, p. 121.

49. See ibid., Chapter 3; Charles S. Maier, *In Search of Stability: Explorations in Historical Political Economy* (New York: Cambridge University Press, 1987), Chapter 2; John Weitz, *Hitler's Banker: Hjalmar Horace Greeley Schacht* (New York: Cambridge University Press, 1987); R. J. Overy, *The Nazi Economic Recovery*; and Silverman, "National Socialist Economics," for analy-

ses of the German economic recovery between 1933 and the start of World War II.

50. Data on per capita income are from Mitchell, *International Historical Statistics*, Table J1, pp. 889–908, for gross domestic product (again based on Hoffman et al., *Das Wachtsum der Deutschen Wirtshaft*), and Table A5, pp. 76–88, for population. In the Maddison data the 1932–38 increase is more modest, but still a very robust 49 percent.

51. Overy, *The Nazi Economic Recovery*, Table V, p. 24.

52. Ibid., Table VII, p. 29.

53. Alexander Gerschenkron, *Bread and Democracy in Germany* (Berkeley: University of California Press, 1943), pp. 4–5. It is noteworthy that Gerschenkron wrote these lines while the outcome of World War II was still in doubt.

54. Lothar Gall, *Bismarck: The White Revolutionary*, translated by J. A. Underwood (Boston: Unwin Hyman, 1990), and Otto Pflanze, *Bismarck and the Development of Germany* (Princeton: Princeton University Press, 1990), give good accounts of Bismarck's role in the creation of the new empire and the shaping of German politics in its early years.

55. Thomas Nipperdey, *Deutsche Geschichte, 1866–1918* (Munich: C. H. Beck, 1983), provides a comprehensive account; also see James J. Sheehan, *German Liberalism in the 19th Century* (Chicago: University of Chicago Press, 1978).

56. In the same vein, the British North America Act of 1867, which served (and with modifications still serves) as Canada's constitution, did not spell out the responsibility of the executive to Parliament. The act contains no mention of a cabinet, nor of the office of prime minister, and until 1982 it did not contain an explicit bill of rights.

57. See Nipperdey, *Deutsche Geschichte*.

58. Geoff Eley, "Liberalism, Europe, and the Bourgeoisie, 1860–1914," in David Blackbourn and Richard J. Evans (eds.), *The German Bourgeoisie: Essays on the Social History of the German Middle Class from the Late Eighteenth to the Early Twentieth Century* (New York: Routledge, 1991), p. 303.

59. Data on per capita income growth are from Mitchell, *International Historical Statistics*. In Maddison's data, real per capita income in 1871 was 15 percent above the 1861 level and 29 percent above 1851.

60. In Maddison's data the 1871–74 growth of real per capita income is 5.3 percent per annum.

61. In the Maddison data real per capita income in 1884 was above the 1874 level, but by only 2.5 percent.

62. See Gerschenkron, *Bread and Democracy in Germany*, Part 1, on the politics of agricultural protection in the nineteenth-century German empire.

63. Oddly, the Anti-Socialist Law did not ban individual Social Democrats from seeking election to the Reichstag, or from serving if elected, and some continued to do so.

64. W. L. Guttsman, *The German Social Democratic Party, 1875–1933: From Ghetto to Government* (Boston: Allen & Unwin, 1981), p. 61.

65. A. J. P. Taylor, *The Struggle for Mastery in Europe, 1848–1918* (Oxford: Oxford University Press, 1971), p. 264.

66. Nipperdey, *Deutsche Geschichte*, Vol. 2, p. 297; Nipperdey's phrase in German is *"Die erste Hochkonjunktur."*

67. See Nipperdey, *Deutsche Geschichte*, and Craig, *Germany.*

68. Election data from Chris Cook and John Paxton (eds.), *European Political Facts, 1848–1918* (Basingstoke, U.K.: Macmillan, 1986), pp. 124–25. It is also significant that after the turn of the twentieth century, as economic growth returned, the anti-Semites' vote share steadily shrank. By 1912, the last prewar election, it was down to just .5 percent.

69. See David Blackbourn, *Populists and Patricians: Essays in Modern German History* (Boston: Allen & Unwin, 1987), Chapters 6 and 10; Geoff Eley, *Reshaping the German Right: Radical Nationalism and Political Change After Bismarck* (New Haven: Yale University Press, 1980); and Roger Chickering, *We Men Who Feel Most German: A Cultural Study of the Pan-German League, 1886–1914* (Boston: Allen & Unwin, 1984).

70. Nipperdey, *Deutsche Geschichte*, Vol. 1, pp. 343–44.

71. Bismarck's state-provided welfare programs built on already existing paternalist programs put in place by German employers as a way to improve worker loyalty and thereby boost productivity. Just as the aim of these private sector programs had been to "bind workers to the company," Bismarck sought to shift workers to reliance on the government-provided scheme, as well as to offer pension and other coverage to workers who previously had none. See Susanne Hilger, "Welfare Policy in German Big Business after the First World War: Vereinigte Stahlwerke AG, 1926–33," *Business History* 40 (January 1998): 50–76; the quotation is from p. 52.

72. Otto von Bismarck, *The Memoirs, Being the Reflections and Reminiscences of Otto, Prince von Bismarck: Written and Dictated by Himself After His Retirement from Office*, translated by A. J. Butler (New York: H. Fertig, 1966).

73. See Erich J. C. Hahn, "The Occupying Powers and the Constitutional Reconstruction of West Germany, 1945–1949," in Erich J. C. Hahn et al., *Cornerstone of Democracy: The West German Grundgesetz, 1949–1989* (Washington, D.C.: German Historical Institute, 1995).

74. For contemporary views by key participants in the process, see Carl J. Friedrich, "Rebuilding the German Constitution" *American Political Science Review* 43 (June 1949): 461–82, and 43 (August 1949), pp. 704–20; and Hans Simon, "The Bonn Constitution and Its Government," in Hans J. Mogenthau (ed.), *Germany and the Future of Europe* (Chicago: University of Chicago Press, 1951).

75. David P. Currie, *The Constitution of the Federal Republic of Germany* (Chicago: University of Chicago Press, 1994), pp. 343–46.

76. See Herbert Giersch, Karl-Heinz Paqué, and Holger Schmieding, *The*

Fading Miracle: Four Decades of Market Economy in Germany (Cambridge: Cambridge University Press, 1992), Chapter 3.

77. On Adenauer's role, see Hans-Peter Schwarz, *Konrad Adenauer: A German Politician and Statesman in a Period of War, Revolution and Reconstruction* (Providence, R.I.: Berghahn, 1995), and Charles Williams, *Adenauer: The Father of the New Germany* (London: Little, Brown, 2000).

78. Per capita income data are from Maddison, *The World Economy*. Mitchell, *Industrial Historical Statistics*, gives no figures for 1939-49.

79. Data are again from Maddison, *The World Economy*.

80. See again, for example, Hahn, "The Occupying Powers and the Constitutional Reconstruction of West Germany."

81. Bark and Gress, *History of West Germany*, Vol. 2, p. 157.

82. For discussions of the post-OPEC inflation and subsequent increase in German unemployment, see Laurence Ball, "Disinflation and the NAIRU," in Christina D. Romer and David H. Romer (eds.), *Reducing Inflation: Motivation and Strategy* (Chicago: University of Chicago Press, 1997); Olivier Blanchard, "The Economics of Unemployment: Shocks, Institutions, and Interactions" (Lionel Robbins Lectures; unpublished manuscript, MIT, 2000); Olivier Blanchard and Justin Wolfers, "The Role of Shocks and Institutions in the Rise of European Unemployment: The Aggregate Evidence," *Economic Journal* 110 (March 2000): 1-33; Stephen Nickell, "Unemployment and Labor Market Rigidities: Europe Versus North America," *Journal of Economic Perspectives* 11 (Summer 1997): 55-74; and Rüdiger Soltwedel, "Employment Problems in West Germany—The Role of Institutions, Labor Law and Government Intervention?," *Carnegie-Rochester Conference Series on Public Policy* 28 (Spring 1988): 153-219.

83. Unemployment data are from the OECD.

84. See, for example, Giersch et al., *The Fading Miracle*, Chapter 4.

85. W. R. Smyser, *The German Economy: Colossus at the Crossroads* (New York: St. Martin's, 1993), p. 186.

86. Data are from Bundesanstalt fur Arbeit, "Labor Market Report, 2000."

87. See Eric Johnson, "Germany Marks Reunification with Holiday Pessimism," United Press International, October 3, 2000.

88. Before 1990 the foreign population of East Germany was 1.2 percent compared to 7.7 percent in the West. Antipathy to foreigners in the former East Germany is not limited to neo-Nazis or other far-right political parties. A poll taken in 2000—again, before the subsequent economic slowdown—showed that 59 percent of supporters of the Party of Democratic Socialism (the former East German ruling party) thought Germany already had too many foreigners, and 45 percent favored abolishing the right to asylum. See Hendrik Paul, "The German PDS Joins the Political Campaign to Limit Immigration," *World Socialism*, January 11, 2001.

89. Alan Cowell, "Party Routed in East; Far Right Enters Assembly," *New York Times*, April 27, 1998, p. A3.

90. Roger Cohen, "Schroder's Party Is Set Back Painfully in 2 State Elections," *New York Times*, September 6, 1999, p. A3.

91. Stephen Kinzer, "A Wave of Attacks on Foreigners Stirs Shock in Germany," *New York Times*, October 1, 1992, p. A1.

92. Stephen Kinzer, "Germany Outlaws a Neo-Nazi Group," *New York Times*, November 28, 1992, p. A1.

93. Ferdinand Protzman, "German Neo-Nazis Firebomb Foreigners' Housing," *New York Times*, August 26, 1992, p. A3.

94. A. M. Rosenthal, "On My Mind: Our German Crisis," *New York Times*, November 24, 1992, p. A15, and Stephen Kinzer, "Germans Hold Suspect in Firebombing That Killed 3 Turks," *New York Times*, November 27, 1992, p. A3.

95. Craig R. Whitney, "Bonn Suspects Neo-Nazi Arson as 5 Turks Die," *New York Times*, May 30, 1993, p. A1, and "2 Questioned in German Arson Deaths," *New York Times*, May 31, 1993, p. A1.

96. Stephen Kinzer, "Stemming the Refugee Tide; Germany's Open Door to Asylum-Seekers Closes," *New York Times*, May 30, 1993, Section 4, p. 2.

97. Bundesamt fur Verfassungschutz, "Rechtsextremistische Skinheads" (August 1998), p. 2.

98. Irina Repke, "Man Muss Sich Behaupten," *Der Spiegel*, April 24, 2000, pp. 58–60, especially figure on p. 60. Despite this strong relationship at the state level, not all of the evidence for Germany supports a connection to unemployment. Alan Krueger and Jörn-Steffen Pischke, for example, found no relationship between underemployment and the incidence of ethnic violence across the different *counties* in Germany, after allowing for whether a county was in the former East or West Germany; see Krueger and Pischke, "A Statistical Analysis of Crime Against Foreigners in Germany," *Journal of Human Resources* 32 (Winter 1997): 182–209.

99. See Marilyn B. Hoskin, *New Immigrants and Democratic Society: Minority Integration into Western Democracies* (New York: Praeger, 1991); Ira N. Gang and Francisco Rivera-Batiz, "Unemployment and Attitudes Towards Foreigners in Germany," in Gunter Steinmann and Ralf E. Ulrich (eds.), *Economic Consequences of Immigration to Germany* (Heidelberg: Physica-Verlag, 1994); and Walter Pierce Woodward, "Hostility Toward Immigrants in Reunited Germany: The Effects of Economic Conditions on Ethnic Intolerance" (unpublished thesis, Harvard University 1999). For contrasting evidence, however, see Jerome S. Legge, Jr., "Antiforeign Sentiment in Germany: Power Theory Versus Symbolic Explanations of Prejudice," *Journal of Politics* 58 (May 1996): 516–27.

100. Woodward, *Hostility Toward Immigrants in Germany*, p. 42.

101. See again ibid.

CHAPTER 12
Economics and Politics in the Developing World

1. Samuel P. Huntington, *Political Order in Changing Societies* (New Haven: Yale University Press, 1968), p. 41.
2. Albert O. Hirschman, "Social Conflicts as Pillars of Democratic Market Society," *Political Theory* 22 (May 1994): 214.
3. Most of the familiar indicators of the quality of people's lives, such as life expectancy, infant mortality, malnutrition, and literacy, show rapid improvement with a country's average income up to the level of about $5,000 per capita, and more modest but still easily visible improvement up to about $10,000 or in some cases even $15,000—in other words, roughly the income of South Korea or Portugal today. Above that level the relationship to average income is typically weak at best.
4. As we have seen from the modern history of Germany, however, persecution and genocide can occur in advanced industrialized countries too.
5. Americans at that time also already enjoyed a higher standard of living than do the citizens of many developing countries today. On the eve of the Civil War, per capita income in America was nearly $3,300 in 2003 dollars, about equivalent to that of Ecuador or Indonesia today—but, even so, greater than the per capita income in nearly half of the world's countries today. The 1860 income estimate for the United States is from Robert E. Gallman, "Real GNP, Prices of 1860, 1834–1909" (unpublished paper, University of North Carolina, undated); international comparisons are from the World Bank, *World Development Report 2005: A Better Investment Climate for Everyone* (Washington, D.C.: World Bank, 2004), Table 1, pp. 256–57.
6. Daniel Bell, *Cultural Contradictions of Capitalism* (New York: Basic Books, 1996), p. 315.
7. Data on per capita incomes (expressed in terms of purchasing power parity, in 2003 dollars) are from *World Development Report 2005*, Tables 1 and 5.
8. Data are from the United Nations Development Programme, *Human Development Report 2004: Cultural Liberty in Today's Diverse World* (New York: United Nations Development Programme, 2004), Tables 7, 9, and 24.
9. Income comparisons are from *World Development Report 2005*, Table 1.
10. Per capita income comparisons are from Angus Maddison, *The World Economy: Historical Statistics* (Paris: OECD, 2003), Table 7c, p. 234.
11. See Elsa Artadi and Xavier Sala-i-Martin, "The Economic Tragedy of the XXth Century: Growth in Africa," World Economic Forum, *African Competitiveness Report*, March 2004, for an analysis of poverty trends in Africa. The poverty line Artadi and Sala-i-Martin use is meant to be the equivalent of the World Bank's standard of *one* dollar a day in 1985 dollars.

12. Primary school completion data are from the World Bank's online *World Development Indicators.*

13. Data on growth of per capita incomes are from *World Development Indicators.*

14. Some years ago it was not uncommon to see the claim that democracy is primarily a Western value, so that to urge democracy on the developing world, or judge developing countries by their progress toward democracy, is simply another form of cultural imperialism. More recently the discussion of such issues has recognized democracy as an intrinsic, universal value. See, for example, Amartya Sen, "Democracy As a Universal Value," in Larry Diamond and Marc F. Platter (eds.), *The Global Divergence of Democracy* (Baltimore: Johns Hopkins University Press, 2001).

15. Data on electoral democracies are from the Freedom House Web site and annual "Freedom in the World" publications.

16. In the modern world people in many countries gravitate to cities for still other reasons as well, including the ability to take advantage of government programs and subsidies; see Edward Glaeser and Alberto F. Ades, "Trade and Circuses: Explaining Urban Giants," *Quarterly Journal of Economics* 110 (February 1995): 195–227. See also Paul Krugman, "Increasing Returns and Economic Geography," *Journal of Political Economy* 99 (June 1991): 483–99; Paul Bairoch, *Cities and Economic Development: From the Dawn of History to the Present* (Chicago: University of Chicago Press, 1988); and Mancur Olson, *The Rise and Decline of Nations: Economic Growth, Stagflation and Social Rigidities* (New Haven: Yale University Press, 1982).

17. As we have seen, how happy citizens of developing countries say they are, in survey studies, depends *negatively* on the prevalence of televisions, radios, and other communications equipment (after allowing for effects due to income levels and health). See again Genevieve Wang, "Foreign Contact, Communication, and Exposure: A Study of Low Life Satisfaction in Developing Nations" (unpublished paper, Harvard University, 2003).

18. In addition, in developing countries whose first intensive exposure to foreign influence was as colonies, people may have further reasons to take a jaundiced view of modernization. See Lucian W. Pye with Mary W. Pye, *Asian Power and Politics: The Cultural Dimensions of Authority* (Cambridge: Harvard University Press, 1985).

19. Samuel Huntington, "Political Development and Political Decay," *World Politics* 17 (April 1965): 386–430; see also Huntington, *Political Order in Changing Societies.*

20. The argument made here parallels that made in Hirschman, "Social Conflicts as Pillars of Market Society." (Hirschman also credits earlier scholars, including Helmut Dubiel, Marcel Gauchet, Bernard Crick, and Dankwart Rustow.) Hirschman, however, appealed to the conflict-raising and -resolving tendencies not of economic development but of "pluralist

market society" more generally. But his emphasis also on wealth creation makes the two arguments highly similar.

21. For an early discussion of the difference between "more-or-less" conflicts and "either-or" conflicts in the context of economic development, see W. Arthur Lewis, *Politics in West Africa* (New York: Oxford University Press, 1965), Chapter 3.

22. Works that reflect a similar theme include Douglas W. Rae and Michael Taylor, *The Analysis of Political Cleavages* (New Haven: Yale University Press, 1970), and Arend Lijphart, *Democracy in Plural Societies: A Comparative Exploration* (New Haven: Yale University Press, 1977). See also several of the essays in Kenneth D. McRae (ed.), *Consociational Democracy: Political Accommodation in Segmented Societies* (Toronto: McClelland and Stewart, 1974), and Gary Marx and Larry Diamond (eds.), *Reexamining Democracy: Essays in Honor of Seymour Martin Lipset* (Newbury Park, Calif.: Sage Publications, 1992).

23. See Dietrich Rueschemeyer, Evelyne H. Stephens, and John D. Stephens, *Capitalist Development and Democracy* (Chicago: University of Chicago Press, 1992).

24. Edward C. Banfield, *The Moral Basis of a Backwards Society* (Glencoe, Ill.: Free Press, 1958).

25. See Gabriel A. Almond and Sidney Verba, *The Civic Culture: Political Attitudes and Democracy in Five Nations* (Princeton: Princeton University Press, 1963).

26. See, for example, Ronald Inglehart, *Culture Shift in Advanced Industrial Societies* (Princeton: Princeton University Press, 1990), Chapter 1 and in particular Figure 1-4, p. 37. One specific recent example of a country where rapid industrialization also bought sharp increases in voluntary associations, informal kinds of cooperation, and other indications of personal trust is Indonesia; see E. Miguel, P. Gertler, and D. Levine, "Did Industrialization Destroy Social Capital in Indonesia?" (unpublished paper, University of California–Berkeley, 2002).

27. Albert O. Hirschman and Michael Rothschild, "The Changing Tolerance for Income Inequality in the Course of Economic Development," *Quarterly Journal of Economics* 87 (November 1973): 544–66.

28. See Crane Brinton, *The Anatomy of Revolution* (New York: Norton, 1938).

29. Alexis de Tocqueville, *The Old Régime and the French Revolution*, translated by Stuart Gilbert (Garden City, N.Y.: Doubleday, 1955), pp. 176–77. Tocqueville continued on to say, "For the mere fact that certain abuses have been remedied draws attention to the others and they now appear more galling; people may suffer less, but their sensibility is exacerbated." Ted R. Gurr, *Why Men Rebel* (Princeton: Princeton University Press, 1970), offers a similar analysis of political upheavals in the modern world.

30. See again Hirschman and Rothschild, "The Changing Tolerance for Income Inequality."

31. The original version of the Freedom House ratings was due to Raymond Gastil. See Raymond Gastil, *Freedom in the World* (New York: Freedom House, 1978).

32. An even broader summary measure, which incorporates additional dimensions of personal liberties like gender equality, marriage institutions, and access to birth control, is the "human rights" rating compiled in more recent years under the sponsorship of *The Economist;* see Charles Humana, *World Human Rights Guide* (New York: Facts on File, 1986), and *World Human Rights Guide* (New York: Oxford University Press, 1992). For the years in which these ratings exist, they closely parallel the Freedom House ratings. (For example, all of the countries to which Freedom House gives its best possible rating for both political rights and civil liberties have ratings between 80 and 100 on the 100-point *Economist* scale, while all of the countries to which Freedom House gives a worst possible rating on both of its measures have *Economist* ratings between 20 and 40.)

33. Iraq was in this category as well, for many years, until 2004 when the country's rating for civil liberties improved somewhat. As of 2004 Iraq still had the lowest possible rating for political rights. (Presumably that too has changed with the elections held in 2005.)

34. The idea that societies with higher living standards are more likely to have political democracy dates back (at least) to Aristotle's *Politics*. In modern times the scholar who has most visibly called attention to this relationship has been sociologist Seymour Martin Lipset. Nearly a half-century ago, Lipset wrote, "Perhaps the most widespread generalization linking political systems to other aspects of society has been that democracy is related to the state of economic development. Concretely, this means that the more well-to-do a nation, the greater the chances that it will sustain democracy." Seymour Martin Lipset, "Some Social Requisites of Democracy: Economic Development and Political Legitimacy," *American Political Science Review* 53 (March 1959): 69–105; quotation on p. 75. Nevertheless, some researchers have questioned the empirical foundation for even this basic proposition; see, for example, Daron Acemoglu, Simon Johnson, James Robinson, and Pierre Yared, "Income and Democracy" (National Bureau of Economic Research, Working Paper 11205, 2005).

35. The values shown for rights/liberties are averages of the 2004 Freedom House political-rights and civil-liberties ratings for each country, converted from the Freedom House seven-point scale to a zero-to-one scale where zero is the worst possible rating and one is the best. The values shown for per capita income (for 2003) are World Bank data, with incomes adjusted for differences in each country's cost of living.

36. See Daron Acemoglu, Simon Johnson, and James A. Robinson, "The Colonial Origins of Comparative Development: An Empirical Investigation," *American Economic Review* 91 (December 2001): 1369–1401, for a discussion of the role played by European settlement. Also see Stanley L.

Engerman and Kenneth L. Sokoloff, "The Evolution of Suffrage Institutions in the New World," *Journal of Economic History*, forthcoming, for an
argument emphasizing the racial and ethnic heterogeneity of the population, and also the inequality of incomes, in different countries' early histories. More generally, Engerman and Sokoloff have argued that processes
involving the evolution of social and political institutions play out over
very long time spans; see also Stanley L. Engerman and Kenneth L.
Sokoloff, "Factor Endowments, Institutions, and Differential Paths of
Growth Among New World Economies: A View from Economic Historians of the United States," in Stephen Haber (ed.), *How Latin America Fell
Behind: Essays on the Economic Histories of Brazil and Mexico, 1800–1914*
(Stanford, Calif.: Stanford University Press, 1997); and Stanley L. Engerman, Stephen Haber, and Kenneth L. Sokoloff, "Inequality, Institutions
and Differential Paths of Growth Among New World Economies," in
Claude Menard (ed.), *Institutions, Contracts, and Organizations: Perspective
from New Institutional Economics* (Northampton, Mass.: Edward Elgar,
2000).

37.   For helpful discussions of this enormous subject, see for example, Seymour
M. Lipset, Kyoung-Ryung Seong, and John C. Torres, "A Comparative
Analysis of the Social Requisites of Democracy," *International Social Science
Journal* 45 (May 1993): 155–75; George F. Kennan, *The Cloud of Danger:
Current Realities of American Foreign Policy* (Boston: Little, Brown, 1977);
Samuel P. Huntington, *The Third Wave: Democratization in the Late Twenti-
eth Century* (Norman: University of Oklahoma Press, 1991); and Robert J.
Barro, *Determinants of Economic Growth: A Cross-Country Empirical Study*
(Cambridge: MIT Press, 1997), Chapter 2. Also see the useful overview in
Seymour Martin Lipset, "The Social Requisites of Democracy Revisited,"
American Sociological Review 59 (February 1994): 1–22.

38.   The *Economist*/Humana human rights rating shows a similar positive rela-
tionship to per capita income; see Peter Boone, "Political and Gender
Oppression as a Cause of Poverty" (unpublished paper, London School of
Economics, 1996).

39.   See John Helliwell, "Empirical Linkages Between Democracy and Economic Growth," *British Journal of Political Science* 24 (April 1994): 225–48,
and Robert Barro, "Democracy and Growth," *Journal of Economic Growth* 1
(March 1996): 1–27.

40.   The values shown for rights/liberties are again the average of the two
Freedom House ratings for 2004. The growth values, from the World
Bank, are averages for 1978–2003. The fact that countries' political rights
and civil liberties are positively related to their *growth* of per capita income
is not just another reflection of the positive relationship between these
freedoms and the level of per capita income. The average Freedom House
rating is significantly related to the country's growth rate even after allowing for the separate effect of the initial level of income.

41. See William Easterly, "Life During Growth," *Journal of Economic Growth* 4 (September 1999): 239–76, for more detailed evidence that growth is related to improvements in individual rights, political democracy, and equality across both class and gender. (By contrast, many of the other indicators that Easterly examined did not show a positive relation to economic growth.)

42. See again the argument of Engeman and Sokoloff that dynamic processes involving political and social institutions play out slowly over time. For just this reason, the force of the relationship between economic growth and political and civil institutions over a much shorter period, like a single decade, is normally weaker than what Figure 12.2 shows. For still shorter periods, like the typical span of just one business cycle, usually no relationship is apparent at all.

43. This paradox is yet another reason why, as we have seen, the relationship between economic growth and the advance of an open society has so many exceptions when observed over any limited time period.

44. Ray Fair, in a series of papers, has documented the effect of economic conditions on voting in American presidential elections. See, for example, Ray C. Fair, "The Effect of Economic Events on Votes for President," *Review of Economics and Statistics* 60 (April 1978): 159–73; "The Effect of Economic Events on Votes for President: 1992 Update," *Political Behavior* 18 (June 1996): 119–39; and "The Effect of Economic Events on Votes for President: 2000 Update" (unpublished paper, Yale University, 2002). Alberto Alesina and Howard Rosenthal have shown a similar effect on congressional elections; see Alesina and Rosenthal, *Partisan Politics, Divided Government and the Economy* (New York: Cambridge University Press, 1995).

45. See Thomas Carothers, "Is Gradualism Possible? Choosing a Strategy for Promoting Democracy in the Middle East" (Carnegie Endowment for International Peace, Democracy and Rule of Law Project, Working Paper 39, 2003).

46. For every year, Przeworski classified each country's government as either a democracy or a dictatorship depending on whether there were elections and whether there was a credible political opposition. (This two-way classification is therefore a simplified version of the Freedom House seven-point political rights rating.) See Adam Przeworski and Fernando Limongi, "Democracy and Development," in Axel Hadenius (ed.), *Democracy's Victory and Crisis* (Cambridge: Cambridge University Press, 1997), Table 9.1, p. 169.

47. See Mike Alvarez, José Antonio Cheibub, Fernando Limongi, and Adam Przeworski, "Classifying Political Regimes," *Studies in Comparative International Development* 31 (Summer 1996): 3–36. Also see Adam Przeworski et al., *Democracy and Development: Political Institutions and Well-Being in the World, 1950–1990* (Cambridge: Cambridge University Press, 2000).

48. See again Przeworski and Limongi, "Democracy and Development."

49. See again Barro, *Determinants of Economic Growth*, Chapter 2.

50. See again Lipset, "Some Social Requisites of Democracy" and "The Social Requisites of Democracy Revisited." Lipset argues that "What new democracies need, above all, to attain legitimacy is efficiency—particularly in the economic arena, but also in the polity" ("The Social Requisites of Democracy Revisited," p. 17).

51. Inglehart, *Culture Shift*, Chapter 1, especially Table 1-1, p. 39.

52. For example, among a group of more than 100 different countries from the 1950s through the early 1980s, there were more than 150 coups or other irregular changes in government; see Charles Lewis Taylor and David A. Jodice, *World Handbook of Political and Social Indicators* (New Haven: Yale University Press, 1983), and Arthur S. Banks, *Cross-Polity Time-Series Data* (Cambridge: MIT Press, 1971) and subsequent data sets compiled by Banks and his associates.

53. See, for example, Samuel E. Finer, *The Man on Horseback: The Role of the Military in Politics* (New York: Praeger, 1962), and Edward Luttwak, *Coup d'Etat: A Practical Handbook* (Cambridge: Harvard University Press, 1979). A closely related idea, which incorporates the thinking outlined in Chapter 4 here, is that coups result from the gap between the living standard people expect and what they actually have; see again Gurr, *Why Men Rebel*. As David Landes observed of the consequences of Russia's industrialization in the latter half of the nineteenth century, "The dreams caught on faster than the technologies and wrenched the country out of sync"; David S. Landes, *The Wealth and Poverty of Nations: Why Some Are So Rich and Some So Poor* (New York: Norton, 1998), p. 269.

54. See John B. Londregan and Keith T. Poole, "Poverty, the Coup Trap, and the Seizure of Executive Power," *World Politics* 42 (January 1990): 151–83. The calculation of reduced probabilities also relies on private correspondence with John Londregan (February 27, 1997); I am grateful for his assistance.

55. Alberto Alesina, Sule Ozler, Nouriel Roubini, and Philip Swagel, "Political Instability and Economic Growth," *Journal of Economic Growth* 2 (June 1996): 189–213, Table 2.

56. This calculation also draws on Londregan and Poole, "Poverty, the Coup Trap, and the Seizure of Executive Power," as further interpreted by John Londregan in private correspondence (February 27, 1997).

57. Alesina et al., "Political Instability and Economic Growth."

58. See again ibid.

59. This calculation again draws on Londregan and Poole, "Poverty, the Coup Trap, and the Seizure of Executive Power," as further interpreted by John Poole in private correspondence (February 27, 1997).

60. See Alberto Alesina and Roberto Perotti, "The Politics of Growth: A Survey of the Recent Literature," *World Bank Economic Review* 8 (September 1994): 351–72.

61. See Edward N. Muller, "Democracy, Economic Development, and Income Inequality," *American Sociological Review* 53 (February 1988): 50–68.

62. W. Arthur Lewis, *The Theory of Economic Growth* (Homewood: R. D. Irwin, 1955), pp. 420–21.

63. Amartya Sen, *Development as Freedom* (New York: Anchor, 1999).

CHAPTER 13
Virtuous Circles, Vicious Circles

1. Mishna Avot 3:17.

2. For example, as political analyst Thomas Carothers observed of many countries in the Arab world, "Although the idea that economic change should precede political change is very appealing, the sticky fact remains that the lack of political reform and political accountability is precisely what undermines efforts to motivate Arab governments to undertake far-reaching economic structual reform." Carothers, "Is Gradualism Possible? Choosing a Strategy for Promoting Democracy in the Middle East" (Carnegie Endowment for International Peace, Democracy and Rule of Law Project, Working Paper 39, 2003), p. 9.

3. There is a large literature addressing the question of how openness *to international trade* affects economic growth, and vice versa; but that is not the notion of openness under consideration here. A useful survey of this other "openness and growth" literature is Sebastian Edwards, "Openness, Trade Liberalization, and Growth in Developing Countries," *Journal of Economic Literature* 31 (September 1993): 1358–93. More recently, see Sebastian Edwards, "Openness, Productivity and Growth: What Do We Really Know," *Economic Journal* 108 (March 1998): 383–98; Jeffrey Frankel and David Romer, "Does Trade Cause Growth?," *American Economic Review* 89 (June 1999): 379–99; and Robert E. Baldwin, "Openness and Growth: What's the Empirical Relationship?," in Robert E. Baldwin and L. Alan Winters (eds.), *Challenges to Globalization: Analyzing the Economics* (Chicago: University of Chicago Press, 2004).

4. Alwyn Young, "Lessons from the East Asian NICS: A Contrarian View," *European Economic Review* 38 (April 1994): 964–73, and Paul Krugman, "Competitiveness: A Dangerous Obsession," *Foreign Affairs* 73 (March–April, 1994): 28–44.

5. This debate in modern form springs from the contribution of Robert Solow; see Robert M. Solow, "Technical Change and the Aggregate Production Function," *Review of Economics and Statistics* 39 (August 1957): 312–20. Examples of recent contributions that attribute most of the observed differences across countries to resource accumulation are N. Gregory Mankiw, David Romer, and David N. Weil, "A Contribution

to the Empirics of Economic Growth," *Quarterly Journal of Economics* 107 (May 1992): 407–37, and, emphasizing differences in efficiency and technology, Peter J. Klenow and Andrés Rodríguez-Clare, "The Neoclassical Revival in Growth Economics: Has It Gone Too Far?," *NBER Macroeconomics Annual* (1997), pp. 73–103, and William Easterly and Ross Levine, "Africa's Growth Tragedy: Policies and Ethnic Divisions," *Quarterly Journal of Economics* 112 (November 1997): 1203–50. For useful recent surveys of this debate, see Romain Wacziarg, "Review of Easterly's *The Elusive Quest for Growth*," *Journal of Economic Literature* 40 (September 2002), pp. 907–18, and Barry P. Bosworth and Susan M. Collins, "The Empirics of Growth: An Update," *Brookings Papers on Economic Activity* (No. 2, 2003), pp. 113–206.

6. Douglass C. North, *Structure and Change in Economic History* (New York: Norton, 1981) and *Institutions, Institutional Change, and Economic Performance* (New York: Cambridge University Press, 1990); the quotation is from *Institutions, Institutional Change, and Economic Performance*, p. 3. See also Douglass C. North and Robert P. Thomas, *The Rise of the Western World: A New Economic History* (Cambridge: Cambridge University Press, 1973). For a more recent treatment of this issue, see Dani Rodrik, "Institutions for High-Quality Growth: What They Are and How to Acquire Them," *Studies in Comparative International Development* 35 (Fall 2000): 3–31. See Daron Acemoglu, Simon Johnson, and James Robinson, "Institutions as Fundamental Causes of Economic Growth," in Philippe Aghion and Steven Durlauf (eds.), *Handbook of Economic Growth* (Amsterdam: Elsevier Science, forthcoming), for a survey of the empirical literature initiated in part by North's ideas. For a contrary view in some key respects, see Edward L. Glaeser, Rafael La Porta, Forencio Lopez-de-Silanes, and Andrei Shleifer, "Do Institutions Cause Growth?," *Journal of Economic Growth* 9 (September 2004): 271–303.

7. Adam Smith certainly thought so: "The theme of the *Wealth of Nations* was that a good *moral* climate would encourage good economic performance, *and* conversely that good economic performance could improve the *moral* climate"; Athol Fitzgibbons, *Adam Smith's System of Liberty, Wealth and Virtue: The Moral and Political Foundations of the Wealth of Nations* (New York: Oxford University Press, 1995), p. 153. For a modern statement of this argument, see, for example, Milton Friedman, *Capitalism and Freedom* (Chicago: University of Chicago Press, 1962).

8. For example, see again Samuel P. Huntington, *Political Order in Changing Societies* (New Haven: Yale University Press, 1968).

9. See, for example, Jagdish N. Bhagwati, *The Economics of Underdeveloped Countries* (New York: McGraw-Hill, 1966).

10. See, for example, statements by Lee Kuan Yew quoted in "Democracy and Growth: Why Voting Is Good for You," *Economist*, August 27, 1994, p. 15, and in Fareed Zakaria, "A Conversation with Lee Kuan Yew," *Foreign*

Affairs 73 (March–April 1994): 109. More generally, see Lee Kuan Yew, *The Singapore Story: Memoirs of Lee Kuan Yew* (Singapore: Singapore Press Holdings, Times Editions, 1998), and *From Third World to First: The Singapore Story, 1965–2000* (New York: HarperCollins, 2000).

11. See Mankiw et al., "A Contribution to the Empirics of Economic Growth."

12. Even with the boost provided by the G.I. Bill, fifty years ago only 33 percent of American high school graduates attended college, and only 16 percent completed a four-year degree. Today 67 percent of all high school graduates go on to get some college education, and 35 percent finish. Data (based on twenty-five- to thirty-four-year-olds, in 1952 and 2003) are from the Census Bureau.

13. See Peter Boone, "Political and Gender Oppression as a Cause of Poverty" (unpublished paper, London School of Economics, 1996).

14. Some researchers have argued that the role of education in furthering economic growth is small, or even negligible; see, for example, William Easterly, *The Elusive Quest for Growth: Economists' Adventures and Misadventures in the Tropics* (Cambridge: MIT Press, 2001). Far more research has supported a significant role for education (and the development of human capital more generally) in economic growth. See, for example, Robert J. Barro, "Economic Growth in a Cross Section of Countries," *Quarterly Journal of Economics* 106 (May 1991): 407–43, and "Education as a Determinant of Economic Growth," in Edward P. Lazear (ed.), *Education in the Twenty-first Century* (Stanford, Calif.: Hoover Institution Press, 2002); Mankiw et al., "A Contribution to the Empirics of Economic Growth"; Jess Benhabib and Mark Spiegel, "The Role of Human Capital and Political Instability in Economic Development," *Journal of Monetary Economics* 34 (October 1994): 143–73; Robert J. Barro and Xavier Sala-i-Martin, *Economic Growth* (New York: McGraw-Hill, 1995); John Helliwell (ed.), *The Contribution of Human and Social Capital to Sustained Economic Growth and Well-Being* (Ottawa: HRDC and OECD, 2001); and Glaeser et al., "Do Institutions Cause Growth?"

15. For example, in 2000 China's Ministry for Public Security drew up a new list of Web sites containing "reactionary material," including Chinese university bulletin boards, Taiwan- and Hong Kong–based pro-democracy political organizations, and such American organizations as Amnesty International and Human Rights in China. In Saudi Arabia, the committee at King Abdul-Aziz City for Science and Technology that serves as the country's official Internet monitor blocks all sites that "violate the social, cultural, political, media, economic, and religious values of the Kingdom of Saudi Arabia." See Joseph Kahn, "China Toughens Obstacles to Internet Searches," *New York Times*, September 12, 2002, p. A3; Michael Dwyer, "China's Leadership Fears It Is Being Caught in a Net," *Australia Financial Review*, June 5, 2000, p. 18A; Frank Langfitt, "Out of Closet, onto Inter-

net," *Baltimore Sun*, February 27, 2000, p. A1; Howard W. French, "Chinese Censors and Web Users Match Wits," *New York Times*, March 4, 2005, p. A8; and Human Rights Watch, "The Internet in the Mideast and North Africa: Free Expression and Censorship" (New York: Human Rights Watch, 1999).

16. Per capita income data are from the World Bank, *World Development Report 2005: A Better Investment Climate for Everyone* (Washington, D.C.: World Bank, 2004), Table 1, pp. 256–57. Literacy data are from United Nations Development Programme, *Human Development Report 2004: Cultural Liberty in Today's Diverse World* (New York: United Nations Development Programme, 2004), Table 1, pp. 139–42.

17. "Nearly all highly educated countries are stable democracies. . . . The least educated countries are overwhelmingly led by long-standing dictators." Glaeser et al., "Do Institutions Cause Growth?" (quotation from pp. 18–19, prepublication version). See also Peter H. Lindert, "Voice and Growth: Was Churchill Right?" *Journal of Economic History* 63 (June 2003): 315–50: "A telltale sign of damage to growth from elite rule is the under-investment of public funds in egalitarian human capital" (quotation from abstract).

18. In the United States, for example, investment in education on average yields an effective after-inflation return of about 10 percent per annum, versus long-run average returns of 7 to 8 percent for stocks and 1 to 2 percent for Treasury bills; Orley Ashenfelter and Cecilia Rouse, "Income, Schooling and Ability: Evidence from a New Sample of Twins," *Quarterly Journal of Economics* 111 (February 1998): 253–84.

19. See Gary S. Becker and Nigel Tomes, "Human Capital and the Rise and Fall of Families," Part 2, *Journal of Labor Economics* 4 (July 1986): S1–S39, for a complete statement of this idea.

20. Data on education (through grade five) are from the World Bank.

21. Although most research indicates a high return to investment in education in developing economies, there is also some evidence suggesting that the return is smaller than usually believed; see Lant Pritchett, "Understanding Patterns of Economic Growth: Searching for Hills Among Plateaus, Mountains, and Plains," *World Bank Economic Review* 14 (May 2000): 221–50, for a summary. Part of the issue is whether education merely responds passively to increases in per capita income; see, for example, Mark Bils and Peter J. Klenow, "Does Schooling Cause Growth or the Other Way Around?," *American Economic Review* 90 (December 2000): 1160–83; Andrew D. Foster and Mark R. Rosenzweig, "Technological Change and Human Capital Returns and Investments: Evidence from the Green Revolution," *American Economic Review* 86 (September 1996): 931–53; and Klenow and Rodríguez-Clare, "The Neoclassical Revival in Growth Economics: Has It Gone Too Far?"

22.   At the same time, merely remaining in school for its own sake is not what
      matters. The quality of the education received is as important, if not more
      so. Although quality of education is harder to measure than years of
      schooling, especially where differences across countries are concerned,
      there is some evidence (based on performance on tests administered inter-
      nationally) that educational quality far outweighs raw quantity in con-
      tributing to economic growth. See Eric A. Hanushek and Dennis W.
      Kimko, "Schooling, Labor-Force Quality, and the Growth of Nations,"
      American Economic Review 90 (December 2000): 1184–1208.

23.   Jose Tavares and Romain Wacziarg, "How Democracy Affects Growth,"
      European Economic Review 45 (August 2001): 1341–78.

24.   Marcella Alsan, David E. Bloom, and David Canning, "The Effect of Popu-
      lation Health on Foreign Direct Investment" (National Bureau of Eco-
      nomic Research, Working Paper 10596, 2004).

25.   Fahim Ahmed, "In Search of Human Development: Evaluating the Role of
      Democracy" (unpublished thesis, Harvard University, 2000).

26.   The literature documenting the role of physical capital accumulation
      in economic growth, including in particular economic development, is
      vast. See, for example, J. Bradford DeLong and Lawrence H. Summers,
      "Equipment Investment and Economic Growth," *Quarterly Journal of
      Economics* 106 (May 1991): 445–502; David A. Aschauer, "Is Public
      Expenditure Productive?," *Journal of Monetary Economics* 23 (March 1989):
      177–200; Mankiw et al., "A Contribution to the Empirics of Growth";
      William Easterly and Sergio Rebello, "Fiscal Policy and Economic
      Growth: An Empirical Investigation," *Journal of Monetary Economics* 32
      (December 1993): 417–58; and Dale W. Jorgenson, "Information Technol-
      ogy and the G7 Economies," *World Economics* 4 (October–December
      2003): 139–69. (For a more skeptical perspective, however, see William
      Easterly and Ross Levine, "Africa's Growth Tragedy: Policies and Ethnic
      Divisions," *Quarterly Journal of Economics* 112 [November 1997]: 1203–50.)
      See again Bosworth and Collins, "The Empirics of Growth: An Update,"
      for a partial review. Some part of the tendency for countries with high
      investment rates to have high growth rates is also due, however, to the pos-
      itive effect of growth on saving and investment; see Franco Modigliani,
      "Life Cycle, Individual Thrift, and the Wealth of Nations," *American Eco-
      nomic Review* 76 (1986): 297–313, and Robert J. Barro, *Determinants of Eco-
      nomic Growth: A Cross-Country Empirical Study* (Cambridge: MIT Press,
      1998).

27.   Saving rate data, for 2003, are from the World Bank's online *World Devel-
      opment Indicators*.

28.   Saving is also nonexistent in countries like Eritrea, Rwanda, and Sierra
      Leone, although there armed conflict is presumably a large part of the
      reason.

29. Mancur Olson forcefully made this argument; see Olson, "Dictatorship, Democracy and Development," *American Political Science Review* 87 (September 1993): 567–76, and "Autocracy, Democracy, and Prosperity," in Richard Zeckhauser (ed.), *Strategy and Choice* (Cambridge: MIT Press, 1991).

30. See, for example, Edward L. Glaeser and Raven E. Saks, "Corruption in America" (National Bureau of Economic Research, Working Paper 10821, 2004). Glaeser and Saks found that the variation across the United States in the prevalence of corruption (as measured by federal convictions for "corrupt practices") mirrors the pattern found across countries, in that corruption is more likely to occur in states where average education and average income are lower.

31. Taxpayers bore $126 billion of this cost, the savings and loan industry the rest. Data are from financial statements of the Federal Deposit Insurance Corporation.

32. See Alberto Alesina and Roberto Perotti, "The Political Economy of Growth: A Critical Survey of the Recent Literature," *World Bank Economic Review* 8 (September 1994): 351–71.

33. See Casey B. Mulligan, Ricard Gil, and Xavier Sala-i-Martin, "Do Democracies Have Different Public Policies than Non-Democracies?," *Journal of Economic Perspectives* 18 (Winter 2004): 51–74.

34. See, for example, Stephen Knack and Philip Keefer, "Institutions and Economic Performance: Cross-Country Tests Using Alternative Institutional Measures," *Economics and Politics* 7 (November 1995): 207–27; Robert E. Hall and Charles I. Jones, "Why Do Some Countries Produce So Much More Output Per Worker than Others?," *Quarterly Journal of Economics* 114 (February 1999): 83–116; and Bradford DeLong and Andrei Shleifer, "Prices and Merchants: European City Growth Before the Industrial Revolution," *Journal of Law and Economics* 36 (October 1993): 671–702. Also see again the useful review in Acemoglu et al., "Institutions as Fundamental Causes of Economic Growth."

35. See for example, Paulo Mauro, "Corruption and Growth," *Quarterly Journal of Economics* 110 (August 1995): 681–712 ; Knack and Keefer, "Institutions and Economic Performance"; Shang-Jin Wei, "Local Corruption and Global Capital Flows," *Brookings Papers on Economic Activity* (No. 2, 2000), pp. 303–54; and R. Gaston Gelos and Shang-Jin Wei, "Transparency and International Portfolio Holdings," *Journal of Finance*, forthcoming.

36. Barro, *Determinants of Economic Growth*, reviews this evidence. In a broader historical context, however, the development of democracy was in some respects parallel to the development of property rights and other elements of the "rule of law." Drawing in part on work by Douglass North, Acumoglu et al. argue that in the sixteenth and seventeenth centuries the

"Netherlands and England moved ahead economically of the rest of Europe precisely because they developed limited, constitutional government. This form of government led to secure property rights, a favorable investment climate and had rapid multiplier effects on other economic institutions, particularly financial markets"; "Institutions as the Fundamental Cause of Economic Growth," p. 67.

37. Timothy Besley and Robin Burgess, "Can Labor Regulation Hinder Economic Performance? Evidence from India," *Quarterly Journal of Economics* 119 (February 2004): 91–134.

38. See Manuela Saragosa, "Brittan Warns on Jakarta's Policy for National Car," *Financial Times*, April 23, 1996, p. 4, and David E. Sanger, "In the Shadow of Scandal, U.S. Challenges a Suharto Project," *New York Times*, June 14, 1997, p. A5.

39. George J. Aditjondro, "Suharto & Sons (and Daughters, In-Laws and Cronies)," *Washington Post*, January 25, 1998, p. C1.

40. Samuel Decalo, *Coups and Army Rule in Africa: Motivations and Constraints* (New Haven: Yale University Press, 1990).

41. In late-nineteenth- and early-twentieth-century America, the increasing availability of clean water was apparently responsible for nearly half of the overall decline in mortality in the cities, and nearly two-thirds of the decline in child mortality and three-fourths of the decline in infant mortality. See David M. Cutler and Grant Miller, "The Role of Public Health Improvements in Health Advances: The 20th Century United States," *Demography* 42 (February 2005): 1–22.

42. See for example, Robert J. Barro and Jong-Wha Lee, "Losers and Winners in Economic Growth," *Proceedings of the World Bank Annual Conference on Development Economics* (1993), pp. 267–97.

43. Fertility data are from the World Bank, *World Development Report 1995: Workers in an Integrating World* (New York: Oxford University Press, 1995), Table 26, pp. 212–13.

44. Population growth data are from the World Bank, *Entering the 21st Century: World Development Report, 1999/2000* (New York: Oxford University Press, 2002), Table 3, pp. 234–35.

45. See Alberto Alesina and Roberto Perotti, "Income Distribution, Political Sustainability, and Investment," *European Economic Review* 3 (June 1996): 113–34; Sebastian Edwards and Guido Tabellini, "Political Instability, Political Weakness and Inflation: An Empirical Analysis," *Advances in Econometrics* 2 (1994): 355–76; and Easterly and Rebello, "Fiscal Policy and Economic Growth: An Empirical Investigation."

46. Data on income distribution are from *Human Development Report 2004*, Table 14, pp. 188–91.

47. Dennis C. Mueller, *Public Choice* (New York: Cambridge University Press, 1979), and William C. Mitchell and Michael C. Munger, "Economic Mod-

els of Interest Groups: An Introductory Survey," *American Journal of Political Science* 35 (May 1991): 512–46, provide useful summaries of this familiar line of thinking.

48. Mancur Olson, *The Rise and Decline of Nations: Economic Growth, Stagflation and Social Rigidities* (New Haven: Yale University Press, 1982).

49. Joseph A. Schumpeter, *The Theory of Economic Development: An Inquiry into Profits, Capital, Credit, Interest and the Business Cycle,* translated by Redvers Opie (Cambridge: Harvard University Press, 1934).

50. Pranab Bardhan, "Symposium on Democracy and Development," *Journal of Economic Perspectives* 7 (Summer 1993): 45–49.

51. See, for example, the discussion of the U.S. budget deficit in Benjamin M. Friedman, *Day of Reckoning: The Consequences of American Economic Policy Under Reagan and After* (New York: Random House, 1988). Another example, from the international area, is the "debt crises" that frequently strike developing countries—perhaps because the public in these countries does not actually regard such phenomena as crises. There was no systematic difference in how democracies and dictatorships responded to the 1980s Latin American debt crisis; see Karen Remmer, "Democracy and Economic Crisis: The Latin American Experience," *World Politics* 42 (April 1990): 315–35.

52. Churchill telegram to Roosevelt, June 11, 1944 (T. 1259/4; Churchill papers, 20/166); cited by Martin Gilbert, *Winston S. Churchill: The Road to Victory, 1941–1945* (Boston: Houghton Mifflin, 1986), pp. 804–5.

53. Life expectancy data are from *Human Development Report 2004*, Table 1, pp. 139–42.

54. See Amartya Sen, "Development: Which Way Now?," *Economic Journal* 93 (December 1983): 745–62, and "Freedoms and Needs," *New Republic*, January 10 and 17, 1994, pp. 31–38. See also Sen, *Poverty and Famines: An Essay on Entitlement and Deprivation* (Oxford: Clarendon Press, 1981); Sen and Jean Drèze, *Hunger and Public Action* (New York : Oxford University Press, 1989); and, most recently, Sen, *Development as Freedom* (New York: Anchor, 2000).

55. Sen, "Freedoms and Needs," p. 34.

56. Jagdish Bhagwati, "Democracy and Development: New Thinking on an Old Question," in *A Storm of Windows: Unsettling Reflections on Trade, Immigration, and Democracy* (Cambridge: MIT Press, 1998), pp. 389, 387.

57. Comprehensive surveys of the empirical literature on this question are almost uniformly inconclusive, showing that the answer depends on what sets of countries and what time periods are under study, what is meant by "democracy," and, especially, what additional influences on economic growth are taken into account. See, for example, Larry Sirowy and Alex Inkeles, "The Effects of Democracy on Economic Growth and Inequality: A Review," *Studies in Comparative International Development* (Spring 1990): 126–57; Adam Przeworski and Fernando Limongi, "Political Regimes and

Economic Growth," *Journal of Economic Perspectives* 7 (Summer 1993): 51–69; Silvio Borner, Aymo Brunetti, and Beatrice Weder, *Political Credibility and Economic Development* (New York: St. Martin's, 1995); and Glaeser et al., "Do Institutions Cause Growth?" Two additional factors account for much of the inability to draw firm generalizations on this important question. First, because economies that lag far behind the existing technological frontier find it easier to grow—they need only copy what others are doing—there is always the danger of mistaking for an ingredient of growth what is really just an indicator of backwardness; see Robert J. Barro, "Economic Growth in a Cross Section of Countries," and Robert J. Barro and Xavier Sala-i-Martin, "Convergence," *Journal of Political Economy* 100 (April 1992): 223–51. Second, economic growth among countries with nondemocratic governments has been extremely mixed. Most democracies have performed better in this regard than the worst dictatorships with the most dysfunctional economies, but not as well as the most successful ones; see Alesina and Perotti, "The Politics of Growth: A Survey of the Recent Literature."

58. Barro provides a careful treatment of this distinction in *Determinants of Economic Growth*.

59. Rodrik, "Institutions for High-Quality Growth," p. 5.

60. See again Tavares and Wacziarg, "How Democracy Affects Growth."

61. Barro, *Determinants of Economic Growth*, Tables 1.1 and 1.2, pp. 13 and 34.

62. See ibid., p. 59

63. Daniel Bell, *The Cultural Contradictions of Capitalism* (New York: Basic Books, 1976).

CHAPTER 14
Growth and Equality

1. *The Politics of Aristotle*, translated by Ernest Barker (New York: Oxford University Press, 1962), p. 182.

2. Simon Kuznets, "Economic Growth and Income Inequality," *American Economic Review* 45 (March 1955): 1–28. For an updated discussion of the ideas behind the "Kuznets curve," see Peter H. Lindert, "Three Centuries of Inequality in Britain and America," in Anthony B. Atkinson and François Bourguignon (eds.), *Handbook of Income Distribution*, Vol. 1 (Amsterdam: Elsevier, 2000).

3. This account of the mechanism underlying the "Kuznets curve" incorporates not only Kuznets's original explanation but also further elements suggested later on by other researchers. For example, Kuznets did not address the role of changing wage differentials due to changing relative scarcity of labor and to the influence of wage differentials themselves on firms' choice of new technologies.

4. Stanley Engerman and Kenneth Sokoloff have further argued that inequality, once it has developed, perpetuates itself (or, at the least, becomes very
   long-lasting) through the working of the political and social institutions
   that it brings into being. See, for example, Stanley L. Engerman and Kenneth L. Sokoloff, "Factor Endowments, Inequality, and Paths of Development Among New World Economics," *Economia* 3 (Fall 2002): 41–102.
   One prominent example today is the Hukou restrictions in China, which
   maintain the country's wide rural-urban wage differentials by precluding
   peasants from relocating from the countryside to the cities; see John
   Whalley and Shunming Zhang, "Inequality Change in China and (Hukou)
   Labour Mobility Restrictions," *Journal of Development Economics*, forthcoming.

5. "Relative to other countries, mid-Victorian Britain (1867–1875) stood out
   as a nation of extreme inequality in landownership, personal net worth,
   and pre-tax incomes." Lindert, "Three Centuries of Inequality in Britain
   and America," p. 180.

6. See Jeffrey G. Williamson, *Inequality, Poverty and History* (Cambridge,
   U.K.: Basil Blackwell, 1991); Jeffrey G. Williamson and Peter H. Lindert,
   "English Workers' Real Wages: Reply to Crafts," *Journal of Economic His-
   tory* 45 (March 1985): 145–53; Klaus Denninger and Lyn Squire, "A New
   Data Set for Measuring Income Inequality," *World Bank Economic Review* 10
   (September 1996), pp. 565–91; William Easterly, "Life During Growth,"
   Journal of Economic Growth 4 (September 1999): 239–76; and Robert J.
   Barro, "Inequality and Growth in a Panel of Countries," *Journal of Eco-
   nomic Growth* 5 (March 2000): 5–32. Barro, for example, estimated that the
   turning point occurs at a per capita income of around $5,000 in today's dol-
   lars—about the income of Algeria or Peru ("Inequality and Growth in a
   Panel of Countries," p. 25). Charles Feinstein has interpreted the evidence
   differently, however, disputing not only the initial widening of inequality
   but also the subsequent narrowing; see Charles H. Feinstein, "Pessimism
   Perpetuated: Real Wages and the Standard of Living in Britain During and
   After the Industrial Revolution," *Journal of Economic History* 58 (September
   1998): 625–58. Similarly, although the evidence found by Michael Roemer
   and Mary Kay Gugerty, and by John Gallup and co-authors, focused on
   how the incomes of the poor compared to incomes in the economy as a
   whole (and therefore did not examine what happens in the upper end of the
   distribution), in neither case does their evidence suggest a widening of
   inequality under economic development; see Michael Roemer and Mary
   Kay Gugerty, "Does Economic Growth Reduce Poverty?" (Harvard Institute for International Development, Consulting Assistance on Economic
   Reform II, Discussion Paper 5, 1997), and John Luke Gallup, Steven
   Radelet, and Andrew Warner, "Economic Growth and the Income of the
   Poor" (Harvard Institute for International Development, Consulting

Assistance on Economic Reform II, Discussion Paper 36, 1999). Roberto Perotti has suggested an explanation under which the kind of pattern suggested by Kuznets may appear in cross-country comparisons even if it does not characterize the time path followed by inequality in most countries considered individually; see Perotti, "Political Equilibrium, Income Distribution and Growth," *Review of Economic Studies* 60 (October 1993): 755–76, especially pp. 770–71. Thorsten Beck and co-authors have found evidence that the development of financial institutions in particular disproportionately boosts the incomes of the poor; see Thorsten Beck, Asli Deminger-Kunt, and Ross Levine, "Finance, Inequality, and Poverty: Cross-Country Evidence" (National Bureau of Economic Research, Working Paper 10979, 2004).

7. See World Bank, *The East Asian Miracle: Economic Growth and Public Policy* (New York: Oxford University Press, 1993).

8. See, for example, Nancy Birdsall, David Ross, and Richard Sabot, "Inequality and Growth Reconsidered: Lessons from East Asia," *World Bank Economic Review* 9 (September 1995): 477–508. See also, on the Korean experience, Jonathan Leightner, "The Compatibility of Growth and Increased Equality: Korea," *Journal of Development Studies* 29 (October 1992): 49–71.

9. Samuel P. Huntington, "The New World Disorder," in Larry Diamond and Marc F. Plattner (eds.), *The Global Resurgence of Democracy* (Baltimore: Johns Hopkins University Press, 1993), p. 22.

10. Prominent examples included Raoul Prebisch, Andre Gunder Frank, and Arrighi Emmanuel. A subsequent literature on the effects of distortionary tariffs referred to "immiserizing growth" in a more specialized sense; see Jagdish Bhagwati, "Immiserizing Growth: A Geometrical Note," *Review of Economic Studies* 25 (June 1958): 201–5, and "Distortions and Immiserizing Growth: A Generalization," *Review of Economic Studies* 35 (October 1968): 481–85; also Harry G. Johnson, "The Possibility of Income Losses from Increased Efficiency or Factor Accumulation in the Presence of Tariffs," *Economic Journal* 77 (March 1967): 151–54.

11. Gallup et al., "Economic Growth and the Income of the Poor," Table 1, and results reported in Table 3. The data on income distributions used in this study are from Denninger and Squire, "A New Data Set for Measuring Income Inequality," updated from the World Bank's 1998 *World Development Indicators* CD-ROM.

12. Gallup and co-authors found a one-to-one relationship for income growth of the lowest one-fifth; Gallup et al., "Economic Growth and the Income of the Poor." Roemer and Gugerty found a one-to-one relationship for the lowest two-fifths, and slightly less than one-to-one for the lowest one-fifth; Roemer and Gugerty, "Does Economic Growth Reduce Poverty?"

13. See Martin Ravallion, Gaurav Datt, and Dominique van de Walle, "Quan-

tifying Absolute Poverty in the Developing World," *Review of Income and Wealth* 37 (December 1991): 345–61, for an early exposition of the $1-per-day standard.

14. Poverty-rate data are from the World Bank.

15. Income data are from the World Bank, *World Development Report 2005: A Better Investment Climate for Everyone* (Washington, D.C.: World Bank, 2004), Table 1, pp. 256–57. The rupee-dollar exchange rate is from the Federal Reserve Board.

16. Xavier Sala-i-Martin "The Disturbing 'Rise' of Global Income Inequality" (National Bureau of Economic Research, Working Paper 8904, 2002). These calculations also allow for inflation since 1985, when the World Bank first proposed the $1-a-day definition of extreme poverty, so that the "$1" standard applied for 1998 is actually $1.40 and the "$2" standard is $2.80.

17. Sala-i-Martin, "The Disturbing 'Rise' of Global Income Inequality." See also Surjit Bhalla, *Imagine There's No Country: Poverty, Inequality and Growth in an Era of Globalization* (Washington, D.C.: Institute for International Economics, 2002).

18. Population data—for 1974 and 1998, the years spanned by Sala-i-Martin's study—are from the Census Bureau.

19. Some observers date the beginning of India's recent growth acceleration to the early 1980s, however. See, for example, Dani Rodrik and Arvind Subramanian, "From 'Hindu Growth' to Productivity Surge: The Mystery of the Indian Growth Transition," *IMF Staff Papers*, forthcoming.

20. See Gaurav Datt and Martin Ravaillon, "Is India's Economic Growth Leaving the Poor Behind?" *Journal of Economic Perspectives* 16 (Summer 2002): 89–108, for a review of the evidence, and the surrounding debate, on poverty in India since the 1991 economic reforms. See also Jean Drèze and Amartya Sen, *India: Economic Development and Social Opportunity* (New York: Oxford University Press, 1995), for a discussion of the role to be played by policies other than economic reforms per se.

21. Elsa V. Artadi and Xavier Sala-i-Martin, "The Economic Tragedy of the XXth Century: Growth in Africa," World Economic Forum, *African Competitiveness Report*, March 2004. See also Martin Ravaillon and Shaohua Chen, "What Can New Survey Data Tell Us About Recent Changes in Distribution and Poverty?," *World Bank Economic Review* 11 (May 1997): 357–82.

22. See again Artadi and Sala-i-Martin, "The Economic Tragedy of the XXth Century."

23. Data on under-five mortality are from United Nations Development Programme, *Human Development Report 2004: Cultural Liberty in Today's Diverse World* (New York: United Nations Development Programme, 2004), Table 9, pp. 168–71, and the World Bank's online *World Development Indicators*.

24. Data on access to improved sanitation are from *Human Development Report 2004*, Table 7, pp. 160–163.

25. Data on immunizations are from *Human Development Report 2004*, Table 6, pp. 156–59, and the World Health Organization, "Department of Immunization, Vaccines, and Biologicals."

26. Data on undernourishment are from *Human Development Report 2004*, Table 7, pp. 160–63, and the United Nations Food and Agriculture Organization, "State of Food Insecurity in the World."

27. Enrollment data are from the UNESCO Statistics Division Web site.

28. Fertility data are from *World Development Indicators*.

29. For useful surveys of the evidence on whether equality or inequality better fosters economic growth, see Roberto Perotti, "Income Distribution, Democracy, and Growth: What the Data Say," *Journal of Economic Growth* 1 (June 1996): 149–87; Roland Benabou, "Inequality and Growth," in *NBER Macroeconomics Annual, 1996*, pp. 11–74; and Barro, "Inequality and Growth in a Panel of Countries."

30. Another early adherent of the view that inequality was essential for growth, for just this reason, was Turgot; see Ronald L. Meek, *Social Science and the Ignoble Savage* (New York: Cambridge University Press, 1976), Chapter 3. Alexander Hamilton thought so too, and one motivation for his policies on the development of financial markets, including the establishment of the first Bank of the United States, was (as the contemporary discussion put it) "to raise up a moneyed class." Prominent twentieth-century economists whose theories supported this kind of role for inequality in promoting saving and investment included John Maynard Keynes, Simon Kuznets, and Nicholas Kaldor.

31. See Jerry Z. Muller, *Adam Smith in His Time and Ours: Designing the Decent Society* (New York: Free Press, 1993), p. 138.

32. An alternative interpretation frames the matter in terms of occupational choice (whether or not to be an entrepreneur), rather than whether to save and invest; see Abhijit V. Banerjee and Andrew F. Newman, "Occupational Choice and the Process of Development," *Journal of Political Economy* 101 (April 1993): 274–98.

33. Williamson, *Inequality, Poverty and History*, Chapter 3; as Williamson concludes, "The Smithian trade-off fails for precisely the period for which it was first designed" (p. 90).

34. Oded Galor and Daniel Tsidden have offered a version of this idea that emphasizes the role of home-provided human capital formation, but the extension to the context of formal schooling is straightforward as long as families cannot readily borrow; see Oded Galor and Daniel Tsidden, "The Distribution of Human Capital and Economic Growth," *Journal of Economic Growth* 2 (March 1997): 93–124.

35. See Perotti, "Income Distribution, Democracy, and Growth," especially Table 13, column 3, p. 179. See also Oded Galor and Joseph Zeira,

"Income Distribution and Macroeconomics," *Review of Economic Studies* 60 (January 1993): 35–52, and Gustav Ranis, Frances Stewart, and Alejandro Ramirez, "Economic Growth and Human Development," *World Development* 28 (February 2000): 197–219.

36. See Oded Galor and Hyoungsoo Zang, "Fertility, Income Distribution, and Economic Growth: Theory and Cross-Country Evidence," *Japan and the World Economy* 9 (May 1997): 197–229. Inequality apparently affects fertility in other ways as well. For example, the fertility difference between educated and uneducated women is also greater in countries where incomes are more unequal; see Michael Kremer and Daniel Chen, "Income-Distribution Dynamics with Endogenous Fertility," *Journal of Economic Growth* 7 (September 2002): 227–58.

37. See again Edward N. Muller, "Democracy, Economic Development and Income Inequality," *American Sociological Review* 53 (February 1988): 50–68.

38. Alberto Alesina and Roberto Perotti, "The Politics of Growth: A Survey of the Recent Literature," *World Bank Economic Review* 8 (September 1994): 351–71; see especially p. 367.

39. Alberto Alesina and Roberto Perotti, "Income Distribution, Political Instability and Investment," *European Economic Review* 40 (June 1996): 1203–28.

40. See Benabou, "Inequality and Growth"; Giuseppe Bertola, "Factor Shares and Savings in Endogenous Growth," *American Economic Review* 83 (December 1993): 1184–98; Torsten Persson and Guido Tabellini, "Is Inequality Harmful for Growth?," *American Economic Review* 84 (June 1994): 600–21; Alberto Alesina and Dani Rodrik, "Distributive Politics and Economic Growth," *Quarterly Journal of Economics* 109 (May 1994): 465–90; and John Londregan and Keith T. Poole, "Does High Income Promote Democracy?," *World Politics* 49 (October 1996): 1–30. In many cases, however, politically motivated discussion greatly exaggerates the disincentive effects of moderate rates of taxation; see the discussion of the U.S. experience during the Reagan era in Benjamin M. Friedman, *Day of Reckoning: The Consequences of American Economic Policy Under Reagan and After* (New York: Random House, 1988). Interestingly, there is some evidence that in the developing world especially large redistributions *in either direction* reduce growth; see Abhijit Banerjee and Esther Duflo, "Inequality and Growth: What Can the Data Say?" *Journal of Economic Growth* 8 (September 2003): 267–99.

41. The need for broader markets in economic development has long been recognized. See, for example, P. N. Rosenstein-Rodan, "Problems of Industrialization of Eastern and South-Eastern Europe," *Economic Journal* 53 (June–September 1943): 202–11, and "Notes on the Theory of the 'Big Push,' " in Howard S. Ellis and Henry C. Wallich (eds.), *Economic Development for Latin America* (New York: St. Martin's, 1961); see also Kevin M.

Murphy, Andrei Shleifer, and Robert W. Vishny, "Industrialization and the Big Push," *Journal of Political Economy* 97 (October 1989): 1003–26.

42. See Robert J. Barro and Xavier Sala-i-Martin, *Economic Growth* (New York: McGraw-Hill, 1995).

43. Stephen Knack and Philip Keefer, "Does Social Capital Have an Economic Payoff? A Cross-Country Investigation," *Quarterly Journal of Economics* 112 (November 1997): 1251–88.

44. Barro, "Inequality and Growth in a Panel of Countries," p. 18. Even the direction of this distinction remains unsettled, however; Roberto Perotti found that the effect of equality on economic growth is positive at all income levels, but more positive for higher-income countries; see Perotti, "Income Distribution, Democracy, and Growth."

45. Data on per capita income and population are from *World Development Report 2005*, Tables 1 and 5, pp. 256–57 and 264.

46. If the first part of Kuznets's hypothesis about how economic growth affects the income distribution is correct—that is, if the early stages of growth systematically lead to wider inequality—then these countries also face the threat of being caught in yet another form of trap, in which growth at low incomes creates inequality while inequality at low incomes retards growth. As we have seen, however, the evidence on Kuznets's hypothesis is less supportive of the early upswing in inequality than of the subsequent downswing.

47. See for example, Joseph E. Stiglitz, *Globalization and Its Discontents* (New York: Norton, 2002). For an alternative view, see Jagdish Bhagwati, *In Defense of Globalization* (New York: Oxford University Press, 2004).

48. Cross-country inequality in per capita incomes almost certainly widened before World War II. Although some estimates suggest that it has continued to do so in recent decades, other work based on different methodologies and data suggests the opposite. See Sala-i-Martin, "The Disturbing 'Rise' of Global Income Inequality," and "The World Distribution of Income, Estimated from Individual Country Distributions" (National Bureau of Economic Research, Working Paper 8933, 2002); Arne Melchior, Kjetil Telle, and Henrik Wiig, *Globalization and Inequality: World Income Distribution and Living Standards, 1960–1988* (Oslo: Royal Norwegian Ministry of Foreign Affairs, 2000); Andrea Boltho and Gianni Toniolo, "The Assessment: The Twentieth Century," *Oxford Review of Economic Policy* 15 (Winter 1999): 1–17; and T. Paul Schultz, "Inequality in the Distribution of Income in the World: How It Is Changing and Why," *Journal of Population Economics* 11 (August 1998): 307–44.

49. Prominent advocates of free trade in early-nineteenth-century Britain included David Ricardo and both James and John Stuart Mill. Douglas A. Irwin, *Against the Tide* (Princeton: Princeton University Press, 1996), Chapters 3–6, provides a useful review of how thinking on the subject evolved during this period.

50. See Michael Bordo, Barry Eichengreen, and Douglas A. Irwin, "Is Global-
    ization Today Really Different than Globalization a Hundred Years Ago?,"
    in Susan Collins and Robert Lawrence (eds.), *Brookings Trade Policy Forum*
    (Washington, D.C.: Brookings Institution, 1999).

51. Not surprisingly in a world of electronic communications, *gross* financial
    flows are far greater today. But net flows are what finance investment, and
    in the pre–World War I era net international capital flows were larger as a
    share of either total income or total saving and investment than they are
    today. Episodes like the late 1990s Asian financial crisis notwithstanding,
    disturbances to financial markets were also more globalized before World
    War I than they are today; see Michael D. Bordo and Antu Panini Mur-
    shid, "Globalization and Changing Patterns in International Transmission
    of Shocks in Financial Markets" (National Bureau of Economic Research,
    Working Paper 9019, 2002).

52. See again Bordo and Murshid, "Globalization and Changing Patterns in
    International Transmission of Shocks in Financial Markets."

53. See Lant Pritchett, "Divergence, Big Time," *Journal of Economic Perspec-
    tives* 11 (Summer 1997): 3–17.

54. See again Jeffrey G. Williamson, "The Impact of the Corn Laws Just Prior
    to Repeal," *Explorations in Economic History* 27 (April 1990); 123–56.

55. Peter H. Lindert and Jeffrey G. Williamson, "Does Globalization Make
    the World More Unequal?" in Michael D. Bordo, Alan M. Taylor, and Jef-
    frey G. Williamson (eds.), *Globalization in Historical Perspective* (Chicago:
    University of Chicago Press, 2003).

56. For evidence that cross-country inequality increased somewhat overall
    during this period, see François Bourguignon and Christian Morris-
    son, "Inequality Among World Citizens: 1820–1992," *American Economic
    Review* 92 (September 2002): 727–44.

57. Lindert and Williamson, "Does Globalization Make the World More
    Unequal?"

58. See again Bourguignon and Morrisson, "Inequality Among World Citi-
    zens: 1820–1992," and Lindert and Williamson, "Does Globalization
    Make the World More Unequal?"

59. See Kevin H. O'Rourke "Globalization and Inequality: Historical Trends,"
    Annual World Bank Conference on Economic Development (2001/2002): 39–67.
    Robert Barro found that a country's openness to international trade widened
    within-country inequality among lower- and middle-income countries
    to a small extent, but narrowed it among high-income countries; Barro,
    "Inequality and Growth in a Panel of Countries." By contrast, Shang-Jin
    Wei and Yi Wu's study of the effect of openness to trade in China found
    that globalization has reduced the country's worrisome urban-rural in-
    come gaps; Chinese cities that are more involved in international trade
    have experienced a greater decline in local urban-rural income differen-
    tials; see Wei and Wu, "Globalization and Inequality: Evidence from

Within China" (National Bureau of Economic Research, Working Paper 8611, 2001). For a useful review of the evidence on different channels by which trade liberalization might affect inequality, see Pinelopi Koujianou Goldberg and Nina Pavcnik, "Trade, Inequality and Poverty: What Do We Know? Evidence from Recent Trade Liberalization Episodes in Developing Countries," *Brookings Trade Forum* (2004): 223–69. See also Gary Burtless, "International Trade and the Rise in Earnings Inequality," *Journal of Economic Literature* 33 (June 1995): 800–16, for a review of earlier evidence.

60. Bourguignon and Morrisson find a continuing increase, but at a much slower rate. Melchior et al., Schultz, Boltho and Toniolo, and Sala-i-Martin all find a decline, although they differ on the timing of the reversal.

61. United Nations Conference on Trade and Development, *Handbook of International Trade and Development Statistics, 1987 and 1995* (New York: United Nations, 1988 and 1997); cited in Lindert and Williamson, "Does Globalization Make the World More Unequal?," note 21.

62. See Bhagwati, *In Defense of Globalization*, for a more comprehensive discussion of "the broadly social effects of economic globalization" (p. 22), including its impact on poverty, immigration, women's rights, culture, the environment, and democracy. See also Michael A. Santoro, *Profits and Principles: Global Capitalism and Human Rights in China* (Ithaca, N.Y.: Cornell University Press, 2000), for a discussion of how foreign investment has affected working conditions and workers' rights in China in particular. Santoro concluded that companies operating in China in higher-technology industries have mostly improved the situation of Chinese workers, while those in lower-technology industries have mostly done the opposite.

63. See Alan B. Krueger, "International Labor Standards and Trade," *Annual World Bank Conference on Development Economics* (1996): 281–302; also "Strategies for Eliminating Child Labour: Prevention, Removal, and Rehabilitation" (unpublished paper, International Labor Organization/UNICEF, 1997).

64. See Kaushik Basu, "Child Labor: Cause, Consequence and Cure, with Remarks on International Labor Standards," *Journal of Economic Literature* 37 (September 1999): 1083–1119.

65. Eric V. Edmonds and Nina Pavcnik, "International Trade and Child Labor: Cross-Country Evidence," *Journal of International Economics*, forthcoming.

66. Few worked outside of agriculture.

67. Eric V. Edmonds and Nina Pavcnik, "The Effect of Trade Liberalization on Child Labor," *Journal of International Economics* 65 (March 2005): 401–19, and Eric V. Edmonds, "Does Child Labor Decline with Improving Economic Status?," *Journal of Human Resources* 40 (Winter 2005): 77–99.

68. On the potential role of different "cultures" in accounting for economic growth, see David S. Landes, *The Wealth and Poverty of Nations: Why Some*

Are So Rich and Some So Poor (New York: Norton, 1999), and the essays in Lawrence E. Harrison and Samuel P. Huntington (eds.), *Culture Matters: How Values Shape Human Progress* (New York: Basic Books, 2000). Gregory Clark and Robert Feenstra have argued that the problem that prevented the poor countries from achieving better growth was (and is) a problem of "employing labor effectively." Specifically, it was (and is) not a problem of getting access to new technologies. See Gregory Clark and Robert Feenstra, "Technology in the Great Divergence," in Bordo et al. (eds.), *Globalization in Historical Perspective.*

69. T. N. Srinivasan, "The Costs of Hesitant and Reluctant Globalization: India," *Indian Economic Review* 38 (July–December 2003): 131–55; quotation from p. 133.

70. See Lindert and Williamson, "Does Globalization Make the World More Unequal?" and Jeffrey G. Williamson, "Winners and Losers over Two Centuries of Globalization" (WIDER Annual Lecture, Copenhagen, 2002). Also see Jeffrey D. Sachs, Andrew Warner, Anders Aslund, and Stanley Fischer, "Economic Reform and the Process of Global Integration," *Brookings Papers on Economic Activity* (No. 1, 1995): 1–118, for evidence of convergence of average incomes among countries pursuing open trade policies but not among those with more closed economies.

71. Lindert and Williamson, "Does Globalization Make the World More Unequal?," p. 250.

72. Ibid., p. 252.

CHAPTER 15
Growth and the Environment

1. World Commission on Environment and Development, *Our Common Future* (New York: Oxford University Press, 1987), p. 8.

2. The phrase "the American century" was first popularized by Henry Luce; see Henry R. Luce, "The American Century," *Life* 10 (February 17, 1941), pp. 61–65.

3. Truman letter of January 22, 1951, reproduced in President's Materials Policy Commission, *Resources for Freedom: A Report to the President* (Washington, D.C.: Government Printing Office, 1952), p. viii.

4. Ibid.

5. Rachel Carson, *Silent Spring* (Cambridge, Mass.: Riverside Press, 1962), p. 6.

6. Ibid., p. 8.

7. Public Law 91–90, Section 101a. See Matthew J. Lindstrom and Zachary A. Smith, *The National Environmental Policy Act: Judicial Misconstruction, Legislative Indifference, and Executive Neglect* (College Station: Texas A&M University Press, 2001), p. 142.

8. See Martin Janicke and Helmut Weidner (eds.), *Successful Environmental Policy: A Critical Evaluation of 24 Cases* (Berlin: Sigma, 1995), p. 147; Michael Skou Anderson and Duncan Liefferink, *European Environmental Policy: The Pioneers* (Manchester, U.K.: Manchester University Press, 1997), p. 162; Uday Desai (ed.), *Ecological Policy and Politics in Developing Countries: Economic Growth, Democracy and Environment* (Albany: State University of New York Press, 1998), p. 129; Baltic Marine Environment Protection Commission, *20 Years of International Cooperation for the Baltic Marine Environment, 1974–1994* (Helsinki: Helsinki Commission, Baltic Marine Environment Protection Commission, 1994), p. 6.

9. Donella H. Meadows, Dennis L. Meadows, Jørgen Randers, and William W. Behrens III, *The Limits to Growth: A Report for the Club of Rome's Project on the Predicament of Mankind* (New York: Universe, 1972). The analysis in *The Limits to Growth* drew importantly on the prior work of Jay W. Forrester, also at MIT, including especially his *World Dynamics* (Cambridge, Mass.: Wright-Allen, 1971).

10. Meadows et al., *The Limits to Growth*, p. 23.

11. Ibid., pp. 45, 48, 46.

12. E. F. Schumacher, *Small Is Beautiful: A Study of Economics as if People Mattered* (London: Blond & Briggs, 1973). Schumacher was at some pains to distance himself from the analysis in *The Limits to Growth*. For example, at one point he flatly stated, "the modern industrial system is not gravely threatened by possible scarcities and high prices of most of the materials to which the M.I.T. study devotes such ponderous attention" (p. 114).

13. Early examples include Wei-Chyung Wang, Joseph P. Pinto, and Yuk Ling Yung, "Climatic Effects Due to Halogenated Compounds in the Earth's Atmosphere," *Journal of the Atmospheric Sciences* 37 (February 1980): 333–38; and J. Hansen, D. Johnson, A. Lacis, S. Lebedev, P. Lee, D. Rind, and G. Russell, "Climate Impact of Increasing Atmospheric Carbon Dioxide," *Science* 213 (August 28, 1981): 957–66. See Spencer R. Weart, *The Discovery of Global Warming* (Cambridge: Harvard University Press, 2003), for a useful historical review of thinking in this area, going back to the work of British researcher John Tyndall in 1862.

14. Walter Sullivan, "Study Finds Warming Trend That Could Raise Sea Levels," *New York Times*, August 22, 1981, p. A1.

15. Philip Shabecoff, "E.P.A. Report Says Earth Will Heat Up Beginning in 1990's," *New York Times*, October 18, 1983, p. A1. The EPA report described in the article was "The Potential Effects of Global Climate Change on the United States" (Washington, D.C.: EPA, 1983).

16. Data on CO_2 emissions are from the World Bank's online *World Development Indicators*.

17. Data on deforestation are from Norman Meyers, *Deforestation Rates in Tropical Forests and Their Climatic Implications* (London: Friends of the Earth Trust, 1989), Table 1 and pp. 12, 28.

18. Data for 1990–2000 are from the U.N. Food and Agriculture Organization, *State of the World's Forests, 2003*.

19. See, for example, Thomas Lekan, *Imagining the Nation in Nature: Landscape Preservation and German Identity, 1885–1945* (Cambridge: Harvard University Press, 2004).

20. See Charles C. Mann and Mark Plummer, *Noah's Choice: The Future of Endangered Species* (New York: Knopf, 1995).

21. Data on total energy consumption in the United States are from the Department of Energy.

22. Data on world petroleum consumption are from the Department of Energy. Data on proved petroleum reserves and oil prices are from *Oil and Gas Journal*.

23. See William D. Nordhaus, "World Dynamics: Measurement Without Data," *Economic Journal* 83 (December 1973): 1156–83, and William D. Nordhaus, Robert N. Stavins, and Martin L. Weitzman, "Lethal Model 2: The Limits to Growth Revisited," *Brookings Papers on Economic Activity* (No. 2, 1992), pp. 1–59, for reviews of *Limits to Growth*.

24. See Barbara Freese, *Coal: A Human History* (Cambridge, Mass.: Perseus, 2003).

25. Jeffrey A. Frankel, "Globalization and the Environment," in Michael Weinstein (ed.), *Globalization: What's New?* (New York: Council on Foreign Relations, 2005), pp. 132–33.

26. See Edward A. Parson, *Protecting the Ozone Layer: Science and Strategy* (New York: Oxford University Press, 2003).

27. Not only has the Senate not ratified the Kyoto Protocol, but in 1997 it adopted—by a vote of 95–0—a resolution saying it would reject any treaty that did not impose emission restrictions on developing countries as well (the Kyoto agreement restricts industrial countries' emissions but not those of developing countries), and that it would also reject any treaty that would cause "serious harm" to the American economy. See the discussion of America's policy position in this area, including the Byrd-Hagel Resolution, in David G. Victor, *Climate Change: Debating America's Policy Options* (New York: Council on Foreign Relations, 2004).

28. See Steven Lee Meyers, "Putin Ratifies Kyoto Protocol on Emissions," *New York Times*, November 6, 2004, p. A7, and Shankar Vedantam, "Kyoto Treaty Takes Effect Today; Impact on Global Warming May Be Largely Symbolic," *Washington Post*, February 16, 2005, p. A4.

29. See, for example, Richard N. Cooper, "Toward a Real Global Warming Treaty," *Foreign Affairs* 77 (March–April 1998): 66; David G. Victor, *The Collapse of the Kyoto Protocol and the Struggle to Slow Global Warming* (Princeton: Princeton University Press, 2001); Thomas Schelling, "What Makes Greenhouse Sense?: Time to Rethink the Kyoto Protocol," *Foreign Affairs* 81 (May–June 2002): 2; William D. Nordhaus, "After Kyoto: Alternative

Mechanisms to Control Global Warming" (unpublished paper, Yale University, 2002); and Robert N. Stavins, "Forging a More Effective Global Climate Treaty," *Environment* 46 (December 2004): 23–30.

30. Desai (ed.), *Ecological Policy and Politics in Developing Countries*, p. 282. See, more generally, Joseph Alcamo (ed.), *Coping with Crisis in Eastern Europe's Environment* (New York: Parthenon, 1992).

31. Data on service sector shares in total output are from *World Development Indicators*.

32. Josh Ederington, Arik Levenson, and Jerry Minier, "Trade Liberalization and Pollution Havens" (National Bureau of Economic Research, Working Paper 10585, 2004).

33. See Kirk Smith, "Fuel Combustion, Air Pollution Exposure and Health: The Situation in Developing Countries," *Annual Review of Energy and Environment* 18 (1993), pp. 529–66, and Subham Chaudhuri and Alexander S. P. Pfaff, "Fuel-Choice and Indoor Air Quality: A Household-Level Perspective on Economic Growth and the Environment" (unpublished paper, Columbia University, 2003).

34. This idea first appeared in a concise form in the World Bank's 1992 *World Development Report*. Other early discussions were Thomas Selden and Daqing Song, "Environmental Quality and Development: Is There a Kuznets Curve for Air Pollution Emissions?," *Journal of Environmental Economics and Management* 27 (September 1994): 147–62, and Gene M. Grossman and Alan B. Krueger, "Economic Growth and the Environment," *Quarterly Journal of Economics* 110 (May 1995): 353–77. A large body of literature has appeared since then, testing this hypothesis. For reviews, see Susmita Dasgupta, Benoit Laplante, Hua Wang, and David Wheeler, "Confronting the Environmental Kuznets Curve," *Journal of Economic Perspectives* 16 (Winter 2002): 147–68; Anastasios Xepapadeas, "Economic Growth and the Environment," in Karl-Goran Mäler and Jeffrey R. Vincent (eds.), *Handbook of Environmental Economics* (Amsterdam: Elsevier, 2003); Jeffrey A. Frankel and Andrew K. Rose, "Is Trade Good or Bad for the Environment? Sorting Out the Causality," *Review of Economics and Statistics* 87 (February 2005): 85–91; and Brian R. Copeland and M. Scott Taylor, "Trade, Growth and the Environment," *Journal of Economic Literature* 42 (March 2004): 7–71.

35. See again Selden and Song, "Environmental Quality and Development," and Grossman and Krueger, "Economic Growth and the Enviroment"; also Nemat Shafik, "Economic Development and Environmental Quality: An Econometric Analysis," *Oxford Economic Papers* (New Series) 46 (October 1994): 757–73; F. G. Hank Hilton and Arik Levinson, "Factoring the Environmental Kuznets Curve: Evidence from Automotive Lead Emissions," *Journal of Environmental Economics and Management* 35 (March 1998): 126–41; and David Bradford, Stephen H. Shore, and Rebecca

Schlieckert, "The Environment Kuznets Curve: Exploring A Fresh Speci-
fication," *Berkeley Electronic Journals in Economic Analysis and Policy,* forthcoming.

36. Grossman and Krueger, "Economic Growth and the Environment."

37. See again Shafik, "Economic Development and Environmental Quality."

38. Data on ambient pollutants are from the Environmental Protection
Agency.

39. Data on forest area and wood volume are from the Department of Agriculture, USDA Forest Service, "Preliminary 2002 Resources Planning Act
(RPA) Assessment Tables," Tables 3, 25.

40. Just as wider access to sanitary drinking water did much to increase
American life expectancy in the first half of the nineteenth century—see
again David Cutler and Grant Miller, "The Role of Public Health
Improvements in Health Advances: The 20th Century United States,"
Demography 42 (February 2005): 1–22—cleaner air has further lowered
infant mortality in more recent decades. Based on a county-by-county
analysis of the American experience, Kenneth Chay and Michael Greenstone have estimated that each 1 percent decline in total suspended particulates results in a .5 percent decline in infant mortality, and that the 1970
Clean Air Act resulted in roughly 1,300 fewer infant deaths by 1972; Kenneth Chay and Michael Greenstone, "Air Quality, Infant Mortality, and
the Clean Air Act of 1970" (National Bureau of Economic Research,
Working Paper 10053, 2003).

41. As the example of automobiles shows, environmental policy at the subnational level can be important as well. The stricter requirements for pollution controls put in place by the state of California in 1966 had a strong
influence on industry standards. Today the industry's active interest in
developing an electronic car stems mostly from requirements that California legislated in 1990, initially scheduled to take effect by 2003 but subsequently delayed.

42. See Susmita Dasgupta, Ashoka Mody, Subhendu Roy, and David Wheeler,
"Environmental Regulation and Development: A Cross-Century Empiri-
cal Analysis," *Oxford Development Studies* 29 (June 2001): 173–87, and
Dasgupta et al., "Confronting the Environmental Kuznets Curve."

43. Scott Barrett and Kathryn Graddy, "Freedom, Growth, and the Environment," *Environment and Development Economics* 5 (October 2000): 433–56,
and Frankel and Rose, "Is Trade Good or Bad for the Enviroment?"

44. Data on CO_2 emissions are again from *World Development Indicators.*

45. Data on current (2003) income are from the World Bank, *World Develop-
ment Report 2005: A Better Investment Climate for Everyone* (Washington,
D.C.: World Bank, 2004), Table 1, pp. 256–57. Data on current life
expectancy are from United Nations Development Programme, *Human
Development Report 2004: Cultural Liberty in Today's Diverse World* (New
York: United Nations Development Programme, 2004), Table 1, pp. 140–43.

Data on historical life expectancy in the United States are from Michael R. Haines, "The Population of the United States, 1790–1920," in Stanley L. Engerman and Robert E. Gallman (eds.), *The Cambridge Economic History of the United States: The Long Nineteenth Century* (New York: Cambridge University Press, 1996–2000), Table 4.3, p. 158. The value given for 1880 is for whites only. The value for 1850 combines separate values for whites and blacks using population weights from *Historical Statistics of the United States, Colonial Times to 1970* (Washington, D.C.: Census Bureau, 1975), Table A 91–104.

46. See David Landes, *The Wealth and Poverty of Nations: Why Some Are So Rich and Some So Poor* (New York: Norton, 1999), Chapter 1, for a discussion of the connection between tropical diseases and economic development. Landes's Table 1.1, p. 10, gives World Health Organization data on the incidence of these and other specific diseases.

47. Xiaoying Ma and Leonard Ortolano, *Environmental Regulation in China: Institutions, Enforcement, and Compliance* (Lanham, Md.: Rowman & Littlefield, 2000), pp. 17, 28; O. P. Dwivedi, *India's Environmental Policies, Programmes and Stewardship* (New York: St. Martin's, 1997), p. 59.

48. On Korea, see Michael C. Howard, *Asia's Environmental Crisis* (Boulder, Colo.: Westview, 1993), p. 28off; on Venezuela, Desai (ed.), *Ecological Policy and Politics in Developing Countries*, p. 212ff; on Brazil and Indonesia, Gordon MacDonald, Daniel L. Nielson, and Marc A. Stern (eds.), *Latin American Environmental Policy in International Perspective* (Boulder, Colo.: Westview, 1997), pp. 93, 212ff; on Kenya, Government of Kenya, Ministry of Environmental and National Resources, *The Kenya National Environmental Action Plan: Report* (1994).

49. See, for example, Alvin K. Klevorick, "The Race to the Bottom in a Federal System: Lessons from the World of Trade Policy," *Yale Law and Policy Review/Yale Journal of Regulation* 67 (Symposium Issue, 1996): 177–86; Peter P. Swire, "The Race to Laxity and the Race to Undesirability: Explaining Failures in Competition Among Jurisdictions in Environmental Law," *Yale Law and Policy Review/Yale Journal of Regulation* 67 (Symposium Issue, 1996): 67–110; and Herman Daly, "Globalization and Its Discontents," in Peter M. Haas (ed.), *Environment in the New Global Economy* (London: Edward Elgar, 2003). See also the reviews of this issue in Daniel C. Esty, "Bridging the Trade-Environment Divide," *Journal of Economic Perspectives* 15 (Summer 2001): 113–30; the introduction to Daniel C. Esty and Damien Geradin (eds.), *Regulatory Competition and Economic Integration* (Oxford: Oxford University Press, 2001); and Jagdish Bhagwati, *In Defense of Globalization* (New York: Oxford University Press, 2004). The idea in the environmental dimension echoes similar concerns about such issues as occupational safety, workers' hours, and child labor.

50. See Josh Ederington, Arik Levenson, and Jerry Minier, "Footloose and Pollution-Free," *Review of Economics and Statistics* 87 (February 2005):

92–99; Muthukumara Mani and David Wheeler, "In Search of Pollution Havens? Dirty Industry in the World Economy, 1960–95," in Per G. Fredriksson (ed.), *Trade, Global Policy and the Environment* (Washington, D.C.: World Bank, 1999); Jean-Marie Grether and Jaime de Melo, "Globalization and Dirty Industries: Do Pollution Havens Matter?" (National Bureau of Economic Research, Working Paper 9776, 2003); Brian R. Copeland and M. Scott Taylor, "Trade, Growth and the Environment" (National Bureau of Economic Research, Working Paper 9823, 2003); and Arik Levenson and M. Scott Taylor, "Unmasking the Pollution Haven Effect" (National Bureau of Economic Research, Working Paper 10629, 2004), for reviews of some of this evidence.

51. *Our Common Future*, p. ix.

52. Ibid., pp. xii, 1.

53. Ibid., p. 8.

54. Ibid., pp. 8, 9.

55. Data on population growth net of immigration are from the United Nations, Population Division, Department of Economic and Social Affairs, "World Population Prospects: The 2002 Revision," based on the "zero-migration variant" projection for 2000–2005. Data on fertility are from *World Development Indicators*.

56. Data on population growth and fertility are from *World Development Indicators*.

57. See Robert J. Barro and Jong-Wha Lee, "Sources of Economic Growth," *Carnegie-Rochester Conference Series on Public Policy* 40 (June 1994): 1–46, and "Losers and Winners in Economic Growth," *Proceedings of the World Bank Annual Conference on Development Economics* (1993), pp. 267–97; and David E. Bloom and Jeffrey Williamson, "Demographic Transitions and Economic Miracles in Emerging Asia," *World Bank Economic Review* 12 (September 1998): 419–55; also Robert J. Barro and Xavier Sala-i-Martin, *Economic Growth* (Cambridge: MIT Press, 2003), Chapter 12.

58. Garrett Hardin, "The Tragedy of the Commons," *Science* 162 (December 13, 1968): 1243–48, quotation from p. 1248.

59. Averages here are weighted by the population in each country.

60. Robert M. Solow, "Sustainability: An Economist's Perspective," in Robert Dorfman and Nancy S. Dorfman (eds.), *Economics of the Environment: Selected Readings* (New York: Norton, 1993), p. 181.

61. Ibid., p. 182. Society may of course choose to preserve a specific physical area in its natural state, but the reason, which is typically aesthetic, is not central to sustainability. And while sustainability certainly encompasses a concern for biodiversity, the argument for protecting any specific individual species is instead that humans have no moral right to extinguish another living species. That argument may be cogent, even compelling, but it does not arise from the principle of sustainable development either.

CHAPTER 16
Economic Policy and Economic Growth in America

1. Alexis de Tocqueville, *Democracy in America*, translated by Henry Reeve (New York: Vintage, 1990), Vol. 2, p. 190.

2. For a comprehensive review of the evidence, see Zvi Griliches, *R&D and Productivity: The Econometric Evidence* (Chicago: University of Chicago Press, 1998), "Introduction," and *R&D, Education and Productivity: A Retrospective* (Cambridge: Harvard University Press, 2000), Chapters 4 and 5.

3. For a recent assessment, see again N. Gregory Mankiw, David Romer, and David N. Weil, "A Contribution to the Empirics of Economic Growth," *Quarterly Journal of Economics* 107 (May 1992): 407–37.

4. See again Dale W. Jorgenson and Kevin J. Stiroh, "Raising the Speed Limit: U.S. Economic Growth in the Information Age," *Brookings Papers on Economic Activity* (No. 1, 2000), pp. 125–235, and Stephen D. Oliner and Daniel E. Sichel, "The Resurgence of Growth in the Late 1990s: Is Information Technology the Story?," *Journal of Economic Perspectives* 14 (Autumn 2000): 3–22.

5. Data on productivity and employment are from the Bureau of Labor Statistics. Data on capital stocks are from the Bureau of Economic Analysis.

6. The fact that the cross-country relationship between capital investment and productivity growth holds up well for investment in equipment, but not for investment in plants, commercial offices, or other buildings, suggests that in many countries businesses tend to undertake construction projects at least in part for noneconomic reasons.

7. See J. Bradford de Long and Lawrence H. Summers, "Equipment Investment and Economic Growth: How Strong Is the Nexus?," *Brookings Papers on Economic Activity* (No. 2, 1992), pp. 157–211. These patterns are readily visible in data from Robert Summers and Alan Heston, "The Penn World Table (Mark 5): An Expanded Set of International Comparisons, 1950–1988," *Quarterly Journal of Economics* 106 (May 1991): 327–68, and from the World Bank's *World Development Indicators*.

8. See McKinsey Global Institute, *Capital Productivity* (Washington, D.C.: McKinsey & Company, 1996), for an analysis of how the American economy manages to be more productive with less capital.

9. Robert J. Barro and Jong-Wha Lee, "International Comparisons of Educational Attainment," *Journal of Monetary Economics* 32 (December 1993): 363–94, and "Losers and Winners in Economic Growth," *Proceedings of the World Bank Annual Conference on Development Economics 1993*, pp. 267–97, provided early evidence for the positive relationship between education and economic growth. Since then a large literature has reconfirmed this finding. Not all of the observed relationship reflects the direct effect of education on productivity, however. One benefit of additional schooling, especially beginning from low levels, is improved health and a correspond-

ing increase in life expectancy; another is a reduced birthrate and therefore slower population growth. These developments also help improve a country's growth prospects, no less than literacy or job skills more narrowly defined. See Robert J. Barro, *Determinants of Economic Growth: A Cross-Country Empirical Study* (Cambridge: MIT Press, 1997), and Roberto Perotti, "Growth, Income Distribution and Democracy: What the Data Say," *Journal of Economic Growth* 1 (June 1996): 148–87.

10. Eric A. Hanushek and Dennis D. Kimko, "Schooling, Labor-Force Quality, and the Growth of Nations," *American Economic Review* 90 (December 2000): 1184–1208.

11. See, for example, Joshua D. Angrist and Alan B. Krueger, "Does Compulsory School Attendance Affect Schooling and Earnings?," *Quarterly Journal of Economics* 106 (November 1991): 979–1014, and David Card and Alan B. Krueger, "Does School Quality Matter? Returns to Education and the Characteristics of Public Schools in the United States," *Journal of Political Economy* 100 (February 1992): 1–40. The literature documenting the relationship between education and earnings is also vast. For a recent review, see David Card, "The Causal Effect of Education on Earnings," in Orley Ashenfelter and David Card (eds.), *Handbook of Labor Economics* (Amsterdam: Elsevier, 1999), Vol. 3.

12. Lawrence F. Katz and Kevin M. Murphy, "Changes in Relative Wages, 1963–1987, Supply and Demand Factors," *Quarterly Journal of Economics* 107 (February 1992): 35–78.

13. See David M. Cutler and Lawrence F. Katz, "Macroeconomic Performance and the Disadvantaged," *Brookings Papers on Economic Activity* (No. 2, 1991) pp. 1–74; Katz and Murphy, "Changes in Relative Wages, 1963–1987"; and David H. Autor, Lawrence F. Katz, and Alan B. Krueger, "Computing Inequality: Have Computers Changed the Labor Market?," *Quarterly Journal of Economics* 113 (November 1998): 1169–1213. Data on earnings differentials for 2003 are from an analysis of Census Bureau data by the Economic Policy Institute.

14. See again Franco Modigliani, "Life-Cycle, Individual Thrift, and the Wealth of Nations," *American Economic Review* 76 (June 1986): 297–313, for an explanation of why an economy that is growing rapidly will therefore do more saving and investment, and Peter J. Klenow and Andrés Rodríguez-Clare, "The Neo-Classical Revival in Growth Economics: Has It Gone Too Far?," *NBER Macroeconomics Annual 1997*, pp. 73–102, for a parallel theory of education responding to economic growth. Even for comparisons among different individuals within a single country, education makes people more productive and therefore increases their earning power, but there are also reasons to think that people who are naturally more intelligent or energetic, or more productive in other ways, are likely to seek more education; see Orley Ashenfelter and David J. Zimmerman,

"Estimates of the Returns to Schooling from Sibling Data: Fathers, Sons, and Brothers," *Review of Economics and Statistics* 79 (February 1997): 1–9.

15. Data on investment rates are from the Bureau of Economic Analysis.

16. Data on real compensation are from the Bureau of Labor Statistics.

17. Data on saving rates are from the Bureau of Economic Analysis. For a discussion of the longer historical experience, see Edward Denison, "A Note on Private Saving," *Review of Economics and Statistics* 40 (August 1958): 261–67, and Paul A. David and John L. Scadding, "Private Savings: Ultra-rationality, Aggregation, and 'Denison's Law,'" *Journal of Political Economy* 82 (March–April 1974): 225–49.

18. Budget data are from the Office of Management and Budget.

19. Congressional Budget Office, "The Budget and Economic Outlook: Fiscal Years 2006 to 2015" (January 2005), Table F-12, p. 145.

20. See, for example, Martin Feldstein, "Clinton's Revenue Mirage," *Wall Street Journal*, April 6, 1993, p. A14, and "Tax Rates and Human Behavior," *Wall Street Journal*, May 7, 1993, p. A14.

21. Congressional Budget Office, "The Budget and Economic Outlook: Fiscal Years 2002–2011" (January 2001), Table 1-1, p. 2, and "The Budget and Economic Outlook: Fiscal Years 2006 to 2015," Table 1-2, p. 3.

22. Office of Management and Budget, *Budget of the United States Government, Fiscal Year 2006* (Washington, D.C.: Government Printing Office, 2005), Table 5-1, p. 343.

23. William G. Gale and Peter R. Orszag, "The Outlook for Fiscal Policy," *Tax Notes*, February 14, 2005, pp. 841–53. The underlying assumptions are that the 2001 and 2003 tax cuts become permanent, that Congress liberalizes the Alternative Minimum Tax, and that real nonentitlement spending increases in step with the U.S. population.

24. Data on budget shares are from the Treasury and the Congressional Budget Office.

25. Board of Trustees, Federal Old-Age and Survivors Insurance and Disability Insurance Trust Funds, *2004 Annual Report* ("2004 Social Security Trustees Report"), Tables IV.B2 and VI.F8, pp. 47 and 178 ("intermediate" projections).

26. Board of Trustees, Federal Hospital Insurance and Federal Supplementary Medical Insurance Trust Funds, *2004 Annual Report* ("2004 Medicare Trustees Report"), Tables I.D1 and II.A5, pp. 4 and 31.

27. See Alan J. Auerbach, William G. Gale, and Peter R. Orszag, "Sources of the Long-Term Fiscal Gap," *Tax Notes*, May 24, 2004, pp. 1049–59, especially Tables 4 and 5, pp. 1053 and 1054.

28. See, for example, James Poterba and Lawrence H. Summers, "The Economic Effects of Dividend Taxation," in Edward I. Altman and Marti G. Subrahmanyam (eds.), *Recent Advances in Corporate Finance* (Homewood, Ill.: R. D. Irwin, 1985), and Laurie Simon Bagwell and John B. Shoven, "Cash

Distributions to Shareholders," *Journal of Economic Perspectives* 3 (Summer 1989): 129–40. See also Alan J. Auerbach, "The Theory of Excess Burden and Optimal Taxation," in Alan J. Auerbach and Martin Feldstein (eds.), *Handbook of Public Economics*, Vol. 1 (Amsterdam: Elsevier Science, 1985).

29. Even after allowing for increasing pension plan coverage as well as the fact that many people who owned corporate equities enjoyed sizable gains in their wealth as a result of the rising stock market (both of which reduced people's need to save directly out of their current incomes), at most it is possible to explain away only part of the 1980s decline in private saving. See David Bradford, "Market Value Versus Financial Accounting Measures of National Saving," in B. Douglas Bernheim and John B. Shoven (eds.), *National Saving and Economic Performance* (Chicago: University of Chicago Press, 1991).

30. Additional life expectancy at age sixty-five in the United States is now 16.4 years for men and 19.4 years for women. In 1940 it was 11.9 years for men and 13.4 years for women. (Data are from the National Center for Health Statistics, National Vital Statistics Reports.)

31. The current schedule for increasing the retirement age calls for a step-up of two months per year until 2009, then a pause, and then a renewed two-months-per-year increase from 2021 to 2027. The estimated reduction in spending is from the CBO's analysis of the proposed (but not enacted) Bipartisan Retirement Security Act of 2004 (H.R. 3821).

32. See, for example, the list given in Henry J. Aaron, "Social Security: Tune It Up, Don't Trade It In," in Henry J. Aaron and John B. Shoven, *Should the United States Privatize Social Security?* (Cambridge: MIT Press, 1999), especially Table 2.2, p. 90.

33. Just what those conditions are is a matter of intense debate. See, for example, the different points of view in Martin Feldstein, "Structural Reform of Social Security," *Journal of Economic Perspectives*, 19 (Spring 2005): 33–55, and Peter A. Diamond and Peter R. Orszag, *Saving Social Security: A Balanced Approach* (Washington, D.C.: Brookings Institution, 2004), especially Chapter 8. Also see again Aaron, "Social Security: Tune It Up, Don't Trade It In."

34. See, for example, Henry J. Aaron, *Serious and Unstable Condition: Financing America's Health Care* (Washington, D.C.: Brookings Institution, 1991), and David M. Cutler, *Your Money or Your Life: Strong Medicine for America's Health Care System* (New York: Oxford University Press, 2004).

35. Lisa Potetz and Thomas Rice provide a useful summary of such proposals in Potetz and Rice, *Medicare Tomorrow: The Report of the Century Foundation Task Force on Medicare Reform* (New York: Century Foundation, 2001). Also see again Cutler, *Your Money or Your Life.*

36. At least half of the growth in American medical spending in recent decades has been the direct consequence of technological change. See Aaron, *Financing America's Health Care*, and Joseph P. Newhouse, "Medical Care

Costs: How Much Welfare Loss?," *Journal of Economic Perspectives* 6 (Summer 1992): 3–21.

37. 2004 Social Security Trustees Report, Table V.A2, p. 78.

38. Data on poverty by age groups are from the Census Bureau.

39. In 2003 the poverty rate for the over-sixty-five population was 10.2 percent. For those under sixty-five it was 12.8 percent.

40. J. K. Iglehart, "The American Health Care System: Medicare," *New England Journal of Medicine* 327 (November 12, 1992): 1467.

41. Angus Campbell, *The Sense of Well-Being in America: Recent Patterns and Trends* (New York: McGraw-Hill, 1981), p. 245; see also Linda K. George, "Economic Status and Subjective Well-Being," in Neal E. Cutler, Davis W. Gregg, and M. Powell Lawton (eds.), *Aging, Money, and Life Satisfaction* (New York: Springer, 1992).

42. Data on Social Security benefits as a share of income are from the National Center for Policy Analysis.

43. Auerbach et al., "Sources of the Long-Term Fiscal Gap," Table 9, p. 1056.

44. Under the existing legislation, the estate tax is to be restored in 2011. Here too few people believe that this is what Congress intended to happen.

45. See William G. Gale and Joel Slemrod, "Rethinking Estate and Gift Taxation: Overview," in William G. Gale, James R. Hines, Jr., and Joel Slemrod (eds.), *Rethinking Estate and Gift Taxation* (Washington, D.C.: Brookings Institution, 2001).

46. Data on estate and gift tax collections are from the Congressional Budget Office, "The Budget and Economic Outlook: Fiscal Years 2005 to 2014," Table F-3, p. 131.

47. Brookings–Urban Institute Tax Policy Center, www.taxpolicycenter.org/commentary/agreement.cfm#agree.

48. Auerbach et al., "Sources of the Long-Term Fiscal Gap." This estimate also assumes that the 2001, 2002, and 2003 tax cuts become permanent and that Congress reforms the Alternative Minimum Tax.

49. David T. Ellwood, "The Sputtering Labor Force of the 21st Century: Can Social Policy Help?" in Alan B. Krueger and Robert M. Solow (eds.), *The Roaring Nineties: Can Full Employment Be Sustained?* (New York: Russell Sage Foundation, 2001). See also Dale W. Jorgenson, Mun S. Ho, and Kevin J. Strioh, *Information Technology and the American Growth Resurgence* (Cambridge: MIT Press, forthcoming), Chapter 6, and J. Bradford DeLong, Claudia Goldin, and Lawrence F. Katz, "Sustaining U.S. Economic Growth," in Henry J. Aaron, James M. Lindsay, and Pietro S. Nivola (eds.), *Agenda for the Nation* (Washington, D.C.: Brookings Institution, 2003).

50. See Eric A. Hanushek, "Further Evidence on the Effects of Catholic Secondary Schooling: Comments," *Brookings-Wharton Papers on Urban Affairs* (2000), pp. 194–97; Francine D. Blau and Lawrence M. Khan, "Do Cogni-

tive Test Scores Explain Higher US Wage Inequality?," *Review of Economics and Statistics* 87 (February 2005): 184–93; and the discussion of this issue in James J. Heckman and Alan B. Krueger, *Inequality in America: What Role for Human Capital Policies?* (Cambridge: MIT Press, 2003).

51. James J. Heckman and Pedro Carneiro, "Human Capital Policy," in Heckman and Krueger, *Inequality in America*, p. 86.

52. Dirk Krueger and Krishna B. Kumar, "US-Europe Differences in Technology-Driven Growth: Quantifying the Role of Education," *Journal of Monetary Economics* 51 (January 2004): 161–90.

53. Data are from the National Center for Education Statistics, *2002 Digest of Education Statistics*, Tables 2, 170.

54. Data are from the *2002 Digest of Education Statistics*, Tables 157, 334, 335.

55. Recent evidence has confirmed these society-wide benefits. More education makes a person more likely to vote, more likely to read newspapers, and more likely to support free speech; see Thomas S. Dee, "Are There Civic Returns to Education?," *Journal of Public Economics* 88 (August 2004): 1697–1720; and Kevin Milligan, Enrico Moretti, and Philip Oreopoulos, "Does Education Improve Citizenship? Evidence from the United States and the United Kingdom," *Journal of Public Economics* 88 (August 2004): 1667–95. Graduating from high school reduces a person's likelihood of being either arrested or incarcerated, with the largest effects for murder, assault, and motor vehicle theft; see Lance Lochner and Enrico Moretti, "The Effect of Education on Crime: Evidence from Prison Inmates, Arrests, and Self-Reports," *American Economic Review* 94 (March 2004): 155–89.

56. Francine D. Blau et al., *The Economics of Women, Men and Work*, 5th ed. (Upper Saddle River, N.J.: Prentice Hall, forthcoming), Figure 4.10a.

57. See Carneiro and Heckman, "Human Capital Policy."

58. Philip Oreopoulis, Marianne E. Page, and Ann Huff Stevens, "Does Human Capital Transfer from Parent to Child? The Intergenerational Effects of Compulsory Schooling" (National Bureau of Economic Research, Working Paper 10164, 2003).

59. See, for example, the poll results cited by Alan B. Krueger, "Inequality, Too Much of a Good Thing," in Heckman and Krueger, *Inequality in America*, pp. 19–20.

60. See, for example, Joshua D. Angrist and Alan B. Krueger, "Does Compulsory School Attendance Affect Schooling and Earnings?" *Quarterly Journal of Economics* 106 (November 1991): 979–1014, and Ashenfelter and Zimmerman, "Estimates of the Returns to Schooling from Sibling Data." Also see again the review of this literature by Card, "The Causal Effect of Education on Earnings."

61. Orley Ashenfelter, Colm Harmon, and Hessel Oosterbeck, "A Review of Estimates of the Schooling/Earnings Relationship, with Tests for Publication Bias," *Labour Economics* 6 (November 1999): 453–70.

62. See again Card, "The Causal Effect of Education on Earnings"; also Pedro Carneiro, James Heckman, and Edward Vytlacil, "Estimating the Rate of Return to Education When It Varies Among Individuals" (unpublished paper, University of Chicago, 2001); David Card, "Estimating the Return to Schooling: Progress on Some Persistent Econometric Problems," *Econometrica* 69 (September 2001): 1127–60; and the results surveyed in Carneio and Heckman, "Human Capital Policy," Table 2.4, p. 150.

63. Data on hourly wages by education of workers are from Lawrence Mishel, Jared Bernstein, and Heather Boushey, *The State of Working America, 2004/2005* (Ithaca, N.Y.: ILR Press, forthcoming), Table 2.17.

64. Card and Krueger, "Does School Quality Matter?"

65. Cross-country comparisons suggest, however, that students forced to stay in school end up more successful economically, and even healthier, than if they had dropped out; see Philip Oreopoulos, "Do Dropouts Drop Out Too Soon? International Evidence from Changes in School-Leaving Laws" (National Bureau of Economic Research, Working Paper 10155, 2003). Even for the United States, there is evidence that increased compulsory schooling reduces rates of teenage childbearing; see Sandra E. Black, Paul J. Deveraux, and Kjele Salvanes, "Fast Times at Ridgemont High? The Effect of Compulsory Schooling Laws on Teenage Births (National Bureau of Economic Research, Working Paper 10911, 2004).

66. See the reviews of the literature on this issue in Edward Zigler and Jeanette Valentine (eds.), *Project Head Start: A Legacy of the War on Poverty* (New York: Free Press, 1979); Ruth Hubbell McKey, *A Review of Head Start Research Since 1970* (Washington, D.C.: Department of Health and Human Services, Head Start Bureau, 1983), and *The Impact of Head Start on Children, Families and Communities* (Washington, D.C.: Department of Health and Human Services, Head Start Bureau, 1985); Sue Bredekamp and Carol Copple (eds.), *Developmentally Appropriate Practice in Early Childhood Programs* (Washington, D.C.: National Association for the Education of Young Children, 1997); W. Steven Barnett, "Benefits of Compensatory Preschool Education," *Journal of Human Resources* 27 (Spring 1992): 279–312; Janet Currie and Duncan Thomas, "Does Head Start Make a Difference?," *American Economic Review* 85 (June 1995): 341–64; and Eliana Garces, Duncan Thomas, and Janet Currie, "Longer-Term Effects of Head Start," *American Economic Review* 92 (September 2002): 999–1012.

67. For example, James J. Heckman, Lance Lochner, Jeffrey Smith, and Christopher Taber, "The Effects of Government Policy on "Human Capital Investment and Wage Inequality," *Chicago Policy Review* 1 (Spring 1997): 1–40, quotation on p. 34, and Carneiro and Heckman, "Human Capital Policy," p. 204. Learning begets learning across generations as well, even when the parents' learning is compulsory. A historical study of the effects of changes in states' compulsory schooling laws shows that increased education of either parent reduces the probability that a child will either

repeat a grade or drop out of school; see again Oreopoulos et al., "Does Human Capital Transfer from Parent to Child?"

68. See Joseph Tierney and Jean Grossman, *Making a Difference: An Impact Study of Big Brothers/Big Sisters* (Philadelphia: Public/Private Ventures, 1995), and the discussion in Carneiro and Heckman, "Human Capital Policy."

69. See the different stances on this question taken by Krueger and by Carneiro and Heckman in Heckman and Krueger, *Inequality in America.*

70. Carneiro and Heckman, "Human Capital Policy," p. 97. See also Stephen V. Cameron and Christopher Taber, "Estimation of Educational Borrowing Constraints Using Returns to Schooling," *Journal of Political Economy* 112 (February 2004): 132–82.

71. See Judith Ann Li, "Estimating the Effect of Federal Financial Aid on Higher Education: A Study of Pell Grants" (unpublished Ph.D. dissertation, Harvard University, 1999). The current maximum grant is $4,050 per year. The government's Perkins program extends loans in a similar way.

72. See Stephen Cameron and James J. Heckman, "Can Tuition Policy Combat Rising Wage Inequality?," in Marvin Kosters (ed.), *Financing College Tuition* (Washington, D.C.: American Enterprise Institute, 1999), and Susan Dynarski, "Does Aid Matter? Measuring the Effects of Student Aid on College Attendance and Completion," *American Economic Review* 93 (March 2003): 279–88. Similarly, the government's "529" and Coverdell tax-advantaged plans to encourage saving for education are most advantageous to the highest-income families; see Susan Dynarski, "Who Benefits from the Education Saving Incentives? Income, Educational Expectations, and the Value of the 529 and Coverdell," *National Tax Journal* 57 (June 2004): 359–83.

73. Thomas J. Kane, "A Quasi-Experimental Estimate of the Impact of Financial Aid on College-Going" (National Bureau of Economic Research, Working Paper 9703, 2003).

74. See Eric A. Hanushek, "The Economics of Schooling: Production and Efficiency in Public Schools," *Journal of Economic Literature* 24 (September 1986): 1141–77, and "Measuring Investment in Education," *Journal of Economic Perspectives* 10 (Autumn 1996): 9–30; and David Card and Alan B. Krueger, "School Resources and Student Outcomes: An Overview of the Literature and New Evidence from North and South Carolina," *Journal of Economic Perspectives* 10 (Autumn 1996): 31–50.

75. Larry Hedges, Richard Laine, and Rob Greenwald reviewed the earlier literature of such studies in Larry V. Hedges, Richard D. Laine, and Rob Greenwald, "An Exchange: Part I: Does Money Matter? A Meta-Analysis of the Effects of Differential School Inputs on Student Outcomes," *Educational Researcher* 23 (April 1994): 5–14.

76. The teachers in these classes were also randomly assigned.

77. See Frederick Mosteller, "The Tennessee Study of Class Size in the Early

School Grades," *The Future of Children: Critical Issues for Children and Youth* 5 (Summer–Fall 1995): 113–27; Alan B. Krueger and Diane M. Whitmore, "Would Smaller Classes Help Close the Black-White Achievement Gap?" in John Chub and Jan Loveless (eds.), *Bridging the Achievement Gap* (Washington, D.C.: Brookings Institution, 2002), and "The Effect of Attending a Small Class in the Early Grades on College-Test Taking and Middle School Test Results: Evidence from Project STAR," *Economic Journal* 111 (January 2001): 1–28; and Alan B. Krueger, "Experimental Estimates of Education Production Functions," *Quarterly Journal of Economics* 114 (May 1999): 497–532, and "Economic Considerations and Class Size," *Economic Journal* 113 (February 2002): 34–63.

78. Janet Currie and Matthew Neidell, "Getting Inside the 'Black Box' of Head Start Quality: What Matters and What Doesn't?," *Economics of Education Review*, forthcoming.

79. See again the contrasting views presented in Heckman and Krueger, *Inequality in America.* Also see Card and Krueger, "Does School Quality Matter?" and "School Resources and Sudent Outcomes," and James Heckman, Anne Layne-Farrar, and Petra Todd, "Human Capital Pricing Equations with an Application to Estimating the Effect of Schooling Quality on Earnings," *Review of Economics and Statistics* 78 (November 1996): 562–610.

80. William Sander, "Expenditures and Student Achievement in Illinois: New Evidence," *Journal of Public Economics* 52 (October 1993): 403–16.

81. James J. Heckman, Anne Layne-Ferrar, and Petra Todd, "Does Measured School Quality Really Matter? An Examination of the Earnings-Quality Relationship," in Gary Burtless (ed.), *Does Money Matter? The Effect of School Resources on Student Achievement and Adult Success* (Washington, D.C.: Brookings Institution, 1996).

82. There are grounds for believing that inflation in the prices of what schools have to buy (especially labor) has been greater than inflation in the economy as a whole, however, and if so the real increase in school spending has been correspondingly less than 3.4 percent per annum. Not only do prices in typical service industries rise faster than in industries producing physical goods, but primary and secondary education in America relies disproportionality on the labor of female workers, whose wage gains have outpaced men's on average over this period. (In addition, in recent decades much of the increase in school spending has gone into extra services for children with "special needs"; but this is a matter of allocation of resources, not overall costs.)

83. Data on school expenditures are from the *2002 Digest of Education Statistics*, Table 166.

84. Data on average class size are from ibid., Tables 2, 4.

85. Eric A. Hanushek and Steven G. Rivkin, "Understanding the Twentieth-Century Growth in U.S. School Spending," *Journal of Human Resources* 32 (Winter 1997): 35–68.

86. See, for example, Eric A. Hanushek and Dale W. Jorgenson (eds.), *Improving America's Schools: The Role of Incentives* (Washington, D.C.: National Academy Press, 1996).

87. One study, however, based on experience in the Texas public schools, suggests that teachers are not responsive to higher salaries anyway; higher pay in some schools than others did not attract teachers with superior qualifications. See Eric A. Hanushek, John F. Kain, and Steven G. Rivkin, "Do Higher Salaries Buy Better Teachers?" (National Bureau of Economic Research, Working Paper 7082, 1999). Other researchers have argued that the entire scale by which primary and secondary school teachers are paid is too low to attract qualified people now that educated American women have far broader occupational opportunities than used to be the case; see, for example, Peter Temin, "Teacher Quality and the Future of America" (National Bureau of Economic Research, Working Paper 8898, 2002).

88. See, for example, the discussion of this issue in Charles Fried, *Saying What the Law Is: The Constitution in the Supreme Court* (Cambridge: Harvard University Press, 2004), Chapter 5.

89. In addition, the evidence is mixed on whether voucher plans, as put into practice, have delivered improvements in such outcomes as participating students' scores on standardized tests. See, for example, the analysis of New York City's school choice program (which involved a series of lotteries for private school scholarships) in Alan B. Krueger and Pei Zhu, "Another Look at the New York City School Voucher Experiment," *American Behavioral Scientist* 47 (January 2004): 658–98. A broader study of voucher programs and charter schools that likewise reached a mostly negative conclusion about the benefits of these innovations is Brian P. Gill, Michael Timpane, Karen E. Ross, and Dominic J. Brewer, *Rhetoric Versus Reality: What We Know and What We Need to Know About Vouchers and Charter Schools* (Santa Monica, Calif.: Rand Corporation, 2001).

90. Because school quality affects the demand for houses in each district, it is often a major factor influencing house prices. See Charles M. Tiebout, "A Pure Theory of Local Expenditures," *Journal of Political Economy* 64 (October 1956): 416–24.

91. New test score results released in 2004 by the Department of Education have cast doubt on the ability of charter schools to deliver improved learning, however. Even after allowance for such factors as urban location, parents' income, and race, students attending charter schools performed less well than did comparable students at regular public schools. See Diana Jean Schemo, "Charter Schools Trail in Results, U.S. Data Reveals," *New York Times*, August 17, 2004, p. A1, and "A Second Report Shows Charter School Students Not Performing as Well as Other Students," *New York Times*, December 16, 2004, p. A32.

92. See, for example, Diana Jean Schemo, "Effort by Bush on Education Hits Obstacles," *New York Times*, August 18, 2004, p. A1, and Sam Dillon, "Bad

School, or Not? Conflicting Ratings Baffle the Parents," *New York Times*, September 5, 2004, p. A1. One recent study has even shown that, within grades, students' progress as measured by standardized tests has slowed since the law took effect; see Greg Winter, "Study Finds Shortcoming in New Law on Education," *New York Times*, April 13, 2005, p. A15.

93. Caroline M. Hoxby, "School Choice and School Productivity (or Could School Choice Be a Tide that Lifts All Boats?)," in Hoxby (ed.), *The Economics of School Choice* (Chicago: University of Chicago Press, 2003).

94. See Mark Schneider, Paul Teske, Melissa Marschall, Michael Mintrom, and Christine Roch, "Institutional Arrangements and the Creation of Social Capital: The Effects of Public School Choice," *American Political Science Review* 91 (March 1997), pp. 82–93; Caroline M. Hoxby, "Does Competition Among Public Schools Benefit Students and Taxpayers?," *American Economic Review* 90 (December 2000): 1209–38; and George M. Holmes, Jeff De Simone, and Nicholas G. Rupp, "Does School Choice Increase School Quality?," *Education Next*, forthcoming.

95. Caroline M. Hoxby, "The Effects of School Choice on Curriculum and Atmosphere," in Susan E. Mayer and Paul E. Peterson (eds.), *Earning and Learning: How Schools Matter* (Washington, D.C.: Brookings Institution, 1999).

96. See, for example, the evidence in Jacob Mincer, "The Production of Human Capital and the Life-Cycle of Earnings: Variations on a Theme," *Journal of Labor Economics* 15 (January 1997): S26–S47.

97. See James J. Heckman, "Is Job Training Oversold?," *Public Interest* 115 (Spring 1994): 91–115, and Heckman et al., "The Effects of Government Policy on Human Capital Investment and Wage Inequality." Experience shows that many employers can, in effect, make workers shoulder part of the cost of their own training by paying lower wages to new or unskilled workers, so that they can go ahead and provide training to new recruits without worrying that they are using their own resources to train their competitors' future employees. See also Jacob Mincer, "Investment in U.S. Education and Training" (National Bureau of Economic Research, Working Paper 4838, 1994).

98. See Gary Burtless, "Are Targeted Wage Subsidies Harmful? Evidence from a Wage Voucher Experiment," *Industrial and Labor Relations Review* 39 (October 1985): 105–14.

99. See the review of these programs in Robert J. LaLonde, "The Promise of Public Sector–Sponsored Training Programs," *Journal of Economic Perspectives* 9 (Spring 1995): 149–68. Under the 1982 Job Training Partnership Act, the government turned over to the states much of the training that had been carried out under the Comprehensive Employment and Training Act program, albeit still with federal financing.

100. See Charles F. Manski and Irwin Garfinkel, *Evaluating Welfare and Training Programs* (Cambridge: Harvard University Press, 1992); Lalonde,

"The Promise of Public Sector-Sponsored Training Programs"; Krueger, "Inequality, Too Much of a Good Thing"; and Carneiro and Heckman, "Human Capital Policy."

101. John Burghardt, Peter Z. Shochet, Sheena McConnell, Terry Johnson, R. Mark Gritz, Steven Glazerman, John Homrighausen, and Robert Jackson, *Does Job Corps Work? Summary of the National Job Corps Study* (Princeton, N.J.: Mathematica Policy Research, 2001).

102. See, for example, the different conclusions drawn by Krueger and by Heckman and Carneiro in Heckman and Krueger, *Inequality in America*.

103. As we have seen, this theme has figured prominently in American thinking since well before the founding of the republic. For a recent discussion in a context explicitly addressing issues of economic policy, see Edmund S. Phelps, *Rewarding Work: How to Restore Participation and Self-Support to Free Enterprise* (Cambridge: Harvard University Press, 1997).

104. See Jeffrey M. Perloff and Michael L. Wachter, "The New Jobs Tax Credit: An Evaluation of the 1977–1978 Wage Subsidy Program," *American Economic Review* 69 (May 1979): 173–79, and Lawrence F. Katz, "Wage Subsidies for the Disadvantaged," in Richard B. Freeman and Peter Gottschalk (eds.), *Generating Jobs: How to Increase Jobs for Less-Skilled Workers* (New York: Russell Sage Foundation, 1998). See also Robert H. Haveman and Barbara Wolfe, *Succeeding Generations: On the Effects of Investments in Children* (New York: Russell Sage Foundation, 1994).

105. Anne Case, Darren Lubotsky, and Christina Paxson, "Economic Status and Health in Childhood: The Origins of the Gradient," *American Economic Review* 92 (December 2002): 1308–34.

106. *Time*, April 14, 1941, pp. 86–87; cited in Alan Brinkley, *The End of Reform: New Deal Liberalism in Recession and War* (New York: Knopf, 1995), p. 128.

Acknowledgments

Principal funding for the research and writing of this book came from the Calvin K. Kazangian Foundation for Economics and from the Curran Foundation. The Hickrill Foundation provided additional support. I am grateful to these three foundations for making this work possible. I am also grateful to Michael MacDowell, to Willard Speakman, and to Frank and Denie Weil, for their help in securing this support and, just as important, their enthusiasm for this inquiry and their personal vote of confidence in it and in me. Harvard University provided two sabbaticals during which I worked on this book and also supported my research with grants from several university funds.

Any intellectual endeavor that self-consciously draws on different disciplines as this one does inevitably reflects the advice and encouragement of many individuals. Living and working in a university community, I have been blessed with a rich collection of colleagues and friends to whom I could turn. Many will find reflections of their influence in these pages.

Two of these colleagues, neither an economist, deserve particular thanks for the help and encouragement they have given me (although, needless to say, neither bears responsibility for what I have written). Daniel Bell, of Harvard's Sociology Department, stimulated my ideas from the very beginning of this inquiry, pointed me in directions I had not known to look, read and insightfully commented on parts of what I had written, and encouraged me throughout. William Hutchison, of the Harvard Divinity School, likewise suggested ideas that were new to me and provided continual support and encouragement. I have been guided by their advice, and strengthened by their friendship.

Similarly, my editor at Knopf, Jonathan Segal, has been helpful and encouraging throughout the writing of this book—reading successive drafts, asking the right questions, and pointing the way to improvements. His efforts have made it a better book. I am also grateful to Robert Barnett for handling arrangements with Knopf on my behalf.

Other colleagues and friends who read and commented on draft chapters of this work include Alberto Alesina, Harold Attridge, Bernard Avishai, Stephen

Bergman, Peter Bernstein, Olivier Blanchard, Derek Bok, Michael Bordo, Adam Broadbent, John Campbell, Robert Carswell, Stefan Collignon, Robert Dorfman, Arthur Dubow, Michael Edelstein, Jason Epstein, Niall Ferguson, Donald Fleming, John Flemming, Robert Frank, Helmut Friedlaender, Wolfgang Gebauer, Edward Glaeser, Claudia Goldin, Neva Goodwin, Richard Grossman, Patrice Higonnet, Albert Hirschman, Stanley Hoffmann, Glenn Hubbard, Richard Hunt, Otmar Issing, Toshiki Jinushi, Serene Jones, Ethan Kapstein, Carl Kaysen, Morton Keller, David Laibson, Charles Maier, Gregory Mankiw, Stephen Marglin, Richard Musgrave, Joseph Nye, Thomas Ogletree, John Olcay, Brendan O'Leary, Torsten Persson, Adam Posen, Rolf Richter, Francis Schott, Anna Schwartz, Tibor Scitovsky, Robert Shiller, Pierre Sicsic, Hamish Stewart, Peter Temin, Charles Tilly, Louis Uchitelle, and David Weil. Others who often went beyond the call of ordinary duty in repeatedly answering questions and providing useful information include Robert Barro, Jared Bernstein, Thomas Senior Berry, David Cutler, Charles Donahue, Richard Easterlin, Jeffrey Frankel, William Gale, Robert Gallman, Henry Gemery, Robert Gordon, Zvi Griliches, James Heckman, Caroline Hoxby, Ronald Inglehart, Howell Jackson, Dale Jorgenson, Lawrence Katz, Charles Kindleberger, Michael Kremer, Alan Krueger, Jeffrey Liebman, Tobias Linzert, John Londregan, Harvey Mansfield, Laurie Matthews, Dwight Perkins, James Poterba, Adam Przeworski, Michael Sandel, Juliet Schor, Amartya Sen, Robert Stavins, Stephen Thernstrom, Richard Tuck, Sidney Verba, Julian von Landesberger, and Jeffrey Williamson. I appreciate their help, and I thank them all.

I have also benefited enormously, during the years I have worked on this project, from the assistance of a series of Harvard students: Eric Fleisig-Greene, Benjamin Hett, Bruce Gottlieb, Jamie Horr, David Kessler, Amanda Kowalski, Matthew Maguire, Richard Mansfield, Michael Morell, Justin Muzinich, Matthew Price, Geoff Rapp, Danny Shoag, Claudia Sitgraves, Stephen Weinberg, and Emma Wendt. They too will recognize the results of their efforts here. Working with young people of this high caliber—both intellectually and personally—is a particular joy of the research process. I appreciated their help when they were students. Most of them have now graduated, and they are my friends.

My longtime secretary, Helen Deas, did her usual excellent job in not only typing and retyping (and again retyping) the manuscript but also keeping track of multiple drafts of sixteen chapters. Her faithful support has consistently underpinned both my research and my teaching. Shelley Weiner also ably and cheerfully pitched in when the volume of work to be done required more than one person to do it.

And, fortunately, there are the constants, the moral anchors, of one's life. A decade ago, asked to write an essay on my approach to "doing economics" for a collection aimed at students and young professionals in the field, I chose to approach the subject at both the intellectual and the moral level. I wrote, in part, "Have an agenda, and know why it matters. . . . My wife and sons come first." The contribution that Barbara, John, and Jeff have made to the effort behind this book has been indirect, but it has been no less valuable—to me—for that. I dedicate the book to Barbara.

Index

A NOTE ABOUT THE AUTHOR

Benjamin M. Friedman is the William Joseph Maier Professor of Political Economy, and formerly chairman of the Department of Economics, at Harvard University. His research and writing have primarily focused on economic policy, and he has frequently advised both policymakers and candidates for public office on economic issues. His book *Day of Reckoning: The Consequences of American Economic Policy Under Reagan and After* received the George S. Eccles Prize, awarded annually by Columbia University for excellence in writing about economics. Most recently, he was the 2005 recipient of the John R. Commons Award, presented every two years by Omicron Delta Epsilon, the International Honor Society for Economics, in recognition of achievements in economics and contributions to the economics profession.

In addition to *Day of Reckoning*, Mr. Friedman is the author or editor of eleven books aimed primarily at economists and economic policymakers, as well as the author of over one hundred articles on economics and economic policy published in numerous journals. He is also a frequent contributor to newspaper op-ed pages and to other publications, especially *The New York Review of Books*.

Apart from his writing and teaching, Mr. Friedman's current professional activities include serving as a director of several American companies, including the *Encyclopaedia Britannica*. He is also a member of the Council on Foreign Relations. He and his wife, Barbara, and their two sons live in Cambridge, Massachusetts.

A NOTE ON THE TYPE

This book was set in Janson, a typeface long thought to have been made by the Dutch-man Anton Janson, who was a practicing typefounder in Leipzig during the years 1668–1687. However, it has been conclusively demonstrated that these types are actu-ally the work of Nicholas Kis (1650–1702), a Hungarian, who most probably learned his trade from the master Dutch typefounder Dirk Voskens. The type is an excellent example of the influential and sturdy Dutch types that prevailed in England up to the time William Caslon (1692–1766) developed his own incomparable designs from them.

Composed by Creative Graphics, Inc.,
Allentown, Pennsylvania

Printed and bound at R. R. Donnelley,
Harrisonburg, Virginia

Designed by Soonyoung Kwon